FLORIDA REAL ESTATE: PRINCIPLES, PRACTICES, AND LICENSE LAWS

FLORIDA REAL ESTATE: PRINCIPLES, PRACTICES, AND LICENSE LAWS

SAM IRLANDER

SOUTH-WESTERN
CENGAGE Learning™

Australia • Brazil • Japan • Korea • Mexico • Singapore • Spain • United Kingdom • United States

Florida Real Estate: Principles, Practices, and License Laws

Sam Irlander

VP/Editorial Director: Jack W. Calhoun

VP/Editor-in-Chief: Dave Shaut

Acquisitions Editor: Sara Glassmeyer

Developmental Editor: Mary Draper

Sr. Editorial Assistant: Adele Scholtz

Sr. Marketing Manager: Mark Linton

Sr. Content Project Manager: Cliff Kallemeyn

Art Director: Ed Donald

Production Technology Analyst: Adam Grafa

Sr. First Print Buyer: Kevin Kluck

Production and Composition: International Typesetting and Composition

For product information and technology assistance, contact us at **Cengage Learning Academic Resource Center, 1-800-423-0563**
For permission to use material from this text or product, submit all requests online at **www.cengage.com/permissions**
Further permissions questions can be emailed to **permissionrequest@cengage.com**

Library of Congress Control Number: 2007939322

ISBN 13: 978-0-324-64113-4

ISBN 10: 0-324-64113-3

South-Western Cengage Learning
5191 Natorp Boulevard
Mason, OH 45040
USA

Cengage Learning products are represented in Canada by Nelson Education, Ltd.

For your course and learning solutions, visit **academic.cengage.com**

Purchase any of our products at your local college store or at our preferred online store **www.ichapters.com**

Printed in the United States of America
1 2 3 4 5 6 7 11 10 09 08 07

In memory of
Herman Irlander
My father, my teacher, my hero.

Brief Contents

Preface xvii

1 THE REAL ESTATE BUSINESS 3

2 LICENSE LAW AND QUALIFICATIONS FOR LICENSURE 15

3 LICENSE LAW AND COMMISSION RULES 31

4 LAW OF AGENCY—RELATIONSHIPS AND DISCLOSURES 43

5 OPERATION OF A BROKER'S OFFICE 63

6 LICENSE LAW: VIOLATIONS, COMPLAINTS, PENALTIES, AND PROCEDURES 79

7 FEDERAL AND STATE LAWS AFFECTING HOUSING 91

8 PROPERTY OWNERSHIP 107

9 TITLE DEEDS AND OWNERSHIP RESTRICTIONS 133

10 PROPERTY DESCRIPTION 161

11 REAL ESTATE CONTRACTS 173

12 REAL ESTATE FINANCE 195

13 MORTGAGE MARKET OPERATIONS 215

14 TITLE CLOSING AND COMPUTATIONS 249

15 VALUATION OF REAL PROPERTY 277

16 RESIDENTIAL CONSTRUCTION AND ENVIRONMENTAL ISSUES 313

17 INVESTING IN REAL ESTATE AND BUSINESS BROKERAGE 337

18 TAXES AFFECTING REAL ESTATE 363

19 THE REAL ESTATE MARKET 383

20 PLANNING AND ZONING 393

MATH BUSTERS GUIDE TO REAL ESTATE MATH 402

ANSWERS TO CHAPTER REVIEW QUESTIONS 408

PRACTICE END-OF-COURSE EXAM 412

ANSWER SHEET FOR MARKING ANSWERS 426

ANSWERS TO END-OF-COURSE EXAM 428

EXAMPLE REAL ESTATE FORMS 434

Glossary 454

Index 470

Contents

Preface xvii

1 The Real Estate Business 3

Key Terms • Learning Objectives

INTRODUCTION TO THE REAL ESTATE BUSINESS 3

OTHER PROFESSIONS THAT RELY ON THE REAL ESTATE BUSINESS 3

REAL ESTATE AND THE NATION'S ECONOMY 4

BROKERAGE SPECIALTY TYPES 5

REAL ESTATE BROKERAGE 6

THE SALES PROCESS AND THE SALES LICENSEE 7

Step 1—Canvassing for Product • Step 2—Canvassing for the Product Buyer/ User • Step 3—Showing the Property • Step 4—Submission and Negotiating of the Offer • Step 5—Execution of a Sales Contract • Step 6—Closing of the Sales Contract • Step 7—Recording Activities

PROPERTY MANAGEMENT 8

APPRAISAL 9

FINANCING AND THE REAL PROPERTY TRANSACTION 9

DEVELOPMENT AND CONSTRUCTION 10

Land Acquisition/Subdividing and Construction

GOVERNMENT'S ROLE 10

Federal Government • State Government • Local Government

PROFESSIONAL ORGANIZATIONS 11

SUMMARY 12

REVIEW QUESTIONS 12

2 License Law and Qualifications for Licensure   15

Key Terms • Learning Objectives

HISTORICAL PERSPECTIVE   15

CATEGORIES OF LICENSURE   15

LICENSURE REQUIREMENTS FOR SALES ASSOCIATE   16

Be Honest and of Trustworthy Character • Complete a FREC-Approved 63-Hour Qualifying Course • Pay the Required Fee • Additional Requirement: Postlicense Education

LICENSURE REQUIREMENTS: BROKER AND BROKER ASSOCIATE   18

Additional Requirement: Postlicense Education

LICENSURE REQUIREMENTS: APPLICATION   19

LICENSURE REQUIREMENTS: EXAMINATION   19

LICENSURE REQUIREMENTS: NONRESIDENT LICENSURE   20

LICENSURE VIA MUTUAL RECOGNITION   20

LICENSE RENEWAL   21

LICENSURE, LICENSE RENEWAL, AND CONTINUING EDUCATION   21

LICENSURE, LICENSE RENEWAL, AND CONTINUING EDUCATION EXEMPTIONS   22

IMPORTANT STATE LAWS   22

LICENSES AND REGISTRATIONS   23

WHO MUST HOLD A REAL ESTATE LICENSE   23

Broker • Broker Associate • Sales Associate

LICENSURE: WHO IS EXEMPT FROM LICENSE LAW?   24

SUMMARY   26

REVIEW QUESTIONS   26

3 License Law and Commission Rules   31

Key Terms • Learning Objectives

GOVERNING BODY AND ENFORCEMENT   31

FUNCTIONS OF THE FLORIDA REAL ESTATE COMMISSION AND THE DIVISION OF REAL ESTATE   32

ADMINISTRATIVE PENALTIES   32

PRACTICING REAL ESTATE WITHOUT A LICENSE   33

COMPOSITION, QUALIFICATIONS, AND COMPENSATION OF THE FLORIDA REAL ESTATE COMMISSION   34

THE DIVISION OF REAL ESTATE (DRE)   35

ADDRESS REQUREMENTS   35

LICENSE PERIODS   35

LICENSE RENEWAL/MILITARY EXEMPTIONS   36

MULTIPLE AND GROUP LICENSES   36

ACTIVE LICENSE VS. INACTIVE LICENSE   36
   Voluntary Inactive • Involuntary Inactive
VOID AND INEFFECTIVE LICENSES   37

REGISTRATION OF PROPRIETARY REAL ESTATE SCHOOLS   38

THE REAL ESTATE EDUCATION AND RESEARCH FOUNDATION   39

SUMMARY   39

REVIEW QUESTIONS   39

4 Law of Agency—Relationships and Disclosures   43

Key Terms • Learning Objectives
LAW OF AGENCY   43
   Statutory Law • Common Law
AGENCY—RELATIONSHIPS DEFINED   44
   Responsibilities to the Principal • Responsibilities to the Customer
TYPES OF AGENCIES   48
   Universal Agency • General Agency • Special Agency
THE FLORIDA BROKERAGE RELATIONSHIP DISCLOSURE ACT   50
   Exemptions to Disclosure Requirements
TYPES OF AUTHORIZED AGENCY RELATIONSHIPS   50
   Nonrepresentation (No Brokerage Relationship) • Single Agent
   Relationship • Transaction Broker Relationship
TRANSITIONING TO ANOTHER AUTHORIZED RELATIONSHIP   56

MAINTAINING RECORDS   57

DESIGNATED SALES ASSOCIATE   57

TERMINATION OF AGENCY   58

SUMMARY   59

REVIEW QUESTIONS   59

5 Operation of a Broker's Office   63

Key Terms • Learning Objectives

THE BROKER'S OFFICE   63

CHANGE OF ADDRESS   63

CHANGE EMPLOYING BROKER   63

BRANCH OFFICES   64

SIGNAGE   64

ADVERTISING   64

ESCROW (TRUST) ACCOUNTS IN FLORIDA   65

Escrow Dispute and Disposition of Funds • Good-Faith Doubt

RENTAL INFORMATION OR RENTAL LISTS   68

LICENSE VERSUS REGISTRATION   69

Permitted Registrations • Entities That May Not Register

SUMMARY   73

REVIEW QUESTIONS   74

6 License Law: Violations, Complaints, Penalties, and Procedures   79

Key Terms • Learning Objectives

PROCEDURES FOR DISCIPLINING LICENSEES   79

THE COMPLAINT PROCESS, PROCEDURES, AND APPEAL   80

Complaint and Investigation • Probable Cause Panel • Formal Complaint • Formal or Informal Hearing • Final Order • Appeal Process

LICENSE LAW VIOLATIONS   83

Revocation/Suspension of Broker's License • Violations and Penalties • The Real Estate Recovery Fund

SUMMARY   87

REVIEW QUESTIONS   88

7 Federal and State Laws Affecting Housing   91

Key Terms • Learning Objectives

INTRODUCTION TO FAIR HOUSING   91

The Civil Rights Act of 1866 • The Civil Rights Act of 1968 • State Law

INTRODUCTION TO FAIR HOUSING VIOLATIONS   93

FAIR HOUSING VIOLATIONS   94

Blockbusting • Improper Listings • Refusal to Show Property to Minorities • Steering • Advertising • Less Favorable Treatment of Minority Buyers • Redlining

ADDITIONAL REGULATIONS   97

THE REAL ESTATE SETTLEMENT PROCEDURES ACT   97

Real Estate Settlement Procedures Act Requirements

FLORIDA HOUSING LAWS   98

The Florida Uniform Land Sales Practices Act • The Florida Residential Landlord and Tenant Act • Leases Covering Residential Dwelling Units

SUMMARY   102

REVIEW QUESTIONS   103

8 Property Ownership   107

Key Terms • Learning Objectives

PROPERTY OWNERSHIP   107

Classification of Property

REAL PROPERTY COMPOSITION   108

Surface Rights • Subsurface Rights • Air Rights

FIXTURES   111

Plants, Trees, and Crops • Legal Determination of a Fixture • Trade Fixtures

TYPES OF ESTATES   114

Freehold Estate • Nonfreehold Estates or Estates Less Than Freehold

FORMS OF OWNERSHIP   119

Sole Ownership • Concurrent Ownership • Partitioning of Ownership • Special Ownership Interests

COMMUNITY OWNERSHIP   123

Condominiums • Cooperatives • Planned-Unit Development (PUD) • Resort Time-Share Developments

SUMMARY   130

REVIEW QUESTIONS   130

9 Title Deeds and Ownership Restrictions   133

Key Terms • Learning Objectives

METHODS OF TRANSFER   133

DEEDS   134

Elements of a Deed

TYPES OF DEEDS   137

General Warranty Deed • Special Warranty Deed • Bargain and Sale
Deed • Quitclaim Deed • Preparation of Deeds

TITLES   139

Public Records • Constructive Notice • Actual Notice • Recording • Torrens
Land Titles • Title Insurance • Owner's Title Insurance • Mortgagee's Title
Insurance

EASEMENTS   142

Easement Appurtenant • Easement in Gross • Party Wall Easement • Licenses
• Creation of Easements • Termination of Easements

ENCROACHMENTS   145

LEASES   146

Basic Principles of Leases • Types of Leases • Contract versus Economic Rent
• Security Deposits • Essentials of a Valid Lease • Termination of a Lease
• Assignment and Subletting

LIENS   153

Mortgage Liens • Tax Liens • Mechanic's Liens • Judgment Liens • Deficiency
Judgment Liens • Categories of Liens • Priority of Liens • Transfer of Encumbered Title

SUMMARY   157

REVIEW QUESTIONS   157

10 Property Description   161

Key Terms • Learning Objectives

METHODS OF DESCRIPTION   161

Recorded Plats • Metes and Bounds • Government Rectangular Survey

BASIC FACTS   166

Introduction

SUMMARY   168

REVIEW QUESTIONS   169

11 Real Estate Contracts   173

Key Terms • Learning Objectives

DEFINITIONS   173

CATEGORIES OF CONTRACTS   173

Expressed versus Implied • Valid versus Void and Voidable • Bilateral versus Unilateral • Executed versus Executory

CONTRACT VALIDITY AND ENFORCEMENT REQUIREMENTS   176

Consideration • Agreement • Legal Objective • Legally Competent Parties

METHODS OF DISCHARGING CONTRACTS   180

Assignment • Novation • Termination

THE STATUTE OF FRAUDS   183

OPTION CONTRACTS   184

Miscellaneous Characteristics of Options

BREACH OF CONTRACTS   185

Remedies for Breach • "Time is of the Essence"

LISTING CONTRACTS   186

CONTRACT OF SALE   187

Disclosures • Earnest Money • Time Limits • Acceptance • Back-up Contract • Binder • Installment Sales Contract

SUMMARY   190

REVIEW QUESTIONS   191

12 Real Estate Finance   195

Key Terms • Learning Objectives

MORTGAGES AND HYPOTHECATION   195

TITLE THEORY   195

LIEN THEORY   197

Lien Theory and the Financing Instruments • Promissory Note • Mortgage

PRIORITY OF LOANS   203

FORECLOSURE   203

Judicial Foreclosure • Deficiency Judgment • Excess from Sale • Statutory Redemption • Deed in Lieu of Foreclosure

TYPES OF LOANS   205

Term Loan • Amortized Loan • Partially Amortized Loan • Budget Loan • Package Loan • Purchase Money Loan • Open-End Loan • Blanket Loan • Graduated Payment Loan • Adjustable Rate Loans • Wraparound Loan • Buydown Loan • Construction Loans • Shared Equity/Participating Loan • Reverse Annuity Loan • Sale and Leaseback

LENDING PRACTICES AND UNDERWRITING RISK   209

SUMMARY   210

REVIEW QUESTIONS   211

13 Mortgage Market Operations   215

Key Terms ● Learning Objectives

FEDERAL RESERVE SYSTEM   215

FEDERAL HOME LOAN BANK SYSTEM   215

FEDERAL DEPOSIT INSURANCE CORPORATION   216

INTERMEDIATION   216

DISINTERMEDIATION   216

PRIMARY AND SECONDARY MORTGAGE MARKETS   216

Primary Mortgage Market ● Secondary Mortgage Market

THE HISTORY OF LOANS   220

Amortized Loans ● Federal Agencies

LOAN DISCOUNTING   221

LOAN-TO-VALUE RATIO   223

CONVENTIONAL LOANS   223

Types of Conventional Loans ● Down Payments ● Private Mortgage Insurance Payments

FHA LOANS (NONCONVENTIONAL)   227

Loan Insurance Programs

203(B)—STANDARD LOAN PROGRAM   228

Loan Insurance ● Cash Investment ● Loan Amount ● Interest Rate ● Discount Points ● Maximum Term ● Closing Costs ● Escrow Accounts ● Loan Processing ● Appraisal ● Restrictions

VA LOANS (NONCONVENTIONAL)   232

Maximum Loan Amount ● Down Payment ● Term and Interest Rate ● Discount Points ● Closing Costs ● Funding Fee ● Escrow Account ● Veteran's Liability ● Appraisal ● Eligible Properties

ASSUMPTION METHODS   235

Assuming and Agreeing to Pay a Loan ● Taking Subject to an Existing Loan ● When to Use an Assumption ● Closing Requirements ● Advantages and Disadvantages

QUALIFYING THE BUYER   239

Underwriting

LOAN CHARGES   243
  Variable Costs • Fixed Costs • Discount Points
SUMMARY   245
REVIEW QUESTIONS   246

14 **Title Closing and Computations**   **249**
  Key Terms • Learning Objectives
TITLE CLOSING   249
CLOSING STATEMENTS   249
  State Transfer Taxes
PRORATING   261
  Property Taxes
PRACTICE EXERCISES   265
  Calculating the Number of Days Prior to the Month of Closing • Calculating the Total
  Number of Days the Seller Is Responsible for Property Taxes • Calculating the Amount
  of Property Tax Due for Each Day of the Year • Calculating the Amount of the Seller's
  Tax Payment at Closing
SALES CONTRACT TO CLOSING   269
  After the Sales Contract Is Signed • Loan Processing • Preparing for Closing
SOLD SIGNS   274

SUMMARY   274
REVIEW QUESTIONS   274

15 **Valuation of Real Property**   **277**
  Key Terms • Learning Objectives
PRINCIPLES OF PRICING AND VALUE   277
  Appraisal versus Pricing • Basic Concepts of Valuation • Elements of Value
  • Physical Characteristics of Land • Principles (Theorems) of Value • Miscella-
  neous Topics • Steps in the Appraisal Process • Market Data (Sales Comparison)
  Approach • Cost Approach (Reproduction) • Income Approach to Pricing •
  Gross Rent Multiplier • Reconciliation
MARKET ANALYSIS   295
  Sources of Information • Effects of Financing • Completing the Market Analysis
REPLACEMENT COST PRICING   304
  Step 1: Estimate Land Value • Step 2: Estimate Replacement Cost • Step 3: Add
  Replacement Cost and Land • Step 4: Deduct Depreciation
SUMMARY   308
REVIEW QUESTIONS   309

16 Residential Construction and Environmental Issues   313

Key Terms • Learning Objectives

FEATURES OF EXTERIOR CONSTRUCTION   313

Footings and Foundations • Framing • Insulation • Ventilation • Exterior Wall Covering • Windows • Roofs

MECHANICAL SYSTEMS AND EQUIPMENT   317

Heating Systems • Types of Fuel • Cooling Systems • Plumbing Systems • Hot Water System • Sewers and Septic Tanks • Electrical System

COMMON CONSTRUCTION TERMS   321

Backfill • Bearing Wall • Commercial Acre • Conduit • Deciduous • Drywall • Elevation Drawing • Energy Efficiency Ratio (EER) • Flashing • Footing • Foundation • Header • Joist • Percolation Test • Plot Plan (Plot Map) • Potable Water • R Value • Rafter • Ridgeboard • Roof • Sheathing • Sill • Soil Pipe • Sole Plate • Stud

RESIDENTIAL LOTS   325

Corner Lots • Interior Lots • T Lots • Cul-de-sac Lots • Key Lots • Flag Lots

ENVIRONMENTAL HAZARDS   328

Radon • Formaldehyde Gas • Asbestos • Lead • Groundwater Contamination • Disclosure Statement • Due Diligence Investigation

SUMMARY   332

REVIEW QUESTIONS   332

17 Investing in Real Estate and Business Brokerage   337

Key Terms • Learning Objectives

REAL ESTATE INVESTMENTS   337

The Licensee Regarded as an Expert • Property Types and Subtypes • Goals of Investments • Advantages of Investing in Real Estate • Disadvantages of Investing in Real Estate • Property Investment Analysis

CALCULATING PRICE AND COMMISSIONS   345

Commission Problems • Investment Problems • Value Problems • Loan Problems

CALCULATING COST AND PRICE   353

Cost Problems • Price Problems

BUSINESS BROKERAGE   356

Comparison to Real Estate Brokerage • Expertise • Sale of a Business • Valuation of a Business

SUMMARY   358

REVIEW QUESTIONS   358

18 Taxes Affecting Real Estate   363

Key Terms • Learning Objectives

TAXATION   363

Ad Valorem Taxes • Special Assessment Taxes

FEDERAL INCOME TAX   369

Active Income • Passive Income • Portfolio Income

FEDERAL INCOME TAX AND REAL PROPERTY   370

Deductions • Tax on Sale of Property • Exclusion of Capital Gains • Capital Gains Tax Rates • Installment Sales • Real Estate Exchanges

SUMMARY   378

REVIEW QUESTIONS   378

19 The Real Estate Market   383

Key Terms • Learning Objectives

PHYSICAL CHARACTERISTICS OF REAL ESTATE   383

ECONOMIC CHARACTERISTICS OF REAL PROPERTY   384

Demand • Supply

INTERPRETING MARKET CONDITIONS   387

Price Levels • Vacancy Rates • Sales Volume

SUMMARY   388

REVIEW QUESTIONS   389

20 Planning and Zoning   393

Key Terms • Learning Objectives

THE HISTORY OF URBAN PLANNING AND ZONING   393

PUBLIC LAND-USE CONTROL   394

Zoning Ordinances • Nonconforming Use • Variance • Special Exception • Master Plan • Local Planning Agency • The Process of Planning • Developments of Regional Impact • Building Codes

PRIVATE LAND-USE CONTROLS   398

Enforcement

SUMMARY   400

REVIEW QUESTIONS   400

MATH BUSTERS GUIDE TO REAL ESTATE MATH   402

ANSWERS TO CHAPTER REVIEW QUESTIONS   408

PRACTICE END-OF-COURSE EXAM   412

ANSWER SHEET FOR MARKING ANSWERS   426

ANSWERS TO END-OF-COURSE EXAM   428

EXAMPLE REAL ESTATE FORMS   434

Glossary   454
Index   470

Preface

Welcome to the fascinating world of real estate. Making career decisions in life is never easy. Decisions are usually filled with questions. In fact, you may even question whether this career decision was appropriate. Relax, you are not alone. If you are the type of person who is looking for a career that is highly lucrative, provides excitement, and involves problem solving, you have come to the right industry. I am pleased to report that after 33 years of transactional real estate experience (and still counting), no two days are ever the same for me. How many folks get to say that about their career?

As is the case with learning of any new subject matter, questions will arise. This book was written to provide you with the answers. You will be faced with industry terms that at times seem as if you are learning a foreign language. Let this book be your guide and interpreter. Learning does not have to be a difficult or unpleasant experience. It should always be rewarding. Every effort went into this publication to ensure that your learning experience is a pleasant one.

This book was written with you in mind. During your career in real estate, you will be faced or challenged with a variety of transactional issues. It would be difficult to imagine that any one book could provide all the answers or solutions. However, this book provides the reader with the necessary essentials required for one to practice real estate in Florida.

As your journey begins through the learning process, we will first examine the various sectors of the real estate industry. Later, we will learn about the regulatory agencies, license law, and the licensing process. As we progress through the remaining sections of this book, you will learn about the principles and practices of the real estate field.

I created what is believed to be a fresh, new, comprehensive Florida real estate book that provides up-to-date content in a crisp and efficient format punctuated with real-world examples. Key terms, summaries and extensive review questions for each chapter allow users to check their understanding. A 100-question practice exam at the end of the book tests student knowledge of key concepts. Two additional online practice exams simulate the actual Florida real estate exam providing critical exam preparation.

Most notably, users will appreciate the *"Coaching Tips"* throughout each chapter enabling them to master the material and confidently pass the Florida real estate salesperson license exam. The book incorporates engaging learning features such as:

- **Crisp, uncluttered format** will engage learners enhancing their success on the Florida real estate salesperson license exam.
- *"Math Buster"* **appendix** provides keen insights to learning and using fundamental math formulas used on the real estate exam.
- *"Coaching Tips"* **highlight** practical application of the key principles using real-life scenarios to fully prepare users for their new real estate careers.

- **Two online practice exams** match the question format used on the actual Florida real estate salesperson license exam.
- **Learning tools** like key terms, chapter summaries and extensive review questions help users successfully master the material.

This preface would not be complete without personally reaching out to thank those whose contributions to this publication were just so valuable. My heart-felt thanks goes out to Sara Glassmeyer whose belief in me resulted in the opportunity to write this book. Additionally, thanks to Mary Draper whose help and guidance was the shining light in development of this publication. In addition, I would like to thank Mark Linton, Senior Marketing Manager, and Cliff Kallemeyn, Content Project Manager, for their contributions to the success of this new textbook. I am also grateful to Dallie Moriarty, Cooke Real Estate School, for her excellent work on the questions and final exams. Finally, I thank the following real estate professionals who provided valuable insights as reviewers: James P. Christie, Christie's School of Real Estate; Joseph R. Ponds, Jr., MemoryQuest, Inc.; Glenn Sudnick, Palm Beach School of Real Estate; and Don Widmayer, American Business College, Inc. Their reviews were invaluable and their comments were incorporated to make this a quality publication.

I close with the following: may the real estate practice that has rewarded and enriched my life over the years be as rewarding to you and yours.

Samuel Irlander

Florida Real Estate: Principles, Practices, and License Laws

Chapter 1

LEARNING OBJECTIVES

After completing this lesson, you will be able to:

- Recognize the different avenues within real estate practice available to you.
- Understand various types and uses of modern-day real property.
- Explain why property management services have grown as well as its importance to absentee owners.
- Explain modern-day development and construction.
- Understand the three phases of residential construction.
- Recognize the Uniform Standards of Professional Appraisal Practice (USPAP).
- Explain licensing requirements for mortgage brokers and mortgage bankers.

The Real Estate Business

INTRODUCTION TO THE REAL ESTATE BUSINESS

This chapter is intended to familiarize the student with the real estate business as a practice. It will also provide the student with a clear understanding of the different choices and areas (including required expertise) for entry into real estate.

Real estate as a profession is a clear and direct response to society's demand for:

- Individual housing
- Commercial space
- Manufacturing space
- Institutional needs

In previous years, population trends have grown and expanded into different areas of the country as well as the state of Florida. Therefore, the ongoing need for qualified and competent industry service providers has increased as well.

OTHER PROFESSIONS THAT RELY ON THE REAL ESTATE BUSINESS

Where federal, state, and local laws can directly affect the procedural considerations of most real estate transactions, there are many other industry nuances that sellers and buyers experience. Therefore, sellers, buyers, landlords, and tenants all have a need for professional assistance.

Due to society's litigious overtones, property transactions have become more sophisticated and complex. The transactions' sophistication and complexity must be addressed and answered. Therefore, the real estate business has expanded to provide the answers. The need for expertise is addressed by various types of service providers. Today, property transactions will probably include a team of professionals whose sole purpose is to assist in completing the transaction. Within any property transaction, you could expect to see one or more service providers assisting with the deal.

The following are just a few examples of transaction-oriented professionals involved with a purchase/sale or lease transaction:

- Real estate agent—Assists a buyer, seller, landlord, or tenant in the acquisition or disposition of real property.
- Attorney—Reviews legal documents primarily for the protection of a buyer, seller, landlord, or tenant.

- Certified public accountant—Advises a buyer, seller, landlord, or tenant as to the income tax ramifications of any transaction.
- Title company—Charges an insurance premium for issuance of title coverage, which is the policy that protects a buyer from defects to the title transferred by the selling party.
- Architect/engineer—Assists the buyer with:
  - Construction/structural design services
  - Decorative services
  - Municipal property violation correction services

Where there may be an array of other service providers involved in any one transaction, this list highlights the transactional players of any given deal.

In order to protect the general public from potential loss because of the acts of others performing certain transactional duties, many of these industries are regulated in some manner. For example, any service provider in a regulated industry is required to responsibly discharge her role within a transaction. The service provider can and will be held accountable for her actions or for failing to deliver the appropriate service within her job role. This may be enforced by the industry's regulatory agency or by the damaged party's rights under a civil lawsuit.

REAL ESTATE AND THE NATION'S ECONOMY

Today, most real estate transactions are performed by licensed real estate professionals. Although real estate involves a variety of different activities and transactions, the most common and active market is residential housing. As a result, the **brokerage** end of the business contains the majority of real estate licensees. Brokerage can be defined as the business of bringing together buyers and sellers or landlords and tenants for a fee. The fee is generally paid in the form of a commission.

Real estate agents are no different than other business people. They perform acquisition and disposition services in exchange for a fee. In many cases, agents are compensated in the form of commission. This will usually result in the broker receiving an agreed-upon percentage of the final sales price. However, this does not preclude the parties from entering into:

- Flat fee arrangements
- Fee for service, as provided
- Any other valuable consideration that is exchanged for services

In Florida, when one performs a real estate act (as defined under the Florida Statutes) for another, for compensation or in anticipation of compensation or any other valuable consideration, he or she must be licensed as one of the following:

- Broker
- Sales associate (within the employ of a broker)

In any Florida **residential transaction**, a licensee may be employed by a buyer, seller, landlord, or tenant as any one of the following:

- Transaction broker
- No representation/facilitator of the transaction
- Single agent working for a seller, buyer, landlord, or tenant (but never more than one party within any residential transaction)

Coaching Tips: **Although this will also be addressed in more detail later, it is important for the reader to understand that in Florida, a residential transaction is defined as any transaction involving the sale or leasing of a property that contains four or fewer units intended for dwelling purposes. This definition is expanded to include ten acres or less of agricultural property.**

Any transaction for the sale or lease of real property containing greater than four units or more than ten acres of agricultural property is considered to be a **commercial transaction**. The purchaser of the property is deemed to be holding same for investment purposes rather than as an owner occupant transaction.

Example

Consider a five-unit residential property where the buyer intends on living in one of the units while leasing out the other four. Regardless of the buyer residing in one unit, this example would still be considered a commercial transaction.

The reader should not confuse the definition of residential property provided within zoning regulations. Under zoning, residential property is a class or category type that defines and determines the property's lawful use.

The reader should also note that from state to state (with some variation), the definition of a residential transaction is used extensively by lending institutions. This enables the lender to determine whether or not the property will be used for owner-occupant purposes. Pursuant to the loan origination process, this enables the lender to determine the appropriate interest rate to charge the borrower. This may be in addition to any other loan underwriting technique that the lender may use.

BROKERAGE SPECIALTY TYPES

The future use of a property determines its type and category. Conventional real property (non-single-purpose/nongovernmental) can be broken down into four basic property group-types. Each property group has various subgroupings. The following best describes how properties are categorized and subcategorized:

- Residential
  - Single-family homes
  - Townhouses
  - Multifamily
    - Cooperative
    - Condominium
    - Rental income producing
- Commercial
  - Office
  - Retail
  - Professional/medical
  - Garage/parking
- Manufacturing
  - Heavy industrial (factories)
  - Light manufacturing
  - Loft/storage (warehouses)
- Mixed-use
  - Flex properties

REAL ESTATE BROKERAGE

The **real estate brokerage** (the business of bringing together buyers and sellers and landlords and tenants for a fee) business consists of two primary services:

- Sales
- Leasing

Everyone needs a roof over their head. It is for that reason that residential real estate tends to be the more active of markets. Real property sales are generated by two driving forces:

- The owner-occupant
- The investor

Some people purchase residential property for the sole purpose of becoming an owner-occupant of the property. The property may be used as a primary residence or as a secondary residence (weekend or vacation home). Others may find an investment haven through real property ownership.

There are many specialties in the real estate brokerage business. A licensee might choose to specialize in any of the following areas:

- Residential—This part of real estate practice contains the most licensees. Chapter 475, Florida Statutes (F.S.), defines residential property as any transaction involving the sale or leasing of a property that contains four or fewer units intended for dwelling purposes. This would include unimproved land or lots to be improved to contain four or fewer units intended for dwelling purposes. The definition is expanded to include ten acres or less of agricultural property. Knowledge in this area will warrant a local awareness of demographics, infrastructure, services and amenities, property taxes, utilities, and countless other items.

- Commercial—These transactions usually involve investment properties. Participating in commercial transactions requires the sales associate be well educated and versed in a variety of other subjects. The licensee must possess an expertise that may or may not arise in a residential transaction. In order to achieve success in this arena, the licensee must have an acute awareness of the valuation process, finance, and leasing markets. Simply put, any licensee involved in this facet of the business must have problem-solving skills.

- Industrial—This field requires a licensee to be familiar with the needs of industry. This includes the understanding of transportation issues, availability of raw materials, and utilities necessary for manufacturing of goods and products. Activity within this area may include independent sites, industrial parks, and unimproved land for future development and expansion.

- **Agricultural/Farm Area**—This specialty area requires skills from the licensee that the previous property types may not require. To best communicate with the constituency in this field, a licensee may need direct knowledge of farming operations and costs. Chapter 475, F.S., defines agricultural property as any property consisting of greater than ten acres.

- Business brokerage—This area of brokerage can be highly lucrative and complicated, and involves a valuation process based upon the income attributable to the business in question. Knowledge and understanding in the use of financial statements becomes critical in achieving success.

Depending on staff size, market, and geographic location, a brokerage firm can take on many forms of operation. For example:

- Small firms consist of sales staff of 1–5 people
- Boutique firms consist of sales staff of 6–19 people
- Mid-size firms consist of sales staff of 20–100 people
- Larger institutional firms consist of greater than 100 people

As the business realizes its specialty area of expertise, it will simultaneously focus its sales promotion and efforts toward that core direction. It is the core business that enables the real estate firm to evolve into a diverse-services organization. In order to accomplish this (not so easy) feat, the brokerage firm needs to identify:

- Their geographic area of coverage
- Specialty services

It is the geographic area and types of specialty services that a firm will provide that enable its sales staff to succeed. Careful selection is required to ensure success. Not all brokers choose urban or central business areas as their primary focus. In rural sections, agriculture and farming fuel both micro- and macroeconomies. Regardless of location or primary area of expertise and servicing, knowledge of the product market becomes essential. This would include assembling and maintaining databases of properties within the selected area as well as information critical to marketing to that area. It is market knowledge that affords the broker the ability to market his services to others seeking those services. Although market knowledge and name recognition through branding becomes critical to the success of an organization, the business tends to be more of a "who you know before you get to show what you know." It is critical to become familiar with individuals or clientele within a constituency. This is usually achieved via networking or actual market activity on the part of the organization.

THE SALES PROCESS AND THE SALES LICENSEE

Real estate is a complicated and sophisticated business. The broker (in most cases) will act as an agent for one party or the other. An agent acts as an intermediary between the parties and performs duties on behalf of the party that the agent represents. The term *agent* is defined as one who transacts business on behalf of another within a relationship of trust. Sales staff work for the broker and provide services to buyers and sellers. This requires expert knowledge. It is essential that the sales associate have a clear understanding of the steps associated with a sales transaction. Therefore, it is important to illustrate the steps associated with a typical sale.

Step 1—Canvassing for Product

As in any sales arena, one needs to match a product to someone who needs the product. This may include the listing of properties for sale or lease, or businesses for sale.

Step 2—Canvassing for the Product Buyer/User

This part of the process tends to be a little more challenging. The sales associate must find the "right lid to fit the right barrel." This is a process of hard work and good marketing skills.

Step 3—Showing the Property

The sales associate requires appropriate knowledge of the product as well as good people-handling skills.

Step 4—Submission and Negotiating of the Offer

This step can be critical to the success of any transaction. Regardless of the agent's opinion of an offer, all offers as directed must be submitted for the other party's consideration.

Step 5—Execution of a Sales Contract

If all has gone well, both parties will sign a sales contract.

Step 6—Closing of the Sales Contract

In this step, the parties to the contract may be charged with the execution of various tasks and responsibilities. Examples include but are not limited to the following:

The buyer

- Arranging for necessary financing to conclude the transaction. This will include:
  - Credit approval and underwriting
  - Property appraisal
  - Property survey
  - Any other item that the lender requires prior to extending a financing commitment

The seller

- Ensuring that she has marketable title
- Deed preparation and any other item required for the closing to occur

Step 7—Recording Activities

If all goes well, the closing takes place and the deed issued to the buyer is usually recorded with the county clerk to provide protection for the buyer against any future claims by others to the property.

PROPERTY MANAGEMENT

The way a property is managed determines the appearance and ultimate success of an investment project. It is truly a hands-on activity. Not all investors that own income-producing properties have the time or the expertise to devote to a project. As a direct result of these **absentee owners**, the need for professional management services has grown dramatically with the popularity of investing in income-producing property.

There are two primary service functions within the **property management** field:

1. Operations—This includes the day-to-day operation of the property. It includes knowledge of mechanical systems, the ability to make repairs, implementing preventative-maintenance measures, and remodeling and decorative upgrades to enhance the property's appearance and desirability to renters.

2. Financial Reporting—Investors in income-producing real property do not invest in "brick and mortar." They purchase and invest in cash-flow operations. It is the property's cash flow that generates the investor's return on his invested capital. *Therefore, real property, like stocks and bonds, act as mere vehicles that house cash flow.* As such, the property manager is charged with the responsibility of reporting the property's financial activity. This may be as often as monthly or bimonthly reports. Financial reporting includes submitting accounting records in the form of general ledger reports. This activity includes collecting rents, annual budgeting, financial analysis, setting profit goals, and recognizing financing opportunities. Financial reporting offers the ownership the ability to make educated and informed decisions concerning the property.

Property management services are compensated in a variety of ways. In most cases, the management firm receives a percentage of the effective gross income (actual income collected after taking into account any vacancy) attributable to the property. Other fee arrangements might include flat fees, annual per square foot amount, or increased income performance requirements. The type of compensation is determined by the property owner and the management firm. The scope of work and how the manager will be compensated is always detailed in the management contract.

APPRAISAL

Appraisal is one of the most vital areas of real estate practice. Appraisal can be defined as an opinion of value that is based upon certain facts as of a given date. That date is referred to as the effective date or as of date. An appraiser is usually hired for the purpose of valuing a property. There are many driving reasons why appraisals are conducted; however, most appraisals are conducted for the purposes of sale or purchase.

In Florida, appraisers are regulated by the Florida Real Estate Appraisal Board. Appraisers are also required to abide by the **Uniform Standards of Professional Appraisal Practice (USPAP)**. Where the Appraisal Board is empowered to regulate the activities of all state-certified, licensed, and registered appraisers, USPAP provides standards for how appraisers accomplish their assignments. Although the definition of a real estate broker under the Florida Statutes includes the right to appraise real property for compensation, unless licensed as an appraiser, a real estate broker may not present herself as a state-certified, licensed, or registered appraiser. More importantly, only state-certified, licensed, and registered appraisers may render appraisals on federally related transactions. This minimizes the type of transactions that a real estate licensee may be involved in. A federally related transaction (as defined by the Federal Institutions Reform Recovery and Enforcement Act of 1989 [FIRREA]) is defined as a real property transaction involving a lending institution insured by the federal government where preparation of an appraisal is required as a precursor for loan consideration and underwriting. This type of transaction includes transaction values of greater than $250,000 where real property is hypothecated (pledged) as security for the repayment of a loan.

In the normal course of conducting business, a real estate broker is often asked by a seller to render an opinion of value by examining recently sold properties, listings of properties currently on the market, and previous expired-listing information. The preparation of a **comparative market analysis (CMA)** provides the seller with vital market information. It is this type of information the seller will use when setting the selling price of his property. Even though the licensee may use similar techniques as an appraiser to determine the value of a property, the two are different. A CMA will primarily focus on the marketing/price setting of a particular property while an appraisal will strictly focus on *value*. This is critical to lenders, sellers, and buyers. This is the primary reason a CMA may never be referred to or represented as an appraisal. Most real estate brokerage firms offer CMAs for free as a selling tool to obtain a listing; however, firms are not prohibited from charging a fee for a CMA.

Appraisers are governed by the rules of ethics covered within USPAP. An appraiser should not have any ownership interest in the appraisal assignment. It should always be an arms-length transaction.

FINANCING AND THE REAL PROPERTY TRANSACTION

If every purchaser of real property could pay cash for the purchase, transactions would be simplified. However, that is not realistic or probable. A majority of purchase and sales transactions involve financing of the property in one way or another. It is critical that the licensee has a good understanding of how financing works. Whereby mortgage brokers in Florida must hold a current and valid mortgage broker license to engage in that practice, a sales associate should know the costs associated with borrowing funds. This can only aid the licensee in successfully concluding a sale.

DEVELOPMENT AND CONSTRUCTION
Land Acquisition/Subdividing and Construction

To quote one of our nation's earliest and wealthiest real estate entrepreneurs, John J. Astor, "Buy by the acre and sell by the lot."

This quote reflects the business of subdividing large parcels of land into smaller ones for sale. There are subdividers and there are builders. Where all subdividers may be builders, not all builders are involved in the subdivision process. This process requires the division and planning (zoning permitting) of larger parcels of land into smaller buildable lots. The ability to create streets and the availability of utilities to the area are prime essentials for any subdivider. It is no secret that development costs exceed the original cost for land. We refer to the costs associated with land acquisition and development as hard costs. Before a subdivision is created and sold, it must be approved by the local municipality. This requires the subdivider to prepare and submit a **plat map of subdivision** for review by the municipality. The plat map acts as a visual rendering of the proposed development. Streets, building lots, water, sewer, and public utilities are often the subject of the rendering. In order to provide municipal service of the common areas (i.e., sanitation, street cleaning), namely the streets, the subdivider will grant the municipality ownership of the streets through a process called **dedication**. Dedication can be defined as private property given by an owner for the public's use. It is important to know that not all dedication of private property is accepted by the municipality. Acceptance by the municipality obligates the public body to provide vital services to that area. In certain places throughout the country, municipalities are only required to accept dedications for mapped streets.

When a subdivision reaches the development stage, developers will most often include and record **restrictive covenants**. These covenants are designed to create a means of conformity within a particular subdivision. Examples include setback requirements, size minimum square footage requirements, property use(s), and in most cases the architectural design of the improvement. These restrictive covenants assure the developer that property value for the sale of the last available lots is realized verses the first one that was sold.

It is at this point that the construction process begins. Construction is performed by a licensed contractor. Residential construction can be seen in three types of residential construction:

1. Speculative homes—The builder constructs these homes in anticipation of an active market without having buyers in hand. Where the spec home may act as a marketing tool for the builder (a model), this is a risky area of the construction business.

2. Tract homes—These are similar to spec buildings. Numerous models are finished with size and design differences intentionally created.

3. Custom homes—These homes contain custom designs and usually include the input of either the buyer or her architect.

With the exception of custom houses, timing is crucial to the developer. The outlay of cash combined with the carrying costs of loans to construct requires a massive marketing campaign to sell these homes. This may call for the developer to enlist and engage the services of outsourced real estate licensees. Not all developers employ in-house sales staff to complete the sale of their inventory.

GOVERNMENT'S ROLE
Federal Government

Real property transactions are influenced by the federal government's activities. There are two direct factors that affect purchase considerations. Interest rates and income tax policies in particular will influence real estate markets nationally. In forthcoming chapters we will learn more about the federal government's influence. We will also take a closer look at some of its agencies, namely, the Internal Revenue Service (IRS), the Department of Veterans Affairs (VA), and the Department of Housing and Urban Development (HUD).

State Government

State government activities range from being vast owners of public property to custodians of coastal property. In addition, the state occupies leased space in privately owned properties. There are three types of transfer taxes paid on the sale of real property. This includes all transfers of property. These taxes are paid to the state. They include:

1. Documentary stamps on the deed

2. Documentary stamps on the note

3. Intangible tax on (new) mortgage money introduced to the transaction

We will discuss this in greater detail in later chapters.

Local Government

Local government's role in real property transactions include the right to:

- Assess property taxes
- Limit the bulk and use of property through zoning regulations
- Issue building permits

PROFESSIONAL ORGANIZATIONS

Professional organizations provide services to their constituents. In most cases, they provide and promote seminars for career building, print and circulate newsletters to their members, and conduct courses in ethics practice as well as other necessary continuing education for the real estate professional. Additionally, organizations like the National Association of Realtors (NAR) and the Florida Association of Realtors (FAR) further provide very important government-lobbying services. It is these services that protect the nature, interests, and integrity of the real estate licensee.

NAR is a national association that on a local basis comprises the board of Realtors. One must apply to become a member. Unfortunately, membership is company based. Therefore, if a company or brokerage is accepted for membership, the licensees of that company or brokerage are required to join as well. Individual membership without company or brokerage membership is currently unavailable. As a large national organization, NAR also has the ability and clout to create affinity group programs. This may include group health coverage, car rental discounts, and many other perks.

Coaching Tips: Throughout this course, you will encounter terminology involving parties to a transaction. You may or may not be familiar with the identity of the party being referenced. A helpful tool to resolve that problem is

The "OR" "EE" Rule.

A good way to remember which party is which in a transaction would be to use the "OR" "EE" rule. Words that end in "OR" are the owners or givers of whatever is owned or being given. Words that end in "EE" are the receivers of whatever is owned and being given.

There are no exceptions to this rule other than one spelling exception. The word *employer* falls under the category of "OR" because it ends in the letter "r." Employers are still the provider of employment.

SUMMARY

The real estate business contains other areas of the trade outside of sales. Even though the sales market tends to be the most active and thereby the most populated part of the real estate industry, an applicant for a real estate license should also be aware of other specialty areas of the real estate profession. In addition, professional organizations are created to service their constituents and strive to enhance the information pool provided on an industry level. They also provide education to licensees. This enables licensees to stay on top of day-to-day nuances and changes that arise.

REVIEW QUESTIONS

1. Charles, a Florida real estate licensee, is employed to appraise property for an FHA loan. Charles:
   a. Can do this if he is a broker.
   b. Cannot appraise property with a real estate license.
   c. Must hold a state appraisal license for this activity.
   d. Must follow the Uniform Standards of Professional Appraisal Practice (USPAP).

2. Which of the following is NOT a residential property transaction?
   a. Sale of a duplex
   b. Sale of three agricultural acres
   c. Sale of a vacant lot in a subdivision
   d. Sale of a ten-unit residential apartment building

3. Property management has grown dramatically as part of the real estate profession in Florida, principally because of:
   a. An increase in the state's population.
   b. The opening of more retail stores.
   c. The rising sale of condominiums.
   d. Absentee ownership and the popularity of investments in income-producing property.

4. The purpose of subdivision restrictive covenants is to:
   a. Control the quality of the homes in order to maintain values within the subdivision.
   b. Limit the maximum of square feet allowed for improvements.
   c. Define the numbers of household composition.
   d. Set the ratio of land cost to development.

5. Which of these statements is FALSE about a comparative market analysis (CMA)?
   a. A CMA may never be referred to as an appraisal.
   b. Licensees use CMAs as marketing tools.
   c. No one may charge for a CMA.
   d. A CMA focuses on the market price of a property.

6. The developer signed over the streets in the subdivision to the city. This is an example of:
   a. Restrictive covenants.
   b. Land acquisition.
   c. Subdividing.
   d. Dedication.

7. The purpose of recording a deed is to:
   a. Fulfill legal requirements.
   b. Protect the rightful property owner against present and future claims of ownership by others.
   c. Prevent liens.
   d. Ensure the title is marketable.

8. A state-licensed appraiser charged a seller "1 percent of the appraised value of the property" as part of the agreement. This action is:
   a. A conflict of interest.
   b. Not a legal practice.
   c. Standard practice in Florida.
   d. A USPAP requirement.

9. ABC Development builds homes and advertises the properties in brochures and newspapers, and on billboards. This is an example of:
   a. Custom building.
   b. Tract building.
   c. Spec building.
   d. Primary market activity.

10. State government affects the real estate industry by establishing:
    a. Zoning laws.
    b. Transfer taxes.
    c. Building moratoriums.
    d. Air-quality standards.

11. A builder wants to find if Mediterranean-style homes are allowed in an existing subdivision. The builder could find this information in the:
    a. Zoning requirements.
    b. Building codes.
    c. Restrictive covenants.
    d. Commerce codes.

12. A real estate licensee can appraise property for compensation for a nonfederally related transaction:
    a. As long as she calls the appraisal a CMA.
    b. Only if she is licensed as an appraiser.
    c. If the licensee is listing the property.
    d. If she does not refer to herself as an appraiser.

13. A business broker in Florida:
    a. Must be a real estate broker.
    b. Holds a business broker license.
    c. Focuses on sales promotion and advertising.
    d. Cannot deal in residential property for others.

14. Teresa just received her first license as a sales associate, and she wants to join the local board of Realtors. Teresa:
    a. Can join by paying a membership fee and quarterly dues.
    b. Can join when her license is activated.
    c. Must be a broker to join the board of Realtors.
    d. Must work for a firm that is a board member.

15. Which of the following is a function of local government?
    a. Property tax
    b. Interest rates
    c. Building codes
    d. Intangible tax

16. A company that reports the financial activity for a particular property and bears the responsibility for maximizing the profit for the property owner is engaged in:
    a. "Farming" the area.
    b. Industrial development.
    c. Property management.
    d. Public accounting.

17. Maria's dad owns four lots in Florida and has moved to another state. The dad asked Maria to sell his lots and promised if she sold three, he would give her the remaining lot. She quickly accepted. She sold two of the lots, but could not sell the third lot. Her dad did not give her the fourth lot. Which of the following is true?
    a. If Maria receives a lot, a license is required.
    b. Maria did this for her dad, so no license is required.
    c. There was no compensation so no license is required.
    d. Maria has broken Florida real estate laws.

18. A real estate licensee who is well versed in transportation issues could specialize in dealing with which of these properties?
    a. Commercial
    b. Industrial
    c. Business
    d. Residential

19. Most firms engaged in the real estate profession in Florida deal with:
    a. Residential properties because it is the most active market.
    b. Industrial properties as more and more industries relocate to Florida.
    c. Commercial properties because this is where the big money is.
    d. Agricultural properties because agribusiness is the largest industry in Florida.

20. A licensed mortgage broker:
    a. Originates loans.
    b. Services loans.
    c. Sells loans for others.
    d. Acts as a financial intermediary who brings borrowers and lenders together for a fee.

Chapter 2

KEY TERMS

broker

broker associate

caveat emptor

compensation

deficiency letter

Florida residency

irrevocable consent to service

license

mutual recognition agreement

nolo contendere

registration

Rule 61J2-26.002

sales associate

LEARNING OBJECTIVES

After completing this lesson, you will be able to:

- Know the purpose of the license law and identify the qualifications for a sales associate's license.
- Identify license application requirements, including nonresident requirements.
- Understand the importance of fully disclosing background information on an application.
- Identify what education is required prior to obtaining a license as well as post-licensing responsibilities.
- Understand the various categories of licensure and identify real estate services.
- Understand the exemptions to license law.
- Appreciate the difference between a license and a registration.
- Understand mutual recognition as it applies to Florida licensure.

License Law and Qualifications for Licensure

HISTORICAL PERSPECTIVE

In 1923 many states, including Florida, enacted license laws governing real estate activities. Prior to this point, the expression **caveat emptor,** the Latin term for "let the buyer beware," was prevalent in the real estate marketplace. However, it wasn't until 1925 that Florida lawmakers created and empowered what is known today as the Florida Real Estate Commission (FREC). The structure and function of FREC will be discussed in Chapter 3.

Generally speaking, licensing laws were originally created primarily to protect the general public against financial losses resulting from acts involving:

- Fraud
- Dishonesty
- Incompetency of individuals transacting on behalf of others

Today, each state in the United States has adopted and enacted its own license law.

License law requires any licensee representing another in a real estate transaction (particularly where **compensation** is involved) to be held at a higher standard than that of the general public. Compensation is defined as a payment, something of value that is tangible or intangible. In essence, the licensee is held accountable for any infraction of the license law. This process is policed through the governing body regulating and enforcing the license law. If necessary, this enforcing body administers disciplinary action on any licensee. Where license law was designed primarily to protect the public against fraud, dishonesty, and incompetency, it is *not* used to prescribe or regulate commission rates charged by service providers such as brokers. License law is also *not* used to protect buyers from sellers.

CATEGORIES OF LICENSURE

FREC has two categories of real estate licenses. The categories are:

1. Broker
2. Sales associate

However, as a subcategory of broker, it should be noted that a broker associate is an individual who has qualified to be a broker but chooses to work under the direction of another broker. This will be discussed later within this chapter.

LICENSURE REQUIREMENTS FOR SALES ASSOCIATE

In order to qualify for a license as a **sales associate** (one who assists a broker in the disposition of his/her business duties) in the state of Florida, you must:

- Be at least 18 years of age
- Hold a high school diploma or equivalent
- Be honest and of trustworthy character
- Be mentally competent
- Successfully complete a FREC-approved 63-hour qualifying course (entitled FREC Course I) through any Florida accredited school authorized by FREC to administer prelicense courses
- Pass the state sales associate license exam with a grade of at least 75 percent
- Obtain the signature of a sponsoring broker on the application
- Pay the required license fee

Let's examine three of these sales associate requirements in more detail.

Be Honest and of Trustworthy Character

In order to be considered honest and of trustworthy character, certain disclosures are required. For example, if the applicant had a problem in the past (e.g., convicted of a crime), honest and trustworthy character can be demonstrated to the licensing body by the applicant's full cooperation and disclosure of all facts that would normally affect the ability to qualify as a licensee. Depending on the applicant's past, the level of cooperation through the applicant's disclosure may be viewed by the regulatory body as an act or sign of that person's character. This may or may not be a mitigating factor in successfully obtaining a real estate license.

An applicant must make full disclosure if the applicant has ever:

- Been convicted of a crime
- Pleaded guilty or **nolo contendere** to a charge (*nolo contendere* means the person does not dispute the charges but does not admit any guilt)

This disclosure applies to any felony, misdemeanor, or traffic offenses (except traffic signal, parking, speeding, or inspection violations). This disclosure is required without regard to whether the applicant was placed on probation, had adjudication withheld, was paroled, or was pardoned. (*Adjudication withheld* means that the person is placed on probation; if probation is successfully completed, the conviction is not entered into the records.) Failure on the part of the applicant to fully disclose such events may render the applicant ineligible to receive a license. If the applicant has fraudulently received a license, failing to make the appropriate disclosures would be grounds for immediate revocation of the license. This type of behavior may subject the individual to other civil or criminal liability, as well as disciplinary action by the appropriate regulatory body.

In addition to disclosing any felony, misdemeanor, or traffic offenses, an applicant must make other disclosures, including if the applicant:

- Has previously operated under another name or alias
- Has ever been denied a license, permit, or registration to practice any regulated profession in Florida or any other jurisdiction

- Has ever had a license, permit, or other registration revoked in Florida or any other jurisdiction
- Is currently residing in a mental health facility or similar institution

We just examined one requirement for obtaining a sales associate's license—being honest and trustworthy.

We will now look at two other requirements—completing a FREC-approved 63-hour qualifying course (entitled FREC Course I) and paying the required fee.

Coaching Tips: **Completion of FREC Course I can be done in a variety of ways:**

- **Online approved course**
- **Classroom**
  - **In English with the class final and state exam in English**
  - **In Spanish with the class final and state exam in Spanish**

Complete a FREC-Approved 63-Hour Qualifying Course

The course breaks down into 60-hours of instruction plus a 3-hour final exam. The passing grade for the state exam is 75 percent, but the passing grade for the course exam is 70 percent. In the event the student fails the final exam, the student is entitled to a one-time retest. This may only be accomplished after waiting for at least a 30-day period from the previous failed exam. The exam (which must be a different exam then that of the first failed exam) must be retaken no later than 1 year from the time of the original exam. If the student does not take the make-up exam within this 1-year period, or takes and fails the make-up exam, the student must repeat FREC Course I.

Pay the Required Fee

FREC charges various licensure fees, such as initial license fees, subsequent renewal fees, and exam fees that are paid directly to the testing vendor (currently Promissor).Because fees are subject to change at any time, please consult the Division of Real Estate (DRE) and the testing vendor at the time of application for the current amount.

Additional Requirement: Postlicense Education

Within the first license cycle following issuance (which may be no less than 18 months or more than 2 years after initial licensure), a licensed sales associate must complete additional FREC-approved education. The licensee is issued a conditional license that is subject to the completion of additional postlicense education. This education must equal a total of 45 hours in order for the sales associate to renew his license. The course can be completed in a classroom environment or online. In either case, the licensee must also pass an examination covering the postlicense course material. If the student fails the final exam, a one-time retest can be taken, but only after waiting for at least a 30-day period from the previous failed exam. The retest must be taken no later than 1 year from the time of the original exam. As another option, the student may choose to retake the postlicense course.

If the licensee fails to complete the course by the end of the first license renewal period, her license becomes null and void. To return to real estate practice, the individual must retake the sales associate's prelicense course (FREC Course I) and pass the state exam.

LICENSURE REQUIREMENTS: BROKER AND BROKER ASSOCIATE

In addition to meeting all of the requirements to obtain a sales associate's license, a broker or broker associate applicant must also:

- Successfully complete FREC Course II, which is an approved 72-hour qualifying course, through any Florida accredited school authorized by FREC to administer prelicense courses. This course can be administered in a classroom environment or online.

  o For any individual who has not held a previous real estate license, this 72-hour course is in addition to the 63-hour sales associate's qualifying course and the mandatory 45-hour sales associate's postlicense course. However, it is important to note that if an applicant has previously held a real estate license in another state, jurisdiction, or country, and if an applicant can prove at least 1 year of active licensing within the previous 5 years from that state, jurisdiction, or country, the applicant is exempt from taking FREC Course I and the sales associate postlicensing courses.

- Successfully pass the state broker license exam with a grade of at least 75 percent

Also, a sales associate licensed in Florida must complete the sales associate's postlicense education as well as hold a current and valid license to be eligible for a broker license.

In addition, an applicant for a broker or broker associate's license must meet a certain experience requirement. This experience requirement is considered satisfied by FREC when the applicant has achieved one of the following:

- Has held a valid and *active* sales associate's license under a broker for at least 1 year within the preceding 5 years, or

- Has held a valid and *active* broker's license for at least 1 year within the preceding 5 years in another state, or

- The applicant has held a valid and active real estate sales associate's license for at least 1 year during the preceding 5 years while in the employ of a governmental agency for a salary and performing the duties as authorized in Chapter 475, F.S.

Coaching Tips: Florida recognizes and accepts the experience of any person who has previously held or is the holder of an active sales associate, broker associate, or broker's license in Florida *or* any other state for at least 1 year within the preceding 5 years.

As just mentioned, to obtain a broker's license, an applicant must have held a valid and active real estate license for at least 1 year during the previous 5 years. You should know that a person holding a valid and active sales associate license for at least 6 months is permitted to *enroll* in FREC Course II (the broker qualifying course). However it should be understood that the person will not be eligible to *receive* a Florida broker's license prior to satisfying the entire 1-year experience requirement.

Additional Requirement: Postlicense Education

Within 2 years after initial licensure, a licensed broker must complete additional FREC-approved education. This education must equal a total of 60 hours in order to renew the broker license. The course can be completed in a classroom or online. In either case, the licensee must also pass an exam covering the postlicense course material. In the event the student fails the final exam, a one-time retest can be taken, but only after waiting for at least a 30-day period from the previous failed exam. The retest must be taken no later than 1 year from the time of the original exam. As another option, the student may choose to retake the postlicense course.

If licensee fails to complete the course by the end of the first license renewal period, the licensee's broker license becomes null and void (this term will be discussed in Chapter 3 in greater detail). If the broker's license becomes null and void and the licensee wishes to act as a *sales associate,* the licensee may do so but only after providing proof of completion of 14 hours of continuing education (described later) within 6 months following expiration of the broker's license. If the licensee wishes to act as a *broker,* the licensee must retake the broker's prelicense course and pass the state broker exam.

Coaching Tips: **The 60-hour broker postlicense education is offered in two separate 30-hour courses.**

LICENSURE REQUIREMENTS: APPLICATION

Any person who wishes to receive a license must complete and submit a completed application form. After the application is submitted, a 30-day period is allowed to check for any errors or omissions on the application. The applicant will be notified that the application was either approved or denied within 90 days. Currently, an approval notification is given to the applicant by Promissor. This notification will also describe the process required for the applicant to sit for the exam.

LICENSURE REQUIREMENTS: EXAMINATION

As mentioned earlier, an applicant for a broker, broker associate, or sales associate's license must pass an examination administered by the state. There is an exam fee, which is paid to the approved testing agency. It is the approved testing agency that will arrange for the individual to sit for a computer-based test. If the applicant fails the exam, the applicant may retake the exam as many times as necessary in order to pass. However, the exam must be passed within the EARLIER of either:

- 2 years from when the applicant was issued a transcript for the successful completion of the prelicense requirements from the approved school
- 2 years from the time of receiving, from FREC, an approved application permitting the applicant to sit for the state exam

---

Coaching Tips: **Currently the law requires electronic fingerprinting. However, an applicant that is a nonresident of Florida should send the DRE fingerprint card to Promissor's Denver office. At present time, the address is:**

Florida Division of Real Estate
c/o Promissor, Inc.
P.O. Box 173679
Denver, CO 80217-0701
As companies do relocate from time to time, the nonresident applicant should contact Promissor to confirm their current address prior to submission of the fingerprint card The required fee should be submitted with the fingerprint card. Due to the constant change in fees, the applicant should check in advance to confirm the fee charged at the time of application.

Applications for licensure are good for 2 years. However, the applicant must take the test at least once within 1 year from the time that the application was approved. Failure to do so will require the applicant to reapply and for the reapplication to be approved before sitting for the state exam.

Each time an applicant retakes the exam, the required examination fee must be paid. There are two types of state exams:

1. The sales associate exam
2. The broker exam

The sales associate exam consists of 100 multiple-choice questions worth 1 point each.

The exam is broken down by category in the following manner:

- 45 questions test Florida real estate law
- 45 questions test principles and practices of real estate
- 10 questions test math skills

The broker exam consists of 95 multiple-choice questions. Ninety questions are worth one 1 point each, while five closing statement questions are worth 2 points each.

The exam is broken down by category in the following manner:

- 40 questions test Florida real estate law
- 45 questions test Florida principles and practices of real estate
- 5 questions test math skills
- 5 questions test the applicant's ability to complete a composite closing statement problem (this is not a typical HUD closing statement)

LICENSURE REQUIREMENTS: NONRESIDENT LICENSURE

Any person considered a nonresident of Florida may apply for a Florida real estate license. A nonresident is anyone who does not physically reside in Florida for the statutory period required to create Florida residency. The establishment of **Florida residency** is covered by **Rule 61J2-26.002**. This rule states that one is a Florida resident after residing in Florida continuously for four calendar months or more within a calendar year. This definition would also include one's intent to reside for four calendar months or more within a calendar year. Residency can be established irrespective of residing in a:

- Hotel
- Rental unit
- Mobile home/recreation vehicle

In order to receive a Florida real estate broker or sales associate license, every nonresident applicant must meet the same requirements as a resident applicant, including:

- Completion of all prelicense requirements
- Passing the state exam
- Paying the required license fee

In addition, a nonresident applicant must file a completed **irrevocable consent to service** form. Consent to service means that the nonresident applicant designates the director of the Florida Division of Real Estate as the recipient of any legal notices against the nonresident. In the event that a legitimate complaint is filed against the nonresident licensee, a copy of the legal notice will be sent to the nonresident. This form also states that any lawsuits against the nonresident licensee may be filed in any county in Florida in which the plaintiff resides. The Irrevocable consent to service form is included in the Forms Appendix

LICENSURE VIA MUTUAL RECOGNITION

If already licensed in another state, a nonresident may be able to obtain a Florida license without taking the prelicense course. This is true for licensees who reside in a state where Florida has a **mutual recognition agreement**.

Under such an agreement, Florida will mutually recognize the education and experience that a licensee has obtained by holding a real estate license in another state. Currently, Florida shares mutual recognition agreements with ten other states.

These states include:

1. Alabama
2. Arkansas
3. Colorado
4. Georgia
5. Indiana
6. Kentucky
7. Mississippi
8. Nebraska
9. Oklahoma
10. Tennessee
11. Connecticut

Mutual recognition is possible only for residents of states that offer Florida residents the same license privileges in exchange. If a licensee from a mutual recognition state wishes to obtain a Florida real estate license, the licensee must:

- Pass a 40-question exam covering Florida real estate law with a grade of 75 percent or higher
- Complete an irrevocable consent to service form
- Submit a fully completed application
- Pay the required license fee
- Submit a certification of license history from her home state, which:
  - Acts as proof of licensure within that state
  - Indicates how she obtained a license in that given state
  - States how long she has held a license (taking into consideration that in some states, records are destroyed after approximately 7 years)
  - Indicates to the DRE whether or not the licensee has had any previous disciplinary action assessed to her license

LICENSE RENEWAL

After a real estate license has been issued, the license must be renewed periodically. The license-renewal period is 2 years.

In Florida and in any calendar year, there are two license-expiration dates:

1. March 31
2. September 30

When an original license is issued, the license will expire on the nearest renewal date under 2 years. After that, the license-renewal period is every 2 years.

For example, an initial license issued on November 1, 2005, will expire on September 30, 2007. Thereafter, the license will expire every 2 years on September 30.

License renewal will be covered in greater detail in Chapter 3.

LICENSURE, LICENSE RENEWAL, AND CONTINUING EDUCATION

As mentioned earlier, the license period is 2 years for brokers, broker associate, and sales associates. Before the end of the first renewal period after initial licensure, a licensee must complete postlicense education (45 hours for sales associates and 60 hours for brokers). However, during the second and all subsequent renewal periods, the licensee has the responsibility to complete all continuing education requirements. *Prior* to renewing or being eligible to renew the license, a licensee must complete at least 14 hours of FREC-approved continuing education courses (unless otherwise exempt under the law).

The continuing education requirement may be accomplished in several ways:

- 14 in-class hours of prescribed and approved education—no end-of-course exam required
- 14 hours of prescribed and approved education satisfied by completing an approved correspondence/distance learning course containing an end-of-course exam with a passing grade of 80 percent or better

The 14 hours of prescribed education break down as follows:

1. 3 hours of core law (Core law includes a review of real estate law as well as updates to current law.)
2. 11 hours of FREC-approved specialty courses (This section is offered by local boards and a variety of real estate schools. If a licensee attends a FREC meeting, he can earn 3 hours [*specialty course hours and not core law hours*] of continuing education credit toward his 14-hour requirement.)

Coaching Tips: **Providers of continuing education courses are required to electronically report to the DRE a student roster of those who have successfully completed the course(s). Reporting must occur:**

- **Within 30 days from the date of course completion, or**
- **By month's end if it is a renewal month**

As of September 2006, the DRE will not issue a renewal unless the licensee has successfully completed the required education. Presently, the DRE will issue the licensee a letter stating that renewal is denied due to insufficient education. In addition, any licensee who has not successfully completed the required continuing education will be issued a **deficiency letter**. This letter informs the licensee that he/she has not completed the required continuing education prior to license renewal.

LICENSURE, LICENSE RENEWAL, AND CONTINUING EDUCATION EXEMPTIONS

Some individuals are exempt from continuing education requirements:

- A licensee who is currently a member of the U.S. Armed Forces is exempt from license-renewal requirements, including continuing education, while serving on active duty. The licensee has up to 6 months from release of duty to renew the license without penalty or loss of license. In addition, if the spouse of any active member of the military (particularly one who is serving active duty in a place outside Florida) is also a current holder of a valid real estate license, both licensees will have 6 months after release from active duty to renew their licenses without loss or penalty. The aforementioned exemption will ONLY hold true if the licensee is not active in the practice of real estate during this period.
- Active members of the Florida Bar are exempt from continuing education requirements. However, they are *not* exempt from the postlicense requirements.

IMPORTANT STATE LAWS

Florida law clearly defines who must be licensed. The student should know that:

- Chapter 455 of the Florida Statutes (455, F.S.) regulates professions and occupations
- Chapter 475 of the Florida Statutes (475, F.S.) is known as the real estate license law

- Chapter 61J2 of the Florida Statutes (61J2, F.S.) provides the rules of the Florida Real Estate Commission as to how real estate activities by a licensee may lawfully occur
- Chapter 120 of the Florida Statutes (120, F.S.) is the Administrative Procedures Act

Where 61J2, F.S. provides the rules for the disposition of a licensee's duties, the licensing and disciplinary process is outlined in Chapter 120.

LICENSES AND REGISTRATIONS

Real estate licenses and registrations are similar to that of motor vehicles licenses. For example, a driver's license is issued only to an *individual* who has successfully completed all education and exams (written and driver's test) to drive a motor vehicle; a registration is thereby issued to the *vehicle* itself. The driver's license allows the individual to operate the vehicle while the registration allows the vehicle to be driven on the roadways.

Real estate **licenses** (permission from the state to operate as a real estate agent) are only given to *individuals*. As we have discovered earlier, in order to obtain a real estate license in Florida, one must complete necessary education as well as qualify to sit for and pass an exam. Therefore, **registrations** are given to business entities. A registration can be defined as the official placement of a real estate brokerage business or practice within the records of the Florida Department of Business Regulation (DBPR). Think of the business entity as the *vehicle* that houses or holds the license for the licensee.

Registrations can include some of the following:

- Business entities
- Offices and branch offices
- Persons registered as officers and directors of real estate corporations
- Persons registered as partners in real estate
  - General partnerships
  - Limited partnerships

Office and branch office registrations result in the issuance of a license to perform activities only at the registered location. Any change in address would require notification to the DRE and require a new registration. Issued licenses resulting from a registration are not transferable.

WHO MUST HOLD A REAL ESTATE LICENSE
Broker

A real estate **broker** is defined as any person, corporation, partnership, limited liability partnership, or limited liability company who performs a real estate act for another, in exchange for or in anticipation of compensation or other valuable consideration.

The following activities require a real estate broker's license:

- Buying, selling, leasing, renting, or exchanging real property
- Buying, selling, leasing, renting, or exchanging business enterprises or business opportunities
- Buying, selling, leasing, renting, or exchanging mineral rights
- Soliciting prospects for any of these functions
- Negotiating for any of these functions
- Advertising for any of these functions

- Appraising real property
- Auctioning real property
- Providing rental lists or rental information

A broker may operate a business under a trade name (fictitious name) by registering that name with FREC. All real estate brokers are responsible for the activities of the broker associates and sales associates within their employ. It is the principal broker's responsibility to continuously supervise the activities of all licensees engaged in real estate activities within her employ. This responsibility is applicable whether the individual is categorized as an independent contractor or as an employee. Independent contractor versus employee status only refers to how income is taxed by the Internal Revenue Service (IRS).

Broker Associate

A **broker associate** is a person who is licensed as a real estate broker but, rather than forming his own business, chooses to work under the name and supervision of another broker. Although the licensee holds a real estate broker's license, he operates within the organization performing sales associate duties and activities on behalf of the broker. A broker associate or sales associate may be issued a license as a professional corporation if the licensee provides FREC with proper authorization from the Department of State. However, this election is for tax and liability purposes and is not intended for the broker associate to run a brokerage company and/or hire other sales associates.

Sales Associate

A **sales associate** is a person associated with a licensed real estate broker who assists in performing services offered by the broker. A sales associate is licensed to work for, and act as a representative of, the broker. A sales associate may be issued a license as a professional corporation if the licensee provides FREC with proper authorization from the Department of State. As stated above, this election is for tax and liability purposes and is not intended for the sales associate to run a brokerage company and/or hire other sales associates. A sales associate performs real estate activities previously described within the definition of a real estate broker. A sales associate must be under constant supervision by a principal broker who is responsible for the sales associate's activities while engaged and registered within the broker's employ.

A sales associate:

- May assist in any of the services performed or to be performed by a licensed broker
- May *only* work in the name of the licensed principal employing broker, an owner/developer, or a governmental agency. However, if the sales associate wishes to become a broker, only employment by a broker counts toward the 1-year experience requirement.
- May *only* work while under the supervision of a licensed principal employing broker
- May *never* accept compensation or any valuable consideration of any type directly or indirectly from anyone other than her principal employing broker

LICENSURE: WHO IS EXEMPT FROM LICENSE LAW?

We just looked at the activities that require a real estate broker's license. However, some individuals are exempt from licensing requirements even though they may perform the services of a broker. Under Florida license law, the following persons are exempt from license law requirements:

- Owners of real property transacting in real estate strictly for their own account
- A corporation, partnership, or other entity when selling, exchanging, or leasing its own property
  - This exemption does not exist if an agent, employee, or independent contractor receives compensation (other than a salary) in the form of commission or the individual is compensated on a transactional basis.
- Anyone who sells cemetery lots
- An attorney-in-fact under a duly authorized power of attorney to carry out a specific real estate transaction
- Those persons appointed or acting under a court order while disposing of those duties under the order (i.e., receiver, trustee in a bankruptcy, etc.)
- A person who is authorized to act as:
  - An executor or administrator of a will
  - A trustee under a deed of trust or trust agreement
- Authorized employees of a government agency, utility company, or railroad, while acting in the conduct of official business
- A salaried employee of an owner of an apartment (or the owner's registered broker) who is employed on the premises to lease the property
- Anyone who rents rooms in public lodging establishments (e.g., hotels and motels) for temporary occupancy
- A salaried employee acting as a manager for a condominium or cooperative who rents individual units, if the units are rented for periods of 1 year or less
- A property management firm or owner of an apartment complex who pays a finder's fee or referral fee to a tenant, if the value does not exceed $50. The finder's fee or referral fee may be cash, credit toward the tenant's rent, or another item of value.
- The owner of a time-share, for the owner's own use and occupancy, who later resells the time-share
- Certified public accountants performing services within the scope of the accounting profession
- A depository institution selling, exchanging, buying, or renting a business enterprise to or from an accredited investor
- An appraiser who is registered, licensed, or certified under Part II of Chapter 475 of the Florida Statutes (the portion addressing appraisers) and who performs appraisals in accordance with that statute
- A full-time graduate student in a FREC-approved college or university program, who is acting under direct supervision of a broker or appraiser and is performing tasks related to the educational program
- Attorneys performing services within the scope of the legal profession
  - However, in Florida, any attorney who seeks to engage personally or employ other sales associates under her supervision must comply with the license law by obtaining a real estate broker's license. To do so, the attorney must meet experience requirements, complete education requirements, pass the state exam, and pay the required fees.
  - In addition, any attorney wishing to operate under any name other than that of the individual must also comply with the Florida Fictitious Name Act by:
    - Paying the appropriate license fees
    - Registering and clearing any fictitious name(s) with the DRE
    - Having the license issued under the registered fictitious name or entity

---

Coaching Tips: In Florida, if an applicant has received a 4-year degree in real estate, he is exempt from pre- and postlicensing requirements. In addition, accepted members into the Florida Bar are exempt *only* from taking the sales associate prelicensing course.

SUMMARY

License laws came about in the early 1920s in order to protect the general public. In order to be a holder of a real estate license in Florida, and in conjunction with all applicable laws, every applicant must qualify through education and testing requirements. Once an individual receives a license, each licensee is charged with the responsibility of completing the required postlicense education. Nonresidents are able to achieve licensing in Florida; however, in addition to all other requirements, the applicant must complete an irrevocable consent to service form, which designates the director of the Florida Division of Real Estate as the recipient of any legal notices against the nonresident. Mutual recognition is an agreement entered into between states allowing residents of one state to receive licenses in the other state. Finally, anyone who performs a real estate act (as defined by state law) must be a holder of a valid real estate license.

REVIEW QUESTIONS

1. Florida real estate laws are passed by the legislature primarily to:
   a. Limit the number of licensees.
   b. Protect buyers from sellers.
   c. Protect the general public.
   d. Protect licensees from fraudulent actions.

2. An applicant for a real estate license must reveal, if relevant:
   a. Maiden name.
   b. Speeding tickets.
   c. Parking tickets.
   d. Proof of citizenship.

3. Michael is licensed in a mutual recognition state and is applying for a Florida real estate license. In order to qualify he must:
   a. Successfully pass a prelicense course.
   b. Complete the postlicensing class.
   c. Pass a 40-question test about Florida laws.
   d. Become a resident of Florida.

4. Kesha is registered as a broker associate. Which statement is true about Kesha?
   a. She has a broker associate license.
   b. Kesha is inactive.
   c. A broker associate license is used to operate a real estate business.
   d. Kesha works for a broker or an owner developer.

5. Which of the following people require a real estate license?
   a. Jim sells cemetery lots for a cemetery association.
   b. Sara receives a salary to manage an apartment complex.
   c. Hugh leases interests in businesses.
   d. Bill helps buyers finance the purchase of condos.

6. Jim is licensed and works for ABC Realty. Jim worked especially hard to sell Ms. Smith's home and she was very grateful. To show her appreciation, Ms. Smith gives and Jim accepts $100 to take his wife out to dinner. According to Florida laws:
   a. This is fine as long as Jim tells his broker.
   b. Jim has violated Chapter 475, F.S.
   c. Ms. Smith is the seller. She can compensate Jim.
   d. Jim must keep written records and report gifts received from clients.

7. A sales associate wants to apply for a broker license. The associate:
   a. Can do this at any time after receiving a sales license.
   b. Can apply after completing a minimum number of transactions.
   c. Cannot apply until 1 year passes after being licensed.
   d. Can apply after working for a broker for 1 year.

8. Diane lives in Tampa and sells homes for XYZ Development Corp. If Diane moves to Georgia and continues to work for the developer, Diane must:
   a. Stop working for the developer in Florida.
   b. Hold a Georgia license to work for the developer.
   c. Do nothing. A license isn't needed to work for a developer.
   d. Within 60 days send the irrevocable consent to service form to the DRE and conform to all nonresident requirements.

9. Fred received his first sales license November 29, 2007. His license expires:
   a. November 30, 2009.
   b. September 30, 2009.
   c. March 31, 2009.
   d. January 31, 2009.

10. A sales associate works during the week for Acme Realty, and shows model homes on weekends for an owner-developer.
    a. This is legal if both employers are registered with FREC.
    b. Only broker associates can have more than one employer.
    c. The associate is engaged in illegal activity.
    d. A license is not required to work for an owner-developer.

11. To qualify as a resident for a real estate license, an applicant must:
    a. Live in Florida for 1 year prior to applying.
    b. Have a Florida mailing address.
    c. Have a Florida driver's license.
    d. Intend to live in Florida for at least 4 months in any calendar year.

12. A sales associate failed to complete the 45-hour postlicensing class. The associate wants to continue to practice real estate in Florida. The associate:
    a. Does not have a license and must start over.
    b. Can pay a $1,000 fine and complete the class after renewal.
    c. Must pay a late fee in order to renew.
    d. Will be disciplined by FREC.

13. In order to renew an initial broker license, the broker:
    a. Must complete 60 hours of broker postlicensing classes and successfully pass the exams.
    b. Can complete 14 hours of continuing education in order to renew.
    c. Must pass another state exam and have an active license.
    d. Cannot have a nonresident license.

14. Julio is an active real estate licensee in another state and he wants to acquire a broker license in Florida. Julio:
    a. Must acquire a Florida sales license before applying for a broker license in Florida.
    b. Must prove he has been actively licensed for at least 12 months in the past 5 years within the state where he is licensed when applying for a Florida broker license.
    c. Cannot apply for a broker license in Florida under any circumstances.
    d. Is a broker in another state so he can apply for a broker license in Florida.

15. Which of these persons is NOT exempt from FREC Course I?
    a. A practicing Florida attorney
    b. A person with a 4-year degree in real estate
    c. Persons paid on commission for renting motel rooms
    d. Anyone who advertises rentals for others

16. Rules and regulations passed by the Florida Real Estate Commission can be found in:
    a. F.S. 455.
    b. Chapter 475, F.S.
    c. Chapter 61J2, FAC.
    d. Florida Statute 83.

17. A California real estate licensee sold two lots she owned in Florida.
    a. The licensee has broken Florida real estate laws.
    b. A real estate license to sell your own property is not required.
    c. Mutual recognition agreements allow this practice.
    d. Sales associates from other states must have a real estate license in Florida. Brokers from other states do not.

18. Jacob has an uncle who helped him sell a vacant lot Jacob owned. This is the second time his uncle has helped him market a property. Jacob's uncle refuses all compensation. What is true about this situation?
    a. No compensation is involved therefore no license is required.
    b. Jacob's uncle must have a real estate license.
    c. Relatives can help other relatives with properties, for a fee without a real estate license.
    d. Both Jacob and his uncle are practicing real estate without a license.

19. Harold failed the exam for FREC Course I a second time. In order to take the exam again, Harold must:
    a. Reapply for the sales license.
    b. Retake the class.
    c. Pay the state an additional fee.
    d. Wait 1 year in order to retest.

20. The decision regarding the acceptance of a licensee's application for licensure is made by the:
    a. Division of Real Estate.
    b. Department of Business and Professional Regulation.
    c. Division of Licensure and Testing.
    d. Florida Real Estate Commission.

Chapter 3

KEY TERMS

active license

canceled

cease to be in force

Department of Business and
   Professional Regulation
   (DBPR)

Division of Real Estate (DRE)

Florida Real Estate Commission
   (FREC)

group license

inactive license

ineffective

involuntary inactive

multiple licenses

prima facie

void

voluntary inactive

LEARNING OBJECTIVES

After completing this lesson, you will be able to:

- Describe the makeup, qualifications, and appointment of the Florida Real
  Estate Commission.
- Know the powers as well as the duties of the Florida Real Estate Commission.
- Know the difference between active and inactive license status.
- Understand the regulations concerning involuntary inactive.
- Grasp the difference between void and ineffective licenses.
- Recognize the difference between multiple and group licenses.
- Know what can cause a license to be invalid.
- Understand what can cause a license to be canceled.
- Know the purpose of the Real Estate Education and Research Foundation.

License Law and Commission Rules

GOVERNING BODY AND ENFORCEMENT

There are two key regulatory agencies related to real estate licensing in Florida. They are the **Florida Real Estate Commission (FREC)** and the **Division of Real Estate (DRE).** FREC is the regulatory body whose purpose is to protect the general public by regulating:

- Real estate brokers
- Broker associates
- Sales associates
- Real estate schools; and
- Instructors

The DRE performs ministerial, administrative and all functions concerning the regulation of the real estate industry.

Today, both FREC and the DRE are administratively part of the **Department of Business and Professional Regulation (DBPR).** The DBPR is charged with regulating licensed professions and professionals within the state of Florida. There are many other departments that fall within the auspices of the DBPR ("Department").

Other divisions contained within the DBPR include:

- The Division of Technology—An outsource provider for exam development.
- The Division of Professions and Regulation—Responsible for administering and regulating professional boards. This division is also charged with the enforcement of regulated businesses.
- The Division of Service Operations and Licensure, which includes units such as:
  - The Bureau of Education and Testing—Oversees education course content and exams for the various regulated professions.
  - Central Intake Unit—Responsible for license application processing.
  - Central Customer Contact Center—Handles public inquiries from the general public.

Let's look at the functions of the Florida Real Estate Commission and the Division of Real Estate.

FUNCTIONS OF THE FLORIDA REAL ESTATE COMMISSION AND THE DIVISION OF REAL ESTATE

In order to simplify the reader's understanding of the functions of FREC and the DRE, it should be noted that they work in tandem with each other. A description of each one's role in licensing of professionals can be explained in the following way.

FREC is empowered by Florida Statutes to protect the general public. This is accomplished by regulating:

- Real estate brokers and real estate brokerage firms
- Broker associates
- Sales associates
- Real estate schools and instructors

The purpose is to foster the education of:

- Real estate licensees
- Permit holders

The powers and duties of FREC fall into three general areas of responsibilities:

1. *Executive powers* to regulate and enforce the license law
2. *Quasi-legislative responsibilities* that include the power to:
   - Enact and revise administrative rules and regulations
   - Interpret questions regarding the practice of real estate
3. *Quasi-judicial responsibilities* that include the power to:
   - Grant or deny license applications
   - Determine license law violations
   - Administer penalties

Although the DRE performs various functions that are related to the regulation of real estate in Florida, the DBPR employs all DRE personnel to support FREC activities.

In essence, FREC performs the required administrative functions required to protect the general public. The functions of FREC include regulating licensees through its ability to:

- Grant or deny a license or registration
- Suspend or revoke a license or registration
- Administer disciplinary action including but not limited to:
  - Fines
  - Other forms of disciplinary action, such as requiring the licensee to sit for education course work in addition to a fine. (This may be a necessary imposed action on the part of FREC in order to educate the licensee to avoid future infractions of license law.)

ADMINISTRATIVE PENALTIES

Violation of state license laws rules and regulations can result in administrative penalties. Penalties include:

- Denial of an application for licensure
- Refusal to renew a license

- Suspension of one's license for a period not to exceed 10 years
- Revocation of a license
- Fines of up to $5,000 for each violation of Chapter 475 (or separate offense) of the Florida Statutes (475, F.S., which applies to the regulation of real estate brokers, sales associates, and schools)
- Fines of up to $5,000 for each violation of Chapter 455 of the Florida Statutes (455, F.S., which applies to business and professional regulation)

In addition to administrative/monetary fines, criminal assessments may be applied for a first-degree misdemeanor. There is one offense that would fall into this category:

- Failing to provide accurate and current rental information

The penalty for these offenses consists of one or both of the following:

- Punishment of up to 1 year in jail
- A $1,000 fine

In addition, any violation of Chapter 475, or any lawful order, regulation, or rule is a second-degree misdemeanor. The penalty for a second-degree misdemeanor is one or both of the following:

- A fine not exceeding $500
- A prison term not to exceed 60 days

PRACTICING REAL ESTATE WITHOUT A LICENSE

Performing unlicensed real estate activities in Florida is a third-degree felony. The DBPR may issue fines of up to $5,000 per count. Violators may also have a cease and desist order issued to them by the DBPR when any statute pertaining to real estate has been violated.

Under Florida license law, any infraction of the law is deemed a misdemeanor. A jail sentence as a result of an infraction may only be administered by a court of law. FREC cannot impose a jail sentence. It is, therefore, FREC's responsibility to inform the attorney general's office if it knows or suspects a crime has been committed.

In addition to the previously mentioned activities, FREC has the following powers and duties:

- Adopt a seal that when placed on official documents will act as **prima facie** (on face value) evidence of the documents authenticity (Chapter 475.10, F.S.).
- Create or change (as the case may be) the rules and regulations that affect brokers, broker associates, sales associates, and authorized licensed real estate instructors (Chapter 475.05, F.S.).
- Create and mandate the required syllabus identifying the minimal and acceptable course content required for a person to hold a real estate license. In addition, FREC has the ability to create rules and regulations as to what schools may offer within approved course content (Chapter 475.04, F.S.).
- Create rules and regulations pertaining to license law that dictate the allowed practices and activities of a licensee. They have the power to discipline licensees (Chapter 475.25, F.S.). FREC is an administrative regulatory body that governs over all licensees under its jurisdiction. It has the power to inspect and audit brokers, broker associates, sales associates, and authorized licensed real estate

schools and instructors (Chapter 475.5016, F.S.). However, it is the DRE that actually carries out the rules, regulations, and policies of FREC.

- Administer the Florida Real Estate Commission Education and Research Foundation. The purpose of this foundation is to promote projects that educate licensees and the public in real estate matters.

- Create license fees and/or other miscellaneous fees associated with the holding of a Florida real estate license. Such fees include exam fees, initial license fees, and any Real Estate Recovery Fund assessment, if necessary. (The Real Estate Recovery Fund will be discussed in greater detail in Chapter 6.)

Coaching Tips: Because fees are subject to change at any time, please consult the DRE when you apply for a real estate license for the most updated amount.

As mentioned previously within this chapter, FREC is required to report all known or suspected criminal activities to the appropriate agencies for further investigation and/or prosecution. As a commission, FREC merely administers the license law (as it applies to all licensees). It is not permitted to impose criminal penal sanctions, such as prison sentencing.

While FREC has the power to create or change the rules and regulations that affect brokers, broker associates, sales associates, and authorized licensed real estate instructors, the DRE actually carries out the rules, regulations, and policies of FREC.

COMPOSITION, QUALIFICATIONS, AND COMPENSATION OF THE FLORIDA REAL ESTATE COMMISSION

The Florida Real Estate Commission is comprised of seven members. The seven members receive minimal compensation in the form of a minimal per diem amount plus any expense reimbursement relating to direct service performed on behalf of the Commission.

The makeup of the seven-member Florida Real Estate Commission consists of:

- Four members that must hold or have held active Florida real estate broker's licenses. An active license must be validly held by each member for a period not less than 5 years prior to serving on the Commission.

- Two members that must be individuals from the general public who have never held or been licensed as either a broker or sales associate.

- One member that must be either an active broker or sales associate. The active license status must be held by this member for at least 2 years prior to serving on the Commission.

At least one of the seven members of the Commission must be 60 years of age or older. The seven members of the Commission are appointed by the governor and serve a 4-year term. Term limits consist of not more than two consecutive terms. Commission meetings are held no fewer than 12 times per year.

The Commission and its members are accountable to the office of the presiding governor. The governor bears the responsibility of supervising the Commission and its members. As a result of their Commission responsibilities and activities, all seven Commission members receive total exculpation (release from blame or liability) from any civil claims that may result while in office and performing Commission service.

We have been looking at the duties and makeup of the Florida Real Estate Commission. Let's move on to another important regulatory entity—the DRE.

THE DIVISION OF REAL ESTATE (DRE)

Whereas the FREC is composed of appointees (individuals appointed by the governor), the Florida DRE is composed of state employees. The DRE is funded by fees assessed by the Commission. Aside from key investigative functions, the DRE also:

- Acts as the record keeper/file cabinet of the DBPR (e.g., maintaining records of each applicant exam, which is required to be kept and may not be disposed of for a period of 2 years subsequent to taking the examination, etc.)
- Provides exams necessary for licensure
- Provides support services to FREC, such as:
  o Legal services
  o Administrative services

Although the state capital of Florida is Tallahassee, the primary offices of both the DRE and FREC are located in Orlando. The DRE makeup consists of the following:

- Whereas Commission members are appointed by the governor, the director of the DRE is appointed by the Secretary of the Department.
- DRE workers are employed by the Department as ancillary to the support of FREC.

The DRE provides FREC with the essential information critical to its ability to carry out, administer, and enforce the license law. Enforcement of the law is a critical and necessary procedure to protect the general public. It is for this basic and primary reason that license law came into effect throughout the nation.

As mentioned previously, the DRE represents one of the divisions within the DBPR. The DRE performs various functions essential for FREC to carry out its duties. The DRE's primary and most important function that assists FREC in carrying out its duties is that of investigative-related services.

The investigative function of the DRE involves screening applicants when FREC is making a determination as to license issuance, as well as the investigation of potential violations by licensees. The DRE does *not* regulate commission rates.

ADDRESS REQUREMENTS

Although one does not need to be a Florida resident to hold a Florida real estate license, Chapter 455.275(1) requires that all licensees maintain an accurate and current mailing address with the DBPR. Post office boxes are deemed acceptable by the DBPR as a valid address. Licensees are required to immediately notify the DBPR of any change in their mailing address. Notification must be sent or received by the DBPR within 10 days from the change of address (rule 61J2-10.038). Failure to do so in a timely manner subjects the licensee to disciplinary action. This would include a citation and a $100 fine. In addition, licensees who do not reside in Florida must execute an irrevocable consent to service. A resident who relocates outside of Florida (becomes a nonresident) has 60 days to comply with all nonresident requirements (see Chapter 2).

LICENSE PERIODS

Unlike other states, Florida has two license issuance/expiration periods. A license will bear an issuance/expiration date of one of the following:

1. March 31
2. September 30

In either of these two cases, the license period is for 2 years with the exception of the first license issuance. The first issuance may be no less than 18 months and no greater than 24 months. This is primarily due to the applicable date of license issue. That date will be March 31 or September 30 of any given year.

LICENSE RENEWAL/MILITARY EXEMPTIONS

In order to renew a license, the required education applicable to that license must be completed. For example:

- A first-time renewal requires the licensee to complete the necessary *postlicense* education *prior to the submission of a renewal form.*
- For all other renewals (after the initial renewal), the licensee must complete 14-hours of prescribed FREC-approved continuing education. As in the initial renewal above, all education must be completed *prior to the submission of a renewal form.*

The licensee's signature on the renewal form acts in the form of an oath that the licensee has completed his education requirement in conjunction with state requirements. Any renewal that occurs after his license has expired subjects the licensee to a late fee.

Some individuals are exempt from renewal requirements. A licensee who is currently a member of the U.S. Armed Forces is exempt from license renewal requirements, including continuing education, while serving on active duty. The licensee will have up to 6 months from release of duty to renew the license without penalty or loss of license. In addition, if the spouse of any active member of the military (particularly one who is serving active duty in a place outside Florida) is also a current holder of a valid real estate license, both licensees will have 6 months after release from active duty to renew their licenses without loss or penalty. The aforementioned exemption will *only* hold true if the licensee is not active in the practice of real estate during this period.

MULTIPLE AND GROUP LICENSES

An owner-developer who owns property in the name of several entities may submit proof that such entities are so connected or affiliated that ownership is essentially held by the same individual(s). Any sales associate or broker associate working for the owner-developer may be issued a **group license**. In this situation, the licensee is considered to hold one license and to be working for one employer.

Florida allows a broker, but not a broker associate or sales associate, to hold more than one license at any one time. In Florida, any broker that holds more than one broker license at one time is termed as a holder of **multiple licenses**. A sales or broker associate may *not* work for more than one broker at any one time or hold more than one Florida license.

It should be noted that any licensee may hold licenses issued by other states.

ACTIVE LICENSE VS. INACTIVE LICENSE

We have previously examined different categories of licenses. In addition to other forms of holding a license in Florida, a licensee may place her license in one of the following two types of statuses:

1. Active status
2. Inactive status

An **active license** is where the licensee is actively engaged in real estate activities as defined by FREC. An **inactive license** is where the licensee is not actively engaged in real estate activities.

There are two forms of inactive licensing:

1. Voluntary inactive
2. Involuntary inactive

Voluntary inactive status exists when a licensee chooses this status; **involuntary inactive** status occurs automatically when a licensee fails to renew his license in a timely manner. This may also occur when a case for summary suspension is brought against a licensee. (Summary suspension will be discussed further in Chapter 6.)

Voluntary Inactive

This status exists when the licensee chooses this type of status. In doing so, the licensee:

- May *not* engage in any real estate activity that is defined as requiring an active license during this voluntary inactivity.
- May remain voluntary inactive indefinitely. This may be done so long as the licensee completes all required postlicense and continuing education (as the case may be) for the period necessary for the licensee to renew her license.
- May reactivate the license at any time by notifying FREC in writing by completing the required form.

Involuntary Inactive

This status occurs automatically when a licensee fails to renew his license in a timely manner (the procedures for renewing a license were discussed earlier in this chapter). The following applies when a licensee's status is involuntary inactive:

- The licensee may *not* engage in any real estate activity that requires an active license.
- The licensee may *not* remain in the involuntary inactive status indefinitely.
- The licensee must reactivate the license within 2 years following entry into the involuntary inactive status or subsequently face the license becoming null and void. Due to the severity of this implication, 90 days prior to the expiration of an involuntary inactive license, the licensee is notified by the DBPR as to this important deadline. Depending on the amount of involuntary inactivity time that has passed, the licensee can redeem and reactivate his license by completing the required continuing education as follows:
  - Fewer than 12 months—The licensee must complete *14 hours* of approved education.
  - Greater than 12 months and up to 24 months—The licensee must complete a *28-hour* FREC-approved education course.
- If the license becomes null and void and the licensee wishes to remain within the real estate industry, he would be required to repeat the entire prelicensing process.

VOID AND INEFFECTIVE LICENSES

A license is **void** when one of the following has occurred:

- The license has been expired for more than 24 months
- The license has been revoked following a disciplinary action

Whereby, void means that the action was involuntary in nature (i.e., failing to renew one's license on a timely basis rendering the license involuntary inactive, and taking no action to activate the license within 2 years subsequent to the inactivity renders that license null and void).

Revocation is an act that always occurs as a result of disciplinary action taken against the licensee. This act permanently removes the individual from the real estate profession as a licensed party. However, licenses are not permanently revoked in the following two exceptions:

1. An applicant for licensure files an application containing false information
2. Failing to complete continuing education requirements prior to executing a renewal for the forthcoming cycle.

A license that is **canceled** is considered void. This may occur when a licensee chooses to no longer conduct real estate activities. Cancellation of a license does not occur as a result of any disciplinary action.

A license is said to be **ineffective** under certain circumstances. This is not to say that a license does not exist; however, predicated on the circumstances specific to that individual, the licensee may not use it. The following are examples of an ineffective license:

- Voluntary inactivity
- Involuntary inactivity
- Revocation of license
- Suspension of license

Licenses that are issued by FREC, **cease to be in force** when notification (within 10 days from either event below has occurred) has not been received by FREC as a result of:

- Any relocation requiring notification of a change of address occurs
- A change of association occurs

REGISTRATION OF PROPRIETARY REAL ESTATE SCHOOLS

In Florida, all schools that intend on offering any type of prelicense curriculum must be registered and issued a permit. Exceptions to this rule include the following accredited institutions:

- Universities
- Colleges
- Community colleges

An owner of a proprietary real estate school must exercise caution when advertising. Any inappropriate advertising may subject the school owner's permit to suspension. Some of these include:

- Inaccurate, false, or misleading statements
- Promises or guarantees of employment where there are none provided by the school
- Providing a student with questions from previous state exams
- Offering refunds to a student who has failed the exam
- Offering a guarantee program for the passage of the state exam if the student enrolls in the school

THE REAL ESTATE EDUCATION AND RESEARCH FOUNDATION

The Real Estate Education and Research Foundation was created to develop and fund programs directly designed to further real estate research and education to both the general public and real estate licensees.

Created in 1985 by the state legislature, this foundation fell under the direct control of FREC. To further education of the real estate issues pertaining to Florida, the foundation seeks information from various people to accomplish its goal. This includes:

- Real estate schools
- Colleges and universities
- Real estate licensees
- The general public

SUMMARY

The Florida DRE provides investigative services, record-keeping services, and exam services and as a result of its functions, the DRE provides FREC with the essential information critical to their ability to carry out, administer, and enforce license law.

Enforcement of the law is a critical and necessary procedure to protect the general public. It is for this primary reason that license law came into effect throughout the nation. Today, each state in the United States has enacted its own license laws.

The FREC in essence:

- Performs the required administrative functions to protect the general public that include regulating licensees through the ability to:
  - Grant or deny a license or registration
  - Suspend or revoke a license or registration
  - Administer fines
  - Impose other forms of disciplinary action that may include but not be limited to items such as:
    - Requiring the licensee to sit for education course work in addition to a fine. This may be a necessary imposed action on the part of FREC in order to educate the licensee to avoid future infractions of license law.

REVIEW QUESTIONS

1. Sal works for ABC Realty in Tampa, Florida, but lives in Palm Harbor. Recently, Sal moved to Lutz, but still works for ABC Realty. Sal:
   a. Has 10 days to register his new address with the DBPR.
   b. Works in the same location. There is no paperwork.
   c. Must register the employer within 10 days.
   d. Has 60 days to notify the DBPR of an address change.

2. John is registered as the broker of record for three different companies. John:
   a. Is in violation of F.S., 475.
   b. Has a group license.
   c. Holds multiple licenses.
   d. Can have only one real estate license in Florida.

3. Jake has legally obtained a group license. This means Jake:
   a. Works for an owner-developer.
   b. Owns and operates more than one business.
   c. Supervises others in real estate matters.
   d. Is the broker of record for several employees.

4. Which of the statements below is FALSE about FREC?
   a. Commissioners only work for the Florida governor.
   b. Four commissioners must own and operate real estate businesses.
   c. One commissioner can work as a sales associate.
   d. Commissioners are employed by the state of Florida.

5. Kim and Kelly are married and both are real estate licensees. Kim was called to active duty with the National Guard, and Kelly left the state as a result. Which statement is true about their license renewals?
   a. Kim is exempt from renewal requirements but Kelly is not.
   b. They must renew their licenses within 6 months of Kim's discharge.
   c. There are no legal exceptions from license-renewal requirements.
   d. The licenses are automatically canceled.

6. Sonia is going to take a break from practicing real estate and informs her broker she will no longer be an employee.
   a. Her sales license will be canceled.
   b. The license is involuntarily inactive.
   c. The broker must report the change in employment.
   d. Sonia must inform the DRE within 10 days of the change.

7. Tyrone let his third licensee expire, but changed his mind 7 months later. In this situation, Tyrone:
   a. Must take FREC Course I and begin again.
   b. May complete a 28-hour continuing education course and reactivate his license.
   c. Has a license categorized as voluntary inactive.
   d. Holds an involuntarily inactive license.

8. Kaitlyn let her third license expire, but reconsidered 13 months later. Kaitlyn:
   a. Must take FREC Course I and begin again.
   b. May complete a 28-hour course and reactivate her license.
   c. Has a license labeled voluntary inactive.
   d. Has a canceled license.

9. George is the only broker for ABC Realty. George's license is suspended. The licenses of the associates registered as George's employees are:
   a. Involuntarily inactive.
   b. Automatically canceled.
   c. Null and void.
   d. Effective.

10. The offices of the Division of Real Estate, part of the Department of Business and Professional Regulation, are located in:
    a. The various real estate districts.
    b. Tallahassee.
    c. Orlando.
    d. Miami.

11. The content of all real estate exams is mandated by the:
    a. Department of Business and Professional Regulation.
    b. Division of Real Estate.
    c. Bureau of Education and Testing.
    d. Florida Real Estate Commission.

12. Broker Frank's broker's license expired 26 months ago. As a result, Frank:
    a. Has a null and void license.
    b. Can reactivate by completing a prescribed 28-hour course.
    c. Lost the broker license, but can practice as a sales associate.
    d. Must pay a late fee as well as the license fee to bring the license up to date.

13. Lila changed her address and has not notified the Florida Real Estate Commission. Lila's license:
    a. No longer exists.
    b. Is involuntarily inactive.
    c. Has been canceled.
    d. Is an effective license.

14. Members of the Florida Real Estate Commission are appointed by the governor for a period of:
  a. 1 year.
  b. 2 years.
  c. 4 years.
  d. 8 years.

15. Members of the Florida Real Estate Commission are currently paid:
  a. $51,000.
  b. Nothing.
  c. On a per diem basis.
  d. Expenses plus $50 a day when on Commission business.

16. One exception to permanent revocation of a license occurs when:
  a. A license was renewed prior to completing the required education.
  b. The cause of revocation was unlawful activity in another state.
  c. The individual can prove a change of character.
  d. A pardon and restoration of voting rights is obtained.

17. Osvaldo's broker lost her license and Osvaldo's license is involuntarily inactive. In order to have a valid real estate license at this point, Osvaldo:
  a. Must take the state-licensing exam again.
  b. Can reassociate with a new broker as an employer.
  c. Must wait 30 days for a new broker to be appointed.
  d. Must file an exception before 30 days pass.

18. The Florida Real Estate Commission's powers and duties would include all the these activities EXCEPT:
  a. Adopting a seal that is evidence in court that a document is legal.
  b. Writing rules that become legal requirements for real estate practitioners.
  c. Revising administrative rules about the practice of real estate.
  d. Keeping the Commission's records.

19. Florida Real Estate Commission meetings require the presence of a quorum of members and must occur:
  a. Biannually.
  b. Quarterly.
  c. Monthly.
  d. Bimonthly.

20. Susan was so busy moving to her new house that she forgot to notify the DBPR of her change of address. When she realized her lapse, she sent in her new address with a sincere letter of apology.
  a. A citation with a $100 fine will be issued.
  b. This is OK because this was an accident.
  c. Susan's license is subject to a 60-day suspension.
  d. The license is involuntarily inactive.

Chapter 4

KEY TERMS

agency

agency coupled with an interest

agent

caveat emptor

consent to transition

customer

designated sales associates

dual agency

fiduciary

general agency

limited confidentiality

limited representation

nonrepresentation

principal (client)

residential sale

single agent

special agency

transaction broker

universal agency

LEARNING OBJECTIVES

After completing this lesson, you will be able to:

- Describe the provisions that directly apply to the Brokerage Relationship Disclosure Act including any exemptions to the act.
- Define a residential transaction.
- Define several terms related to an agency relationship.
- Characterize three types of agency relationships.
- Describe the duties owed under the various authorized agency relationships.
- Specify the methods by which an agency can be created.
- Describe the ways an agency can be terminated.
- Describe the disclosures that are required by each agency relationship.
- Describe a designated sales associate and the required disclosures of a designated sales associate in a nonresidential transaction.

Law of Agency– Relationships and Disclosures

LAW OF AGENCY

On October 1, 1997, Florida enacted the Florida Brokerage Relationship Disclosure Act. The act has since been modified and amended several times. The Florida Brokerage Relationship Disclosure Act was created to provide clarity to the consumer about the relationships between licensees and buyers and sellers in real estate transactions. This was achieved via required disclosures on the part of a licensee.

Any person who transacts business activities on behalf of another is commonly referred to as an **agent**. The activities of an agent are regulated and governed by the law of agency.

Most of our real estate terminology is derived from the old English feudal system. As a result of time and progress, laws concerning how agency relationships are derived and treated stem from two primary types of prevailing law:

1. Statutory Law
2. Common Law

Statutory Law

Statutory law is a derivative of the legislative procedure toward creation of law. It is law that is enacted via state legislature. Any person working on behalf of another, as an agent, will fall under the auspices of the state law of agency. In addition to the aforementioned, Florida Real Estate Commission (FREC) rules will also come into play and will dictate how an agent may operate within an agency relationship in Florida.

Common Law

Where statutory law is legislatively enacted and created, common law is derived from case law, or in other words, from the courts. Cases heard by the courts resulted in judgments. Today, it is these judgments that guide us in interpreting agency activities as well as dispute resolution. Irrespective of common law, the student should be aware that statutory law can supercede that of common law.

FIGURE 4.1

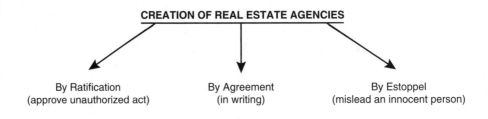

CREATION OF REAL ESTATE AGENCIES

By Ratification
(approve unauthorized act)

By Agreement
(in writing)

By Estoppel
(mislead an innocent person)

AGENCY—RELATIONSHIPS DEFINED

An agent is someone who is hired to transact business on behalf of another.

An agent:

- Is employed by another person
- In some cases, has the legal authority to act on behalf of and bind that person
- Has the authority to exercise some degree of discretion while acting for the other person

Some examples of agents would include:

- A real estate broker acting for a homeowner to sell a home
- A lawyer representing a client
- An investment manager who invests someone else's money

The person who hires or appoints an agent to act on her behalf is called the **principal** or the **client**. The **customer** is the third party in a transaction. An **agency** is the name for the relationship created between the agent and the principal. An agency relationship is created by employing the agent under a contract (see Figure 4.1). For example, when a real estate broker obtains a listing to sell a home, the broker has an agency that allows him to act for the homeowner. Please note that the term *agency* does not refer to a business but to the relationship between the agent and the principal (see Figure 4.2).

The principal/client is:

- The party who hires the licensee
- The party with whom the licensee enters into an authorized brokerage relationship

Responsibilities to the Principal

When an agency relationship is created, the agent takes on fiduciary responsibilities to the principal. As a result of these fiduciary responsibilities, the agent is often referred to as a **fiduciary**. This means that the agent:

- Owes loyalty to the principal
- Must act in the principal's best interest

FIGURE 4.2

REAL ESTATE AGENCY

Principal		Agent		Third party
Seller	Appoints →	Real Estate Broker	To find →	Buyer

An agent's responsibilities to the principal consist of the following:

- Loyalty
- Obedience
- Disclosure
- Accountability
- Care
- Confidentiality

Let's look at these responsibilities in more detail.

Loyalty

In an agency relationship, the agent's fiduciary responsibilities include providing the principal with undivided loyalty. This means that the interest of the principal comes before all others. The interests of the agent are secondary to that of the principal. Let's examine this duty of loyalty as it applies to a real estate agent.

If an agent works for a seller, the agent occupies a position of trust that requires loyalty to the seller. This means that the agent must always act in the best interest of the seller. It further requires placing the seller's interest above all others including those of the agent. To safeguard the interests of the seller, the law prohibits several specific acts that would represent a failure to be loyal to the seller. An agent is prohibited from:

- Making a secret profit
- Violating the seller's confidence
- Failing to disclose the purchaser's identity
- Acting as a dual agent
- Acting in an undisclosed dual capacity
- Holding an offer to purchase

An agent is prohibited from receiving any additional fee or profit over and above the commission *unless* it is done with the knowledge and consent of the seller.

Example

A seller lists a house for sale for $100,000 with a broker. A purchaser wants to buy the house for a lower price and offers the broker $500 if the broker convinces the seller to sell the house for $95,000. The broker may not legally accept such an offer.

Obedience

The agent must follow all of the principal's instructions as long as the instructions are:

- Legal
- Ethical
- Reasonable

Coaching Tips: When a principal insists that an agent obey the performance of an illegal act, the agent is directed to withdraw completely from the relationship. In addition, the agent may not substitute his judgment or opinion for that of the principal.

Disclosure

The agent is required at all times to fully disclose to all interested parties within a transaction all material facts concerning or affecting (adversely or otherwise) the value of the property in question. This disclosure must take place prior to the parties entering into a contract of sale and purchase. Failure to disclose will result in disciplinary action against the licensee committing the violation. *All* offers, written or otherwise, must be submitted promptly. When more than one written offer is received, all offers must be submitted in one sitting. The agent may present the offers in any order she deems fit for the principal. The agent is not allowed to hold one offer in the expectation of receiving another offer later, even if it would be a better offer.

Accountability

An agent is responsible for an accounting and/or the remittance of all valuable consideration belonging to others that is entrusted to the agent. This further includes maintaining:

- Appropriate books and records
- Evidence of all receipts or expenditures from an agent escrow (trust) account

Care

The agent should not be negligent in the disposition of his obligations within the relationship. The broker is a licensed professional and, as such, is expected to exert due diligence in performing on the principal's behalf. Failure to do so is considered negligence. When a licensee is acting on behalf of a principal, the licensee must exercise extreme care when disposing of his duties. The agent must possess skill while simultaneously exercising required diligence.

Confidentiality

When information concerning the principal is entrusted with the agent, the agent may not divulge to another party any information that would be deemed sensitive in nature to the principal without the principal's prior consent. In particular, this would include any information that could or would adversely affect the principal's position within a transaction.

Coaching Tips: **A good rule to follow is** *never say or mention anything concerning the principal in her absence that you would not mention or say in her presence.*

One convenient memory device for remembering the fiduciary responsibilities that an agent owes to a principal under an agency relationship is to remember the mnemonic LOW PAIN:

- *L*oyalty to the principal
- *O*bedience to the principal
- *W*ritten offers must be submitted
- *P*ersonally act for the principal
- *A*ccount for all monies
- *I*nform the principal of all material facts
- *N*ot be negligent

Responsibilities to the Customer

The customer in a transaction:

- May be a potential buyer or seller of real property
- May or may not be represented by a real estate licensee

As you learned earlier, the agent always has a fiduciary responsibility to his principal. In addition to the responsibilities to the principal, the agent (broker) is bound by certain duties to third parties. When dealing with third parties, also termed *customers*, the agent's responsibilities are more limited than those owed to the principal. This is primarily due to the agency relationship that exists between the principal and the agent. As previously mentioned, an agent must provide undivided loyalty to his principal. However, the agent also owes the following primary responsibilities to the customer:

- Honesty
- Fair dealing
- Accountability
- Full disclosure

These responsibilities are always required of an agent in dealing with a third party. The third party is usually a prospective buyer with whom the broker deals. When dealing with a buyer, the seller's agent should:

- Deal:
  ○ Honestly
  ○ Fairly
  ○ In good faith
- Account for all funds that are entrusted to her
- Disclose all material facts known to agent concerning:
  ○ The value of the property
  ○ The desirability of the property

In Florida, the precedent-setting court case *Johnson vs. Davis* provides that a *seller* of residential property (property that includes one- to four-family units) is required to disclose to a buyer any known defects to or within the property that would affect the value of that property. In addition, Florida statutes require that a real estate *licensee* disclose to all interested parties within the transaction any known or suspected defects to the property or its condition that would affect the value of that property. This disclosure must take place prior to the parties entering into a contract of sale and purchase.

As just mentioned, all material facts about the subject property must be communicated to the prospective buyer. Facts must be disclosed even if they are detrimental to the principal (the seller). This applies to all material facts that are known to the broker or should have been known to the broker. Some sellers have the mistaken notion that selling a property "as is" relieves them of any obligation to disclose defects. This is not the case.

Selling "as is" does *not* mean that the seller or her agent has the right to withhold any information about known defects that might affect the buyer's decision to buy. When a property is sold "as is," it only means that the seller is selling without agreeing to correct any known defects that exist. In the past, the real estate brokerage profession operated in a legal environment that can be succinctly described by the legal phrase **caveat emptor** which is Latin for "let the buyer beware." Caveat emptor, or buyer beware, describes a general legal environment in which the burden of obtaining information about a property was almost entirely the buyer's responsibility, not the seller or her agent. Under caveat emptor, for example, an agent working for the seller was under no obligation to voluntarily disclose pertinent information about a property to the buyer. The agent was bound only to tell the truth when he said anything about the property, but was not obligated to say anything. If the buyer wanted to obtain pertinent information about the property, it was her responsibility to get it herself. During the last half of the twentieth century, caveat emptor was gradually replaced by an environment that was much more favorable to the buyer. In today's environment, the broker has a much greater responsibility to safeguard the interests of the buyer as the customer, even if the broker represents the seller as the client.

As previously stated, when a licensee enters into an authorized agency relationship:

- The licensee is referred to as an agent who is hired to transact business on behalf of another.
- An agent is governed by strict laws and rules concerning that relationship.
- A customer may or may not be represented by a real estate licensee.
- A principal is always represented by a licensee.

Coaching Tips:

- An agent transacts on behalf of his principal and no one else within the same transaction.
- The principal or the client employs the agent to bring the customer to the bargaining table.
- The customer is the third party to the transaction that the agent is hired to bring to the principal.
- If the principal is the buyer, the customer is the seller.
- If the principal is the seller, the customer is the buyer.
- All of these statements apply to transactions involving leased spaces as well.

When an agency relationship is created, the agent takes on what are referred to as fiduciary responsibilities. These responsibilities will be discussed in greater detail further within this chapter. A fiduciary is best defined as someone within an agency relationship who is granted a position of the highest form of trust. The agent is then considered a fiduciary. Because an agent is defined as one transacting business on behalf of another (usually for compensation of some sort), the term *fiduciary* is synonymous with that of an agent. Therefore, it is safe to conclude that all agents are fiduciaries. It is the fiduciary's job to ensure that the interests of her principal are maintained when dealing with others. It is for this reason that an arm's-length relationship should exist with third parties. In this type of situation, the term *caveat emptor* certainly applies to those third parties.

TYPES OF AGENCIES

When we examine the various types of agents, it is important to note that the level or scope of authority extended to an agent is the sole determining factor as to which type of agency category the relationship falls within. Therefore, there are three major types of agencies:

1. Universal
2. General
3. Special

Universal Agency

In a **universal agency**, the agent is given the legal authority to transact matters of *all* types for the principal. Universal agencies are extremely rare and discouraged by the courts because the agent's powers are so broad. One of the few examples of this type of agency has become more visible recently in professional sports. Many athletes are hiring universal agents who have the authority to:

- Negotiate salary with a team owner
- Select and manage all the player's investments
- Negotiate endorsement contracts

Another example of a universal agent is a person responsible for taking care of an elderly family member who no longer can look after herself. This may include:

- Handling of bank accounts
- Sale of real and/or personal property
- Any other matter requiring decision or action

General Agency

The second type of agency is a **general agency**. A general agent is authorized to act for the principal in a specific business or trade. Unlike a universal agency where the universal agent transacts on all matters for his principal, a general agency allows the agent to transact on all matters concerning one or more matters. Some examples of general agency include:

- A real estate sales associate who is a general agent for the broker in the real estate business
- A property manager who manages property for the owner
- A sales representative in any field who sells products for a company

Special Agency

The third type of agency is a **special agency**. In a special agency, the agent is authorized to perform a specific act or transaction. A very narrow scope of authority is granted to the agent. Some examples of special agency include:

- A real estate broker who is authorized to sell a home
- A person who has power of attorney to sign a deed for someone

In the first example, the agent merely receives the assignment of bringing prospective buyers to the table for her seller. Unlike the universal and the general agent, a special agent may not bind the principal within this relationship. Special agents operate within a narrow scope of authority. This agency relationship is created by the listing agreement. It also is limited to one transaction—selling the property.

Coaching Tips: There is a fourth type of agency category that exists called an agency coupled with an interest. Although this agency is not as common as the previous three, the student should have a practical understanding of its existence as well as its meaning. This type of relationship exists when an agent has some form of interest within the property in question.

For example, a developer wishes to construct an office building for income-producing purposes. Whereby construction and completion dictates the project obtain some form of financing, the developer engages the agent to procure financing in exchange for the exclusive right to lease and manage the property upon its completion. Obviously, the appointment cannot legitimately commence prior to construction and completion of the building. Provided that the agent is successful in arranging financing of the project, this type of agency relationship:

- Is nonterminable by the death of the developer/principal
- May not be revoked by the principal

Coaching Tips:

- A universal agency is the broadest in scope of the different agency types.
- A general agency is more limited than a universal agency.
- A special agency is much more limited than a general or universal agency.
- Power of attorney can create a universal or general agency.
- A broker under a listing agreement has a special agency with his principal.

THE FLORIDA BROKERAGE RELATIONSHIP DISCLOSURE ACT

Practically speaking, there has been confusion on the part of the general public as to whose interests are being served in any given real property transaction. Anyone who has previously engaged the services of a real estate agent may at some point have felt that same confusion. As a result of this confusion and to meet the needs of the general public, Florida enacted laws that clearly define the responsibilities of agents within an authorized agency relationship. When a licensee is engaged in any type of authorized brokerage relationship, Chapter 475 imposes definite duties and obligations on the part of a licensee to make adequate disclosures concerning the relationship and duties afforded to the parties in a transaction. Although, the aforementioned applies to all transactions, disclosure requirements apply only to residential transactions as defined by Florida law. Next, we will define some of the important terms concerning the Florida Brokerage Relationship Disclosure Act. The act covers agency and nonagency relationships as they pertain to a residential sale in Florida.

A **residential sale** is defined as any of the following:

- The sale of improved land used as one- to four-family dwelling units
- The sale of unimproved land intended for use as one- to four-family dwelling units
- The sale of farm/agricultural land of up to ten acres

Exemptions to Disclosure Requirements

As mentioned previously, the disclosure requirements of the Florida Brokerage Relationship Disclosure Act (which were just described) apply to residential sales only.

The disclosure requirements do *not* apply to:

- Nonresidential transactions
- Auctions
- Appraisals
- Transactions involving the rental or leasing of property, unless an option to purchase property with one to four residential units is given
- Transactions involving business enterprises or business opportunities, unless the property has one to four residential units

TYPES OF AUTHORIZED AGENCY RELATIONSHIPS

In Florida, a buyer, seller, landlord, or tenant has only three choices concerning representation. A real estate licensee may only transact as one of the following:

1. A nonrepresentative (no brokerage relationship)
2. A single agent for either a buyer or a seller
3. A transaction broker

The buyer or seller, in conjunction with the broker, must decide which option best serves the parties. We will look at each of these options individually.

As of October 1, 1997, **dual agency** relationships are no longer permitted within the state of Florida. A dual agency relationship is defined as a relationship in which the agent represents both the buyer (or lessee) and the seller (or lessor) within the same transaction. Therefore, the licensee (a dual agent) has an agency relationship with both the buyer (lessee) and seller (lessor). Dual agency results in a very dangerous situation for the licensee because of the inability on the licensee's part to provide certain responsibilities to both parties within the transaction at the same time. To say the least, "No one can serve two masters." That is, in a dual agency relationship, it is highly improbable that the licensee can serve both parties with the same undivided loyalty and confidentiality. It is for these reasons that the Florida legislature and regulators have passed laws that have totally *outlawed dual agency* as an authorized and acceptable type of relationship in Florida. In fact, Florida is the first state in the union to totally outlaw this type of agency relationship. Therefore, dual agency is *never* legal in Florida. It is illegal for any agent to represent both parties in the same transaction as a single agent.

As mentioned previously, in Florida, there are three authorized relationship types:

1. Nonrepresentation (no brokerage relationship)
2. Single agency
3. Transaction broker relationship

Next, we will go over the features of these types of relationships and the disclosures that licensees must make in each situation. Keep in mind that these disclosures apply to residential sales transactions only. In these types of transactions, disclosure forms are issued in writing; however, the signature of the party receiving the disclosure is not required. In the event that the recipient of the disclosure form refuses to sign, the licensee should make a note of the party's refusal to sign the form, write the party's name(s) and the date, and save in his files for a period of not less than 5 years. This would apply if a contract was formed. The only disclosure form that requires the principal's signature at all times is the **consent to transition** to transaction broker relationship. From time-to-time the need may arise for a licensee to change his/her relationship with a principal, therefore, the consent to transition form is used to apprise a principal of the agent's need to transition to another authorized form of agency relationship. Prior to any transition on the part of a licensee, the written consent of the principal is required.

Nonrepresentation (No Brokerage Relationship)

In Florida (as in other states), buyers, sellers, landlords, and tenants *are not required* to employ and engage the services of a real estate licensee. Therefore, if any of the above parties chooses not to employ the services of a licensee under a single agent or transaction broker relationship, the licensee takes on the role of a facilitator to the transaction. In this role, the licensee is free to enter into any compensation agreement with any party without fear of creating a single agent or transaction broker relationship.

At this point, it would be important to note that *compensation or a compensation agreement does not constitute an agency relationship* nor does it dictate that the paying party is owed any fiduciary responsibilities by the licensee. Agency relationships are created via agency agreements. Those agreements may be implied or expressed (this will be covered in greater detail in Chapter 11).

In essence, compensation does not dictate who the licensee owes her allegiance to. A licensee's responsibility is to dispose of her obligations under an agency agreement.

Example

You are hired as a buyer's broker under a single agent relationship agreement. Within the compensation paragraph of the single agent agreement, the buyer requires that "all compensation resulting from any transaction under that agreement is to be paid by the seller of the property that the buyer ultimately selects."

In this scenario, the buyer hires the licensee to procure the new premises on his behalf under a buyer broker/single agent relationship agreement. However, within the agreement, the buyer requires that the licensee seek compensation from the selling party. Assuming the selling party ultimately pays the fee, the licensee is hired by the buyer and therefore is required to deliver to the buyer no less representation than that called for within the single agent relationship. The licensee would owe the selling party nothing other than the duty of fair and honest practice.

In a **nonrepresentation** relationship, the broker owes the party the following duties:

- Accountability—The licensee is responsible for a full accounting of all funds belonging to others that are entrusted to her possession.

- Fair and honest practice—The licensee must be fair and honest in the manner that information is exchanged to a customer.

- Full disclosure of property defects—The licensee is compeled and required to fully disclose any known fact that could materially affect the value of the property. In addition, the licensee may not withhold information that would be considered to materially affect the value of the property or could materially affect or sway the decision-making process of the customer had the information been disclosed or made readily available prior to a decision. This includes the disclosure of material facts that are not readily observable to the customer.

In a nonrepresentation relationship, the broker is not obligated to provide loyalty, which is considered one of the fiduciary duties that a broker owes to a principal under a single agency relationship. Under a single agency relationship, a broker would owe full fiduciary duties to a principal.

To summarize, in a nonrepresentation (no brokerage) relationship, *the broker owes* the party the duties of accountability, fair and honest practice, and full disclosure of facts that could materially affect the value of the property. *The broker is not obligated to provide* loyalty or confidentiality, which are considered fiduciary duties a broker owes to a principal under a single agency relationship.

Nonrepresentation (No Brokerage) Relationship Disclosure Requirements

In Florida, prior to showing a property and when no brokerage relationship exists, a licensee is required to provide the customer (either a buyer or seller) with a disclosure form entitled No Brokerage Relationship Notice. This important notice informs the potential buyer or seller that he is not being represented, nor will he be represented, by the licensee providing the notice until the parties enter into an agreement creating an authorized agency relationship. Therefore, at inception of this relationship, this disclosure form *must* be provided to a buyer or a seller at the earlier of:

- At first substantive contact (where confidential information about the buyer or seller is given or exchanged)
- Prior to showing the property

All licensees are required to provide a buyer or seller with a written No Brokerage Relationship Notice disclosure form, the contents of which are prescribed by law. (A copy of this form is included in the Forms Appendix at the end of the book.)

The disclosure itself is not required if:

- It has been determined that the buyer or seller is being represented by another broker as one of the following:
  - A single agent
  - A transaction broker
- Any of the following *does not occur* at an open house:
  - Negotiations of any type concerning the subject property
  - Exchanging of any confidential information
  - Obtaining a submission of an offer to purchase by the purchaser
  - Entry into an agency agreement
- Meetings with buyers or sellers where no discussions concerning any of the above open house issues arise or enter the discussion
- Responding to questions concerning an advertised listing(s)

A licensee who is an agent of a seller must disclose the agency relationship in writing to any potential buyers with whom she is working. This may be accomplished by the licensee giving a copy of the No Brokerage Relationship Notice to the buyer. The disclosure must be in writing. Verbal disclosure may prove adequate in court in some cases, but written disclosure is always a better and safer approach. When speaking on the telephone, it is best to make an immediate verbal disclosure followed by a written disclosure prior to showing property. Although a nonrepresentation relationship bears duties and responsibilities on the part of the licensee, these responsibilities will differ from those of a fiduciary relationship (which will be discussed next).

Single Agent Relationship

In a **single agent** relationship, a licensee represents either a buyer or a seller *but never both* within the same transaction. The seller-broker agency (single agent for the seller) was the first kind of agency to develop. The buyer-broker agency (single agent for the buyer) was developed more recently and is becoming increasingly common. Florida recognizes both types of agency relationships. In Florida, a single agent relationship is defined as a relationship bearing *full fiduciary* responsibilities on the part of a licensee. When a licensee has full fiduciary responsibilities, the highest form of trust should exist between the principal and his agent. An agent who is not careful in the disposition of his duties under this type of relationship may be the subject of disciplinary actions, such as civil suits and penalties. When a single agency relationship is created and ultimately entered into, the person hiring the licensee is called the principal/client and the licensee is referred to as the single agent.

Coaching Tips: It is actually the *broker* or the legally registered brokerage firm that is the agent for the principal (buyer or seller). Any sales associate or broker associate registered under the broker is an agent for the broker and a subagent for the principal (buyer or seller). All such licensees have a fiduciary duty to the principal and must represent the principal's best interests. It should also be noted that under a single agent relationship, the principal is responsible for the acts of the agent/licensee.

When an authorized single agent relationship is created and entered into, the licensee owes her principal/client the following fiduciary duties:

- *Fair and honest practice*—The licensee must be fair and honest in the manner that information is exchanged to a principal.
- *Care*—A licensee is considered a professional and, as such, must dispose of her responsibility with the utmost skill, care, and diligence.

- *Confidentiality*—The licensee must *at all times* keep the confidence of any sensitive information that is entrusted to the licensee by her principal and should avoid at all costs any relationships that would adversely affect her principal.

- *Loyalty*—The licensee must place the needs and interest of her principal above those of all others including those of the agent.

- *Obedience*—The agent should always obey the legal and reasonable instructions of her principal.

- *Accountability*—The licensee must account for all funds belonging to others entrusted to her possession.

- *Full disclosure*—The licensee must fully disclose to her principal all facts and information that could materially affect the transaction or the value of the property. This includes the disclosure of material facts that are not readily observable.

- *Submitting all offers*—The licensee must promptly present any and all offers and counteroffers.

Prior to, or at the time of, entering into a single agent relationship with a principal, a licensee must provide the principal with a Single Agent Notice disclosure form, the contents of which are prescribed by law. (A copy of this form is included in the Forms Appendix at the end of the book.) This disclosure may be a separate disclosure document or it may be included as part of another document, such as a listing or an agreement for representation. When it is included within another document, the notice must be of the same size type, or larger, as other provisions of the document and must be conspicuous in its placement to advise customers of the duties of a single agent. Also, the first sentence must be printed in uppercase bold type.

The Single Agent Notice disclosure form must be given at the earlier of:

- The time of entry into a single agent relationship with a principal
- The showing of the property

Coaching Tips: In 2006, the Single Agent Notice disclosure form was amended to eliminate the Important Notice section.

Transaction Broker Relationship

The third type of authorized relationship in Florida is the **transaction broker** relationship. In a transaction broker relationship, the broker provides **limited representation** to one or both parties to the transaction. The broker does not represent either party in a fiduciary capacity or as a single agent. Rather, the broker provides a limited form of nonfiduciary representation to the buyer, seller, or both. *Since July 1, 2003, under Florida law, it is presumed that a licensee is acting as transaction broker unless a single agent or no brokerage relationship is established in writing with a customer.* In a transaction broker relationship, a buyer or seller is not responsible for the acts of the licensee. In other words, the buyer or seller does not have vicarious liability resulting from the acts of a licensee. In addition, within this relationship, the parties to the real estate transaction give up their rights to the undivided loyalty of a licensee. This aspect of limited representation allows the licensee to facilitate a real estate transaction by assisting both the buyer and the seller, but the licensee will not work to represent one party to the detriment of the other party when acting as a transaction broker to both parties.

Consumers are not required to hire agents or enter into fiduciary relationships. If either a buyer or a seller hires an agent, he may not require a relationship that bears full fiduciary responsibilities like that of a single agent relationship. That is, he may be in need of only limited services. In this case, the transaction broker relationship may be appropriate. A transaction broker relationship imposes only limited representation responsibilities on the part of the licensee. In this type of relationship, there is *no* fiduciary relationship created; therefore, both the buyer and seller become *customers* of the transaction broker. In other states, a transaction broker is more commonly known and referred to as a *facilitator*. Compensation for services may or may not be equivalent to a brokerage commission. A broker may only be compensated for the agreed-upon service being provided.

In the transaction broker relationship, the transaction broker is not totally relieved of responsibilities to both parties. In fact, the transaction broker has several duties, including:

- *Accountability*—The licensee is responsible for a full accounting of all funds belonging to others that are entrusted to her possession.
- *Care*—A licensee is considered a professional and, as such, must dispose of her responsibility with the utmost skill, care, and diligence.
- *Disclosure of property defects*—The licensee is compeled and required to fully disclose any fact known to the licensee that could materially affect the value of the property. In addition, the licensee may not withhold information that would be considered to materially affect the value of the property or could materially affect or sway the decision-making process of the customer had the information been disclosed or made readily available prior to a decision. This includes the disclosure of material facts that are not readily observable to the customer.
- *Fair and honest practice*—The licensee must be fair and honest in the manner that information is exchanged to a customer.
- *Submitting all offers*—The licensee must promptly present any and all offers and counteroffers.
- **Limited Confidentiality**—The licensee's duty of confidentiality is limited. The licensee may not disclose to one party what she knows about the other. Specifically, the licensee cannot disclose that the seller will accept a lower price than the list price, that the buyer will pay a greater price than offered, that either party will agree to financing terms other than those offered, or the motivation of either party for buying or selling the property.

Any other duties required by the parties may be created by agreement with the transaction agent.

Prior to, or at the time of, entering into an agreement for representation, a licensee must provide the principal with a Transaction Broker Notice disclosure form, the contents of which are prescribed by law. (A copy of this form is included in the Forms Appendix at the end of the book.) This disclosure may be a separate disclosure document or it may be included as part of another document, such as a listing or an agreement for representation. When it is included within another document, the notice must be of the same size type, or larger, as other provisions of the document and must be conspicuous in its placement to advise customers of the duties of limited representation. Also, the first sentence must be printed in uppercase bold type.

The Transaction Broker Notice disclosure form must be given at the earlier of:

- The time of entry into an agreement for representation with a customer
- The showing of the property

Coaching Tips: In 2006, the Transaction Broker Notice disclosure form has been amended to eliminate the following:

- The Important Notice section
- The section that states, "Florida law requires that real estate licensees operating as transaction brokers disclose to buyers and sellers their role and duties in providing a limited form of representation."

In addition, the Transaction Broker Notice disclosure will no longer be required after July 1, 2008. Also, changes in Florida law expanded the definition of a transaction broker. The law now states:

- A buyer or seller (within this relationship) is not responsible for acts committed by a licensee.
- The parties relinquish their rights as it applies to the duty of the agent to provide undivided loyalty.
- Any licensee working in this capacity may not favor one party to the detriment of the other party within that transaction.

TRANSITIONING TO ANOTHER AUTHORIZED RELATIONSHIP

In Florida, a broker or legal registered brokerage entity may *transition* from a single agent relationship with either a buyer or a seller to a transaction broker at any time as long as:

- The broker provides the proper disclosure form entitled Consent to Transition to Transaction Broker
- The principal to whom this situation applies (either the buyer or the seller as the case may be) has fully consented to the transition prior to the agent making the actual transition
- The principal's permission is evidenced by his signature on the Consent to Transition to Transaction Broker disclosure form

The licensee will be disciplined if she transitions to a different relationship before the events listed above have occurred.

The Consent to Transition to Transaction Broker disclosure form may be a separate disclosure document or it may be included as part of another document, such as a listing or an agreement for representation. (A copy of this form is included in the Forms Appendix at the end of the book.) When it is included within another document, the notice must be of the same size type, or larger, as other provisions of the document and must be conspicuous in its placement to advise customers of the duties of limited representation. Also, the first sentence must be printed in uppercase bold type.

Let's look at an example of a transition to another authorized relationship. This example involves an in-house transaction.

Example

Potential Situation—XYZ Realty is a single agent for Seller Smith. XYZ Realty is also a single agent for Buyer Baker. Buyer Baker is interested in Seller Smith's property. Although this type of situation may seem innocent, it can be very dangerous if not handled lawfully. The danger specifically lies in the creation of an *unlawful* dual agency. In this situation, a sales associate employed by XYZ Realty *cannot* show Seller Smith's property to Buyer Baker because a broker cannot represent both the buyer and the seller in the same transaction (dual agency). As previously mentioned, dual agency is illegal in Florida.

Lawful Solution—One way for the broker to proceed with this transaction legally would be for the broker/brokerage entity to transition from a single agent relationship to that of a transaction broker. The broker would be required to transition from a single agent relationship to that of a transaction broker with both the buyer and seller *prior to* the buyer inspecting the property. Any attempt to show the property to the buyer prior to a lawful transition occurring would be an infraction of the license law. Doing so would create a dual agency and subject the licensee to severe disciplinary action.

MAINTAINING RECORDS

If a transaction results in a written sales contract, the broker is required to maintain copies of the disclosure forms in a transaction file for at least 5 years. Record maintenance requirements apply to:

- All residential transactions (as defined by 475, F.S.) to include:
  - Closed transactions
  - Transactions that do not close; the following should be included in the broker's files:
    - The purchase contract
    - Any escrow documents and bank statements referencing the purchase contract
    - Agency disclosure forms
- All nonresidential transactions that utilize designated sales associates (see the next section)

DESIGNATED SALES ASSOCIATE

We have already looked at the authorized brokerage relationships that apply to *residential sales* transactions. Now, let's look at a special agency situation that is permitted in *nonresidential* transactions.

Earlier in this chapter, you learned that a *residential sales* transaction is defined as one of the following:

- The sale of improved land used as one- to four-family dwelling units
- The sale of unimproved land intended for use as one- to four-family dwelling units
- The sale of farm/agricultural land of up to ten acres

If a transaction does not fall under these definitions of a residential sales transaction, it is considered *a commercial or nonresidential sales transaction even if it involves residentially zoned property.* This would be the case in a property containing greater than four dwelling units.

In a *nonresidential* sales transaction, if the buyer and the seller desire the services of the same real estate broker to act as a fiduciary single agent to both parties, the broker may appoint **designated sales associates** to act as single agents for the parties. That is, the broker may designate one sales associate to act as a single agent for the buyer and a different sales associate to act as a single agent for the seller. In this case, the broker is not considered a dual agent, but a neutral party.

The designated sales associate situation is *only permitted if:*

- A request for such representation is made by both parties
- Both parties can demonstrate that their asset holdings are valued in excess of $1,000,000
- The broker acts strictly on an advisory level to both designated sales associates within the organization
- The broker only uses any confidential information disclosed by either designated sales associate in order to properly advise the sales associates on how to proceed in a lawful and appropriate manner

A designated sales associate has the same duties as a **single agent**, including the disclosure requirements (described earlier in this chapter). In addition, a Designated Sales Associate Disclosure Notice must be provided.

TERMINATION OF AGENCY

The agency relationship created by a listing agreement is automatically terminated when a sale of the property is completed. In addition, there are several other ways in which a listing agreement can be terminated (see Figure 4.3). One good way to remember the methods by which an agency can be terminated is to remember the mnemonic READIE:

- *R*evocation or renunciation
- *E*xpiration of the listing period
- *A*greement of the parties
- *D*eath of either party
- *I*ncapacity of either party
- *E*xtinction of the property

Revocation or renunciation—The principal may decide to revoke the agency and terminate the listing. However, this does not relieve the principal from the obligation to pay a commission if the property is sold during the original listing period. For example, the owner may "take the property off the market" and terminate the agency, but the principal must pay a commission if it is sold during the listing period.

Expiration of the listing period—If the property does not sell during the listing period, the listing agreement automatically terminates.

Agreement of the parties—If both parties mutually agree, the listing agreement can be terminated.

Death of either party—If the principal or broker dies, the listing agreement is automatically terminated.

Incapacity of either party—The listing agreement is terminated if either party is declared legally incompetent, declares bankruptcy, or if the broker loses his license.

Extinction of the property—If the property is destroyed, the listing agreement is terminated.

These six ways of terminating a listing can be classified as occurring through one of the following:

- Acts of the parties
- Acts of law

To remember which method of termination falls into which category, use the following graphic illustrations:

> The first three categories are classified as "acts of the parties":
>
> - Revocation or renunciation
> - Expiration of the listing period
> - Agreement of the parties

FIGURE 4.3

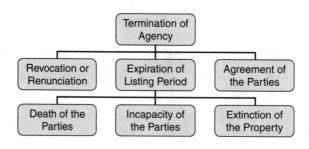

The remaining three categories are classified as "acts of law":

- Death of either party
- Incapacity of either party
- Extinction of the property

To remember which category is which, remember that the "D" in "DIE" stands for "death" of either party, which is termination by an "act of law."

SUMMARY

There are three types of agents: universal, general, and special. Under Florida law, it is presumed that a licensee is acting as unless a single agent or nonrepresentation relationship is established in writing with a customer.

- In a *single agency* relationship, an agent represents one party.
- An agent who represents only buyers is a single agent for the buyer (a buyer's agent).
- An agent who represents only sellers is a single agent for the seller (a seller's agent).
- Dual agency refers to a relationship in which the agent represents both the buyer (or lessee) and the seller (or lessor) within the same transaction.
- Dual agency is *never* legal in Florida.
- In a nonrepresentation relationship, the broker owes the party the duties of accountability, fair and honest practice, and full disclosure of facts that could materially affect the value of the property.
- Neither a buyer nor a seller is obligated or required to enlist the efforts or services of a real estate licensee. Therefore, in this situation, the licensee merely acts as a *facilitator* in concluding the sale.
- In a *single agency* relationship, the broker owes full fiduciary duties to her principal.
- In a s*ingle agency* relationship, a licensee represents *either* a buyer or a seller but never both in the same transaction.
- In a *single agency* relationship, the broker owes full fiduciary duties to his principal.
- In a *transaction broker* relationship, the duty of confidentiality is limited.
- In a *transaction broker* relationship, the broker provides limited representation to one or both parties to the transaction.

REVIEW QUESTIONS

1. The brokerage relationship disclosure requirements are relevant to the:
   a. Sale of a business.
   b. Lease of a single-family home.
   c. Sale of a residential apartment complex.
   d. Sale of three agricultural acres.

2. Only a transaction broker would owe customers:
   a. Loyalty.
   b. Limited confidentiality.
   c. Obedience.
   d. Full disclosure.

3. A seller listed a lot with Jones Real Estate for $100,000. A buyer calls the company and asks if the seller will take $30,000. The company:
   a. Should tell the buyer to raise the offer.
   b. Doesn't have to present verbal offers.
   c. Must present all offers to the seller.
   d. Can use its own discretion in the matter.

4. A company represents a buyer and a seller as a transaction broker. As an associate presents a low offer to the seller, the associate tells the seller the buyer would pay more. The company:
   a. Has violated limited confidentially and can be sued.
   b. Is obligated to reveal this to the seller.
   c. Must be loyal to the seller.
   d. Has violated the duty of confidentiality to the buyer.

5. A company has a nonrepresentation relationship with a buyer. Which of the following duties does the company owe?
   a. Loyalty
   b. Accounting for all funds
   c. Skill, care, and diligence
   d. Presenting all offers in a timely manner

6. Written disclosures regarding the duties in each type of brokerage relationship apply to:
   a. All real estate transactions.
   b. All residential transactions.
   c. Residential leases and sales.
   d. Residential sales as defined by Florida law only.

7. A signature on the written notices is:
   a. Important but not required.
   b. Only required on the Consent to Transition forms.
   c. Only required on Single Agent Notice forms.
   d. Always required.

8. Under Florida law, it is presumed that all licensees are transaction brokers unless a single agent or nonrepresentation relationship notice is established in writing.
   a. Therefore, the written Transaction Broker Notice is not obligatory.
   b. Even so, the written Transaction Broker Notice must be given in all residential transactions.
   c. However, the written Transaction Broker Notice must be given in residential sales.
   d. If the firm advertises "Transaction Broker (Brokers)," the written notice is not mandatory.

9. When buyers and sellers have $1,000,000 or more in assets, a designated sales associate:
   a. Represents the broker's interest in residential sales.
   b. Is a subagent for the broker.
   c. Is appointed as a single agent by single agent brokers.
   d. Is appointed by the broker, at the request of the parties to the transaction, as a single agent for the buyer or seller in a nonresidential transaction.

10. Which of these will NOT terminate a brokerage relationship?
    a. The offer is withdrawn.
    b. The broker renounces the relationship.
    c. The principal renounces the relationship.
    d. The broker dies.

11. Broker Beth is a single agent for the seller. The seller tells Broker Beth the garage roof leaked in the last rain, but there is no visible evidence. The seller asks Broker Beth not to mention the leak. Beth's legal obligation is to tell buyers:
    a. The roof does not appear to leak.
    b. Nothing unless someone asks about leaks.
    c. The roof has developed a leak.
    d. Nothing because licensees in a single agent relationship owe principals obedience.

12. A real estate licensee has a legal obligation to tell all prospective buyers before or at the time of showing a property that:
    a. Two owners ago, there was a murder in the house.
    b. The residents in the neighborhood are predominantly Hispanic.
    c. The shutters do not meet the Miami-Dade wind codes.
    d. The seller allegedly has AIDS.

13. A transaction broker for a customer owes all of the following duties EXCEPT:
    a. Using skill, care, and diligence in the transaction.
    b. Dealing honestly and fairly.
    c. Limited confidentiality, unless waived by a party.
    d. Full disclosure.

14. A real estate firm is the single agent for a seller. A buyer offers to purchase the seller's property for more than the listing price and will pay in cash. The buyer insists on an answer today, or the buyer will buy a different property. The seller can't be found. In this situation, the broker:
    a. Must accept the offer because it is in the seller's best interest.
    b. Cannot say yes, no, or maybe.
    c. Can accept the offer, conditional to the seller's signature.
    d. Legally must reject the offer.

15. As a single agent broker, Acme Realty can represent:
    a. Buyers only.
    b. Sellers only.
    c. Both buyers and sellers if they are in the same transaction.
    d. Both buyers and sellers, but not if they are in the same transaction.

16. Sherman Homes is the single agent for Seller Jim and Buyer Mary. Jim's home is perfect for Mary. How can Mary see Jim's house?
    a. Jim can sign a waiver allowing Mary to see the house.
    b. Mary can sign a waiver allowing herself to see the house.
    c. Before Buyer Mary may see the home, both Jim and Mary must sign the consent form to allow Sherman Homes to transition from a single agent relationship to a transaction broker.
    d. Mary can't see Jim's house under any circumstances.

17. It would be appropriate to give the No Brokerage Relationship Notice to:
    a. Sellers who are represented by other companies.
    b. Persons attending an open house.
    c. All persons who ask about the price of the house.
    d. A for-sale-by-owner when showing your buyer the home.

18. Vivian has signed a listing agreement with your company to sell her house, but Vivian doesn't want to sign the Transaction Broker Notice. What are you going to do?
    a. Be polite, but insist on a signature.
    b. Put a note in the office files that Vivian accepted the relationship but didn't want to sign.
    c. You can accept the listing, but you can't be Vivian's transaction broker.
    d. You can sign the notice; this will suffice.

19. Brokerage relationship disclosure documents that result in a written contract to buy or sell residential property, even if the transaction didn't close, must be:
    a. Kept for a period of 3 years.
    b. Kept for a period of 5 years.
    c. Replaced with electronic files or CDs.
    d. Kept confidential.

20. A transaction broker for buyers or sellers:
    a. Must represent either a buyer or seller, but not both in the same transaction.
    b. Does not represent either party in a fiduciary capacity.
    c. Represents principals in residential transactions.
    d. Can work for one party's interest over the other.

Chapter 5

KEY TERMS

arbitration

blind ad

commingle

conflicting demands

conversion

corporation

deposits

double taxation

earnest money

escrow (trust) account

escrow disbursement order (EDO)

general partnership

good-faith doubt

interpleader

limited liability company

limited liability partnership

limited partnership

mediation

ostensible partnership

point of contact information

sole proprietorship

trade name

LEARNING OBJECTIVES

After completing this lesson, you will be able to:

- Describe the provisions of the license law related to operating a real estate business, including:
  - Broker offices and branch offices
  - Signage
  - Advertising
  - Escrow (trust) accounts
  - Rental information or rental lists
- Describe the types of business entities that may register as a real estate brokerage.
- Describe requirements for change of address and change of employment.
- Understand the procedures for the disposition of escrowed funds when conflicting demands occur.

Operation of a Broker's Office

THE BROKER'S OFFICE

All Florida brokers must establish and maintain a principal place of business that must be registered with the Division of Real Estate (DRE). Florida law defines and requires the broker's principal office to be contained or housed within a stationary building containing one or more enclosed rooms. Therefore, a mobile home does not qualify under these definitions. However, a mobile home resting on a permanent foundation does qualify and fall within the guidelines.

CHANGE OF ADDRESS

If a broker's or real estate school's business address changes, the DRE must be notified of the address change in writing within 10 days of the change. (A license ceases to be in force until the DRE receives this notification.)

The broker or school must file a notice of the change of address, along with the names of any sales associates or instructors who are no longer employed by the brokerage or the school. The notice of the change of address also acts to change the address of each sales associate or instructor. In essence, the broker or school is notifying the DRE of any agents or instructors who will not be moving to the new address with the broker or the school. The licenses of those who choose not to go with the broker or the school revert to involuntary inactive. They remain involuntary inactive until they reassociate with another broker or school.

Similarly, if a licensee changes his current residential address, the DRE must be notified of the change in writing within 10 days. Failure to do so can and most probably will result in disciplinary action that includes fines and/or license suspension.

CHANGE EMPLOYING BROKER

Also, if a sales associate changes employing brokers, the DRE must be notified of the change in broker within 10 days on a prescribed form. The sales associate's license ceases to be in force until the DRE receives such notification. When a sales associate transfers from one employing broker to another, the sales associate is *not* permitted to remove or copy any transaction records from the previous employer. The records belong to the employing broker, not the sales associate, even if the sales associate was involved in the transaction.

BRANCH OFFICES

If a broker operates more than one office, each additional location must be registered as a branch office. A temporary shelter, located on the grounds of a subdivision being sold by the broker, is *not* considered a branch office if the purpose of the shelter is strictly protection from the weather. However, the shelter *is* considered a branch office and must be appropriately registered if one or both of the following occurs:

- Transactions are closed in the shelter
- Sales associates are permanently assigned to the shelter

SIGNAGE

The broker's place of business must have a sign. This includes the broker's principal office as well as any branch offices. The sign must be easily observed and read by anyone who is about to enter the office. Each sign must contain, at a minimum, the following information:

- The name of the broker
- Any fictitious name or **trade name** (as registered with the Florida Real Estate Commission). A trade name is a fictitious name other than one's own name used to conduct one's business
- The words "licensed real estate broker" or "lic. real estate broker" following the broker's name

If the firm is a partnership or corporation, the sign must also include the name of the partnership or corporation and at least one of the brokers. The inclusion of any broker associates' or sales associates' names is the broker's decision. Should the broker opt to list either one or both classes of licensed individuals, the broker is cautioned to make a clear distinction between the broker and any affiliated licensees.

Example

Sunshine State Real Estate Services
Theodore Sunshine—Licensed Real Estate Broker
Wilma Morrison—Broker Associate
Harry Thompson—Sales Associate

You should be aware that the broker's address is *not* required on the sign.

The licensee is cautioned to observe both zoning and license laws governing the operation of a real estate brokerage business from a residence. In this type of situation, the signage requirements are not relaxed or excused. In addition to any signage requirements, the licensee is cautioned to adhere to accessibility laws such as the Americans with Disabilities Act (ADA). This would apply to any principal office or branch office, as well as any office in a residence. Any violation can and most probably will result in disciplinary action against the licensee.

ADVERTISING

A broker is prohibited from placing any advertisement that is false or misleading. This applies to all types, methods, and vehicles of advertising, including but not limited to:

- Newspapers
- Magazine ads
- Fliers

- Television
- Radio
- Internet
- Billboards
- Yard signs
- Benches

Furthermore, it is unlawful for a broker to place an ad without indicating that the advertiser is a licensed real estate broker. That is, all ads must contain the name of the brokerage firm. An ad that does not include the brokerage firm name is called a **blind ad**. Blind ads are not only unlawful; they also subject the licensee to disciplinary action. Blind ads mislead the general public by lacking disclosure that the advertiser is a real estate licensee. All advertising must be worded in such a manner that a reasonable person would know the ad was placed by a real estate licensee. If the name of any contact person appears within an ad, the ad must *always* include the person's surname. Ads with only a contact person's first name are prohibited. The licensee's last name must appear as it appears on her license and as it is registered with the DRE.

When advertising on the Internet, the name of the brokerage firm must appear immediately above, below, or adjacent to the name of the **point of contact information**. The point of contact information means the method by which the brokerage firm or licensee may be contacted and includes any of the following:

- E-mail address
- Mailing address
- Street address
- Phone number
- Fax number

Coaching Tips: Many brokers like to place "sold" signs on properties as a means of advertising. There was a time when a "sold" sign could not be placed on a property prior to closing without the seller's consent. That rule was repealed in October 2002. Currently, a licensee may place any of the following types of signs:

- Sold
- Sale Pending
- Contract Pending
- Under Contract

ESCROW (TRUST) ACCOUNTS IN FLORIDA

Licensees are often entrusted with **deposits**, which is defined as money or other valuable consideration belonging to others. We will now take a look at the laws and requirements that must be followed in such situations. It is important to note that the single most common license infraction leading to cancelation or revocation of one's license occurs while mishandling other people's money. The purpose of an **escrow or trust account** is to hold the funds of others that have been entrusted to the broker. In Florida, when a licensee handles funds belonging to others in the normal course of business, the licensee must immediately deposit those funds in the broker's escrow (trust) account. Let's look at what is meant by *immediately.*

In Florida, *immediately* means the following:

- To the sales associate—When funds belonging to others are entrusted to a sales associate or broker associate, the licensee must immediately place those funds in the possession of his broker. In this case, *immediately* means within the next business day following receipt.

- To the broker—When funds belonging to others are received by the broker, the broker must immediately deposit the funds into her escrow (trust) account. In this case, *immediately* means no later than the close of banking business on the third business day following receipt of the money. This time period begins on the day the *sales associate* or *broker associate* received the funds.

Example

On Monday, a sales associate receives an **earnest money** deposit from a buyer. Earnest money refers to a deposit paid by a prospective buyer to show his intention to go through with the sale. The sales associate must turn the funds over to her broker by Tuesday (assuming there are no holidays). The broker must deposit the funds into an escrow (trust) account by Thursday—the third day after the funds were received by the sales associate (again, assuming there are no holidays). Failure to do so will result in a citation, fine, and/or other administrative penalty assessed to the licensee.

When a broker receives funds belonging to others in a real estate transaction, the broker must *not* **commingle** the funds. Commingling refers to mixing funds belonging to others with the broker's personal funds or business funds. If the broker deposits such funds into a business operating account, it would be considered commingling. There is one exception permitted under the license law. A broker is permitted to maintain up to $5,000 of personal or brokerage funds in the broker's property management escrow account and up to $1,000 in his sales escrow account. (In the event of any legal proceeding concerning a broker's escrow account, the disbursement of escrowed funds must not be delayed due to any dispute over the personal or brokerage funds that may be present in the account.)

The broker must avoid **conversion**. Conversion occurs if the broker unlawfully takes funds belonging to others for her own personal use. For example, a broker using such funds to pay for a personal trip is considered conversion.

Escrow funds must be deposited in one of the following ways:

- In a savings bank, commercial bank, or credit union
- In a Florida title company that has trust powers
- With an attorney admitted into the Florida Bar (if specified in the contract)

The broker may have as many escrow accounts as needed provided that the following requirements are met:

- The broker is a signatory on any and all accounts.
- The broker makes available to the Department of Business and Professional Regulation (DBPR) any records associated with the escrow accounts for examination and audit by the DBPR.
- The records are kept for a minimum of 5 years from conclusion of activity on any transaction. However, if the records of the broker were the subject of any lawsuit, the broker must retain the records for an additional period of 2 years subsequent to the conclusion of the lawsuit, but in no event less than 5 years. This may ultimately mean that the broker retain these records for as much as 7 years.

In the event that there is an error in an escrow account, the broker is given a reasonable amount of time to correct the error if there is no shortage of funds and the error poses no significant threat of economic harm to the public.

A broker's escrow account may be an interest-bearing or noninterest-bearing account. Before placing funds in an interest-bearing escrow account, all parties must agree in writing, and the written agreement must specify who will be paid the interest.

Escrow Dispute and Disposition of Funds

It is not uncommon for a dispute to arise concerning how funds that are held by a broker are distributed. That is, **conflicting demands** may be made upon the escrowed funds when two parties (such as a buyer and a seller) do not agree as to how the funds should be disbursed. In this unfortunate event, the licensee must immediately notify her broker of the conflicting demands. The broker must follow strict rules, regardless of the demands made by the parties. These rules are described next.

First, the broker is required to notify the Florida Real Estate Commission (FREC) in writing within 15 days of the last demand made by either party for a distribution. Within the notification, the broker may request that FREC issue an **escrow disbursement order (EDO)** instructing the licensee to distribute the funds to one party or the other. FREC may or may not issue an EDO. If not, the broker has three disposition options (which must be initiated within 30 days following the last request by either party for funds held in escrow):

1. Mediation
2. Arbitration
3. Litigation

Coaching Tips: Within 15 business days, the broker must send notification to FREC and within 30 business days institute one of the three settlement procedures following a good-faith doubt **as to how to disburse disputed escrow funds. While good faith can be defined as:**

- A willing party's desire to transact business.
- Good-faith doubt is when the broker questions or doubts the parties willingness and desire to transact business. When this occurs, law requires the licensee to institute one of the settlement procedures mentioned above. Please note that this must be accomplished within the time requirements established by FREC. For example, a broker notifies FREC in writing 9 days following the receipt of a dispute. In this case the broker has only 21 days to initiate a settlement procedure.

Let's discuss the three disposition options.

Mediation

Mediation occurs when parties who are unable to agree among themselves seek the assistance of a third party (a mediator) for the purpose of providing a recommended non-binding solution. FREC rules require this process to be completed within 90 days following the last request by either party for funds held in escrow, or the licensee must then institute one of the other disposition options.

Arbitration

Arbitration occurs when parties who are unable to agree among themselves seek the assistance of a third party (one or more arbitrators) who formulates a decision that is binding on all the parties involved. Prior to arbitration, each party must submit to the arbitrator or arbitration panel, as the case may be, that they will be bound by the decision. As a general note concerning this type of proceeding, arbitrator decisions are usually upheld in court and are very difficult to overturn through appeal. However, as a last resort, the broker may submit a dispute to litigation.

Litigation

Litigation may involve an **interpleader**, in which the broker deposits the funds with the courts and petitions the courts to decide on the disbursement. If the petition is accepted, the courts decide on the outcome of disbursement and which party receives the funds. This process ultimately relieves the broker of any further responsibility regarding the disputed funds.

Use the mnemonic LAME to remember the procedures for the disposition of escrowed funds when there are conflicting demands:

- *L*itigation
- *A*rbitration
- *M*ediation
- *E*scrow disbursement order

Good-Faith Doubt

We just looked at the steps a broker may take when conflicting demands are placed on funds held in the broker's escrow account. These same procedures may also be followed if the broker has a good-faith doubt as to who is entitled to receive the funds. Good-faith doubt means the broker doubts the parties' intention to conduct business honestly and to perform their duties under the contract. The situations that may cause a broker to have good-faith doubt are listed below.

Good-faith doubt may exist in the following situations:

- Closing of the transaction has passed, and the broker has not received instructions (either conflicting or identical) from all parties concerning disbursement of the funds.
- Closing of the transaction has not passed, but one party has expressed an intention not to go through with the transaction, and the broker has not received instructions (either conflicting or identical) from all parties concerning disbursement of the funds.

If the broker has a good-faith doubt as to who is entitled to receive the funds, the broker must notify FREC in writing within 15 days, and must initiate one of the following procedures within 30 days:

1. Request that FREC issue an escrow disbursement order (EDO) instructing the licensee to distribute the funds to one party or the other
2. Submit the matter to mediation
3. Submit the matter to arbitration
4. Submit the matter to a court of law

RENTAL INFORMATION OR RENTAL LISTS

Some real estate licensees are involved in selling rental information to prospective tenants. Anyone who furnishes rental information or rental lists for a fee is subject to rules concerning such lists. The individual must provide the purchaser of the list (the prospective tenant) with an agreement or receipt. The agreement must state that if the party is unable to successfully achieve a rental from that list, upon the demand of the party purchasing the list, the licensee must return at least *75 percent* of the amount paid for the rental information list within *30 days*. If a rental list is found to be outdated or inaccurate, the purchaser of the list would be entitled to a full refund. In addition, if the list is found to be intentionally outdated or inaccurate, a license infraction has occurred and the licensee will be disciplined. This would be considered a first-degree misdemeanor. This would subject the licensee to license suspension or revocation, a fine of $1,000, and/or the potential of imprisonment for up to 1 year.

LICENSE VERSUS REGISTRATION

It is important to understand that real estate licenses are *only* issued to qualified *individuals* and not to *business entities*. Thus, *an individual receives a license, while a business entity receives a registration.* The qualifications for a real estate *license* in Florida were covered in Chapter 2. We mentioned then that in order for an individual to receive a real estate license in Florida, an applicant must do the following three things:

1. Successfully complete prelicense education
2. Submit a fully completed application along with the necessary license fee
3. Successfully sit for and pass the Florida state examination

As you can see from these licensing requirements, no one other than an individual person can accomplish items 1 and 3 above. Business entities cannot sit for prelicense courses or take exams. It is for this reason that those entities are required to *register* with FREC.

Permitted Registrations

The following types of business entities are permitted to register with the DBPR as *legally registered brokerage entities:*

- Sole proprietorships
- Partnerships
  - General partnerships
  - Limited partnerships
- Limited liability partnerships
- Corporations
- Limited liability companies

Each type of business entity will be discussed by covering its formation and composition.

Sole Proprietorships

A **sole proprietorship** is a business where the sole owner is the individual licensee. A sole proprietor may do one of the following:

- Do business under his name
- Do business under a d/b/a (doing business as) name, *but not an incorporated name,* so long as the d/b/a is registered with FREC

A sole proprietorship bears unlimited liability. That is, the sole proprietor is personally responsible for *all* the debts of the business that exceed the assets. If a lawsuit results from a real estate transaction, not only are the company assets at risk, but the owner's real and personal property are at risk as well. In addition, a sole proprietor is responsible for any and all other licensees within her employ. This includes routine daily supervision of all sales staff directly employed by the sole proprietor/broker. A sole proprietor does not pay taxes as a business. Rather, a sole proprietor pays individual income taxes on any income earned in any given tax year.

Partnerships

The next type of business entity that may register as a real estate broker is the partnership. There are two types of partnerships:

1. General partnerships
2. Limited partnerships

General Partnerships

A **general partnership** is formed when two or more partners comprise the business entity. The partnership is created by an express or implied agreement between all partners. Each partner bears joint and several liability for the other partners and for the partnership. Joint and several liability means each member of a group may be held individually liable for the acts of the entire group. This includes monetary obligations of the partnership and/or partners. Each partner bears unlimited liability for the debts of the partnership. Each partner may bind and obligate the other. For example, if one partner incurs expenses on behalf of the partnership, all other partners may be liable for those expenses, even if they were unaware of them.

If the partnership performs any real estate act as defined under Florida law, at least one of the partners in a general partnership is required to have an active broker license. Any other partner who will perform a real estate act for compensation must also hold an active broker's license. Sales associates and broker associates may never be registered as partners in a general partnership.

The partnership name must receive a registration from FREC. Any change in the registration (such as resignation, termination, or death of a registered partner) must be reported to FREC. In the event that the only active broker/partner resigns, dies, or is terminated, in order to maintain the registration of the partnership, the broker must be replaced within 14 calendar (not business) days or the partnership's registration will be canceled. In the event there is more than one active broker within the partnership and one of the active brokers resigns, dies, or is terminated, the broker may be replaced by another active broker. At that point, no change in the registration occurs. However, irrespective of any of these circumstances, FREC must be notified of the substitution.

We just looked at the features of a general partnership. Another type of partnership is the limited partnership.

Limited Partnerships

A **limited partnership** can be created with one or more *general partners* and one or more *limited partners*. *General partners* make decisions and actively participate in the operation of the business. *Limited partners* are not permitted to make decisions or otherwise participate in the operation of the business. Limited partners may not perform an active managerial role in the day-to-day operation of the partnership; they are strictly *passive* investors. In effect, limited partners are silent partners.

A limited partnership is formed by a written agreement that must be filed with the Florida secretary of state. Each general partner bears *unlimited* liability. Each limited partner bears *limited* liability—up to the amount the partner has invested. If the partnership performs any real estate act as defined under Florida law, at least one of the general partners is required to have an active broker's license. Any other general partner who will perform a real estate act for compensation must also hold an active broker's license. Sales associates and broker associates may not be general partners in a limited partnership. The partnership name must receive a registration from FREC.

Any change in the registration (such as resignation, termination, or death of a general partner) must be reported to FREC. In the event that the only active broker/general partner resigns, dies, or is terminated, in order to maintain the registration of the partnership, the broker must be replaced within 14 calendar (not business) days or face cancelation of the partnership's registration. In the event there is more than one active broker/general partner and one of the active brokers resigns, dies, or is terminated, the broker may be replaced by another active broker. At that point, no change in the registration occurs. However, irrespective of any of these circumstances, FREC must be notified of the substitution. Limited partners are not required to register with FREC.

Ostensible Partnerships

Another type of partnership is the **ostensible partnership**, which is an entity that appears to be a partnership but is not a real partnership. That is, the parties act like a partnership exists, when in fact, one does not. Because ostensible partnerships are deceitful, such entities are prohibited. When brokers that operate separate entities share space (which is common), their business should be separate from the other. This will avoid the perception of an ostensible partnership. Each party's identity should be separate and distinct from the other.

Limited Liability Partnerships

Another type of business entity that may register as a broker is a **limited liability partnership**. It's important to distinguish limited liability partnerships from partnerships. A limited liability partnership is like a regular limited partnership, but with one big difference—it does not have unlimited personal liability. Under a limited liability partnership, a partner is not liable for negligent acts committed by another partner. A partner is, however, liable for his own negligent acts. A limited liability partnership must file with the Florida secretary of state. The entity name must include either the words "Registered Limited Liability Partnership" or "LLP" at the end of the entity name.

Corporations

A **corporation** is defined as a legal person/entity organized under the laws of Florida or another state. A corporation may include one or more people. Individuals become part-owners (shareholders or stockholders) by purchasing stock in the corporation. The shareholders elect a board of directors who manage the corporation while looking out for the shareholders' best interest. Officers run the day-to-day operations of the corporation. Corporations offer individual asset protection to its officers and shareholders. This means that the corporation is responsible for its obligations.

For example, if a creditor sues a corporation for money, the corporation itself has to pay if it loses the lawsuit. However, if the corporation does not have enough money to pay the creditor, the creditor may *not* look to the officers or shareholders of the corporation to pay what the corporation could not.

Corporations, unlike the previously discussed entities (partnerships), are subject to **double taxation**. When a corporation earns money, it can make a profit. These profits must be reported to the IRS and taxes paid. When the corporation pays out dividends from its profits to its shareholders, the payments are considered income to the shareholders and also must be reported to the IRS and taxes paid. The net effect is double taxation—the money is taxed once on the profits of the corporation and once on the dividends paid to its shareholders. As a further note, the IRS has determined that a corporation can only pay or distribute a dividend after having made a profit. A corporation is deemed to be a legal person that stands on its own as a separate entity from its shareholders—therein lies the reasoning behind double taxation.

Corporations are formed under a document called *articles of incorporation*. The articles of incorporation address the purpose and rules of operation of the corporation. A corporation can be either a domestic or a foreign corporation.

A *domestic* corporation is formed in and under the laws associated with the state of formation (e.g., a corporation formed under Florida laws in Florida would be a domestic corporation).

A *foreign* corporation is formed in and under the laws associated with another state (e.g., a corporation doing business in Florida but that was formed under the laws of another state).

A corporation may also be for profit or not for profit. If the corporation will operate as a real estate brokerage entity, the corporation must be registered with FREC. The corporation must provide FREC with necessary proof showing a legal corporate formation exists. If the corporation will operate as a real estate brokerage entity, at least one of the officers or directors must hold an active real estate broker's license (the qualifying or principal broker). Any other officers or directors who engage in brokerage activities must hold active broker's licenses. Sales associates and broker associates *may never be officers or directors of the corporation.* In addition, this means a sales associate or broker associate may not be designated a title (after her name) that would normally indicate that she is an officer of a corporation.

If there is only one active broker in a corporation, any change in the status of the active broker (resignation, termination of employment, or death) must be reported to FREC and a replacement broker must be registered within 14 calendar (not business) days. Failure to do so can result in cancelation of the corporation's registration. Cancelation of a registration of any legal entity renders the licenses held under that registration involuntarily inactive. If the corporation has more than one active broker, the corporation's registration would not be affected by the resignation, termination, or death of one of the active brokers.

Limited Liability Companies

The last type of business entity that may register as a broker is the **limited liability company**, which was created recently as an allowed organizational form of legal entity. The characteristics of this type of business entity are summarized next.

Limited liability companies are basically hybrids of corporations and partnerships. A limited liability company has full liability protection to the same degree as a corporation. However, unlike corporations that have shareholders and profit that is subject to double taxation, a limited liability company has *members* and has profit that is not subject to double taxation. Rather, like partnerships, limited liability companies enjoy profit that is taxed once. Money comes into the company. The company pays no taxes on the income. The limited liability company then pays distributions out to its members, who must then report the income to the IRS and pay income tax on it. Thus, the entity does not pay taxes, only its members do.

Remember the following:

- A limited liability company does not have shareholders, it has members.
- A limited liability company does not have officers, such as a president, vice-president, etc. It has titles, such as a managing member.
- The entity name must include either the words "Registered Limited Liability Company" or "LLC" at the end of the entity name.

Entities That May Not Register

We just looked at the types of business entities that are permitted to register as real estate brokers. There are also some legal entities that are *not* permitted to register as real estate brokerage entities:

- Joint ventures
- Trusts
- Corporation sole
- Associations

Joint Ventures

A joint venture is not a legal entity; it is more of an arrangement that is usually designed for one specific project. The combining of two or more parties in a joint venture does not constitute a formation of a new legal person/entity. It is an arrangement that usually terminates at the end of that project. This does not prohibit the parties to work together in another arrangement and it sometimes can lead to new future partnerships. Let's look at an example of how this arrangement can come about.

Example

Developer Max and developer Ian attend an auction. Both have the intention of purchasing the same property. Rather than competing and bidding against each other (resulting in overpayment for the property), they decide to joint venture the project and purchase the property together.

There are times whereby two separate real estate brokers are working as coagents to the same principal. This may be by choice of the brokers to combine their efforts and expertise to vie for an assignment that the other could not necessarily obtain alone. Then again, the principal may have two favored real estate brokers that work in different offices and cannot decide whether to grant the assignment to one or the other. The principal asks the two separate brokers to work together. In that situation, both brokers work as one agent to the principal.

Trusts

A trust engages in transactions that involve its own property. Acquisition and disposition of real property is on behalf of the trust and its beneficiaries. This is the primary reason why a trust may not register as a real estate brokerage.

Corporation Sole

A corporation sole is typically a religious organization like a church. It is a not-for-profit entity.

Associations

Associations usually own or are responsible for operating a cooperative or a condominium. They are created for that purpose.

SUMMARY

Licensees, unless they are real estate brokers, must work under the license and supervision of a broker or developer. Real estate brokers are required to have a stationery office and register that office with the DBPR. Blind advertising is illegal. Escrow laws were created to protect the owner of the funds that are being held by another. In Florida, a broker may act as an escrow agent and is governed by strict rules concerning escrow accounts.

A broker must decide how to organize her business. A broker may do so through a variety of legal entity formation options. An understanding of each of these options becomes essential when choosing the right form and vehicle in operating the broker's business. Individuals receive licenses while legal business entities receive registrations. In each entity situation, if there is only one active broker, any change in the status of the active broker (resignation, termination of employment, or death) must be reported to FREC and a replacement broker must be registered within 14 calendar (not business) days or face cancelation of the registration.

REVIEW QUESTIONS

1. A buyer gave a binder deposit to a sales associate on Friday. This money must be turned over to his/her broker by:
   a. The end of Friday.
   b. The end of Monday.
   c. The end of Tuesday.
   d. The end of Wednesday.

2. The buyer and seller are quarreling over repairs for termite damage as required in the contract, and each has demanded the escrow deposit because of breach. The broker must:
   a. Notify FREC before 15 business days pass.
   b. Follow the seller's written instructions.
   c. Advise the parties to consult attorneys.
   d. Ask the DRE to issue an escrow disbursement order.

3. Sylvia Black works for Acme Realty and she is sending out calendars to neighborhoods where she would like to obtain listings. These calendars must contain:
   a. Sylvia's work address and phone numbers.
   b. The name of Sylvia's broker.
   c. Sylvia's business card, which indicates she is a broker associate.
   d. The words "Acme Realty."

4. Jane has personalized the yard signs for her listings by placing toppers that state "Call Jane!"
   a. This is not legal unless Jane is the broker.
   b. This is a legal and common practice.
   c. This is OK if Jane's last name is on the sign.
   d. This is OK if the firm's name is on the sign.

5. The buyer gives an associate a binder deposit on Friday. The money must be in the broker's escrow account no later than:
   a. Before the end of Monday.
   b. Before the end of Tuesday.
   c. Before the end of Wednesday.
   d. Before the end of Thursday.

6. The buyer came to the office on Friday and gave the binder deposit directly to the broker. The money must be placed in the broker's escrow account no later than:
   a. The end of Monday.
   b. The end of Tuesday.
   c. The end of Wednesday.
   d. The end of Thursday.

7. Louise places an ad for Acme Realty in the local newspaper. The ad describes the property, gives the price, and states "For more information, call 555-2111."
   a. Louise cannot place ads for her broker.
   b. This is an example of institutional advertising.
   c. This ad constitutes a blind advertisement.
   d. There is nothing illegal about the situation.

8. Both the buyer and the seller have demanded the escrow deposit. The broker notified FREC in writing 7 days later. How many days does the broker have to institute a settlement procedure?
   a. 30 days
   b. 23 days
   c. 15 days
   d. 13 days

9. Which statement is true about an office sign?
   a. No sign is required if the firm operates out of a private home.
   b. The office address is a sign requirement.
   c. The names of all partners in a real estate partnership must be on the sign.
   d. "Licensed Real Estate Broker" must be on the sign.

10. Which entity CANNOT be registered as a real estate broker?
    a. Corporation sole
    b. Nonprofit corporation
    c. General partnership
    d. Limited partnership

11. Two brokers own and operate separate real estate businesses. They are going to join together to oversee the rehabbing of an apartment building into condos, at which time they are going to market the condos. This:
    a. Is a partnership and must be registered with FREC.
    b. Joint venture, a temporary arrangement, is not registered with FREC.
    c. Requires a written agreement that is filed with the Department of State.
    d. Is an ostensible partnership with shared liability.

12. General Realty stores its office records in a storage facility at another location.
    a. All records must be kept on the premises for a period of 5 years.
    b. This is legal if the records are not destroyed.
    c. As long as the records are available, they can be in another place.
    d. The records must be available to auditors for at least 7 years.

13. The seller refuses to pay the broker's $5,000 commission. The broker is holding $5,000 in escrow for this transaction. The broker:
    a. Can take the $5,000 in lieu of the commission.
    b. Can hold up closing until the seller agrees to pay.
    c. Is allowed to place a $5,000 lien on the property.
    d. Can sue the seller in a court of law.

14. Which of these statements about a limited partnership is FALSE?
    a. The limited partnership agreement must be filed with the Florida Department of State.
    b. The limited partnership must be registered with FREC.
    c. The limited partners can be associates.
    d. Associates can be registered as licensed general partners.

15. When forming a general partnership as a real estate business:
    a. The general partnership agreement must be filed with the Florida Department of State.
    b. The general partners must hold real estate licenses.
    c. One general partner must be licensed as a broker.
    d. All general partners must be licensed as brokers.

16. Which statement is true concerning real estate brokerage trust funds?
    a. The broker may not place personal funds into an escrow account.
    b. The broker must dispense the interest if the funds are in an interest-bearing account.
    c. Interest-bearing accounts are not legal for trust accounts.
    d. A Florida attorney can hold the escrowed funds.

17. If only one partner in a general partnership has a broker license, and the license is suspended:
    a. The partnership is dissolved and must be reformed.
    b. A new active licensed broker must be substituted for the previous one prior to the passing of 14 days.
    c. The loss must be reported to FREC.
    d. All partners in a real estate partnership must be licensed as brokers.

18. Super Sales Realty has agreed to market a builder's homes. Sales associates are assigned to the model homes and potential buyers arrive at a designated location in response to the ads. The agents are using one of the model homes as a central place to meet the buyers and hand out sales brochures. When a buyers wants to make an offer, the agents take the buyer to the company's principal office to complete the paperwork.
    a. The model home is considered to be a branch office because buyers know to arrive at the location.
    b. This is a branch office because agents are assigned to the location.
    c. This is not a branch office because contracts and negotiations are signed and held elsewhere.
    d. An office sign must be placed on or about the entrance.

19. The escrow records of Surefire Sales were audited. Records showed that in June, the escrow account held $1,003 of the broker's personal funds.
    a. The broker is guilty of commingling.
    b. The broker has committed fraud.
    c. There is no illegality; the amount was less than $5,000.
    d. This is OK because the records are accurate and complete.

20. Jim works for Broker Smith and Jim receives 50 percent of the money he generates for the company. After a closing, Broker Smith calls Jim and apologizes for spending Jim's share of the commission to pay the office rent.
    a. Smith is guilty of fraud.
    b. This is legal if Smith pays Jim later.
    c. Jim can charge Smith with conversion.
    d. All money belongs to the broker. Jim is out of luck.

21. Which of the following is the only first-degree misdemeanor in the practice of real estate?
    a. Practicing without a license
    b. Failing to follow laws regarding rental lists
    c. Violating the Time Share Act
    d. Violating the laws regarding advance fees

Chapter 6

KEY TERMS

citation

complaint

formal complaint

legally sufficient

letter of guidance

notice of noncompliance

probable cause

probable cause panel

recommended order

revocation

summary (emergency) suspension

LEARNING OBJECTIVES

After completing this lesson, you will be able to:

- Identify acts that are considered license law violations.
- Describe how to report violations.
- Describe the steps involved in investigating complaints against licensees and conducting hearings.
- Understand how complaints are investigated.
- Understand how complaint hearings are conducted.
- Describe what constitutes a valid complaint.
- Describe the composition and makeup of the probable cause panel.
- Describe the reasons why an application for licensure would be denied.
- Describe the causes and events leading to license suspension or revocation.
- Understand the purpose of the Real Estate Recovery Fund, eligible and noneligible parties, and their ability to petition the fund.
- Explain the penalties associated with license law infraction, including first- and second-degree misdemeanors.

License Law: Violations, Complaints, Penalties, and Procedures

PROCEDURES FOR DISCIPLINING LICENSEES

In Florida, the disciplinary procedure begins with various aspects and parts of state law. Any licensee that bears the misfortune of disciplinary action taken against his license will be subject to state laws that cover each of the following:

- The investigative process
- The hearing process

  These laws include:

- Chapter 120, F.S.
- Chapter 455, F.S.
- Chapter 475, F.S.
- Chapter 61J2

  The Division of Real Estate (DRE) acts on broad powers. These powers are given to the Department of Business and Professional Regulation (DBPR) by the Florida legislature to investigate any legally sufficient complaint against any Florida licensee (person) or registrant (business) that has violated any state:

- Rule
- Regulation
- Statute

  The allegation does not have to involve real estate or occur in Florida. The term **legally sufficient** means that if the allegation were true, a rule, regulation, or statute has been violated. Therefore, the DRE is charged with the responsibility to investigate:

- All applicants for licensure by:
  - Verifying information contained on the application
  - Performing background checks
- All complaints that are received against a licensee

- Any licensee who is believed to have broken any state or license laws in the absence of a complaint from the general public

This investigative procedure and process is necessary for Florida Real Estate Commission (FREC) to carry out its role as a prosecuting unit. Let's take a look at the complaint process and the respective role that each unit of state government takes within this process.

THE COMPLAINT PROCESS, PROCEDURES, AND APPEAL

Complaint and Investigation

Because the license law was enacted to protect the health and welfare of the general public from losses resulting from those acting on behalf of others, the DBPR and the FREC respond very seriously to any **complaint** made by the general public against a licensee. A complaint can be defined as an allegation to a violation of a rule or law

Any written complaint that is legally sufficient and filed with the DBPR will be investigated. This is true even if the complaint was filed anonymously. In Florida, there is a statute of limitations for filing a complaint against a licensee. The complaint must be filed within one of the following time frames:

- Within 5 years after the act (the alleged violation)
- Within 5 years after the act was discovered or should have been discovered

In all cases, a copy of the complaint must be sent to the licensee. If a complaint is made and later the complainant withdraws the complaint, the DBPR may continue with the investigation. As previously mentioned, if the DBPR believes that a licensee has violated the license law or any other state law and there is no complaint from the general public, the DBPR (on its own initiative) may conduct its own investigation into the matter. Once a licensee is brought up on allegations of license law infractions or other complaints against that licensee, the infraction review process begins. Let's examine this process.

When a complaint against any one or more licensees has been duly made and appropriately filed with the DBPR, the complaint itself will be examined to verify its validity. To establish the validity of a complaint, the DBPR must establish whether or not there is any indication that state laws have been broken or if any rules of either the DBPR or FREC have been violated.

Coaching Tips: If a violation is minor and is the licensee's first offense, the DBPR has the authority to issue a notice of noncompliance. The notice identifies the violation and describes steps the licensee must take to comply with the law. If the licensee fails to comply, disciplinary procedures may proceed. An example of a minor violation is failing to maintain the proper office sign.

In the event the DBPR establishes that a complaint is valid, the DBPR is required to investigate the matter. During the investigation, depositions may be taken and subpoenas may be issued for the attendance of witnesses and/or the production of relevant documents.

Probable Cause Panel

At the end of the investigation, the DBPR creates a report that is submitted to a **probable cause panel**. The panel consists of two appointed members of FREC who are appointed by the Commission Chair. In the event that a panel cannot be formed in a timely manner by the Commission Chair, they are appointed by the DBPR. The decision as to whether probable cause exists is made by a majority vote.

Unlike Commission meetings, probable cause meetings are not open to the public. In fact, Commission members who do not serve on the panel are restricted from the panel meeting. This ensures a licensee will receive fair treatment under the laws that govern the disciplinary procedure.

At this point, the panel must decide within 30 days from receiving the investigation report whether or not **probable cause** exists (in this case, defined as reasonable grounds for prosecution of a licensee). This will be based upon the facts of the report submitted by the DBPR. This becomes the sole objective for the panel. Generally, a decision is reached within 30 days; there may be instances whereby the panel can ask for more time or for more information in order to render a decision.

If the panel determines that there is no existence of probable cause, one of the following occurs:

- The case is dismissed via a **letter of guidance** (a letter that suggests action or actions to be taken concerning the subject)
- The DBPR elects to pursue the matter further on its own. If this occurs:
  - The matter is immediately referred to FREC
  - FREC will determine whether or not the matter requires further investigation. Within this process the FREC may involve and retain one or both of the following:
    - Outside legal assistance
    - Private investigators

If the panel determines that probable cause does exist, the disciplinary process continues.

Coaching Tips: Complaints do not become public until one of the following occurs:

- **10 days after probable cause is determined**
- **10 days after the licensee waives her confidentiality privilege**

Formal Complaint

The DBPR is required to file a **formal complaint** against the respondent licensee. The formal complaint lists the charges set forth against the respondent licensee. The licensee then has a prescribed period of time to either accept or reject the charges set forth within the complaint. A licensee who responds to a formal complaint (in a timely manner) has three choices:

1. The licensee can meet with a DRE attorney and request a stipulation (settlement of penalty). The stipulation must be approved by FREC. The licensee may appear with or without legal representation.

2. The licensee can choose to not dispute the charges and elect to have an informal hearing held at an open Commission meeting. In this choice, the probable cause panel will not participate. Some agreement can be reached, at which point the matter will draw to an end.

3. The licensee can dispute the allegations set forth and request a formal hearing. In the event that any material fact of the allegation(s) is disputed by the licensee, a formal hearing is mandatory.

The Florida Division of Administrative Hearings (DOAH) will appoint an administrative law judge (ALJ) to preside over the formal hearing. The ALJ must be a member of the Florida Bar for at least the previous 5 years. In addition, the ALJ may not be a judge in the traditional sense. In order to give this procedure more weight, the current title of *administrative law judge* was changed from the previous title of *hearing officer*. At the conclusion of the formal hearing, the ALJ will issue a **recommended order** to FREC. The recommended order includes:

- Case findings
- A conclusion
- The recommended penalty

Should the licensee fail to respond to the formal complaint within the statutory allowed period of time, a default judgment will be entered against a licensee. When this occurs, the penalty usually will result in license revocation. This is a permanent removal from the practice itself.

If the charges contained are accepted, this ultimately results in a final order setting forth the action to be taken against the respondent licensee. If the charges contained are not accepted, a hearing is then scheduled.

Formal or Informal Hearing

The hearing may entail informal or formal proceedings. During an informal hearing, the licensee presents his case, typically at a Commission meeting (probable cause panel members are excused). Following the hearing, the parties may resolve the issue. However, if the parties cannot agree as to how to settle the matter, a formal hearing is held.

A formal hearing takes place before an administrative law judge. At the formal hearing, the respondent licensee will be given a chance to present her defense against the allegations contained within the complaint. The process is similar to how a case is tried in either civil or criminal court, wherein each party presents her facts and witnesses. This process is conducted within the rules of the courtrooms and not within the rules of the DBPR, DRE, or FREC.

At the conclusion of the hearing process, the presiding judge will draft an order recommending any applicable restitution and penalty to be assessed against the respondent licensee. The presiding judge will forward the conclusive order to the DBPR for further action and enforcement.

Final Order

FREC considers the judge's recommended order and issues a final order. Issuance of the final order brings conclusion to the case against the licensee. In addition to the final order, FREC can ask the secretary of the DBPR to issue a **summary (emergency) suspension**. FREC may accept, modify, or reject the recommended order. Thus, although the DBPR investigates complaints, FREC issues the final order. The final order:

- Must be in written form
- Must detail the charge(s)
- Must be inclusive of determination of facts found through the case hearing
- Must list the action taken against the licensee
- Must advise the licensee that the final order may be appealed
- Takes effect 30 days from entry

FREC must promptly report to the proper prosecuting authority any criminal violation of any statute relating to the practice of a real estate profession regulated by FREC.

Coaching Tips: If a violation poses an immediate danger to public health or safety, a hearing for summary suspension (emergency suspension of a license) may be held. In this situation, the final order must be issued by the DBPR secretary or his legal representative. If a summary suspension is ordered, the order must be followed with a formal suspension or revocation hearing. In addition, a licensee may continue to practice his profession up to the day the final order takes effect.

Appeal Process

If a respondent licensee disagrees with the final order issued by FREC, the licensee has the right under the Florida Statutes to appeal the order by requesting a judicial (court) review. It is this appeal method that allows the respondent licensee to challenge the findings of regulatory agencies such as the DBPR. In the event of any miscarriage of justice resulting from the disciplinary process, this final appeal process gives a respondent licensee a chance to overturn the decision. If the decision is in fact overturned, the licensee's privilege and ability to practice real estate is restored.

The Steps of the Complaint Process

1. The complaint is submitted to the DBPR.

2. Investigation of the complaint commences and the licensee is notified of the investigation.

3. A probable cause panel reviews the case to determine the existence of probable cause.

4. Drafting of a formal complaint commences if probable cause exists.

5. Formal or informal hearings commence.

6. Final order (judgment) is achieved bringing the case to a close.

7. The appeal process (via the courts) begins.

LICENSE LAW VIOLATIONS

License law infractions will result in disciplinary action against a licensee. The following list of actions identifies just a few of the violations that result in immediate disciplinary action such as denial, revocation, and/or suspension of a real estate license by FREC:

- Obtaining a license through material misstatements on a license application
- Engaging in fraud, dishonesty, or misrepresentation in a business transaction
- Being found guilty of, or pleading nolo contendere to, a crime involving moral turpitude and failing to disclose same
- Failing to maintain principal office or branch office entrance signs as required
- Failing on the part of the broker to register any branch office
- Failing on the part of the broker to properly register a trade or fictitious name
- Failing to supervise either of the following:
  - A broker associate
  - A sales associate registered with that broker/brokerage
- Advertising in a false and/or misleading manner
- Placing a blind advertisement
- Failing to account for or to deliver to a person escrowed property as required by law
- Failing to make a timely deposit of monies belonging to others requiring deposit into the broker's escrow/trust account

- Failing to review trust account procedures to ensure accurate compliance with the law
- Failing to provide necessary disclosure forms concerning:
  - Single agent relationships
  - Transaction broker relationships
  - Consent for transitioning from a single agent relationship to another relationship
- Failing to include a definite date of expiration, description of the property, price and terms, fee or commission, and signature of the principal in a written listing agreement; or failing to give a copy to the principal
- Entering into any listing agreement that contains an automatic renewal clause
- Paying a fee or commission for a real estate activity to an unlicensed person, even if only for a referral (paying a commission to a broker licensed in another state is acceptable)
- In the case of a sales associate, accepting a commission or compensation from anyone other than his employing broker
- In the case of a broker, employing a sales associate who is not properly licensed

Revocation/Suspension of Broker's License

Revocation of one's license represents a *permanent* removal from the real estate practice, while suspension results in a less permanent or temporary penalty. Under Florida law, if a broker's license is revoked and/or suspended, the licenses of all licensees employed under that broker automatically become involuntarily inactive. However, those affected licensees may reassociate and apply for a license with another broker willing to sponsor the individual.

Example

Broker Betty's license is suspended. Sales Associate Sam was employed by Broker Betty. Sales Associate Sam may reassociate and apply for a license with another broker willing to sponsor him. Sales Associate Sam cannot open his own real estate business. Also, Sales Associate Sam is not required to retake the state exam.

Coaching Tips: A license is considered *ineffective* when it has been suspended or canceled or when it is inactive. A license is considered *void* when it has expired or has been revoked.

Violations and Penalties

There are three types of penalties for license law violations:

1. Administrative penalties, which are imposed by FREC
2. Criminal penalties, which are imposed by a court of law
3. Civil penalties, which are also imposed by a court of law

   Let's take a closer look at these types of penalties.

Administrative Penalties

The FREC is authorized to:

- Deny a license
- Suspend a license for not more than 10 years
- Revoke a license
- Place a licensee on probation

- Impose a fine not to exceed:
  - $5,000 for each violation of Chapter 475 of the Florida Statutes (475, F.S.)—real estate brokers, sales associates, and schools
  - $5,000 for each violation of Chapter 455 of the Florida Statutes (455, F.S.)—business and professional regulation
- Issue a citation

Citations

On a daily basis, DBPR investigators are out in the field and may randomly inspect and audit:

- Real estate licensees
- Real estate brokerage businesses
- Real estate schools

While conducting a routine inspection, a DBPR investigator has the authority (for certain minor violations) to issue a **citation** to a licensee. The citation identifies the violation and the penalty (e.g., fine, order to complete educational courses, etc.). Common offenses that could be cited include:

- Blind advertising (advertising without clearly identifying that the advertiser is a real estate broker/licensee)
- Inappropriate handling of escrow accounts such as
  - Not signing reconciliation statements
  - Not dating the statements

When a citation has been issued, the licensee has 30 days to respond to the allegations contained within the citation. The licensee may choose to accept the citation in lieu of going through the hearing process described earlier. Should this occur, the citation results in a final order. At that point, the matter concludes. However, should the licensee decide that he prefers to dispute the allegations contained within the citation, he must reply in writing within the 30-day period. When the citation is responded to within the appropriate time frame, a formal hearing may be held.

In addition to the citation, other administrative penalties include:

- Issuing a notice of noncompliance
- Placing a licensee on probation
- Depending on the infraction, requiring a licensee to sit for education course(s) in addition to a monetary penalty

Criminal Penalties

In addition to administrative penalties imposed by FREC, a licensee may be subject to criminal penalties imposed by the courts. Most violations of Chapter 475 of the Florida Statutes are considered second-degree misdemeanors and penalties include one or both of the following:

- A fine of up to $500
- Imprisonment for up to 60 days

It is important to note that legal entities such as corporations cannot be jailed and therefore may suffer extreme fines as a result of a crime. All fines are determined in a court of law. FREC is not empowered to impose fines for criminal activities; however, any such activity must be reported to the appropriate authorities responsible for investigating crimes.

Penalties for first-degree misdemeanors include one or both of the following:

- A fine of up to $5,000
- Imprisonment for up to 1 year

Also, there is one violation that is considered a third-degree felony:

- Operating as any of the following without holding a valid and active license:
  - A broker
  - A broker associate
  - A sales associate

Penalties for nonlicensed activity consist of:

- $5,000 fine per offense and/or up to 5 years in jail
- A cease and desist order issued by the DBPR against the violator as well as impose fines of up to $5,000 per count
- Commencement of a criminal case (in criminal court) against the offender by the state district attorney

Civil Penalties

Civil penalties may be imposed by the courts if an individual performs real estate services without a license. In this case, the courts may deny the individual the right to receive compensation for the service.

The Real Estate Recovery Fund

The Real Estate Recovery Fund has been established to reimburse members of the public for monetary losses suffered when real estate licensees violate the license law. If a person is adversely affected by the actions of a real estate licensee, the aggrieved person may go to court to obtain a judgment against the licensee and ask for damages. If the judgment is issued and damages awarded, that person must first file a writ of execution to recover damages by liquidating the assets of the offending licensee. If this does not recover of all damages awarded, as a last resort, the injured person may seek to recover the remaining damages out of the Real Estate Recovery Fund. An action for recovery of damages must be brought within 2 years of the violation or discovery of the violation.

When payment is made out of the Real Estate Recovery Fund to satisfy a judgment against a licensee, the license of the person against whom the claim is made is automatically suspended. The licensee may also be subject to other disciplinary action. In order to restore the license to its previous status, the licensee must repay the full amount paid from the fund plus interest.

There are, however, exceptions to the previously stated penalties. Let's look at one potential scenario.

Example

An escrow dispute arises between a buyer and a seller concerning the disbursement of escrowed funds. In this transaction, the funds are held by the broker in her escrow fund. Upon first notice of conflicting demands for the escrowed funds, the broker acts appropriately and follows the necessary procedures dictated by license law.

To resolve the matter, the licensee is required to:

- Notify FREC within 15 days from the last conflicting demand for escrowed funds
- Request that FREC issue an escrow disbursement order (EDO), which, if issued by FREC, should be complied with by the licensee

An EDO is issued by FREC and directs the licensee to disburse the escrowed funds to a particular party within the transaction. The broker complies with the EDO and is later sued in civil court by the opposing party to the transaction. A judgment is awarded in civil court and is issued against the licensee. At a later point, payment from the Real Estate Recovery Fund is made on behalf of the licensee. In this case, *no action* is taken against the licensee. A licensee who is directed by FREC to act in accordance with an EDO, and does so, will:

- Not be required to repay the fund
- Not have her license disciplined

The limit of payment from the fund for multiple judgments or settlements against a single licensee cannot exceed $150,000. The limit of payment for damages for a single transaction cannot exceed $50,000, regardless of the number of claimants.

The minimum balance for the fund has been established at $500,000. If the balance in the fund drops below $500,000, each licensee will be charged a special Recovery Fund fee when applying for initial licensure and when renewing a license. If the balance exceeds $1,000,000, the special fee will be discontinued until the balance falls below $500,000.

None of the following would be eligible to petition the fund:

- A person who is licensed attempting to recover for damages resulting from a transaction in which he acted as a licensee
- A spouse of an offending licensee
- An individual who at the time of offence and sustained loss was operating without a valid real estate license
- A licensee who committed acts while on inactive status
- A corporation, branch office, or partnership, except through its individual licensees

SUMMARY

The DBPR investigates complaints in order to determine whether or not a complaint is deemed legally sufficient enough to proceed in a case against any licensee. If a complaint is found to contain investigative grounds for charging a licensee, the matter is turned over to FREC. A probable cause panel, which consists of two appointed members, is created next. Should the panel find that probable cause exists, a hearing is scheduled, which may be formal or informal. An administrative law judge presides over the hearing and issues a recommended order. FREC issues the final order specifying the action to be taken against the licensee. The DBPR would issue a final order only in the case of a summary suspension. At this point the case is closed. The licensee may appeal the final order through the courts.

The Real Estate Recovery Fund acts as a last resort to recover damages suffered via the actions of licensees. The fund may only be petitioned after first obtaining a judgment in civil court. Only certain people are eligible to petition the fund. The limit of payment from the fund for damages for multiple judgments or settlements against a single licensee is $150,000. The limit of payment for damages for a single transaction is $50,000, regardless of the number of claimants. The minimum balance for the fund is $500,000. If the balance of the Real Estate Recovery Fund exceeds $1,000,000, any special recovery fund fees charged to licensees will be discontinued.

REVIEW QUESTIONS

1. A complaint against a licensee was filed and investigated. The next step in the complaint process will be:
   a. The formal complaint.
   b. An informal hearing.
   c. A stipulation.
   d. Probable cause determination.

2. Punishment for a first-degree misdemeanor is a:
   a. Fine of up to $500 and/or up to 60 days in jail.
   b. Fine of up to $1,000 and/or up to 1 year in jail.
   c. Fine of up to $5,000 and/or up to 3 years in jail.
   d. Fine of up to $5,000 and/or up to 5 years in jail.

3. FREC authorized payment of $7,000 from the Real Estate Recovery Fund because of wrongdoing by a licensee. Which of the following actions would result against the licensee's license?
   a. Notice of noncompliance
   b. Summary suspension
   c. Automatic suspension
   d. Probation

4. A broker followed FREC's escrow disbursement order but was successfully sued by the other party. The broker must pay $40,000 in damages, plus $5,000 court costs and $7,000 in attorney fees. FREC will authorize payment from the the Real Estate Recovery Fund of:
   a. Nothing.
   b. $40,000.
   c. $50,000
   d. $52,000.

5. Mary holds a sales license in Florida. Mary purchased some land and the property was misrepresented. Mary successfully sued the buyer's agent and was awarded a judgment for $30,000 plus $20,000 in punitive damages. The agent then declared bankruptcy, and a court-ordered asset search confirmed there are no assets to pay the judgment. Mary:
   a. Cannot collect from the Real Estate Recovery Fund because she has a license.
   b. Cannot collect from the Real Estate Recovery Fund because the agent declared bankruptcy.
   c. Can collect $30,000 from the Real Estate Recovery Fund because she was the buyer.
   d. Can collect the entire $50,000 from the Real Estate Recovery Fund.

6. The DBPR is authorized in the field to immediately issue:
   a. Citations.
   b. Emergency suspensions.
   c. Administrative penalties.
   d. Fines of up to $1,000.

7. Joan is an associate for True Sales Brokerage and she was issued a citation by mistake. As a result, Joan:
   a. Must pay the fine and file a protest.
   b. Can only sue in a civil court.
   c. Can petition the DRE for a formal hearing.
   d. Can file a written dispute of the citation within 30 days.

8. The brokerage sign was not placed near the entrance and an investigator issued a notice of noncompliance. How long will the firm have to take corrective action?
   a. 10 days
   b. 15 days
   c. 30 days
   d. 45 days

9. A broker who concealed a leaky roof was found guilty of misrepresentation and fraud in a brokerage transaction. The broker could be subject to:
   a. Administrative punishment.
   b. Civil penalties.
   c. Imprisonment by a court of law.
   d. Administrative, civil, and criminal action.

10. The most FREC will authorize as payment from the Real Estate Recovery Fund for one licensee is:
    a. $25,000.
    b. $50,000.
    c. $75,000.
    d. $150,000.

11. What is the source of the money in the Real Estate Recovery Fund?
    a. The Foundation Trust Fund
    b. Administrative fines
    c. The state general fund
    d. Licensing fees

12. The DBPR is authorized to initiate an investigation of a complaint if:
    a. The act happened in Florida.
    b. The complaint is signed.
    c. The complaint is found to be legally sufficient.
    d. The complaint involved real estate activity.

13. A licensee received a formal complaint and does not dispute the charges. She decides her best course of action is to hire an attorney and meet with a DBPR attorney to negotiate any possible punishment. If an agreement is reached that is satisfactory to both parties, the agreement is termed a:
    a. Stipulation.
    b. Final order.
    c. Recommended order.
    d. Citation.

14. In the complaint process, a recommended order is issued by the:
    a. Florida Real Estate Commission.
    b. Secretary of the DBPR.
    c. Administrative law judge.
    d. Director of the DRE.

15. The Florida Real Estate Commission decides on the appropriate punishment in each disciplinary case. This is a final order and would NOT include:
    a. Placing the respondent on probation.
    b. Assigning fines and imprisonment.
    c. Suspending the license for up to 10 years.
    d. Permanent revocation of a license.

16. Julia set up a business to sell apartment seekers lists of possible units available to rent in the surrounding area. Julia does not have a license. Julia can be found guilty of a:
    a. Felony of the first degree.
    b. Felony of the second degree.
    c. Felony of the third degree.
    d. Misdemeanor of the first degree.

17. The word *license* in real estate includes all of the following EXCEPT:
    a. Permit.
    b. Registration.
    c. Certification.
    d. Stipulation.

18. An audit of the firm's escrow records revealed that in May of last year, the broker failed to sign the monthly reconciliation. As a result:
    a. No action will be taken. This was an honest mistake.
    b. The broker will receive a citation.
    c. The firm will receive a notice of noncompliance.
    d. The auditor will issue a formal complaint.

19. Broker Jones devised a land investment scam and enticed ten doctors to participate. When the scheme fell apart, each doctor individually sued the broker and received a $1,000,000 judgment against the broker, amounting to a total of $10,000,000 dollars. The broker declared bankruptcy and the court confirmed the judgments could not be collected. The doctors asked to be compensated from the Real Estate Recovery Fund. The Florida Real Estate Commission will authorize the payment of:
    a. $50,000 to each doctor.
    b. $75,000 to each doctor.
    c. $150,000 to each doctor.
    d. $50,000 split by the ten doctors.

Chapter 7

KEY TERMS

actual eviction

blockbusting

constructive eviction

Division of Land Sales,
    Condominiums, and Mobile
    Homes

familial status

property report

public accommodation

Real Estate Settlement
    Procedures Act (RESPA)

redlining

seven-business day right
    ?of rescission

steering

subdivided lands

LEARNING OBJECTIVES

After completing this lesson, you will be able to:

- Describe the provisions of the Civil Rights Act of 1866.
- Describe the provisions of the Civil Rights Act of 1968.
- Define the terms *steering* and *blockbusting*.
- Explain how an individual can enforce either Fair Housing Act.
- Recognize ways to avoid fair housing violations in your day-to-day practice.
- Identify several areas in which fair housing violations are most likely to occur.
- Describe some additional regulations related to fair housing opportunities.
- Describe the provisions of the Florida Uniform Land Sales Practices Act and the Florida Residential Landlord and Tenant Act.

Federal and State Laws Affecting Housing

INTRODUCTION TO FAIR HOUSING

There are two primary federal laws relating to fair housing:

1. The Civil Rights Act of 1866
2. The Civil Rights Act of 1968 (Also known as the Fair Housing Act of 1968)

Let's look at the provisions of each of these laws.

The Civil Rights Act of 1866

The Civil Rights Act of 1866 prohibits all discrimination on the basis of race in the purchase, sale, lease, or other conveyance of real or personal property. The Civil Rights Act of 1968 covers housing only. The Civil Rights Act of 1866 covers race only.

The Civil Rights Act of 1968

The second law is the Civil Rights Act of 1968, also known as the Fair Housing Act of 1968. This act also makes it illegal to discriminate in the purchase, sale, lease, or other conveyance of real property. The Fair Housing Act later was amended in 1974 and again in 1988.

This act differs from the Civil Rights Act of 1866 in two ways:

1. It extends the criteria on which discrimination is prohibited to the following:
   - Race
   - Color
   - Religion
   - Sex
   - National origin
   - **Familial status** (families with children under the age of 18 and pregnant women)
   - Handicapped individuals—physically and mentally
2. It covers discrimination related only to housing.

The Fair Housing Act prohibits the following acts of discrimination when they are based on race, color, religion, sex, or national origin:

- Refusing to sell, rent, negotiate, accept a purchase offer, or otherwise deal with any person
- Changing the terms or conditions for buying or selling
- Changing the terms or conditions for financing the sale of property
- Advertising that housing is available to only some buyers, or otherwise excluding some buyers
- Claiming that housing is not available for inspection, rent, or sale when it actually is available
- Excluding access to real estate services, such as multiple-listing services, or brokers' associations

In addition to the discriminatory acts just presented, there are two additional types of discriminatory acts that deserve special attention because they make up the majority of the complaints against licensees under the Fair Housing Act of 1968. These are:

1. Steering
2. Blockbusting

Steering

Steering refers to the practice of influencing potential buyers to buy only in certain areas or neighborhoods on the basis of race, color, religion, sex, or national origin. Steering includes:

- Directing minority buyers away from certain areas
- Directing minority buyers toward predominantly minority areas or areas of changing makeup

Steering accounts for most of the complaints filed under the provisions of the Fair Housing Act of 1968.

Blockbusting

Blockbusting, also referred to as *panic selling*, is the illegal practice of inducing owners to sell their properties by using information about changes or expected changes in the makeup of the neighborhood.

For example, a licensee might attempt to induce a homeowner to sell her home by claiming that the racial makeup of the neighborhood is about to change, and that this change would cause property values to fall, schools to deteriorate, or crime to increase.

Any inducement such as this is blockbusting and is illegal under the Fair Housing Act of 1968.

Properties Covered

The Fair Housing Act of 1968 applies to the sale, lease, or other conveyance of the following types of housing:

- Any single-family home owned by a private individual when:
  - A real estate broker is used
  - Discriminatory advertising is used
- Single-family housing not owned by individuals

- Single-family housing owned by an individual who:
  - Owns more than three houses
  - Sells more than one house in 24 months (other than his own)
- Multiple-family dwellings of five units or more
- Multiple-family dwellings of four or fewer units *if* the owner does not live in one of the units

---

Coaching Tips: **While some categories of housing are not covered in the Fair Housing Act of 1968, they are still covered under the Civil Rights Act of 1866, which makes it illegal to discriminate on the basis of *race* under any circumstances. This is true as a result of *Jones v. Mayer*, a significant court case that upheld the Civil Rights Act of 1866.**

Exemptions

We just looked at the properties covered by federal fair housing laws. Under the federal fair housing laws, certain exemptions are provided and exist under defined circumstances. The following are some of the exemptions:

- A dwelling containing one- to four-family housing where the property owner resides in one of the units. Please note that this exemption does not apply in either one of the following instances:
  - The services of a real estate licensee is used
  - Discriminatory advertising has been used
- Facilities reserved only for their respective membership of private organizations and not for use by or with the general public
- Facilities of or within a house of worship or other religious sector that are strictly for the benefit of their constituents

Enforcement

Any individual who feels discriminated against may take action to enforce the fair housing laws. There are various ways, on a federal level, that someone can enforce the Fair Housing Act of 1968, such as:

- Filing a written complaint with the Department of Housing and Urban Development (HUD) in Washington, D.C.
- Filing an action in court (U.S. District Court, or a state or local court)
- Filing a complaint with the U.S. attorney general

The Civil Rights Act of 1866 can *only* be enforced by filing a suit in federal court.

State Law

On a state level, Florida has its own fair housing law. In fact, certain provisions of state law are more restrictive in many ways than federal laws. In other ways, federal laws are more restrictive than state laws. Whenever there is a conflict between the state and federal laws, the rule to follow is: *The more restrictive provision will normally prevail over the other.*

INTRODUCTION TO FAIR HOUSING VIOLATIONS

Previously, you learned about the major provisions of fair housing laws. It is important to know what these laws provide to ensure fair housing opportunities for everyone. It is also very important for you to understand how to conduct your business in compliance with fair housing laws. Now, you will learn about some of the practical situations in which the issue of fair housing can arise, as well as some general practices to follow to ensure that you comply with the law.

FAIR HOUSING VIOLATIONS

A licensee has violated the law if equal service is denied to anyone on the basis of race, color, religion, ancestry, sex, national origin, familial status, or handicap. If a licensee violates the law in this manner, the licensee may be subject to severe penalties including:

- Loss of license
- Civil damages and penalties
- Criminal prosecution, fines, and imprisonment

In order to ensure that you do not violate fair housing laws, you should do two things:

1. Fully understand your responsibilities under fair housing laws
2. Constantly monitor your own actions to ensure that they are in compliance with the law

As you evaluate your actions, it is important that you look both at the *effects* of your actions and at your *intent*. It is not sufficient that your *intention* is not to violate the law. It is possible that your actions may result in a violation, even if that is not your intent. There are several areas (some that we have covered) in which violations of the fair housing law are most common:

- Blockbusting
- Improper listings
- Refusing to show property to minorities
- Steering
- Advertising
- Less favorable treatment of minority buyers
- Redlining

Note that the first two violations occur while working with a seller, while the last five occur while working with a buyer. Let's look at each of these in more detail.

Blockbusting

There are two situations in which a charge of blockbusting is most likely to be made:

1. When a sales associate attempts to get a listing by conveying information about a minority group in the neighborhood or coming into the neighborhood
2. When a sales associate uses an intensive solicitation campaign (e.g., phone calls, letters, door-to-door canvassing) in a neighborhood whose makeup is changing (in terms of one or more minority groups)

Let's look at a sales associate inducing a sale by conveying information about a minority group.

Putting It to Work

Example 1

A sales associate was trying to get a listing on the Smiths' house by convincing them to sell and move somewhere else. The sales associate stated to the Smiths that a Hispanic family had bought a house down the street from them.

This is a violation of the law because the sales associate stated that a change was occurring in the racial makeup of the neighborhood *in order to induce the Smiths to sell.*

Improper Listings

There are two categories of improper listings you should guard against:

1. Refusing to accept a listing because the owner is a minority
2. Accepting a listing from a seller who attempts to place restrictions on selling to one or more minority groups

Let's look at an example for each of these.

Putting It to Work

Example 1

An Asian owner called a sales associate and asked to have his home listed for sale. The home was located in the Chinese section of town. When the sales associate learned of the location of the home, he turned the listing down. He stated that he did not know much about that part of town, but knew that buyers had often had difficulty getting loans for homes in that area.

Was there a violation? Yes. The sales associate's refusal to list the home was found to be based on the owner's race and the racial makeup of the neighborhood. The fact that loans had been difficult to get was irrelevant and is using someone else's discrimination as an excuse. The effect is the same—racial discrimination. A sales associate must make the same effort to sell property owned by a minority as she would make to sell property owned by a nonminority.

Example 2

An owner wants to sell his home, but only to an African American person. He contacts a sales associate who has several listings in the area and asks her to sell the home for him, but only to an African American.

Can the sales associate legally do this? No. The sales associate must comply with fair housing laws even if the seller does not. She should tell the owner that she may accept the listing *only* if he lifts the restrictions, and that he may be violating the law.

Refusal to Show Property to Minorities

It is a violation of the law to refuse to show property to a person because that person is a member of a minority group.

Let's look at an example.

Putting It to Work

Example 1

A Hispanic sales associate was showing a young, Caucasian, divorced mother properties for sale. When the woman asked about a property in a predominantly Hispanic neighborhood, the sales associate refused to show the property and attempted to discourage her, by saying, "Don't you think you would enjoy living in another area better? I think it would be more suitable for your family situation."

Is there a violation? Yes. This is clearly a case of refusing to show property based on race.

Steering

Steering refers to the practice of influencing which neighborhood a buyer buys in, in either one of the following ways:

- Directing a minority buyer *toward* minority or changing neighborhoods
- Directing a nonminority buyer *away* from minority or changing neighborhoods.

Let's look at an example.

Putting It to Work

Example 1

A sales associate was showing a businessman several homes. The buyer was looking through the sales associate's multiple-listing book when he spotted a home he particularly liked. When the sales associate saw which home he liked, she commented: "I don't think you will like that area. It is changing." The sales associate was aware that the neighborhood had recently become integrated.

Was there a violation? Yes. The sales associate's comment referred to a change in the racial makeup of the neighborhood. The sales associate was steering the buyer away from this neighborhood.

Advertising

Discrimination in advertising is prohibited by fair housing laws and must be avoided, even if the discrimination is not intentional.

Putting It to Work

Example 1

A sales associate placed the following ad:
"Oriental families notice bargain-priced agent's home."

Was there a violation? Yes. Even though the agent claimed that the reference to "oriental families" was done only to point out the oriental design, the advertisement referred to the racial makeup of potential buyers.

Less Favorable Treatment of Minority Buyers

A charge of less favorable treatment of a minority buyer usually occurs because a sales associate does one of the following:

- Insults or ignores a minority buyer
- Refers a minority buyer to a licensee of the same minority group
- Does not use his best efforts to close a sale
- Gives preference in submitting a nonminority buyer's offer over a minority buyer's offer
- Treats minority buyers differently in terms of financial matters

Let's look at an example.

Putting It to Work

Example 1

Just before closing, a listing broker found out that the buyers on a property were African American. He immediately called the company that was to provide a termite clearance letter and told the company to raise the cost of the letter from the previously stated price of $175 to $380. Because of the increased cost of the termite letter, the sale did not close.

Was there a violation in this situation? Yes. The listing broker discriminated against the buyers. He discouraged their purchase by artificially raising the price of the termite letter.

Redlining

Redlining is the practice of discriminating when making loans in a neighborhood because of the makeup of the neighborhood in terms of race, color, religion, national origin, or sex. Redlining refers to either refusing to make loans in such neighborhoods or making loans at less favorable terms. Redlining also applies to the issuance of insurance policies. For example, an insurance company refuses to issue a homeowners policy because the property is located in a declining neighborhood.

ADDITIONAL REGULATIONS

Earlier in this chapter, you learned about fair housing laws. You should also be aware of some additional regulations that are related to fair housing, such as:

- Civil Rights Act of 1964—This act prohibits discrimination in housing programs that receive federal funding.
- Equal Credit Opportunity Act—This act prohibits discrimination in the credit-application process based on race, color, religion, sex, national origin, marital status, or age, or because the individual receives income from a public-assistance program. This act requires a lender to originate a loan merely on credit worthiness.
- Americans with Disabilities Act—Title III of this act prohibits discrimination based on disability by places of **public accommodation** and commercial facilities. (Places of public accommodation are privately owned businesses and nonprofit organizations open to the public.) This act applies to:
  o Properties available to the public that were built after 1990
  o Properties available to the public that were rehabbed after 1990
  o Multifamily housing built after 1990 whereby a certain percentage of units must be wheelchair accessible
- State and local laws—Some state and local laws prohibit discrimination based on additional classes or categories of individuals.

In addition, the Code of Ethics of the National Association of Realtors (NAR) prohibits discrimination. According to the NAR Code of Ethics, when providing real estate services, a Realtor is prohibited from discriminating against individuals because of their race, color, religion, sex, handicap, familial status, or national origin. An individual who believes he has been discriminated against by a Realtor may file a complaint with the local Board of Realtors. The Board of Realtors is authorized to take disciplinary action against a Realtor if the board determines that a violation has occurred.

THE REAL ESTATE SETTLEMENT PROCEDURES ACT

The **Real Estate Settlement Procedures Act (RESPA)** was passed by Congress in 1974 and later revised in 1996. RESPA's purpose is to regulate financial institutions that originate loans secured by mortgages for housing transactions. RESPA applies to federally financed residential property transactions. It does not apply to:

- Seller financed properties
- Commercial transactions

RESPA serves the following purposes:

- Provides the buyer/borrower with a more expeditious advance disclosure of settlement costs

- Provides the buyer/borrower protection from expensive settlement costs resulting from egregious practices

- Provides the buyer/borrower with the settlement process costs in a timely manner

- Provides the buyer/borrower with the closing services at the lender's actual cost. This eliminates kickback and referral fees that may increase the cost to the buyer/borrower for the closing services.

Real Estate Settlement Procedures Act Requirements

The provisions of the Real Estate Settlement Procedures Act (RESPA) require that the lender must:

- Provide a good-faith estimate of the costs of borrowing to the buyer/borrower within three business days from the time of a completed loan application

- Send the buyer/borrower a booklet entitled *Guide to Settlement Costs*, which is a buyer's guide to settlement costs

- Show the buyer/borrower the Uniform Settlement Statement prior to closing as follows:

  ○ The form must be available *on request* from the buyer. (The lender is not required to show it to the buyer unless requested to do so.)

  ○ It must be made available one business day before closing.

  ○ It must include an itemized list of charges to the buyer.

This information is helpful in that it shows the buyer an itemized listing of all charges, which determines the amount of money that the buyer will be required to pay at closing. Note, however, that the Uniform Settlement Statement provided to the buyer need not be *complete* under the provisions of RESPA. RESPA only requires that whatever is complete as of one business day prior to closing must be shown to the buyer if requested.

FLORIDA HOUSING LAWS

Previously in this chapter, we looked at the federal fair housing laws. Now we will go over two state laws related to housing:

1. The Florida Uniform Land Sales Practices Act
2. The Florida Residential Landlord and Tenant Act

The Florida Uniform Land Sales Practices Act

The Florida Uniform Land Sales Practices Act (Chapter 498 of the Florida Statutes) covers and deals primarily with required disclosures as they apply to subdivisions (or **subdivided lands**). Under this act, a subdivision is defined as any land to be subdivided into 50 or more lots or interests. The purpose of the act is to provide potential buyers with adequate information about the property. The agency responsible for regulating the sale of land contained within a subdivision in Florida is the **Division of Land Sales, Condominiums, and Mobile Homes**. This division is a part of the Department of Business and Professional Regulation (DBPR).

According to the Florida Uniform Land Sales Practices Act, a person cannot sell subdivided land unless she has a valid registration for the sale of the subdivided land. Prospective buyers of the land must be given a public offering statement. The public offering statement is a document that fully discloses the characteristics of the subdivided land, including:

- A description of the land
- An identification of any encumbrances, liens, easements, or restrictions
- A statement of the taxes
- Other information required to ensure full disclosure

Anyone entering into a contract for the purchase of subdivided property covered under the Florida Uniform Land Sales Practices Act has a **seven-business day right of rescission**. That is, the buyer is permitted to cancel a sales contract within seven days of signing it. *This right of rescission does not apply to anyone (a builder) who is in the business of purchasing subdivided land for the sole purpose of building on the lots.*

There is also a federal law that regulates the sale of subdivided land. This federal law is called the Interstate Land Sales Full Disclosure Act, which requires that certain disclosures be made to potential buyers and that each buyer be given a period during which he may cancel the sales contract and receive a full refund. Under this act, the disclosure document that must be provided to purchasers is referred to as a **property report**.

The Florida Residential Landlord and Tenant Act

The Florida Residential Landlord and Tenant Act was originally designed to define the relationship between a landlord and a tenant.

Specifically, the act was designed to define that relationship as it would apply *only* to a residential property containing dwelling units. The following terms are specifically defined under the act:

- Landlord—the property owner/lessor
- Tenant—the legal occupant/lessee under a mutually executed lease agreement within a rental property
- Dwelling—any property where one or more persons legally reside

In order to have a valid enforceable contract, the agreement must contain all the essential elements necessary to make that contract enforceable. An enforceable contract is one that will stand up in court. (Contracts are discussed in much greater detail in Chapter 11.) One of those essential elements of an enforceable contract is a competent party. A lease is considered a contract. In Florida, no persons under the age of 18 years old are considered to be competent parties. Therefore, in order to have an enforceable lease agreement, the lessee must be 18 years of age or older.

Leases Covering Residential Dwelling Units

When a lease covering a residential dwelling unit (as defined under Florida Statutes) is entered into between a landlord and tenant, each party to the lease has performance obligations to the other party. Let's take a look at these obligations, beginning with the landlord's obligations.

Landlord's Requirements under a Lease

The landlord's requirements under a lease include:

- Maintaining the demised premises (*Demised premises* refers to the property that has been leased.)
- Properly handling security deposits and rent paid in advance

Let's go over each of these responsibilities.

Maintaining the Demised Premises

A landlord has duties with regard to the day-to-day maintenance of the rental property. A landlord is required to:

- Provide a unit for rental that meets all codes relating to rental property in Florida
- Provide the following simple yet necessary services in operating the property:
  - Properly functioning systems for heat and hot water
  - Trash removal (from the property itself)
  - Extermination
  - Maintenance of the structure and its grounds at least within minimum standards required for habitation

Handling Security Deposits and Rent Paid in Advance

Chapter 83.49, F.S., deals with the appropriate measures concerning the handling and disposition of deposits and advance rents. Deposits are not limited to only security deposits, but also include items such as:

- Pet deposits
- Any contractual deposits that were agreed to in advance by the landlord and tenant
- Damage deposits
- Advance rents

Generally, upon execution of a residential lease, the tenant will deposit with the landlord:

- The first and last months' rent
- A security deposit in the amount of one or more months' rent

The security deposit is designed to protect the owner against a number of possible tenant-related losses resulting from the tenant's occupancy. Possible losses include nonpayment of rent or damage to the dwelling unit by the tenant or the tenant's visitors. Under the Florida Residential Landlord and Tenant Act, the landlord is required to place deposits received from the tenant within a separate bank account. The account:

- Must be held and maintained within a Florida institution
- May be an interest bearing or noninterest bearing account
  - If the account is held as an interest-bearing account, the tenant is required to receive either 75 percent of that annual interest amount or an annual simple interest rate of 5 percent.
- Must be held separate from the landlord's operating account
  - The landlord may not use the account's funds, pledge the funds as collateral, or commingle the funds. Commingling refers to mixing funds belonging to others with personal funds.

In lieu of holding funds in a separate account, the landlord may post a bond in the amount of $50,000 or the amount of the security deposits/advance rents, whichever is less. In this situation, the landlord is required to pay the tenant interest at an annual simple interest rate of 5 percent. No later than 30 days after the landlord receives any security deposit and/or advance rents, the landlord must:

- Notify the tenant as to how these funds are being held on deposit
- Provide the tenant with the name and address of the institution holding these funds

At the end of a lease, the landlord has certain obligations regarding the handling of security deposits that have been placed in her possession. When the lease term expires, the landlord is required to:

- Notify the tenant in writing within 30 days indicating that the landlord intends to retain part or all of the deposit currently in the landlord's possession

- Indicate the reason for retention of the funds

- Send this notice via certified mail for proper delivery

- Allow the tenant 15 days thereafter to either agree or disagree with the contents of the claim

If the tenant challenges the landlord's claim to the deposit, the outcome of the challenge will be decided in court. At such time, the losing party will be responsible for paying the other's costs and expenses associated with either bringing the action or defending the claim.

In the event that the landlord has not imposed any claims on the deposits, the landlord must deliver these funds to the tenant within 15 days from termination of the lease. In addition, through a doctrine of laches (meaning, "assert your rights or lose them"), if the landlord has remained silent on any claim or imposition on the deposit for longer than 30 days, she loses the right to any further claim on the deposit.

We have been looking at the obligations of the landlord under a lease. Now, let's go over the obligations of the tenant.

Tenant's Requirements under a Lease

The Florida Residential Landlord and Tenant Act requires a tenant to continuously use his best efforts toward maintaining the demised unit in accordance with any and all relevant housing codes. This includes, but is not limited to:

- Complying with sanitary codes as they apply to dwelling units

- Maintaining the interior unit plumbing fixtures

- Maintaining the interior unit air-conditioning

- Maintaining the interior unit appliances

- Following any other rules and regulations contained within the lease or dwelling complex

- Providing the landlord with any reasonable access allowed under state laws or necessary for the performance of the landlord's responsibilities under the lease

Terminating a Lease

A lease can be terminated by the tenant or by the landlord. A member of the U.S. Armed Forces may terminate a lease under the following circumstances:

- When the member of the U.S. Armed Forces is stationed 35 miles or more from the rental property (as a direct result of orders)

- When the member of the U.S. Armed Forces is involuntarily or prematurely discharged or released from active duty

Terminating the lease would entail the following process:

- Providing the landlord a written notice of the intent to terminate the tenancy at least 30 days following the landlord's receipt of the notice to terminate. A letter should be included with the notice to terminate from the commanding officer as proof of written verification of the tenant's military service orders.

- At termination, the tenant would be liable for the pro-rata portion of rent due up to the date of termination

Termination by Tenant

Landlords are required to provide a tenant with a habitable unit or living complex. That is, the property must meet certain minimum standards. From time to time, the landlord and tenant will disagree as to what is considered to be minimum standards. **Constructive eviction** occurs when the landlord causes or permits a situation to occur that makes it impossible for the tenant to enjoy the premises under the terms of the lease. However, because a valid and enforceable lease exists between the landlord and tenant, the tenant must first:

- Notify the landlord in writing as to the defect/default item to the property
- Allow the landlord the ability to correct said defect/default within 7 days *prior to* constructive eviction

Termination by Landlord

Conversely, a landlord may find himself with a nonperforming tenant. This usually results from nonpayment of rent but can result from other types of tenant default (e.g., disturbing other tenants by creating too much noise). When rent is involved, the landlord may terminate the lease by providing a 3-day notice to the tenant, which will demand either the rent in question or that the tenant deliver physical and legal possession of the demised premises to the landlord. If the tenant willfully vacates, the landlord is still required to do one of the following:

- Refund the security deposit in its entirety within 15 days of the vacating of the premises
- Properly notify the tenant if any security deposit will be retained by the landlord

If the tenant fails to vacate the premises, the landlord's only option is to seek **actual eviction**. Actual eviction refers to the legal removal of the tenant from the leased property because she violates some provision of the lease.

A landlord may not simply evict a tenant without going through a specific eviction process. The eviction process requires judicial intervention. This means that the landlord must obtain a judgment from the courts prior to removing the tenant and/or the tenant's belongings from the unit. The following steps must be taken during the eviction process:

- The tenant must receive notice of the demand for possession of the property in writing.
- The landlord must file an eviction complaint with the appropriate county court.
- If the complaint is not answered by the tenant in a timely manner, a default judgment is entered in favor of the landlord.
- If the complaint is contested by the tenant, the case will be heard before the court to determine a judgment on the matter.
- If the judgment is awarded to the landlord, a writ of possession is executed by the sheriff.
- It is only at this point that the landlord (with the sheriff's assistance) may physically and legally remove any remaining tenant possessions from the unit.

SUMMARY

Federal and state housing laws affect sellers, buyers, landlords, and tenants. These laws also affect how a licensee must service and deal with the general public. The services that are offered by a real estate brokerage should not differ from one person/party to another. Testers are members of programs that enforce the rights of home-seekers. Their mission is to determine whether the information or services that come out of a licensee's office is influenced by race. Therefore, licensees should avoid any practice that can be perceived as a violation of State or Federal Housing laws. In addition, the licensee is urged to attend Fair Housing seminars and courses that cover this material.

REVIEW QUESTIONS

1. Broker Bill is a business broker and has a contract to sell a candy store. The owner instructed Bill to refrain from showing the business to racial minorities. What is true about this situation?
   a. Bill represents the owner and must honor the owner's request.
   b. The owner can do this, but Bill cannot.
   c. This violates the Civil Rights Act of 1866.
   d. This violates the Civil Rights Act of 1968.

2. A couple of Asian descent asks you to show them properties only in Asian neighborhoods. You:
   a. May honor this request.
   b. Would be guilty of blockbusting.
   c. Would be guilty of redlining.
   d. Would be guilty of steering.

3. A landlord collects the last month's rent from a tenant as a requirement of the lease. In this situation:
   a. The landlord can post a bond and spend the money.
   b. The money can be placed in an interest-bearing account and the landlord can keep the interest.
   c. The money must always be kept in a noninterest-bearing account.
   d. If an interest-bearing account is used for the deposit, the landlord must pay the tenant 7 percent simple interest.

4. How long does a landlord in Florida have to notify the tenant of the location of advance fees collected and held by the landlord?
   a. All tenants must be informed about the money before 15 days pass.
   b. The tenant must be notified in writing; no time limit exists.
   c. If the money leaves Florida, the landlord has 60 days.
   d. Tenants must be informed in writing within 30 days of paying the fees.

5. Forrest owns and lives in one unit of a duplex and is interviewing prospective tenants for the other unit. Forrest questions the applicants about their religious beliefs. Which of the statements is true regarding the situation?
   a. Forrest is in violation of the Civil Rights Act of 1866.
   b. Religion is a protected status. No one can do this.
   c. Forrest is exempt from fair housing requirements.
   d. This is legal only because Forrest lives in the property.

6. Sure Fire Insurance refuses to write insurance policies for homes in Palm Shores because minorities live there. This is an example of:
   a. Redlining.
   b. Steering.
   c. Blockbusting.
   d. Channeling.

7. A private club has maintained a clubhouse and rental rooms on the beach for more than 70 years. Only club members can rent the club's rooms. The club's rental restrictions:
   a. Predate fair housing laws and are grand-fathered in.
   b. Violate fair housing laws in the Civil Rights Act of 1968.
   c. Are legal because private clubs are exempted.
   d. Are legal if the club accepts minorities as members.

8. Fran owns a vacant rental unit in a Spanish-speaking neighborhood in Tampa. She decides to advertise the vacancy in a Spanish-language newspaper in Tampa.
   a. The choice is Fran's to make.
   b. Fran is guilty of steering.
   c. The neighborhood is Spanish-speaking; this is an example of redlining.
   d. This is legal as long as the ad isn't discriminatory.

9. Joseph has a new listing in a neighborhood in St. Petersburg. One of the features of the neighborhood is a beautiful Catholic church. The church building is a local landmark and is often featured on postcards and pictures in the papers. Joseph places an ad in the paper that states the home for sale is "near St. Mary's." This is an example of:
   a. A common practice in real estate ads.
   b. Discrimination prohibited as redlining.
   c. Landmarks and can be referred to in ads.
   d. Steering.

10. In a large apartment complex, it is policy to place married couples in one building and singles in another on the theory that the singles party and create noise. This policy:
    a. Is an example of steering.
    b. Is not steering but does violate fair housing laws.
    c. Does not violate any laws.
    d. Is discrimination based on familial status.

11. The law that requires lenders to provide borrowers with a good-faith estimate of closing costs is the:
    a. Equal Credit Opportunity Act.
    b. Real Estate Settlement Procedures Act.
    c. Civil Rights Act of 1968.
    d. Consumer Credit Protection Act.

12. The Equal Credit Opportunity Act prevents discrimination in lending based on:
    a. Marital status.
    b. Familial status.
    c. Handicap status.
    d. Credit status.

13. Geneva applied for a loan to purchase a new home. The lender talked about closing costs and loan features. Geneva left the office without the special information from HUD that suggests what reasonable closing costs might be. The lender's actions:
    a. Violated the Equal Credit Opportunity Act.
    b. Are entirely legal.
    c. Violated RESPA
    d. Can be prosecuted by HUD.

14. It is the policy of management of an apartment complex to place families with children in the building near the playground equipment.
    a. Management has violated fair housing laws.
    b. This is legal if the parents are informed.
    c. The policy is legal if the parents agree with the placement.
    d. Marital status is not protected in housing. This policy is legal.

15. Steve is 85 years old and has an above-average income and an excellent credit rating. Steve applied for a 30-year loan to buy a vacation condo, but the lender said a 15-year loan was the only loan Steve could qualify for.
    a. At his age, Steve is glad for any loan at all.
    b. The lender has no legal obligation to lend money.
    c. Age is a protected status in lending decisions.
    d. Fair housing laws protect age in residential property.

16. A Presbyterian church sponsors a retirement home for retired Presbyterian ministers and their spouses. No other persons can lease the units.
    a. This is discrimination in housing based on religion.
    b. Religions have a special exemption in fair housing requirements.
    c. Churches can be granted fair housing exemptions on a state-by-state basis.
    d. Religious discrimination is not addressed in fair housing laws.

17. The Interstate Land Sales Full Disclosure Act differs from the Florida Uniform Land Sales Practices Act in that:
    a. Florida's law exempts builders with 100 or more lots.
    b. The federal law lets purchasers cancel within 7 days.
    c. The federal law applies to builders with 50 lots or more.
    d. The federal law requires the subdivision be registered with HUD.

18. An African American couple called the realty firm and asked to inspect a house the firm just listed. The listed home is located in an African American neighborhood.
    a. This is an example of steering.
    b. Showing the couple the listing is redlining.
    c. You must show the couple all the listings in this price range.
    d. You can show the couple the house.

19. Prospective buyers of time-shares in Florida:
    a. Can cancel the purchase from a developer within 15 days.
    b. Must be given a public offering statement.
    c. Are only leasing the property.
    d. Would never receive a deed.

20. Eviction is a judicial process in Florida and must be carried out by the courts. The first step in a legal eviction is notification of the tenant. This could be accomplished by any of the following EXCEPT:
    a. Mail the notice to the tenant.
    b. Post the notice on the door.
    c. Knock on the door and hand the notice to the tenant.
    d. Pay the sheriff's department to notify the tenant.

21. In Florida, the Florida Landlord and Tenant Act states that if a landlord is informed in writing by a tenant of any failure to maintain the building in compliance with all health, building, and local codes, the landlord must:
    a. Make the required repairs in 7 days or face prosecution.
    b. Make the required repairs in 15 days or face prosecution.
    c. Make the required repairs in 30 days or face prosecution.
    d. Respond to the tenant in writing within 15 days of the notice.

Chapter 8

KEY TERMS

bundle of rights

chattel

common property

concurrent ownership

cond-op

condominium

cooperative

declaration of condominium

elective share

estate at will

estate for years

estate in severalty

estates in land

exempt property

fee

fee simple absolute

fee simple defeasible

fee simple estate

fixtures

freehold estate

holdover tenant

homestead

joint tenancy

land

leased property

leasehold

leasehold estates

life estate pur autre vie

life estates

monthly maintenance

owners association

partition

personal property

personalty

property

proprietary lease

real estate

real property

remainderman

reversionary interest

right of survivorship

separate property

statutory life estates

tenancy at sufferance

tenancy at will

tenancy by the entirety

tenants in common

time-shares

Property Ownership

After completing this lesson, you will be able to:

- Define real property based on the definition in Chapter 475, F.S.
- Know the physical components of real property.
- Know the four tests courts use to determine if an item is a fixture.
- Know the difference between real property and personal property.
- Understand the bundle of rights associated with real property ownership.
- Understand the principal types of estates (tenancies) and describe their characteristics.
- Understand the features associated with the Florida Homestead Law.
- Know the difference between condominiums, cooperatives, and time-shares and the ability to describe the four main documents associated with condominiums.

PROPERTY OWNERSHIP

Classification of Property

Most of our real estate terminology is derived from the old English feudal system of property ownership. The feudal system dates as far back as the Renaissance period. In simple terms, this system of property ownership meant that land ownership was a vested interest held only by the Crown. To this day, the United Kingdom, as well as worldwide British mandates and territories, still subscribe to this system of property ownership. Therefore, if the Crown was the only party with land ownership rights and interests, noblemen or lords (as they were called) received a grant/gift of land from the Crown. In essence, this grant was the Crown's reward to the nobility for loyalty and service.

This system of property ownership later evolved to what is known today as the allodial system. The difference between the two systems is simple:

- Feudal system—**Land** (the ground and all permanent attachments) ownership vests only with the Crown. The Crown acts as the grantor by granting only possession of the property to the nobleman who in turn becomes the grantee. The nobleman only has a possessory right in the property but not ownership in the land. This directly resembles **leased property** as we know it today. In essence, the estates were reversionary and defeasible. This meant that at any point, the Crown, who was the sole owner of the land, would be able to recapture the granted property. Therefore:

o Land is owned by the Crown and not by the individual(s)

o Individuals possessed rights for their lifetime only

o Individuals did not possess an inheritable estate

Coaching Tips: **It is important to point out that property ownership is comprised of two components:**

1. **The** fee, **which represents the direct ownership within the land**
2. **The** leasehold, **which represents the possessory right to the land and improvement(s)**

Based on this, it was possible then, as it is now, that one party could have ownership/vested rights within the land or the fee, while another party received a leasehold interest in the property.

• Allodial system—The feudal system evolved into the allodial system. Under the allodial system, the purchaser received more than just a possessory right to the property. This system provided vesting/ownership rights to the land and any improvements to the property. These rights are greatly limited by the rights of government. However, under this system:

o Land vests with the individual owner(s) of the property

o The owners possess an inheritable estate

REAL PROPERTY COMPOSITION

There are two categories of interests held in land:

1. Interests held by government
2. Interests held by individuals

Interests held by individuals are referred to as **estates in land**. An estate in land is the degree, quantity, nature, and extent of one's interest in the land. The term *estate in land* refers to an individual's interest in the land and not to the land itself or the physical properties of the land. Therefore, an estate in land is the interest held in land (real property or real estate).

The term **property** refers to the rights of ownership. The term *estate* means ownership in property. What type of property or estate one holds can be defined by the two types of property referred to within our system:

1. **Real property** or **real estate**—Real property is land and all things attached to and affixed to it. This would include ownership in the

   • Fee (land)
   • Leasehold (improvements)

The permanence of any attached item (i.e., house, wood deck, etc.) to the land makes that item real property. Although at its inception, an improvement made to real property may have been personal property, the manner by which the improvement was attached to the land categorizes it as real property.

FIGURE 8.1

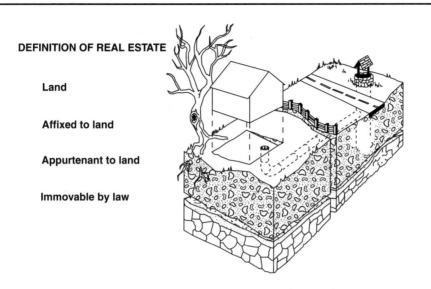

DEFINITION OF REAL ESTATE

Land

Affixed to land

Appurtenant to land

Immovable by law

Coaching Tips: Chapter 475.01, F.S., defines real property in the following manner: "Real property" or "real estate" means any interest or estate in land and any interest in business enterprises or business opportunities, including any assignment, leasehold, subleasehold, or mineral right; *however, the term does not include any cemetery lot or right of burial in any cemetery; nor does the term include the renting of a mobile home lot or recreational vehicle lot in a mobile home park or travel park.* (See Figure 8.1.)

---

2. **Personal property**—Personal property includes all other property other than real property. Personal property is also known as **chattel** or **personalty**. As a helpful guide, if it is moveable, it is personal property.

There are two categories of chattel:

1. Chattel personal
2. Chattel real

An item of chattel personal is an item of personal property that is moveable and is not attached to or associated with the real property. This includes items such as:

- Automobiles
- Tools
- Furniture
- Boats
- Clothing
- Money

An item of chattel real is an item of personal property that is not moveable or is attached to or associated with the real property. It may consist of tangible property or an intangible interest. Examples of chattel real that are considered to be tangible property include:

- Trade fixtures
- Emblements (crops)
- Mortgages

FIGURE 8.2

Bundle of rights

- Leases
- Options
- Easements

Aside from the title aspect to ownership in real property, ownership comes with other legal rights. These legal rights are termed as the **bundle of rights**. (See Figure 8.2.) The bundle of rights include rights of:

- Use/enjoyment—Includes the ownership's right to use the property in any lawful manner prescribed by law.
- Possession—The inception of this right commences on the day that title passes to the rightful owner. It includes the right of ingress (entry) and egress (exit) of one's property. It further includes the property owner's right to benefit from any income attributable to the property derived from rent.
- Improvement—This right allows the property owner to improve the property through the addition of constructing improvements to the land. This right is regulated by local zoning and building codes.
- Exclusion—This right allows the property owner to control who may enter the property. It also allows the property owner to enforce her rights against any unlawful trespass by another.
- Disposition—This right allows the property owner to sell, lease, mortgage, license, or gift all or a portion of the property to another.

Let's examine the bundle of rights as they apply to the owner. There are three basic physical rights that are attributable to real property ownership: surface rights, subsurface rights, and air rights.

Surface Rights

Included in surface rights are water rights, which consist of:

- Littoral rights—Those rights that occur when land adjoins a stationary body of water such as oceans, lakes, or seas. They are generally navigable bodies of water.
- Riparian rights—Those rights that occur when land adjoins rivers, streams, or other flowing bodies of water. They are usually nonnavigable bodies of water.

When land joins a flowing body of water, the owner has the right to limited, non-exclusive use of the water out of the watercourse (i.e., river or stream). The owner does not own the water itself, but may use it for reasonable purposes.

The boundary of the property carrying riparian rights depends on whether the river or stream is navigable or not. If it is navigable (meaning boats can travel on it), the land owner's property ends at the high water mark. If it is not navigable, the land owner's property ends at the middle of the watercourse (i.e., river or stream).

Doctrine of Prior Appropriation

The riparian rights of an owner in some states are limited by the doctrine of appropriation. This doctrine states that the first owner to divert water for his own use may continue to do so, even if it is not fair to other owners along the watercourse.

A littoral right is the right of a landowner to use the water in a lake, ocean, or sea that adjoins her property. The landowner may use or enjoy the water touching her land provided she does not alter the water's position by artificial means.

Surface rights extend from border to border of any property.

Other terms and factors that affect land ownership bearing littoral or riparian rights include:

- Accretion—The gradual build-up to a shoreline or bank of a waterway
- Alluvion—The build-up of land by accretion
- Erosion—The loss of land resulting from the elements
- Reliction—The increase of land resulting from the permanent receding of a body of water

Subsurface Rights

Included within these rights are:

- Oil
- Gas
- Mineral rights

Subsurface rights extend to the center of the earth's core.

Air Rights

Air rights are defined as the total legal bulk of an improvement made to land. The total size of the improvement is regulated by local zoning ordinances.

It is important to note that some properties are not built (within the existing improvement) to the full extent that zoning permits and, as such, unused development rights remain. In certain cases, this may permit the owner of these unused development rights to further enlarge the improvement or allow by means of transfer (under certain conditions prescribed by local zoning ordinances) of those same rights to another neighboring or adjacent property. Historic/landmark property is a typical example of an unused air rights candidate. Where historic/landmark districts within a municipality may impede further development of that property, the unused building rights become an asset that can be sold and transferred.

Given the rights discussed above, it would not be unimaginable for a property owner (whose sole interest was in the surface rights) to sell his subsurface and air rights to two separate parties. This scenario creates three separate ownerships within the property rights of one parcel of land.

FIXTURES

Fixtures are special categories of real property. They can be items that were initially real property or personal property. When permanently attached to the real property, a fixture becomes a part of the real property via utility and permanence of the object to the property.

Example

A tree is severed into wood and subsequently used to build a wood deck attached to a home. The original tree is categorized as real property via its roots. Once severed, it becomes personal property. When that same wood is attached to a home as a deck, it reverts back to real property.

In any real property transaction, buyers and sellers can often confuse the difference of what is a fixture versus what is personal property. The classic example would be the heirloom chandelier. Illumination receptacles are commonly referred to as light fixtures. Although they can be easily removed (with little or no damage to the property), the manner of their attachment and adaptation to the property has made light fixtures the subject of lawsuits within a purchase and sale contract. In order to avoid these problems, the sales associate may wish to review with the seller a punch list of items that would not be included in the sale of the property.

Plants, Trees, and Crops

Plants, trees, and crops growing on real property represent a special category of property. They can be either real or personal property under certain conditions. Their classification will depend on whether they are considered to be one of the following:

- Fructus naturales
- Fructus industriales

Fructus naturales are plants that are considered to be part of land, including:

- Trees
- Cultivated perennial plants (such as orange or apple trees)
- Uncultivated vegetation of any kind (such as naturally growing shrubs, bushes, etc.)

Fructus industriales are plants that are cultivated annually. They are considered to be personal property. They are also referred to as emblements. They include cultivated crops such as corn, wheat, or vegetables.

Coaching Tips: **Fructus naturales are plants that grow naturally without help from humans. They are considered real property.**

Fructus industriales are plants that are cultivated by humans and depend on humans for their existence and growth. They are considered personal property. They are also referred to as emblements.

Legal Determination of a Fixture

Courts apply the following three tests when faced with determining whether or not an item is considered a fixture:

1. Method of attachment
2. Adaptability of the improvement to the property
3. Intent or agreement of the parties

Coaching Tips: **In some cases, the courts may even use a fourth test to make a determination as to whether an item is a fixture. The "relationship between the parties" becomes another method of dispute resolution.**

Method of Attachment

Observance of how an improvement is made and ultimately attached aids in determining whether or not an item is classified as a fixture. If the removal of the item will result in damage to the property, it is usually classified as a fixture and a permanent part of the real property.

Adaptability of the Improvement to the Property

A close examination of how an item adapts to the real property can also determine whether or not an item is considered a fixture. Sometimes it is difficult to determine whether an item is permanently attached or not.

Example

A room-sized air-conditioner may or may not be permanently attached. In cases such as these, it is necessary to look at whether the item has been adapted to the building. If the air-conditioning unit is window mounted, it would not be considered a fixture. Conversely, if the unit is wall mounted (wall unit cut out), it would probably be considered a fixture.

As another example, if storm windows are a standard size that could be used on other standard windows, the storm windows probably would not be considered a fixture. However, if the storm windows are custom fit to the windows, they would probably be considered a fixture. The custom-fit window directly adapts to conform to the house.

Kitchen cabinets are deemed to be fixtures. Aside from the fact that they are an essential item within any kitchen (their adaptability to the room), removal would cause considerable damage. They also represent a design feature necessary to the room.

Intent or Agreement of the Parties

It is obvious that "good agreements make for good friends." When an agreement is made in advance, determining whether an item is deemed a fixture or personal property is simplified. Defining ownership of improvements that are made by a tenant in a lease will certainly avoid a landlord/tenant dispute at lease expiration. Listing items to be removed within a contract of sale will also avoid a dispute between buyer and seller.

Trade Fixtures

A special category of fixtures deals with fixtures used in a trade or business. Trade fixtures are items that are installed and used in the conduct of one's business. Therefore, when items are attached to or installed in real property for business purposes, the item(s) are considered personal property and may be removed at the end of a lease (which is more commonly the case) or at time of sale. They are deemed to be personal property items of the enterprise. For this to occur, two conditions are met:

1. The items must be removed *prior* to lease expiration.
2. The property is returned or restored to its original condition upon removal of the items.

Example

Department stores utilize wall units and shelving to display their inventory for sale. Their method of attachment to the property is generally permanent in nature. Whereby, we define a fixture as any item that when removed will result in damage to the property, the wall units and shelves were initially installed with the intent that the interested party would have the right to remove them at time of sale or lease expiration.

The issue of whether an item is real property (fixture) or personal property is important in a number of situations:

- When property is sold:
  - A fixture, because it is real property, is sold as part of the property being sold.
  - Personal property is not sold as part of the real property and thereby remains the property of the selling party.

FIGURE 8.3

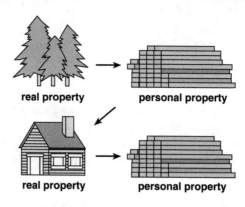

- When property taxes are assessed:
  - A fixture contributes to the value of the property in the form of an improvement. Generally speaking, when an improvement extends the life of the property or adds value through its utility, the item of improvement will cause higher property assessments. To the property owner, this translates into property tax increases.
- When property is appraised:
  - A fixture adds to the value of the property.
  - Personal property does not add to the value of the property.
- When insurance is issued on real property:
  - Fixtures are covered under the real property coverage.
  - Personal property is not covered or covered separately.

  See Figure 8.3 for an illustration of real property and personal property.

Tests for Fixtures Mnemonic Device—MAI
    *M*ethod of attachment
    *A*daptability of the improvement
    *I*ntent or agreement between the parties

TYPES OF ESTATES

There are two types of estates within the property system:

1. Freehold estates (ownership of the property)
2. Nonfreehold estates or estates less than freehold (leaseholds/leased property)

Freehold Estate

The first type of estate in land is called a **freehold estate**. A freehold estate corresponds to what is commonly known as ownership interest in land (the fee). It is:

- An interest in land that may be held for an indefinite period of time. This includes property that is held for a lifetime (life estate) or longer.
- An entitlement to the holder to both the rights of:
  - Ownership
  - Possession

As a memory device, the term *freehold* represents the owner's ability to "freely hold a parcel of property" for as long as deemed appropriate by that owner.

There are several types of freehold estates:

- Fee simple estates, including:
  ○ Fee simple absolute
  ○ Fee simple defeasible
- Life estates

Some of the estates listed bear limitations and thereby create "variations to the theme." Let's examine the composition of these different variations.

Fee Simple Estate

As written earlier, property can be broken down into two parts:

1. Fee—Represented as ownership in the land and all rights contained therewith.
2. Leasehold—Offers ownership (of a limited duration) and comes in the form of rights of possession within the improvement(s) to the fee. The giver of the lease-hold is known as the lessor and has a reversionary right within the property upon expiration of the lease (the leasehold).

A **fee simple estate** is the most comprehensive and simplest form of property ownership; it is ownership in land itself. Historically, before improvements were made to a property, the ownership process began with unimproved land. Therefore, the simplest and highest form of ownership came in this form. The importance of this type of estate is shown in the text regarding Rockefeller Center in New York City that directly follows.

Today, it is not uncommon to see property broken down with two separate parties involved:

1. The land owner (fee owner)
2. The developer/investor (holding a leasehold interest to the land)

We can conclude that not all land owners are developers and not all developers are land owners. With this thought in mind, major developments exist today that began as leasehold development.

Example

In the early twentieth century, a 16 million square foot commercial space develop-ment was created in New York City in what is known today as Rockefeller Center. This development included Radio City Music Hall. At its inception, the Rockefeller family donated the land under Rockefeller Center to Columbia University. While the land (or fee simple) was donated to Columbia University, the Rockefeller family reserved a long-term leasehold (in excess of 50 years) that enabled them to construct numerous office and entertainment structures. As a result of restructuring in the mid-1990s, today, both fee and leasehold are owned by the various owners who have purchased these properties.

The primary characteristics of a fee simple estate are as follows:

- They are held for a lifetime or longer.
- Fee simple property ownership includes the right of inheritability (can be willed to heirs).
- **Fee simple absolute** is the most preferred, common, and desirable form of owner-ship. Fee simple absolute is the most complete form of ownership and the type

that most property owners possess. It is not a defeasible estate. A fee simple absolute has three primary characteristics:

1. It is the least restricted form of property ownership.
2. It is limited only by government's rights of eminent domain, taxation, police power, and escheat.
3. It is a nondefeasible estate. This means that it cannot be defeated (overcome) by another individual against the owner's will under any circumstances.

- **Fee simple defeasible** is lesser in its desirability insofar as ownership of real property is concerned. This type of ownership bears conditions or is conditional on whether or not certain or specific events occur. Property is transferred to another with certain conditions. In the event that these conditions are violated, the property owner's rights of ownership can be defeated with a right of reentry by the previous party. This type of estate can be determined by examination of the title being conveyed. Words that reference "but if" are usually followed by the conditions of title being conveyed.

Example

Mrs. Black gave her property to a charity organization "for as long as it is used for elderly housing." The estate owned by the charity is a fee simple defeasible. In the event that the property is used for anything other than the stated conditions, title to the property reverts to Mrs. Black or her heirs.

Life Estates

The primary characteristics of **life estates** are as follows:

- They are held for a lifetime (but not longer).
- They are not inheritable and therefore may not be willed to heirs. There is one exception to the rule that life estates are not inheritable A **life estate pur autre vie** is the exception and it is based on the lifetime of a third party. Therefore, it is inheritable only if the life tenant dies prior to that of the named third party whose life the life estate was predicated on. For example, "A" gives a life estate pur autre vie to "B" for the life of "C". Later, "B" dies and wills the life estate pur autre vie to "D". As long as "C" is alive, "D" will be able to benefit from the inherited life estate. That life estate would continue until the death of the third party occurred. It is for this reason that a life estate pur autre vie is the exception.
- They are always reversionary estates or interests. This simply means that the original grantor receives ownership and all rights associated therein upon the death of the life tenant who is the grantee. In other words, the death of the life tenant/grantee automatically terminates the life estate and all possessor rights associated therein.

Voluntary Life Estates

Voluntary life estates are created by a voluntary act of the grantor. All of the life estates presented so far are voluntary in nature. There are three types of voluntary life estates:

1. Life estate in remainder, in which ownership of the fee simple estate reverts to a third party upon the death of the life tenant. The third party named to receive the fee simple estate is called the **remainderman** (see Figure 8.4a).
2. Life estate in reversion, in which ownership of the fee simple estate reverts to the grantor or her heirs upon the death of the life tenant (see Figure 8.4b).
3. Life estate by reservation, is where ownership is transferred to another, and the selling party reserves or keeps a life estate for the rest of the selling party's life. Upon death of the selling life estate party, possession and use reverts to the buyer (see Figure 8.4c).

FIGURE 8.4

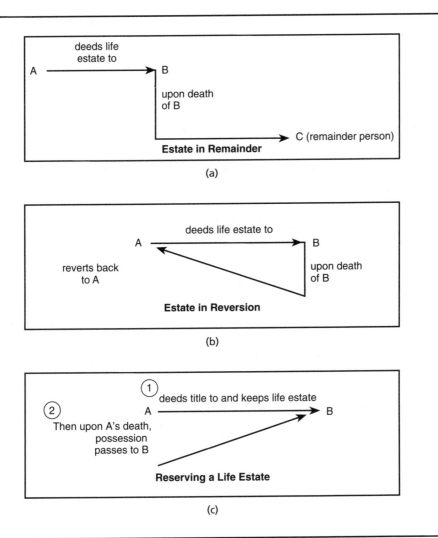

Estate in Remainder

(a)

Estate in Reversion

(b)

Reserving a Life Estate

(c)

Statutory Life Estates

It is important to point out that in some states, some life estates are created *not* by voluntary action, but by law. These type of life estates are called **statutory life estates**. There are three types of statutory estates:

1. Dower—A wife's right to receive, upon the death of her husband, a share of all property held or owned by the husband during the marriage.

2. Curtesy—A husband's interest in the property owned by his wife at the time of her death.

3. Homestead protection—Provides a life estate to a widow or widower. It should be noted that this is not the same thing as a homestead tax exemption.

Nonfreehold Estates or Estates Less Than Freehold

Before we discuss nonfreehold estates or estates less than freehold, let's first review the differences between freehold estates and nonfreehold estates or estates less than freehold. The easiest way to remember the difference is as follows:

- Freehold estate means *ownership*.

- Nonfreehold estates or estates less than freehold means *rental or leased property*.

Nonfreehold estates or estates less than freehold are also called **leasehold estates**. This applies to any property that is leased by a tenant. Where freehold estates are considered real property, nonfreehold estates or estates less than freehold are considered personal property.

Some basic terminology related to nonfreehold estates or estates less than freehold includes:

- The holder of nonfreehold estates or estates less than freehold is called the *tenant* or *lessee.*

- The property owner granting this estate is called the *landlord* or *lessor.*

  The rights of the parties to the lease include the following:

- The tenant or lessee may occupy and use the property exclusively as long as he has a valid lease, abides by the terms and conditions provided within the lease, pays rent on time, and is not in default of any of the terms or provisions therein.

- The landlord or lessor cannot occupy or use the property until the lease has expired and the landlord/lessor has obtained legal possession of the property.

- During the lease term, the landlord/lessor is said to possess a **reversionary interest** in the property leased. This provides for the right to reclaim and regain legal possession of the property at the end of the lease term.

Types of Nonfreehold Estates or Estates Less Than Freehold

There are three categories of leasehold estates:

1. Estate for years
2. Estate at will
3. Estate at sufferance

Estate for Years

An **estate for years** is a lease that has a specified starting and ending date. In spite of its name, it does not necessarily have to be for more than 1 year. In fact, it can be for any duration—as little as 1 day to many years. However, this would be predicated upon the specified duration stipulated within the lease.

Estate at Will

An **estate at will** is also referred to as a **tenancy at will** or, in Florida, a tenancy without a specified term. Simply put, it may be terminated by either lessor or lessee at any time (at will). Otherwise, it is a normal landlord-tenant relationship.

Coaching Tips: Some states place limitations on estates at will. Generally, these limitations tend to deal with notice requirements to terminate, requiring minimum notice periods from either party. For example, in order to terminate a month-to-month tenancy at will, Florida law requires that either party to the lease provide the other with notice of the intent to cancel the lease not less than 15 days prior to the end of that monthly period.

Estate at Sufferance or Tenancy at Sufferance

An estate at sufferance or **tenancy at sufferance** occurs when a tenant remains in possession beyond her legal tenancy without the consent of the landlord/lessor. In this situation, the tenant/lessee is referred to as a **holdover tenant** or a tenant at sufferance. In this situation and if done in a timely manner, a tenant at sufferance or holdover tenancy

FIGURE 8.5

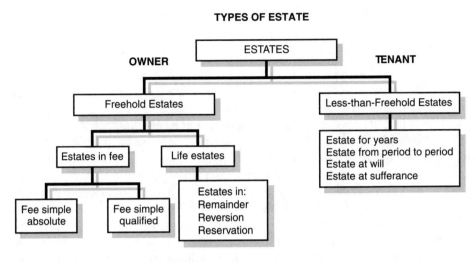

TYPES OF ESTATE

can be evicted. However, if a tenant has the landlord's permission to remain in possession of the leased property after the initial term expires, this is a tenancy at will rather than a tenancy at sufferance. (See Figure 8.5.)

Entitles Holder to:	Freehold Estate	Estate Less Than Freehold
Entitles Holder to:	Ownership and Possession	Possession Only
Duration:	Lifetime or Longer	Less than a Lifetime

FORMS OF OWNERSHIP

There are two basic forms of property ownership:

1. Sole ownership
2. Concurrent ownership

Sole Ownership

Sole ownership or ownership in property by one person is called an **estate in severalty**. The word *severalty* sounds like it should mean ownership by several people, but that is not the case. In fact, the root word of severalty is *sever.* A means of remembering this would be to think of severed ownership. Any freehold estate can be held in severalty.

Concurrent Ownership

Any ownership held by two or more persons in property is called **concurrent ownership**. There are four types of concurrent estates/ownership:

1. Joint tenancy (with rights of survivorship)
2. Tenancy in common
3. Tenancy by the entirety
4. Community property

In each of these types of concurrent ownership, each co-owner holds an undivided interest in the property as a whole verses separate parts of the property.

Joint Tenancy

In order to create this type of ownership, more than one party to the transaction is required. Therefore, any two or more persons may hold title as joint tenants. The primary distinguishing characteristic of **joint tenancy** is the fact that it carries the rights of survivorship. Survivorship means that when a joint tenant dies, her share or interest within the property automatically goes to any surviving joint tenant or tenants. The share or interest does not go to any heirs of the deceased joint tenant. The reason for this is the survivorship provision within the title to this vesting. Due to the survivorship provision, a joint tenancy is not willable or inheritable. Survivorship rights supercede and have full priority over any dower or curtesy rights. During the life of a joint tenant, the joint tenant may sell to whomever is willing to buy his interest within the property. However, upon the death of the joint tenant and in the absence of a sale during his life, the deceased tenant's share will always equally inure to the benefit of any remaining joint tenants.

Creation of a joint tenancy with rights of survivorship requires the presence of four unities:

1. Unity of time—All joint tenant owners must acquire the property at the same time.

2. Unity of interest—All joint tenant owners must hold equal degrees (shares) of interest (i.e., four parties each having a 25 percent interest in the property at time of purchase).

3. Unity of title—All joint tenant owners must acquire title in the same way. This must be in the form of one single title to the whole property (undivided interest).

4. Unity of possession—All joint tenant owners must hold an undivided interest in the possession of the whole property.

Coaching Tips: **A helpful tool and mnemonic device is PITTS:**

- *Possession* (unity of)
- *Interest* (unity of)
- *Time* (unity of)
- *Title* (unity of)
- *Survivorship* (rights of)

There are two important remaining points to discuss concerning joint tenancy:

1. As previously mentioned, a joint tenant may sell to anyone she chooses to during her life. This may be done without the consent of the other joint tenant owners. However, any new owner who is outside of the initial acquisition, becomes a tenant in common with the remaining living original joint tenants/co-owners.

2. Corporations may *never* hold ownership as joint tenants with rights of survivorship. Corporations have what is referred to as perpetual life. Therefore, it is safe to assume that a corporation will always outlive the joint tenant. It is for this primary reason that corporations may not hold title to property in this fashion. Corporations may hold property either in severalty or as tenants in common with others.

Tenancy in Common

Any two or more persons may hold title to property as **tenants in common**. Where the unity of possession is required, unlike joint tenancy, each tenant holds a separate title to his undivided interest within that subject property. A co-owner may sell his share within the property at anytime and to anyone with or without the other's consent. Rights of survivorship do not exist within this type of title holding. Therefore, a tenancy in common bears the rights of inheritability. In addition, co-owners may hold equal or unequal shares within the property ownership. Unlike joint tenants, the unity of interest is not required.

Coaching Tips: In most states, when there are two or more owners of a property and no specific form of concurrent ownership is suggested or indicated, the owners by default are presumed (by law) to be tenants in common. Specifically, such is the case within Florida.

Joint Tenancy		Tenancy in Common
YES	Possession (Unity of)	YES
YES	Interest (Unity of)	NO
YES	Time (Unity of)	NO
YES	Title (Unity of)	NO
YES	Survivorship	NO

Tenancy by the Entirety

Tenancy by the entirety can be compared with joint tenancy. It is a special form of joint tenancy. The primary difference lies with the relationship of the parties. Tenancy by the entirety is solely reserved for husband and wife relationships. It requires the following:

- The four unities of joint tenancy, namely:
  - Possession
  - Interest
  - Time
  - Title
- A fifth unity is called the unity of person. It is limited to ownership held jointly by husband and wife who are considered to be one person. As such, each spouse owns an undivided interest in 100 percent of the property. This tends to protect either spouse from a forced sale resulting from judgments against one but not the other.

Tenancy by the entirety normally carries the inherent **right of survivorship**. The right of survivorship can be defined as:

- The right of a surviving party to the property of a deceased party.
- This is an inherent characteristic of joint tenancy relationships and tenancy by the entirety.
- It is only recognized in about half of the states in the United States, including Florida.

Under this holding of title, neither spouse may encumber the property or sell the property without the consent of the other. However tenancy by the entirety may be terminated by any of the following:

- Joint action of husband and wife
- Divorce
- Death of either spouse

Community Property

Community property is based on the concept that each spouse has an equal interest in any property *acquired* during marriage. Property acquired before the marriage or received after the marriage through a will or gift does not qualify as community property. Florida is not a community property state.

Partitioning of Ownership

Holders of concurrent estates/ownership have an undivided interest in the property. In some cases, this interest can be separated by **partition**. Partition is the dividing of common interests into separate interests owned in severalty. Joint tenancy and tenancy in common can be partitioned; however, tenancy by the entirety cannot. Partitioning can occur by two methods:

1. Partition in kind—The property itself can be subdivided and split among the owners.
2. Partition at law—The property can also be sold and the proceeds divided among the owners.

   In addition, portioning can be brought about in either one of two ways:

1. The co-owners can agree voluntarily to the partition.
2. One or more co-owners can ask the courts to partition the property if the owners cannot agree among themselves.

Special Ownership Interests

There are also some special ownership interests in Florida, including:

- Elective share
- Exempt properties
- Homestead

Elective Share

Elective share deals with the rights of a surviving spouse who has been excluded from the deceased spouse's will. In this situation, by law, the surviving spouse is entitled to a share of the decedent's estate. At present time, the elective share in Florida is 30 percent of the net estate. This does however bear some exclusions.

   A spouse who was included in a will may also have rights if the share provided for under the will is less than the spouse stood to receive under state law. In this case, the spouse may be entitled to an elective share. For this to happen, the elective share must be greater than the share provided for within the decedent's will.

Exempt Properties

Another property right is referred to in Florida as **exempt property**. Exempt property refers to personal property that a spouse is automatically entitled to when the other spouse dies. In Florida, exempt property includes household items such as furniture and appliances with value of up to $10,000 plus automobiles. Such property may not be seized or sold by a creditor to satisfy a debt.

Homestead

Florida state law provides for an owner-occupant of a home to be eligible to receive **homestead** status. To be eligible, the homeowner must reside in the home and have legal title to the property as of January 1 of any given year. The homeowner must also file for the homestead exemption. It is the declaration of one's residence as a home-stead that entitles the property owner to certain protections as well as benefits.

The purpose behind the homestead is to ensure that families with unsecured debts cannot be removed from their homestead as a result of a forced sale of the property. The creation of a homestead will protect and relieve the property owner from all debts that may result in a forced sale of the property *except* debts resulting from:

- Unpaid real property taxes
- Any unpaid special assessments
- Recorded mortgages
- Vendor liens, wherein the seller holds a lien on property when the sale involves a purchase money mortgage
- Construction liens, such as mechanics and materialman's liens, wherein a supplier of labor or materials places a lien on the property if the labor materials are not paid for

Liens are claims on the property of another. This subject will be discussed in greater detail in Chapter 9.

Homestead Exemption

Florida homestead law currently allows the owner of a property that qualifies as a home-stead to receive an annual property tax exemption. With few exceptions, this does not mean that a qualified homestead will pay zero property tax. It simply provides for a credit against the property tax bill up to the amount of the exemption. At present time, the maximum exemption is $25,000.

The application of the exemption is then used to calculate one's annual property tax bill. The tax bill is calculated by deducting the homestead exemption amount (be it a partial or full homestead) from the assessed valuation applied to the property by the municipality assessor. Assuming no further exemptions are available to the property owner, the difference between the gross assessment and the homestead deduction acts as the net assessment. The net assessed value is then multiplied by the appropriate tax rate for the area. Let's look at an example of this application:

Example

$100,000 Assessed Value of Property (prior to homestead deduction)
− 25,000 Homestead Exemption
$75,000 Assessed Value Subject to Property Tax

COMMUNITY OWNERSHIP

So far, we have covered various forms of ownership of individual parcels of real prop-erty. Next we will examine ownerships in situations where communities of property are involved. (This is different from the concurrent ownership category called *community property.*)

Other than detached housing, there are four types of property ownership vehicles that one can purchase in a community:

1. Condominiums
2. Cooperatives
3. Planned-unit developments
4. Resort time-sharing developments

In community ownership, individual owners surrender some of their property rights in exchange for certain benefits of community living. In each form of community ownership, it is helpful to think of the community as a "city within a city" that has all the requirements for:

- Some form of self-government of the citizens
- Assessments or common area maintenance (CAM) to fund the operation of the community
- The provision of services

Condominiums

The first form of community ownership is called a **condominium**. A condominium is a form of individual fee ownership of a unit within a multifamily development property. The distinguishing features of a condominium are:

- Ownership of separate property
- Common property

The individual unit owner holds two types of interest in a condominium:

1. A fee simple title to the individual unit. Ownership of a condominium unit on the tenth floor of a high-rise tower is no different than that of single-family home ownership. Just like the owner of a single home property, the condominium unit owner receives a deed for the property.
   - These individual units are called **separate property**.
2. An undivided interest (shared ownership) in the remaining elements in the development as tenants in common.
   - These remaining areas are better known as common areas.

Separate property consists of the individual dwelling units. Technically, a dwelling unit consists of only the four walls. This includes space between the walls, floor, and ceiling of the unit.

Common property is everything else, including:

- Land
- Interior and exterior walls
- Any other improvements such as pools and tennis courts
- Hallways and stairs
- Recreation areas and landscaping
- Parking lots

In Florida, a condominium may be created by either one of the following ways:

1. New construction
2. By conversion of a rental property to condominium ownership

Generally speaking, condominiums, by design, are more likely to be new construction as opposed to a conversion of rental property. Any type of private development can be organized as a condominium. How the property will be used has no affect on whether it can be organized in condominium form. The following are a few examples of properties that may be organized as condominiums:

- High-rise buildings
- Garden apartments
- Townhouse developments
- Warehouses
- Office buildings
- Detached single-family dwellings

Enabling legislation must be passed by the state in order for a condominium development to exist. This type of legislation bears different names in different states, including:

- Horizontal Property Act
- Strata Title Act
- Condominium Act

In each of the aforementioned cases, legislature provides for horizontal subdivision of the air space above the land into cubicles called air lots. Each unit within the development occupies one air lot.

In Florida, both the sales and the day-to-day operations of condominiums must comply with the Florida Condominium Act. Compliance is set forth within Chapter 718 of the Florida Statutes, or 718, F.S.

As previously stated, title to a condominium comes in the form of a deed. The deed that covers the entire property is called the master deed. By splitting the fee (land) title to the air space above the land, each separate unit owner is able to receive a deed to his unit. Remember, real property is always transferred from one person to another by deed. This is the instrument used for transferring real property from one party to another. Once recorded, these deeds give their owners:

- Fee simple title to their unit
- An undivided interest in the land and other common areas of the property, held as tenants in common with others

Condominium ownership rights are as desirable as that of private home ownership. These ownership rights give the owner the right to:

- Sell without association approval
- Sublease without association approval. However, associations do require a right of first refusal on any subleasing or sale. If this association right is exercised, it must be at the identical terms as those offered to a tenant or buyer. Some associations have restrictions and/or limitations on subleasing.
- Gift (with no occupancy restrictions or constraints)
- Will to heirs (with no occupancy restrictions or constraints)

This type of ownership and community living arrangement requires some form of governing authority within the development. This is achieved through the creation of an **owners association**. As ownership in each individual unit vests with the unit owner, each unit owner automatically becomes a member of the association. The association is normally organized as a not-for-profit corporation. An owners association has the duty to control, regulate, and maintain all of the common areas.

The association may elect a board of managers and/or a third-party property management company to run the day-to-day activities of the condominium. Condominium fees (called *common charges*) are assessed to provide money and liquidity to pay for such things as:

- Maintenance of common areas
- Insurance
- Management and legal fees
- Property tax on common areas
- Reserves for future capital expenditure

These common charges are based, predicated, and derived on proportionate share of total expenses in running the association's operations. Similar to rental income-producing property, common charges are paid monthly. Each unit owner receives a separate property tax bill from the municipality. Each unit owner is charged with the responsibility of paying the tax bill directly to the governing municipality. As in single-family housing, property taxes form a lien on the property until the taxes are paid. Failure to pay the taxes will ultimately result in *in rem proceedings* (foreclosure proceeding for unpaid property tax).

Financing for each unit is exclusively arranged by the individual unit owner. There is no joint liability between owners for loans on the individual units. Any mortgage resulting from a borrowing (specifically) for the common areas are achieved by the owners association (who acts as the mortgagor).

Maintenance of the condominium areas are handled as follows:

* Common area maintenance and repairs are the responsibility of the owners association.

* Individual unit owners bear the responsibility for maintenance and repairs to each respective unit.

Condominium Creation

In order to create a condominium, the Florida Condominium Act (Chapter 718 of the Florida Statutes, or 718, F.S.) provides for the creation and/or submission of certain documents such as:

* **Declaration of condominium**—The instrument used to create the condominium.

* Bylaws—Dictate how the owners' association may run the facility.

* Plat map—Provides the legal description required for each unit as well as its location within the development.

* Conveyance document—Used for deeding title to the condominium.

In addition, on a primary sale, the developer is required to provide a disclosure statement to each buyer. This is intended to advise the buyer of the right to rescind any contract to purchase within the later of *15 days* of signing the contract or of receiving all condominium documents. In the event of a resale from a previous owner (outside of the developer of the project) of an existing condominium unit, the buyer only receives a *3-day* right of rescission from the time of signing the contract and receiving all required condominium documents.

In the resale case above, any real estate licensee holding a deposit from a prospective purchaser of a condominium unit who acts on her right of rescission within the allotted lawful time period, is required to promptly refund in full to the purchaser all deposits previously held by the licensee.

Cooperatives

Another form of community ownership is a **cooperative**. In a cooperative, title to the land, building, and all other improvements to the property are held by the cooperative. The cooperative is organized as a not-for-profit corporation. Anyone who purchases within a cooperative is only purchasing shares of stock in the corporation. Where the cooperative corporation holds fee simple ownership to the land and improvements made to the land, the stockholder is only given shares of stock and an occupancy agreement that conveys rights of occupancy to the respective unit. This agreement is called a **proprietary lease**. Only shareholders are permitted by the cooperative to occupy the unit. Although the issuance of a proprietary lease may resemble a lease for rental property, the monthly payment by the shareholder(s) is not made in the form of rent; it is made and referred to as **monthly maintenance**. The cooperative corporation is responsible for payment of:

* Any payments required by a lender for the underlying mortgage (if any)

* Property tax for the entire property (shareholders do not receive individual tax bills nor do they pay property tax direct to the charging municipality)

- Repairs and maintenance
- Management expenses

Each unit shareholder pays their proportionate share in one fixed monthly fee termed *maintenance*. The unit proportion toward maintenance is generally calculated on a per share basis. Shares are allocated to each unit. Allocation of how many shares are issued to each unit is derived by:

- Square foot size of the unit versus the overall property bulk (size)
- Location in the property
- Exposure (certain facing exposures are more desirable than others)
- Floor height within the property (i.e., second floor versus twentieth floor)
- Views and outdoor space (terraces or balconies)

As a short informational note, *terraces* are defined (in most areas) as the outdoor space built above another unit's living space. A *balcony* is defined as an extension protruding out over airspace. Balconies do not have a living area below the floor of the balcony.

The cooperative occupants are composed of all shareholders to the cooperative. The shareholders elect a board of directors who are charged with running the day-to-day activities of the cooperative. In almost all cases, rights associated with a shareholder in a cooperative will bear a *more restrictive* living arrangement than that of a condominium.

Cooperative boards, at their sole discretion, may do the following:

- Screen new shareholder purchases
- Reject any sale that a shareholder may propose
- Grant their approval and consent to the transfer of shares and issuance of a new proprietary lease
- Deny or consent to any subleasing
- Charge a flip tax to the selling shareholder at the time of sale (This is usually an income-generating device for the cooperative to build their financial property reserves. In many cases, this may amount to approximately 2 percent of the selling price.)

In Florida, activities concerning formation and disclosure issues are governed by the Cooperative Act (Chapter 719 of the Florida Statutes, or 719, F.S.). The act requires disclosure of the following related to cooperatives:

- A legal description of the property
- Description of the common areas associated with the property
- Title held
- Liens
- Easements
- Outstanding or pending lawsuits as they relate to the cooperative
- Judgments related to the cooperative
- Manager of the property
- Date of completion (if not substantially completed)
- Operating statements and budgets
- Sale and resale procedures

As a further note, cooperatives are organized as not-for-profit entities (Chapter 617 F.S.). Prior to December 20, 2007 cooperatives were restricted by law by the IRS from receiving more than 20 percent of their operating budget from passive-income activities.

This was (prior to the change in law) more commonly referred to as the 80/20 rule. Active income (80 percent) was defined as the maintenance collected from unit shareholders while passive income (no more than 20 percent) was derived from investment income-producing activities such as:

- Collection of rents on cooperative owned, such as:
  - Retail space(s)
  - Garage rents
  - Cellular antennae(s)
  - Satellite dish
  - Vending machine income
  - Any other income-producing vehicle attributable to the property outside of maintenance

As of December 20, 2007 Congress passed HR3648, the Mortgage Forgiveness Debt Relief Act of 2007, and the 80/20 law has been repealed and amended to read as follows:

- At all times during the taxable year, 80% or more of the total square footage of the corporation's property is used or available for use by the tenant-shareholders for residential purposes or purposes ancillary to such residential use; or
- if 80% or more of the cooperative's gross income is derived from tenant-shareholders; or
- 90% or more of the corporation's expenditures paid or incurred during the taxable year are paid or incurred for the acquisition, construction, management, maintenance, or care of the corporation's property for the benefit of the tenant-shareholders.

Prior to December 20, 2007 and the change in law concerning the 80/20 rule, in other states a hybrid of condominiums and cooperatives emerged. This hybrid is called a **cond-op.**

A cond-op begins as condominium property. A developer sought to solve the former 80/20 issue by retaining ownership in the commercial portion of the property. The developer sells the residential units to individuals while reserving and retaining the commercial parts of the property for future income-producing purposes. This income benefits only the developer while indirectly solving the 80/20 issue for the property. The end result becomes:

- Condominium ownership in the land by the condominium owners association (representative of the residential units)
- Condominium ownership in the land by the developer for the commercial spaces such as:
  - Retail spaces
  - Garage facility
- The residences are structured as a cooperative setup with condominium bylaws
  - This allows the cooperative shareholder condominium flexibility concerning sales and subleasing.
  - From an income tax point of view, a cooperative offers higher tax benefits with respect to maintenance than that of a condominium.
  - The extra benefit usually is a result of a per share deduction of the interest attributable to the underlying mortgage that generally exists in a cooperative and not in a condominium.
  - Tax deductibility creates a marketing tool for the developer concerning sales of residential units.
  - The 80/20 issue is eliminated (now eliminated by new legislature).

Planned-Unit Development (PUD)

A planned-unit development (PUD) will normally consist of individually owned homes within a community ownership of common areas. The common areas are often developed as recreational areas. The ownership of common areas in a PUD differs from that of a condominium.

In a condominium:

- The individual unit owners own the common areas as tenants in common.
- The owners association is responsible for maintenance of the common area only.

In a PUD:

- The community association owns the common areas and the unit owners own a share of the association.

PUDs are created by local zoning laws rather than state laws. There is usually a trade-off involved in the development of the property:

- The developer is allowed to build on smaller lots, thus increasing the density of the homes.
- In exchange, the developer is required to create and develop the common areas (often as recreational areas).

In a condominium, each unit owner in a planned-unit development owns the land, the air above the land, and the unit itself. Because the unit owner owns the air above the land, vertical stacking is not possible. As a result, the most common forms of buildings are single-family detached dwellings or attached townhouses.

Resort Time-Share Developments

Time-sharing is a method of dividing up and selling a living unit for a specified period each year. **Time-shares** are almost exclusively resort-type properties, such as hotels, condominiums, townhouses, villas, recreational vehicles parks, and campgrounds. The primary advantage to time-sharing resort property is that it becomes possible to afford a vacation retreat that could not otherwise be afforded.

Time-share developments may be organized in three ways:

1. The right-to-use format gives the buyer the right to occupy a unit within the development for a specified time (usually 1 week) each year for a specified number of years (usually up to 40 years, after which the interest in the property reverts back to the developer).
2. The interval ownership format gives the buyer the right to fee simple ownership of a unit along with other buyers and the use of the property for 1 week each year.
3. The club plan gives the buyer a membership in a club that owns the property and the right to use the property for 1 week each year.

Like condominiums and cooperatives, the Florida Time-Share Act (Chapter 721 of the Florida Statutes, or 721, F.S.) is designed to protect the general public from suffering economic loss due to lack of seller/developer disclosures.

The Florida Time-Share Act requires that:

- Any sales associate selling time-shares hold a current and valid real estate license.
- The seller/developer disclose that the buyer has a right to rescind any contract to purchase a time-share at the later of within 10 days of signing a contract or receiving the public offering statement. The public offering statement contains certain required disclosures as well as a permit authorizing the developer to sell time-shares.

Timeshares that are registered with the Securities and Exchange Commission (SEC) are exempt from the Florida Time-Share Act.

SUMMARY

Real property or real estate is land and all improvements permanently attached to the land. Real property can be held by individuals and operating business enterprises. There are two types of estates: freehold (owned) or nonfreehold (leased). Title may be held in several ways. There is sole ownership and ownership held in conjunction with others. Sole ownership is held in severalty while ownership held with others or concurrent owners have various vesting options available to the owning party. There are various other vehicles of ownership other than single family detached housing. This would include condominiums, cooperatives, PUD's and time shares. The licensee must have a clear understanding as to differences concerning the variety of ownership vehicles.

REVIEW QUESTIONS

1. Margo owns a one-third interest in a property and she received a deed for her interest. One of Margot's cousins owns a one-sixth interest. Margo can sell her one-third, give it away, or leave it in a will. Margo's interest is a:
   a. Tenancy by the entireties.
   b. Leasehold estate.
   c. Tenancy in common.
   d. Joint tenancy.

2. Which of the following items would most likely be personal property?
   a. Chandelier
   b. Doorbell
   c. Ceiling fan
   d. Refrigerator

3. One of the advantages of declaring a homestead in Florida is protection from forced sale for:
   a. Mortgage liens.
   b. Tax liens.
   c. Credit card debts.
   d. IRS liens.

4. Purchasers of condominiums in Florida must be given required disclosures before or at the time of signing a purchase contract. The documents include:
   a. The Public Offering Statement.
   b. A declaration.
   c. Management fees.
   d. Proprietary lease.

5. Jose gave a house to his stepmother for as long as she lives. After Jose's stepmother dies, Jose's sons will own it. The stepmother's interest is a:
   a. Reversionary estate.
   b. Remainder estate.
   c. Life estate.
   d. Fee simple estate.

6. Florida law that states "a form of ownership of real property wherein legal title is vested in a corporation or other legal entity" and "beneficial use is evidenced by an ownership in the association and a lease" best describes:
   a. Cooperatives.
   b. Time-sharing.
   c. Condominiums.
   d. Estates in severalty.

7. Suzie and Jack are married and own a home in both their names. They have children who are their legal heirs. Suzie dies.
   a. Jack owns the home outright.
   b. Jack owns a half-interest in the home; the children own their mother's half.
   c. Ownership would depend on Suzie's will.
   d. Jack has a life estate in the home and the children are vested remaindermen.

8. Rebecca has complete and absolute ownership of two vacant lots in a nearby subdivision. Rebecca is married to Brad. Rebecca's interest is a(n):
   a. Joint tenancy.
   b. Estate by entireties.
   c. Fee simple estate, ownership in severalty.
   d. Remainder estate.

9. In order to calculate the real property tax that contains a homestead exemption, the homestead exemption is:
   a. Subtracted from the assessed value.
   b. A limit of what the property taxes can be.
   c. Exempted from property taxes on certain homes.
   d. Available for all homeowners.

10. Alice agreed that her tenant could live in the unit through April of next year. The tenant's estate is a(n):
    a. Tenancy by entireties.
    b. Estate for years.
    c. Tenancy at will.
    d. Tenancy at sufferance.

11. The tenants' lease expired, and the tenants are still living in the unit. This is a(n):
    a. Tenancy by entireties.
    b. Estate for years.
    c. Tenancy at will.
    d. Tenancy at sufferance.

12. The list of property rights that constitute title in Florida would NOT include:
    a. Exclusion.
    b. Possession
    c. Severalty.
    d. Disposition.

13. Which of the following estates features survivorship?
    a. By the entireties
    b. Tenancy in common
    c. Estate in severalty
    d. Estate for years

14. Which of these statements about a planned-unit development (PUD) is FALSE?
    a. PUDs allow for commercial use like grocery and drug stores.
    b. Doctors' offices are a permissible use within the development.
    c. Homes are clustered within large green spaces.
    d. Industrial parks are an allowed PUD idea.

15. How can you tell if an item is a fixture?
    a. The item is too large to move.
    b. How the item is installed.
    c. The item is used as part of a business.
    d. The item provides a necessary function, such as a stove.

16. Joe's lot is on the beach. When there is a storm, waves deposit more sand, so Joe's lot is getting bigger. This process is called:
    a. Reliction.
    b. Erosion.
    c. Alluvion.
    d. Accretion.

17. Fern purchased a farm and later discovered an oil company has a right to sink wells on a part of the farm's pastures. Fern cannot exclude the equipment. Fern's purchase did not include the:
    a. Surface rights.
    b. Air rights.
    c. Subsurface rights.
    d. Surface and subsurface rights.

18. Cathy's interest in an orange grove is an estate in severalty. This means Cathy:
    a. Is not the only owner.
    b. Must have a tenancy in common.
    c. May be a joint tenant.
    d. Does not share the ownership.

Chapter 9

KEY TERMS

abstract of title

acceptance

acknowledgment

actual notice

adverse possession

assignment

chain of title

condemnation

constructive notice

covenant of further assistance

covenant of seisin

covenant of warranty of title
(covenant of warranty
forever)

deed

deed restrictions

delivery

doctrine of laches

easement

eminent domain

encroachment

escheat

fee

general lien

general warranty deed

graduated lease

grant

grantee

granting clause

grantor

gross lease

ground lease

habendum clause

index lease

leasehold

lien

lis pendens

marketable title

net lease

percentage leases

quiet enjoyment

quitclaim deed

recourse loans

sandwich lease

special warranty deed

specific lien

sublease

title

title opinions

Torrens system

Title Deeds and Ownership Restrictions

LEARNING OBJECTIVES

After completing this lesson, you will be able to:

- Describe the process of transferring title to real property by use of a deed.
- Explain the following types of deeds:
  - General warranty deed (full covenant and warranty deed)
  - Special warranty deed
  - Bargain and sale deed
  - Quitclaim deed
- Describe the necessary elements that would constitute a valid and enforceable deed.
- Understand the difference between constructive notice and actual notice.
- Describe the different restrictions that can be placed on ownership:
  - Private
  - Governmental
- Describe the different title insurance policies.
- Recognize the variety of lease types that are used in residential and commercial transactions.

METHODS OF TRANSFER

In real estate, the **title** is the sum of all facts or evidence of ownership. When title is transferred between parties, the process is referred to as alienation. Alienation can be either voluntary or involuntary:

- Voluntary alienation—The willful transfer of the property with the consent and control of the owner.

FIGURE 9.1

COURT ACTION

Partition action
Foreclosure action
Bankruptcy
Escheat
Eminent domain

- ○ During life this is accomplished via a deed.
- ○ At death, this is accomplished via a valid will.
- Involuntary alienation—The unwillful transfer of the property against the wishes and control of the owner.
  - ○ During life, this is accomplished as follows (see Figure 9.1):
    - Court judgment
    - Foreclosure action
    - Bankruptcy
    - At death, this is accomplished through **escheat** (due to no existence of a valid will or remaining heirs to accept the property, the property goes to the state).
    - **Eminent domain** (a public taking of private property through the process known as **condemnation**)
    - **Adverse possession** (a lawful taking of another's property based on specific conditions and requirements; usually a private taking). In Florida, a person who attempts this form of acquiring property must fulfill the following conditions:
      - □ Open and notorious occupation of the property belonging to another in the color of title
      - □ Must be continuous occupation for seven or more years
      - □ While possessing the property of another, the adverse possessing party has paid the property taxes for same

There are several ways that title to real property can be transferred:

- Deed
- Inheritance
- Adverse possession
- Acts of nature

We just looked at public restrictions that may be placed and affect real property ownership. Now let's examine private restrictions on real property that would include:

- **Deed restrictions** (restrictions on the ownership of private property that are contained in deeds)
- Liens
- Easements
- Leases

Deeds are the most common method used to convey title while the holder of the title is alive. Inheritance is the process of conveying title after the holder of the title has died. (This will be covered later in this chapter.)

DEEDS

A **deed** is an instrument that is used to convey and transfer the ownership interest in real property from one or more parties to another. A deed is used to convey any fee estate, any life estate, or certain easements.

Coaching Tips: It is imperative to understand that possessing a deed does not necessarily constitute legal ownership in the real property. A deed (which is only an instrument of paper) reflects legal ownership only when the deed has been accepted for recording by the county clerk's office. The county clerk only accepts valid deeds for recording.

Florida requires that all deeds be in written form. In addition, the Statute of Frauds requires that all deeds:

- Be in writing
- Be signed by the grantor in order to transfer title

In order to record the deed in the public records, **acknowledgment** is usually required. Acknowledgment means that the **grantor** (seller) must acknowledge his signature to the **grantee** (buyer). This is achieved by the grantor signing the deed before a notary public. The notary acts as a legal witness for hire. The notary's role is to witness the signature of the grantor (only after presentation of appropriate ID). This witnessing is a determination and testament to the grantee that the grantor is who he is claiming to be (the rightful owner of the property). In order to record the deed, the document must be acknowledged. Otherwise, it will not be accepted by the county clerk. Only the *grantor* acknowledges a deed.

Coaching Tips: **Some deeds contain deed restrictions. This can be deemed as the most common form of private restriction on ownership of real property. These restrictions are found in deeds. Once these restrictions are in place and recorded, enforcement becomes critical on the part of property owners or these restrictions may be vacated via** the doctrine of laches **(the use and enforcement of one's rights or loss of same resulting from lack of enforcement and assertion of those rights). Therefore it is up to the subdivision, unit owners or any other party benefiting from the restriction to enforce same. In particular, a purchaser of property should pay close attention to restrictions contained within a deed.**

Examples of common deed restrictions would be:

- A minimum set-back requirement from an adjacent neighbors property line
- A minimum square footage required to construct living space

As you just learned, when *real property* is sold or otherwise conveyed, the ownership is transferred through the use of a document called a deed. When *personal property* is sold or otherwise conveyed, this is done through the use of a document called a bill of sale. When a home is sold, for example, the ownership of the land and its improvements (real property) are transferred with a deed. If any personal property is sold at the same time, such as furniture, tools, etc., it must be transferred in a separate bill of sale. The actual act of conveying ownership of real property is called a **grant**. There are two parties to a deed:

1. Grantor—The party who transfers title (the seller).
2. Grantee—The party to whom the title is transferred (the buyer).

Elements of a Deed

As noted previously, deeds *must be written*. In addition, to be considered valid and enforceable, they *must* include the following seven elements:

1. Competent grantor—The grantor must be legally competent. In most states, this means that the grantor must be of:
   - Legal age (18 in Florida)
   - Sound mind
   In many states, the grantee:
   - Must also be of sound mind
   - Does not have to be of legal age (a minor can be the grantee)
   In Florida, the grantee does not have to be of sound mind. A mentally incompetent person can be the grantee; however, due to a lack of legal capacity as a competent party, the grantee may be unable to convey title as a grantor to another without assistance from some form of guardian.

2. Consideration—The deed must state that consideration was given by the grantee to the grantor. The consideration can be either one of the following:

   • Valuable consideration—Money or its equivalent.

   • Good consideration—One not expressed in monetary terms, such as love and affection.

   In Florida, the actual amount of consideration does not need to be stated. Often, a nominal amount is stated, such as, "One dollar and other good and valuable consideration."

3. Words of conveyance—These words indicate the intent of the grantor to transfer title. The words *grant* and *convey*, either alone or in combination, are commonly used in the conveyance. Another name for the words of conveyance is the **granting clause**.

Coaching Tips: **The granting clause is just one derivative of the feudal system of the medieval/Renaissance period in English history. In this period and time, the Crown owned all the lands, the peasants were tenants and occupants of the land, and title to land and property were granted by the Crown to the king and queen's noblemen.**

---

4. Property description—The deed must adequately describe the property being conveyed. Any legally recognized method of description can be used. A street address is not acceptable as it does not identify the property boundaries and is subject to change.

5. Name of grantor and grantee—Both names must be stated on a deed for purposes of chain of title. The **chain of title** is similar to a bicycle chain containing links. Each link represents a previous or current owner. This allows interested parties to research the public records for the purposes of identifying the correct owner of record. (If the deed is to be recorded, the addresses of the grantor and grantee must be provided along with their names.) A fictitious name may be used by the grantee. If a fictitious name is used, the deed is still valid, but the *same* name must be used when the property is later transferred to another person to preserve the chain of title.

6. Grantor's signature—A deed must be signed by the grantor in order to be valid. The signature of the grantee is *not* required. Some states require that the grantor's signature be witnessed. In Florida, grantor's signature must be witnessed by two people.

7. Delivery and acceptance—To be valid, a deed must be delivered by the grantor to the grantee and accepted by the grantee. **Delivery** does not have to be a physical act of "handing over" the deed. If the grantor indicates by her actions that she intends for the grantee to own the property, then delivery has occurred. Delivery of a deed is presumed to have occurred if one of the following takes place:

   • The deed is found in the possession of the grantee.

   • The deed is recorded.

   Acceptance is presumed to have occurred if the grantee:

   • Retains the deed

   • Records the deed

   • Encumbers the title

   • Performs any other act of ownership

   To be valid, a deed must be delivered during the grantor's lifetime.

Coaching Tips: **The Seven Essential Elements of a Deed**

1. **Competent grantor**

2. **Consideration**

3. **Words of conveyance**

4. Property (legal) description

5. Name of grantor and grantee

6. Grantor's signature

7. Delivery and acceptance

Nonessential Element

One element found in most deeds, but *not required,* is the **habendum clause**. If the habendum clause is included, it contains the type of estate being granted. The habendum clause tells the extent of interest transferred.

TYPES OF DEEDS

We have just discussed the essential elements needed to constitute a valid and enforceable deed. Now let's examine the types of deeds that may be used to convey real property.

There are several types of deeds:

- General warranty deed (full covenant and warranty deed)
- Special warranty deed
- Bargain and sale deed
- Quitclaim deed

These types of deeds are all commonly used and accepted instruments of conveyance in Florida. These deeds differ primarily in the guarantees (warranties) provided about the title being conveyed. Guarantees are provided through covenants included in the deed. The covenants (which are promises) are the means by which the grantor agrees to defend the title against the claims of all other persons.

General Warranty Deed

The **general warranty deed**, also called the full covenant and warranty deed, is the most common form of deed. A general warranty deed provides the greatest guarantee about the title being conveyed and contains the following covenants:

- Covenant of seisin
- Covenant against encumbrances
- Covenant of quiet enjoyment
- Covenant of further assistance
- Covenant of warranty of title

Covenant of Seisin

In the **covenant of seisin**, the grantor warrants that he is the owner of the property and that he has the right to convey the property.

Covenant Against Encumbrances

In the covenant against encumbrances, the grantor warrants that there are no encumbrances on the property that are not mentioned in the deed.

Coaching Tips: A covenant against encumbrances does not state that there are no encumbrances on the property, only that all encumbrances that exist are stated in the deed.

Covenant of Quiet Enjoyment

In a covenant of quiet enjoyment, the grantor warrants that the grantee will enjoy the property free of claims by anyone else.

Coaching Tips: Quiet enjoyment **is often confused and should not be mistaken for peace and quiet. This clause in a deed or in a lease deals only with the issue of title and/or rights associated with the estate.**

Covenant of Further Assistance

This obligates the grantor to perform any acts necessary to protect the title being conveyed to the grantee. The **covenant of further assistance** is also called the covenant of further assurance.

Covenant of Warranty of Title

A **covenant of warranty of title (covenant of warranty forever)** ensures that the grantor will bear the expense of defending the title against the claims of others. There is no time limit on a covenant of warranty of title.

Special Warranty Deed

The **special warranty deed** is used when the grantor is unable or unwilling to include all the covenants just discussed. It includes only one covenant, the covenant against encumbrances. In effect, the grantor warrants against her own acts. The grantor warrants that she has not encumbered the property beyond those encumbrances stated in the deed. The grantor does not warrant that someone else had not encumbered the property prior to her assuming ownership.

Coaching Tips: **In some states, like New York, the special warranty deed is called the bargain and sale deed with covenant.**

The special warranty deed is often used when the grantor is acting as an agent, or fiduciary, for a principal, such as a trustee or executor of a will. The agent is willing to warrant that he has not encumbered the property, but is not willing or able to provide any other warranties.

Bargain and Sale Deed

A bargain and sale deed conveys the grantor's interest in the property, but contains *no warranties* about the state of the title. It *implies* that the grantor has a claim to, or an interest in, the property, but does not provide this warranty.

Quitclaim Deed

The **quitclaim deed** contains *no warranties* to title, either expressed or implied. In simple terms, it can be defined to be an instrument of release (as it may apply to any claim). The quitclaim deed simply conveys whatever interest the grantor held at the time of conveyance. The grantee has no recourse to the grantor if the title proves to be defective. The quitclaim deed is not inferior to any other deed in terms of its ability to transfer title. It is different only in that it provides no warranties about the status of the title.

The quitclaim deed may be used to transfer *any* type of estate, including fee simple and life estates. Normally, however, it is used to convey or release minor interests in real estate for the purpose of clearing title defects or clouds on a title. For example, it may be used by anyone who held a lien that had since been satisfied, in order to release the owner from the lien. It is also an instrument commonly used to convey real property from one family member to another.

Coaching Tips: **The different types of deeds that have just been covered provide different types of guarantees (in the form of warranties) about the title being conveyed. They *do not* convey different "amounts" of title or different "degrees" of title. The "amount" or "degree" of title conveyed is determined by the type of estate being conveyed, such as a fee simple estate, a life estate, etc.**

Preparation of Deeds

State law determines who may prepare a deed. In some states, attorneys must prepare a deed while other states allow the property owner to prepare the deed. Some states allow a real estate broker to prepare a deed on which she acted as agent for the sale.

It is important to note that the unauthorized practice of law by any real estate licensee is a licensing offense and will subject the licensee to disciplinary action. The licensee is therefore cautioned to limit her activities to just filling in blanks within preprinted forms previously prepared and approved by an attorney admitted to the state bar or by the agent's principle.

Acknowledgment of Deeds

In order to be admissible for public records, a deed must be acknowledged in most states. Acknowledgment is a formal declaration of the following:

* The person signing the document is the person named in the document.
* The signing of the deed is a free and voluntary act.

Acknowledgment is done before an authorized official, usually a notary public, who is responsible for ensuring that the person signing the deed is the grantor named in the deed.

Coaching Tips: **The acknowledgment is the declaration made by the grantor, not the certification by the notary public. The deed must be signed by the *grantor*. Acknowledgment is the grantor's statement of his ability to convey, not the certification of the notary public.**

TITLES

In real estate, the title is the sum of all facts on which ownership is founded.

An **abstract of title** includes:

* A full summary of all instruments affecting the title to a property, such as deeds, wills, grants, etc.
* A statement of all liens and encumbrances affecting the property and their present status.

No single document proves title to property. Title to a property is based on an evaluation of the abstract and other instruments indicated by the abstract.

Marketable title is one that is free of reasonable doubt as to ownership.

Chain of title is the record of ownership transactions that connects the present owners to the original source of title.

One method of determining marketable title is through a title opinion. **Title opinions** are made and given by attorneys. In essence, the attorney scrutinizes in a careful manner the abstract of title. The opinion letter or certificate of title opinion, as it is more commonly known, will indicate any encumbrances, liens, or easements that affect the property. Although the certificate of title is an acceptable instrument for determining marketable title, one should be cautioned that the certificate is merely an opinion of the title based on a review of the abstract and is not in any way a guarantee.

Public Records

Before the enactment of the Statute of Frauds in England in 1677, ownership of a parcel of land was largely determined on who was in physical possession of the land. Possession gave notice of ownership. After 1677, written deeds were required to show transfer of ownership from one owner to another. Public records were instituted to record deeds so that no disputes would arise about who held the most current deed. It also provided a means of search and research of the public records by interested parties concerning any recorded parcel of property. Public records can be examined by anyone at any time as desired.

Constructive Notice

Since 1677, two ways to give notice of a claim or right to land (ownership) have evolved:

1. By recording documents in the public records that give written notice to that effect
2. By physically occupying the property

According to law, if an interested party wants to determine ownership, the party must do the following:

- Examine the public records.
- Look at the property itself to see who occupies it.

    Constructive notice combines these two ideas:

1. People give notice by public recording and occupancy.
2. It is presumed that anyone interested in the property has inspected both the records and the property itself to determine ownership.

Actual Notice

Constructive notice is based on a *presumption* that the records and property have been inspected. **Actual notice** is specific knowledge based on what you have *actually* seen, heard, read, or observed.

Recording

Instruments affecting title (such as deeds) are recorded in the jurisdiction in which the land is situated. They are usually recorded at the county level, sometimes at the city level, but never at the state level. Recordation is a privilege allowed by the law, and is not required by law. Recordation allows owners to give public notice of their claim to ownership.

Torrens Land Titles

The **Torrens system** is a system of registered land titles, called Torrens land titles. Very few states use this system. In states that do, the Torrens system is used to:

- Verify ownership of property using a single document.
- Establish the status of title including any existing encumbrances other than tax liens.

The Torrens system does not require an additional title search to determine ownership, since title verification is based on a single document. In order for the Torrens system to be used in a state, it requires enabling legislation known as a Torrens Title Act. The steps needed to establish a Torrens land title are:

1. A quiet title action is filed in court. This asks the court to ascertain the true condition of the title.
2. The court determines the condition of the title.
3. The court orders the registrar of titles to issue a Torrens title certificate to the property.

The Torrens title certificate identifies the:

- Exact boundaries of the property
- Name of the title holder
- Encumbrances on the title

Once a title is registered, any subsequent liens or encumbrances must be entered on the registrar's copy of the certificate of title in order to give constructive notice. When registered land is conveyed, the grantor gives the grantee a deed. The grantee presents the deed to the registrar of title who destroys the old certificate and issues a new one naming the grantee as owner. The Torrens system exists in several states, but its use is extremely rare. It is the principal or only system used in about ten states.

Title Insurance

Title insurance is an insurance policy that protects the insured against a loss that might be sustained by a defective title or any liens or encumbrances. In general, title insurance protects against such defects in title as:

- Forged documents
- Undisclosed heirs
- Documents filed incorrectly
- Mistakes in legal interpretation of wills
- Gaps in the chain of title

The two most common types of title insurance are:

1. Owner's title insurance
2. Mortgagee's title insurance

Contrary to popular belief, the vast majority of title insurance policies issued are for the mortgagee's title insurance. These policies cover losses suffered by the mortgage company, not the buyer.

Owner's Title Insurance

Owner's title insurance names the owner as the insured. It is issued in an amount equal to the acquisition cost of the property. Some policies include an inflation clause that increases the amount of coverage as the property appreciates in value. Owner's title insurance remains in force for as long as the *owner or the owner's heirs* retain an interest in the property. Owner's title insurance is terminated only when the owner or the owner's heirs no longer have any interest in the property. The title insurance process is shown in Figure 9.2.

Mortgagee's Title Insurance

A mortgagee's title insurance policy is issued in an amount equal to the original balance on the mortgage loan. The coverage decreases as the loan is amortized (paid off) and terminates when the loan is fully paid.

FIGURE 9.2

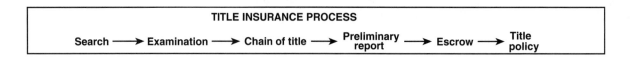

TITLE INSURANCE PROCESS

Search ⟶ Examination ⟶ Chain of title ⟶ Preliminary report ⟶ Escrow ⟶ Title policy

Both owner's and mortgagee's title insurance are single premium policies. The mortgagee's title insurance policy premium is paid only once—when the policy is issued. Because the amount of coverage provided by the mortgagee's policy is lower, it costs slightly less. This is due to the fact that the amount being financed is less than the total purchase price (which includes the property owner's down-payment)

EASEMENTS

So far you have learned about three general types of interests in real property:

1. Government interest
2. Individual interest—freehold and nonfreehold estates
3. Business interest

There are three remaining categories of interests in land:

1. Easements
2. Encroachments
3. Liens

An **easement** is the right to use or occupy the property of another in a limited way. The right to cross another's property (easement) can also be termed as a right of way. The holder of an easement does not have any ownership in the property, or even possession of the property, only the use of the property for a specific purpose. An easement is not an estate in land.

Easements can be categorized into three types:

1. Easement appurtenant
2. Easement in gross
3. Party wall easement

Easement Appurtenant

An easement appurtenant requires two or more properties, usually adjacent to each other, called:

1. A dominant estate (or dominant tenement)
2. A servient estate (or servient tenement)

The easement is the right of the owner of the dominant estate to use the property of the servient estate. The owner of the servient estate grants the easement.

An easement appurtenant runs with the land. This means the following:

- The easement becomes a part of the land itself (the dominant estate).
- If the owner of the *dominant estate* dies or sells the property, the easement remains with the dominant estate.
- If the owner of the *servient estate* dies or sells the servient estate, the easement remains with the dominant estate. (See Figure 9.3.)

FIGURE 9.3

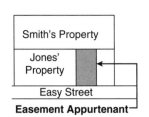

Easement Appurtenant

FIGURE 9.4

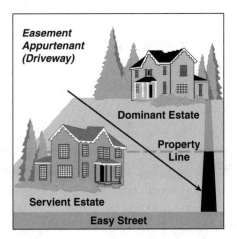

Easement in Gross

An easement in gross involves only one property, the servient estate. There is no dominant estate. The holder of the easement in gross has the right to use part of the servient estate for a specific purpose (see Figure 9.4). Some examples of easements in gross include easements for telephone lines, sewer lines, gas lines, power lines, and ditch easements for storm runoff. All of these are examples of easements held by a business or the government, and are called commercial easements. Commercial easements belong to the government or business, and are not attached to a parcel of land (like an easement appurtenant), so there is no dominant estate. The servient estate is the land on which the business or government has a right of use. All future owners of the servient estate are bound by the easement. Commercial easements are assignable (transferable). For example, one telephone company may sell or transfer its easement for phone lines to another telephone company.

A second type of easement in gross is a personal easement in gross. This type of easement is similar to a commercial easement in gross, except that:

• The holder is a person, not a business or government.

• A personal easement in gross terminates with the death of the holder.

• The holder cannot transfer the easement.

Example

John grants Bill an easement to cross his property to get to his favorite fishing spot on a lake.

Party Wall Easement

A party wall easement exists when a single wall that forms part of two buildings is located on a lot line. In this case, each owner owns the half of the wall on her property plus an easement in the other half of the wall on the adjacent property. An example would be a wall between two adjacent units in a fee simple townhouse development.

Licenses

A license is a personal privilege to use another's land in a limited manner. A license is *not* a right or interest in land, but it is covered here because it is similar to and often confused with a personal easement in gross. The following are the primary differences between a license and a personal easement in gross:

- A license must be terminable at the will of the person who granted it (licensor).
- A personal easement in gross cannot be revoked.

    A license (like a personal easement):

- Cannot be assigned (transferred to another).
- Terminates on the death of either party or the sale of the property owned by the person granting the license, or upon the expiration of the license that was granted for a prescribed period of time.

    A very common example of a personal license is a license to hunt on another's property. Easements appurtenant and commercial easements in gross are transferable. Personal easements in gross and licenses are not transferable.

Creation of Easements

Easements can be created in five different ways:

1. Private grant—A written agreement between the landowner and the easement holder. This is the most common method of creation.
2. Prescription—The acquisition of an easement by continuous, hostile, uninterrupted possession for a period set by law. (In Florida, it is 20 years.) The process of achieving an easement by prescription bears a direct resemblance to the process of achieving adverse possession. In each case, a taking or use of another's property occurs without remuneration. The difference is that in easement by prescription, you acquire an easement. In adverse possession, you acquire ownership of the property itself. (Adverse possession was described earlier in this chapter.)
3. Condemnation—The acquisition of an easement by the government under the power of eminent domain.
4. Reservation—Occurs when a landowner reserves, or retains for himself, the easement in a deed that conveys title to the land to another party.
5. Necessity—Prevents a landowner from becoming landlocked, which means having no way to reach a street or road. This arises when an owner sells a parcel of land that has no access to a road, but owns adjacent property that does have road frontage. Necessity requires the creation of an easement on that property to reach the property without frontage. The seller cannot sell the property and refuse to grant the easement.

Coaching Tips: Use the mnemonic POPCORN to remember the five different ways easements can be created:

- *Private grant*
- *O*
- *Prescription*
- *Condemnation*
- *O*
- *Reservation*
- *Necessity*

Coaching Tips:

- Deed restrictions limit the use of property.
- Prescription involves the adverse use of property.
- Reservation refers to reserving or retaining an easement in a deed.
- Condemnation is the process used by the government to acquire easements under eminent domain.
- Adverse possession is used to acquire title to property. It is not a method of creating an easement.

Note that it is *not necessary* for an easement to be in writing to be created. For example, an easement may be created by prescription by simply using the servient estate for a period of time prescribed by law.

Termination of Easements

Easements can also be terminated in five different ways:

1. Release—The party holding the easement gives a written release to the owner of the servient estate, usually in the form of a quitclaim deed.
2. Abandonment—The party holding the easement fails to use it for a sufficient period to raise the presumption of release.
3. Vacation—This is termination by court order when the need for the easement no longer exists.
4. Merger—This occurs when the dominant and servient estates are combined or come under one ownership.
5. Expiration—Expiration occurs if the easement was created for a specified period of time.

ENCROACHMENTS

An **encroachment** is an unauthorized intrusion of a building, fixture, or other improvement on the land of another. (See Figure 9.5.) An encroachment can constitute either one of the following:

- A trespass if it encroaches on the land.
- A nuisance if it violates the neighbor's airspace.

FIGURE 9.5

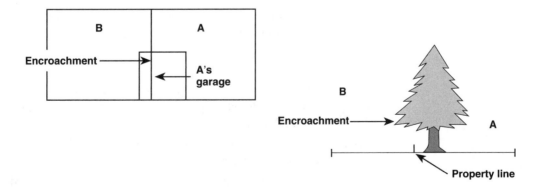

For example, a fence built by Smith is located 2 feet onto Jones's property. This constitutes a trespass. The limbs of a tree on Jones's property extend 15 feet over Smith's property. This constitutes a nuisance.

Encroachments can be discovered in two ways:

1. Survey—A survey will definitely disclose the existence of an encroachment, even if it cannot be detected by casual observation.

2. Observation—Some encroachments are obvious and can be detected by simply looking at the property.

Encroachment disputes that cannot be resolved between the owners involved may be settled by the court, which may do of the following:

• Order the removal of the encroachment.

Coaching Tips: **In Florida, if a property owner builds a fence or other structure that encroaches onto the land belonging to a neighbor, and this condition lasts for seven or more years, an implied easement is created.**

LEASES

In Chapter 8, we looked at three types of estates in land created by leases:

1. Estate for years
   • An estate for years is a lease that has a defined, prescribed, and fixed lease term. It contains a predetermined commencement and expiration date.
   • Upon expiration of the fixed term, the lease will either terminate and the tenant will relocate or the lease may be renewed/extended through a new agreement at either the same rent or at a newly negotiated rent.
   • This lease type is not terminable upon either the sale of the property or the death of either party to the transaction.

2. Estate at will
   • An estate at will has no definite term.
   • Vulnerability exists on the part of both parties regarding rent increase or decrease.
   • Either party to the transaction has the chance to change the terms of the deal.
   • An estate at will can be terminated by notifying the other party as to the intent to cancel.
   • In order to terminate this type of estate in Florida, proper notice must be given. For example, in order to terminate a month-to-month tenancy at will, Florida law requires that either party provide the other with notice of the intent to cancel the lease not less than 15 days prior to the end of that monthly period.

3. Tenancy at sufferance
   • Tenancy at sufferance occurs when a previous leasehold estate is terminated and the tenant/lessee refuses to return possession of the demised premises (leased property) to the landlord/lessor.
   • A tenant at sufferance is most commonly referred to as a holdover tenant. The tenant is not considered a trespasser.
   • A tenant is considered to be at sufferance usually due to the landlord's failure to issue the existing tenant a renewal/lease extension.

Basic Principles of Leases

A lease is a contract by which one person is given the right to occupy or use the property of another. A lease:

- Can be either written or oral to be valid and enforceable.
- Requires the payment of rent by the tenant to the landlord.
- Can be for a definite or indefinite period of time.

    The Statute of Frauds requires that:

- Leases for more than 1 year must be written to be enforceable.
- Leases for 1 year or less that are oral are enforceable.

    Parties to a lease consist of the following two parties:

1. The landlord is called the lessor. The landlord is usually the owner, but this is not always the case. For example, a landowner (or the owner of the fee) net leases land to another. The party who leases the land under a long-term ground lease later develops the land with a building (office or residential units). The developer then has the right to lease out the offices or residential units to others, however, the developer may only do so up to the term the developer has leased the land from the landowner.
2. The tenant is called the lessee.

    Real property is broken down into two components:

1. The land, also referred to as the **fee**.
2. The improvement affixed to the fee, referred to as the **leasehold**.

    A leasehold is the interest or estate in land that a tenant acquires by virtue of a lease. Real estate law treats a leasehold as personal property (as you learned earlier in Chapter 8). However, in most states, the *licensing law* treats a leasehold as real property. This treatment allows licensing law to regulate the activities of those involved in the leasing of property as a business.

Types of Leases

There are several different types of leases that are commonly used in residential and commercial transactions. These specific types of leases can be associated with any of the three leasehold estates just reviewed. The different types of leases will be covered next.

    As the application of a lease is required within a particular transaction, a variety of different lease types are available to the landlord for use, such as the following:

- Gross lease
- Net lease
- Percentage lease
- Ground lease
- Graduated lease
- Sandwich lease
- Index lease

Coaching Tips: While an index lease may at times be tied into an inflationary index such as the consumer price index (CPI), it is really a gross lease that allows the landlord to increase rents resulting from increases of operating expenses and property taxes. These increased expenses and taxes become operational and property tax pass-throughs that increase the rent to the tenant. The base rent is paid as written in the gross lease with "additional rent" payments within the lease covering the increased cost of the landlord's operating expenses.

Gross Lease

In a **gross lease**:

- The tenant pays a fixed monthly rent only.

- In residential leases, the landlord pays all expenses of ownership, operation, and maintenance, including such things as taxes, insurance, utilities, etc., whereas, in commercial lease transactions, the landlord provides within the lease for the pass-through of increased property expenses over a base amount. This is usually expressed within the lease rider clause as a base year. The landlord (via lease clause) has the right to pass-through to the tenant the increased cost of operations and property taxes that occur over the base year amount. The tenant pays these costs in the form of additional escalated rent. This is still considered a gross lease by commercial property terms.

- In Florida, all leases involving residential multifamily properties are gross leases. However, it is not uncommon for a tenant to pay his own unit-related utility costs.

Net Lease

In a **net lease**:

- The tenant pays a fixed monthly rent, *plus some or all* of the expenses associated with the property, such as taxes, insurance, utilities, etc.

- The landlord pays only those expenses not paid by the tenant.

If the property is not a single-tenant property, the portion of the expense that the tenant or tenants would be responsible for is based and predicated on the tenant's ratio of occupied space in relation to the total building area. This is commonly referred to as the tenant's proportionate share.

For example, a tenant occupies 10,000 square feet of space in a building that totals 100,000 square feet. In this case, the tenant would occupy 10 percent of the property and would therefore be responsible for 10 percent of the expenses.

Coaching Tips: To help remember which lease is a gross lease and which lease is a net lease, remember that the lease is being described from the landlord's point of view:

- A gross lease to the landlord means that expenses have to be deducted from the payment the landlord receives.

- A net lease to the landlord means that expenses do not have to be deducted from the payment received from the tenant. The money received is *net* to the landlord.

   In addition, terms such as *triple net* and *double net* are slang expressions used to communicate that a certain item or all items are net of rents. This slang terminology comes up within *net lease* transactions and is not really the textbook terminology. The correct expression is simply *net* of some or all of the expenses. However, students should be familiar with the slang terminology as well.

Percentage Lease

Percentage leases are commonly used for retail establishments in shopping malls. The landlord receives a percentage of the gross sales of the business as part or all of the rent. When a shopping mall is successful, it is common for the retailer to pay a higher minimum base rent plus a higher percentage of sales. The percentage of gross sales can be from either one of the following:

- The first dollar representing sales.

- When the retailer exceeds an agreed-upon gross sales dollar amount. The gross sales dollar amount threshold is usually representative of the retailer's breakeven on store operational costs. In some markets, the term is commonly referred to as the *natural breakeven.*

The percentage lease is most common with publicly listed stock exchange companies versus mom-and-pop operations. It is easier to audit a public company for gross sales than a privately owned mom-and-pop enterprise.

Example

A retail tenant will pay $5,000 per month representing the minimum base rent being charged. This will be paid whether or not the retailer sells its product. In addition, the retailer will pay to the landlord an amount of 5 percent of all sales over the natural breakeven. The rent would be calculated as follows:

- Step one:
  - Annualize the monthly rent: $5,000 × 12 = $60,000 per annum.
- Step two:
  - Divide the annual rental by the percentage of sales: $60,000 ÷ 0.05
  - The result is $1,200,000 of sales equals the natural breakeven.
  - Therefore 5 percent of any sale over that amount goes to the landlord as additional rent over and above the $5,000 minimum monthly base rent.

Ground Lease

A **ground lease** is a long-term lease of land. Certain landowners (or fee owners) prefer to avoid becoming developers of property. In some cases, this is due to:

- Lack of knowledge or expertise required to develop the property.
- Lack of funds to develop the property.
- Capital, market, or construction risks.
- The desire to collect ground rent (as an annuity) from those seeking to take on the aforementioned risks.

Generally speaking, ground leases typically require that the lessee construct a building or an improvement on the land. This type of lease (although it is categorized as a ground lease) takes the form of a net lease. This will require the lessee/developer to pay for property taxes, insurance, and any other expenses associated with the land and ultimate improvements to the land. However, bear in mind that if improvements result in an income-producing property, the lessee/tenant will keep the rent proceeds achieved from the improvement.

Graduated Lease

In a **graduated lease**, the tenant pays a fixed rent for an initial period but the rent increases at specific intervals thereafter. A graduated lease can be used in a variety of situations:

- For long-term leases:
  - To cover increased general cost of living
  - Merely to protect the owner's ability to capitalize on improved market conditions that result in higher rents
- For a retail store in a shopping center or mall where a clientele has not yet been established
- To attract a tenant in slow market conditions:
  - The landlord will start the tenant's lease at a cheaper rental rate at lease inception.
  - However, the rental rate will increase incrementally over the term of the lease so the tenant will pay a higher rate at the tail end of the lease.

○ Psychologically, because the tenant will pay the higher rental rate, it becomes easier for the landlord to renew the tenant at even a higher rent then the previous rental rate.

A graduated lease is also called a step-up lease.

Coaching Tips: You should be aware that commercial leases bear longer terms than that of residential leases. Therefore, landlords may be faced with good or bad market conditions at any time. Therefore, a landlord may prefer starting a tenant at a lower rent that will graduate even higher over the term of the lease. At the end of the initial lease term, the landlord will generally experience easier lease renewal negotiations to maintain the higher rent (or even receive a rent increase). The landlord's reasoning is that psychologically the tenant (exclusive of market conditions) is accustomed to paying the higher amount.

Sandwich Lease

A **sandwich lease** occurs when a leased property is subleased. When property is subleased, the original lessee (the tenant) becomes the lessor to the new tenant (the sublessee). The original lessee (the sublessor) is *sandwiched* between the landlord and the new tenant, the sublessee. An easier way to view this arrangement would be to identify the parties in other terms. Assume the following party names:

• The Property Owner/Landlord is the Overlandlord

• The Original Primary Tenant is the Overtenant

• The New Tenant/Sublessee is the Undertenant

Example

The Overlandlord prime leases to the Overtenant who in turn subleases to the Undertenant. The Overtenant is sandwiched between the Overlandlord and the Undertenant. It should be noted that this directly resembles what we term as a **sublease**.

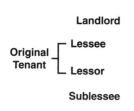

Index Lease (Modified Gross Lease)

An **index lease**, also known as a modified gross lease, contains a provision for future rent increases based on increased operating costs to the landlord (for taxes, insurance, utilities, janitorial services, etc.). It contains an escalator clause that provides for the rent increase based on some economic indicator called an index. There is usually a cap on the allowable annual rent increase. This type of lease is usually used for long-term commercial leases.

Contract versus Economic Rent
Contract Rent

Contract rent is the amount of rent the tenant must pay the landlord under the terms of the lease contract.

Economic Rent

Economic rent is the amount of rent the property *could* be rented for on the open market at a given time if it were available for rent. At the time the lease contract is signed, the economic rent and the contract rent are the same. As the lease matures, the economic rent will often exceed the contract rent.

Security Deposits

Generally, upon execution of a residential lease, the tenant will give a security deposit to the landlord. The security deposit is designed to protect the owner against a number of possible tenant-related losses resulting from the tenant's occupancy. Possible losses include nonpayment of rent or damage to the dwelling unit by the tenant or the tenant's visitors. (The provisions of the Florida Residential Landlord and Tenant Act dictating how security deposits are to be handled was discussed in Chapter 7.)

Essentials of a Valid Lease

For a lease to be considered a valid and enforceable lease, it must contain the following essential elements:

- Competent parties—the lessor and lessee. (In Florida, a person must have reached the age of 18 to be considered a competent party.)
- An adequate legal description of the property. (A formal legal description is not required, so a street address is acceptable.)
- An agreement to convey possession rights by the lessor to be accepted by the lessee (the demising clause).
- Signatures—The lease should be signed by both parties.

    In addition, a lease should include the following:

- Provision for payment of rent (the consideration)
- The term of the lease to include
  - The starting date and ending date, along with the total duration of the lease.
  - The exact lease term indicated in years, months, and days.

    In addition, the rent should always be expressed in annual amounts payable in equal monthly installments. Failure to do so may result in a month-to-month tenancy verses that of a multiyear lease.

Example

Jones (lessor) enters into a 1-year lease with Smith (lessee) on January 1 for a monthly rental of $500. In late May of the same year, Smith notifies Jones of his intent to vacate at the end of the following month (June 30 of that year). Smith vacates and Jones seeks unpaid rent from July through December, only to find out that Smith had a month-to-month lease and no additional rent was due.

    In order for Jones to have collected the remaining July through December rent, Jones needed to properly state in the lease that it was a 1-year lease "at an *annual* rental of $6,000 to be paid in equal monthly installments of $500 in advance at the first of each monthly period."

Termination of a Lease

A lease can be terminated in the following ways:

- Expiration—If the original term of the lease expires, the lease is terminated.
- Mutual agreement—Both landlord and tenant can agree to terminate a lease.
- Destruction or condemnation of the property—If property is destroyed, damaged, or condemned to the point that it cannot be used, the lease is terminated.
- Breach of contract—If either party violates the terms of the lease, the lease may be terminated at the discretion of the other party; however, it is always best to allow the courts to decide the appropriate course of action. For example:
  - If a tenant uses the property for a purpose that violates the lease, the landlord may elect to terminate the lease and evict the tenant.
  - If the landlord for a commercial property violates a noncompetition clause in the lease by leasing another storefront in the same shopping center to a competitor of the tenant, the tenant may elect to terminate the lease.

A breach of the terms of a contract may also result in eviction of the tenant. There are two types of eviction:

1. Actual eviction—The legal removal of the tenant from the leased property because the tenant violates some provision of the lease.

2. Constructive eviction—This occurs when the landlord causes or permits a situation to occur that makes it impossible for the tenant to enjoy the premises under the terms of the lease. For example, if a landlord allows the water in an apartment to be shut off, leaving the tenant without water, the landlord has caused constructive eviction.

There are some significant situations under which a lease is *not* terminated. A lease for years is not terminated by:

• The death of either party—Should either party die during the lease period, the deceased party's estate is bound by the terms of the lease.

• The sale of the property—If the property is sold during the lease period, the new owner becomes the lessor and is bound by the lease contract.

Coaching Tips: Both a tenancy at will and tenancy at sufferance *are* terminated by the death of either party or the sale of the property.

Assignment and Subletting

A tenant may assign or sublet leased property unless otherwise prohibited in the lease. **Assignment** is the transfer of *all* rights that the tenant (assignor) holds in the property to another (assignee). The new tenant, the assignee, once approved by the landlord, becomes primarily liable for performance (payment of rent) under the lease contract. Unless a novation (substitution) of obligation occurs or the original tenant receives a release from the obligation, the original tenant (the assignor) remains secondarily (ultimately) liable.

A sublessor is the original tenant who sublets to a new tenant when property is subleased. Subletting is the transfer of *some but not all* of the rights and interests in the leased property held by the original master tenant or overtenant. The original tenant (the sublessor) retains some reversionary rights, the right to retake possession of the property after the new tenant (the sublessee or undertenant) vacates. Unlike the assignment, regardless of the overlandlord consenting to the sublease, the original tenant (or overtenant) remains solely liable to the landlord for performance under the lease contract (payment of rent). The sublessee is liable only to the original lessee, not to the landlord. The subtenant is also not a direct tenant of the landlord and as such, has no parity with the property owner. (See Figure 9.6.)

 FIGURE 9.6

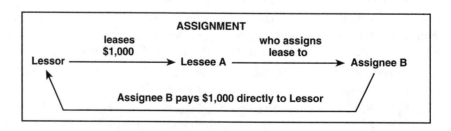

ASSIGNMENT

Lessor ——leases $1,000——→ Lessee A ——who assigns lease to——→ Assignee B

Assignee B pays $1,000 directly to Lessor

LIENS

Previously, you learned about several types of interests in real property and encumbrances to property ownership. Now you will learn about the last type of encumbrance, called a lien.

A **lien** is a legal hold or claim for the repayment of debt/owing that:

- One person has upon the property of another.
- Is used as security for a debt.

There are two parties to a lien. The lienor is a person who has a right of lien upon the property of another. The lienee is a person whose property is subject to a lien.

There are several types of liens that you should know about:

- Mortgage liens
- Tax liens
- Mechanic's liens
- Judgment liens
- Deficiency judgment liens

Mortgage Liens

A mortgage lien is created when a property owner borrows money using the property as collateral. The property is pledged and used as security by the lender for the repayment of the loan. The lien is the instrument through which the lender's interest in the property is secured. In essence, until the loan is repaid to the lender, the borrower continues to own the property while the lender maintains and holds a lien on the property.

Coaching Tips: **The process of pledging the property as collateral is also known as hypothecation.**

Tax Liens

There are five major types of tax liens:

1. Ad valorem property tax liens
2. Special district assessment/property tax liens
3. Federal income tax liens (issued and placed by the Internal Revenue Service)
4. Estate/inheritance tax liens
5. Corporate tax liens

Ad Valorem Tax Liens

Ad valorem taxes are normally referred to as property taxes that are assessed according to the value of the property. An ad valorem tax lien is levied and attached on a property at the beginning of each tax year. That same lien is removed only when payment for that tax period has been received and credited. When someone fails to pay the ad valorem taxes that have been assessed on a property, collection procedures are instituted by either one of the following:

- The municipality
- In some cases, individuals or entities that purchase municipal tax liens

In most municipalities, the tax liens are sold to investors. This saves municipalities the wasteful use of public funds to pay for legal fees, court costs, and the time required for judicial tax foreclosure and sale of the property.

Either a municipality or an investor initiates a procedure to collect on the lien via a foreclosure sale of the property. This procedure is the collection process for any outstanding amounts plus interest and penalties.

Special District Assessment/Tax Liens

Special assessment taxes are assessed on certain properties only in order to pay for improvements for those properties affected. An example would be a special assessment tax to pay for street lights in a neighborhood at the owners' request. When special assessment taxes are assessed, a tax lien is placed on the property. When the taxes are paid, the lien is removed.

Federal Income Tax Liens

Federal income tax liens arise when federal income taxes are not paid.

Estate/Inheritance Tax Liens

Upon the death of an individual or entity, taxes are levied on all personal property and real property in the form of a tax lien.

Corporate Tax Liens

The Internal Revenue Service (IRS) requires that all corporations pay corporation taxes on all annual profits derived by that corporation through its operations.

Coaching Tips: Income tax liens, estate/inheritance tax liens, and corporate tax liens all fall into the category of general liens. That is, these liens apply to *all* property, both real and personal, of the lienee. General liens will be described in more detail later in this chapter.

Mechanic's Liens

A mechanic's lien protects those people who supply labor or materials in the construction or improvement of buildings. If the labor or materials are not paid for, the person supplying them has the right to place a lien against the property for which the labor or materials were supplied. In Florida, a mechanic's lien must be filed and recorded with the circuit court clerk within *90 days* after the completion of the work or the furnishing of the last materials in order for the lien to have priority over any mortgage liens established after the labor or materials were initially supplied. To enforce a claim against a mechanic's lien, a lienor must file a lawsuit in court within *1 year.* In order to give notice of her claim and to protect her lien from expiration while the suit is pending, the lienor may file a notice of **lis pendens** in the public records.

Judgment Liens

When a person wins a lawsuit against another person in court to receive monetary damages, the person winning the suit is awarded a judgment. When the judgment is recorded in the public records, it becomes a judgment lien against all the property, both real and personal, of the defendant (the loser of the lawsuit). Thus, judgment liens are considered to fall within the category of general liens. If the lienee (the loser of the suit) does not voluntarily pay the amount of the damages awarded by the court, the court will issue a writ of execution that directs the sheriff to sell enough of the lienee's property to pay the damages and the cost of the sale.

It should be noted that judgment liens are general liens and attach to all real and personal property of the lienee.

Deficiency Judgment Liens

A deficiency judgment arises when a property is foreclosed on and sold to satisfy a debt. If the proceeds from the sale of the property are not sufficient to satisfy the outstanding balance on the debt, the mortgagee may obtain a deficiency judgment. This judgment serves as a lien on all of the mortgagor's assets. If the mortgagor fails to pay the remaining balance on the property, the lien is enforced like any other judgment lien. The mortgagor's property, both real and personal, can be sold to pay off the remaining balance. Mortgage liens are voluntary liens. This is to mean that the borrower/property owner is willingly allowing the lien to be placed on his property in exchange for the money loaned by the lender. This will be discussed later in this chapter.

It is important to note that not all mortgages give the lender the right to a deficiency judgment. Mortgage loans that are **recourse loans** (those where the borrower personally guarantees the repayment of the borrowed amount) versus those mortgage loans that are nonrecourse (those where the borrower *does not* personally guarantees the repayment of the borrowed amount). For the loan to be nonrecourse, it will usually have an exculpation clause. This clause basically says that the bank will only look to the collateral property for repayment of the debt. Deficiency judgment liens are general liens and attach to all real and personal property of the lienee.

Categories of Liens

Deficiency judgment liens can be categorized in two ways:

1. Voluntary versus involuntary
2. General versus specific

Voluntary liens are liens created by an agreement of the parties. An example would be a mortgage lien.

Involuntary liens are created by the operation of law. Examples would include:

- A tax lien from failure to pay property
- Taxes
- A mechanic's lien for failure to pay for work done
- A judgment lien or a deficiency judgment lien

Involuntary liens are also called statutory liens. (See Figure 9.7.)

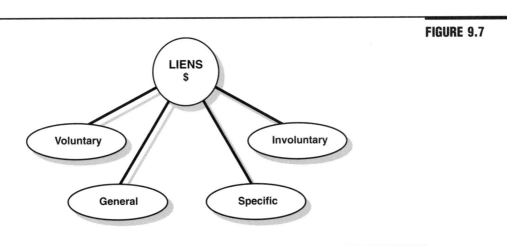

FIGURE 9.7

A **general lien** is one that attaches to *all* property owned by the lienee. Examples of general liens include:

- Federal income tax lien—A statutory lien that can occur when federal income taxes are not paid.
- Judgment lien—A statutory lien that results from court action brought against the lienee.
- Deficiency judgment lien—A statutory lien that results when the proceeds from a foreclosure sale are insufficient to satisfy the outstanding indebtedness.

A **specific lien** attaches only to a specific property identified in the lien. Examples of specific liens include a:

- Property tax lien when taxes are not paid.
- Mortgage lien when a mortgage is used in financing.
- Mechanic's lien when work done is not paid for.

Coaching Tips: General Lien versus Specific Lien

- General liens attach to all property owned.
- Specific liens attach only to a specific property.
- Specific liens are also called special liens.

Voluntary Lien versus Involuntary Lien

- Voluntary liens are created by an agreement between parties.
- Involuntary liens are created by an act of law.
- Not all general liens are involuntary liens.
- Statutory liens are created by the operation of law.

Priority of Liens

When two or more liens exist, it becomes important to determine the priority of liens. In most states, priority is determined by race statutes. In general, race statutes give priority on the basis of the date of recordation of a lien in the public records. The first to be recorded has priority. There are two exceptions to this rule:

1. Real property tax liens take priority over all other liens on a given property, regardless of when they were recorded. Both ad valorem tax liens and special assessment tax liens have priority over all other types of liens.

Coaching Tips: Federal income tax liens *do not* have any special priority. They take priority on the date of their recordation just like any other lien other than a property tax lien.

---

2. A mechanic's lien takes priority on the basis of one of the following:
   - When the work began.
   - When the materials were delivered, *not* the date the mechanic's lien was recorded.

Transfer of Encumbered Title

A lien is an encumbrance on the title to the real property to which it attaches. To transfer the title, one of the following must occur:

- The lien is satisfied.
- The lien is assumed by the person to whom the title is being transferred (the grantee).

SUMMARY

Real property like other personal property can be transferred from one person to another. Real property is transferred by deed while personal property is transferred by bill of sale. There are various deed instruments that are accepted as transfer instruments. The ownership in real property may come with private (deed restrictions) or public restrictions (such as zoning). Whereas an estate (ownership in real property) is conveyed to another by deed, possession rights to property are transferred by lease. There are a variety of leases that are used (as applicable). Liens are claims on the property of another for repayment of an indebtedness. Liens are either voluntary or involuntary. They also fall into two categories of liens; general or specific. Title searches help to identify liens that exist on property.

REVIEW QUESTIONS

1. An effective deed is one that has been:
   a. Signed by a competent grantee.
   b. Acknowledged.
   c. Signed by a competent grantor.
   d. Signed by the grantor and grantee.

2. A deed that would carry the least legal liability for a grantor is a:
   a. Special warranty deed.
   b. General warranty deed.
   c. Quitclaim deed.
   d. Bargain and sale deed.

3. Anna paid cash for her orange grove. She took her deed home and put it in a safe place. This action:
   a. Is not legal.
   b. Is legal, but courts will favor a recorded deed.
   c. Is legally equal to recording the deed.
   d. Is called constructive notice.

4. The bargain and sale deed is characterized by the covenant of seisin. This clause in a deed:
   a. Promises the grantor is the legal owner.
   b. Warrants the title is clear.
   c. Guarantees the grantor has not ruined the title.
   d. States the price that was paid for the property.

5. The clause in a deed that promises the grantor will defend the grantee's right to own the property is the:
   a. Covenant of no encumbrances.
   b. Covenant of warranty forever.
   c. Covenant of quiet enjoyment.
   d. Covenant of further assurance.

6. The clause in a deed that warrants the title while the grantor has owned the property, but does not warrant title from claims prior to the grantor's ownership, is the covenant of:
   a. Seisin.
   b. No encumbrances.
   c. Quiet enjoyment.
   d. Warranty forever.

7. If the sale contract is silent regarding the deed the seller will provide the buyer at closing, in Florida the seller must provide the buyer with a:
   a. Quitclaim deed.
   b. Bargain and sale deed.
   c. Special warranty deed.
   d. General warranty deed.

8. A valid deed in Florida must be:
   a. Executed with two witnesses.
   b. Acknowledged.
   c. Signed by a grantee.
   d. Recorded.

9. A list of everyone who has ever owned a property from the time the property was first conveyed through a patent from a president until the present owner is:
   a. An opinion of title.
   b. A chain of title.
   c. An abstract of title.
   d. A lis pendens.

10. An opinion of title in Florida can be issued by:
    a. An attorney.
    b. A broker.
    c. A title company.
    d. Anyone.

11. Local townspeople have been crossing a farmer's field to get to a good fishing spot on the river for more than 20 years. This access to the farmer's land is:
    a. Illegal trespass.
    b. An encroachment.
    c. An implied easement.
    d. An easement by prescription.

12. Susan is an avid gardener and takes pride in her flowerbeds. When she came home, she discovered workers from the power company had entered her gated backyard and damaged her flowers in order to get to the power poles behind her fence. Under these circumstances, this surprise entry constituted:
    a. An encroachment on her property.
    b. An easement in gross.
    c. Illegal entry; Susan can sue.
    d. An easement by prescription.

13. An owner's title insurance policy:
    a. Is issued for an amount no greater than the debt and is transferable.
    b. Is issued for an amount no greater than the purchase price and is not transferable.
    c. Is a legal requirement in Florida when purchasing real property.
    d. Is issued to protect the lender.

14. Jane's aunt, Mary, died. While helping her mother clear out her aunt's home, Jane discovered a deed for the house signed by her aunt with two witnesses deeding the house to the Red Cross. Mary died without a will, and has a son, John. Who owns Mary's house?
    a. The Red Cross owns the house.
    b. By escheat, the state owns Mary's house.
    c. Mary's son, John, owns his mother's house.
    d. Jane's mother, Mary's sister, owns the house.

15. The deed to Solomon's lot and house states the house must be painted sage green so long as the building stands. This is an example of a:
    a. Deed restriction.
    b. Requirement Solomon can waive.
    c. Whim by a former owner that is not legal.
    d. Subdivision covenant.

16. Jerry pays $1,000 per month to live at an apartment. Jerry's apartment developed a leak in the roof. Jerry called the owner to come fix the roof right away. Jerry's lease is a:
    a. Gross lease.
    b. Net lease.
    c. Percentage lease.
    d. Ground lease.

17. The storefront merchant in a successful mall must pay a fixed amount of money for occupying the space. In addition, the merchant must pay a share of the mall owner's taxes, insurance, and other operating expenses for the property. The merchant's lease is:
    a. Unconscionable and can be rescinded.
    b. A percentage lease.
    c. A net lease.
    d. A gross lease.

18. The right of a government to take private property when needed for a public purpose is called:
    a. Escheat to the state.
    b. Condemnation.
    c. Eminent domain.
    d. A public grant.

19. The East to West Railroad Company is planning a new route through George's farm. George strongly objects to this action and the price he is being paid. Which of the following statements is true?
    a. George can commence an action in court to dispute the amount of compensation he is being paid for his farm.
    b. A court can give George and injunction to stop the railroad.
    c. George can sue the railroad for damages.
    d. George can simply refuse to sell.

20. Which of the following liens will be paid first?
    a. A property tax lien filed on January 1, 2007.
    b. A mechanic's lien filed on December 1, 2006.
    c. A special assessment lien filed on February 12, 2006.
    d. A mortgage lien filed on March 26, 2007.

Chapter 10

KEY TERMS

base line

benchmarks

block

check

correction lines

government rectangular survey system

legal descriptions

lots

metes and bounds

monument

point of beginning (POB)

principal meridian

range

sections

tier

township

township lines

LEARNING OBJECTIVES

After completing this lesson, you will be able to:

- Explain the three legal methods of describing property.
- Describe the process of transferring title to real property by use of a deed.
- Explain the informal method of describing property.
- Describe the major elements of each approach to property description.
- Solve problems relating to the government survey system.

Property Description

METHODS OF DESCRIPTION

There are four methods of describing property:

1. Recorded subdivision plat maps
2. Metes and bounds
3. Government rectangular survey
4. Informal reference, such as street address or locally recognized name

For the purpose of transferring title, only the first three are legally acceptable. These three are called **legal descriptions**.

The fourth method, informal reference:

- Is not accurate enough for title transfer.
- Can be used in a listing because no transfer of title is involved (but it is best to use a legal description).

Only the three legal description methods can be used for deeds and any other contracts involving title transfer.

Recorded Plats

The first method of legal property description is called recorded plats. A plat is simply a map of a subdivision. Plats are usually created by a developer or subdivider when a parcel of raw land is subdivided into building lots. As a helpful tool, think of subdividing as "buying by the acre while selling it by the lot." Plats are recorded in the public land records when the subdivision is created, along with a list of any restrictive covenants that will apply to the subdivision. After a plat is recorded, any property located in the subdivision can be identified by reference to the recorded plat.

The plat (map) of a subdivision of land describes the property by breaking it down into units called blocks and lots. A **block** is the largest unit within a subdivision. Each block is subdivided into individual **lots** that houses are built on. The plat also shows the boundaries of all streets and easements in the subdivision and any other relevant details of the subdivision.

Metes and Bounds

The second method of legal property description is called **metes and bounds**. *Metes* means distance and *bounds* means direction. The metes and bounds method is the oldest method of legal description. The best way to understand a metes and bounds description is to think of it as a set of instructions you would give someone on how to walk around the outside boundaries of the property.

For example, you might tell someone, "Start at the well and go north for 100 feet to the creek. Then turn right and go east for 150 feet to a large oak tree. Then turn right and go south for 100 feet to a large rock. Then turn right and go 150 feet back to the well."

This is an example of a simple metes and bounds description using natural monuments. The natural monuments used were the well, the creek, the large oak tree, and the rock. As you saw in the example, a **monument** is an object that is used to define a corner of a parcel of property. (A corner is any place where you change direction while walking around the property.)

A monument may be:

- A natural monument—A natural object such as a tree or rock, like the ones used in the example.

- A permanent monument—A man-made object such as an iron pin driven into the ground or a concrete marker placed by a surveyor.

The metes and bounds method using natural monuments was used primarily in the past when surveyors were not generally available or when land was plentiful and inexpensive. The metes and bounds method using permanent monuments is commonly referred to today as a survey of property and is used as the primary method of description in many states. Metes and bounds descriptions are very useful in describing parcels of property that are irregular in shape, because they can describe *any* property by using directions of travel, distance of travel, and monuments. The advantage of permanent monuments is that permanent monuments last longer and are not as likely to be moved. However, even permanent man-made monuments may be occasionally moved or destroyed. To protect against this possibility, metes and bounds descriptions are tied to what are called permanent reference markers. A permanent reference marker (PRM) is a precisely identified location that is identified by reference to latitude and longitude. Permanent reference markers are also referred to as **benchmarks**.

A metes and bounds description *must* always begin at a point of beginning.

The **point of beginning (POB)** is:

- Identified as the POB on the plat.
- Usually marked by an iron pin placed by the surveyor.

The POB must be precisely identified. If the location of the POB is vague or unclear, the resulting legal description is invalid, which means that the contract or deed based on the description may be void. From the POB, the boundaries of the parcel are described using the direction and distance of travel from a permanent monument, or the location and distance between natural monuments. The description must always return to the POB. Any description that does not return to the POB is defective (invalid), which means that the contract or deed based on the description may be void.

With the metes and bounds method, direction is typically measured using compass directions. Compass directions are expressed in degrees, minutes, and seconds. There are 360 degrees in a circle, 60 minutes in a degree, and 60 seconds in a minute. Compass directions also involve the directions north, south, east, and west. A direction begins by indicating whether the primary direction is north or south, then rotating the appropriate number of degrees, minutes, and seconds to either the west or the east. The maximum number of degrees is 90. (See Figure 10.1.)

Example

- South 45 degrees west indicates a direction that is halfway between due south and due west.
- North 89 degrees east indicates a direction facing almost due east (90 degrees east would be due east).

FIGURE 10.1

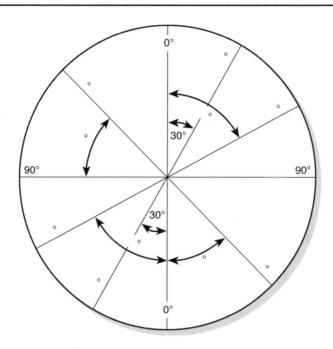

When a metes and bounds description is used, errors are possible and the actual distance between monuments may be different from the distance given in the metes and bounds description. When this happens, the *actual* distance *takes precedence* over the distance stated in the metes and bounds description.

Government Rectangular Survey

The third method of legal property description is called the **government rectangular survey system**, which was established by Congress in the mid to later 1780s. It has been applied in most states since that date, with few exceptions. The states where the government rectangular survey system is used are primarily in the West and Midwest and a few states in the South, such as Florida. It has not been applied to those states that were formed prior to the mid 1780s, including the original 13 states and a few others.

Each **principal meridian** is intersected by only one **base line**. Throughout the United States, there are 36 different intersecting principal meridians and base lines. In Florida, the principal meridian and base line intersect in Tallahassee. As a result, it is named the Tallahassee Principal Meridian and Base Line. The overall size of each system varies from system to system. The outermost boundaries of a system are irregular in shape and often conform to the border between states.

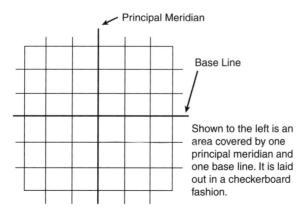

Principal Meridian

Base Line

Shown to the left is an area covered by one principal meridian and one base line. It is laid out in a checkerboard fashion.

Guide Meridians

Due to the earth's spherical shape, the north/south meridian lines respectively meet at the north or south poles. As a result, the parallel north/south lines that meet at the respective poles require a solution. Therefore, guide meridians (north and south lines) are drawn every 24 miles to the east and west of the principal meridian. These lines end every 24 miles from the principal meridian and provide the offset necessary (approximately 50 feet away) to correct for the spherical shape of the earth.

Correction Lines

Correction lines are made up of east/west lines situated every 24 miles to the north and south of the base line. A **check** is the 24-mile square that is achieved through the intersecting guide meridians.

Ranges and Tiers

Here is the best way to remember the difference between a range and a tier:

- A **range** runs north and south. All three words—*range, north,* and *south*—have *five* letters.
- A **tier** runs east and west. All three words—*tier, east,* and *west*—have *four* letters.
  - A tier is also referred to as a **township**.

  Thus, the term *township* refers to both of the following:

1. A square parcel of land formed by the intersection of range lines and **township lines**. Township lines are lines that are drawn every 6 miles north and south of a base line thereby forming east and west parcels of land
2. A row of townships running east-west.

  As a helpful tool, think of as the following:

- West is to the left of the principal meridian.
- East is to the right of the principal meridian.
  - Tiers run east to west (tier, east, and west all have *four* letters).
- North is above the base line.
- South is below the base line.
  - Ranges run north to south (range, north, and south all have *five* letters).

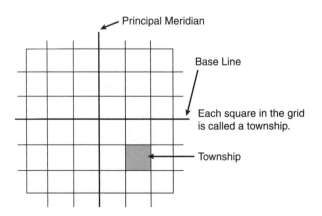

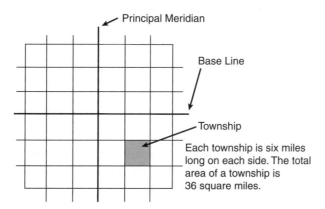

Principal Meridian

Base Line

Township

Each township is six miles long on each side. The total area of a township is 36 square miles.

There is one special situation that results in **sections** that have slightly different measurements from the normal measurements just presented. Because of the curvature of the earth's surface, the dimensions of some townships must be corrected (usually the townships contained along the northwest perimeter of the drawn guide meridians). Because of this correction, some of the sections along the northwest borders of a township are smaller than the rest. These sections are about 50 feet narrower than the other sections. This occurs as a result of correction lines that are drawn every 24 miles to the west and east of the principal meridian. This correction accounts for the curvature of the Earth particularly at the north and south poles where meridian lines meet.

Sections

Each township contains 36 sections. Each section measures 1 mile square. Each section within a township is represented by a number from 1-36. Section 1 is always found in the northeast corner of a township. The numeric progression is westward of section 1 until section 6. Section 7 is found directly to the south (below) of section 6 and continues eastward until section 12. Section 13 is found directly to the south of section 12 and continues westward until section 18. This numeric progression of sections continues in the exact same manner as just described until section 36 is reached. Section 36 is always found in the southeast corner of a township.

HINT: If you draw a horizontal line that follows the numeric progression, the line would resemble a continuous letter "S"

When writing or identifying a legal description of a section:

* The appropriate section number appears first.
* The tier, referenced by its number and direction, appears second.
* The range number and direction appears last.

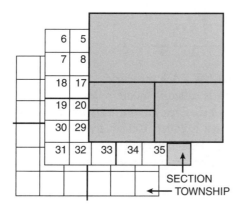

SECTION
TOWNSHIP

Example

Section 14, Tier 14 South (T14S), Range 4 West (R4W), of the Tallahassee Principal Meridian and Base Line.

BASIC FACTS

Introduction

Throughout this chapter, you will be presented with a summary of some basic math relationships that are involved in the government survey system. The presentation of these facts will consist simply of a set of statements of equivalent values.

Example

1 section = 640 acres

Before we begin working with the basic facts for the government survey system, we need to cover one general math concept.

Let's begin with the figure below. Let's assume that the figure represents a square parcel of land that measures 4 miles on each side.

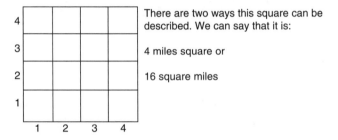

There are two ways this square can be described. We can say that it is:

4 miles square or

16 square miles

Let's look at the difference in these two descriptions.

Notice that each side of the square is 4 miles long. One way it can be described is to say that it is 4 miles square.

If the square measured 3 miles on each side, it would be described as 3 miles square.

A square that measured 10 miles on each side would be described as 10 miles square.

The other way to describe the parcel shown below is 16 square miles. This description simply states the area of the square.

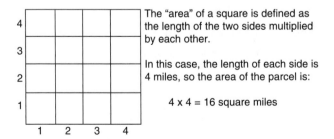

The "area" of a square is defined as the length of the two sides multiplied by each other.

In this case, the length of each side is 4 miles, so the area of the parcel is:

4 x 4 = 16 square miles

A square parcel that has sides measuring 3 miles would have an area equal to 3 miles × 3 miles, which is called 9 square miles.

A square parcel that has sides measuring 10 miles would have an area equal to 10 miles × 10 miles, which is called 100 square miles.

In the remainder of this lesson, we will practice working with two sets of basic math facts relating to the government survey system. Before we begin with the first set, let's review the major units of measurement in the government survey system.

The checkerboard layout that is formed around the intersection of a baseline and a principal meridian is illustrated next.

The checkerboard is divided into units called townships, as shown in the figure below:

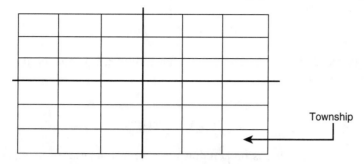

Now, let's look at the first set of basic math facts relating to the government survey system:

1 township = 6 miles by 6 miles

1 township = 6 miles square

1 township = 36 square miles

1 section = 1 mile square

1 section = 1 square mile

1 section = 640 acres

1 township = 36 sections

6	5	4	3	2	1
7	8	9	10	11	12
18	17	16	15	14	13
19	20	21	22	23	24
30	29	28	27	26	25
31	32	33	34	35	36

Township

The size of a section is important when trying to determine the number of acres in a tract of land (see Figure 10.2). As mentioned previously, each section represents 1 square mile and contains 640 acres. Sections can be broken down into smaller parcels.

FIGURE 10.2

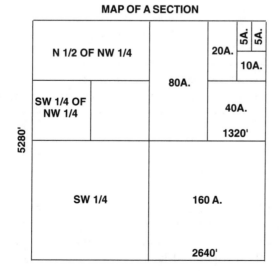

MAP OF A SECTION

For example, a section can be broken down into quarter sections. Each quarter section contains 160 acres:

$$640 \text{ acres} \div 4 = 160 \text{ acres}$$

Each quarter section can then be broken down further. One quarter of one quarter of a section contains 40 acres:

$$640 \text{ acres} \div 4 = 160 \text{ acres}$$
$$160 \text{ acres} \div 4 = 40 \text{ acres}$$

Similarly, if the section is broken down further, one quarter of one quarter of one quarter of a section contains 10 acres:

$$640 \text{ acres} \div 4 = 160 \text{ acres}$$
$$160 \text{ acres} \div 4 = 40 \text{ acres}$$
$$40 \text{ acres} \div 4 = 10 \text{ acres}$$

Assume that you want to determine the size of a tract of land. If you know the tract of land consists of the northeast quarter of section 6, you would calculate the size as follows:

$$640 \text{ acres} \div 4 = 160 \text{ acres}$$

Let's look at another example.

A tract of land consists of the southwest quarter of the northeast quarter of section 6. In this situation, the size of the tract is calculated as follows:

$$640 \text{ acres} \div 4 = 160 \text{ acres}$$
$$160 \text{ acres} \div 4 = 40 \text{ acres}$$

The tract contains 40 acres:

$$640 \text{ acres} \div 4 = 160 \text{ acres}$$
$$160 \text{ acres} \div 4 = 40 \text{ acres}$$

Now, let's look at another set of basic math facts relating to the government survey system:

$$1 \text{ acre} = 209 \text{ feet } 209 \text{ feet}$$
$$1 \text{ acre} = 209 \text{ feet square}$$
$$1 \text{ acre} = 43{,}560 \text{ square feet}$$

$$1 \text{ mile} = 5{,}280 \text{ feet}$$
$$1 \text{ mile} = 320 \text{ rods}$$
$$1 \text{ rod} = 16.5 \text{ feet}$$

Coaching Tips: **One acre is not exactly 209 feet square (209 feet × 209 feet). It is actually 208.71 feet square, but for convenience we will round this measurement off to 209.**

SUMMARY

In order for a parcel of improved or unimproved land to be conveyed from one party to another, a formal legal description of that parcel must be referenced. This legal description provides the boundaries of any parcel in question. There are various acceptable methods for the legal description of land. This includes the government rectangular survey system, metes and bounds, and recorded plats.

REVIEW QUESTIONS

1. What method of legal description is only used in subdivisions?
   a. Government survey system
   b. Lot and block method
   c. Metes and bounds
   d. Tax ID method

2. What section is due south of section 2?
   a. Section 12
   b. Section 11
   c. Section 3
   d. Section 8

3. Where is section 31 located in every township?
   a. The northeast corner
   b. The northwest corner
   c. The southeast corner
   d. The southwest corner

4. Which of these legal descriptions contains 2.5 acres?
   a. The SW ¼ of the SE ¼ of the NE ¼, section 11, T1S, R1E
   b. The SW ¼ of the SE ¼ of the NE ¼ of the NE ¼, section 11, T1S, R1W
   c. The SW ¼ of the SE ¼, and the NE ¼ of the NW ¼
   d. The S ½ of the SW ¼

5. Calculate the number of acres in the NW ¼ of the SE ¼ and the S ½ of the SE ¼.
   a. 40 acres
   b. 80 acres
   c. 100 acres
   d. 120 acres

6. Which legal description has been in use the longest?
   a. Metes and bounds
   b. Lot and block
   c. Government survey system
   d. Natural monument system

7. What is the most critical feature of the metes and bounds legal description?
   a. Use of natural monuments
   b. Presence of permanent monuments in the landscape
   c. An accurate POB
   d. Guide meridians

8. What compass direction is directly opposite of N 40°E?
   a. N 40°W
   b. S 40°E
   c. S 40°W
   d. N 80°E

9. What township is directly east of T3N, R4E?
   a. T2N, R4E
   b. T4N, R4E
   c. T3N, R5E
   d. T3N, R3E

10. Which method of legal description is the most accurate?
    a. Metes and bounds
    b. Lot and block
    c. Government survey system
    d. Subdivision plat system

11. The south boundary of section 12, T2N, R3W is:
    a. 8 miles north of the baseline.
    b. 6 miles north of the baseline.
    c. 10 miles north of the principal meridian.
    d. 10 miles north of the baseline.

12. The traditional measure of a homestead, based on the government survey system, was:
    a. 640 acres.
    b. 320 acres.
    c. 160 acres.
    d. 40 acres.

13. Which of the statements is FALSE?
    a. A section is a one-mile square.
    b. A section covers one square mile.
    c. There are 36 sections in a township.
    d. A section contains 36 acres.

14. Deanna purchased one-half of a section and gave one-quarter of that section to her son, Charles. How many acres did Charles receive?
    a. 320 acres
    b. 160 acres
    c. 80 acres
    d. 40 acres

15. Guide meridians and corrections lines are placed every:
    a. Mile.
    b. 6 miles.
    c. 12 miles.
    d. 24 miles.

16. How many square feet are in one acre?
    a. 640
    b. 26,780
    c. 43,560
    d. 87,120

17. In Florida, where do the principal meridian and baseline intersect?
    a. Orlando
    b. Tallahassee
    c. Jacksonville
    d. Green Swamp

18. A vertical strip of land, 6 miles wide and parallel to the principal meridian, is a:
    a. Range.
    b. Township tier.
    c. Section.
    d. Check.

19. In the government survey system, a fragmented piece of land that is not entirely square that was on the gulf, for example, is called a:
    a. Check.
    b. Plot.
    c. Government lot.
    d. Benchmark.

20. The requirement for a legal description is:
    a. It must be sufficient that a surveyor could find it.
    b. The street address must accompany the description.
    c. Enough for the local county standards.
    d. An official street address will do.

Chapter 11

KEY TERMS

assignment
attorney-in-fact
bilateral contract
competent
contract
exclusive right to buy
executed contract
executory contract

expressed contract
implied contract
liquidated damages
meeting of the minds
novation
option contract
rescission of a contract
Statute of Frauds

Statute of Limitations
unenforceable
unilateral contract
valid contract
void contract
voidable contract

LEARNING OBJECTIVES

After completing this lesson, you will be able to:

- Define *contract* and differentiate between the following types of contracts:
  - Expressed and implied
  - Valid, void, and voidable
  - Bilateral and unilateral
  - Executed and executory
- Describe the four requirements for a valid contract:
  - Consideration
  - Agreement
  - Legal objective
  - Legally competent parties
- Explain the methods by which contracts can be discharged.
- Define the Statute of Frauds and how the provisions of the Statute of Frauds affect contracts.
- Identify several characteristics of option contracts.
- Recognize what activities constitute a breach of contract.
- Identify remedies for a breached contract.
- Describe the major characteristics of four types of contracts used in real estate:
  - Contract of sale
  - Back-up contract
  - Binder
  - Installment contract

Real Estate Contracts

DEFINITIONS

A **contract** is an agreement between two parties. It can be an agreement to do something, or not to do something. If it is an agreement *not* to do something, it is called a contract for forbearance.

In general, contracts can be written or oral. Although the validity of an oral contract without proper witnesses is difficult to prove, oral contracts in Florida are enforceable. However, the **Statute of Frauds** dictates and requires that all contracts involving either the purchase of or sale of any parcel of real property *must* be in writing to be enforceable. An oral contract is called a parol contract.

CATEGORIES OF CONTRACTS

Contracts can be categorized in four ways:

1. Expressed versus implied
2. Valid versus void and voidable
3. Bilateral versus unilateral
4. Executed versus executory

Each of these categories will be covered in this chapter.

Expressed versus Implied

An **expressed contract** is one in which the intent of the parties is stated (expressed) in the contract itself. An expressed contract can be either written or oral.

Example

(1) A contract to sell real estate is an expressed contract because the intent of the seller to sell and the buyer to buy is stated in the contract; (2) a verbal lease on an apartment for 3 months is an expressed contract because the parties verbally state their intent.

An **implied contract** is one in which the intent of the parties is not stated but is indicated by their actions.

Example

If you order food in a restaurant, your actions (ordering the food) imply a contract on your part to pay. The acceptance of the order by the waiter implies that the restaurant will deliver food in return for your money.

Valid versus Void and Voidable

From a legal standpoint, there are three types of contracts:

1. Valid
2. Void
3. Voidable

A **valid contract** is one that is legally sufficient and meets all the essential requirements of the law to create a contract between two or more persons.

A valid contract can be either enforceable or unenforceable:

- Enforceable—A valid contract that can be enforced in a court of law.
- **Unenforceable**—A contract that cannot be enforced in a court of law. An unenforceable contract is valid until challenged in court.

An unenforceable contract is usually one that is valid but is *not written,* and therefore cannot be enforced in court. Such is the case concerning the transfer of real property from one party to another. In real estate, some contracts must be written to be enforceable, while others do not need to be written, such as an open listing agreement.

As required by the Statute of Frauds and with no exceptions, all contracts for the purchase or sale (in part or in whole) of any parcel of real property must be in written form to be considered valid and enforceable. This issue will be covered in more detail later in this chapter.

A **void contract** is one that is not recognized legally and has no legal effect. From its inception, the agreement lacks one or more of the necessary essential requirements for the creation of a valid and enforceable contract. For example, a contract to perform any unlawful or illegal act is void from inception. It lacks the requirement of a legal objective. (The requirements for a valid contract, including legal objective, will be described in detail later in this chapter.)

It is important to understand the following:

- A void contract is not binding on either party.
- Even though a void contract may seem to be a contract, it is not a contract at all.

A **voidable contract** is one that is capable of being voided by *one* of the parties to the contract. It is binding on one party to the contract only and is *valid* until action is taken by one party to make it void.

Although the contract seems to be valid on the surface, it may lack one or more necessary essential requirements for the creation of a valid and enforceable contract. For example, a contract for the purchase and sale of real property involving a minor as either the buyer or the seller is a voidable contract. Because the minor is not considered to be a competent party, only the minor may void the contract. See Figure 11.1.

Bilateral versus Unilateral

The third way of categorizing contracts is in terms of the nature of the commitments made by the parties to the contract. Contracts are said to be either bilateral or unilateral.

A **bilateral contract** is one in which *both* parties promise to give up something or to perform in such a manner as required by the agreement. A promise is exchanged for a promise (see Figure 11.2).

FIGURE 11.1

LEGAL EFFECTS OF CONTRACTS

✓ VALID
  binding and enforceable

✓ VOIDABLE
  one party can cancel due to fraud, duress, or
  undue influence, but the other side cannot cancel

✓ UNENFORCEABLE
  appears valid, but cannot be enforced in court

✓ VOID
  no legal effect, no contract

Example

A real estate sales contract is a bilateral contract. Both parties promise to give up something. The seller promises to give her home to the buyer. In return, the buyer promises to give money to the seller.

Coaching Tips: **A bilateral contract is like a two-way street. This means that it is not an agreement whereby only one party is required to act in accordance with the promises contained in the contract (an option to purchase where a seller must sell but the buyer is not required to purchase). A bilateral contract requires that both parties act on the promises contained in the contract, ultimately to the benefit of both parties (a buyer's promise to buy and a seller's promise to sell).**

A **unilateral contract** is one in which only *one* party promises to give up something. A promise is exchanged for some act or performance by the other party (see Figure 11.2).

Example

A sales bonus offered to a salesperson is a unilateral contract. The company promises to pay a bonus if sales targets are met, but the salesperson does not promise to meet those goals.

Coaching Tips: **A unilateral contract is like a one-way street. It is an agreement that benefits only one party to the transaction.**

FIGURE 11.2

TYPES		OF CONTRACTS
UNILATERAL	=	PROMISE FOR AN ACT
BILATERAL	=	PROMISE FOR A PROMISE
EXPRESSED	=	VERBAL OR WRITTEN
IMPLIED	=	CREATED BY ACTIONS
EXECUTORY	=	SOME ACTION NEEDED
EXECUTED	=	COMPLETED CONTRACT

Most real estate agreements are expressed bilateral contracts.

One of the best examples of a unilateral contract in real estate is the **option contract**. An option is a contract that gives someone the right but not the obligation to buy a property. Under an option contract, the property owner gives a potential buyer the right to buy the property at a prescribed price for a prescribed time period (the option period). To ensure that the option received is considered valid and enforceable, the potential buyer gives the property owner valuable and substantial consideration for the option period. During the option period, the buyer may purchase the property if he chooses to, whereby the owner would have to comply and sell at the agreed-upon price. However, the property owner cannot force the buyer to purchase the property.

The option creates a "one-way street" or a one-party promise—the owner promises to sell (if the buyer chooses to buy), but the buyer does not promise to buy.

Executed versus Executory

The fourth way of categorizing contracts is in terms of whether or not they have been completed. Contracts are said to be either executed or executory.

An **executed contract** is one in which all requirements of the contract have been fulfilled and the parties have done what they agreed to do in the contract. In essence, all interested parties to the transaction have fully performed (see Figure 11.2).

Example

When a real estate sales contract is closed or settled, it is executed.

Coaching Tips: Don't confuse an executed contract with executing a document. Executing a document simply refers to the process of signing the document.

An **executory contract** is one in which some or all requirements have not yet been completed (see Figure 11.2).

Example

A real estate contract that has been signed by both parties but has not closed is an executory contract because all the requirements of the contract have not been completed (e.g., transfer of title, payment of purchase price, etc.).

CONTRACT VALIDITY AND ENFORCEMENT REQUIREMENTS

There are four elements that are required for a contract to be valid. These four elements can be remembered by the mnemonic CALL. A valid contract CALLs for these four requirements:

1. Consideration
2. Agreement
3. Legal objective
4. Legally competent parties

Coaching Tips: In order for a contract involving the transfer of any interests in real property to be enforceable in Florida, the Statutes of Frauds requires that the contract be an agreement in written form.

Consideration

The first requirement of a valid contract is consideration. Consideration is a promise that someone makes to give up something of value. In a typical home sale, the seller promises to give up her home and the buyer promises to give the seller money (the purchase price).

Coaching Tips: In a real estate contract, consideration is *not* the earnest money, but the exchange of the purchase price (or something else of value) for real property.

Example

A painter signs a contract in which he promises to paint a house (a consideration) in exchange for money (a consideration).

There are two types of consideration:

1. Valuable consideration—Anything that has a monetary value such as money, services, merchandise, etc. (The *promise* of something that has monetary value is also considered valuable consideration, such as a buyer's promise to pay the purchase price and a seller's promise to sell real property.)

2. Good consideration—Something of worth that does not have a monetary value such as love, affection, or good will.

Good consideration is involved when a person gives real property as a gift. In this case valuable consideration (real property) is exchanged for good consideration (love and affection).

Agreement

The second requirement of a valid contract is mutual agreement or mutuality. This is sometimes called a **meeting of the minds** or offer and acceptance. This means that there must be a mutual agreement on the provisions of the contract.

Coaching Tips: You will encounter a variety of legal terms that end in the letters OR and EE. Here is a helpful tip in identifying and remembering the parties and their role within the situation:

- OR at the end of a word is the owner of, or giver of, whatever is owned and is given. An example of this is offeror. The offeror is the owner of or giver of the offer or counteroffer. As you will learn later in this chapter, the offeror can be either the buyer or the seller.

- EE at the end of a word is the receiver of, or recipient of whatever has been given. An example of this is offeree. The offeree is the receiver or recipient of the offer or counteroffer. The offeree can be either the buyer or the seller.

   There are generally no exceptions to this rule; however, there is one spelling exception, which is employer. The ER ending is treated as if it had an OR ending, therefore, providing the same definition as the OR. The employer is still the owner of the employment.

For mutual agreement to be achieved, three general conditions must be met:

1. One party (the offeror) must make an offer to the other party (the offeree).
2. The offeree must accept the offer.
3. The offeree must communicate the acceptance to the offeror.

If the offeree chooses not to accept the original offer of the offeror, he may make a counteroffer, which is a new offer substituted for the original offer. The counteroffer extinguishes the original offer. A counteroffer automatically terminates the original offer and constitutes a totally new offer, even if only one minor item is changed in the counteroffer.

It is important to understand that an offer *can* be withdrawn, even if was accepted, if it is not communicated or delivered. An offer *can't* be withdrawn after acceptance is communicated or delivered. Only the person who made the offer can withdraw it.

The second condition for accomplishing a mutual agreement is that *none* of the following may occur:

- Intentional misrepresentation
- Innocent misrepresentation
- Mistake

Intentional Misrepresentation

Intentional misrepresentation is an act intended to deceive someone in order to get her to give up something of value. It can result from intentionally giving false information or withholding relevant information.

Intentional misrepresentation results in fraud. Examples of fraud include:

- A seller tells a buyer that the property he is selling is zoned commercial when he knows that it is zoned residential.
- A seller is aware that the roof of her house leaks but conceals this fact from the buyer.

When fraud occurs, the injured party has the option to rescind (cancel) the contract or to leave it in effect.

Innocent (Unintentional) Misrepresentation

Innocent misrepresentation is the giving of incorrect information by one party *without* the intent to deceive.

Example

A prospective home buyer asks the seller if the city bus stops near the house, and the seller says "yes" without realizing that this service had been discontinued the week before.

In the case of innocent misrepresentation, although it may not be intentional on the part of the injuring party, the injured party has the option to rescind (cancel) the contract if it is done in a timely manner. In the event the innocent misrepresentation occurs due to the act or acts of a licensee, the licensee may be exposed to very serious civil liabilities. Furthermore, and perhaps even more important, the licensee will be the subject of disciplinary action by the Florida Real Estate Commission (FREC). When an individual receives a license, he is considered (in the eyes of the regulatory agency) as being an expert. The general public views licensees in the same light. Therefore, when proceeding with a real property transaction, it is important to realize that any misstatement(s), particularly a misstatement that results in a financial or other loss by a customer, subjects the licensee to severe disciplinary action by FREC.

Coaching Tips: **To avoid any unpleasant experiences concerning misstatements, it is always good practice to remember the following: If you tell the truth, you don't need a good memory.**

Mistake

A mistake is an error in the facts of a transaction that occurs:

- Mutually by both parties
- Unintentionally
- Without negligence

Example

A buyer is given directions to look at a property for sale, and the buyer goes to see the property alone. He mistakenly looks at the wrong vacant property and writes a contract to buy. After closing, the seller and the buyer discover the error. In this case, the buyer thinks he is buying one property, and the seller thinks she is selling another. In the case of a mutual mistake such as this, the contract is void because there is no mutual agreement.

The third condition that must be met to achieve mutual agreement is that the offer and acceptance must be genuine and freely given. There can be no duress or undue influence used to obtain agreement. Duress is forcing someone to do something against his will. Undue influence is taking unfair advantage of someone.

If a contract is obtained under either of these conditions, the injured party has the option to rescind (cancel) the contract or leave it in effect. Thus, it is voidable.

Legal Objective

The third requirement for a valid contract is that it must have a legal purpose. It cannot call for any action that violates the law. A contract whose objective is illegal is void, and cannot be enforced in court.

Legally Competent Parties

The fourth requirement for a valid contract is that the parties to the contract must be legally **competent**. There are three primary categories of people who are *not* legally competent:

1. Minors
2. Intoxicated persons
3. Insane persons

The first group of individuals who are not legally competent are minors. A minor is a person who has not reached the legal age requirement (age of majority). In Florida, the legal age (the age of majority) is 18. Most contracts with minors are voidable, so long as the minor elects to void the contract while still a minor or within a reasonable period after reaching the age of majority. (The definition of a *reasonable period* is determined by the courts.)

The second group of individuals who are not legally competent are intoxicated persons. A contract made by an intoxicated person is typically voidable.

The third group of individuals who are not legally competent are insane persons. An insane person is an individual of unsound mind who has been declared incompetent by the court and has been appointed a guardian. Such individuals cannot enter into contracts. Any contract signed by an insane person is void. If a person who has no guardian signs a contract and is *later* judged to be incompetent *at the time of the signing,* the contract is voidable.

FIGURE 11.3

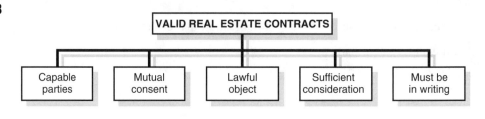

Coaching Tips: Parties who are not legally competent are not precluded from receiving personal property from a legally competent party. If a person not legally competent desires to sell personal property, that person would be required to do one of the following:

- Reach the age of majority (if a minor).

- Not be intoxicated at the time of entry to a contract for the purchase and sale of real or personal property.

- Have a court-appointed guardian perform the transaction on his behalf.

Most individuals who do *not* fall into one of the three categories just covered are considered competent to enter into contracts on their own behalf. In addition, two other categories of entities enter into valid contracts:

1. Attorneys-in-fact

2. Corporations

An **attorney-in-fact** is someone who has been granted power of attorney limited to a specific transaction named in a document. A contract entered into by an attorney-in-fact is valid when the power of attorney has been properly granted.

Corporations are considered to be artificial, or legal, persons and may enter into valid contracts. However, the contract must be executed and carried out in a manner that is consistent with the corporation's prescribed methods. The law is designed in such a manner that a corporation is treated as a legal person and/or entity in itself. Like an individual, a corporation has its own separate identity. Its identity stands separate and apart from that of its shareholders who bear no corporate responsibilities on a personal level. A corporation is issued a separate tax identification number, which is not unlike that of an individual Social Security number.

See Figure 11.3 for valid real estate contracts.

METHODS OF DISCHARGING CONTRACTS

Most contracts are discharged by performance of the contract requirements (i.e., they are executed). This is always the preferred way. However, some alternatives exist, such as the following:

- Assignment

- Novation

- Termination

Assignment

Assignment is the transfer of one's interest in a executory contract to another person. Executory contracts can be assigned unless prohibited in the contract. Executed contracts cannot be assigned because they have been fully performed already.

Example

Deeds are executed contracts and cannot be assigned.

Novation

Novation involves substituting a new contract for an old contract or substituting a new party for an old party under an existing contract. Novation is also a means of general release from previous contractual obligations. Examples of novation would include:

- Assumption of an existing mortgage whereby the lender officially releases the original borrower for the substitution of the new borrower/home buyer.
- An assignment of a master lease by the master tenant whereby the overlandlord/property owner officially releases the original master tenant for the substitution of the new assigned master tenant.

    The following items are facts about the assignment of contracts:

- The person who assigns her interest is the assignor.
- The person to whom the interest is assigned is the assignee.
- Once the assignment is made, the assignee becomes primarily liable for fulfillment of the contract.
- However, unless there is a novation agreement relieving the assignor of liability, the assignor remains ultimately liable (contingent liability) if the assignee fails to perform as required.

    The following is an example of contingent liability in a transaction:

- The landlord leases space (the overlease) to the tenant who in turn, subsequently, subleases the demised space or unit to the subtenant.
- Although the subtenant accepts responsibility to make all the rental payments to the sublandlord who in turn pays the landlord, the sublandlord still retains liability for total performance under the overlease to the landlord.
- A mortgage assumption by a new buyer without a novation/release agreement would also constitute a contingent liability to the seller/original borrower. In the event that the new buyer defaulted on the loan, the seller/original borrower would be secondarily responsible to the lender for repayment of the loan.

Coaching Tips: **A sublease is also known as a sandwich lease. The tenant is sandwiched between the subtenant and the landlord (previously discussed in Chapter 9).**

    As previously discussed, novation is the substitution of a new contract between two parties that terminates and replaces an old contract, or the substitution of new parties for an existing contract. However, the difference between assignment and novation is related to the withdrawing party's liability. With assignment, the *assignor* is still ultimately liable for performance. With novation, the withdrawing party is released from liability.

Example

When a buyer assumes an existing loan from a seller, novation occurs if the original borrower is released and a new party is substituted in the mortgage note contract.

Termination

Termination can occur in a variety of ways, such as the following:

- Mutual agreement of the parties
- Expiration of time

- Rescision of a voidable contract
- Operation of law

Mutual Agreement of the Parties

Simply put, the interested parties to a contract unanimously decide that the contract should be terminated, possibly due to a number of unforeseen events that arise in any transaction.

Expiration of Time

Many contracts have time limitations or restrictions. If a time limitation or restriction expires, the rights associated with the contract terms expire.

Example

Landlord Ian leases an apartment to Tenant Max for a period of 1 year. At the end of that lease term, all rights of possession to the apartment by Tenant Max terminate (if not renewed) and possession reverts back to Landlord Ian.

Example

Buyer Max is granted a 3-month option to purchase Seller Ian's home. Seller Ian agrees to sell to Buyer Max for $500,000. Buyer Max agrees to pay Seller Ian $5,000 for the 3-month option and Seller Ian agrees. The 3-month anniversary of the option comes and Buyer Max fails to buy the home. Buyer Max's $5,000 option fee to Seller Ian is forfeited and the option is terminated via the expiration of time.

Coaching Tips: **Remember that an option is used for the purposes of buying time.**

Rescision of a Voidable Contract

Rescision of a contract can be defined as voiding or canceling the contract, whereby, the parties to the contract are placed back in their original positions prior to the creation of the contract.

Operation of Law

Operation of law can be defined as the voiding of a contract resulting from:

- The impossibility of the parties performing under the contract due to:
  - Discovery or the existence of fraud
  - Expiration of the Statute of Limitations concerning the nature of the contract
- Other causes of operation of law include the following:
  - Destruction of the property
  - Bankruptcy of either party
  - Death of one of the parties

If one of the parties to a contract dies, the contract is terminated only if it requires an act that only the deceased person could perform. In the absence of a provision to the contrary, real estate sales contracts are *not* terminated by the death of one of the parties. The contract is binding on the deceased person's estate, regardless of whether it is the buyer or seller who dies.

The Uniform Vendor and Purchaser Risk Act covers cases where real property involved in a sales contract is destroyed. If the property is destroyed *before* either possession of the property or title to the property has passed to the buyer (while the contract is executory), the *seller* is at risk. This means that if the property is destroyed while the contract is executory, the buyer is not obligated to go through with the sale and is entitled to his money back.

THE STATUTE OF FRAUDS

The Statute of Frauds is a state law that states, among other things, that some real estate contracts must be in writing to be enforceable. According to the Statute of Frauds in Florida, the following types of valid real estate contracts must be written to be legally enforceable:

- Deeds
- Real estate sales contracts
- Options
- Leases for more than 1 year
- Listings for more than 1 year

According to the Statute of Frauds in Florida, the following types of valid real estate contracts are enforceable if they are oral:

- Leases for a period of 1 year or less
- Listings for a period of 1 year or less

Status of Oral Contracts

	VALID	ENFORCEABLE
Open Listings	YES	YES
Leases – 1 year or less	YES	YES
Sales Contracts	YES	NO
Leases – over 1 year	YES	NO
Exclusive Listings	NO	NO
Options	NO	NO
Debt Instruments (Mortgages)	NO	NO
Deeds	NO	NO

Status of Oral Contracts

	VALID	ENFORCEABLE
Open Listings	YES	YES
Leases – 1 year or less	YES	YES
Sales Contracts	YES	NO
Leases – over 1 year	YES	NO

Status of Oral Contracts

	VALID	ENFORCEABLE
Open Listings	YES	YES
Leases – 1 year or less	YES	YES
Sales Contracts	YES	NO
Leases – over 1 year	YES	NO

Status of Oral Contracts

	VALID	ENFORCEABLE
Open Listings	YES	YES
Leases – 1 year or less	YES	YES
Sales Contracts	YES	NO
Leases – over 1 year	YES	NO

OPTION CONTRACTS

As explained earlier, an option is a contract that gives the right to buy a property but does not require the receiver of the option to buy the optioned property. For this reason, an option contract falls under the category of a unilateral contract. As previously learned in this chapter, a unilateral contract is where only one party is required to perform.

Example

Mr. Green owns a parcel of undeveloped property. Mrs. White is considering the possibility of building a shopping center on that property, but is also looking at other sites. In order to give herself some time to make up her mind and to ensure that Mr. Green's property will not be bought by someone else in the meantime, Mrs. White might decide to purchase an option to buy Mr. Green's property. If she does, the option contract that she signs will allow her to purchase the property during the option period *if she so chooses*. Mr. Green, the owner of the property, cannot force Mrs. White to purchase the property, but he must sell to her if she chooses.

In this example, Mr. Green, the owner, is the optionor because he *gives* Mrs. White the option to buy his property. Mrs. White, the potential buyer, is the optionee because she *receives* the option (the right to buy the property).

In general, the optionor is the owner of the property, the one who gives an option to someone. The optionee is the person who receives an option to buy someone else's property.

An option contract gives an **exclusive right to buy**. This means that no one other than the person holding the option (the optionee) can buy the property during the option period. In effect, an option is a way of protecting your right to buy a property for a certain period of time while preventing anyone else from buying it. The period the option is in effect *must* be specified in the option contract. The option contract must include a specific ending date. The option contract must also specify the sales price of the property *when it is signed*. It is not acceptable to wait until the optionee decides to buy the property (exercise the option) to set a sales price. During the period the option is in effect, the optionee (the potential buyer) has the right to *exercise* the option. Exercising the option means the optionee chooses to buy the property as provided for in the option contract. Only the optionee can exercise the option because the optionee is the one who holds the right to buy. When the optionee exercises her option to buy, the option contract automatically becomes a sales contract for the sale of the property.

When an option is signed the optionee *must* pay a valuable consideration (money or its equivalent) to the optionor. In Florida, in order for an option to be valid and enforceable, there must be adequate (substantial) consideration exchanged. An option contract with only token or nominal consideration is considered unenforceable. In effect, the optionee is buying the right to purchase the property under the terms of the option. Usually, if the option is exercised and the property is purchased, the money paid by the optionee for the option right is applied to the purchase price, but this is subject to negotiation before the option is signed. If the option to buy is not exercised, the money paid to obtain the option is forfeited.

Miscellaneous Characteristics of Options

An option contract must contain all the essential elements of a valid contract. As a result, when the option is exercised it automatically becomes a binding sales contract. The listing broker on an optioned property is not entitled to a commission until the option is exercised. Options are assignable unless prohibited in the option contract.

Let's examine what interest exists in the property encumbered by an option contract:

- During the option period, the optionor retains title and all rights to the property.
- The optionee has no legal rights in the property under the option contract.
- Once the option is exercised, the buyer has equitable title.

Let's also examine the categorizing of option contracts:

- Until an option is exercised, it is an executory contract. Once exercised, it is an executed contract.
- Because only one party is obligated under an option contract, it is a unilateral contract.

An option differs from a right of first refusal in that a right of first refusal:

- Is a right to have the first opportunity to buy the property if and when it becomes for sale.
- Has *no* predetermined price for buying the property.
- Has *no* fixed time to purchase the property.

However, with an option contract:

- The optionee has an *exclusive* right to buy the property.
- There must be a predetermined price for the property.
- The option must be in effect for a fixed period of time.

When an optionee holds an option to buy a property, the optionor (the owner) may sell the property during the option period. However, the option remains in effect and must be honored by the new owner. The optionee can compel the new owner to sell the property under the terms agreed to by the previous owner.

BREACH OF CONTRACTS

A breach of contract occurs when one party fails to live up to his contractual obligations. When this occurs, the other party (either buyer or seller) is referred to as the innocent party. The innocent party under a breach of contract has certain rights that can be used to remedy the breach of contract. A breach of contract does not relieve either party of their obligations under the contract and does not terminate the contract. A breach of contract will generally involve litigation between the aggrieved parties. However, let's take a look at some remedies that are available to the parties.

Remedies for Breach

Whenever a breach of contract occurs, the aggrieved party has certain rights. In order to remedy a breach, the innocent party has the right to do the following:

- Partial performance—The innocent party may accept partial completion of the contract as satisfactory.
- Rescision—The innocent party may rescind (cancel) the contract unilaterally, or the parties may mutually agree to rescind. Rescision is the opposite of specific performance, whereby, the parties are placed back into their original position as if the contract never existed.
- Sue for specific performance—The innocent party may sue the other party in court to carry out the requirements of the contract as written.
- Sue for damages—The innocent party may go to court to pursue a judgment for monetary damages. The amount is determined by the courts and would be based upon the facts concerning the case
- Liquidated damages—The parties may determine in advance a sum to be paid to the innocent party in the event of a breach. Normally in residential and commercial sales transactions, the deposit tendered by a buyer serves as the liquidated damages resulting from a default by the buyer

---

Coaching Tips: In general, when a suit for specific performance is sought as a remedy for a breach of contract:

- A buyer can usually win a suit for specific performance under a valid contract.
- A seller may have more difficulty in winning a suit for specific performance because normally the seller can be adequately compensated by monetary damages.

Liquidated Damages

A sales contract may include a statement that if the buyer breaches the contract, the seller may demand forfeiture of the earnest money deposit as **liquidated damages**. However, this may prevent the seller from suing for additional monetary damages. The innocent party must take action to remedy the breach of contract within a specific time period set by the **Statute of Limitations**. This is an example of the doctrine of laches. Laches are rights that one has inherent in any situation; however, if those rights are not asserted or exercised in a timely manner, one will lose those rights. In essence, use them (assertion of rights) or lose them.

"Time is of the Essence"

As you work with contracts, you may encounter the phrase "time is of the essence." This phrase means that the contract must be performed on or before the date specified in the contract. A party who fails to meet the deadline is guilty of a breach of contract.

LISTING CONTRACTS

In Florida, there are four types of listing agreements that are commonly used. The four types include:

1. Exclusive right to sell listing—Of the four listing agreement types, for the broker, this listing agreement is the most desirable arrangement. In this type of agreement, the seller appoints one agent to transact business on their behalf with the intent of achieving a successful conclusion (the sale of the property). During the term of this type of agreement, regardless of which party succeeds in the sale of that property, the broker will be compensated. This would include a sale that is effectuated by others such as:

   1. Any other broker
   2. The seller
   3. A family member
   4. Any other person or entity

2. Exclusive agency listing—In this type of agreement and as in the case above, the seller still appoints one agent to transact business on their behalf with the intent of achieving a successful conclusion (the sale of the property). However, this listing agreement provides the seller with a reservation to sell the property on his/her own. Should that occur, the exclusive agency broker is not compensated. In the event any other cooperating party effectuates a sale, the exclusive agency broker is compensated under the agreement.

3. Open listing—In essence, open listings are properties that are for sale by owner (FSBO). The owner may attempt the sale of the property without the use of a real estate licensee or they may engage one or more agents to effect a sale. In either case, in this type of listing agreement, the property owner will only compensate the party who is the procuring cause within the transaction. This arrangement is the least desirable for the broker.

4. Net listing—A net listing is where a seller is seeking a stated amount as the final purchase price. The purchase price does not include the broker's compensation for a successful conclusion to that transaction. Therefore, the broker markets the property at an agreed upon listing price that is greater than the net amount the seller wishes to receive. The licensee is cautioned that any amount retained by the licensee as net compensation should reflect a customary amount commensurate with the services provided. Otherwise, the licensee's compensation may be viewed as "unjust enrichment."

Example

A seller enters into a net listing with a broker. The net amount that the seller is desirous of is $100,000. This amount does not include a provision for the broker to be paid, therefore, the seller and the broker agree to list the property at $130,000. The property sells for $125,000. Under these conditions the licensee is entitled to a brokerage fee of $25,000, however, the seller may find this amount to be excessive in relationship to transactions of similar type.

In most states, net listing agreements are unlawful. In Florida, net listings are legal. Due to fraud and potential deception that may arise out of these relationships, regulators would discourage a licensee from accepting and entering into this type of relationship.

CONTRACT OF SALE

A contract of sale is a written agreement wherein a seller agrees to sell and a buyer agrees to buy real estate on the terms and conditions set by the contract. A contract of sale is commonly called a sales contract. It is the contract that is signed when a buyer offers to buy a house from a seller. When both seller and buyer sign a sales contract, a binding agreement on the sale has been reached, but the actual transfer of the property does not occur at that point. The actual transfer of ownership of the property occurs at a later date after a process called a closing or settlement. The reasons for having a sales contract followed by a closing at a later date include:

- The buyer needs time before a transaction is completed to determine whether the seller has good title and the legal right to convey title.
- The buyer needs time to arrange financing.
- The contract determines the duties and obligations of the parties to the sale at closing.

    Each real estate sales contract must contain certain information, such as:

- Names of the parties to the contract
- Description of the property being sold
- Date, time, and location of closing
- Purchase price and financing terms
- Amount of earnest money or binder deposit being held and by whom
- Type of deed
- Any personal property that will be included in the sale
- Broker(s) associated with the transaction (if applicable)
- All required disclosures

Disclosures

State and federal laws require that prior to or at the time of signing a real estate sales contract, the buyer must be provided with following disclosures:

- Radon gas disclosure
- Lead-based paint disclosure

- Energy-efficiency disclosure
- Condominium or cooperative disclosure
- Homeowner association disclosure
- Property tax disclosure
- *Johnson v. Davis Property Defect*

Radon Gas Disclosure

Radon is a colorless, odorless toxic gas that is the by-product of the natural decay of uranium. Radon gas enters a building from the ground through openings around plumbing or through cracks in the foundation.

Radon gas is hazardous because it can cause damage to the lungs; it is also a known carcinogen. Florida state law requires that *all contracts* for purchase and sale of real property contain a disclosure statement explaining what radon is and the disclosure must be provided to a buyer prior to or at the time of signing a sales contract.

Lead-Based Paint Disclosure

Lead-based paints were used in most homes built before 1978. Exposure to lead can cause serious health problems, especially in children and pregnant women. Federal law requires the disclosure of known information on lead-based paint before the sale of most housing built before 1978. Sellers must also provide buyers with a federally approved pamphlet titled *Protect Your Family from Lead in Your Home.* Sellers must also allow the buyer a 10-day period to test for lead-based paint. Sellers, however, are not required to pay for this testing.

Energy-Efficiency Disclosure

According to the Florida Building Energy-Efficiency Rating Act, a potential buyer must be provided with a brochure explaining that the buyer has the option to obtain an energy-efficiency rating on the building and that the energy-efficiency rating may qualify the buyer for an energy-efficient mortgage. This brochure must be provided to the buyer prior to or at the time of signing a sales contract.

Condominium or Cooperative Disclosure

If the property being sold is a condominium or cooperative, any disclosures required under the Florida Condominium Act or the Florida Cooperative Act must be provided.

Homeowner Association Disclosure

The purpose of a homeowner association is often to maintain and improve local properties and property values. Such associations may enforce restrictive covenants, which are agreements that may limit the use and physical features of property. If a property is subject to a mandatory homeowner association, the buyer must be provided with a disclosure statement concerning the association, any restrictive covenants, and any assessments (fees). Licensees have a responsibility to provide or make available to a purchaser all information concerning this matter.

Property Tax Disclosure

Florida law requires that a seller provide a prospective buyer with a disclosure of the tax levied on the subject property. The disclosure must be made to the buyer prior to the execution of a contract for purchase and sale. The purpose of the disclosure is to inform the buyer of the current tax levied on the property in the year of sale, and to note that this tax is not a representation of the future tax following the year of sale.

Johnson v. Davis/Property Defect

Johnson v. Davis was a precedent-setting case in Florida regarding residential transactions. This case held sellers of residential property accountable and responsible for disclosure of material defects (that are known to the seller) affecting the value of the property. Prior to *Johnson v. Davis,* the theory of caveat emptor (let the buyer beware) was a standard practice in residential transactions. Now, sellers must disclose all material defects to the property. In addition, *Rayner v. Wise Realty Co. of Tallahassee* required that sellers disclose to licensees the condition of the property.

Earnest Money

Earnest money is paid by the buyer at the time the sales contract is signed. Although there are no state or federal laws that require a deposit under the purchase and sale contract, it is a good business practice. The following are reasons why deposits are part of customary practice within these transactions:

* An earnest money deposit shows good faith on the part of the buyer and increases the likelihood that the buyer will perform her obligations under the contract.
* In the event of a buyer's default under the terms of the contract, earnest money usually acts as the liquidated damages to the seller.

Coaching Tips: Earnest money is *not* the consideration in the contract. (The consideration is the promise to pay the purchase price for the property.)

If earnest money is held by a broker, the broker is required to place the money into his escrow (trust) account immediately. As we learned in Chapter 5, *immediately* is defined as:

* For the broker:
  * No later than the close of banking business on the third business day following receipt of the earnest money deposit (weekends and holidays not included).
* For the sales associate and broker associate:
  * Any deposit entrusted to a sales associate or broker associate must be delivered to her broker no later than the end of business of the next day from receipt of the money.

Time Limits

When a contract is offered, it usually includes a specific time period in which a response must be made by the offeree. If the offer is not accepted in that time, the offer terminates. If no stated period for a response is included, the offer terminates after a reasonable time. (The courts ultimately determine what is a *reasonable time.*)

Acceptance

The contract offer must be accepted *exactly* as it is written. Any change in the offer, no matter how minor, automatically *terminates* the original offer and constitutes a counteroffer.

Back-up Contract

A back-up contract is a contract of sale accepted by the seller with the stated understanding that the seller has already accepted a prior offer.

Binder

A binder is a short purchase contract used in some states to secure a real estate transaction until a more formal contract can be prepared by an attorney. Binders may or may not be enforceable.

Installment Sales Contract

An installment sales contract may also be referred to as a:

- Land contract
- Contract for deed
- Contract for title

An installment contract is a contract of sale under which:

- The seller retains title and holds the deed.
- The purchaser takes possession while installment payments are being made.

An installment contract is often used when the seller provides financing for the sale but is not sure of the buyer's ability to pay. The seller retains title, thus eliminating the need for foreclosure in the case of default. If the buyer defaults, he forfeits all payments and can be evicted like a rental tenant. In some states, an installment contract is used most commonly for resort-type property. *Legally,* the seller is the property owner:

- The seller holds legal title.
- The buyer holds equitable title until the property is paid for.

Practically, the buyer is the owner of the property. The buyer:

- Pays property taxes.
- Deducts interest payments for tax purposes.
- Claims any depreciation if the property is income-producing.

Types of Contracts

Contract of Sale	Deed
Back-up Contract	Deed of Trust
Binder	Lease
Installment Contract	Listing Contract
	Mortgage

Coaching Tips: **To remember how installment sales contracts work, view this kind of transaction as identical to a *layaway plan* for the purchase of real property.**

In a layaway plan of personal property:

1. **Installment payments are made for the full cost of the item in question.**
2. **The retailer retains possession of the item as collateral for the full payment of the purchase price.**
3. **When all installment payments have been made, the retailer will transfer the ownership of the item by issuing a bill of sale. Of course, in a real estate transaction the deed is received as the transfer of ownership instrument.**

SUMMARY

Contracts are legal documents. Preparing a legal document is considered practicing law, and only attorneys are permitted to draft these documents. Because most real estate licensees are not attorneys, most licensees cannot prepare legal documents such as deeds and mortgages. Doing so would be considered unauthorized practice of law and subject the licensee to both civil liability in addition to disciplinary action by the Florida Real Estate Commission. This includes the addition of riders to a contract. However, there are certain types of contracts that licensees are permitted to prepare, including sales contracts and listing contracts. Licensees are not permitted to draft an option contract. However, licensees are allowed to fill in the blanks in a preprinted, "form" option contract that has been prepared by an attorney.

REVIEW QUESTIONS

1. Which of the following best describes the Statute of Frauds?
   a. It sets standards for fraudulent behavior.
   b. It states contracts must have termination dates.
   c. It requires competent parties for contracts.
   d. All transfers of real estate in part or in whole must be in writing to be enforceable.

2. Which of these contracts is an exception to the Statute of Frauds?
   a. A lease agreement for 6 months
   b. A 13-month listing agreement
   c. A statutory deed
   d. Any unilateral contract

3. Broker Andrew agreed to sell his neighbor's house within the next 4 months at a 3 percent commission and Andrew and the neighbor shook hands on the deal. Andrew sold the house 3 months later for $320,000, but the neighbor refused to pay the fee. According to the Statute of Frauds, Andrew:
   a. Should have had his neighbor sign a listing agreement.
   b. Can sue, but will have no expectation of prevailing in court.
   c. Can expect Florida courts to force his neighbor to pay.
   d. Can sue his neighbor for fraud.

4. Which of these contracts is NOT an exception to the Statute of Frauds?
   a. A 12-month lease agreement
   b. An oral sale contract where the buyer has moved into the home
   c. A 6-month lease agreement
   d. A 13-month listing agreement

5. The Statute of Limitations for a parol contract is:
   a. 1 year.
   b. 3 years.
   c. 4 years.
   d. 5 years.

6. The broker for ABC Realty posted a notice on the office bulletin board that stated the first agent to sell three houses in the next calendar quarter will receive a $3,000 bonus. This is an example of a(n):
   a. Bilateral contract.
   b. Unilateral contract.
   c. Parol contract.
   d. Illegal compensation.

7. Harmon had a buyer in his car and knocked on the door of a for-sale-by-owner. Harmon identified himself as a real estate licensee and asked if the seller would show them the house. Harmon brought an offer from the buyer that the seller accepted, but the seller refused to pay Harmon a commission. If Harmon sues, he:
   a. Cannot expect to collect any money.
   b. Could possible lose his license.
   c. Should find another line of work.
   d. Can expect to be paid a reasonable sum.

8. The sales contract is expected to close on the 30th of the month. On the 29th, the contract is considered to be a(n):
   a. Executory contract.
   b. Voidable contract.
   c. Unilateral contract.
   d. Exclusive right of sale contract.

9. Which of the following is NOT a remedy for a breach of contract?
   a. A suit for specific performance
   b. Collection of liquidated damages
   c. A suit to rescind on the breach
   d. Operation of law

10. An adult signed a written contract with a minor. This means:
    a. The contract is illegal.
    b. The adult can walk away.
    c. The contract is void.
    d. The contract is voidable.

11. Which of these is NOT an essential element of a valid and enforceable contract?
    a. Competent parties
    b. Signed and witnessed
    c. Consideration
    d. Legality of object

12. A seller says she wants your real estate company to sell her home. However, she is also talking to her cousin about buying the home. If she sells to her cousin, she doesn't want to pay the commission. This describes a(n):
    a. Exclusive agency listing.
    b. Open listing.
    c. Net listing.
    d. Exclusive right of sale listing.

13. The seller has signed a listing stating the seller will accept any offer that provides the seller with a stated minimum amount. This listing is a(n):
    a. Exclusive agency listing.
    b. Open listing.
    c. Net listing.
    d. Exclusive right of sale listing.

14. One real estate company is given a listing. No matter who sells the property, the listing broker will be paid. This is a(n):
    a. Exclusive agency listing.
    b. Open listing.
    c. Net listing.
    d. Exclusive right of sale listing.

15. Millie and Gary are thinking of leasing a home that was built in 1972. Before they can sign the lease agreement:
    a. They must be provided with and sign the lead-based paint disclosure.
    b. They must have the home inspected for lead-based paint.
    c. The seller must pay for a lead-based paint inspection.
    d. All lead-based paint must be contained or removed.

16. A meeting of the minds (an essential element of a contract) comes about:
    a. When the offer is made in writing.
    b. When the contract is signed by the offeror.
    c. When the offeree signs the contract.
    d. When the acceptance is communicated.

17. Bernie signed a contract to purchase a house and was scheduled to close the sale on the 30th of the month. Bernie's friend, Celia, begged Bernie to let her buy the house instead, so Bernie assigned the contract to Celia. 1 week before closing, Celia changed her mind about buying. In this circumstance:
    a. Celia will have to buy the house.
    b. The contract is void.
    c. Bernie will have to buy the house.
    d. The seller doesn't have to sell.

18. Which of these actions will terminate a contract?
    a. The seller dies.
    b. The contract is assigned without a novation.
    c. There is no binder deposit.
    d. The contract is not in writing.

19. In Florida, only an attorney can prepare contracts. However, which of these contracts can be legally prepared with a real estate license?
    a. Deeds
    b. Notes
    c. Leases
    d. Options

20. Which of the following laws states that contracts without agreed-upon termination dates are not binding in perpetuity?
    a. The Statute of Frauds
    b. The Statute of Limitations
    c. The Operation of Law
    d. The Legal Contract Standards Law

21. Which statement is true regarding the radon gas disclosure?
    a. The disclosure must be a separate document.
    b. If radon gas is found, the seller must fix it.
    c. All property must be inspected for radon gas.
    d. The buyer can choose to ignore the warning.

Chapter 12

KEY TERMS

acceleration clause	hypothecation	prepayment clause
amortized loan	index plus a margin	prepayment penalty
assumption	interest	promissory note
balloon payment	lien theory	reconveyance clause
certificate of estoppel	lines of credit	statutory redemption
deed in lieu of	lis pendens	subject to the mortgage
foreclosure	mortgage	subordination clause
deferred interest	mortgagee	takeout loan
deficiency judgment	mortgagor	term loan or straight
due on sale clause	negative amortization	loans
equity	PITI	title theory
home equity loans	power-of-sale clause	wraparound mortgage

LEARNING OBJECTIVES

After completing this lesson, you will be able to:

- Know what a mortgage is and how it is used.
- Know what hypothecation of mortgages is and why it is used.
- Know the two theories of hypothecation.
- Know what a promissory note is and how it is used.
- Know the purpose and function of clauses in the promissory note.
- Know the essential and optional elements of a mortgage.
- Know which loans usually contain alienation clauses.
- Know how the priority of loans is determined.
- Understand the process of foreclosure.
- Know about an additional security instrument—a deed of trust.
- Know several types of loans used in financing real property.
- Know the characteristics of these loans.
- Know the situations in which many of these loans are used.

Real Estate Finance

MORTGAGES AND HYPOTHECATION

A mortgage provides security for a note through a process called hypothecation. **Hypothecation** means that the real property is put up as security for a loan *without* surrendering possession of the property. In essence, the **mortgage** is the instrument that places the property (by the borrower) as *collateral* for securing the repayment of the loan. Therefore, it would be safe to remember that a mortgage is collateral.

Whenever a property is hypothecated as security for a loan, the following occurs:

• The owner retains possession of the property.

• The lender uses the property as security by holding a mortgage on the property.

It is interesting to note that the Spanish word *hypoteca* is the word describing a mortgage.

There are two different legal theories concerning the manner in which real property is hypothecated. These theories determine the legal practice used in different states for dealing with real property hypothecation. The two theories are:

1. Title theory
2. Lien theory

TITLE THEORY

The mortgage is commonly used to secure notes on real property in more than half of the United States, including Florida. In most of the remaining states, the instrument that is used to secure real property notes is called the deed of trust or trust deed. In a **title theory** state, there are three parties to a loan secured by real property:

1. Trustor (property owner/borrower)
2. Trustee (neutral third party appointed by both the borrower and the lender to hold the naked title)
3. Beneficiary (lender)

Under the title theory approach, there is no such instrument known as a mortgage. The instrument that is used in place of a mortgage (which is only used in a lien theory state) is called a trust deed or deed of trust. In this type of loan, the trustor (borrower) actually conveys/transfers legal title to the property to the beneficiary (lender).

The beneficiary and trustor give the title to the trustee, whose sole responsibility within the transaction is to hold the naked title in trust for one party or the other until one of the following events occurs:

- Upon full satisfaction of the repaid loan, title is reconveyed to the trustor.
- In the event of a default under the terms of the note and the lapse of any statutory redemption period, title is transferred to the beneficiary.

A trust deed provides security for a note. Trust deeds are the instruments used in place of a mortgage. This type of instrument is applicable in states that subscribe to the title theory within the financing of real property.

In a trust deed, there are two clauses that create the primary difference between the trust deed and a mortgage:

1. The reconveyance clause
2. The power-of-sale clause

The **reconveyance clause** requires the trustee to reconvey the title to the trustor (the borrower) when the loan has been paid in full. This reconveyance is done with either one of the following:

- A release deed (a type of quitclaim deed)
- A marginal release

The marginal release is a notation of satisfaction written in the margin of the trust deed in the public records. See Figure 12.1.

The **power-of-sale clause** provides for nonjudicial foreclosure. It allows the property to be sold at public auction in the event of default by the borrower without going to court. The sale is called a trustee's sale. The power-of-sale clause (and its resulting nonjudicial foreclosure) is the primary difference between lien theory and title theory.

Coaching Tips: The title given to and held by the trustee is referred to as naked title. The naked title is held by the trustee as security for the beneficiary until the debt is paid. During the borrowing period and as long as the trustor/borrower is not in default under the terms and conditions of the trust deed, the beneficiary is not permitted to hold or possess the naked title. That is the primary reason for the neutral third party in this transaction, namely the trustee. This is termed *naked title* because the trustor/borrower has literally signed the deed to the property in the favor of the beneficiary. When the debt is paid in full, the trust deed becomes null and void and the trustee is then required, through the use of a reconveyance deed, to transfer the property back to the trustor unencumbered. This is the equivalent of a satisfaction of repayment of the debt. During the borrowing period, the borrower holds equitable title in the property while the trust deed is in effect.

FIGURE 12.1

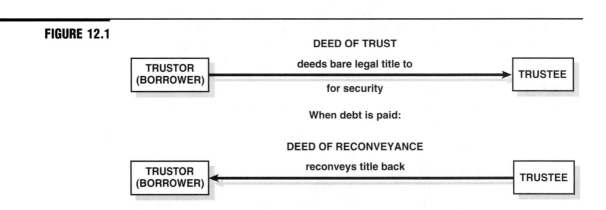

DEED OF TRUST

TRUSTOR (BORROWER) — deeds bare legal title to / for security → TRUSTEE

When debt is paid:

DEED OF RECONVEYANCE

TRUSTOR (BORROWER) ← reconveys title back — TRUSTEE

Coaching Tips: In title theory states:

- There is no mortgage—a trust deed is used.
- The borrower is called the trustor.
- The lender is called the beneficiary.
- The neutral third party is called the trustee.
- The trustee is appointed by the lender and borrower.
- The trustee holds the naked title to the property while the note is in effect.
- The trustee reconveys the property back to the trustor upon satisfaction of the terms associated with the note and trust deed.

LIEN THEORY

In a **lien theory** state, a transaction consists of:

- Two parties
- Two instruments used within the transaction

Under the lien theory approach to mortgage hypothecation, it is important to understand the following:

- The legal title remains in the possession of the borrower.
- The mortgage held by the lender creates a lien on the title in favor of the lender.

Coaching Tips: As is the case with the majority of the states in the union, *Florida is a lien theory state.*

Lien Theory and the Financing Instruments

When real property is sold utilizing any type of financing, two primary documents are always involved in the financing process:

1. The promissory note
2. The mortgage

Coaching Tips: A note that is secured by a mortgage is known as a secured note, while a note that is not secured by a mortgage is known as an unsecured note.

Promissory Note

A **promissory note** is the instrument whereby the borrower promises to repay money borrowed from the lender. The note acts as the following:

- Prima facie (on face value) evidence of the borrowing. This simply means that the note by itself is evidence of the borrower's debt to the lender.
- It states the terms under which the borrower agrees to repay the loan, such as:
  - The annual interest rate
  - The term of the loan
  - The type of loan (e.g., interest only, fully amortized, partially amortized)
- It is also deemed a negotiable instrument.

A negotiable instrument means that the ownership of the instrument can be transferred to another person, either by sale or gift. A mortgage provides security for repayment on a note. It acts as the collateral. As previously stated, it secures the note with the collateralized property.

Coaching Tips: **Think of it this way—unless a lender is comfortable with the collateralization of the loan, the lender will not be willing to arrange financing on the purchase of the real property.**

A promissory note, or note, may contain whatever specific terms are agreed to by the borrower and lender. The note will always contain two primary clauses:

1. A prepayment clause
2. An acceleration clause

Prepayment Clause

The **prepayment clause** contained within the mortgage will provide the borrower with the ability to prepay the outstanding principle balance (in part or in whole), either with or without a penalty. However, there are four possible scenarios that can arise concerning the prepayment clause within a mortgage:

1. The note may not be prepaid at all.
2. The note may not be prepaid for a fixed period (lock-in clause); however, subsequent to the lock-in period, it may be prepaid.
3. The note may be prepaid with *no* penalty at any time.
4. The note may be prepaid, but a penalty must be paid for doing so.

In this case, the penalty is called a **prepayment penalty**. Whereas, a prepayment *clause* is required in a mortgage, the penalty becomes optional on the part of the lender. Some commercial loans are issued subject to the lender receiving *yield maintenance*. This means that the borrower may prepay the outstanding balance in part or in whole at any time; however, the penalty for prepaying would equal the total amount of interest that the lender would have received had that loan lived to its maturity.

Acceleration Clause

The **acceleration clause** allows the lender to demand full and immediate payment (accelerate the payment) if the borrower fails to meet all terms of the note. The acceleration clause also allows the lender to couple other clauses contained within the mortgage document. For example, by invoking the alienation clause (or due on sale clause, described later), when a property secured by a nonassumable mortgage is sold, the acceleration clause will also come into play. The lender accelerates the remaining principal balance of the loan upon the closing of title. When the acceleration clause is invoked, the lender is said to *call in* the note.

Although the promissory note is evidence of the existence of the loan, it is essentially only a promise to repay a loan. It does not provide any collateral as security that the loan will be repaid. Because of this, the lender will require that a mortgage be executed to provide this security.

Mortgage

A mortgage is an instrument that provides collateral as the security for a loan. It is used in conjunction with a promissory note. As mentioned previously:

- A note without a mortgage means the note is unsecured.
- A mortgage without a note is meaningless because a mortgage is simply security for a note.

Essential Elements

There are a number of elements that may appear in a mortgage instrument, but the following will always appear:

- The parties to the mortgage
- A granting clause
- A defeasance clause

Parties to the Mortgage

There are two parties to the mortgage:

1. The borrower—The borrower is called the **mortgagor** because the borrower gives/conveys the mortgage (collateral or security) to the lender.
2. The lender—The lender is called the **mortgagee** because the lender is the one to whom the mortgage (collateral or security) is given/conveyed.

Coaching Tips: **A good way to remember which party is which in a mortgage is to remember the OR and EE rule. Words that end in OR are the owners or givers of whatever is owned or being given. Words that end in EE are the receivers of whatever is owned or being given.**

Granting Clause

The granting clause in a mortgage:

- Is similar to the granting clause contained within a deed.
- Transfers legal title from the borrower, in title theory states.
- Creates a title lien, in lien theory states.

Defeasance Clause

The defeasance clause in a mortgage:

- Is the right of the mortgagor (borrower) to defeat the lien held by the mortgagee by fulfilling all the terms and conditions of the loan.
- Makes the mortgage null and void when paid in full.

Optional Elements Contained within a Mortgage

A mortgage may also contain the following:

- One or more covenants, which are promises made by the mortgagor to the mortgagee.
- An alienation clause (also known as a due on sale clause)

Covenants

There are several covenants that may be included in a mortgage, such as:

- Covenant to pay taxes—The borrower promises to keep all taxes paid as the taxes come due. In most if not all loans secured by a mortgage, the lender will usually impound an amount necessary to cover the property tax payment. This impounded amount is over and above the monthly payment for principle and interest. The portion of the additional payment is placed into an interest-bearing escrow account benefiting the borrower. The lender pays the property tax for the borrower from that account. This event does not occur when a borrower can demonstrate 100 percent prepayment of the taxes. The lender is concerned that the property tax is always current. As previously learned, property tax liens come before all others. This could defeat the lien perfected by the lender.

- Covenant of insurance—The borrower promises to keep the property adequately insured during the life of the mortgage. As in property taxes, the lender will usually impound an amount necessary to cover the property insurance payment. This impounded amount is over and above the monthly payment for principle and interest and property taxes. As in the case of the taxes, the portion of the additional payment is placed into an interest-bearing escrow account benefiting the borrower. The lender pays the property insurance premium for the borrower from this account. This event does not occur when a borrower can demonstrate 100 percent prepayment of the annual property insurance premium. The lender is concerned that the property insurance is always current. This will protect the lender's lien in the event of fire/casualty issues to the property.

- Covenant against removal—The borrower promises not to remove any of the improvements to the property, which would reduce its value as collateral. Any removal or addition to the property will generally require the lender's prior written consent.

- Covenant of good repair—The borrower promises to maintain all improvements in good repair and not to permit them to deteriorate. This is also a concern for the lender. A lender is more concerned with the retention of the property's value than anything else. In the event of a borrower default on the terms of the mortgage, the property's value will ultimately be the lender's only form of outstanding balance recovery.

- Covenant of reentry—The borrower promises to allow the lender to enter the premises at reasonable hours to ascertain that all other covenants are being adhered to. The lender rarely exercises this right.

Should the mortgagor (borrower) fail to adhere to these covenants, the mortgagee (the lender) may invoke the acceleration clause and demand full and immediate payment.

Alienation Clause (Due on Sale Clause)

The word *alienate* means "to transfer," such as transferring property from one to another. The alienation clause permits the mortgagee to call in the note if the mortgagor transfers the property either through sale or gift. This clause is commonly referred to as the **due on sale clause**. It is used to prohibit the **assumption** of the mortgage loan by a buyer or the use of a **wraparound mortgage**.

As a memory device, think of the alienation clause as *alienating* the rest of the world from the benefits of the loan, thereby, making the loan unassumable by any other person outside of the original borrower.

Acquiring Property with Existing Mortgages

Before the 1960s, few mortgages included an alienation (due on sale) clause. Because of the rapid rise of interest rates since that time, alienation clauses have become common. Today, virtually all conventional (nongovernment) loans include an alienation clause that enables the lender to require the loan be paid in full upon the alienation (transfer) of the ownership. Alternatively, the lender may choose to increase the interest rate on the assumed loan to the current market rate. Before 1986, Federal Housing Administration (FHA) loans were freely assumable and did not require the new borrower to qualify for the loan. Before 1988, Department of Veterans Affairs (VA) loans were freely assumable and did not require the new borrower to qualify. In 1986 for FHA loans and 1988 for VA loans, changes were made that placed some restrictions on the assumption of these loans. Now both FHA and VA loans may require the buyer to qualify to assume the loan.

Changing Loan Balance

Often, the most troublesome part of dealing with a loan assumption is the fact that the loan balance on the assumed loan changes between the time a sales contract is signed and the closing of the sale. This problem occurs when the purchaser agrees to buy the property at a fixed price by assuming a loan. The difference in the selling price and the remaining balance is the amount of cash that the buyer must pay the seller. The problem arises when the buyer doesn't realize that the amount of cash that she will have to pay may increase if the loan does not close right away. Let's look at why this happens.

Example

The buyer agrees to buy a property for $100,000 by assuming the seller's loan. At the time the contract is signed, the situation looks like this:

Sales price	$100,000
Remaining balance	−80,000
Cash required	$ 20,000

By the time the sale is closed, the situation may look like this:

Sales price	$100,000
Remaining balance	−79,000
Cash required	$ 21,000

The difference in the cash required at closing, which the buyer did not expect, results because the payments made on the loan between the signing of the sales contract and the closing date reduced the remaining principal. (The amount of reduction used in this example is larger than normal in order to illustrate the point.)

Because of this situation, there are two ways a loan assumption can be handled:

1. A loan assumption with price to control
2. A loan assumption with cash to control

The situation described above is an example of a loan assumption with price to control. In other words, *price to control* means that the selling price will be set, and the selling price (along with the changing loan balance) will *control* the amount of cash to be paid by the buyer. In a loan assumption with cash to control, the buyer and seller do not agree on a fixed sales price. Instead, they agree that the buyer will pay the seller a fixed amount of cash and assume the remaining loan balance as of the date of closing.

The situation as of the date of the contract and closing would look like this:

Date of Contract		Date of Closing	
Remaining balance	$80,000	Remaining balance	$79,000
Cash to be paid	$20,000	Cash to be paid	$20,000
Sales price	$100,000	Sales price	$99,000

The contract calls for a fixed amount of cash to be paid, which remains at $20,000. The loan balance decreases by the time the closing occurs. The result is that the actual selling price at closing is less than the amount it would have been if the sale had closed the day the contract was signed. In this situation, the amount of cash paid is set at a specific amount that does not change. The remaining loan balance and the actual sales price *do* change between the time of the signing of the sales contract and the closing date. As a result, the amount of cash paid controls the selling price, and this situation is referred to as *cash to control.*

Subject to the Mortgage

Subject to the mortgage is the direct opposite of assumption. In a subject to the mortgage transaction, the buyer is not assuming the loan, the buyer is merely making the payments associated with that loan. In order for this arrangement to occur, the existing loan must not contain a due on sale clause. In this arrangement, the seller (as the original borrower):

• Will give up possession of the property to the buyer.

• Transfers the deed for the property to the buyer.

• Remains contingently liable for performance on the loan.

The buyer merely makes the payment for the loan. In the event of a default by the buyer, the seller is responsible to the bank. The buyer has no relationship whatsoever with the bank.

On closing of the deal and on the closing statement, *documentary stamps on the note as well as the intangible taxes are not computed* (closing statements will be discussed in Chapter 14).

This arrangement should not be confused with a contingency on receiving financing on a purchase and sale contract.

Other Mortgage Documents

The **certificate of estoppel** is a document that is completed by a *borrower* to acknowledge the full amount of the debt that the borrower owes. It is usually used when a lender is about to sell the mortgage note and the purchaser wants to verify the amount and terms of the note as well as the borrower's acknowledgment of the debt. Estoppel certificates are also used by owners of income-producing property. Most, if not all, leases require that the tenant periodically execute estoppel certificates in the favor of the landlord. These certificates are used in two primary instances:

1. When the owner is selling the property
2. When the owner is placing debt on the property

In the first instance above, the buyer would normally require the seller to certify the rent roll or the income proceeds received from the rentals. Investors purchase income, not the brick and mortar. The improvement is merely the vehicle that houses the income. Therefore, the only instrument that allows the seller to oblige the buyer is the estoppel certificate. This certificate is ultimately executed by each tenant.

In second instance above, the lender requires the certificate for the same reason as in the first instance, except that the lender is not purchasing the property. The lender is originating a loan predicated upon the income stream to that property.

Coaching Tips: In a lease, an estoppel certificate is defined as the document that provides a certification by a tenant to their landlord that:

• The lease is in full force and effect.

• The amount of rent currently being paid is in fact the rent being paid.

• The amount and form of security deposit currently being held by the landlord is acknowledged as correct.

• The tenant has no offsets, credit, or defenses to the payment of rent.

PRIORITY OF LOANS

Loans usually take priority based on the date on which they are recorded in the public records. For example:

- What is commonly referred to as a *first mortgage* is the one that was recorded first for a particular property. Another name for a first mortgage is a *senior mortgage.*
- What is commonly referred to as a *second mortgage* is the one that was recorded second for a particular property. Another name for any mortgage recorded after a senior mortgage is a *junior mortgage.*

The exception to this rule would be a clause that waives the right to priority. This clause is called a **subordination clause**. For example, this is the clause within a lease that states that the rights of the leasehold interest are secondary to that of a previous or subsequent lien or interest in the real property. A subordination clause is a major requirement by all lenders on income-producing property. Institutional lenders do not take second or subsequent lien positions when originating loans.

FORECLOSURE

Foreclosure is a legal procedure that is implemented when a borrower defaults on a loan secured by real property. The property is sold in order to satisfy the debt. There are two types of foreclosures:

1. Judicial foreclosure
2. Nonjudicial foreclosure

Judicial Foreclosure

Judicial foreclosure is the most common form of foreclosure. It requires that the lender go to court to foreclose. The foreclosure proceeding serves two purposes:

1. The lender obtains possession of the property.
2. The equity of the owner/borrower is liquidated.

In order to conduct a foreclosure sale, liquidation of the owner/borrower's equity of the property becomes as important as obtaining possession. The foreclosure proceeding provides the vehicle for the lender to subsequently conduct a foreclosure sale. The proceeds from the foreclosure sale will go toward satisfying (in part or in whole) the unpaid note amount. The foreclosure process includes the following nine steps:

1. The mortgagee/lender invokes the acceleration clause thereby making the entire balance due.
2. A title search on the property is conducted.
3. A notice of **lis pendens** is filed that informs the public that there is an action pending.
4. A lawsuit is filed.
5. If the court rules in favor of the lender, a public auction is held to sell the property. A public notice advertises the sale of the property by public auction.
6. Once the sale is completed, the court clerk is then required to file the certificate of sale with the court. Assuming all has proceeded in accordance with the laws governing the foreclosure sale and the highest possible price has been obtained, the court will approve the sale.
7. The lender is paid from the proceeds of the sale.
8. The buyer receives the title.
9. Any monies that are left over from the foreclosure sale after satisfying all outstanding liens against the property are then given to the mortgagor/borrower.

In most states, the sale of foreclosed property is usually conducted by the county sheriff, and is often called a sheriff's sale. At the sheriff's sale, the lender will usually bid the principal amount remaining on the loan because of the following reasons:

- A lower bid by anyone else would not satisfy the outstanding balance of the loan.
- The lender would be paying itself for the loan.

All bidders other than the lender must pay cash.

Deficiency Judgment

Loans secured by mortgages are originated in one of two forms:

1. Recourse loans
2. Nonrecourse loans

When a recourse loan is originated, the borrower is personally guaranteeing full performance in the repayment of the note. This type of loan contains a clause within the mortgage called the deficiency clause. which allows the lender to recover from the defaulting borrower the difference between the proceeds from the foreclosure sale versus the outstanding note balance.

If a foreclosure sale recovers less than the outstanding balance amount, the lender would seek a **deficiency judgment** from the courts to enforce a deficiency clause. If a deficiency judgment is obtained, the lender may seek recovery of the differential from the original borrower. The amount of the deficiency judgment is limited to the amount of the outstanding debt that is not recovered.

Nonrecourse loans contain a clause commonly referred to as an exculpation clause. This clause removes any personal guarantee and performance on the part of the borrower. Therefore, the lender may only look to the property for recovery of the unpaid principle balance and not to the borrower for any proceeds resulting from the borrower's default on the loan.

Coaching Tips: A deficiency judgment clause would only appear in a recourse loan.
A nonrecourse loan would contain an exculpatory clause, which means that the lender may only look to proceeds of the property (if any) as repayment for any unpaid debt resulting from foreclosure on the borrower.

Excess from Sale

If the property sells for *more* than the debt, the excess amount goes to the satisfaction of any other secured and recorded liens. If there are no other outstanding recorded unpaid liens on the property, the remaining money is given to the mortgagor (the owner who defaulted).

Statutory Redemption

Some states give a borrower a period of time after foreclosure to repay the debt and take back ownership of the property. This is called **statutory redemption**. As in most lien theory states, Florida law provides for redemption rights *only* up to the time of the foreclosure sale.

Deed in Lieu of Foreclosure

In some cases, the borrower may avoid foreclosure by signing the property over to the lender. This is done using a document called a **deed in lieu of foreclosure**. (A deed in lieu of foreclosure is also commonly referred to as a *friendly foreclosure.*) The instrument conveys all rights, title, and interest held by the borrower to the lender. This action must be approved by the lender in advance before the borrower may use this approach.

TYPES OF LOANS

The following are basic terms that you'll find in many loans:

- Principal—The amount of money borrowed
- **Interest**—The money paid for the privilege of using the lender's principal (payment of *rent* for the use of another's money).
- Term—The period of time over which the loan is repaid.
- Principal balance—The amount of the principal that is owed at a given point in time.
- **Equity**—The difference between the market value of a property and the principal balance on any loans against it. At the time of purchase, equity is equal to the down payment.

There are many types of loans and more are being developed continually. Figure 12.2 identifies some of the more established types of loans that you will encounter.
Each of these will be defined in this chapter.

Term Loan

Term loans or straight loans were used for financing real estate prior to the Depression and are experiencing a resurgence in popularity today. There are two primary characteristics to this loan type:

1. Payments during the term of the loan cover interest only. No principal reduction occurs through the loan payments.
2. The principal is paid in full at the end of the term of the loan. This is known as a **balloon payment**.

Amortized Loan

An **amortized loan** is one in which both principal and interest are paid during the term of the loan. Payments are for the same total amount throughout the term of the loan. Part of each payment covers the interest due for the previous installment period (usually a

---

FIGURE 12.2

Types of Loans

Term	Graduated Payment
Amortized	Adjustable Rate
Partially Amortized	Wraparound
Budget	Buydown
Package	Construction
Purchase Money	Shared Equity/Participation
Open-End	Reverse Annuity
Blanket	Sale and Leaseback

month), and the remaining amount goes toward the repayment of the principal (debt reduction). Over the amortization period (the term), the following occurs:

- The payment amount going to interest decreases.
- The payment amount going to principal increases.

By the end of the term of the loan when the final loan payment is being made, the entire borrowed principal amount is repaid in full.

Partially Amortized Loan

A partially amortized loan is similar to a fully amortized loan with one exception: At the end of the term, there is still a balance due on the principal amount. (The installment payments were not significant enough to retire the original principal amount.)

The remaining principal balance is paid in one lump sum at the end of the term. The partially amortized loan is often referred to as a balloon loan (mortgage). This lump sum payment is commonly called a balloon payment. In Florida, with this type of loan, the lender is required to state within the loan document the amount of the final principal balance (balloon payment) to be made by the borrower.

Budget Loan

A budget loan is an amortized loan that also includes an amount to cover the taxes and insurance on the property in each payment. Each payment includes the amount for principal and interest plus one-twelfth of the estimated annual taxes and insurance cost. This type of loan is often referred to as a **PITI** loan, which stands for:

- *P*rincipal
- *I*nterest
- *T*axes
- *I*nsurance

All FHA and VA loans are budget loans. Also, lenders who loan more than 80 percent of the value on a conventional loan often require a budget payment.

Package Loan

A package loan is a budget loan that also includes a provision for an installment payment on some article of personal property. Thus, a package loan is secured by both real and personal property. An example of a package loan would be a condominium in a resort area that is secured by the condo (real) and the furnishings (personal). This gives the borrower the advantage of financing those items at a lower rate of interest by including them in a package with the home loan.

Purchase Money Loan

This is a loan from the seller to the buyer of real property to finance all or part of the purchase price of the property. It is more commonly referred to as *seller financing*. No money changes hands because the buyer gives the seller a promissory note and a mortgage (or other security instrument) for the amount of the loan. This is often referred to as *taking back* a mortgage or *carry back financing*. This type of loan is often used when the seller finances part of the purchase price in the form of a second mortgage (or a junior mortgage), but it can be used with loans of first priority (or a senior mortgage), or any lower priority as well.

Open-End Loan

This is a loan under which the borrower can obtain additional money during the term of the loan. It is often used in **home equity loans**. Home equity loans are mortgage loans (usually 2nd mortgages) to property owners up to a prescribed limit. The property is pledged as collateral toward the repayment of the loan. It is also used in **lines of credit**. A line of credit is funds that a borrower obtains from a lender where draws on the line of credit are limited up to a prescribed amount. The property is not pledged as collateral for repayment of the loan. An open-end loan normally occurs when the borrower reduces the principal balance amount. At that point, the lender allows the borrower to further borrow or draw down additional principal loan amounts. The lender issues to the borrower a line of credit that can be borrowed, all or in part, at the demand of the borrower. When the loan is repaid, all or in part, the remaining credit line can be reborrowed. This also resembles revolving credit card debt.

Blanket Loan

This is a loan under which more than one property is used as security for a single loan. A blanket loan is most commonly used in subdivided properties or subdivisions. The mortgage will usually contain a partial release clause. This clause permits single properties to be released from the mortgage as the principal balance is reduced. The principal balance reduction amount is generally arrived at by agreement between the borrower and the lender.

Example

Subdivider Max purchases six acres for the purposes of subdividing the land into six separate one-acre lots. Max finances the purchase of the six-acre parcel with one blanket mortgage. He later subdivides the acreage into lots. At this point, he has six lots covered by one loan. In order for Max to sell one or more of these lots to others, he must have a partial release clause. This clause requires the lender to release its lien on each lot. This way, the individual lots may transfer unencumbered to the buyer.

Graduated Payment Loan

One common type of graduated payment loan is the FHA, Title II, Section 245 loan, commonly referred to as a Section 245 loan. In this type of amortized loan, the payments are set low initially, and then gradually increase over the first 5 or 10 years of the loan.

In the early years of the loan, the repayment schedule may result in **negative amortization** (negative amortization occurs when the loans principal balance increases with each installment payment rather than decreasing with each installment payment). Negative amortization means the following:

• The scheduled loan payment is not large enough to cover all the interest due.

• The unpaid interest each month is added to the principal balance.

The result is that the principal balance increases each month, rather than decreasing as in a regular amortized loan. As the amount of the scheduled payment increases each year, the amount of negative amortization decreases until it reaches zero. The principal balance then begins to decrease with each payment.

Adjustable Rate Loans

With an adjustable rate loan (also known as an adjustable rate mortgage, or ARM), the rate of interest may change over the term of the loan. The rate is keyed to an index, such as the price of U.S. Treasury bills. As the price of the index changes, the interest rate on the loan changes at preset intervals. The index must be readily verifiable by the borrower but not under the control of the lender. The interest rate on the loan is equal to the **index plus a margin**, which is a fixed number of percentage points (usually 1–3 percent, which is also expressed as 100–300 basis points). For example, if the Treasury bill index was 7 percent and the margin was 2 percent, the interest rate on the loan would be 9 percent. Margin or spread as it is also commonly called is representative of the lender's profit for loan origination. Adjustments to the interest rate usually have certain limitations, such as:

- Adjustments are made at the end of each adjustment period, usually 1–3 years in length.
- Most adjustments have a limit (or cap) on the interest rate increases.
  - Periodic interest rate cap—The maximum amount the interest rate can increase in one adjustment period.
  - Lifetime cap—The maximum amount the interest rate can increase over the life of the loan (usually about 5–6 percent).

Adjustable rate loans may also have a payment cap that limits the amount of the increase in the monthly payment. This can sometimes result in negative amortization as in a graduated payment mortgage.

Wraparound Loan

A *wraparound loan* can only be used when there is no alienation (due on sale) clause on an existing loan. It is therefore an assumable mortgage. The characteristics of this loan type are the following:

- The first loan is assumed by the buyer.
- The seller usually makes the loan to the buyer as a second loan on the property.
  - The second loan resembles a purchase money mortgage as it is originated out of the seller's equity in the property at time of origination (defined earlier as *seller financing*).
- A new loan is created but the existing loan also stays in effect.
- The buyer's loan requires payments on an amount greater than the original principal on the old loan.
- Out of this payment, the seller continues to make the payments on the original loan, and pockets any difference.
- A wraparound loan is only feasible when the interest rate on the seller's existing loan is more favorable than that available to the buyer on a new market rate loan.

Buydown Loan

This is a loan in which the seller (often a builder) prepays an amount of money in order to reduce the interest that would normally be paid in the first few years of the loan (usually 1–3 years). Buydowns became popular in the 1970s when interest rates climbed dramatically. Buydown loans are not as common as they were in the past but are used in some instances. A more recent development is called the *lender-funded buydown*. With a lender-funded buydown, the lender charges an overall interest rate that is slightly higher than the standard rate but allows the buyer to pay a lower rate during the first few years of the loan.

Construction Loans

Construction loans are short-term loans (also known as interim loans) made to the owner or builder for constructing a building. The lender advances money from the loan as construction takes place. The construction loan is paid off when permanent financing is obtained on the property. The permanent financing is commonly referred to as the **take-out loan**. Because the loan is secured by a partially completed improvement, a construction loan is considered risky for the lender. Because of the added risk, construction loans usually carry an interest rate higher than that of permanent financing. These types of loans are generally originated by commercial banks, which prefer short-term loans over permanent long-term financing.

Shared Equity/Participating Loan

With a shared equity loan (also known as a shared appreciation loan), the buyer receives favorable loan terms from the lender. These terms would probably include below market interest rates on the borrowed funds. In exchange, the lender receives a portion of the appreciation from the property, usually when the property is sold or refinanced, or in the case of income-producing properties, the lender shares in the net operating income as a dividend. The end payment to the lender is sometimes referred to as **deferred interest**.

Reverse Annuity Loan

A reverse annuity loan allows a homeowner to borrow against the equity in his home. The borrower receives monthly payments from the lender, and a gradual debt builds up against the property. The debt must be repaid to the lender on a specified date or when a specified event occurs, such as the sale of the home or the death of the borrower. Reverse annuity loans are often used by retirees who have built up equity in their homes and wish to continue their residency in the same home, but need additional income to meet living expenses.

Sale and Leaseback

In a sale and leaseback arrangement, the property owner sells the property to an investor. The investor then leases the property back to the original owner. This type of arrangement is often used by an owner of commercial property who wants to free up capital to use for other purposes while simultaneously achieving tax deductions from the capital gains achieved through the sale. The deduction is by the rent payments made for the continued occupancy. It should be noted that this is not a borrowing instrument or loan type. It is an alternative means of raising money through the equity in the property that is already owned.

See Figure 12.3 for a summary of key terms associated with mortgages.

LENDING PRACTICES AND UNDERWRITING RISK

Lenders have certain requirements when originating a loan that will include real property as the security for repayment on a note. Although lenders have different ways of underwriting risk, there are a few common elements one can find when applying for a loan with any lender, such as:

- Employment verification—Lenders are required to verify an applicant's current employment and in some cases previous employment history. This process helps the lender to establish the borrowing party's ability to repay the loan.
- Tax returns—Generally, lenders look at the current tax return or previous 2 years of tax returns. This will verify the applicant's employment as well as wages.
- Credit check—Lenders routinely perform credit checks to determine the quality of the borrower's ability to repay the loan.
- Appraisal—In order to determine a property's true value, a lender will always conduct an appraisal.
- Loan-to-value ratio (LTV)—The LTV is the relationship between the borrowed amount versus the value of the property. Please note that *all* originated loans are based upon *the lesser of* the purchase price or the appraised value.

FIGURE 12.3

Mortgages at a Glance

- In a **term or straight loan**, interest is only paid *during* the term of the loan. In a *term* loan, the principal is paid in one payment at the end of the term of the loan.

- **Amortized loans** have equal monthly payments that consist of the required principal and interest that leave the borrower with a zero principal balance upon payment of the last installment of the loan.

- **Partially amortized loans** include both partial principal and interest payments. The last remaining payment is called a **balloon payment**.

- **Package loans** are secured by both real and personal property.

- A **purchase money loan** is made by the seller. It is seller financing.

- An **open-end loan** lets the borrower borrow more money on the same loan. It resembles a line of credit.

- A **blanket loan** covers more than one property.

- In an **adjustable rate loan**, margin is the amount added to the index to get the interest rate on the loan. An adjustable rate loan changes with changes in an index. The periodic interest rate cap is the limit for one adjustment period. The lifetime cap is the most it can increase during the loan term.

- In a **sale and leaseback** arrangement, the property owner sells the property to an investor who then leases the property back to the original owner. Commercial property owners often use sale and leaseback arrangements to free up capital.

- With a **shared equity** arrangement, the lender offers the borrower favorable loan terms in exchange for a share of the appreciation from the property.

- With a **buydown**, a party (possibly the seller, builder, or lender) prepays an amount of money in order to reduce the interest that the buyer pays in the first few years of the loan.

- In a **reverse annuity loan**, the borrower receives monthly payments from the lender, and a gradual debt builds up against the property.

It should also be noted that by law, banks may not originate greater than loan-to-value ratios of 80/20 without charging a premium for mortgage insurance. This premium applies to any amount that exceeds the 80 percent borrowed amount ratio. For example, a buyer requires 90 percent financing with a 10 percent down payment (or initial investment, as it is sometimes called). Whereby a lender quotes an interest rate of 7 percent on the 80 percent loan portion, the borrower will pay a higher interest rate amount for the overage amount. That interest premium disappears when the LTV reaches 80 percent or below.

SUMMARY

Whether one purchases a home or invests in income-producing property, financing usually is involved. The lending documents and their contents become critical aspects for both the success of the home owner and the investor. Remember that Florida is a lien theory state that encompasses a two-party, two-instrument transaction. The two parties are the mortgagor/borrower and the mortgagee/lender. The two instruments are the promissory note acting as evidence of the borrowing, and the mortgage acting as the collateral/security pledged by the mortgagor/borrower to repay the loan. There are many loan options to fit the needs of the borrower. Prior to a lender originating a loan, the borrower must pass certain qualifying lender requirements. These requirements must meet loan underwriting standards.

REVIEW QUESTIONS

1. In a title theory state:
   a. The borrower holds the title.
   b. The mortgagor holds the title.
   c. The trustee holds the title.
   d. The title company holds the title.

2. In a lien theory state, such as Florida:
   a. The lender holds the property until the note is paid.
   b. The buyer owns the property; while the lender has a lien.
   c. The borrower gets a mortgage to buy the property.
   d. The buyer owns the mortgage and the lender owns the note.

3. Mortgages, like stocks and bonds, are negotiable instruments. When mortgages are sold in the secondary market, the selling of the mortgage is accomplished via:
   a. Assignment of mortgage.
   b. Hypothecation.
   c. The subordination agreement.
   d. A letter of estoppel.

4. The clause contained in a mortgage that can effect whether or not a loan may be paid off prior to its maturity date is best described as:
   a. An exculpatory clause.
   b. The prepayment clause.
   c. The due on sale clause.
   d. A prepayment penalty clause.

5. The clause in a mortgage that requires a new buyer to find her own financing is the:
   a. Subordination clause.
   b. Exculpatory clause.
   c. Alienation/due on sale clause.
   d. Prepayment penalty clause.

6. The defeasance clause in a mortgage requires the lender to:
   a. Pay the debt in full when the property is sold.
   b. Record a satisfaction of mortgage when the note is paid off in full.
   c. Pay the entire balance in case of default.
   d. Precollect taxes and insurance.

7. When Tudor Investment purchased a mortgage from Jack's Finance, the company ordered a letter of estoppel. This document:
   a. Legally transfers the ownership of the mortgage.
   b. Legally establishes the remaining balance of the loan.
   c. Notifies the buyer of the new owner of the mortgage.
   d. Allows the investor to change the interest rate.

8. A buyer is in default on the note. This allows the lender to:
   a. Commence with a foreclosure proceeding.
   b. Sell the property to someone else.
   c. Sue for all of the back payments that are owed.
   d. Seize the property in lieu of the debt.

9. Foreclosure is a judicial process and is lengthy and expensive to the lender. Once the foreclosure has begun, the buyer has a right to stop the foreclosure by paying all back payments, the interest on the money that is owed, and the expenses the lender has paid in the foreclosure process. This right to stop foreclosure and regain the ownership of the property is known as:
   a. The right to reinstate.
   b. The acceleration clause.
   c. The receivership clause.
   d. The equity right of redemption.

10. A monthly payment for real property that includes payments for insurance and taxes as well as scheduled repayment of the debt is known as:
    a. PITI.
    b. Wraparound payment.
    c. Taxes and insurance,
    d. PMI.

11. A property sale in which the seller holds the title until the buyer has completed the stated requirements in the contract is known as a:
    a. Wraparound mortgage.
    b. Lease with an option to buy.
    c. Contract for deed.
    d. Reverse annuity mortgage.

12. When Jackson defaulted on the note he signed in order to purchase a resort hotel, the lender had the property sold through a foreclosure proceeding. The sale didn't bring enough money to satisfy the note. The lender had no further recourse and absorbed the loss because of a clause in the mortgage known as the:
    a. Subordination clause.
    b. Acceleration clause.
    c. Exculpatory clause.
    d. Satisfaction of mortgage.

13. In the purchase of real property, the instrument that acts as evidence of the borrowing and obligates the mortgagor for the debt is the:
    a. Mortgage.
    b. Note.
    c. Letter of estoppel.
    d. Alienation clause.

14. In a fully amortized mortgage, the portion of the monthly payment that pays interest to the lender:
    a. Increases each month by a regular amount.
    b. Increases each month in a nonregular way.
    c. Decreases each month by a regular amount.
    d. Decreases each month in a nonregular way.

15. In a partially amortized mortgage, monthly payments contain interest and a portion of the principal. At the end of the stated term, the rest of the debt is due. The payment is referred to as a(n):
    a. Balloon payment.
    b. Acceleration payment.
    c. Open-end loan.
    d. Package mortgage.

16. Allen borrowed $50,000 and pledged his home as security. When he paid the loan down to $40,000, he borrowed $10,000 again. Allen probably has a(n):
    a. Purchase money loan.
    b. Package loan.
    c. Open-end loan.
    d. Reverse annuity loan.

17. Which of these loans could prove beneficial for an older couple?
    a. Open-end loan
    b. Reverse annuity loan
    c. Adjustable rate loan
    d. Package loan

18. In an adjustable rate loan, the components that comprise the interest rate are:
    a. Margin and spread.
    b. Index and cap.
    c. Index and points.
    d. Margin and index.

19. Steele wants to buy a small pizza restaurant. He wants the lender to finance the purchase of the restaurant equipment as well as the land and the building. If the lender agrees to the loan, this will be a:
    a. Purchase money loan.
    b. Wraparound loan.
    c. Package loan.
    d. Buydown loan.

20. The buyer signed a note to the seller and gave the seller a mortgage as part of the price to purchase the property. This is a:
    a. Purchase money loan.
    b. Reverse annuity loan.
    c. Wraparound loan.
    d. Buydown loan.

Chapter 13

KEY TERMS

closing costs	loan-to-value ratio (LTV)	primary mortgage market
conforming loan	mortgage bankers	private mortgage insurance
discount points	mortgage brokers	(PMI)
discount rate	mortgage company	purchase money mortgage
disintermediation	Office of Thrift Supervision	(PMM)
entitlement	open-market operations	reserve requirements
intermediation	origination fee	secondary mortgage market

LEARNING OBJECTIVES

After completing this lesson, you will be able to:

- Identify some important entities that influence real estate financing including the Federal Reserve System, the Federal Home Loan Bank System, and the Federal Deposit Insurance Corporation.
- Define two concepts involved in real estate financing: intermediation and disintermediation.
- Describe the major sources of real estate loans in the primary mortgage market.
- Explain the difference between the primary and secondary loan markets and the functions of the secondary market.
- Describe the three major government components of the secondary mortgage market and their functions.
- Define loan discounting and identify its role in the secondary mortgage market.
- Define loan-to-value ratio and understand how it is used.
- Appreciate some of the primary fees involved in taking out a loan.
- Know who can pay the fees with different types of loans.
- Know the major features of the FHA-insured loan program, including:
  - Loan insurance, determination of cash investment, and loan amount
  - Interest rate, discount points, maximum term, closing costs, and escrow accounts
  - Loan processing, appraisals, and restrictions
- Explain what a guaranteed VA loan is and how the guarantee works.
- Know the major features of VA-guaranteed loans, including:
  - Maximum loan amount, down payment, loan term, and interest rate
  - Discount points, closing costs, funding fee, escrow account, and veteran's liability
  - Restrictions on VA loans

Mortgage Market Operations

FEDERAL RESERVE SYSTEM

The Federal Reserve System (the Fed) is the central banker of the United States. The Fed is responsible for the ebb and flow of the country's money supply. The Fed is composed of 12 privately owned regional Federal Reserve banks and a vast number of member commercial banks. The Fed sets **reserve requirements** for its member commercial banks. The reserve requirements set forth the amount of funds that the member banks must maintain on deposit at any one time. The Fed uses reserve requirements to control the country's money supply. That is, the Fed can decrease the money supply by increasing the reserve requirement (which reduces the amount of money in circulation). Conversely, the Fed can increase the supply of money by decreasing the reserve requirement (thereby increasing the amount in circulation). Reserve requirements also affect the amount of leverage that banks may use at any time to generate funds for loans. The greater the reserve requirement, the less funds available for loans. Due to the scarcity of money in these times, this directly affects interest rates.

Another method to control the money supply that the Fed can institute is **open-market operations**. This is where the Fed buys and sells securities. A tightening of the money supply occurs through the sale of securities by the Fed. (Funds from the sales are held by the Fed, reducing the money supply.) Conversely, an increase in the money supply occurs when the Fed buys securities.

Another means for the Fed to tighten or loosen the money supply is by raising or lowering the **discount rate**, which is the interest rate the Fed charges to its member banks for borrowing funds. The higher the rate the Fed charges its member banks, the greater the cost of those funds to individual borrowers. As a result, the number of borrowers is greatly reduced.

FEDERAL HOME LOAN BANK SYSTEM

Whereas the Fed governs over commercial banks, the Federal Home Loan Bank System (FHLB) is the regulatory body that governs over savings associations (also known as savings and loan associations [S&Ls]). Like the Fed, the FHLB also has 12 district member savings associations. The FHLB acts as a provider of reserve credit for the member savings associations, thereby ensuring mortgage fund availability. Member savings associations are chartered through and regulated by the **Office of Thrift Supervision**.

FEDERAL DEPOSIT INSURANCE CORPORATION

The Federal Deposit Insurance Corporation (FDIC) insures individual accounts up to $100,000 per account that are held within its member institutions. The FDIC is run by a board of governors. Its powers are derived through the Deposit Insurance Fund and two of its subsidiaries, Savings Association Insurance Fund and the Bank Insurance Fund.

INTERMEDIATION

Intermediation occurs when thrift institutions (commercial banks and savings associations) receive inflows of money into savings accounts. The purpose on the part of the depositor is to achieve high-yielding returns on the investment. These savings in turn are used to invest in larger investment projects. Intermediation results in funds being available for mortgages.

DISINTERMEDIATION

Disintermediation occurs when those same thrift institutions experience the opposite effect. That is, depositors withdraw their savings in order to achieve higher yielding returns on invested capital within alternative investment vehicles. Disintermediation results in a scarcity of money available for mortgages.

Coaching Tips: When thrift institutions (commercial banks and savings associations) *receive* inflows of money into savings accounts, it is called intermediation.

Disintermediation occurs when depositors *withdraw* their savings in order to achieve higher yielding returns on invested capital within alternative investment vehicles.

PRIMARY AND SECONDARY MORTGAGE MARKETS

There are two major components to the market that provide the source of funds for real estate financing:

1. The primary mortgage market
2. The secondary mortgage market

Primary Mortgage Market

The **primary mortgage market** is the part of the market where lenders originate loans. These lenders include:

- Savings and loan associations
- Commercial banks
- Insurance companies
- Mortgage companies
- Mortgage brokers
- Mutual savings banks
- Municipal bonds
- Credit unions
- Pension, endowment, and trust funds

There are five major sources of loans for *residential* real estate in the primary mortgage market:

1. Savings and loan associations
2. Mortgage companies
3. Mortgage brokers
4. Commercial banks
5. Private lenders (including sellers)

Savings and Loan Associations

Savings and loan associations (S&Ls) make loans primarily on residential property. Historically, *S&Ls have made the majority of all residential real estate loans;* however, in the 1990s, mortgage companies became the primary supplier of such loans. The funds for the loans they make come from their depositors.

Mortgage Companies

A **mortgage company** (mortgage banker) makes loans, using its own money, and then sells the loans to long-term investors. Once the loans have been sold, the mortgage company often retains the servicing of the loan (collects payments, keeps records, etc.) in return for a fee, such as 0.25 of 1 percent of the outstanding loan balance. Because mortgage companies sell their loans in the secondary mortgage market, they primarily make government-backed mortgages (such as Veterans Affairs [VA] and Federal Housing Administration [FHA] loans). These loans can be easily sold in the secondary mortgage market. However, mortgage companies have also become active in conventional loans. *Since the early 1990s, mortgage companies have become the largest originators of residential real estate loans.*

Mortgage Brokers

Mortgage brokers are often confused with **mortgage bankers**. Mortgage bankers are defined as a company or an individual that originates loans to others with their own funds and with the intent on selling those loans to investors. Mortgage brokers do not typically loan their own money, and they usually do not service the loans themselves.

Mortgage brokers bring together borrowers and lenders for a fee, usually based on a percentage of the loan. The lender then makes the loan directly to the borrower, and the mortgage broker has no further role.

Commercial Banks

Like S&Ls, commercial banks also obtain funds from depositors to make loans. Commercial banks primarily make short-term loans, such as business loans and real estate construction loans. These loans are usually higher risk loans and carry higher interest rates.

Historically, commercial banks have been the primary source for short-term residential real estate loans, such as construction loans, interim loans, or second mortgage loans. Interim loans, often called *swing* or *bridge* loans, are made to buyers who are buying a new home but haven't sold their existing home. The interim loan replaces the equity that they will eventually receive from the sale of their existing home. Historically, commercial banks rarely made long-term residential loans. However, this trend is changing, and commercial banks have become a significant source of residential loans.

Private Lenders

Private lenders are individual citizens who make loans, and include two major categories:

1. Individuals who are in the business of making first or second mortgage loans.
2. Sellers who assist in financing the sale of their own property.

Of these, the most common private lender is a seller who is selling her own property. Sellers are also the source most preferred by buyers. Seller financing is particularly attractive to a buyer if the seller has a large equity in the property being sold or new financing is not available or desired by the buyer. Seller financing is commonly referred to as a **purchase money mortgage (PMM)**.

The five sources of residential financing just described will meet your buyer's needs for residential financing in most situations. However, there may be other sources that may be appropriate in some cases. You should consult your broker for information on these other sources, or if those listed earlier do not meet your needs in a particular situation.

Coaching Tips:

1. Prior to the 1990s, S&Ls were the largest source of residential real estate loans. Since that time, mortgage companies have become the largest source of such loans.
2. Mortgage brokers don't make loans. They bring borrowers and lenders together for a fee.
3. Savings and loan associations are primary lenders, but not private lenders.

The lenders just covered are the major sources of *residential* real estate loans. In addition to these lenders, there are two additional sources of loans in the primary mortgage market that provide loans for nonresidential real estate:

1. Insurance companies
2. Municipal bonds

Insurance Companies

Insurance companies invest premiums paid by their policyholders. They usually specialize in large-scale projects, such as commercial and industrial properties. Insurance companies rarely make loans on residential properties.

Municipal Bonds

Municipalities can issue bonds for real estate purposes. The interest paid to investors to obtain the funds is tax exempt. The bonds usually carry interest rates 1 to 2 percent below market rates. Banks and S&Ls use their deposits to make loans. Origination fees cover operational expenses and profit.

As previously discussed, there are two major components to the market that provides the source of funds for real estate financing: the primary mortgage market and the secondary mortgage market.

You have already learned about the primary mortgage market where loans are originated (see Figure 13.1). At this point, you will learn about the secondary mortgage market.

Secondary Mortgage Market

The secondary market should not be confused with where the general public seeks a second mortgage. The **secondary mortgage market** provides an outlet where those who originate loans may sell their loans in order to secure capital to make more loans.

- The primary mortgage market is where loans are originated.
- The secondary market is where these same loans are sold in lots.
- Commercial banks primarily make short-term loans such as commercial and construction loans.
- Savings and loan associations and mortgage companies primarily make long-term residential loans.
- Mortgage companies originate loans and sell the loans in the secondary market.
- Mortgage brokers don't make loans. They bring borrowers and lenders together for a fee.
- Higher risk carries higher interest rates.

FIGURE 13.1

Primary Mortgage Market at a Glance

See Figure 13.2. The purpose of the secondary market is to provide liquidity for the primary market. It is the ultimate source of a large percentage of the money used for real estate loans. There are several major institutions in this market, including:

- Fannie Mae (Federal National Mortgage Association [FNMA])
- Ginnie Mae (Government National Mortgage Association [GNMA])
- Freddie Mac (Federal Home Loan Mortgage Corporation [FHLMC])

Fannie Mae

The Federal National Mortgage Association (FNMA) is commonly referred to as Fannie Mae. It is the oldest and largest institution in the secondary market. It was started as a government-owned corporation in the 1930s. In 1968, it became a private, for-profit corporation, owned by stockholders and operated independently of the government.

Fannie Mae sells bonds to obtain money to buy loans. It buys and sells FHA, VA, and conventional loans to and from sources in the primary market. It buys more mortgages than any other entity.

Ginnie Mae

The Government National Mortgage Association (GNMA) is commonly referred to as Ginnie Mae. It was created by the government when Fannie Mae became private. It is a federal agency in the Department of Housing and Urban Development (HUD). It provides funds primarily by guaranteeing the payment of securities sold to the public and backed by mortgages. The mortgages are insured by the FHA or guaranteed by the VA.

FIGURE 13.2

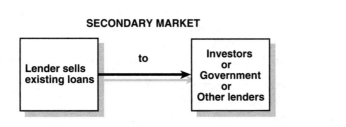

SECONDARY MARKET

FIGURE 13.3

Secondary Market at a
Glance

- Ginnie Mae (GNMA) is the Government National Mortgage Association.
  - Ginnie Mae guarantees securities issued by others.
  - Ginnie Mae is a part of HUD
  - Ginnie Mae was formed when Fannie Mae became a private organization.
- Fannie Mae (FNMA) is the Federal National Mortgage Association.
  - Fannie Mae is a federally chartered private corporation.
- Freddie Mac (FHLMC) is the Federal Home Loan Mortgage Corporation.
  - Freddie Mac was the third government chartered organization.
  - Freddie Mac issues its own securities.
- HUD is a federal agency.
- FHA and VA are branches of federal agencies.
- The FHA insures FHA loans made by qualified lenders.
- The VA guarantees VA loans.
- The VA guarantees loans made by lenders.

Freddie Mac

The Federal Home Loan Mortgage Corporation (FHLMC) is commonly known as Freddie Mac. It is a private corporation created by Congress in 1970. Its primary purpose is to increase the supply of residential financing by purchasing loans. It now deals primarily in conventional mortgages and, to a lesser extent, FHA and VA mortgages. Its funds come from packaging the mortgages it buys into securities and selling those securities to private investors in the general public.

Figure 13.3 summarizes the major institutions of the secondary market.

Now that you have learned something about the major institutions in the secondary mortgage market, let's take a look at how the secondary market functions. Let's begin with a brief history of loans in real estate.

THE HISTORY OF LOANS

Amortized Loans

One major development in real estate finance after the Depression was the introduction of amortized loans. Amortized loans offered a number of advantages over straight loans, such as the following:

- They were typically made for a longer term (15–20 years), which lowered the total annual payment.
- They allowed payments to be made monthly, not annually like straight loans, making it easier to budget for and make payments.
- Each monthly payment covered not only the interest due, but also included an amount applied toward the repayment of the principal. This meant that the borrower would have completely paid for the property at the end of the loan, rather than having to come up with the full principal payment as in the case of a straight loan.

Because of these more liberal repayment terms, amortized loans increased the demand for loans by making home ownership possible for more people, and also helped reduce the number of foreclosures on financed property. Because of this, amortized loans were very popular with lenders as well as buyers.

Federal Agencies

Another major development in real estate finance after the Depression was the creation of two new agencies by the federal government:

1. The Federal Housing Administration (FHA)
2. The Federal National Mortgage Association (FNMA, or Fannie Mae)

Because of the importance of a strong housing market to the economic recovery needed after the Depression, the federal government created these agencies to increase the money supply available for residential loans. Let's briefly look at these agencies.

Federal Housing Administration

The first agency created by the federal government to assist in the financing of real estate was the Federal Housing Administration (FHA). The purpose of the FHA is to insure loans made by private lending institutions, such as savings and loan associations and mortgage companies. By providing insurance that protects the lender against losses when a borrower defaults, the FHA reduces the lender's risk. This encourages lenders to make loans on real estate that they might not make otherwise, thus increasing the supply of money available for real estate loans. The FHA has several different loan programs that are designed for different types of properties and different categories of borrowers. The FHA's most popular loan program is the FHA 203(b) loan. This is the basic FHA loan program for residential property for one to four families. The FHA 234(c) loan is the popular program used for condominium housing.

Fannie Mae

After the Depression, the federal government also created the Federal National Mortgage Association (FNMA), commonly referred to as Fannie Mae. Its original purpose was to purchase loans made by lenders that were insured by the FHA. The creation of Fannie Mae helped solve one of the biggest problems that limited the availability of funds after the advent of amortized loans. With amortized loans, the lender was not able to recoup money as fast as with straight loans because amortized loans were made for much longer terms. Consequently, lenders had less money to loan to borrowers. The federal government addressed this problem by creating Fannie Mae, whose purpose was to purchase FHA-insured loans from lenders who originated the loans. When these loans were purchased from the lender, the lenders in effect received their money back from Fannie Mae, and were able to loan the money again to another borrower. This had a dramatic effect on the availability of funds for real estate loans. The creation of Fannie Mae was the first step in the development of what has come to be called the secondary mortgage market, whose primary purpose is to purchase loans from lenders who originate them. The lenders who originate the loans sold to the secondary mortgage market collectively make up what is referred to as the primary mortgage market. Fannie Mae is still the world's largest agency engaged in the purchase of loans from lenders in the primary mortgage market.

LOAN DISCOUNTING

The term *discounting* refers to selling a loan for less than the face value. Let's look at how this process works and why it is important.

The owners of a property may be faced with taking a second mortgage (purchase money mortgage [PMM]) in order to sell their property. If they need cash, they might induce an investor to purchase the note by offering the note at less than value.

Example

A seller takes back a $10,000 PMM in the sale of his home. To convert this note to cash, he could attempt to sell this asset to an investor. To induce the investor to buy, the seller may offer the note for $9,000. The investor would receive interest on $10,000 and will ultimately be paid back $10,000 on only a $9,000 investment. The process of discounting ultimately increases the yield (return on investment) for the purchaser of the loan. The same basic process occurs when a primary lender sells a loan to the secondary market. If a lender anticipates it will have to discount a loan to sell it to the secondary market, the lender will charge discount points to the borrower to make up the difference. This process will, hopefully, keep the lender in business so people can continue to borrow money to purchase things.

Discount points are actually just prepaid interest paid at closing. As you have just seen, by charging a loan discount in the form of discount points, the lender is able to increase its yield (or earnings) on the loan, while still being able to sell the loan in the secondary market at a discount. A lender is said to *discount the loan* when it charges discount points. Each discount point is equal to 1 percent of the loan amount.

For example, if a lender charges two discount points, the fee is 2 percent of the loan amount. Four discount points would be 4 percent of the loan amount. The *loan discount* is the actual dollar amount by which the loan is discounted.

For example, if three discount points are charged on a $50,000 loan, the loan is said to be discounted by $1,500, which is $50,000 multiplied by 3 percent (0.03). One discount point is equivalent in yield to the lender to $\frac{1}{8}$ of one percentage point in interest. When a lender charges discount points, the additional fee increases its yield on the loan, as you learned earlier. As a general rule, each discount point paid at closing increases the lender's yield by approximately the same amount as increasing the interest rate on the loan by $\frac{1}{8}$ of 1 percent.

For example, if a lender charges two discount points, this is roughly equivalent to raising the interest rate on the loan by $\frac{1}{4}$ of 1 percent (0.0025). This means that a loan at 10 percent with two discount points is equivalent (in terms of the lender's yield) to a loan at 10.25 percent with no discount points.

Let's apply this rule to a VA loan made by a lender. If the interest rate on a VA loan is 9 percent and the prevailing market rate on conventional loans is 9.75 percent, the difference in the interest rates is 0.75 percent, or $\frac{3}{4}$ percent. (This difference of $\frac{3}{4}$ percent expressed in eighths of a percent is $\frac{6}{8}$ percent.) Because one discount point is equivalent to $\frac{1}{8}$ percent, the lender would have to charge six discount points on the VA loan to earn a comparable yield on a VA loan and a conventional loan (or to be able to sell the loan in the secondary market).

The interest rates on two loans differ by $\frac{1}{2}$ percent. How many points would the lender need to charge on the one with the lower interest rate to get an equivalent yield on the two loans? As you have just seen, discount points affect the yield the lender receives on a loan, and the lender's ability to sell it in the secondary market.

Because of this, discount points may be charged or not charged on a loan, depending on a number of factors, including:

• What the lender can make on other investments.

• The amount a secondary lender is willing to pay for the loan at a given interest rate.

Factors such as these make up the forces of supply and demand for loan funds. These forces of supply and demand determine whether discount points will be charged, and if so, the number of points charged.

When loan money is plentiful in the secondary market (secondary lenders are more willing to buy loans) and borrowers are scarce, discount points tend to decrease or disappear. When loan money is limited and there are many borrowers, points tend to reappear or go up.

In general, the number of discount points charged by lenders on real estate loans is a good reflection of market conditions for financing in the community. When discount points are charged, the supply is low and the demand is high. When discount points are not charged (or are low), the supply of money is high and the demand is low.

Because of supply and demand, which affects the availability of loan money as well as the interest rates and discount points charged by lenders, it is important for you as a licensee to constantly monitor the market for loan funds. You should check with the lenders you work with at least weekly so that you will have current information at all times.

LOAN-TO-VALUE RATIO

The **loan-to-value ratio (LTV)** is used to set a limit on how much money can be loaned on a particular property. It is expressed as a percentage and is computed in either of two ways:

1. The amount of the loan is divided by either the sales price, or
2. The amount of the loan is divided by the appraised value of the property, whichever is smaller.

Example

The sales price of a property is $100,000. The property is appraised at $105,000. In this example, the loan amount is divided by the sales price ($100,000) because the sales price is less than the appraised value ($105,000). The maximum LTV allowed by lenders varies for different types of loans.

CONVENTIONAL LOANS

A conventional loan is one that is not issued, insured, or guaranteed by a government agency. Interest rates on conventional loans are negotiated with the lender. Closing costs and discount points charged on conventional loans may be paid by either the buyer or seller. Conventional loans are divided into different types based on their LTV. The LTV is simply the amount of the loan divided by the sales price or the appraised value, whichever is smaller. While loans of varying ratios may be available, for purposes of this course, conventional loans will have LTV of 80 percent, 90 percent, or 95 percent, unless otherwise stated. The LTV allowed is usually no more than 80 percent unless private mortgage insurance is obtained. Typically, if private mortgage insurance is obtained, conventional loans can be made up to a LTV of 95 percent. Loans with private mortgage insurance are called insured conventional loans. **Private mortgage insurance (PMI)** acts just like FHA insurance, except that the insurance is provided by a private insurance company, not a government agency. PMI protects the lender against losses if the borrower defaults on the loan. PMI is usually required by a lender if the LTV exceeds 80 percent. The borrower pays an insurance premium for PMI, usually 1 percent or less at the origination of the loan, and less than 1 percent annually. Once the LTV is reduced below 80 percent, the PMI can usually be dropped.

Coaching Tips:

1. **The LTV is usually limited to 80 percent unless mortgage insurance is obtained.**
2. **The LTV allowed can be higher than 80 percent if PMI is obtained to cover the amount over 80 percent of the value.**
3. **With PMI, the LTV may be as high as 90 or 95 percent.**

Previously, you learned some of the characteristics of conventional loans. Now, you will learn more about the following aspects of conventional loans:

- The different types of conventional loans
- Down payments and how they are calculated
- PMI payments

Types of Conventional Loans

Conventional loans have different features based on their LTV. The most common categories of conventional loans are 80 percent, 90 percent, and 95 percent LTV loans. This does *not* mean that a loan must be made that is *exactly* 80 percent, 90 percent, or 95 percent of the sales price. It only means that the conventional loan will have different characteristics depending on whether the loan is considered to be an 80 percent, 90 percent, or 95 percent loan. When a conventional loan is made for an amount that is not exactly 80 percent, 90 percent, or 95 percent of the sales price, the following guidelines apply:

- A loan for which the loan amount is less than 80 percent is considered an 80 percent loan.
- A loan for which the loan amount is more than 80 percent but less than 90 percent is considered a 90 percent loan.
- A loan for which the loan amount is more than 90 percent but less than 95 percent is considered a 95 percent loan.

For example, a property is sold for $82,000 and the buyer makes a down payment of $6,000. What type of conventional loan would the buyer obtain?

Step 1: Determine the loan amount:

$$\$82,000 - \$6,000 = \$76,000$$

Step 2: Divide the loan amount by the sales price:

$$\$76,000 \div \$82,000 = 92.7 \text{ percent}$$

Because the loan amount is greater than 90 percent, it is considered to be a 95 percent loan. Let's look at another example.

A property is sold for $70,000 and the buyer makes a down payment of $16,000. What type of conventional loan would the buyer obtain?

Step 1: Determine the loan amount:

$$\$70,000 - \$16,000 = \$54,000$$

Step 2: Divide by the sales price:

$$\$54,000 \div \$70,000 = 77.1 \text{ percent}$$

Because the loan amount is less than 80 percent, the loan is considered to be an 80 percent loan. Let's look at a third example.

A property is sold for $120,000 and the buyer makes a down payment of $17,000. What type of conventional loan would the buyer obtain?

Step 1: Determine the loan amount:

$$\$120,000 - \$17,000 = \$103,000$$

Step 2: Divide by the sales price:

$$\$103,000 \div \$120,000 = 85.8 \text{ percent}$$

The loan amount is 85.8 percent, which is greater than 80 percent but less than 90 percent, so the loan is considered to be a 90 percent loan.

Down Payments

Many times a borrower makes the minimum down payment and chooses to obtain the largest loan he can qualify for. When this is the case, the category of loan selected (80 percent, 90 percent, or 95 percent) determines the loan amount. From the loan amount, it is then necessary to calculate the amount of the down payment. The procedure for calculating the down payment in this situation requires two steps.

Step 1: Determine the dollar amount of the loan.

Step 2: Subtract the loan amount from the sales price to get the down payment.

Different lenders have different policies on how to determine the exact amount of a loan as a percentage of the sales price. Let's look at an example to see how this is handled.

A buyer is applying for an 80 percent loan on a property that is selling for $76,400. Eighty percent of $76,400 is $61,120. Some lenders would make the loan for exactly that amount. Other lenders would round the amount off to the next lowest $100 and make the loan for $61,100. In addition, FHA approves loans in increments of $50. Many lenders that make FHA loans, however, make loans only in increments of $100.

Step 1. Determine the dollar amount of the loan.

Because of these differences, it is best to adopt a policy of always rounding the loan amount *down* to the next lowest $100. This ensures that the contract you write will be acceptable to any lender. Let's look at an example.

A property is being sold for $110,500 with a 90 percent conventional loan. What is the loan amount?

First multiply $110,500 by 90 percent:

$$\$110,500 \times 0.90 = \$99,450$$

Next, round *down* to the next lowest $100:

$$\$99,450 = \$99,400$$

The loan amount is $99,400.

Step 2. Calculate the down payment.

Once the loan amount is determined, subtract the loan amount from the sales price to get the down payment. Let's look at an example.

A property is being sold for $87,500 with a 95 percent conventional loan. What is the down payment?

First, calculate the loan amount:

$$\$87,500 \times 0.95 = \$83,125$$

Round *down* to the next lowest $100:

$$\$83,125 = \$83,100$$

The loan amount is $83,100.

Last, subtract the loan amount from the selling price:

$$\$87,500 - \$83,100 = \$4,400$$

The down payment is $4,400.

Private Mortgage Insurance Payments

As you learned earlier, conventional loans of 90 percent and 95 percent usually require that the borrower obtain private mortgage insurance. Some lenders may require PMI on 80 percent conventional loans in some cases as well. PMI is insurance that protects the *lender* against default by the buyer on a *conventional* loan. It requires the payment of a premium, which is usually calculated as a percentage of the loan amount. PMI is charged to the borrower when a new loan is originated, but the payment of the PMI premium is negotiable, and it may be paid by either the buyer or seller. When the seller pays the PMI, it must be paid in cash at closing. When the buyer pays the PMI, it may be paid in one of the following three ways:

1. It may be paid in cash at closing.

2. It may be financed along with the mortgage payment.

3. It may be paid partially in cash at closing with the rest financed along with the mortgage payment.

The method used to calculate the amount of the PMI payment depends on whether it is paid in cash or financed. Let's look first at the case where the PMI is paid in cash at closing. The calculation is the same regardless of whether the buyer or the seller makes the payment. The exact amount of the PMI premium varies from lender to lender.

For purposes of illustration, we will use the following values for PMI:

90 percent loans—2 percent

95 percent loans—2.5 percent

The amount of the PMI when paid in cash is determined by multiplying these percentages by the amount of the loan. For example, a 90 percent loan is obtained by a buyer on a property selling for $88,500. What is the amount of the PMI premium?

Step 1. Determine the amount of the loan:

$$\$88,500 \times 0.90 = \$79,650$$

Step 2. Round down to the next lowest $100:

$$\$79,650 = \$79,600$$

This is the final loan amount.

Step 3. Multiply the loan amount by 2 percent because this is a 90 percent loan:

$$\$79,600 \times 0.02 = \$1,592$$

The amount of the PMI premium is $1,592.

Here's another example. A $60,000 home is financed with a 95 percent conventional loan. Using the rates for PMI given earlier, what is the amount of the PMI premium?

Step 1: Determine the amount of the loan:

$$\$60,000 \times 0.95 = \$57,000$$

Step 2: Calculate the PMI amount using a 2.5 percent rate:

$$\$57,000 \times 0.025 = \$1,425$$

You learned earlier that a buyer may pay part of the PMI in cash at closing, with the rest financed along with her monthly mortgage payment. In this situation, the amount of the monthly payment is calculated using a standard factor. The exact factor used varies from lender to lender, but for study purposes in this course, we will use a value of ¼ percent. Note that the factor used is ¼ percent (or 0.0025). Do not confuse this amount with 2.5 percent (or 0.025), which is used to determine the PMI on a 95 percent loan when the PMI is paid in full at closing.

This factor (¼ percent or 0.0025) is used to determine the *annual* amount of premium to be paid. The amount of the *monthly* payment is calculated from the annual amount.

Let's look at an example.

A 90 percent conventional loan is used to purchase a home for $80,000. The buyer will pay part of the PMI at closing and finance the rest. What is the amount of the *monthly* PMI payment?

Step 1: Determine the loan amount:

$$\$80,000 \times 0.90 = \$72,000$$

Step 2: Determine the amount of the *annual* premium, using the factor mentioned above:

$$\$72,000 \times 0.0025 = \$180$$

Step 3: Divide the annual premium by 12 to get the monthly premium:

$$\$180 \div 12 = \$15.00$$

The *monthly* payment for PMI is $15.00.

Let's look at another example.

A new home is purchased for \$66,900 using a 95 percent conventional loan. The buyer will pay part of the PMI at closing and finance the rest. What is the monthly PMI payment?

Step 1: Determine the loan amount:

$$\$66,900 \times 0.95 = \$63,555$$

Step 2: Round down to the next lowest \$100:

$$\$63,555 = \$63,500$$

Step 3: Determine the annual premium:

$$\$63,500 \times 0.0025 = \$158.75$$

Step 4: Determine the monthly premium:

$$\$158,75 \div 12 = \$13.23$$

FHA LOANS (NONCONVENTIONAL)

The second major category of loans you should be familiar with is FHA loans. The FHA loan programs are administered through the Federal Housing Administration (FHA). Since 1965, the FHA has been an agency within HUD. The three main purposes of the FHA are to:

1. Promote improved housing standards
2. Assist in the stabilization of the mortgage market
3. Provide mortgage loan insurance

Note that the FHA does *not* make loans itself or provide housing.

Loan Insurance Programs

The most familiar function of the FHA is to provide loan insurance programs. The FHA *insures* loans made by private lenders that meet certain guidelines and standards. The FHA mortgage insurance protects the lender against losses resulting from default by the borrower. The money that provides the FHA insurance protection to lenders comes from the insurance premiums that are paid on each loan insured by the FHA. The premium charged by the FHA is called the mortgage insurance premium (MIP). We will look at the MIP in more detail later in this chapter.

The FHA has several different loan programs that are designed for different types of properties and different categories of borrowers. These programs include the following:

- Section 203(b)—Standard loan program
- Special terms for veterans
- Section 245—Graduated payment loan program

Section 203(b)—Standard Loan Program

The Section 203(b) program is the basic FHA loan insurance program for residential property for one to four families. Most FHA loans are limited to owner-occupied properties. The characteristics of the Section 203(b) loan program will be covered later in this chapter. However, before looking at this program in detail, let's look briefly at two other FHA loan programs.

Special Terms for Veterans

The FHA program for veterans is similar in purpose to VA loans, but is administered by FHA, not the VA. The FHA program provides lower down payment loans for veterans.

There is a maximum loan amount that is different for high-cost and low-cost areas. These loan limits may change frequently, so you should check with a lender for the current limits. The veteran must pay a down payment that is calculated in the following way:

0 percent on the first $25,000 of the sales price

5 percent on the amount between $25,000 and $125,000

10 percent of everything over $125,000

Section 245—Graduated Payment Loan Program

The Section 245 program is designed to assist first-time buyers who might otherwise be unable to buy because of rising prices. Its main feature is that the monthly payments on the loan are lower in the first year of the loan and increase over a period of years until the final payment level. The Section 245 graduated payment loan (GPM) program is limited to single-family, owner-occupied houses. The maximum loan term is 30 years. There is a maximum loan amount that is different for high-cost and low-cost areas. These loan limits may change frequently, so you should check with a lender for the current limits. The Section 245 GPM program currently has several different plans that provide different schedules for increasing the loan payment. Each plan differs in terms of the amount of the increase each year and the number of years to reach the maximum payment amount:

	% Yearly Increase	Years to Reach Maximum Payment
Plan I	2.5%	5
Plan II	5%	5
Plan III	7.5%	5
Plan IV	2%	10
Plan V	3%	10

Of these plans, Plan III is the most common.

203(B)—STANDARD LOAN PROGRAM

Now that we have looked briefly at the types of loan programs available through the FHA, let's look at the characteristics of the basic loan insurance program, the Section 203(b) loan program.

Loan Insurance

The 203(b) loan program promotes home ownership by providing insurance for loans on residential real estate. The FHA does not loan money. It insures loans made by primary lenders against losses due to default. Here's how the FHA loan insurance program works:

• The borrower holding an FHA-insured loan defaults on the loan.

• The lender forecloses.

• The property is sold.

• If the proceeds of the sale are less than the outstanding balance on the loan, the FHA pays the lender the difference.

To pay for losses such as these, the FHA charges all borrowers a MIP on FHA-insured loans. In 1991, the FHA began requiring borrowers to pay an up-front payment at closing and monthly payments over a period of years to cover the MIP. However, the regulations governing the payment of the MIP have been subject to frequent change over the past few years. Therefore, you may want to contact your lender to keep up-to-date on the MIP and its payment. The up-front and monthly MIP payments depend on the LTV and the term of the loan.

For example:

LTV	30-Year Loans	15-Year Loans
Below 90%	1.50% up front plus 0.5% monthly	1.50% up front no monthly premium
90%–95%	1.50% up front plus 0.5% monthly	1.50% up front plus 0.25% monthly
over 95%	1.50% up front plus 0.5% monthly	1.50% up front plus 0.25% monthly

Cash Investment

All FHA-insured loans require a cash investment, which includes the down payment. The minimum down payment required on an FHA-insured loan is typically less than that required for a conventional loan, which is one of the major advantages of an FHA-insured loan for the buyer. Depending on the situation, the borrower may be allowed to purchase a home with a total-cash investment as low as 3 percent of the sales price or appraised value, whichever is less.

Loan Amount

The maximum loan amount on an FHA-insured loan is set by the FHA. The maximum amount differs for high-cost and low-cost areas and varies from county to county. The loan limits may vary frequently, so you should contact a lender for assistance when dealing with FHA-insured loan amounts.

Another distinguishing feature of FHA-insured loans is that the FHA allows the loan amount to be based on the appraised value (or sales price) *plus* a percentage of the estimated closing costs. This allows the buyer to finance part of the closing costs and pay the costs over the life of the loan rather than having to pay cash for those costs at closing. The formula that the FHA uses for determining the loan amount when the buyer finances all or part of the closing costs has been changed several times in recent years and currently involves a fairly complex set of calculations. However, you should remember that the minimum cash investment the borrower can make is 3 percent of the sales price or appraised value, whichever is less.

The LTV for an FHA-insured loan varies depending on the amount of the loan and whether the property is located in a high-cost area or a low-cost area. The LTV is typically greater than 95 percent. The formula for determining the LTV for a specific situation has changed in recent years and currently involves a fairly complex set of calculations. If you would like additional information about FHA-insured loans, you should contact a lender.

Interest Rate

Prior to December 1983, HUD set the maximum allowable interest rate on FHA-insured loans. The interest rate on FHA-insured loans is now determined by negotiation between each individual borrower and lender, and the rates are affected by market conditions, just as conventional rates are.

Discount Points

Loan discount points may be charged on FHA-insured loans. When discount points are charged on an FHA-insured loan, the points may be paid by either the buyer or the seller, or they may be split between the buyer and seller. Historically, the interest rate on FHA-insured loans has been lower than on comparable conventional loans. Because of this, lenders usually charge a loan discount to increase their yield on the loan to be comparable to a conventional loan with a higher interest rate. The loan discount is charged in the form of discount points, with one point equal to 1 percent of the loan amount.

Maximum Term

The maximum loan term for an FHA-insured loan is 30 years.

Closing Costs

The closing costs on FHA-insured loans generally include the same items as conventional loans. The closing costs are often paid by the seller. However, closing costs may also be paid by the buyer.

Escrow Accounts

All FHA-insured loans require that escrow accounts be established and that monthly payments for taxes and insurance be made into the escrow accounts. As with conventional loans, these escrow accounts are established at closing through the payment of escrow items.

Loan Processing

The time required for processing an FHA-insured loan varies from lender to lender and with market conditions. It usually takes longer to process an FHA-insured loan than a conventional loan.

Appraisal

The property that is financed with an FHA-insured loan must meet certain standards that are specified in the FHA minimum property requirements (MPRs). Whether the property meets these standards is determined by an appraisal of the property. Appraisals for property on FHA-insured loans are conducted by fee appraisers, which are FHA-approved independent appraisers who conduct appraisals for a fee. An appraisal made for an FHA-insured loan, serves two purposes:

1. It establishes the value of the property for loan purposes.
2. It serves as a conditional commitment to the borrower.

The *conditional commitment* means that the FHA is making a commitment to the borrower to insure a loan on the property *as long as the borrower qualifies for the loan* under the lender's qualifying requirements. The first purpose of the appraisal is to determine the reasonable value for the property. The appraisal for an FHA-insured loan is ordered by the lender who will make the loan, not the borrower. FHA charges an appraisal fee, which must be paid in advance when the appraisal is ordered. The fee must be paid in cash. No form of credit is allowed by either the buyer or seller. Once the value of the property is determined and the conditional commitment is issued, the maximum amount that can be insured by the FHA on that property is set. The conditional commitment will also specify any repairs that must be made to the property before a loan will be insured by the FHA. The repairs must be sufficient to bring the property in compliance with the minimum property requirements.

When an FHA appraisal is ordered, the results of the appraisal will be given only to the lender, not the borrower. The appraisal is good for a specific period of time as follows:

- Existing properties—The appraisal is valid for 6 months.
- Proposed construction—The appraisal is valid for 12 months.

When a buyer seeks to obtain financing that is insured by the FHA, the sales contract is usually contingent on an FHA appraisal greater than or equal to the sales price. If such a contingency exists but the appraised value is less than the sales price in the signed contract, the buyer has four options:

1. Void the contract and request a return of the earnest money.
2. Pay the difference in the appraised value and the sales price in cash.
3. Renegotiate the sales price with the seller so that it does not exceed the appraised value.
4. Request a reconsideration of the FHA appraisal.

Let's look at some of these in more detail.

The borrower may pay more for a property than the FHA appraisal, but the total amount of the price above the allowable loan amount must be paid in cash. (Second mortgages are rarely approved by the FHA.) For example, a house is appraised for $60,000 and the allowable loan amount is $57,500. If the buyer pays $60,000 for the house, the down payment is $2,500. If the buyer pays $65,000 for the house, the down payment must be at least $7,500 ($65,000 − $57,500). While this is a possible solution, it is not used often, because few people are willing to pay more than the appraised value. The borrower may also request that the appraisal be reconsidered. If this is done, the borrower must have a basis for a claim that the appraisal is too low, in the form of information on comparable properties in the same area. The information on these comparables must include several specific items that are beyond the scope of this course. Consult the FHA when dealing with a case such as this.

Restrictions

There are certain restrictions that apply to FHA-insured loans.

First, the buyer generally must have cash for the entire down payment; however, in rare cases, the FHA may allow a second mortgage at the time the loan is made, but this is possible only with the knowledge and consent of the FHA. After the loan is made, second mortgages may be added by the owner or by a later buyer who assumes the loan. Periodically, there may even be a program available allowing the seller, or some other party, to make the down payment.

The second type of restriction is in the clauses allowed in the loan:

- Prepayment penalties are prohibited by law.
- The loan may contain a prepayment clause, but the clause must not contain a penalty for prepayment.
- Due on sale clauses are also prohibited.

Because due on sale clauses are not allowed in FHA-insured loans, this means these loans are assumable. However, changes have placed limits on the assumption of FHA-insured loans. Let's look at these changes next.

In the past, anyone could assume an FHA-insured loan without qualifying. However, changes in the regulations now require that the buyer qualify for the loan under certain conditions:

- For loans made prior to December 15, 1989, a buyer is *not* required to qualify to assume the loan.
- For loans made after December 15, 1989, a buyer is required to qualify to assume the loan.

VA LOANS (NONCONVENTIONAL)

The Department of Veterans Affairs (VA), formerly known as the Veterans Administration, is also a U.S. government agency that provides assistance in the financing of housing. It was established by the federal government as an independent agency by the Serviceman's Readjustment Act of 1944, also called the GI Bill of Rights, and commonly referred to as the GI Bill. It was enacted to provide assistance to veterans who served in World War II and their surviving spouses.

The VA promotes home ownership for eligible veterans of military service by providing loan guarantees to lenders. The guarantee is different from an insurance program such as the FHA in that losses are funded directly out of federal tax funds. Because guarantee funds come directly from tax funds, no insurance premium is paid by anyone.

VA loans are guaranteed, not insured. Here's how the guarantee works:

- The veteran borrower defaults on the VA loan.
- The lender forecloses.
- The property is sold.
- If the proceeds from the sale are less than the outstanding balance on the loan, the VA pays the difference, *up to certain limits,* which are covered next.

Coaching Tips: **The VA also has the option to buy the property from the lender and market the property itself.**

The limits on the amount of VA guarantee are as follows:

- Loan amount of $45,000 or less: 50 percent of the loan amount is guaranteed.
- Loan amount greater than $45,000 up to $144,000: 40 percent of the loan amount is guaranteed or $36,000, whichever is less, but not less than $22,500.
- Loan amount greater than $144,000: 25 percent of the loan amount is guaranteed up to the maximum guarantee of $104,250.

The guarantee covers losses not recovered by foreclosure sale. The loan can be for any amount. A veteran's **entitlement** is the amount of guarantee she is eligible to receive on a guaranteed loan. The maximum entitlement is $104,250 (the maximum guarantee). The veteran may use all, or only part, of her entitlement in a given transaction. If she uses only part of the entitlement, and sells the home by assumption without paying off the original loan, she may use the remaining entitlement on another home (the amount of veteran's full entitlement less the amount already used). If she sells the home and pays off the original VA loan, the full entitlement is restored, and may be used to buy another home.

Maximum Loan Amount

There is no maximum amount for a VA loan set by law. In general, however, lenders will not loan more than four times the guaranteed amount, or $417,000 (4 × $104,250). The veteran may buy a home for more than $417,000 with a VA loan, but the lender will require a down payment, usually 25 percent of the amount above $417,000.

Down Payment

One of the most distinguishing characteristics of a VA loan is that no down payment is required. (The LTV is equal to 100 percent.) Note, however, that a veteran *may* pay a down payment if he chooses to do so. The veteran must also qualify for the payments on a VA loan as on any other loan.

Term and Interest Rate

The maximum term for a VA loan is 30 years. The VA used to set a maximum allowable interest rate for VA loans. However, the VA no longer sets a maximum rate. The interest rate on a VA loan is now a matter of negotiation between the veteran and the lender, just as it is for FHA loans.

Discount Points

Historically, the interest rate on VA loans has been below the prevailing market rate for conventional loans, and VA loans have required the payment of what is called a loan discount. A loan discount is actually prepaid interest that raises the yield on the loan to the lender. The amount of the loan discount is expressed as discount points, or simply points. One discount point is equal to 1 percent of the loan amount. Historically, to protect the veteran's interest, the VA would not allow the veteran to pay the discount points on a VA loan, except in cases of refinancing. However, this has changed, and the veteran is now allowed to pay the discount points. With a VA loan, discount points may be paid by the veteran, or they may be paid by others such as the seller or a builder as well.

Closing Costs

The closing costs on a VA loan generally include the same items as a conventional loan. The closing costs may be paid by either the buyer or seller, and quite often they are paid by the seller.

Funding Fee

VA-guaranteed loans usually require the payment of a funding fee when the loan is originated. The funding fee is paid into a guarantee and indemnity fund, which is used to offset claims under the guarantee program. The amount of the funding fee depends on the amount of down payment made by the veteran as follows:

Down Payment	Funding Fee
No down payment	2.00 percent of loan amount
5 percent down payment	1.50 percent of loan amount
10 percent down payment	1.25 percent of loan amount

These amounts are for first-time users. Subsequent loans have a higher funding fee requirement. These funding fee amounts are for regular veterans; amounts are higher for individuals who have served in the military reserves. The funding fee can be paid by either the buyer or seller. The amount of the funding fee can be included in the loan amount and paid from the loan proceeds. The funding fee may be waived if the veteran has a service-connected disability. Like discount points or closing costs, the funding fee on a VA loan may be paid by either the buyer or seller.

Escrow Account

The monthly payments on a VA loan must include an amount that is paid into an escrow account to cover the annual property taxes and homeowner's insurance. The escrow account is established at closing when the borrower is required to pay several monthly escrow payments in advance. The amount of payment required varies with the time of year the closing occurs. After closing, the borrower must pay an amount into the escrow account each month, along with the principal and interest on the mortgage payment. The amount of the monthly escrow payment for taxes and insurance is equal to 1/12 of the total annual property tax and insurance bills. When these escrow payments are included in the monthly mortgage payment, the loan payments are referred to as PITI payments; PITI stands for principal, interest, taxes, and insurance. This is also known as a budget mortgage or budget payment.

Veteran's Liability

If a veteran defaults on a VA loan, she is liable to the VA for any losses the VA must pay as a result of the default. If another buyer assumes a VA loan, the veteran remains liable for any losses (unless she is released by the VA). If another *veteran* assumes a VA loan, it is possible to transfer the VA entitlement and the liability for VA losses to the new buyer, thus freeing up the original veteran's entitlement. This can be done only with VA approval. As on FHA loans, there are certain restrictions on VA loans.

VA loans may not include a prepayment penalty. Additionally, VA loans may not contain an alienation (due on sale) clause, so they can be assumed with no increase in the interest rate. Most VA loans made prior to March 1, 1988, can be assumed by any buyer without qualifying. However, for VA loans made on or after March 1, 1988, the VA requires that buyers qualify when assuming the loans.

Appraisal

A property that is financed with a VA loan must meet certain standards set by the VA. An appraisal of the property determines whether or not those standards are met. The appraisal must be conducted by a VA-approved fee appraiser. The VA appraisal report is called a certificate of reasonable value (CRV). An appraisal made for property on a VA loan serves three purposes:

1. It determines the acceptability of the property for a VA loan.
2. It establishes the value of the property for loan purposes.
3. It identifies any repairs that might be needed to qualify for a VA loan.

The value established by the appraisal is the maximum loan amount that can be loaned on a 100 percent VA-guaranteed loan. The loan amount cannot be greater than the appraised value in the CRV. To obtain a VA appraisal, the veteran requests the appraisal through the lender who will make the loan. The lender then requests the appraisal in writing from the VA. The VA charges an appraisal fee, which must be paid in advance when the appraisal is ordered. The fee must be paid in cash. No form of credit is allowed by either the buyer or seller. A VA appraisal is good for a specific period of time as follows:

• Existing properties—The appraisal is valid for 6 months.
• Proposed construction—The appraisal is valid for 12 months.

When a buyer seeks to obtain VA financing, the sales contract is usually contingent on a VA appraisal greater than or equal to the sales price. When such a contingency exists and the appraised value is less than the sales price in the signed contract, the buyer has four options:

1. Void the contract and request a return of the earnest money.
2. Pay the difference in the appraised value and the sales price in cash.
3. Renegotiate the sales price with the seller so that it does not exceed the appraised value.
4. Request a reconsideration of the VA appraisal.

Let's look at some of these in more detail.

The borrower may pay more for a property than the VA appraisal, but the total amount of the price above the appraised value must be paid in *cash*. (Second mortgages are *not* allowed if the sales price exceeds the appraised value.) For example, a house is appraised for $104,250, which is the maximum loan amount on a 100 percent loan. If the price of the house is $109,250, the veteran must make a down payment of at least $5,000 ($109,250 − $104,250). While this is a possible solution, it is not often used because few people are willing to pay more than the appraised value. The borrower may also request that the appraisal be reconsidered. If this is done, the borrower must have a basis for a claim that the appraisal is too low, in the form of information on three comparable properties in the same area. The information on these comparables must include several specific items that are beyond the scope of this course. Consult the lender when dealing with a case such as this.

Eligible Properties

VA-guaranteed loans may be used to finance loans on residential property for one to four families that will be occupied by the veteran. They may *not* be used by investors to finance rental property. In general, the LTV can be 100 percent for a VA loan, which means that the veteran is not required to make a down payment. However, in some situations, a lower LTV is required (meaning the veteran must make a down payment).

The VA does not permit loans to exceed the appraised value of the home. If the sales price exceeds the appraised value, the difference must be paid in cash. The VA does not set a maximum loan amount. However, in general, lenders will not loan more than four times the amount of the VA guarantee available to the veteran. (The amount of the veteran's guarantee is also called the veteran's entitlement.) Thus, if the veteran's entitlement is $104,250, the maximum loan on which the lender will allow an LTV of 100 percent is $417,000 (4 × $104,250). The amount of entitlement varies with the loan amount and has been increased by the VA over the years. To obtain current guarantee amounts, contact the VA or a lender who provides VA loans.

ASSUMPTION METHODS

In order to finance a property that is being purchased, a buyer can assume the seller's existing loan. In this situation, the buyer usually pays the seller a down payment equal to the seller's equity in the property and agrees to take over the seller's mortgage loan. There are actually two slightly different legal methods of doing this. The difference in the methods is small but very important. These two methods are called:

1. Assuming and agreeing to pay a loan
2. Taking (the property) subject to an existing loan

Assuming and Agreeing to Pay a Loan

This is the most common method of assuming a loan. In this method, the *purchaser* becomes ultimately liable for the payment of the loan after it is assumed. If the purchaser defaults, the lender will foreclose on the seller. If there is a deficiency after the property is sold (the property sells for less than the balance owed), the seller can then obtain a judgment against the purchaser for the amount of the deficiency. In some cases, the seller may sign a loan modification agreement with the lender that makes the purchaser personally liable for the payment of the debt, even without a judgment by the seller.

Taking Subject to an Existing Loan

In taking subject to an existing loan, the purchaser *does not* become liable for the payment of the debt as he does under an assumption and agreement to pay.

If the purchaser states that he wants to purchase by taking subject to the existing loan, you should do the following:

- Inform the seller that the purchaser will not be liable for repayment of the loan.
- Seek competent legal advice to obtain additional information about the legal problems involved in this situation.

There are other potential problems you should be aware of when a purchaser wants to purchase property by assuming a loan, such as limitations imposed by other clauses in the loan and a changing loan balance.

Limitations from Other Clauses

In many situations, other clauses in the seller's loan may affect the ability to assume the loan or the conditions required to assume it. For example, an alienation (due on sale) clause may specify the following:

- The loan may not be assumed and must be paid in full if transferred to someone else.
- The loan may be assumed, but the interest rate increases.
- The loan may be assumed, but the purchaser must qualify (meet the lender's financial requirements) to assume the loan.

Changing Loan Balance

A loan assumption is often troublesome because the loan balance on the assumed loan changes between the signing of a sales contract and the closing of the sale. One problem occurs when the purchaser agrees to buy the property at a fixed price by assuming a loan. The difference in the selling price and the remaining balance is the amount of cash that the buyer must pay the seller. The buyer often doesn't realize that the amount of cash that she will have to pay may increase if the loan does not close right away. Let's look at why this happens.

A buyer agrees to buy a property for $100,000 by assuming the seller's loan. At the time the contract is signed, the situation looks like this:

Sales price	$100,000
Remaining balance	−80,000
Cash required	$20,000

By the time the sale is closed, the situation may look like this:

Sales price	$100,000
Remaining balance	−79,000
Cash required	$21,000

The difference in the cash required at closing, which the buyer did not expect, results from the fact that the payments made on the loan between the signing of the sales contract and the closing date reduced the remaining principal. (The amount of reduction used in this example is larger than normal to illustrate the point.) Because of this situation, there are two ways a loan assumption can be handled:

1. A loan assumption with price to control
2. A loan assumption with cash to control

The situation described above is an example of a loan assumption with price to control. In other words, *price to control* means that the selling price will be set, and the selling price (along with the changing loan balance) will *control* the amount of cash to be paid by the buyer.

In a loan assumption with *cash to control,* the buyer and seller do not agree on a fixed sales price. Instead, they agree that the buyer will pay the seller a fixed amount of cash and assume the remaining loan balance as of the date of closing.

There is no right or wrong way to structure a loan assumption. Either one of these two methods can be used. The method to use in any particular situation can be negotiated between the seller and buyer. If you have a buyer who wants to purchase property using a loan assumption, be sure to explain to both the buyer and seller the impact of each of these methods so no one is surprised at closing.

In many cases, when a buyer assumes a seller's loan, the seller's equity is greater than the amount the buyer has available for a down payment. In this situation, a seller may accept a note (a promissory note) as part of the payment for the seller's equity. This type of purchase is referred to as a seller taking a second mortgage. The loan (note) is referred to as a purchase money mortgage. This kind of financing arrangement can be used in either one of the two types of loan assumptions discussed above.

Coaching Tips: If the first mortgage note on the property being sold is an uninsured conventional mortgage, the lender may not allow the seller to take a second mortgage when the loan is assumed if the remaining loan balance is more than 80 percent of the current appraised value.

When to Use an Assumption

When considering the use of a loan assumption as a method of financing, it is important to consider if a loan assumption is appropriate. The first step when considering an assumption is to *always* determine from the lender whether the loan can be assumed. For most conventional loans made in the last several years, a loan may be assumed *as long as the buyer qualifies* for the loan just as she would on a new loan. However, never assume that this is the case. You should obtain information from the lender about the assumption of the loan when you obtain a listing on the property.

For loans that can be assumed, the most important factor that affects the ability to sell a home with a loan assumption is the LTV for the outstanding balance on the loan. The higher the ratio, the lower the down payment, and therefore the buyer will likely want to assume the loan. Properties that have assumable loans with low seller's equity in the property (low down payment required) should be relatively easy to sell. As the LTV decreases, and the required down payment increases, the marketability of the home using a loan assumption decreases. Some of the conditions under which a buyer is more likely to consider purchasing a home using a loan assumption include the following:

• The seller will finance part of the selling price.

• Mortgage money is not available.

• The buyer is unable to get a new loan.

• The property has declined in value.

• There is a difference in interest rate.

Let's look at each of these conditions briefly.

One factor that can substantially impact the likelihood of selling a property with a loan assumption is the owner's willingness to finance part of the purchase. This is particularly true if the LTV is low, thus requiring a large down payment. The larger the down payment required, the more difficult it is to sell with a loan assumption. However, if the seller is willing to finance part of the down payment, the loan assumption becomes a much more attractive financing alternative.

Loan assumptions also become very attractive financing alternatives during conditions of tight money supply. When new loan money is not readily available, buyers have fewer options for financing, and loan assumptions can offer an opportunity to obtain a loan that could not be obtained otherwise.

In some cases, a borrower may be in a position to afford a loan, but for some reason, cannot qualify for a new loan. For example, the borrower may be recently self-employed and not have adequate income verification to qualify. In this situation, a loan assumption may be the borrower's only opportunity to obtain a loan.

In some special cases, a loan assumption may be the best financing alternative because the value of the property has declined, and a new loan could not be obtained for an amount greater than the existing loan balance.

Finally, loan assumptions are often an attractive financing alternative when they have an interest rate that is substantially below the current market rate for new loans. However, most conventional loans are no longer assumable at the rate at which they were initially made. Most conventional loans now include an alienation clause that permits the lender to raise the interest rate if the loan is assumed.

Closing Requirements

The closing process for a loan assumption is faster and cheaper than the closing process for a new loan. On a loan assumption, the lender will typically require the following items:

- A loan transfer fee—This fee is substantially below the cost of obtaining a new loan.
- Warranty deed—A copy of the warranty deed conveying the property to the buyer must usually be supplied to the lender at closing.
- Insurance—A fire insurance policy in the buyer's name must also be supplied to the lender at closing.
- Escrow account—The buyer and seller must agree for the seller to "sell" the escrow account to the buyer or transfer it to the buyer in lieu of prorating the escrow funds.

Advantages and Disadvantages

There are a number of potential advantages available to both the buyer and seller with a loan assumption. The advantages to the seller include the following:

- The costs of closing the loan are substantially lower, so the seller might be able to sell the home for less than with a new loan, and still realize the same profit.
- The lender might agree to release the seller from liability under the loan under some conditions.
- If both the seller and buyer are veterans, the seller might be able to transfer the entitlement on the property to the buyer, thus freeing up his own eligibility for another VA loan. This requires VA approval.

The advantages of a loan assumption to a buyer include the following:

- The possibility of a lower interest rate, with savings in interest expense, if the interest rate on the assumed loan is below the current market rate.
- Substantially lower closing costs than on a new loan.
- Less time to close because of the reduced requirements for loan documents and processing.
- Less personal liability in some cases. If the borrower takes the loan subject to the existing loan, as discussed earlier in this chapter, the buyer has no personal liability for the repayment of the loan.

Conversely, there are certain disadvantages of a loan assumption to both buyer and seller:

- Buyer disadvantages—A loan assumption might require a large down payment. Also, the buyer may not be able to offer a loan assumption when the property is sold to a future buyer. The longer the loan is held after assumption, the lower the loan-to-value ratio becomes, increasing the size of the required down payment. If the property increases in value, this problem becomes even greater.

- Seller disadvantages—Unless the seller is released from liability when the loan is assumed, the seller remains ultimately liable for the loan until it is paid off. If the new owner defaults, the lender may sue the original owner as well as the owner in default. In addition, a seller may have difficulty obtaining a new loan if she is still liable for a loan that has been assumed.

QUALIFYING THE BUYER
Underwriting

Underwriting is a term you will hear often when working with buyers that are trying to obtain a loan. Underwriting is the process of evaluating two things:

1. The value of the property as collateral for a loan.
2. The buyer's ability to make the down payment and repay the loan.

The purpose of evaluating these two items is to determine whether the lender is willing to make a loan to the buyer, and if so, the amount of the loan the lender is willing to make. Before we look at the process of underwriting, let's look at how the standards for underwriting are determined.

There are three primary sets of guidelines you will encounter:

1. The FHLMC or Freddie Mac guidelines
2. The FHA guidelines
3. The VA guidelines

Let's look at each set of guidelines in more detail.

Freddie Mac Guidelines

You will most likely encounter the guidelines developed by Freddie Mac. The Freddie Mac guidelines were developed for use with any loans purchased by Freddie Mac from a lender in the primary mortgage market. Because Freddie Mac is the largest purchaser of conventional loans in the secondary mortgage market, these guidelines are often used lenders when making conventional loans. It is important to understand that when a lender in the primary mortgage market makes a conventional loan, the lender is free to use any underwriting guidelines it chooses. However, if a lender desires to sell a mortgage in the secondary mortgage market, the lender must make the loan under the guidelines required by the secondary market. For loans sold to Fannie Mae or Freddie Mac, the guidelines developed by Freddie Mac must be used in making a conventional loan. These guidelines are often called the FNMA/FHLMC guidelines, because they are used by Fannie Mae as well. Any loan approved under these guidelines is called a **conforming loan**. Because of the requirement of using the FNMA/FHLMC guidelines for loans to be sold in the secondary market, most lenders have adopted those guidelines for all their conventional loans.

There are four major factors used to qualify a buyer under the FNMA/FHLMC guidelines:

1. The borrower's income
2. The borrower's net worth and available assets
3. The credit history of the borrower
4. Documentation of relevant information

The last two factors, the credit history of the borrower and the documentation of information, are generally the same to qualify for all loans. The first two factors, the borrower's income and the borrower's net worth and available assets, will be covered next.

Borrower's Income

The borrower's income is a major factor in evaluating a loan application because that income largely determines the borrower's ability to repay the loan. In evaluating the borrower's income, the lender will determine the amount of the borrower's stable monthly income. This amount is the borrower's base monthly income (for both husband and wife), plus any acceptable secondary sources of income, such as bonuses, commissions paid in addition to regular income, overtime pay, part-time employment, Social Security payments, interest earned on savings and/or investments, and alimony or child support. In order to determine whether secondary sources of financing will be accepted in evaluating the borrower's ability to repay a loan, the lender will evaluate the reliability of the income as well as the extent to which it will likely continue on an ongoing basis. When properly documented, secondary sources of income, such as bonuses, overtime pay, commissions paid on a regular basis, and part-time employment, are usually acceptable as part of the borrower's qualifying income. Other secondary income, such as alimony and child support payments, may or may not be acceptable, depending on the reliability of the payments, the qualifications of the person making the payments, and the time period over which they will be paid. Some sources of secondary income, such as unemployment or welfare payments, are almost never allowed as part of the borrower's stable monthly income because they are considered to be temporary income and, therefore, not reliable over time.

The borrower's employment record is also used to evaluate the borrower's income. Generally, the longer a borrower has been continuously employed by the same employer, the more favorable the record. Frequent changes in employment are generally perceived as a negative factor, unless they demonstrate a pattern of improvement in employment. The anticipated stability of continued employment is also a factor, so the identity and stability of the employer may also be considered. The final element in evaluating the borrower's income is the use of financial ratios to directly evaluate the borrower's ability to repay a loan. Under the FNMA/FHLMC guidelines (and the FHA and VA guidelines), there are two ratios used for evaluation purposes:

1. The ratio of the mortgage payment to stable monthly income (which is also known as the ratio to monthly housing obligations)
2. The ratio of all installment debts to stable monthly income (which is also known as the ratio to monthly total obligations)

The first ratio is that of the monthly mortgage payment to the stable monthly income. Under FNMA/FHLMC guidelines, the amount of the mortgage payment should not exceed 28 percent of the borrower's stable monthly income. For example, if the borrower's stable monthly income is $2,000, the mortgage payment should not exceed $560, which is 28 percent of $2,000. If the mortgage payment exceeds 28 percent of the stable monthly income, the borrower's income is not considered adequate for the repayment of the loan.

The second ratio is that of the borrower's total monthly installment debt payments to the stable monthly income. Under FNMA/FHLMC guidelines, the amount of the total monthly debt payments should not exceed 36 percent of the stable monthly income. For example, if the borrower's stable monthly income is $2,000, the total debt payments should not exceed $720, which is 36 percent of $2,000. If the total debt payments exceed 36 percent of the stable monthly income, the borrower's income is not considered adequate to meet all debt requirements and repay the loan. This second ratio between total monthly installment debt payments and the stable monthly income is often referred to as the total debt service ratio.

Net Worth and Assets

The second major factor considered in qualifying the buyer is the buyer's net worth and the assets she has available to make the down payment and to provide adequate reserves. The buyer's net worth is the difference between her total assets and her total liabilities. It is a value that provides a good indicator of the borrower's overall financial strength. If a borrower has a high net worth, it can offset some weakness in one or both of the ratios just covered. The borrower must have enough cash among her assets to pay the down payment required on a loan. The most common type of conventional loan requires a down payment of 20 percent of the purchase price, or the appraised value, whichever is less. Conventional loans may also be made that require only a 10 percent or 5 percent down payment in some cases. These loans require the payment of private mortgage insurance. When a substantial part of the borrower's net worth is in the form of liquid assets, such as savings, money market certificates, etc., it provides additional strength to the borrower's ability to repay a loan because these assets are readily available to meet financial demands in emergencies. Under FNMA/FHLMC guidelines, the borrower is required to have available a minimum amount of highly liquid assets (cash or its equivalent) equal to mortgage payments for two months. This amount must be available over and above the amount needed for the down payment and any costs of closing the loan.

FHA Guidelines

Income Ratios

On April 13, 2005, HUD increased the allowable debt ratio for manually underwritten loans from 29/31 to 31/43. For an FHA loan, the ratio of the monthly mortgage payment to the stable monthly income should not exceed 31 percent. The ratio of the total monthly installment debts to the stable monthly income should not exceed 43 percent.

The debt ratios represent the relationship between an individual's income and his expenses. These ratios are generally seen as two numbers like 31 over 43 or 31/43. The first number, 31, represents the relationship between the borrower's income and his new housing expense of rent and/or PITI (principal, interest, taxes, insurance, and/or any homeowner dues).

The second number, 43, represents the total monthly payment obligations, including housing expenses and all other debt such as credit cards, loans, and child support.

Down Payment

The amount of the down payment on an FHA loan is equal to the sales price less the loan amount. The formula that the FHA uses to determine the loan amount has changed several times in recent years and currently involves a complex set of calculations. Because of this, we will not cover the calculations in this course. However, you should remember that the minimum cash investment the borrower can make is 3 percent of the sales price or appraised value, whichever is less.

VA Guidelines

Underwriting

The guidelines to qualify for a VA loan are considerably different from the qualification guidelines for FNMA/FHLMC and FHA loans. For example, the VA considers what is called the residual income available after taxes are deducted. The specifics of qualifying for VA loans will not be covered in this course. You should consult your broker or a lender when qualifying a buyer for a VA loan. In addition to the financial ratios used to qualify buyer for a VA loan, it is important to determine whether a buyer is eligible for a VA loan. Generally, a buyer who is eligible for a VA loan is a veteran who has served one of the following:

- A minimum of 90 days extended active duty in war time, including World War II, Korea, and Vietnam
- 181 days in peacetime prior to September 8, 1980
- 2 years in peacetime after September 7, 1980

There is a list of specific dates from September 16, 1940, through the present and the number of days of service required during those times in order to qualify for a VA loan. You are not required to know this list of dates and the amount of service required. However, you should be aware that the days of service differ for different periods. You should consult your broker or a lender designated by your broker for a determination of eligibility.

There are two remaining factors important in the underwriting process, the credit history of the borrower and the documentation of the information supplied to the lender. The requirements for each of these are the same for all qualification guidelines.

Credit History

The borrower's credit history is an important factor in determining whether the borrower qualifies for a loan. A buyer who has consistently met his credit obligations on a timely basis is considered a good risk for a loan. The borrower must show all his current debts on the loan application. If a borrower attempts to hide a debt by failing to list it on the loan application, the loan may be denied. The lender will also obtain the borrower's credit report from a credit reporting agency, and occasionally will contact the borrower's creditors.

Documentation

The last factor in the underwriting process is documenting the information provided to the lender. There are two categories of documentation that may be required, depending on the nature and amount of the loan:

1. Regular documentation
2. Alternative documentation

Regular Documentation

Regular documentation refers to the level of documentation usually required on loans with a loan-to-value ratio of 80 percent or higher. Under regular documentation requirements, the lender will require at least three sources of documentation. The first is a verification of employment (VOE) form filled out by the borrower's employer that verifies the borrower's salary and length of employment. The second is a verification of deposit (VOD) form filled out by all financial institutions where the borrower has an account. The purpose of this form is to verify the availability of the cash needed to close the loan. The third is a credit report, which the lender will request from a credit reporting agency. Both the verification of employment and verification of deposit forms must be mailed by the employer or bank to the lender. These verifications may not be hand delivered or mailed by the borrower or a real estate agent.

Alternative Documentation

Alternative documentation is often available on loans of up to 90 percent of the sales price. Under alternative documentation, the verification of employment may be replaced by two current pay stubs and the borrower's W-2 tax form for the previous year. These are supplied to the lender by the borrower. The verification of deposit may be replaced by the borrower's three most recent bank statements, which are supplied to the lender by the borrower. With alternative documentation, the lender also requires a full credit report, just as with regular documentation.

Appraisal

There is one final documentation requirement for all loans. All loans require that the lender have a current appraisal of the property so the lender can establish the property's value. Regardless of the loan type, mortgage loans tend to be originated based on the amount that is the lesser of the purchase price or the appraised value.

Maximum Loan Amount

Another underwriting topic we need to cover is how the maximum loan amount for which a borrower can qualify is determined. Often, it is important for a buyer to know the maximum size loan she can obtain. This is determined by the following factors:

- The maximum amount of cash available for the down payment (and any other closing costs required)
- The maximum monthly loan payment the borrower can qualify for

These factors may limit the amount of the loan that a buyer might obtain. For example, a buyer might have $10,000 available as a down payment. The maximum loan amount he could obtain depends on the type of loan. On a conventional loan, the maximum loan amount would be determined by the loan-to-value ratio:

- 95 percent loan—the maximum loan amount would be $190,000
- 90 percent loan—the maximum loan amount would be $90,000
- 80 percent loan—the maximum loan amount would be $40,000

With any of these conventional loans, the maximum loan amount might be reduced by the buyer's ability to qualify for monthly payments. For example, if a buyer made a down payment on a 90 percent loan of $90,000 at an interest rate of 9.5 percent for 30 years, she would have to qualify for monthly payments of $756.77. If the buyer could not qualify for such a payment, the maximum loan amount would be reduced. The maximum amount a buyer can qualify for on a loan may be determined by:

- The cash available for a down payment
- The ability to qualify for the monthly payment

LOAN CHARGES

Charges are incurred when a buyer takes out a loan for real property. The term **closing costs** includes a number of different loan charges that vary from lender to lender. There are two types of closing costs: variable costs and fixed costs. Variable closing costs are those that vary with the amount of the loan. Typically, variable costs are assessed as a percentage of the loan amount. The following are included in variable costs:

- Lender's title insurance
- Origination fees

Fixed closing costs are those that are assessed as a fixed fee and do not vary with the amount of the loan, including:

- Appraisal fee
- Attorney's fees (could also be variable if charged on an hourly basis)

- Credit report fee
- Survey
- Recording fees
- Pictures
- Amortization schedule

Let's take a look at some of the different items included in closing costs.

Variable Costs

Title insurance is a variable cost. The title insurance policy protects the lender against any loss that results from defects in the title. Title insurance that protects the lender is called lender's title insurance or mortgagee title insurance, and is always required by the lender but is not required by law. The buyer may also elect to obtain a purchaser's or fee title insurance policy, which protects against losses due to defects in the title. Unless this type of policy is obtained independently by the buyer, there is no such coverage provided in a typical closing procedure. The fees for title insurance are typically assessed as a specified fee per $1,000 of the loan amount.

Another type of variable closing cost is the **origination fee**. The origination fee is charged by the lender for processing the loan. It covers primarily the administrative costs to do the paperwork on the loan such as filling out forms, and reviewing credit reports and appraisals. Origination fees are usually a percentage of the loan amount. On FHA and VA loans, the origination fee is limited to 1 percent of the loan amount. The origination fee may be paid by the buyer or the seller on all loans, including FHA, VA, and conventional loans.

Fixed Costs

Fixed closing costs include the following:

- Appraisal fee—This fee covers the cost of having the property appraised by a qualified appraiser. The appraisal is conducted so lender can determine if the property provides adequate security for the loan. The buyer or seller may also obtain an independent appraisal of the property if desired, but the fee for such an appraisal is not included in the closing costs.
- Attorney fees—Attorney fees are fees to pay for legal services provided to the lender in closing the loan. The services provided usually include checking the title, preparing the various documents for closing, and conducting the closing meeting itself. Usually the attorney who conducts the closing meeting represents the lender, and the fees for this service are included in the closing costs. The attorney fees are usually a fixed amount ($400 and up).
- Credit report fee—This fee covers the cost of the credit report that the lender uses to evaluate the credit risk posed by the borrower. The seller may also insist on a credit report if his existing loan is assumed or if the seller extends credit to the buyer in the form of a purchase money mortgage.
- Survey—A survey may also be required by a lender; if it is, the fee for the survey is a fixed closing cost. Different lenders have different policies on when they require a survey. Some always require them; some only require a survey when there is a potential problem or for certain types of properties. Always check with a specific lender to determine its policy on surveys. The cost of the survey is determined by the surveyor and varies with the type of survey, size of property, and type of property.

FIGURE 13.4

REAL ESTATE FINANCING PROCESS

- Recording fee—This is a fee charged by the county for recording documents in the public records. These fees are often in the range of $15 to $50.
- Pictures—Some lenders require pictures of the property being financed.
- Amortization schedule—Some lenders provide a printout or chart of the payment schedule, which shows such things as a month-by-month breakdown of interest and principal paid. The cost is usually about $10.

The payment of loan costs is normally the responsibility of the buyer because these costs are associated with obtaining a loan. However, the payment of these costs is negotiable between the buyer and seller, and either or both may pay closing costs. Also, local custom may determine who pays for specific items. Any sales contract should clearly specify who is to pay any or all of the closing costs.

Discount Points

Another fee often paid at closing is discount points. Earlier in this chapter, you learned the definition of discount points and what role they have in the financing process. On conventional, FHA, and VA loans, either the buyer or the seller may pay the discount points. Prior to 1993, the VA required that someone other than the buyer pay the discount points on new VA loans except in cases of refinancing by the veteran. Now, however, the veteran (the buyer) is allowed to pay the discount points on any VA loan. All loan costs may be paid by the buyer or seller on all loans.

There is one additional charge on VA loans—the VA funding fee. This fee is used to fund the expenses of operating the VA. The amount of the fee varies with the amount of the down payment and the military status of the veteran (e.g., active status, veteran, reservist). It may be paid by the buyer or seller. If the veteran is disabled, the funding fee may be waived.

Figure 13.4 summarizes the real estate financing process.

SUMMARY

Loans are originated in the primary mortgage market; these same loans are bought and sold by others in the secondary market. As previously mentioned, the secondary market operations should not be confused with secondary financing on a property.

There are two types of loan options available to qualified borrowers. These options are either conventional mortgages or nonconventional mortgages. While nonconventional mortgages are government guaranteed, conventional mortgages are not. Nonconventional mortgages would include FHA and VA loans.

Points are charged to enhance the yield to the lender. One point represents 1 percent of the loan amount and is considered as prepaid interest.

REVIEW QUESTIONS

1. The majority of the commercial banks in the United States:
   a. Are regulated by the Office of Thrift Supervision.
   b. Are members of the Federal Reserve System (the Fed).
   c. Belong to the Federal Home Loan Bank System.
   d. Are privately owned and are largely unregulated.

2. The definition of a discount rate is:
   a. The prime rate given to a bank's best borrowers.
   b. The interest rate the Fed charges its member banks for borrowing money from the Fed.
   c. The general interest rate the Fed sets for primary lenders.
   d. Interest primary lenders charge borrowers to increase the lenders' profits.

3. When the Fed raises the reserve requirement, the supply of money in the economy:
   a. Remains unchanged.
   b. Decreases.
   c. Increases.
   d. Costs less to borrow.

4. The Fed is selling securities. The supply of money in the economy:
   a. Remains unchanged.
   b. Is decreased.
   c. Is increased.
   d. Costs more to borrow.

5. Fifth Federal Savings and Loan advertises itself as a "Member of the FDIC." This means:
   a. Deposits are insured up to $100,000 per branch location.
   b. Deposits are insured up to $100,000 per account on deposit.
   c. Deposits are insured up to $100,000 per banking institution.
   d. The federal government will replace all deposits if the banking institution fails.

6. The news from the stock market is unusually good, and depositors are withdrawing their money from banks and savings associations in order to buy stocks. This action by depositors has resulted in:
   a. Disintermediation.
   b. A decrease in interest rates.
   c. Intermediation.
   d. More money available for mortgages.

7. The primary mortgage market:
   a. Is regulated by the Federal Home Loan Bank System.
   b. Is regulated by the Fed.
   c. Originates loans with qualified borrowers.
   d. Buys mortgages from lenders.

8. The largest originators of residential real property loans are:
   a. Mortgage bankers.
   b. Mortgage brokers.
   c. Mortgage companies.
   d. Commercial banks.

9. The oldest participant in the secondary market is:
   a. The Federal National Mortgage Association.
   b. The Government National Mortgage Association.
   c. The Federal Home Loan Mortgage Corporation.
   d. The Federal Home Loan Bank System.

10. Which institution acts as a guarantor for mortgage-backed securities that are sold to the general public?
    a. The Federal National Mortgage Association
    b. The Government National Mortgage Association
    c. The Federal Home Loan Mortgage Corporation
    d. The Federal Home Loan Bank System

11. The institution created by Congress for the primary purpose of buying conventional loans from savings associations is:
    a. The Federal National Mortgage Association.
    b. The Government National Mortgage Association.
    c. The Federal Home Loan Mortgage Corporation.
    d. The Federal Housing Administration.

12. A lender charged 6 percent interest for a loan plus two discount points. The approximate yield to the lender is:
    a. 5 ¾ percent.
    b. 6 ¼ percent.
    c. 6 ½ percent.
    d. 7 percent.

13. Ramon has qualified to purchase a new home for $300,000. The loan is a 90 percent conventional loan and the lender is charging 2½ points. What will the points cost Ramon on this loan?
    a. $5,000
    b. $6,000
    c. $6,750
    d. $7,500

14. Which of the following statements is FALSE regarding the FHA 203(b) loan?
    a. The FHA guarantees the loan and sets the interest rates for borrowers.
    b. The FHA insures the loan and the borrower pays for the insurance.
    c. Limits are set by law and depend on the location.
    d. The FHA requires the borrower to make a minimum 3 percent cash investment.

15. Which of the following statements is FALSE regarding the VA loan?
    a. The VA guarantees the loan and there are no loan limits set by law.
    b. The VA loan is so secure to the lender that generally no down payment is required.
    c. The VA can make loans directly to active duty personnel, veterans, and spouses.
    d. The VA regulations state the veteran cannot be charged points on the loan.

16. If a veteran defaults on a VA loan, the maximum guarantee to the lender is:
    a. One-fourth of the value of the home up to $60,000.
    b. One-half of the value of the home up to $60,000.
    c. One-fourth of the value of the home up to $89,912.
    d. One-fourth of the value of the home up to $104,250.

17. The VA loan:
    a. Always contains a due-on-sale clause.
    b. Eligibility is established by the Department of Veteran Affairs.
    c. Cannot be used for refinancing, construction, or repairs.
    d. Cannot be used for improvements to existing homes.

18. The FHA government agency:
    a. Requires the borrower to pay a one-time upfront mortgage insurance premium.
    b. Will process loans to build houses.
    c. Will automatically cancel the mortgage insurance premium on a condo after loan-to-value reaches 78 percent.
    d. Will not authorize adjustable rate mortgages.

# Chapter 14

KEY TERMS

arrears
credit
debit
prorating

LEARNING OBJECTIVES

After completing this lesson, you will be able to:

- Define title closing.
- Identify the types of information included on a closing statement.
- Distinguish between debits and credits.
- Prorate the payment of certain items when completing the settlement statement.
- Describe your duties immediately after a contract is signed.
- Describe your duties in preparing for closing.

Title Closing and Computations

TITLE CLOSING

A title closing is the consummation of a real estate transaction, when the seller delivers title to the buyer in exchange for payment of the purchase price by the buyer.

CLOSING STATEMENTS

When preparing for closing, one of the most important facts to determine is how much money is exchanged between the buyer and seller. There are many items that must be accounted for. For example:

- The seller usually must pay off any existing loans.
- The amount of the property tax bill must be divided proportionately between the buyer and the seller.
- The property may be rented, and any prepaid rent or deposits must be accounted for.
- The buyer usually must make a down payment on new financing.
- The buyer or seller must also pay the costs of taking out the new loan.

In the remainder of this chapter, we will look at how these and other financial items are handled for the closing. For closing, the details of the financial elements of the transaction are summarized in documents called closing statements or settlement statements. Separate closing statements are usually prepared for the seller and the buyer. These documents list all the items to be paid and received by the buyer or seller and give the total amount that the buyer pays and the seller receives when the transaction is completed. On the next few pages you will find a condensed version of a closing statement. For the sake of explanation, both the buyer's and seller's closing statements are combined into one document.

Coaching Tips: **The deposit must appear twice on the closing statement. The deposit is given to the selling agent at the time the offer is tendered. As a result, it is being held in trust by the seller's agent or the closing agent. Therefore, the second place that the deposit would appear would be in the broker's/closing agent section of the statement (not shown here).**

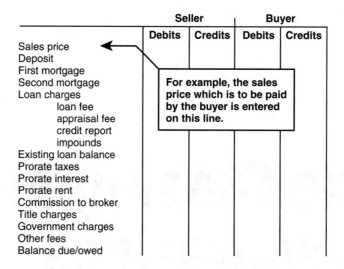

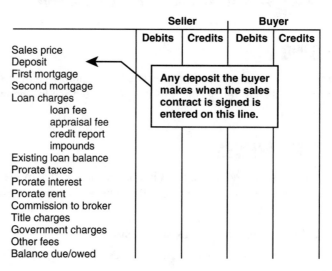

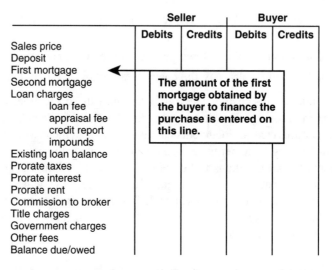

Coaching Tips: **The mortgage must appear twice on the statement as well. When a newly originated loan is acquired through a lending institution, the loan amount is a credit for the buyer on her statement; however, the mortgage would also appear (as in the case of the deposit) in the broker's/closing agent section of the statement (not shown here).**

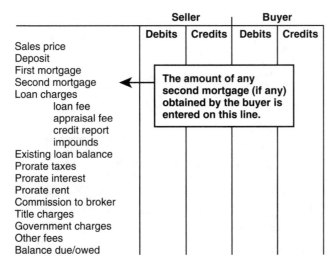

As you already know, the second mortgage is generally seller financing. As such, the seller receives a debit for the amount loaned to the buyer to complete the transaction. The buyer who receives the loan from the seller receives a credit entry.

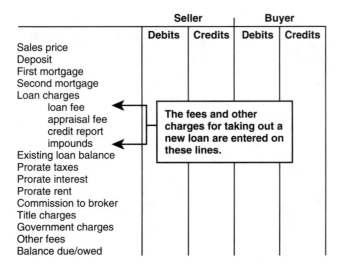

Loan charges are generally expense items that are charged to either the buyer or the seller. In the figure above, the expense items would probably be charged to the buyer because *the benefiting party in relation to an item generally bears the responsibility of paying for that item.*

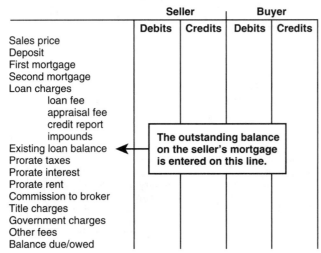

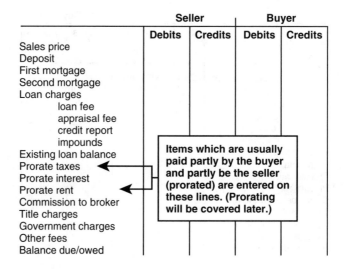

	Seller		Buyer	
	Debits	Credits	Debits	Credits
Sales price				
Deposit				
First mortgage				
Second mortgage				
Loan charges				
loan fee				
appraisal fee				
credit report				
impounds				
Existing loan balance				
Prorate taxes				
Prorate interest				
Prorate rent				
Commission to broker				
Title charges				
Government charges				
Other fees				
Balance due/owed				

Items which are usually paid partly by the buyer and partly be the seller (prorated) are entered on these lines. (Prorating will be covered later.)

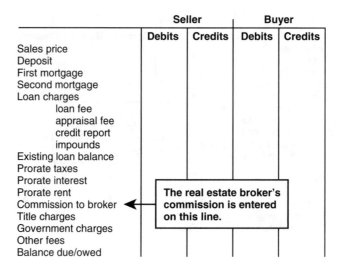

	Seller		Buyer	
	Debits	Credits	Debits	Credits
Sales price				
Deposit				
First mortgage				
Second mortgage				
Loan charges				
loan fee				
appraisal fee				
credit report				
impounds				
Existing loan balance				
Prorate taxes				
Prorate interest				
Prorate rent				
Commission to broker				
Title charges				
Government charges				
Other fees				
Balance due/owed				

The real estate broker's commission is entered on this line.

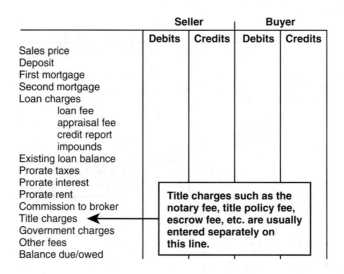

	Seller		Buyer	
	Debits	Credits	Debits	Credits
Sales price				
Deposit				
First mortgage				
Second mortgage				
Loan charges				
loan fee				
appraisal fee				
credit report				
impounds				
Existing loan balance				
Prorate taxes				
Prorate interest				
Prorate rent				
Commission to broker				
Title charges				
Government charges				
Other fees				
Balance due/owed				

Title charges such as the notary fee, title policy fee, escrow fee, etc. are usually entered separately on this line.

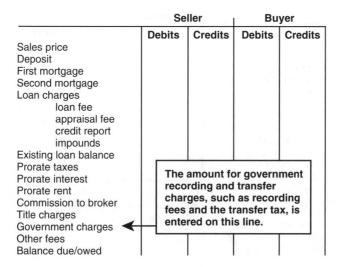

	Seller		Buyer	
	Debits	Credits	Debits	Credits
Sales price				
Deposit				
First mortgage				
Second mortgage				
Loan charges				
loan fee				
appraisal fee				
credit report				
impounds				
Existing loan balance				
Prorate taxes				
Prorate interest				
Prorate rent				
Commission to broker				
Title charges				
Government charges				
Other fees				
Balance due/owed				

The amount for government recording and transfer charges, such as recording fees and the transfer tax, is entered on this line.

State Transfer Taxes

There are three types of state transfer taxes:

1. State documentary stamps (deed)

   - Customarily paid by the seller
   - The formula for calculating the tax is $0.70 per $100 (or any fraction thereof) of the full purchase price

2. State documentary stamps (notes)

   - Customarily paid by the buyer
   - The formula for calculating the tax is $0.35 per $100 (or any fraction thereof) of all new and assumed mortgaged notes (does not apply to *subject to mortgages*)

3. Intangible tax (paid on recorded mortgages)

   - Customarily paid by the buyer (paid only on *new money* that is introduced to the transaction; does not apply to assumed mortgages or subject to mortgages)
   - The formula for calculating the tax is $0.002 (i.e., 2 mills) × new mortgage amount(s)
   - Converting mills to decimals

$$\frac{10}{1000} = \frac{1}{100}$$

	Seller		Buyer	
	Debits	Credits	Debits	Credits
Sales price				
Deposit				
First mortgage				
Second mortgage				
Loan charges				
loan fee				
appraisal fee				
credit report				
impounds				
Existing loan balance				
Prorate taxes				
Prorate interest				
Prorate rent				
Commission to broker				
Title charges				
Government charges				
Other fees				
Balance due/owed				

Other fees, such as survey and pest inspection fees, are entered on this line.

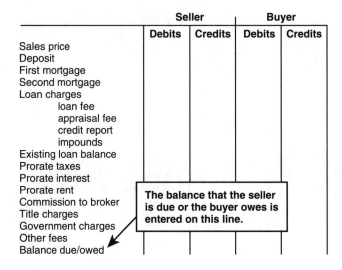

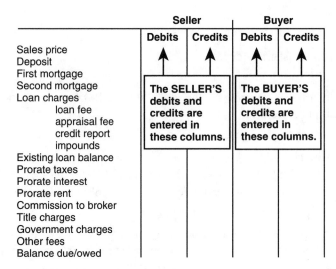

The purpose of completing the closing statements is to account for all details of financial elements of the transaction. There are many parties who have a financial interest in the closing of the transaction, including but not limited to:

- The buyer
- The seller
- The real estate broker(s) involved
- The lender on the seller's existing loan
- The lender on the buyer's new loan
- The escrow company
- The title insurance company

After completing the closing statements, all of these parties will have a clear accounting of the money they are due to receive or the money they must pay. For the buyer and seller, the amount due or owed is shown at the bottom of the statement under "Balance due" or "Balance owed." Let's now look at how the entries on the closing statements are made for each item.

When an item is entered on the closing statement for either the buyer or seller, we must first determine whether the item is a debit or a credit. Note below that both the buyer and seller have columns labeled "Debits" and "Credits" on their sides of the closing statement.

	Seller		Buyer	
	Debits	Credits	Debits	Credits
Sales price				
Deposit				
First mortgage				
Second mortgage				
Loan charges				
loan fee				
appraisal fee				
credit report				
impounds				
Existing loan balance				
Prorate taxes				
Prorate interest				
Prorate rent				
Commission to broker				
Title charges				
Government charges				
Other fees				
Balance due/owed				

A **debit** can best be thought of as a *payment* by someone to someone else. A **credit** is money that is *received* by someone from someone else. To determine who receives a credit or debit on an item, you must establish who owes or who is paying versus who is owed or who is receiving

The party who owes receives an entry in the "Debits" column, while the party who collects the payment receives an entry in the "Credits" column.

Coaching Tips: Think of debits and credits as you would your own personal checkbook. When you receive money (a deposit entry), the bank credits your account and your account balance increases. When you pay a bill and the check is presented to your bank for payment, your checkbook balance is debited or, in other words, results in a balance reduction.

Now, let's look at a typical real estate sales transaction to see which items are debits and which are credits to the buyer and the seller. First, we need to make an assumption that will help us in this situation. To determine the debits and credits on a closing statement, we will *always assume* that the *first step* in *any* transaction is the buyer paying the seller the full sales price in cash. This, of course, will not always be the case, but this assumption will make it much easier to understand debits and credits.

For example, a seller is selling her home to a buyer for $100,000. Remember, we *assume* that the buyer will pay the seller $100,000 in cash, regardless of how the buyer will actually pay for the home. The buyer's first payment of the sales price is entered as *debit* to the buyer. (Remember, a debit is a *payment*.)

Now, let's enter that debit to the buyer on a blank closing statement.

	Seller		Buyer	
	Debits	Credits	Debits	Credits
Sales price			$100,000	
Deposit				
First mortgage				
Second mortgage				
Loan charges				
loan fee				
appraisal fee				
credit report				
impounds				
Existing loan balance				
Prorate taxes				
Prorate interest				
Prorate rent				
Commission to broker				
Title charges				
Government charges				
Other fees				
Balance due/owed				

We enter the sales price as a debit to the buyer by entering it here.

Because the buyer pays the sales price *to the seller,* we must also enter the sales price on the seller's half of the settlement statement. The seller receives the sales price as a payment; because the receipt of money is a *credit,* we enter the sales price as a credit to the seller.

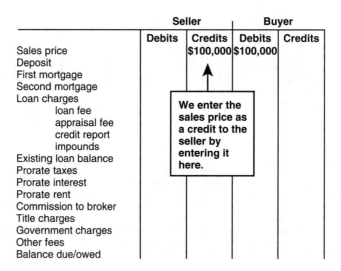

Once the seller receives the sales funds from the buyer, the seller will pay for various items, such as:

- The balance on an existing first mortgage
- The real estate broker's commission
- Escrow fees
- Title insurance
- Transfer taxes on the transference of the deed (based upon the total purchase price)

Because these are *payments* by the seller, these are entered as *debits* to the seller on the seller's half of the settlement statement, as shown next.

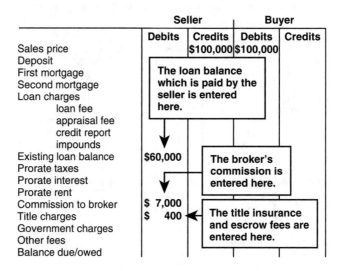

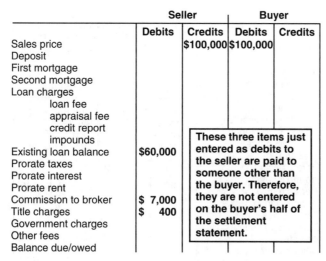

	Seller		Buyer	
	Debits	Credits	Debits	Credits
Sales price		$100,000	$100,000	
Deposit				
First mortgage				
Second mortgage				
Loan charges				
loan fee				
appraisal fee				
credit report			These three items just	
impounds			entered as debits to	
Existing loan balance	$60,000		the seller are paid to	
Prorate taxes			someone other than	
Prorate interest			the buyer. Therefore,	
Prorate rent			they are not entered	
Commission to broker	$ 7,000		on the buyer's half of	
Title charges	$ 400		the settlement	
Government charges			statement.	
Other fees				
Balance due/owed				

Now, let's look at two items that are paid by the seller *to the buyer*. The first of these is the deposit that the buyer made when the sales contract was signed. Because this was paid by the buyer to the seller *prior* to closing, the seller is still holding the buyer's deposit at the closing. Because the buyer will pay the entire sales price to the seller at closing, the seller must return the amount of the deposit to the buyer at closing. Because the buyer's deposit is paid by the seller back to the buyer, it is entered on both the seller's and the buyer's settlement statements. It is entered on the seller's statement as a *debit* because the seller *pays* the deposit back to the buyer. It is entered on the buyer's statement as a *credit* because the buyer *receives* the deposit back from the seller. These entries are shown on the next settlement statement.

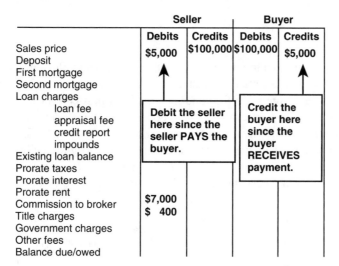

	Seller		Buyer	
	Debits	Credits	Debits	Credits
Sales price		$100,000	$100,000	
Deposit	$5,000			$5,000
First mortgage				
Second mortgage				
Loan charges				
loan fee			Credit the	
appraisal fee	Debit the seller		buyer here	
credit report	here since the		since the	
impounds	seller PAYS the		buyer	
Existing loan balance	buyer.		RECEIVES	
Prorate taxes			payment.	
Prorate interest				
Prorate rent				
Commission to broker	$7,000			
Title charges	$ 400			
Government charges				
Other fees				
Balance due/owed				

If the property is rented, the second item that the seller pays to the buyer is any prepaid rent that the seller has received. For example, let's suppose that a rental property is being sold and the tenant has prepaid the rent through the end of June. Closing will take place on the last day of May. In this situation, the seller has received a full month's rent that should go to the buyer because the buyer will own the property during the month of June. This situation is handled at closing as follows

- The seller has received the June rent in advance and therefore must make a payment to the buyer for the amount of the rent.
- This payment is entered as a *debit* to the seller.
- The buyer receives the rent payment from the seller, so the amount of the rent is also entered as a *credit* to the buyer.

These entries are illustrated in the next settlement section.

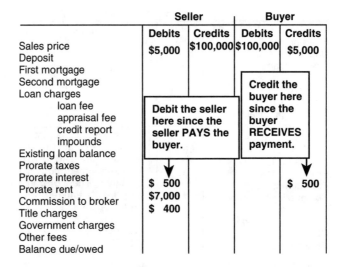

	Seller		Buyer	
	Debits	**Credits**	**Debits**	**Credits**
Sales price	$5,000	$100,000	$100,000	$5,000
Deposit				
First mortgage				
Second mortgage				
Loan charges				
loan fee				
appraisal fee				
credit report				
impounds				
Existing loan balance				
Prorate taxes				
Prorate interest	$ 500			$ 500
Prorate rent	$7,000			
Commission to broker	$ 400			
Title charges				
Government charges				
Other fees				
Balance due/owed				

Debit the seller here since the seller PAYS the buyer.

Credit the buyer here since the buyer RECEIVES payment.

Coaching Tips: **The amount of the prepaid rent must often be prorated. This means that each of the two parties will receive part of the prepaid rent. In the previous example, no proration is needed.**

The last items we will cover are those that are paid by the buyer to someone other than the seller, including:

- Loan origination fees
- Structural pest control report
- Escrow fees
- Recording fees

The buyer might have to pay for many other expenses at closing, but all expenses would be handled on the settlement statement in the same manner. For simplicity, we will cover only loan origination fees and the structural pest control report.

Loan origination fees are charged to the borrower by the lender for making the new loan on the property. Let's assume that the amount of these fees is $3,500. These loan origination fees are paid by the buyer, so they are entered as a *debit* on the buyer's settlement statement. Because these fees are paid to the lender, not the seller, there is *no* corresponding entry on the seller's settlement statement. This entry is illustrated next.

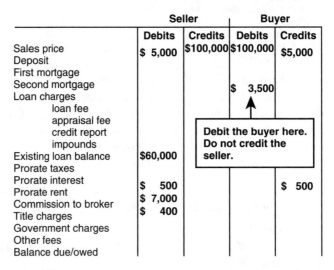

	Seller		Buyer	
	Debits	**Credits**	**Debits**	**Credits**
Sales price	$ 5,000	$100,000	$100,000	$5,000
Deposit				
First mortgage				
Second mortgage			$ 3,500	
Loan charges				
loan fee				
appraisal fee				
credit report				
impounds				
Existing loan balance	$60,000			
Prorate taxes				
Prorate interest	$ 500			$ 500
Prorate rent	$ 7,000			
Commission to broker	$ 400			
Title charges				
Government charges				
Other fees				
Balance due/owed				

Debit the buyer here. Do not credit the seller.

If the cost of the structural pest control report is paid by the buyer, it is handled in the same way. The buyer pays this cost to the pest control company, so the amount is entered on the buyer's settlement statement as a *debit*. There is no corresponding entry on the seller's statement because the payment is not made to the seller. This entry is illustrated next.

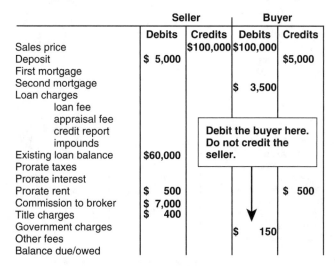

We need to look at one final situation—a loan assumption. Earlier, we covered the situation in which the seller pays off an existing loan when the loan is closed. In that situation, the existing loan amount is entered as a *debit* to the seller because the seller pays that amount at closing to the lender. When an existing loan is assumed by the buyer, the situation is different.

When a loan is assumed, the seller does not pay off the balance on the existing loan. Instead, the balance that is owed is transferred to the buyer, who assumes the obligation to repay the balance on the loan. In this case, the existing loan balance is still a *debit* to the seller because the loan balance must be satisfied (paid) in some way. In an assumption, the balance is paid by transferring the obligation to the buyer. Now the *buyer* has an entry for the loan balance on the buyer's settlement statement. The balance on the loan is entered as a *credit* to the buyer because the buyer actually *receives* an amount from the lender toward the purchase price that is equal to the balance on the existing loan.

Once all the relevant debits and credits have been entered on the seller's and buyer's settlement statements, how much each party must pay or will receive at closing can be determined. This is done by subtracting the total amount of all debits from the total amount of all credits for each party. Let's look at this computation for both parties, beginning with the seller. The next illustration shows a condensed summary of all the debits and credits for both the buyer and seller for the examples we have covered so far.

Total Seller Credits

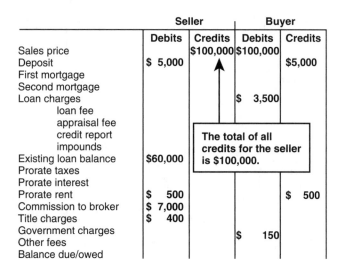

Total Seller Debits

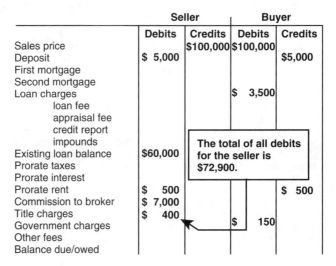

	Seller Debits	Seller Credits	Buyer Debits	Buyer Credits
Sales price		$100,000	$100,000	
Deposit	$ 5,000			$5,000
First mortgage				
Second mortgage				
Loan charges			$ 3,500	
loan fee				
appraisal fee				
credit report				
impounds				
Existing loan balance	$60,000			
Prorate taxes				
Prorate interest				
Prorate rent	$ 500			$ 500
Commission to broker	$ 7,000			
Title charges	$ 400			
Government charges			$ 150	
Other fees				
Balance due/owed				

> The total of all debits for the seller is $72,900.

Check That Seller Will Receive at Closing

	Seller Debits	Seller Credits	Buyer Debits	Buyer Credits
Sales price		$100,000	$100,000	
Deposit	$ 5,000			$5,000
First mortgage				
Second mortgage				
Loan charges			$ 3,500	
loan fee				
appraisal fee				
credit report				
impounds				
Existing loan balance	$60,000			
Prorate taxes				
Prorate interest				
Prorate rent	$ 500			$ 500
Commission to broker	$ 7,000			
Title charges	$ 400			
Government charges			$ 150	
Other fees				
Balance due/owed		$ 27,100		

> By subtracting $72,900 (debits) from $100,000 (credits), we find that the total the seller will receive at the close of escrow is $27,100.

Now, let's look at the same computation for the buyer.

Total Buyer Credits

	Seller Debits	Seller Credits	Buyer Debits	Buyer Credits
Sales price		$100,000	$100,000	
Deposit	$ 5,000			$5,000
First mortgage				
Second mortgage				
Loan charges			$ 3,500	
loan fee				
appraisal fee				
credit report				
impounds				
Existing loan balance	$60,000			
Prorate taxes				
Prorate interest				
Prorate rent	$ 500			$ 500
Commission to broker	$ 7,000			
Title charges	$ 400			
Government charges				
Other fees			$ 150	
Balance due/owed		$ 27,100		

> The total of all credits for the buyer is $5,500.

Total Buyer Debits

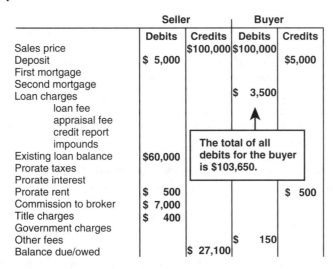

	Seller		Buyer	
	Debits	Credits	Debits	Credits
Sales price		$100,000	$100,000	
Deposit	$ 5,000			$5,000
First mortgage				
Second mortgage				
Loan charges			$ 3,500	
loan fee				
appraisal fee				
credit report				
impounds			*The total of all debits for the buyer is $103,650.*	
Existing loan balance	$60,000			
Prorate taxes				
Prorate interest				
Prorate rent	$ 500			$ 500
Commission to broker	$ 7,000			
Title charges	$ 400			
Government charges				
Other fees			$ 150	
Balance due/owed		$ 27,100		

Check Needed from Buyer at Closing

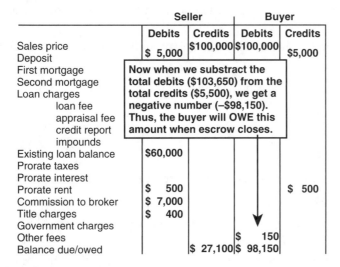

	Seller		Buyer	
	Debits	Credits	Debits	Credits
Sales price		$100,000	$100,000	
Deposit	$ 5,000			$5,000
First mortgage				
Second mortgage		*Now when we substract the total debits ($103,650) from the total credits ($5,500), we get a negative number (–$98,150). Thus, the buyer will OWE this amount when escrow closes.*		
Loan charges				
loan fee				
appraisal fee				
credit report				
impounds				
Existing loan balance	$60,000			
Prorate taxes				
Prorate interest				
Prorate rent	$ 500			$ 500
Commission to broker	$ 7,000			
Title charges	$ 400			
Government charges				
Other fees			$ 150	
Balance due/owed		$ 27,100	$ 98,150	

What is owed (debits) is subtracted from what is received (credits).

PRORATING

Prorating is the concept that the buyer and seller should pay the expenses or receive the financial benefits of owning a property for the part of the current year that they owned the property. When a cost item is prorated, for example, this means simply that part of the cost will be paid by the seller and part of the cost will be paid by the buyer. **Prorating** is the process of determining how much of the item will be paid by the buyer and how much will be paid by the seller, based on how long each party will own the property.

Before we look at prorating in more detail, let's cover some basic points about the process. The *closing day* is when ownership is transferred from the seller to the buyer, as illustrated using the time line shown here.

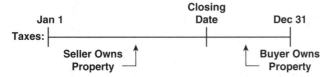

The seller owns the property before the day of closing. The buyer owns the property after the day of closing. But who owns the property on the day of closing?

On the day of closing, the seller actually owns the property for part of the day (before all the paperwork is signed), and the buyer owns the property for part of the day (after the paperwork is signed). To avoid computing the costs for part of a day for the seller and part of the day for the buyer, the general rule for the purpose of prorating costs is *the buyer owns the property on the day of closing for the entire day*. This means that the buyer is responsible for all expenses of ownership on the day of closing. (In some cases, the seller is assumed to own the property for the entire day of closing.)This item becomes a function of negotiation.

Another concept related to prorating is the beginning and ending dates that a prorated item is in effect:

- Beginning date—The first date that a prorated item is in effect.
- Ending date—The last date that a prorated item is in effect.

For example, property taxes are normally paid for the calendar year from January 1 through December 31. In this situation, January 1 is the beginning date for property taxes, and December 31 is the ending date.

From these facts, we can state that the period of ownership, with respect to any item to be prorated, is as follows:

- Seller's period of ownership—The time from the beginning date through the day before the closing date.
- Buyer's period of ownership—The time from the day of closing through the ending date.

The three major cost items that must be prorated on the date of closing are:

1. Property taxes
2. Homeowner's insurance
3. Mortgage interest

For each of these items, the period over which they are prorated may differ:

1. *Property taxes* are prorated over the calendar year for which taxes are due.
2. *Homeowner's insurance* is prorated over the actual period for which the policy was in effect (usually 1 year).
3. *Mortgage interest* is prorated over the month during which the closing occurs.

A typical situation for the proration of each of these items is illustrated next.

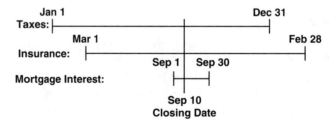

Note that each item is prorated over a different time period. The proration period corresponds to the period over which a particular item is paid.

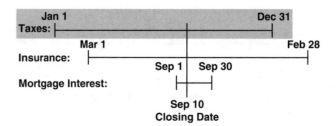

For example, taxes are paid and prorated over the calendar year from January 1 (beginning date) through December 31 (ending date).

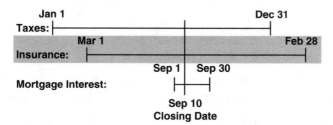

The homeowner's insurance is paid and prorated over a period of 1 year beginning on March 1 and ending on February 28 (the dates the policy is in effect).

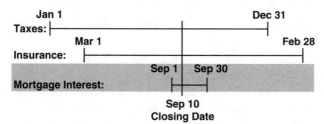

Mortgage interest is paid monthly and is prorated for the month of closing only. The beginning date for this proration is September 1 and the ending date is September 30.

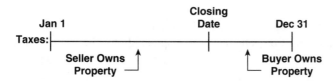

In each of these situations, the seller is responsible for the item's cost from the beginning date to the day before the closing date. The buyer is responsible for each item on the day of closing to the ending date.

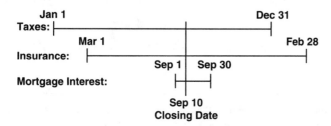

Prorating each of these items is based on different periods of time but involves the same process. Later in this chapter, we will cover the process of prorating taxes in detail. Right now, we will cover some general issues involved in the proration of property taxes.

Property Taxes

Property taxes are assessed for a 12-month tax year. Property taxes are based on a calendar tax year that runs from January 1 through December 31.

In Florida, although taxes are assessed on real property on the first day of any calendar year, these taxes are typically paid in **arrears**. This means taxes can be paid at the end of the tax year without penalty. Thus, in most situations, property taxes have not been paid by the seller prior to the date of closing. If the seller has not paid property taxes prior to closing, the seller must pay her prorated share of property taxes due on the date of closing, as illustrated next.

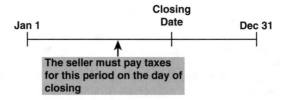

In order to determine the amount of taxes the seller must pay, we first prorate the seller's tax payment. In this situation, we prorate the seller's tax bill using the following three steps:

1. Determine how many days out of the year the *seller* will own the property.
2. Determine how much tax is due for each day (calculation of the daily rate).
3. Calculate the seller's tax payment from these two numbers (multiply the daily rate by the number of days that the *seller* owned the property).

Here is an example to illustrate how a seller's prorated share of the tax payment is calculated.

Assume that a seller has not paid annual property taxes of $877 prior to closing, and the closing date is March 13. Because the seller has not paid the taxes, the amount of tax payment the seller is responsible for must be calculated. This requires four steps.

Step 1: Calculate the number of days the seller was responsible for the tax bill *prior to the month of closing*. To do this, add up the total number of days in each month as follows:

January	31 days
February	+28 days
Total	59 days

Step 2: Add the number of days the seller is responsible for taxes in the month of closing. The number of days the seller is responsible for the taxes is always the same as the day before closing occurs. (The buyer is responsible for the day of closing.)

59 days (from the first step)
+12 days (March 13 closing date)
71 days = Total number of days the seller is responsible for paying the taxes

Step 3: Determine the amount of taxes for each day of the year as follows:

Annual tax bill ÷ 365 days

In this case, the annual tax bill is $877. The computation in this case is:

$877 ÷ 365 = $2.4027 per day

Coaching Tips: **Once you determine the daily rate, *do not round it off*. Rounding the number at this point will cause the total to be in error. Remember, we are multiplying the number of days against an actual calculated daily rate. A rounding off of the daily rate will result in a proration that is either greater or less than the actual proration would normally be. For example: if the daily rate in Step 3 was rounded off to the nearest penny, we would multiply 71 days (as shown in Step 4) x $2.40. The product would equal a proration of $170.40 and not $170.59 as the correct proration is shown in the calculation in Step 4.**

Step 4: Multiply the number of days the seller is responsible for the taxes by the amount of the tax per day, as follows:

71 days × $2.4027 = $170.59

In this case, the seller is responsible for a prorated amount of $170.59 for her share of the tax bill. Because she has not paid the taxes prior to closing, the seller must pay this amount at closing.

Coaching Tips: Proration rule—When taxes are not paid in advance, prorate seller's share to be paid to the buyer.

PRACTICE EXERCISES
Calculating the Number of Days Prior to the Month of Closing

Assume that taxes are paid based on a calendar-year basis from January 1 through December 31.

1. A seller has *not* paid the property taxes before closing, which occurs on April 25. For how many days is the seller responsible for taxes *prior to the month of closing*?

   31 days in January

   28 days in February

   <u>31</u> days in March

   90 total days *prior to the month of closing*

2. A seller has *not* paid the property taxes before closing, which occurs on March 21. For how many days is the seller responsible for taxes *prior to the month of closing*?

   31 days in January

   <u>28</u> days in February

   59 total days *prior to the month of closing*

Calculating the Total Number of Days the Seller Is Responsible for Property Taxes

1. A seller has *not* paid the property taxes before closing, which occurs on April 17. For how many days is the seller responsible for taxes *for the entire tax year*?

   31 days in January

   28 days in February

   31 days in March

   <u>16</u> days in April (closing April 17)

   106 *total* days

2. A seller has *not* paid the property taxes before closing, which occurs on March 3. For how many days is the seller responsible for taxes *for the entire tax year*?

   31 days in January

   28 days in February

   <u>2</u> days in March (closing March 3)

   61 *total* days

3. A seller has *not* paid the property taxes before closing, which occurs on February 2. For how many days is the seller responsible for taxes *for the entire tax year*?

31 days in January

<u>1</u> day in February (closing February 2)

32 *total* days

Calculating the Amount of Property Tax Due for Each Day of the Year

1. The annual property taxes on a property being sold are $1,026. What is the amount of tax due per day?

$1,026 \div 365 = $2.8110

2. The annual property taxes on a property being sold are $652. What is the amount of tax due per day?

$652 \div 365 = $1.7863

Calculating the Amount of the Seller's Tax Payment at Closing

1. A seller has *not* paid the property taxes of $738 before closing, which occurs on April 2. What is the amount of the seller's prorated tax payment at closing?

Step 1: Calculate the appropriate number of days

31 days in January

28 days in February

31 days in March

<u>1</u> day in April

91 total days

Step 2: Calculate the daily rate

$738 \div 365 = $2.0219

Step 3: Calculate the seller's prorated tax payment at closing

$2.0219 \times 91 = $183.99

2. A seller has *not* paid the property taxes of $944 before closing, which occurs on March 20. What is the amount of the seller's prorated tax payment at closing?

Step 1: Calculate the appropriate number of days

31 days in January

28 days in February

<u>19</u> days in March (closing March 20)

78 total days

Step 2: Calculate the daily rate

$944 \div 365 = $2.5863

Step 3: Calculate the seller's prorated tax payment at closing

$2.5863 \times 78 = $201.73

In the proration exercises, the 365-day method is applied, which uses the actual number of days in the proration period.

A second method of proration is called the 30-day-month method. This method assumes that there are 12 months in a year and each month has 30 days. Let's go over one of the previous examples, but this time the 30-day-month method will be applied.

1. The seller has not paid the taxes of $877 prior to closing, and the closing is on March 13. What is the total amount of the seller's prorated tax payment due at closing?

Step 1: Determine the number of months the seller was responsible for the tax bill *prior to the month of closing.* In this case, the seller is responsible for 2 months prior to the month of closing (January and February).

Step 2: Calculate the amount of taxes for each *month* of the year as follows:

$877 ÷ 12 months = $73.0833 per month

Step 3: Multiply the number of *months* the seller was responsible for the tax bill prior to closing (Step 1) by the amount of the tax per *month* (Step 2), as follows:

$73.0833 taxes per month × 2 months = $146.1666

This is the amount the seller's owes for the period prior to the month of closing. We still need to calculate the amount the seller owes for the month of closing.

Step 4: Determine the *number of days* the seller is responsible for taxes *in the month of closing.* In this example, the seller is responsible for 12 days in March. (The buyer is responsible for the day of closing.)

Step 5: Calculate the amount of taxes for each *day* of the month. To do this, you divide the number of taxes per month (from Step 2) by 30 days, as follows:

$73.0833 taxes per month ÷ 30 days = $2.4361 per day

Step 6: Multiply the number of *days* the seller was responsible for taxes in the month of closing by the amount of the tax per *day,* as follows:

$2.4361 taxes per day × 12 days = $29.2332

We now know the amount the seller owes for the month of closing. To arrive at the *total* amount the seller owes for taxes, we must add this value to the amount the seller owes for the months prior to closing (Step 3).

Step 7: *Add Step 3 to Step 6 to calculate the total amount* of the seller's prorated tax payment due at closing:

$146.1666 + $29.2332 = $175.3998

The seller is responsible for a prorated amount of $175.40 for his share of the tax bill.

In this chapter, *two methods* for prorating expenses at closing were discussed:

1. The 365-day method
2. The 30-day-month method

For purposes of this course, you should always use the 365-day method, unless instructed otherwise. See Figure 14.1.

FIGURE 14.1

TIME METHODS OF PRORATION

- **The 365-day method** uses the actual number of days in the proration period.
- **The 30-day-month method** assumes that there are 12 months in the year and each month has 30 days.
  - There is no method called the 12-month method.
  - There is no method called the 30-month method.

CLOSING STATEMENT SECTIONS AND ENTRIES

There are three sections and parties in a closing statement:

1. **Seller**
2. **Buyer**
3. **Escrow/closing agent**

There are three sections for entries in a closing statement:

1. **Transactional entries**
2. **Proration entries**
3. **Expenses/closing costs**

ITEMS THAT REQUIRE SINGLE ENTRY ON THE CLOSING STATEMENT ITEMS THAT ARE ALWAYS DEBITS AND NEVER CREDITS

Expenses:

- Legal fees—each party pays their own attorney
- Title insurance—usually paid by the buyer
- Broker commission(s)—customarily paid by the seller
- Miscellaneous items—paid by the benefiting party (as applicable)
- Recording fees
  - Deed—generally paid by the buying party
  - Mortgage—generally paid by the buying party
- Documentary stamps
  - Deed—generally paid by the selling party
  - Note—generally paid by the buying party
  - Intangiable—generally paid by the buying party

ITEMS THAT REQUIRE DOUBLE ENTRY ON A CLOSING STATEMENT

Transactional information:

- **Sales price**
  - The buyer pays the sale price.
  - The seller receives money from the sales price; therefore, you must also credit the seller.
- **Deposit**
  - The buyer receives the deposit (credit).
  - The seller pays (returns) the deposit (debit).
- **Newly originated first mortgage (by a third-party lender)**
  - The buyer receives the loan from the lender as a credit.
  - The seller does not receive it; it is given to the escrow/closing agent.

FIGURE 14.1
(*Continued*)

- **Assumed first mortgage (by buyer from seller)**
  - The seller pays the loan (debit) by transferring her remaining balance to the buyer.
  - The buyer also receives the loan balance as a credit.
- **Second mortgage (originated as seller financing)**
  - The buyer receives the loan from the seller (who in this case acts as the lender) as a credit.
  - The seller issues the loan (from his equity) and receives a debit entry.

Prorations:

- **Property taxes (unpaid by seller)**
  - The seller pays, so it is a debit.
  - The buyer receives seller's portion of unpaid taxes, so it is a credit.
- **Property taxes (paid** *in advance* **by seller)**
  - The buyer pays his portion of the taxes following closing, so it is a debit.
  - The seller receives the buyer's portion of taxes, so it is a credit.
- **First mortgage interest (assumed) paid in advance of closing by seller**
  - Buyer pays (debit) buyer's portion of interest for month of closing.
  - Seller receives (credit) buyer's portion of interest for month of closing.
- **First mortgage interest (originated by third-party lender)**
  - Interest to lender is usually treated as a one-time expense (debit) to the buyer.
- **Second mortgage interest (normally seller financing)**
  - Buyer pays (debit) seller/lender the interest for month of closing.
  - Seller receives (credit) buyer's interest for month of closing.
- **Rent**
  - The seller pays (debit) prepaid rent due the buyer for month of closing.
  - The buyer receives the prepaid rent (credit) portion from the seller.
- **Insurance (assumption of seller's unused policy)**
  - Buyer pays (debit) seller the buyer's portion of remaining policy.
  - Seller receives (credit) buyer's portion of remaining policy.

SALES CONTRACT TO CLOSING

When you are an agent involved in the sale of property, the signing of the sales contract does not end your responsibilities. Between the signing of the contract and the day the sale is closed, your specific duties are determined by your broker's policy and by your relationship to the parties to the transaction (i.e., single agent for buyer or seller, transaction broker, or no brokerage relationship). Depending on the situation, you may continue to work with the buyer, the seller, and/or the lender to ensure a successful closing.

In the remainder of this chapter, we will look at some of the steps that take place from the signing of the sales contract to the day of the closing. We will also look at duties an agent has at each of these steps.

There are three major periods during the time between the signing of the sales contract and the day of closing:

1. The period immediately after the sales contract is signed

2. The loan application process

3. The preparation for closing

After the Sales Contract Is Signed

Immediately after the sales contract is signed by all parties, make sure that each party to the transaction receives a copy of the signed contract at the time of signing. The following parties should receive a copy of the signed contract:

- The seller
- The buyer
- Your broker
- The cooperating broker, if there is one

If there is a contingency in the sales contract, it is also your responsibility to make sure that everything possible is done by each party to fulfill the conditions of the contingency. For example, if the contract is made contingent on the buyer's ability to obtain new financing, you should monitor the buyer's application process to ensure that it progresses in a timely manner. (During this process, you must make sure your actions comply with the requirements of the Florida Brokerage Relationship Disclosure Act, described earlier in Chapter 4.) While it is best to try to avoid having contingency clauses in a contract, in some situations they cannot be avoided.

In addition to the contingency relating to new financing, there are other situations in which a contingency clause is likely to be involved, including:

- Loan assumptions
- Inspections of the property
- Repairs to the property
- Appraisals of the property
- Surveys of the property
- A termite inspection
- The sale of the buyer's present home

Loan Assumptions

Loan assumptions often involve contingency clauses because many loans now require that the buyer qualify for the loan in order to assume it. When you have a listing on a property for which a loan can be assumed, you should determine at the time you take the listing whether or not the lender will require an application from the buyer to assume the loan. This will allow you to advise any buyer in advance that an application will be required. Note that you should also advise the lender at the time you take the listing that the seller intends to offer the existing loan to a buyer on a loan assumption. In the case of a loan assumption on a Veterans Affairs (VA) loan in which the seller wants to be released from liability on the loan, you should ensure that the buyer cooperates with the lender and the VA in completing the release process.

Inspections of the Property

A contract may be contingent on an inspection of the property (for example, by a spouse or a home inspector). If a home inspection is required, you should make sure that the inspection takes place as soon as possible. Failure to do so can result in costly delays because the property is tied up until the contingency is resolved, and cannot be sold to anyone else. In the event that the contingency is not satisfied successfully, valuable time in getting the property back on the market will be lost.

Repairs to the Property

In addition, the contract may be contingent on the seller making repairs based on the results of a home inspection. Your obligation in dealing with this situation is to ensure that any actions required by the seller are completed in a timely manner (at least by the closing date). This might require you to provide the names of individuals who can do the work, but you should not order the work done yourself. Always have the seller order the work.

Appraisals of the Property

Another very common situation is a contingency on the appraisal of the property for a certain value. In fact, with most loans, such a contingency is required. When an appraisal is required, it is your responsibility to ensure it is completed in a timely fashion. To that end, you should cooperate fully with the appraiser, even if you are only asked to unlock the property for the appraiser. When you are asked to assist an appraiser, remember you should neither ask the appraiser what the appraisal value is nor attempt to influence the appraisal in any way.

Surveys of the Property

At the lender's or buyer's request, a contract may also require that a survey of the property take place before closing.

A Termite Inspection

Assisting the parties in complying with the contract might also include ensuring that a wood infestation inspection is completed and that a report is submitted to the closing agent. An inspection, a clearance letter, or a termite bond might be required in different situations. Any of these items may be required by the buyer, the lender, or by a government agency such as the Federal Housing Administration (FHA) or the VA.

When any of these items are required, you should be aware that different forms and procedures are required by different sources. For example, the forms required for a clearance letter are different for the VA and the FHA. A termite bond that can be transferred from the seller to the buyer might be acceptable to some (but not all) conventional lenders, but is not allowed with VA and FHA loans.

Sale of the Buyer's Present Home

A contract may also be contingent upon the sale of the buyer's present home. In this situation, if you are an agent for the seller, it is your responsibility to obtain information about the sale of homes in the area where the buyer's home is located so that your seller can make an informed decision about whether such a contingency is a good idea. If you are an agent for the buyer, you should do everything possible to assist the buyer in the sale of her home, including listing the property for sale if it is not already listed or referring the buyer to another broker (if entering into a listing with the buyer would conflict with your relationship with the seller).

Loan Processing

Once you have completed your responsibilities immediately after the contract is signed, the next period of the closing process begins—the processing of the buyer's loan. During this period of the closing process, you may be working with the seller, the buyer, and/or the lender who will provide the financing.

The processing of the buyer's loan involves the following elements:

- The selection of a lender
- The loan application
- Homeowner's insurance

Selecting a Lender

The first step to obtain financing is the selection of a lender. It is important to understand who has the right to make this selection. A broker does not have the right to select the lender. The determination of who has the right to select the lender depends on whether the selection is specified in the sales contract or made after the contract is completed. The seller has the right to stipulate in a sales contract that the buyer must use a particular lender. For example, the seller may be a builder who entered into a contract with a lender to provide permanent financing in exchange for providing the construction loan. The seller may stipulate in the contract that only this lender may be used by the buyer. If a seller includes a stipulation in the contract that a particular lender must be used and the buyer signs the contract, the buyer must use the stipulated lender. The other option is to decline to sign the contract if the buyer does not want to be bound to a particular lender.

In another situation, a seller might stipulate in a contract that the buyer use the lender who made the seller's existing loan on the property. This might occur when the lender agrees to waive a prepayment penalty on the seller's loan if the buyer obtains a new loan from that lender. If the buyer signs the contract, the buyer is bound to use the seller's lender. If the buyer does not want to use the seller's lender, the buyer can decline to sign the contract.

Once a contract is signed by both the seller and the buyer, and the contract does not specify a particular lender, the buyer can choose which lender to use. In this situation, the seller may only request that a particular lender be used.

Loan Application

The second major step to obtain financing is the loan application itself. If you are working with the seller, you should keep the seller informed of the progress on the application. For example, you should let the seller know whether the buyer has submitted an application for a loan. The contract may stipulate the time period in which this should be done. You should also inform the seller as to whether or not the buyer is making a good-faith effort to comply with the contract. Failure to submit forms to the lender in a timely manner may indicate that the buyer is not making such an effort. Finally, you should let the seller know the results of the buyer's loan application immediately. If you are working with the buyer, you could ensure that all forms required of the buyer are submitted in a timely manner.

In addition, you have the obligation to assist in resolving any problems that might arise. For example:

- If the appraisal is completed, and the property does not appraise at the required value, you should assist the seller and buyer in finding an alternative solution, or in renegotiating the contract as necessary.
- If the buyer fails to qualify, the contract may need to be renegotiated. For instance, if the buyer fails to qualify for a 90 percent loan, the seller might want to consider providing a purchase money loan for 10 percent of the sales price. The buyer could then apply for an 80 percent loan.

Homeowner's Insurance

During loan processing, the buyer must obtain a homeowner's insurance policy with the lender named as the payee. It may take several days for the policy to be issued, so you should inform the buyer of this fact so she will have adequate time to obtain the policy before closing. In addition, you should follow up to ensure that the policy has been obtained prior to closing.

Coaching Tips: When financing is provided by a lender, that lender will always require the borrower to obtain homeowner's insurance to secure the lender's lien. This will protect the lender (as well as the borrower) against any casualty issue such as:

- Fire
- Vandalism
- Theft
- Destruction
- Mold
- Storm damage

Preparing for Closing

The third major period of the closing process is preparing for the closing itself. You have three primary responsibilities in this area:

1. Providing information to the closing agent
2. Coordinating the date and time of the closing
3. Preparing the buyer and/or seller for closing

Providing Information to the Closing Agent

The closing agent must receive a true and current copy of the sales contract. The closing agent needs the sales contract in order to complete a title search and to prepare the closing statements showing how much money the seller will receive and how much the buyer will pay.

In addition, the closing agent needs a copy of the buyer's hazard insurance policy. If the insurance policy will be paid at closing, the closing agent will need to know the amount of the premium that will be paid. The closing agent also needs a copy of any termite clearance letter or report, if required, and the cost if it is to be paid at closing.

Coordinate the Date and Time of Closing

To prepare for the closing, you also need to coordinate the date and time of the closing, which may be set after the buyer's new loan or loan assumption lien has been approved by the lender. Before setting a date and time, you should consider both the provisions of the contract and the schedules of the closing official, the buyer, the seller, and any brokers involved.

Prepare the Buyer and Seller for Closing

Your last duty in preparation for closing is to prepare the buyer and/or the seller for the closing. This includes two specific tasks:

1. Inform the parties of the date, time, and place of the closing as much in advance as possible to ensure that they can be there.
2. Inform the buyer and/or seller of what to expect at closing.

Perhaps the greatest obstacle to a successful closing is a surprise at the closing table. You should do everything possible to avoid any such surprises. One helpful way to eliminate surprises is to review blank copies of all forms used at closing with the buyer and/or seller. Another way is to discuss all forms that will require a signature. The most important task, however, is to complete the closing statement as accurately as possible, and review it with the buyer and/or seller.

You should also remember that the provisions of the Real Estate Settlement Procedures Act (RESPA) require that the lender must show the buyer the Uniform Settlement Statement prior to closing as follows:

- The form must be available *on request* from the buyer. (The lender is not required to show it to the buyer unless requested to do so.)
- It must be made available one business day before closing.
- It must include an itemized list of charges to the buyer.

This information is helpful because it shows the buyer an itemized listing of all charges, which determines the amount of money the buyer will be required to pay at closing. Note, however, that the Uniform Settlement Statement provided to the buyer need not be *complete* under the provisions of RESPA. RESPA only requires that whatever is complete as of one business day prior to closing must be shown to the buyer if requested.

SOLD SIGNS

The last topic we will discuss in this chapter is the provision of the law regarding "Sold" signs. Previously, the Florida Real Estate Commission indicated that placing a "Sold" sign on a property prior to closing, without first obtaining the seller's consent, was false advertising. This rule has been changed. *Licensees now have their choice of placing either a "Sold" sign or a "Sale Pending" sign.*

SUMMARY

Customarily (with certain exceptions), a real estate broker's compensation is generally predicated on the closing and passing of title. In addition to the listing and selling process, in Florida and in many states, the broker may undertake the role of escrow and closing agent on the transaction.

The broker prepares the closing statement and delivers it to the interested parties to the sale. The declaration and responsibility to pay the required state transfer taxes is included in the statement. These taxes should not be confused with real property tax. There are three transfer taxes in Florida: (1) transfer tax on the deed (based on the full purchase price); (2) transfer tax on the notes (based upon new borrowed funds or assumed mortgages); and (3) intangible tax (solely based on new financing that is introduced to the transaction and that does not apply to assumed mortgages).

REVIEW QUESTIONS

1. A buyer contracted to pay $50,000 for a small rental property. The buyer included $5,000 with the offer, which the broker is holding in escrow. The lender agreed to the assumption of an existing $35,000 mortgage and will lend another $10,000 as a new second mortgage. Calculate all of the transfer taxes due to the state for this transaction.
   a. $122.50
   b. $177.50
   c. $350.00
   d. $527.50

2. How will the earnest money deposit appear on the closing statement?
   a. Credit to the buyer, debit to the seller
   b. Credit to the seller, debit to the buyer
   c. Credit to the buyer only
   d. Credit to the seller only

3. Unpaid property taxes would appear on a closing statement as:
   a. Debit seller, credit buyer.
   b. Credit seller, debit buyer.
   c. Debit to the seller only.
   d. Debit to the buyer only.

4. Mary purchased a lot in a subdivision for $50,030. Calculate the documentary stamps on the deed that the seller will be charged for.
   a. $350.70
   b. $350.21
   c. $175.10
   d. $100.00

5. How would prepaid rent appear on the closing statement?
   a. Debit buyer, credit seller
   b. Debit seller, credit buyer
   c. Credit seller only
   d. Credit buyer only

6. A buyer will obtain a new second mortgage for $73,000 as part of the price for a property. What are the documentary and intangible taxes to the state on the new loan?
   a. $912.50
   b. $511.00
   c. $401.50
   d. $255.50

7. How does the purchase price appear on a closing statement?
   a. Credit seller, debit buyer
   b. Debit seller, credit buyer
   c. Credit to the seller only
   d. Debit to the buyer only

8. A listing agreement specified the seller will pay the listing broker 6 percent of the sales price. A sales associate who works for the listing broker listed and sold the property for $200,000. What is the amount of the commission that will appear on the closing statement?
   a. $12,000
   b. $7,200
   c. $6,000
   d. $4,800

9. As a rule of thumb, how does the state documentary stamp tax on the deed appear on the closing statement?
   a. Debit seller, credit buyer
   b. Credit seller, debit buyer
   c. Debit seller only
   d. Debit buyer only

10. A property owner collected rent for June on June 1. The rent for the month was $900. The owner sells the property and the day of closing is June 12. The day of closing is charged to the buyer. Calculate the proration.
    a. Debit buyer $540, credit seller $540
    b. Debit seller $540, credit buyer $540
    c. Debit buyer $570, credit seller $570
    d. Debit seller $570, credit buyer $570

11. When the transfer of a property closed, the state documentary stamp tax on the deed was $1,050; the state documentary stamp tax on the note was $420: and the intangible tax on the mortgage was $240. What was the purchase price of the property?
    a. $100,000
    b. $120,000
    c. $150,000
    d. $300,000

12. A buyer agreed to pay $125,000 for a property. The purchase includes financing at a LTV ratio of 80/20. In addition, the buyer must pay $3,000 in closing costs. The broker is holding $5,000 in escrow. How much additional cash must the buyer bring to closing?
    a. $15,000
    b. $20,000
    c. $23,000
    d. $25,000

13. How are unpaid property taxes entered on the closing statement?
    a. Debit to the seller only
    b. Debit to the buyer only
    c. Credit to seller and debit to buyer
    d. Credit to buyer and debit to seller

14. If a bank will make a 90 percent LTV loan on a house valued at $75,000 and $2,300 is paid as earnest money, how much additional cash must be brought to closing?
    a. $7,500
    b. $7,270
    c. $6,750
    d. $5,200

15. In Alachua County, a 27.5 acre parcel sold for $4,100 per acre. What is the documentary stamp tax on the deed?
    a. $225.50
    b. $394.25
    c. $789.25
    d. $789.60

Chapter 15

LEARNING OBJECTIVES

After completing this lesson, you will be able to:

- Differentiate between an appraisal and pricing.
- Distinguish between value and market value.
- Identify the economic and physical characteristics of land that affects market value.
- Describe the basic principles that determine market value.
- Describe the basic steps in the market data (sales comparison) approach to pricing.
- Identify the situations in which the market data approach is used most often.
- Explain the basic steps in the cost approach to pricing.
- Recognize the situations in which the cost (cost-depreciation) approach is used most often.
- Differentiate between replacement cost and reproduction cost.
- Define the three types of depreciation.
- Know the basic steps in the replacement cost approach to pricing property: estimating land cost, estimating replacement cost, and adjusting for depreciation.
- Describe the basic steps in the income approach to pricing and identify situations in which the income approach is used.
- Explain the basic steps in the gross rent multiplier approach and describe several uses of this approach.

Valuation of Real Property

PRINCIPLES OF PRICING AND VALUE
Appraisal versus Pricing

Before we discuss property pricing, you need to understand the distinction between the process of appraising a property and the process of pricing a property. An **appraisal** is a formal estimation of the value of real property. In most states, only a certified or licensed appraiser can make an appraisal of property.

In some situations, a real estate licensee may be called upon to help determine an appropriate price for a property. For example, a real estate licensee may be asked to assist a seller in determining a suitable price for a property or to assist a buyer in evaluating a price offered by a seller. In this course, we will refer to this pricing assistance as a **comparative market analysis (CMA)**. A CMA focuses on pricing while the focus of an appraisal is always on the *value* of whatever is being appraised.

When a real estate licensee creates a CMA, the result is a recommended *price* for a property, *not an appraisal.* In fact, under Chapter 475 of Florida state law, a real estate licensee is prohibited from calling a CMA an appraisal, unless the licensee is a licensed or certified appraiser.

As of October 2005, Chapter 475 is breaks down into four parts:

- Part 1 affects real estate brokers, sales associates, and schools.
- Part 2 affects appraisers.
- Part 3 is known as the Commercial Real Estate Sales Commission Lien Act.
- Part 4 is known as the Commercial Real Estate Leasing Commission Lien Act.

Under the definition of Part l, a licensee is permitted to perform an appraisal so long as it is not considered a federally related transaction. However, there are certain rules and procedures to consider such as the following:

- A licensee may not appraise a property if it is valued above $250,000.
- If the licensee accepts an appraisal assignment as authorized under Chapter 475:
  - The licensee must follow the **Uniform Standards of Professional Appraisal Practice (USPAP)**.
  - A violation of USPAP results in one of the following:
    - $5,000 fine
    - License suspension
    - License revocation

In order to perform an appraisal that falls under the definition of a federally related transaction, the individual preparing the report must be either a state-certified or licensed appraiser. A **federally related transaction** is any transaction that includes or involves a financial institution insured or regulated by the federal government.

Appraisers must always conform to the USPAP. USPAP sets forth the procedures an appraiser must follow while performing appraisal services. Real estate licensees performing pricing duties (CMAs) are not required to conform to any of the provisions contained in USPAP. An organization called the Appraisal Standards Board is responsible for the development of USPAP. An organization called the Appraisal Qualifications Board (AQB) is responsible for setting the qualifications for certified and licensed appraisers. Both the Appraisal Standards Board and the AQB are part of a nonprofit organization called the Appraisal Foundation.

When an appraisal is conducted by a licensed appraiser, the result is an estimate of value of the property. The major difference between an appraisal and a CMA is that an appraisal will use definite and distinct principles of valuation applied by using the three approaches to value:

1. Sales (market) comparison approach

2. Cost (reproduction) approach

3. Income approach

In every appraisal that is conducted, the three approaches to valuation are applied. It is only within the **reconciliation** step of the appraisal process that one of the three approaches is given weight over the other two to determine the appraiser's final estimate of value. The most heavily weighted approach tends to be the approach most applicable to the property's category type and/or utility within the marketplace. It is also that approach that is said to clearly define the problem (the type of value being sought) to the appraisal.

A CMA, although similar in nature to that of the sales (market) comparison approach, only measures a property's value in an active marketplace where similar properties are currently being listed, have failed to sell within the prescribed listing period, or have already sold.

In any of the cases discussed, a CMA requires an active marketplace, while an appraisal conducted by a licensed or certified appraiser does not need an active marketplace to determine an estimate of value.

When a real estate licensee assists a client in pricing a property, the result is a suitable price usually achieved by performing a CMA. As mentioned earlier, unless the licensee is either a certified or licensed state appraiser, a licensee may never call a CMA an appraisal. However, the same factors that affect the market value of a property also determine the appropriate price for a property. Because of this, it is important for real estate licensees to have considerable knowledge about the principles of valuation, which are covered in this chapter. Keep in mind, however, that these principles will be used only as a basis for pricing, not a formal appraisal process.

In Florida, there are three categories of appraisal licensing and designation:

1. Certified general appraiser—permitted to appraise all real property.

2. Certified residential appraiser—permitted to appraise all residential real property consisting of one to four units.

3. Registered trainee appraiser—must operate at all times under the direct supervision of either a certified or state-licensed appraiser.

In each of these categories there are specific required courses that the appraiser must successfully complete.

Basic Concepts of Valuation

Licensees are more involved in the valuation of real estate then they may realize. For this reason, the importance of valuation is stressed to the licensee. Licensees are often asked the question: "What is my property worth?" In order for a licensee to accurately, professionally, and properly respond to this question, the licensee must understand the concepts of valuation. If the valuation of a property is misjudged, the following may occur:

- The licensee may be disciplined by the Florida Real Estate Commission (FREC) for overestimating or underestimating the property's value while disposing of his responsibilities to a principal. The law of agency requires a licensee to exercise care as a professional and expert in real estate and to provide full disclosure as to a property's true value.

- Both the principal's and the licensee's time might be wasted trying to sell a property that has been overpriced for market conditions.

For the reasons just mentioned, it is important for licensees to understand the basic concepts of valuation. These concepts are described next.

Valuation is an impartial estimate or opinion of the value of a parcel of property. It is based on specific data that can be used to support and defend the estimate or opinion of value. It is usually required when real property is:

- Sold or exchanged
- Financed
- Condemned
- Taxed
- Insured
- Partitioned
- Subject in a divorce

The *value* of a parcel of property is the present worth of all rights to current and future benefits of ownership. There are many types of value that can be appraised, including:

- Market (most common value)
- Book (more commonly used in the valuation of businesses)
- Insurable (value used to replace a loss)
- Assessed (value used for property tax determination)
- Condemnation (value of property subject to taking by the government)
- Salvage (value of damaged real or personal property)

These different types of value need not be the same because they are used for different purposes. By far, the estimate of value used most often in real estate transactions is the **market value or fair market value**.

Market value is the price that an informed, willing seller would accept, and an informed, willing buyer would pay if:

- The buyer or seller is not under any pressure to buy or sell.
- A reasonable amount of time is allowed for market exposure.
- The transaction is an arm's length transaction, meaning that neither the buyer nor the seller bears relation to the other and that each party is dealing from equal bargaining positions.

Market value is a theoretical value that can only be estimated. The *market price* is the actual amount for which a property sells. Under ideal circumstances, the market price equals the market value, but this is not always the case.

FIGURE 15.1

VALUATION AT A GLANCE

- Valuation determines a market value.
- Valuation can determine an assessed value.
- Valuation results in an estimated value.
- The selling price may be different from the value.
- The listing price may be different from the value.

The term **cost** is usually synonymous with production, or the cost to produce an improvement. It is important to note that cost may or may not equal market price or market value. Either may be significantly less resulting from depreciation.

Depreciation is attributable to a loss of value of any kind resulting from any or all of the following three events:

1. Functional obsolescence (outdated layout, lighting, columns, etc.)
2. Physical deterioration (usually representative of poor maintenance and preventative maintenance programs)
3. Economic/external obsolescence (declining neighborhoods, adverse zoning changes, high interest rates, etc.)

Both functional obsolescence and physical deterioration are losses in value and are conditions that exist within the property line. Economic/external obsolescence is a loss in value and is a condition that exists outside the property line.

Figure 15.1 lists key facts about valuation.

Elements of Value

In order to have value in the real estate market, the following four basic elements must exist:

1. *D*emand
2. *U*tility
3. *S*carcity
4. *T*ransferability

These basic elements of value can be remembered by the mnemonic DUST.

Demand

Demand for property means that someone has a desire to own or use the property. If demand is to have an effect on the value of property, it must be accompanied by purchasing power. If someone desires a property but doesn't have the financial ability to act on that desire, there is no effective demand for the property. When someone has a desire for property and the purchasing power to act on that desire, the resulting demand for the property contributes to its value.

Utility

Utility means usefulness. If land has usefulness, it has utility. If land is useful, this usefulness contributes to its value. The most basic kinds of uses for real property include:

- Providing shelter
- Providing the opportunity for income, either as an investment or through business activities
- Agricultural uses

   The utility (usefulness) of property is affected by zoning ordinances and building restrictions because these limit the uses of property.

Scarcity

The scarcity of land also contributes to its value. If the supply of land were unlimited, it would have less value. The scarcity of land must be accompanied by some demand if the scarcity is to have an effect on the value of land. For example, if desert land was scarce, it would probably not go up much in value, because there is little demand for it. On the other hand, the scarcity of land in the downtown area of a major city contributes greatly to its value because there is a demand for it.

Transferability

The transferability of real property also affects its value. If the ownership of property cannot be transferred from one person to another, it does not have as much value. The degree of transferability of land can be affected by a number of factors, including liens, judgments against the owner, and clouds on the title. Legal problems such as these that affect the transferability of property can affect its value.

   Utility, scarcity, demand, and transferability create value as shown in Figure 15.2.

Physical Characteristics of Land

Land has very significant physical properties that affect its value. Land is:

- Immovable
- Indestructible
- Nonhomogeneous

FIGURE 15.2

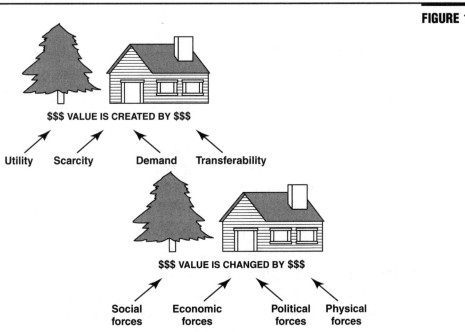

Let's look at what each of these means and how it affects value.

First, land is immovable. Because land cannot be moved, it can never be transported. The significance of this characteristic of land is that the market for real estate is a local one. The economic factors that affect the value of land will be localized to the area around where the property is located. Because land cannot be moved, location is very important. People have preferences for certain areas, and these preferences determine the value of land. A preference for certain areas is referred to as **situs**.

Second, land is indestructible. Barring catastrophic events of unforeseen proportions, land will always remain where it is. This gives comfort to the owner of property that ownership will provide value of some permanence.

Last, land is nonhomogeneous. If land were homogeneous, it would all be alike. Obviously, this is not the case. Because every parcel of land is different, land is said to be nonhomogeneous. This nonhomogeneity means that any two properties will always have some factors that contribute to a preference for one property over the other. This means, for example, that if a seller defaults on the sale of a property to a buyer, the issue of how to compensate the buyer for the loss of that unique property is not a simple one. Similarly, this characteristic of nonhomogeneity comes into play when property is taken under eminent domain and the owner is entitled to compensation for the loss.

Principles (Theorems) of Value

The value of property is a theoretical number that is affected by many factors. The major factors that affect value are summarized in the form of seven basic principles or theorems:

1. Anticipation
2. Substitution
3. Highest and best use
4. Competition
5. Supply and demand
6. Diminishing and increasing returns
7. Conformity

Principle of Anticipation

The principle of anticipation is based on the concept that a buyer will buy property in anticipation of future benefits. No one enters an investment or purchase to lose money. An investor or buyer anticipates that the purchase will have greater value as time goes on. For example:

- An investor will buy in anticipation of future financial return on the investment.
- A homeowner will buy in anticipation of enjoying the shelter provided by a home as well as future financial gains.

This principle plays an integral role in the income approach (described in detail later in this chapter).

Principle of Substitution

The **principle of substitution** states that the maximum value of a property is determined by the cost to buy or build a similar property that is of equal utility and desirability because one property can *substitute* for another. In other words, a smart investor would not pay more for a property with equal utility that they could purchase for less. For example, if two equally desirable homes are for sale in the same neighborhood and one is priced higher than the other, the lower priced one will generally sell first. Because the two homes are substitutable, the lower priced one represents the same value for a lower price, and therefore, will likely sell first.

Principle of Highest and Best Use

This principle states that the greatest value of a parcel of land is determined by its **highest and best use**. The highest and best use is the legal and feasible use that generates the highest possible land value attributable to that use. There are two types of highest and best use analyses:

1. Site as vacant
2. Site as improved

In both types, the appraiser uses the knowledge obtained by a study of alternative site uses. The highest and best use of a site will be determined by the improvement placed or constructed onto that site that will yield the highest residual (left over) value to the site itself. In other words, when both the site and improvements are separated, what is left over is the site's value. For example, a 25-year-old home at the intersection of two major roads has value as a residence. However, due to recent changes in zoning, it probably has a higher value if it was used for commercial purposes, thereby creating its highest and best use. Real estate professionals should always be mindful of this principle of value and the fact that the *current* use of property may not be its highest and best use. However, in many urban environments, the current use of the site is usually its highest and best use.

Coaching Tips: It is important to understand the difference between the terms *land* and *site*. *Land* is what exists before any entitlements to that parcel are in place; *site* is when the owner has assembled all entitlements and the site is then ready to be developed.

Principle of Competition

The principle of competition says that when substantial profit is made, competition is encouraged. For example, if investors are making substantial profits by building rental property, more investors are likely to begin building similar properties to compete for the demand that exists for that type of housing.

Principle of Supply and Demand

This principle states that the value and price of property are affected by both supply (the availability of property to be purchased) and demand (the desire and ability of people to acquire property).

As supply increases relative to demand, prices tend to decrease. As supply decreases relative to demand, prices tend to increase. For example, it is generally true that when fewer homes are available for sale, the prices of homes go up.

Some of the factors that influence *demand* for real estate include:

- Consumer income
- Consumer preferences and taste
- Population size and household composition (*Household* is defined by the U.S. Census Bureau as the people who occupy a separate housing unit.)
- Availability of mortgage credit (Because most purchasers of residential property use borrowed money for the purchase, the availability of mortgage credit is important.)

Some of the factors that influence the *supply* of real estate include:

- Availability of land
- Availability of materials
- Availability of skilled labor (e.g., plumbers, electricians, carpenters, etc.)
- Availability of construction loans and financing

A buyer's market is one in which there are not enough buyers to buy all the property offered by sellers. This is called a buyer's market because supply and demand forces favor the buyer. A seller's market is one in which there are not enough sellers to meet the demand for property by buyers. This is called a seller's market because supply and demand forces favor the seller. To assess the market conditions, a real estate professional can review the following market indicators:

- The number of recent sales
- The recent sales prices
- The number of building permits issued for new construction
- Vacancy rates for rental properties—The vacancy rate is the percentage of units that are unoccupied. A typical vacancy rate for rental units is 5 percent. If the vacancy rate decreases (as occupancy increases), rents are likely to increase, and renters often become motivated to buy homes.

Principle of Diminishing and Increasing Returns

This principle refers to the fact that, at some point, the additional cost to upgrade a property does not produce a corresponding increase in overall value. For example, a home is located in an area near an airport that has just been constructed. It would probably not be prudent to remodel the house because the proximity to the new airport will likely limit the value of the house as a residence. That is, the cost to remodel may be $25,000, but the corresponding increase in value may be only $10,000. In this case, the remodeling is referred to as an **over-improvement**.

Principle of Conformity

This principle states that the maximum value of a property is attained when the property conforms to the usage and style of neighboring property. For example, a contemporary style home that sells for $200,000 in a neighborhood of similar homes would likely sell for less than that in a neighborhood of traditional homes selling for $100,000. This principle is the basis for zoning regulations that require all property in a given zone to conform to the usage, size and style, prescribed for that zone.

Miscellaneous Topics

There are two remaining miscellaneous topics to be covered that relate to the appraisal of property:

1. Assemblage versus plottage
2. Regression versus progression

Assemblage versus Plottage

Assemblage refers to the process of combining two or more adjacent properties into one tract of land. For example, a developer might purchase several residential homes, remove the houses, combine the lots into one parcel, and build a shopping center on it. This would be assemblage.

FIGURE 15.3

Assemblage versus Plottage

- Assemblage is the act of combining the properties.
- Plottage is the increase in value that occurs when properties are combined.

Regression versus Progression

- Regression means that neighboring properties lower the value of a given property.
- Progression means that neighboring properties raise the value of a given property.

Plottage refers to any *increase in value* for a tract of land formed by combining two or more parcels. For example, the property bought by the developer just described is probably worth more when the lots are combined than when they are separate. This represents plottage.

Regression versus Progression

Regression is a principle of appraisal that states that the value of a higher valued property is decreased if it is located among properties of lower value. For example, a house that costs $150,000 to build will have a lower value if it is in a neighborhood of $90,000 homes than if it were in a neighborhood of similar $150,000 homes.

Progression is just the opposite. It states that the value of a lower-valued property is increased if it is located among properties of higher value. For example, a house that costs $85,000 to build will be worth more if it is in a neighborhood of $130,000 houses.

Figure 15.3 summarizes the differences between assemblage and plottage, and regression and progression.

Steps in the Appraisal Process

In all appraisals, there are seven basic steps that an appraisal will follow:

1. Define the problem
2. Preliminary analysis, data selection, and collection
3. Highest and best use analysis
4. Estimate of land value
5. Application of the three approaches (including the market data approach)
6. Reconciliation of value indication
7. Provide the final estimate of value

Now we will examine each of the steps that are used in the market data approach.

Market Data (Sales Comparison) Approach

The market data approach is based on a comparison of the **subject property** (the property being appraised) to similar properties that have recently sold. As with other approaches to appraisal, it assumes the basic principle of substitution in the purchase of real property. The market data approach is also called the **sales comparison approach**.

Step 1: Define the Problem

The first step in all appraisals is to define the problem. This requires the appraiser to understand the type of value being that is being sought by the appraisal. For example, if the appraisal will be used for purpose of real property tax reduction, the appraiser will need to determine the assessed value of the property. When the appraisal will be used for financing purposes, the appraiser will need to determine the property's market value. Once the appraiser has defined the value being sought, she will proceed to the next step in the market data approach.

Step 2: Data Selection and Collection

Locate and gather information on similar properties that have sold recently in the same neighborhood or area. These similar properties are called **comparables** (comps). The data compiled on comparables include:

- Date of sale
- Sale price
- Location
- Terms of sale
- Physical characteristics
- Amenities (extra features that add value).

Step 3: Determining the Highest and Best Use

Highest and best use is performed to determine which use will produce the greatest value attributable to the land. This step requires the appraiser to examine other alternative legal uses in comparison to the current use of the property. The purpose of this step is to determine whether the current use for the subject property is in fact the property's highest and best use. There are two types of highest and best use analysis.

1. Highest and best use as vacant—this approach is applied when land is unimproved. The appraiser will compare alternative legal uses for the property to determine which use provides the highest value from that use attributable to the land. For example if a property is zoned for commercial use, the appraiser will probably compare all commercial uses (offices, retail, hotel/motel) to determine which of those uses produce the greatest land value

2. Highest and best use as improved—as in the highest and best use analysis as vacant, this analysis views the current use of the property to determine if in fact that use is still the highest and best use as improved. Remember, in this case the land is not vacant. The land contains a previously built improvement. Therefore, the primary difference between the two highest and best use approaches is that this analysis requires the appraiser to consider demolition costs of the current improvement toward a determination of that property's highest and best use.

Step 4: Estimate the Value of the Land

At this point the appraiser establishes the land value by comparing land values of other previously sold properties. Land comparables are always available. Regardless of the type of property sold all sales include underlying land. Therefore the appraiser evaluates previous sales to determine land value.

Step 5: Application of the Three Approaches and the Adjustment Process

As was stated earlier in this chapter, all appraisals incorporate application of all three approaches toward value determination. However in doing so, we have to first compare the comparables to the subject property and make adjustments in the price of the comparables for any differences. Comparables are to be adjusted in the following manner and sequence:

1. Transactional adjustments, which include financing terms such as seller financing (which tends to be less expensive than conventional financing) and sales conditions.
2. Locational adjustments, which include differences in the lot location such as a corner versus a rear lot.
3. Physical adjustments, which include differences in the comparables to the subject property such as a two-car garage versus a one-car port, or a pool versus no pool.

Coaching Tips: It is important to know that the appraiser *never adjusts the subject property of the appraisal for differences.* The appraiser *always makes the adjustments to the comparables* thereby making them resemble (as closely as possible) that of the subject property.

Step 6: The Reconciliation Process

Reconcile all the data from the comparables and arrive at a price for the subject property. In this process, the appraiser reviews all value indications derived directly from the application of all three approaches.

Step 7: Reporting the Value

The appraiser will then prepare the appraisal report noting her indication of value.

The market data approach, shown in Figure 15.4, is the most widely used approach to pricing. It is given the most weight of the three approaches in determining a suitable price for residential property and vacant lots.

Cost Approach (Reproduction)

The market data approach is widely used to determine a price for a property for which comparables are readily available. This requires an active marketplace. For some types of properties, the market data approach is not useful because of the lack of comparables that have sold recently. For example, school buildings, fire stations, courthouses, and highway bridges are not sold often enough to provide adequate data for a market data approach to pricing. These properties are termed *special-use* or *single-purpose properties*. In these cases, the pricing approach often used is the cost approach. The cost approach to pricing determines an appropriate price for property based on the current cost of reproduction or replacement of the improvements. In essence, the appraiser creates a comparable of the subject property by comparing it to a replica or not-exact replica of itself. We refer to this process as one of the following:

- Reproduction cost
- Replacement cost

Reproduction cost is the cost to produce an exact replica of the original subject property, using the same materials and construction techniques as the original.

Replacement cost is the cost to replace the improvements with another building that performs the same function and utility but is not an exact replica of the subject property. This process is also the basis for most insurers of real and personal property. Replacement refers to a building with the same function.

The steps in the cost approach to pricing are as follows:

- Step 1: Estimate the reproduction cost (new) of the improvement(s).
- Step 2: Estimate and subtract the accrued depreciation from reproduction cost (new) resulting from functional obsolescence, physical deterioration, and economic/external obsolescence.

FIGURE 15.4

**Example Using
Market Approach**

Assume that the subject property is a medium-quality, 25-year-old, three-bedroom home, with a two-car garage. The square footage for the home is 1,300 square feet. The appraiser locates three similar homes that have recently sold in the neighborhood at fair market prices. All have identical square footage and number of rooms.

Comparables

Data	Comparable A	Comparable B	Comparable C
Price paid	$223,900	$221,500	$216,000
Location	better than subject property	equal to subject property	equal to subject property
Lot size	equal to subject property	larger than subject property	smaller than subject property
Overall condition	better than subject property	equal to subject property	worse than subject property

Dollar Adjustment Factors per the Opinion of the Appraiser

Location difference	$1,000
Lot size difference	$1,500
Overall condition difference	$3,000

Adjustments

Data	Comparable A	Comparable B	Comparable C
Price paid	$223,900	$221,500	$216,000
Location	−1,000	0	0
Lot size	0	−1,500	+1,500
Overall condition	−3,000	0	+3,000
Price comparables would have sold for if they were like the subject home	$219,900	$220,000	$220,500

- o Only the improvements are depreciated.
- o Land is never depreciated because it never wears out. The types of depreciation will be covered later in this chapter.
- • Step 3: Estimate and add the value of the site.

  The cost approach to pricing can be summarized in the following formula:

  Reproduction cost (new)
  −Accrued depreciation
  +Value of land
  = Estimated price

Because people are reluctant to pay more for a given property than it would cost to build it new, the reproduction cost (new) is often used because it tends to set the upper-most limit to value.

The replacement cost approach to pricing requires an estimate be made of the cost to replace the improvements. This can be done in three ways:

1. The square foot method
2. The unit-in-place method
3. The quantity survey method

The Square Foot Method

The steps in this approach are as follows:

- Step 1: Obtain the construction cost of a similar building recently constructed.
- Step 2: Convert the cost of construction to cost per square foot.
- Step 3: Multiply the cost per square foot times the number of square feet in the building whose price is being determined.

A variation of this method is the cubic foot method, which uses cost per cubic foot rather than cost per square foot. The cubic foot method is used for buildings like warehouses that don't have standard ceiling heights.

The Unit-In-Place Method

The steps in this approach are as follows:

- Step 1: Estimate the installed cost of each major unit of the building that is being priced, such as the foundation, walls, roof, windows, doors, etc.
- Step 2: Add the cost of all the units that make up the building plus contractor profit and overhead.
- Step 3: The total estimated cost is the estimated price for the property.

The Quantity Survey Method

The steps in this approach are as follows:

- Step 1: Estimate the cost of all materials (by individual item price) and the cost of all labor.
- Step 2: Add the cost of all materials and labor.
- Step 3: Add the builder's profit or return on investment.
- Step 4: The total estimated cost is the estimated price for the property.

This method is very time consuming and is seldom used by appraisers. See Figure 15.5 for a summary of pricing methods.

FIGURE 15.5

PRICING METHODS AT A GLANCE

- The quantity survey method uses the total cost of all labor and materials.
- The square foot method uses the size of a building to estimate its cost.
- The unit-in-place method is based on the total cost of all major elements.
- The quantity survey method is the most accurate but is used the least.
- The square foot method is used the most but is the least accurate.

FIGURE 15.6

DEPRECIATION AT A GLANCE

1. Physical Deterioration
- Physical deterioration is wear and tear from age.
- Physical deterioration arises from forces within the property.
- Physical deterioration can be categorized as curable or incurable.

2. Functional Obsolescence
- Functional obsolescence arises from forces within the property.
- Functional obsolescence comes from outdated features.
- Functional obsolescence can be categorized as curable or incurable.
  - Broken windows are typically classified as curable.
  - Removing support columns are considered incurable

3. Economic or External Obsolescence
- Economic obsolescence comes from factors outside the property.
- Economic obsolescence comes from factors outside the property and therefore is considered incurable.

Of these three methods, the square foot method is used the most often but is the least accurate.

The unit in place method is more accurate than the square foot method but also more difficult than the square foot method.

The quantity survey method is the most accurate and the most difficult of the three, but is used the least because of its difficulty.

Depreciation

As you learned earlier in this chapter, in the cost approach to pricing, depreciation is subtracted from the estimated reproduction (or replacement) cost before determining the price for the property. (Because the cost approach involves the calculation of depreciation, this approach is also known as the cost-depreciation approach.) There are three different types of depreciation considered in the pricing process (see Figure 15.6):

1. Physical deterioration
2. Functional obsolescence
3. Economic (external) obsolescence

Physical Deterioration

Physical deterioration is the wear and tear that results from normal use. For example, a frame house that needs a new coat of paint is suffering from physical deterioration.

Functional Obsolescence

Functional obsolescence is the reduction in value due to outdated features of the property, including:

- Closets that are too small
- Ceilings that are too high or low
- Too few bathrooms
- Inadequate wiring
- Outdated design or architecture

Functional obsolescence also includes any loss in value due to an over-improvement to the property. An over-improvement is also referred to as superadequacy.

Both physical deterioration and functional obsolescence can be categorized as curable or incurable. Both curable and incurable defects can be corrected, but the difference is whether it is economically feasible to correct the defects. A defect is considered **curable** if it is economically feasible to correct the problem. A defect is considered **incurable** if it is *not* economically feasible to correct the problem.

Economic (External) Obsolescence

The first two categories of depreciation were physical deterioration and functional obsolescence. Both of these types of depreciation arise from the characteristics of the property itself. The third category of depreciation is economic (external) obsolescence. It differs from the first two categories of depreciation in that it represents depreciation that arises from factors outside the property itself. Due to the fact that the value loss is attributable to external forces—outside the property line—economic (external) obsolescence is always said to be incurable.

Examples of economic obsolescence include:

- Changes in the makeup of the surrounding area
- Environmental impacts like noise pollution from an airport
- Changes in highways that serve the property
- The closing of a major business nearby

Figure 15.7 illustrates the cost approach for determining the price of a property.

Income Approach to Pricing

Previously, you learned about the first two approaches to pricing—the market data approach and the cost approach. Now, we will cover the third major approach to pricing—the income approach. See Figure 15.8.

The income approach is used primarily for income-producing properties such as:

- Office buildings
- Apartment buildings
- Retail properties
- Mixed-use properties

This approach is not normally suited to single-family dwellings, even those that are strictly rental properties. The income approach determines the annual income a property is expected to produce and converts that into a price for the property through a process known as capitalization.

Capitalization

Capitalization is the process for converting future income into current value, which is used to determine a price for a property. It can also be defined as the present worth of the property based upon the income produced by that property. Any of the following formulas are used to determine value through the capitalization of income:

$$Income = Rate \times Value$$
$$Rate = Income \div Value$$
$$Value = Income \div Rate$$

This formula is most commonly known as IRV.

FIGURE 15.7

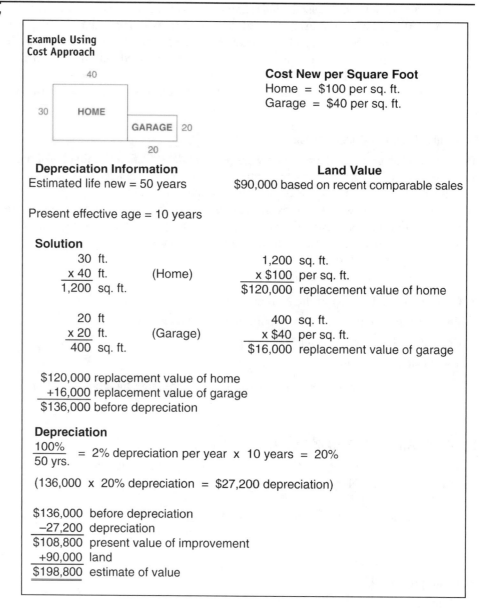

Example Using Cost Approach

Cost New per Square Foot
Home = $100 per sq. ft.
Garage = $40 per sq. ft.

Depreciation Information
Estimated life new = 50 years

Present effective age = 10 years

Land Value
$90,000 based on recent comparable sales

Solution

```
   30  ft.                          1,200  sq. ft.
 x 40  ft.        (Home)          x $100  per sq. ft.
1,200  sq. ft.                  $120,000  replacement value of home


   20  ft                          400  sq. ft.
 x 20  ft.       (Garage)        x $40  per sq. ft.
  400  sq. ft.                  $16,000  replacement value of garage
```

```
$120,000  replacement value of home
 +16,000  replacement value of garage
$136,000  before depreciation
```

Depreciation

$$\frac{100\%}{50 \text{ yrs.}} = 2\% \text{ depreciation per year} \times 10 \text{ years} = 20\%$$

(136,000 x 20% depreciation = $27,200 depreciation)

```
$136,000  before depreciation
 −27,200  depreciation
$108,800  present value of improvement
 +90,000  land
$198,800  estimate of value
```

In each of these formulas, *income* refers to *net operating income* and *rate* refers to the *capitalization rate.* In order for the process of overall capitalization to occur, net operating income (NOI) must be determined. The appraiser must reconstruct an annual income and expense operating statement for the subject property.

In order to construct an annual income and expense operating statement, licensees must understand the following formulas:

$$PGI - V\&C + OI = EGI$$
$$EGI - OE = NOI$$

We will look at the terms in these formulas, beginning with the first formula:

$$PGI - V\&C + OI = EGI$$

PGI stands for potential gross income. This is accomplished when the property in question is fully leased.

FIGURE 15.8

**Example Using
Income Approach**

The property is a clean, but modest, 15-unit apartment with fair market rents of $700 per unit. The estimated factor for vacancies and collection loss is 5%.
Annual operating expenses include:

Property taxes	$9,450
Insurance	$1,000
Management and accounting	$10,000
Repairs and others	$12,000

The capitalization rate selected by the appraiser is 10%.

Solution

Potential gross income	$126,000	($700 x 15 units x 12 months)
Less vacancies and collection losses	−6,300	($126,000 x 5%)
Effective gross income	$119,700	
Less annual operating expenses	−32,450	($9,450 + 1,000 + 10,000 + 12,000)
Net operating income	$87,250	

$$\frac{\text{Net operating income}}{\text{Capitalization rate}} = \frac{\$87,250}{10\%} = \$872,500 \text{ Estimate of value}$$

If the capitalization rate selected had been 9%, the value would be:

$$\frac{\$87,250}{9\%} = \$969,444$$

If the capitalization rate were 11%, the value would be:

$$\frac{\$87,250}{11\%} = \$793,181$$

Observe this rule: *The higher the capitalization rate, the lower the value.* Therefore, you can see that the selection of the appropriate capitalization rate is very critical! *The selection of an inappropriate capitalization rate can greatly distort value.*

V&C stands for vacancy and collection losses. There are times in any calendar or fiscal year when a vacancy arises or a tenant(s) does not pay his rent. Vacancy and collection losses are usually expressed in percentage terms of the PGI (e.g., 5 percent).

OI stands for other income that may be derived from sources outside of the residence or office rents, such as retail rents, parking revenue or rents, and vending machines, such as washer/dryer income. In commercial leases, OI can represent reimbursed increases in the cost of operating the property. This item is referred to in a commercial lease as additional rent.

EGI stands for **effective gross income**. As you saw in the formula on the previous page, EGI is determined by subtracting V&C and adding OI.

Now, let's take a look at the second formula:

$$EGI - OE = NOI$$

EGI was calculated using the first formula provided.

In every income-producing property, there are costs associated with operating that property. These costs are broken down into two categories:

1. Fixed expenses, which include *only* the following:
   - Real property taxes
   - Property insurance
2. Variable expenses, which include items such as the following:
   - Maintenance
   - Repairs
   - Payroll
   - Garbage removal
   - Reserves for replacements

The OE is then subtracted from the EGI; the result is the important NOI.

As mentioned previously, the NOI is used in the capitalization process:

$$Value = Income \div Rate$$

After calculating NOI, the desired capitalization rate must be determined. The capitalization rate is the rate of return on investment desired by the investor, expressed as a percentage. For example, if an investor wants a return of 10 percent on an investment, the capitalization rate would be 10 percent or 0.10. Using the formula above, one can then capitalize the income in order to derive the property's value.

Thus, the final step is to capitalize the net income by dividing it by the capitalization rate to get a price for the property. In simple terms, this concept lets the seller, buyer, and appraiser of income-producing real property determine the following:

- For a seller—How much to sell the property for.
- For a buyer—How much to pay to purchase the property and its income.
- For an appraiser—How much to value the property based on the purpose of the appraisal.

Example

Assume that an investor wants a return on an investment of 10 percent. A property under consideration generates an annual net income of $42,000. What price could the investor pay for the property according to the income approach at the capitalization rate of 10 percent?

Answer:

$$Value = Income \div Rate$$
So in this case, $42,000 \div 0.10 = \$420,000$.

Based upon the above financial model and with a capitalization rate of 10 percent, the property generating an income of $42,000 would support a maximum sale/purchase price of $420,000. If the investor bought the property for $420,000, she would receive $42,000 in net income, which represents a return on investment of 10 percent—the desired return.

The only remaining points you should remember are:

- As the capitalization rate increases, the price of the property decreases.
- As the capitalization rate decreases, the price of the property increases (see bottom of figure 15.8).

Gross Rent Multiplier

We have just covered the three major approaches to pricing—the market data, cost, and income approaches. These are all formal approaches to pricing. There is one remaining technique of property pricing—the **gross rent multiplier (GRM)** technique. The GRM is *not* a formal approach to pricing. However, it can be another form of analysis within the income approach. It is used informally in selected applications involving income-producing property. Its primary use is for an investor who is evaluating several properties and wants a simple and quick way to *eliminate* some properties from consideration before doing formal price determinations. To use the GRM to get an informal estimate of price, complete the following steps:

- Step 1: Identify comparable properties that have been sold recently and determine their gross monthly income.
- Step 2: Divide the price of each property by its gross monthly income. The answer is the GRM.
- Step 3: Average the GRMs for all the comparable properties.
- Step 4: Multiply the gross monthly rent for the subject property by the average GRM from Step 3. The answer is the estimate of price for the subject property.

The advantage of the GRM technique is that it is quick and easy. The disadvantage is that it uses the gross rent and doesn't take into consideration any rent losses or operating expenses. As a result, it is not a very precise or reliable estimate of price.

Reconciliation

All the approaches to pricing that can be applied to a property should be used to determine that property's price. This is not always possible, however. When more than one approach is used, the greatest weight is given to the approach that is best suited to that property. The process of arriving at a final estimate of value when more than one approach is used is called reconciliation.

See Figure 15.9 for a summary of the three approaches to appraisal and Figure 15.10 a-c for a Uniform Residential Appraisal Report.

MARKET ANALYSIS

One of the most important tasks a licensee performs in servicing a listing is assisting a seller or buyer in determining an appropriate price for a property. This may be required when listing a house for sale, assisting the seller in setting a listing price, or assisting a buyer in determining the price for a contract offer. A market analysis is the technique that is used most often to determine a price for a property. A market analysis is a practical method of determining a reasonable estimate of a price at which a home will sell.

When a licensee completes a market analysis to assist a client in pricing a property, the result of the process is simply a determination of a suitable price, not an appraisal or an estimate of the value of the property. Often, when a real estate licensee determines a suitable price for a property on behalf of a client, the licensee does so in a situation in which the property may also be appraised by a licensed appraiser. For example, when a seller lists a property for sale, a licensee may assist the seller in setting a price at which the property is offered for sale. When a buyer is found, the lender will require that an appraisal of the property be conducted before making a loan to the buyer.

FIGURE 15.9

THE THREE APPROACHES TO APPRAISAL AT A GLANCE

- The cost approach uses an estimate of the cost of construction as a basis for determining the price for a property.
  - The cost approach is used when comparables are not available.
  - A reproduction is an exact replica of a building.
  - Depreciation is used in the cost approach.
  - Current building costs are used in the cost approach.
  - Land is never depreciated. Only improvements are depreciated.
- The direct-sales comparison is another term for the market data approach.
  - The market data approach is used for residential property.
  - In order to derive value, the process compares recently sold properties known as comps to that of the subject property.
  - Comparables are used in the market data approach.
  - Market data approach is used most for residential property.
- The income approach uses income generated as a basis for determining the price for a property.
  - The income approach is used for income-producing property.
  - Net income is used in the income approach to pricing.
  - Net income is based on the future income after expenses attributable to the property or projected net income derived from a proforma statement.
  - The income approach uses a process called capitalization.
  - As the capitalization rate increases, the price of the property decreases.
  - The gross rent multiplier (a monthly factor) approach is an INFORMAL means of comparing income properties.
  - The gross income multiplier (an annual factor) is an INFORMAL means of comparing income properties.

The licensee's opinion of a suitable price may differ from a value that results from an appraisal for a number of reasons, including the following:

- Appraisals are usually made for a lender to determine the value of the property as security for a loan. The licensee's opinion is related to a sales price for the property. These are affected by different influences.

- An appraisal for loan purposes is based on the unencumbered value of the property, which means that the status of existing loans has no impact on the estimate of value. The licensee's opinion as to price should take financing issues into consideration because existing financing can affect the ability to sell a home as well as its price.

Principals should understand why the licensee's opinion as to price and an actual appraisal of the property may differ. In addition, before making use of a market analysis, or the information obtained in the process, licensees should check with their broker to determine the broker's policy on conducting a market analysis and to receive training the broker may provide in this area. Now, let's look at the process for completing a market analysis approach to pricing.

To complete a market analysis, you will be seeking to determine the fair market value for the property, which is defined as the price at which a willing seller will sell and a willing buyer will buy, when neither the seller nor the buyer is under abnormal pressure to act.

FIGURE 15.10

UNIFORM RESIDENTIAL APPRAISAL REPORT   File No. _____

SUBJECT / Property Description

Property Address		City		State	Zip Code
Legal Description			County		

Assessor's Parcel No. _____ Tax Year _____ R.E. Taxes $ _____ Special Assessments $ _____

Borrower _____ Current Owner _____ Occupant: ☐ Owner ☐ Tenant ☐ Vacant

Property rights appraised ☐ Fee Simple ☐ Leasehold Project Type ☐ PUD ☐ Condominium (HUD/VA only) HOA $ _____ /Mo.

Neighborhood or Project Name _____ Map Reference _____ Census Tract _____

Sale Price $ _____ Date of Sale _____ Description and $ amount of loan charges/concessions to be paid by seller

Lender/Client _____ Address _____

Appraiser _____ Address _____

NEIGHBORHOOD

Location ☐ Urban ☐ Suburban ☐ Rural
Built up ☐ Over 75% ☐ 25-75% ☐ Under 25%
Growth rate ☐ Rapid ☐ Stable ☐ Slow
Property values ☐ Increasing ☐ Stable ☐ Declining
Demand/supply ☐ Shortage ☐ In balance ☐ Over supply
Marketing time ☐ Under 3 mos. ☐ 3-6 mos. ☐ Over 6 mos.

Predominant occupancy: ☐ Owner ☐ Tenant ☐ Vacant (0-5%) ☐ Vac.(over 5%)

Single family housing PRICE $(000) / AGE (yrs): Low / High / Predominant

Present land use %: One family __ / 2-4 family __ / Multi-family __ / Commercial __

Land use change ☐ Not likely ☐ Likely ☐ In process To: _____

Note: Race and the racial composition of the neighborhood are not appraisal factors.

Neighborhood boundaries and characteristics: _____

Factors that affect the marketability of the properties in the neighborhood (proximity to employment and amenities, employment stability, appeal to market, etc.): _____

Market conditions in the subject neighborhood (including support for the above conclusions related to the trend of property values, demand/supply, and marketing time -- such as data on competitive properties for sale in the neighborhood, description of the prevalence of sales and financing concessions, etc.): _____

PUD

Project Information for PUDs (If applicable) -- Is the developer/builder in control of the Home Owners' Association (HOA)? ☐ Yes ☐ No
Approximate total number of units in the subject project _____ Approximate total number of units for sale in the subject project _____
Describe common elements and recreational facilities: _____

SITE

Dimensions _____ Topography _____
Site area _____ Corner Lot ☐ Yes ☐ No Size _____
Specific zoning classification and description _____ Shape _____
Zoning compliance ☐ Legal ☐ Legal nonconforming (Grandfathered use) ☐ Illegal ☐ No zoning Drainage _____
Highest & best use as improved: ☐ Present use ☐ Other use (explain) View _____ / Landscaping _____

Utilities	Public	Other	Off-site Improvements	Type	Public	Private	
Electricity	☐		Street		☐	☐	Driveway Surface ___
Gas	☐		Curb/gutter		☐	☐	Apparent easements ___
Water	☐		Sidewalk		☐	☐	FEMA Special Flood Hazard Area ☐ Yes ☐ No
Sanitary sewer	☐		Street lights		☐	☐	FEMA Zone ___ Map Date ___
Storm sewer	☐		Alley		☐	☐	FEMA Map No. ___

Comments (apparent adverse easements, encroachments, special assessments, slide areas, illegal or legal nonconforming zoning use, etc.): _____

DESCRIPTION OF IMPROVEMENTS

GENERAL DESCRIPTION	EXTERIOR DESCRIPTION	FOUNDATION	BASEMENT	INSULATION
No. of Units ___	Foundation ___	Slab ___	Area Sq. Ft. ___	Roof ☐
No. of Stories ___	Exterior Walls ___	Crawl Space ___	% Finished ___	Ceiling ☐
Type (Det./Att.) ___	Roof Surface ___	Basement ___	Ceiling ___	Walls ☐
Design (Style) ___	Gutters & Dwnspts. ___	Sump Pump ___	Walls ___	Floor ☐
Existing/Proposed ___	Window Type ___	Dampness ___	Floor ___	None ☐
Age (Yrs.) ___	Storm/Screens ___	Settlement ___	Outside Entry ___	Unknown ☐
Effective Age (Yrs.) ___	Manufactured House ___	Infestation ___		

ROOMS	Foyer	Living	Dining	Kitchen	Den	Family Rm.	Rec. Rm.	Bedrooms	# Baths	Laundry	Other	Area Sq. Ft.
Basement												
Level 1												
Level 2												

Finished area **above** grade contains: _____ Rooms; _____ Bedroom(s); _____ Bath(s); _____ Square Feet of Gross Living Area

INTERIOR	Materials/Condition	HEATING	KITCHEN EQUIP.	ATTIC	AMENITIES	CAR STORAGE:
Floors	___	Type ___	Refrigerator ☐	None ☐	Fireplace(s) # ___ ☐	None ☐
Walls	___	Fuel ___	Range/Oven ☐	Stairs ☐	Patio ___ ☐	Garage ___ # of cars
Trim/Finish	___	Condition ___	Disposal ☐	Drop Stair ☐	Deck ___ ☐	Attached ☐
Bath Floor	___	COOLING	Dishwasher ☐	Scuttle ☐	Porch ___ ☐	Detached ☐
Bath Wainscot	___	Central ___	Fan/Hood ☐	Floor ☐	Fence ___ ☐	Built-In ☐
Doors	___	Other ___	Microwave ☐	Heated ☐	Pool ___ ☐	Carport ☐
		Condition ___	Washer/Dryer ☐	Finished ☐		Driveway ☐

Additional features (special energy efficient items, etc.): _____

COMMENTS

Condition of the improvements, depreciation (physical, functional, and external), repairs needed, quality of construction, remodeling/additions, etc.: _____

Adverse environmental conditions (such as, but not limited to, hazardous wastes, toxic substances, etc.) present in the improvements, on the site, or in the immediate vicinity of the subject property.: _____

Freddie Mac Form 70 6/93   PAGE 1 OF 2   Fannie Mae Form 1004 6/93

(a)

(Continued)

FIGURE 15.10 *(Continued)*

UNIFORM RESIDENTIAL APPRAISAL REPORT

Valuation Section   File No.

COST APPROACH

ESTIMATED SITE VALUE .... = $ _____

ESTIMATED REPRODUCTION COST-NEW-OF IMPROVEMENTS:

Dwelling _____ Sq. Ft. @$ _____ = $ _____
_____ Sq. Ft. @$ _____ = _____
= _____
Garage/Carport _____ Sq. Ft. @$ _____ = _____
Total Estimated Cost New .... = $ _____
Less   Physical   Functional   External
Depreciation _____ _____ _____ =$ _____
Depreciated Value of Improvements .... =$ _____
"As-is" Value of Site Improvements .... =$ _____
INDICATED VALUE BY COST APPROACH .... =$ _____

Comments on Cost Approach (such as, source of cost estimate, site value, square foot calculation and for HUD, VA and FmHA, the estimated remaining economic life of the property): _____

SALES COMPARISON ANALYSIS

ITEM	SUBJECT	COMPARABLE NO. 1		COMPARABLE NO. 2		COMPARABLE NO. 3	
Address							
Proximity to Subject							
Sales Price	$		$		$		$
Price/Gross Living Area	$	$		$		$	
Data and/or Verification Source							
VALUE ADJUSTMENTS	DESCRIPTION	DESCRIPTION	+(–)$ Adjust.	DESCRIPTION	+(–)$ Adjust.	DESCRIPTION	+(–)$ Adjust.
Sales or Financing Concessions							
Date of Sale/Time							
Location							
Leasehold/Fee Simple							
Site							
View							
Design and Appeal							
Quality of Construction							
Age							
Condition							
Above Grade Room Count	Total Bdrms Baths	Total Bdrms Baths		Total Bdrms Baths		Total Bdrms Baths	
Gross Living Area	Sq. Ft.	Sq. Ft.		Sq. Ft.		Sq. Ft.	
Basement & Finished Rooms Below Grade							
Functional Utility							
Heating/Cooling							
Energy Efficient Items							
Garage/Carport							
Porch, Patio, Deck, Fireplace(s), etc.							
Fence, Pool, etc.							
Net Adj. (total)		+ – $		+ – $		+ – $	
Adjusted Sales Price of Comparable			$		$		$

Comments on Sales Comparison (including the subject property's compatibility to the neighborhood, etc.): _____

ITEM	SUBJECT	COMPARABLE NO. 1	COMPARABLE NO. 2	COMPARABLE NO. 3
Date, Price and Data Source, for prior sales within year of appraisal				

Analysis of any current agreement of sale, option, or listing of subject property and analysis of any prior sales of subject and comparables within one year of the date of appraisal:

INDICATED VALUE BY SALES COMPARISON APPROACH _____ $ _____
INDICATED VALUE BY INCOME APPROACH (If Applicable) Estimated Market Rent $ _____ /Mo. x Gross Rent Multiplier _____ = $ _____

This appraisal is made ☐ "as is" ☐ subject to the repairs, alterations, inspections or conditions listed below ☐ subject to completion per plans & specifications.
Conditions of Appraisal: _____

Final Reconciliation: _____

RECONCILIATION

The purpose of this appraisal is to estimate the market value of the real property that is the subject of this report, based on the above conditions and the certification, contingent and limiting conditions, and market value definition that are stated in the attached Freddie Mac Form 439/FNMA form 1004B (Revised _____).
I (WE) ESTIMATE THE MARKET VALUE, AS DEFINED, OF THE REAL PROPERTY THAT IS THE SUBJECT OF THIS REPORT, AS OF _____
(WHICH IS THE DATE OF INSPECTION AND THE EFFECTIVE DATE OF THIS REPORT) TO BE $ _____

APPRAISER:
Signature _____
Name _____
Date Report Signed _____
State Certification # _____ State
Or State License # _____ State

SUPERVISORY APPRAISER (ONLY IF REQUIRED):
Signature _____ ☐ Did ☐ Did Not
Name _____ Inspect Property
Date Report Signed _____
State Certification # _____ State
Or State License # _____ State

(b)

File No. _____

DEFINITION OF MARKET VALUE: The most probable price which a property should bring in a competitive and open market under all conditions requisite to a fair sale, the buyer and seller, each acting prudently, knowledgeably and assuming the price is not affected by undue stimulus. Implicit in this definition is the consummation of a sale as of a specified date and the passing of title from seller to buyer under conditions whereby: (1) buyer and seller are typically motivated; (2) both parties are well informed or advised, and each acting in what he considers his own best interest; (3) a reasonable time is allowed for exposure in the open market; (4) payment is made in terms of cash in U. S. dollars or in terms of financial arrangements comparable thereto; and (5) the price represents the normal consideration for the property sold unaffected by special or creative financing or sales concessions* granted by anyone associated with the sale.

*Adjustments to the comparables must be made for special or creative financing or sales concessions. No adjustments are necessary for those costs which are normally paid by sellers as a result of tradition or law in a market area; these costs are readily identifiable since the seller pays these costs in virtually all sales transactions. Special or creative financing adjustments can be made to the comparable property by comparisons to financing terms offered by a third party institutional lender that is not already involved in the property or transaction. Any adjustment should not be calculated on a mechanical dollar for dollar cost of the financing or concession but the dollar amount of any adjustment should approximate the market's reaction to the financing or concessions based on the appraiser's judgment.

CERTIFICATION AND STATEMENT OF LIMITING CONDITIONS

CERTIFICATION: The Appraiser certifies and agrees that:

1. The Appraiser has no present or contemplated future interest in the property appraised; and neither the employment to make the appraisal, nor the compensation for it, is contingent upon the appraised value of the property.

2. The Appraiser has no personal interest in or bias with respect to the subject matter of the appraisal report or the participants to the sale. The 'Estimate of Market Value' in the appraisal report is not based in whole or in part upon the race, color, or national origin of the prospective owners or occupants of the property appraised, or upon the race, color or national origin of the present owners or occupants of the properties in the vicinity of the property appraised.

3. The Appraiser has personally inspected the property, both inside and out, and has made an exterior inspection of all comparable sales listed in the report. To the best of the Appraiser's knowledge and belief, all statements and information in this report are true and correct, and the Appraiser has not knowingly withheld any significant information.

4. All contingent and limiting conditions are contained herein (imposed by the terms of the assignment or by the undersigned affecting the analyses, opinions, and conclusions contained in the report).

5. This appraisal report has been made in conformity with and is subject to the requirements of the Code of Professional Ethics and Standards of Professional Conduct of the appraisal organizations with which the Appraiser is affiliated.

6. All conclusions and opinions concerning the real estate that are set forth in the appraisal report were prepared by the Appraiser whose signature appears on the appraisal report, unless indicated as 'Review Appraiser'. No change of any item in the appraisal report shall be made by anyone other than the Appraiser, and the Appraiser shall have no responsibility for any such unauthorized change.

CONTINGENT AND LIMITING CONDITIONS: The certification of the Appraiser appearing in the appraisal report is subject to the following conditions and to such other specific and limiting conditions as are set forth by the Appraiser in the report.

1. The Appraiser assumes no responsibility for matters of a legal nature affecting the property appraised or the title thereto, nor does the Appraiser render any opinion as to the title, which is assumed to be good and marketable. The property is appraised as though under responsible ownership.

2. Any sketch in the report may show approximate dimensions and is included to assist the reader in visualizing the property. The Appraiser has made no survey of the property.

3. The Appraiser is not required to give testimony or appear in court because of having made the appraisal with reference to the property in question, unless arrangements have been previously made therefor.

4. Any distribution of the valuation in the report between land and improvements applies only under the existing program of utilization The separate valuations for land and building must not be used in conjunctions with any other appraisal and are invalid if so used.

5. The Appraiser assumes that there are no hidden or unapparent conditions of the property, subsoil, or structures, which would render it more or less valuable. The Appraiser assumes no responsibility for such conditions, or for engineering which might be required to discover such factors.

6. Information, estimates, and opinions furnished to the Appraiser, and contained in the report, were obtained from sources considered reliable and believed to be true and correct. However, no responsibility for accuracy of such items furnished the Appraiser can be assumed by the Appraiser.

7. Disclosure of the contents of the appraisal report is governed by the Bylaws and Regulations of the professional appraisal organizations with which the Appraiser is affiliated.

8. Neither all, nor any part of the content of the report, or copy thereof (including conclusions as to the property value, the identity of the Appraiser, professional designations, reference to any professional appraisal organizations, or the firm with which the Appraiser is connected), shall be used for any purposes by anyone but the client specified in the report, the borrower if appraisal fee paid by same, the mortgagee or its successors and assigns, mortgage insurers, consultants, professional appraisal organizations, any state or federally approved financial institution, any department, agency, or instrumentality of the United States or any state or the District of Columbia, without the previous written consent of the Appraiser; nor shall it be conveyed by anyone to the public through advertising, public relations, news, sales, or other media, without the written consent and approval of the Appraiser.

9. On all appraisals, subject to satisfactory completion, repairs, or alterations, the appraisal report and value conclusion are contingent upon completion of the improvements in a workmanlike manner.

Date: _____   Appraiser(s) _____

Freddie Mac
Form 439 JUL 86-1   MCS, Richardson, Texas 75082 (214) 699-7783   Fannie Mae
                                                                                                     Form 1004B JUL 86-1

(c)

For example, a home sold at a foreclosure sale would not meet these requirements for a fair market value because there were abnormal circumstances to the sale that would affect the price.

The fair market value for a property is determined by the actions of people. Earlier, you learned that the principle of substitution means that the appropriate price of a property is established largely by the price of similar properties that are substitutable for the property you are pricing. This is true because of people's actions. If a buyer can purchase a substitutable property for a lower price, she will normally do so. Therefore, a property will not normally sell for a higher price than that paid for similar, or substitutable, properties. These facts are the basis for the market analysis approach to pricing a property. A market analysis is simply a structured method to determine what people have been willing to pay for homes that are similar to, and substitutable for, the property you are pricing. The logic of the approach is that if homes in the same general neighborhood with similar features have sold for a certain price, then the property you are pricing should sell for approximately the same price. The most basic element of this approach, then, is to determine what similar properties in the same general neighborhood have sold for.

Before we look at the step-by-step process to complete a market analysis, let's take a look at sources of information that are available to determine what similar properties have sold for.

Sources of Information

There are several primary sources of information you should be familiar with, such as:

- Multiple-listing services
- Professional reporting services
- Company records
- Observation of the neighborhood
- Homes currently on the market

Multiple-Listing Services

Most multiple-listing services (MLSs) provide their members with regular publications that contain information on properties currently for sale, as well as those that have recently sold and listings that expired without a sale. These publications can be extremely useful sources of information on the selling price of homes. Usually, these publications also contain not only the selling price of properties, but the method of financing and the length of time the property was on the market before it sold. Both of these are useful items in completing a market analysis.

Coaching Tips: **MLSs may publish the price for which a property was first under contract. This may differ from the actual closing price. You should determine the policy of the MLS of which your firm is a member. When necessary, contact the listing broker to determine an actual closing price for a property you use in a market analysis.**

Professional Reporting Services

There are also national and local firms that compile data on real estate properties that sell this information to brokerage firms. Their information usually comes from public records or from appraisers and appraisal firms who subscribe to their service. The type of information from services such as these can differ, and may range from limited information, such as name, address, date of sale, and selling price, to more detailed information, such as square footage, number of rooms, age, type of construction, condition of the property, amenities, and the type of financing.

Company Records

Another source of information is your brokerage firm's records. Many firms keep detailed records of transactions in which their company was involved. If your company is active in the area in which you are doing a market analysis, these records can be very helpful. Also, you may be able to obtain information from other companies' records in exchange for providing information from your company's records.

Neighborhood Observation

Regardless of where you obtain your primary information for a market analysis, you should always ride through the neighborhood to get a first-hand look at the neighboring properties. This will give you valuable information about characteristics of relevant properties, such as architectural style, condition of the house, landscaping, and the lot size. This information will help you determine which properties are most comparable to the property you are pricing.

Homes Currently on the Market

You should also consider the asking price for homes currently on the market. Because these homes have not yet sold, the prices are not as useful as the actual selling price. The primary use for such information is to assess the competition from other available homes.

Effects of Financing

When you complete a market analysis, you will have to consider the effect of different methods of financing on the price of property. The type of financing can significantly affect the price at which a property will sell. Financing that makes it easier to buy a property (or otherwise benefits the buyer) will usually increase the price of the property. For example, two similar houses are for sale. Owner A wants all cash and will not pay any closing costs or discount points. Owner B will finance part of the sale, requires only a small down payment, and will charge an interest rate that is two percentage points below the market rate. Of these two houses, Owner B's will almost surely sell for a higher price because of the more favorable financing available.

There are five general rules of thumb that will help you adjust the price of a property based on the type of financing:

1. An all-cash sale will result in the lowest price. (Cash is always in limited supply.)

2. The next lowest price will be on a loan assumption. (The cash down payment is usually larger than a down payment on a new loan.)

3. The next lowest price is on a conventional loan on which the buyer must pay all points and closing costs. (The price will likely increase if the seller pays some or all of these.)

4. The next to highest price will be a house that has an Federal Housing Administration (FHA) or Veterans Affairs (VA) loan on which the seller pays the discount points, and especially if the seller pays the closing costs also.

5. The highest price will occur when financing is available on the best possible terms, as in the example given earlier.

The impact of the financing considerations can be illustrated in the following example.

Example

You are pricing a property in a neighborhood where there were two recent comparable sales. House A sold for $53,000 with VA financing on which the seller paid

6 points. House B sold for $50,000 with a conventional loan on which no discount points were required. If your seller is not prepared to pay any of the closing costs and/or points for the buyer, the price of the property should be closer to $50,000 than $53,000. If the seller is willing to pay some of these costs, the price could be closer to $53,000 than $50,000 because the previous sale at $53,000 included the payment of such costs.

Because of the effects of factors such as financing on the price of property, it is always best to adhere to the following rule to the maximum extent possible: *Always use the properties for a market analysis that have the fewest differences you can find from the subject property.* This minimizes the need to make adjustments to the price of the comparable properties based on these differences. Let's now take a look at the step-by-step procedure to complete a market analysis.

Completing the Market Analysis

The market analysis process involves the following six steps:

1. Obtain information on the subject property.
2. Obtain information on comparable properties.
3. Fill in the worksheet.
4. Make adjustments for differences.
5. Attach "weights" to the adjusted prices.
6. Consider current and expired listings.

Subject Property Information

Prior to entering information in the worksheet you will use to complete a market analysis, the first step is to compile information about the subject property. The properties that you use to determine the price of your subject property are called comparable properties, or comps. When selecting your comparables, keep in mind the following:

- The more comparables you have, the better, but you need at least three to five comparables for a valid assessment.
- The more similar the comparables are to the subject property, the better
- The more recent the sale, the better; use properties sold in the last 6 months, if available.
- Properties with prices significantly above or below other comparables should not be used because this usually means some abnormal factor was involved.

Obtain Information on Comparable Properties

After you obtain the information listed on your worksheet for your subject property, you should obtain the same information on your comparables, *plus* the following information:

- The listing price and terms
- The number of days the property was on the market before it sold
- The actual selling price and terms

One of the guidelines for selecting comparable properties is to use properties that are as similar as possible to the subject property. The definition of what is *as similar as possible* will depend on the situation.

Example

You are pricing a 15-year-old, brick ranch home with seven bedrooms, two baths, and a double carport. You find that five homes have sold in the neighborhood within the last 6 months. One of these is a two-story, one is a split-level, and three are ranch style. In this situation, you should use only the ranch-style houses in your analysis.

In the previous example, if you had found six ranch homes, your criteria for selection could have been even more specific.

For example, if one ranch was frame construction, one was stucco, and four were brick, you would use only the four brick ranches because these are more similar to your subject property.

If you were even more fortunate and found that three of the brick ranch houses had the same number of rooms as your subject property, then you could have used only those three because of their similarity to the subject property. In general, you should be as selective as you can in choosing the comparables, and still have at least three to work with.

Fill in the Worksheet

Once you have selected your comparables and you have information on each one, begin to enter information on your worksheet. First, enter the basic information about each of the comparables you selected in the top section of the worksheet. Once you have done this, you are ready for the next step in the process—making adjustments.

Making Adjustments

The objective in making adjustments is to adjust the price of each *comparable* property so that the price of that comparable more accurately reflects the features of the subject property. When making adjustments, you *always* adjust the price of the comparable to bring it in line with the subject property. You *never* adjust the price of the subject property. (You determine the price of the subject property from the adjusted comparables, which will be covered in a later step.)

Example

You find that a comparable property is identical to your subject property except the comparable property has a fireplace and your subject property does not. In this case, the price of the comparable is slightly higher because it has a feature that the subject property does not. Another way of looking at this is that the subject property will probably not sell for quite as much as the comparable because it lacks a feature that the comparable property has. When this is the case, you must *subtract* an estimate of the value of the fireplace from the price of the *comparable* property. This makes it more comparable by taking out the value of the extra feature.

Let's look at the opposite situation.

Example

You find a comparable property that is identical to your subject property except that it does not have a fireplace and your subject property does. In this case, the price of the comparable property is slightly *lower* because it lacks a feature that your subject property has. Another way of looking at this is that your subject property will probably sell for a little more than the comparable because it has an extra feature not found in the comparable property. When this is the case, you must *add* an estimate of the value of the fireplace to the price of the *comparable* property. This makes it more comparable by adding the value of the extra feature to the price of the comparable.

There is a rule that might help you remember how to adjust the price of the comparable in situations such as these: If the *comparable* is *inferior* to the subject property, you *add* to the price of the comparable.

Remember this rule by the mnemonic CIA:

- *C*omparable
- *I*nferior
- *A*dd

If you remember the CIA rule, then you also know that if the comparable is *superior* to the subject property, you *subtract.*

In order to make actual adjustments of the type we have just covered, you will need to know an approximate value for each feature that differs in the subject and comparable properties. For example, if you need to subtract the value of a fireplace from the comparable property, you obviously need to know the fireplace's value.

This is an aspect of market analysis that requires some input from your broker. Because values for features such as these can vary depending on the location of the property as well as many other factors, you should ask your broker for guidance in selecting these values. In this course, these values will be given whenever you need them to complete a market analysis problem.

Assigning "Weights"

Once you have adjusted the price of each comparable, the next step is to assign a "weight" to each comparable. The purpose of the weight is to reflect your assessment of the similarity of each comparable to the subject property. A property that is more similar to the subject property should be given a higher weight than one that is less similar to the subject property. Weights are assigned using percentages.

REPLACEMENT COST PRICING

The market data approach is the best and most convenient method for pricing property when data on the sale of comparable properties are readily available. For some types of properties, the market approach is not very useful because of the lack of comparables that have recently sold. For example, homes in rural areas, homes in a neighborhoods where the market has been inactive, and specialty homes that are unique because of design or age are all difficult to price because of the lack of adequate comparables. In these cases, the pricing approach that is often used is the *cost approach*. The cost approach to pricing gives an estimated price for a property based on the current cost of replacing or reproducing the improvements.

Reproduction cost is the cost of precisely duplicating the original structure, using the same materials and construction techniques as the original.

Replacement cost is the cost of replacing the improvements with another building that performs the same function but is not an exact replica of the subject property.

Of these two types of cost approaches, the replacement cost approach will be the most useful to you, and the one that we will cover in the remainder of this lesson. The reproduction cost method is not as useful because changes in building techniques, styles, and designs over the years make it almost useless to consider reproducing a particular building exactly as it was built originally.

The replacement cost approach is based on providing a new structure that has the same utility as the property being evaluated, but using building methods more appropriate to the time the appraisal is made.

Reproduction is often difficult or impossible because of changing techniques and availability of materials.

The replacement cost approach is based on the following formula:

$$
\begin{array}{rl}
 & \text{Value of land} \\
+ & \text{Replacement cost} \\
- & \underline{\text{Depreciation(based on improvements only)}} \\
= & \text{Estimated price}
\end{array}
$$

In order to understand how to use this approach to pricing, we need to look at each part of the formula separately. The process is very simple if we take it one step at a time. The four steps in the replacement cost approach to pricing are as follows:

- **Step 1:** Estimate the price of the land as if it were vacant.
- **Step 2:** Estimate the replacement cost of the improvements (i.e., buildings) on the land.
- **Step 3:** Add the price of the land and the cost to replace the building.
- **Step 4:** Make deductions for depreciation on the building (the land is not depreciated).

Step 1: Estimate Land Value

The first step of the replacement cost approach to pricing is to determine the price of the land as if it were vacant. There are two ways to do this. The first is to use the market data approach that you learned about earlier in this chapter. This would require obtaining data on the sale of comparable vacant lots. If adequate data on comparables are not available, the next best approach to determine the price of the land is to ask one or more knowledgeable and reputable builders in the area to tell you what they would pay for the property as a building site if it were available. As an example, let's assume that you have talked with the appropriate knowledgeable builders and found that the land for a subject property has a value of $30,000.

Step 2: Estimate Replacement Cost

The second step in the process is to estimate the cost to replace the building. This can be done in three ways:

1. The square foot method
2. The unit-in-place method
3. The quantity survey method

Each of these approaches has been covered; here is a summary of the relative merits of each of these methods.

The square foot method is the easiest to complete but the least accurate.

The unit in place method is more accurate than the square foot method and also more difficult to complete than the square foot method.

The quantity survey method is the most accurate and the most difficult of the three. It is used the least because of its difficulty.

Even though the square foot method is not as accurate as the other methods, it is the most useful approach because of its simplicity and ease of use. We will cover this method in the remainder of this chapter. However, you should always keep in mind that the results of this method are not generally as reliable as those for the market comparison method, or for other types of replacement cost methods.

Now let's take a look at how to complete a replacement cost estimate of price using the square foot method. There are three steps involved in using the square foot method. Because these are all part of Step 2 in the overall process, we will label them as substeps.

Here are the substeps in the square foot method:

1. Determine cost factors that are the cost of construction per square foot for each major element of the house.
2. Determine the actual square footage in each major element of the house being priced.
3. Multiply the cost factors from Step 1 by the number of square feet in each major element from Step 2 to get an estimate of the cost to replace the building.

Determine Cost Factors

The first substep in the square foot method is to determine the cost factors that represent the cost of construction per square foot for the major elements of a house. This is the most important step in the entire pricing process because it has the biggest impact on the final price estimate. Because of this, it is important to obtain the best estimates possible for the cost of construction per square foot. The best method for determining the cost per square foot is to ask one or more reputable builders who have experience building properties of similar style and quality in the area of the subject property. An experienced builder will have fairly accurate estimates of the cost of construction per square foot readily available. If you do not know any builders with these qualifications, ask your broker to recommend one or more. If neither you nor your broker is able to identify an appropriate builder, another possible source is a cost estimate handbook that provides replacement cost factors. Ask your broker for help in finding one.

Let's assume that you have contacted three reputable builders with appropriate experience in the area, and have found that the cost of construction appropriate for the different elements of a house are:

- First-floor heated area—$50 per square foot
- Second-floor heated area—$25 per square foot
- Garage—$30 per square foot
- Basement—$15 per square foot

The most expensive element of the house is the first-floor heated area because, by convention, the cost of the foundation and roof go with the first-floor construction. The second-floor heated area is less expensive because it does not require another roof, and the floor is less expensive than the foundation. The basement and garage are the least expensive areas because they require less interior finish work, plumbing, electrical work, etc.

Determine Actual Square Footage

The second substep in the square foot method is measuring the actual square footage of the major elements of the house. The square footage should be calculated by measuring the *outside* dimensions of the house. (It is a good idea to have a 100-foot metal tape measure for doing this.) In measuring these dimensions, it is also a good idea to make a sketch of the floor plan of the house to use in recording your measurements and calculating the square footage.

The easiest way to determine the square footage is from a sketch or floor plan. First, divide the floor plan into smaller segments so that each segment is a rectangle for which you can determine the length of each side. Once your sketch has been divided into rectangles, determine the square footage of each rectangle and add up the square footage for each one to get the total square footage.

Using the example below, to get the total square footage for the house, total the amounts for the different elements as follows:

480 sq. ft.	Garage
2,432 sq .ft.	First-floor heated area
+1,440 sq. ft.	Second-floor heated area
4,352 sq. ft.	Total square footage

Determine Replacement Cost

Once you know the actual square footage for the house, the final substep is to calculate the cost to replace it. To do this, we need our cost factors from Step 1, and the total square footage for each element of the house that we calculated in Step 2. Then multiply the square footage for each category by the cost per square foot for that category to determine the estimated replacement cost for each category. To get the total estimated replacement cost for the entire house, add up the numbers. The final estimate of the cost to replace the house is $172,000.

Step 3: Add Replacement Cost and Land

Once you have determined the value of the land and calculated the cost to replace the building, add these two values together. This gives the total estimated cost of the land and buildings before depreciation is deducted. In our example, this is done as follows:

Value of land	$ 30,000
Estimated replacement cost	$172,000
Total	$202,000

Step 4: Deduct Depreciation

The next step in the process is to deduct for the effects of depreciation. The value of almost any existing house will be less than the cost to replace it because of the effects of depreciation.

Previously, you learned that there are three major types of depreciation:

1. Physical deterioration
2. Functional obsolescence
3. Economic (external) obsolescence

Let's review each of these types briefly.

Physical Deterioration

This is the wear and tear that results from normal use. For example, a frame house that needs a new coat of paint is suffering from physical deterioration.

Functional Obsolescence

Functional obsolescence is the reduction in value due to outdated features of the property, such as:

- Closets that are too small
- Ceilings that are too high or low
- Too few bathrooms
- Inadequate wiring
- Outdated design or architecture

Economic (External) Obsolescence

This is the loss of value due to external conditions and might include such situations as:

- Changes in the makeup of the surrounding area
- Environmental impacts like noise pollution from an airport
- Changes in highways that serve the property
- The closing of a major business nearby

Both physical deterioration and functional obsolescence arise from the characteristics of the property itself. Economic obsolescence represents depreciation that arises from factors outside the property. To estimate the depreciation for a given property, we must consider the effects of each of these types of depreciation.

The type of depreciation that is most common is physical deterioration, or the wear and tear from normal use. We can estimate the amount of such depreciation using a method called the cost to repair. The first step in this procedure is to make a careful inspection of the property, making note of any items that need repair or replacement. For example, you might find that a house needs a new coat of paint, a new roof, or new carpet. Once you have identified all such items, you can then determine the cost to repair by contacting local contractors and/or the appropriate building supply companies for estimates. The total of the estimates for all such repairs is the total estimate for depreciation using the cost to repair method.

The other types of depreciation—functional obsolescence and economic obsolescence—are more difficult to deal with. Functional obsolescence, also referred to as loss in value due to changing consumer demands, usually results from the way a property is designed and built. That is, functional obsolescence is not caused by repairs that are needed, but results from changes in consumer preferences. Similarly, economic obsolescence is depreciation that cannot be solved through repairs because it arises from factors outside the property. A general decline in values in a neighborhood due to commercial construction nearby is difficult to quantify in the absence of market data on the sale of comparable properties. Specific methods for dealing with these types of depreciation are beyond the scope of this course; you should consult with your broker for methods to deal with them when the need arises.

Once you have estimated the amount of depreciation for the house you are pricing, subtract this amount from the replacement cost estimate from Step 3. In the case of our example, let's assume that we inspected the property and found the need for repairs that totaled $16,000.

We would then calculate the final estimated price for the property as follows:

Replacement cost + land	$202,000
Less depreciation	$ 16,000
	$186,000

The final estimated price for the house is $186,000.

SUMMARY

Valuation is a critical part of real estate practice. It involves the three approaches to appraisal: the sales comparison/market data approach, cost approach, and the income approach.

In addition, licensees perform comparative market analysis (CMA) to determine marketing pricing. This should never be called or confused with an appraisal. Appraisals strictly focus on value.

Various parties to a transaction are dependent on the valuation process. This includes buyers, sellers/landlords, lenders, and other interested parties to a transaction. When a seller is considering listing her property with a licensee, the seller is generally more concerned with the value of her property for marketing purposes. Therefore it is important that the licensee know how to perform the CMA. Licensees should use appraisals (when available) to help them price property.

REVIEW QUESTIONS

1. The most probable price a property should bring in an open market is the:
   a. Median value.
   b. Sale price.
   c. Market value.
   d. Exchange value.

2. A comparable property sold for $100,000. The comparable property is in better condition than the subject property (a value of $13,000). However, the comparable property has fewer square feet than the subject property ($10,000 for square feet). What is the adjusted value of the comparable property?
   a. $123,000
   b. $103,000
   c. $ 97,000
   d. $ 87,000

3. Home prices have increased 6 percent in the last year. A comparable property sold 8 months ago. What is the adjustment to the comparable property?
   a. Minus 6 percent
   b. Plus 6 percent
   c. Minus 4 percent
   d. Plus 4 percent

4. An appraiser made an adjustment because the home had a poor traffic pattern. This is an example of:
   a. Curable physical deterioration.
   b. Functional obsolescence.
   c. Incurable physical deterioration.
   d. External obsolescence.

5. Expenses on a property are $12,920. What is the monthly net income if the property is purchased for $209,000 with a rate of return of 12 percent?
   a. $38,000
   b. $25,080.
   c. $3,167
   d. $2,090

6. In the income capitalization approach to value, which of these would NOT be an operating expense?
   a. Mortgage payment
   b. Hazard insurance
   c. Electric bill
   d. Reserves for replacement

7. An investment property produces $48,000 annual net operating income. The prospective investor wants a 12 percent return. What is the value of the property?
   a. $25,000
   b. $33,000
   c. $300,000
   d. $400,000

8. An investment property has a potential gross income of $60,000. There are no vacancies. Annual expenses are $30,000. With a return of 20 percent, what is the value of the property?
   a. $60,000
   b. $90,000
   c. $150,000
   d. $300,000

9. Effective gross income is a result of:
   a. Net operating income divided by an appropriate capitalization rate.
   b. Potential gross income minus vacancy and collection losses.
   c. Net operating income divided by the price.
   d. Before tax income minus the debt service.

10. A building that is 5 years old has a reproduction cost of $100,000. The economic life of the property is 25 years. Using the cost depreciation approach, what is the building's estimated value?
    a. $20,000
    b. $80,000
    c. $100,000
    d. $120,000

11. Which of the following characteristics is NOT a requirement to create value?
    a. Supply
    b. Transferability
    c. Demand
    d. Utility

12. An appraiser made an adjustment because the roof shingles are curling from exposure to the tropical sun. This is an example of:
    a. Functional obsolescence.
    b. Curable external obsolescence.
    c. Incurable external obsolescence.
    d. Physical deterioration.

13. In an appraisal, the appraiser would assign a greater mathematical weight to the sales comparison approach for:
    a. A community college.
    b. The police station.
    c. A vacant lot zoned for residential use.
    d. An industrial property.

14. In an appraisal, the basis of all three approaches to value is:
    a. The square foot approach.
    b. Depreciation of existing improvements.
    c. The principle of substitution.
    d. Loss in value for any reason.

15. A homeowner built a $60,000 pool in a neighborhood of homes that sell for $120,000. This is an example of:
    a. External obsolescence.
    b. An over-improvement.
    c. Functional obsolescence.
    d. Progression.

16. A contractor charged a homeowner $57,000 to remodel the home's kitchen. This is an example of:
    a. Market value.
    b. Cost.
    c. Consumer price index.
    d. Assemblage.

17. Which type of cost would be used to estimate the value of a church building?
    a. Effective cost
    b. Historical cost
    c. Replacement cost
    d. Estimated cost

18. In an appraisal, an adjustment was made to a home's value because the adjacent neighborhood is in disrepair. This is an example of:
    a. Functional obsolescence that is curable.
    b. Physical deterioration that is curable.
    c. Incurable physical deterioration.
    d. External obsolescence.

19. Which statement is FALSE regarding a appraisal?
    a. Land is estimated separately from the improvements.
    b. Land is valued for its highest and best use as though vacant.
    c. Land is valued for its highest and best use as improved.
    d. Land is depreciated in the cost depreciation approach.

Chapter 16

LEARNING OBJECTIVES

After completing this lesson, you will be able to:

- Describe several features of exterior construction, including:
  - Footings and foundations
  - Framing
  - Insulation
  - Ventilation
  - Exterior wall coverings
  - Windows
  - Roofs
- Describe systems and equipment used in a residential property, such as:
  - Heating systems and cooling systems
  - Plumbing systems and hot water systems
  - Electrical systems
- Understand basic terms and concepts used in construction.
- Identify several types of residential lots.
- Appreciate the environmental hazards that can affect real property.
- Describe guidelines a real estate licensee should follow to avoid legal problems related to environmental hazards.

Residential Construction and Environmental Issues

FEATURES OF EXTERIOR CONSTRUCTION

Footings and Foundations

A footing is a concrete base or support under a foundation wall. It is made by pouring the concrete into a trench dug into the ground. The trench is wider than the foundation wall so that the weight of the foundation is distributed over a larger area of ground. The purpose of the footing is to provide support for the building and to prevent settling or shifting. The foundation is then constructed on top of the footing. There are three types of foundations:

1. Slab-on-grade—Slabs are flat pieces of concrete that rest on the ground or on footings that provide support.

   Note: With very few exceptions, basements are not typical in Florida. This is due to the fact that most of Florida is at or below sea level, therefore, the water table is high and prevents the installation of basements.

2. Basement—A basement floor is constructed similarly to a slab.

3. Crawl space—Crawl spaces are similar to basements except that the height from the floor to the joists is less. Crawl spaces provide protection from flooding and also access to heating ducts, plumbing pipes, and wires.

Framing

Framing refers to the underlying structure of a building. Although steel framing is occasionally used, most residences are built with wood-frame construction. There are several types of framing, including:

- Platform framing
- Balloon framing
- Post-and-beam framing

Platform Framing

With platform framing, each story of the building is built as a separate unit. Each story then serves as a platform for the next story. Platform-frame construction is the most common type of framing.

Balloon Framing

With balloon framing, each wall stud runs the entire height of the building, from the floor of the lowest story to the roof of the building. This is different from platform framing, where separate, shorter wall studs are used for each story. That is, a wall stud for the first story runs from the floor of the first story to the ceiling of that story. A wall stud for the second story runs from the floor of the second story to the ceiling of that story.

Post-and-Beam Framing

With post-and-beam framing, beams that support the building rest on posts or columns rather than bearing walls. Post-and-beam framing is used in contemporary style homes. Often, the framing remains exposed for decorative purposes.

A real estate professional should make note of any problems with the framing. The following problems may indicate structural defects:

- Bulging exterior walls
- Sticking doors and windows
- Sloping floors
- Large cracks developing on the foundation, walls, or ceiling

If defects are suspected, professional consultants may be called in to confirm this opinion.

Coaching Tips: **Framing**

- **Post-and-beam framing—Beams that support the building rest on posts or columns rather than bearing walls.**
- **Balloon framing—Each wall stud runs the entire height of the building, from the floor of the lowest story to the roof of the building.**
- **Platform framing—Each story of the building is built as a separate unit and serves as a platform for the next story.**

Insulation

Insulation is just as important in warm climates to keep the heat out of the home as it is in cold climates to keep the heat in the home. There are several types of insulation:

- Loose-fill—Insulating materials that can be put in place by hand.
- Blanket and batt—Insulation, usually made of fiberglass, available in rolls (blankets) or sheets (batts).
- Sprayed-on—Insulating materials that are sprayed on surfaces.
- Foil—Insulating sheets with aluminum foil backing that reflects heat.
- Rigid—Rigid panels of insulation.
- Foam—Insulating materials that are mixed with a foam and poured or sprayed into place.

The standard method to rate the effectiveness of insulation materials is the **R value**. The R stands for resistance to heat flow. The higher the R value for a particular insulation material, the better the insulation effect. The Department of Energy has established insulation recommendations for homes. The recommended levels of insulation, expressed in R values, differs for different areas of the house (e.g., under the roof, inside exterior walls, etc.) and varies from one locale to another due to differences in climate.

Ventilation

If moisture builds up in spaces that are not ventilated, rot and decay may occur. Ventilation is crucial to prevent water condensation. Air flow is needed in the attic, behind the wall covering, and through the basement or crawl space. This air flow may be obtained by providing holes of varying sizes, which are protected with screens to keep out insects and small animals. The ventilation system may also include attic, basement, kitchen, and bathroom fans.

Exterior Wall Covering

To construct an exterior wall, sheathing is attached to the studs. Common sheathing materials include boards, plywood, pressed board, or wallboard. The sheathing is then covered with waterproof building paper. The exterior finish materials of the walls (siding) are applied on top of the building paper. A wide variety of exterior wall coverings exist, including wood, aluminum, stone, stucco, or masonry.

Windows

There are various window styles available. Some of the most common styles of windows include:

- Single-hung windows
- Double-hung windows
- Horizontal sliding windows
- Casement windows
- Jalousie windows
- Fixed windows

Single-Hung Window

This type of window consists of two sashes, one of which can be raised or lowered to open or close the window. A sash is a frame made of wood, steel, aluminum, or vinyl that holds a pane of glass.

Double-Hung Window

A **double-hung window** consists of two sashes, both of which slide vertically allowing the window to be opened at the top and bottom.

Horizontal Sliding Window

A **horizontal sliding window** consists of sashes that slide horizontally to open or close the window.

Casement Window

A **casement window** consists of a hinged sash that can be opened by swinging the sash outward.

Jalousie Window

This type of window consists of horizontal, overlapping, glass louvers that pivot to open or close (similar to window blinds).

Fixed Window

A **fixed window** consists of a sash that cannot be opened.

Coaching Tips: Windows at a Glance

- A fixed window consists of a sash that cannot be opened, but can be raised or lowered to open or close the window.
- A single-hung window consists of two sashes, only *one* of which can be raised or lowered to open or close the window.
- A double-hung window consists of two sashes, *both* of which slide vertically allowing the window to be opened at the top and bottom.
- A casement window consists of a hinged sash that can be opened by swinging the sash outward.
- A jalousie window consists of horizontal, overlapping, glass louvers that pivot to open or close.
- A fixed window consists of a sash that cannot be opened.

Roofs

The most common types of roof construction are:

- Trusses
- Joists and rafters
- Joists alone
- Post and beam

Trusses

Trusses are framing units that are assembled at a factory and usually consist of several triangle-shaped sections. The shape allows the trusses to support the weight of the roof across a long area. (Interior load-bearing walls may be unnecessary with trusses.) With trusses, hurricane clips are often used. Hurricane clips are metal strips that are nailed and secure the rafters to the top horizontal wall plate.

Rafters and Joists

Rafters are sloping parallel beams that support the roof while joists are horizontal parallel beams located below the rafters. The ceiling is attached to the joists.

Joists Alone

In some situations, the roof is supported directly by the joists, such as with a flat roof.

Post and Beam

With post-and-beam roofing, beams that support the roof rest on posts or columns. The roof is supported by the beams and posts, rather than bearing walls or trusses.

Once the framing for the roof has been constructed, the roof sheathing is attached. Common roof sheathing materials include boards, plywood, or pressed board. Roofing materials are attached to the sheathing. Most residential roofs consist of asphalt shingles.

To construct an exterior wall, sheathing is attached to the studs. The sheathing is then covered with waterproof building paper. The exterior finish materials of the walls (siding) are applied on top of the building paper.

Figure 16.1 summarizes the elements of construction.

FIGURE 16.1

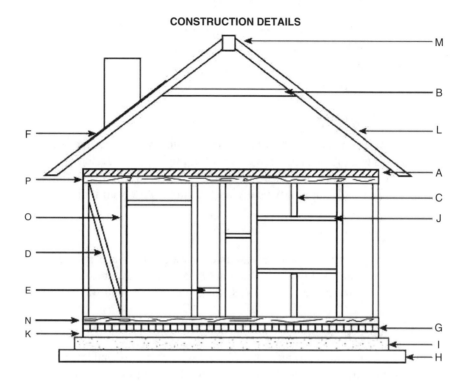

CONSTRUCTION DETAILS

A   CEILING JOIST. Horizontal beams supporting ceiling
B   COLLAR BEAM. A beam that connects opposite rafters above the floor
C   CRIPPLES. Short vertical piece 2 × 4 above or below an opening
D   DIAGONAL BRACE. A brace across corner of structure to prevent swaying
E   FIRE STOP. Short board or wall between studs to prevent fire spreading
F   FLASHING. Metal sheet usually around chimney to prevent water seepage
G   FLOOR JOIST. Horizontal beams supporting floor
H   FOOTING. Base or bottom of a foundation wall
I   FOUNDATION. The supporting portion of structure resting on footing
J   LINTEL. A horizontal board over a door or window, also called header
K   MUDSILL. Perimeter board anchored directly to foundation
L   RAFTERS. Boards designed to support roof loads
M   RIDGE BOARD. Highest board in the house supporting upper ends
N   SOLE PLATE. Usually 2 × 4 on which wall and studs rest
O   STUDS. Vertical boards 2 × 4 supporting the walls every 16″ (on center)
P   TOP PLATE. A horizontal board fastened to upper end of studs

Other Construction Terms
    Board Foot = used to measure lumber, contains 144 cubic inches
    R–VALUE = ranking of insulation materials
    EER = Energy Efficiency Rating

MECHANICAL SYSTEMS AND EQUIPMENT

The following is a summary of the major mechanical systems described in this section:

- Heating system
- Cooling system
- Plumbing system
- Hot water system
- Electrical system

Heating Systems

There are many types of heating systems, including systems that utilize:

- Warm air
- Water
- Steam
- Electricity

Warm Air

Warm (or hot) air heating systems typically utilize some type of blower to distribute heated air to rooms in a building through ducts. Heated air enters the rooms through registers. A space heater is another type of warm air heating system. A space heater is a small unit that typically uses a fan to blow warm air into a room.

Water

Another type of heating system uses water. Hot water is held in a boiler. Electric circulators are used to pump the heated water through pipes into radiators or into additional pipes embedded in the floors, walls, or ceilings, and the heat is transferred into rooms.

Steam

Steam heat is produced by a boiler with a firebox underneath it. When water boils, the pressure builds and forces the steam through pipes into radiators.

Electricity

Electricity can be either a fuel to heat air or water in a furnace or a direct source of heat itself. Resistance elements convert electricity into heat. These resistance elements are embedded in the floors, walls, and ceilings in the area being heated.

Coaching Tips: **Heating Systems**

- **Warm (or hot) air heating systems:**
  - Utilize some type of blower to distribute heated air to the rooms of the building through ducts.
  - Distribute heated air into the rooms through registers.
- **Hot water systems:**
  - Hold hot water in a boiler.
- **Steam systems:**
  - Produce steam heat by a boiler.
- **Electric systems:**
  - Uses resistance elements, which convert electricity into heat. These resistance elements are embedded in the floors, walls, and ceilings.

Types of Fuel

There are several types of fuel, including coal, fuel oil, natural gas, electricity, and solar energy. In the past, coal was the most popular fuel source. Today, most coal systems are obsolete. Fuel oil is popular in certain areas of the United States, mainly the Northeast and Northwest. At one time, fuel oil was competitively priced, but recently it has become expensive. Fuel oil requires an on-site storage tank. Natural gas, which can be delivered by a pipeline, does not require any storage tanks. Natural gas has typically been the most economical fuel in most areas of the country.

Another fuel source is electricity. Because electric systems require no furnace or ducts, they are the least expensive to install. However, the electricity needed to run such systems can be expensive. Solar energy, which comes directly from the sun, is still the least developed source of heat. However, as the technology advances, and as other fuel sources are depleted, the use of solar energy may increase.

Cooling Systems

In the past, buildings were cooled with windows and/or fans. Now, most newly constructed buildings have an air-conditioning system. Types of air-cooling systems include:

- Window units
- Central air-conditioning
- Heat pumps

Window Air-Conditioning Units

To cool a single room or small area, a window air-conditioning unit can be installed easily and plugged into a regular outlet.

Central Air-Conditioning

Central air-conditioning systems may be custom-made or factory-assembled packages that are connected at the residence. The condenser unit is placed outside the house. The condenser transforms refrigerant gas into a cool liquid. A pipe runs from the condenser to the air-handling unit inside the house. The air-handling unit, which consists of an evaporator and a fan, is connected to ducts that distribute cool air throughout the house.

Heat Pumps

Heat pumps are actually used for both heating and cooling. A heat pump is basically a reversible air-conditioning unit. A heat pump takes heat from the outside air or ground and distributes it inside to warm the house in winter. Conversely, the system extracts warm air from inside the house to cool the house in summer. Heat pumps are most efficient in areas with mild winters, including Florida.

Plumbing Systems

A plumbing system has two purposes:

1. To supply adequate clean water to the home
2. To remove waste from the home

The pipes carrying clean water must be strong enough to sustain the pressure necessary for water to flow through them. Pipes that remove waste typically do not use pressure and, therefore, must be angled downward so that waste travels into the sewer system.

Water Supply

There are various sources of water, including:

- Municipal (public-supplied water)
- Well water (private wells on a property)
- Private company

In all cases, water must meet the standards provided by the U.S. Department of Health. According to the Federal Housing Administration (FHA), public water should be used when it's available.

Hot Water System

A hot water system is a necessity. The supply is usually generated in a separate hot water heater, which is powered by electricity, gas, or oil. Additionally, hot water may be supplied from furnace heat. Hot water heater tanks vary in size. The size needed depends on the number of residents and the recovery rate for the unit (the time it takes to heat water). Standard hot water tanks range from 30 to 80 gallons.

Sewers and Septic Tanks

As mentioned earlier, in addition to supplying clean water to a home, a plumbing system must also remove waste from the home. There are several types of systems for removing waste. The preferred method is a municipal sewer system. Another alternative is a septic system.

A septic system is a private system that includes a large concrete septic tank buried in the ground. Waste material enters one end of the tank through a drain line coming from the house. Inside the tank, the waste separates into three parts:

1. Solid waste, which sinks to the bottom
2. Grease, which rises to the top
3. The remaining waste, which is liquid

The septic tank contains bacteria, which decompose the solid wastes and grease. Relatively clear liquid flows out the opposite end of the tank into a distribution box that directs the liquid into a network of buried perforated pipes called a leaching field. The liquid flows into the ground and is absorbed.

Electrical System

Electricity is carried by transmission lines from power plants to homes. Electricity enters a home at a service entrance, where the electricity flows through a meter to a distribution panel. The distribution panel distributes the electricity throughout the home. The distribution panel has a master switch that can be used to cut off all electric service in the house in the event of an emergency.

The panel also contains a master fuse or a master circuit breaker that will automatically shut off the entire system if there is a power overload. A fuse is a piece of wire or metal that will melt and stop the current when the flow of electricity exceeds the prescribed amount. A circuit breaker is a switch that automatically turns off when the flow of electricity exceeds the prescribed amount.

The distribution panel feeds the incoming electricity to separate branch circuits. Each individual circuit is also protected by a fuse or a circuit breaker. In the event of an overload, it automatically shuts off without tripping the main fuse or circuit breaker. A typical panel box has 12 to 16 fuses or circuit breakers.

Electricity is measured in terms of amperes (or amps) and volts. Amps represent the amount of electricity; volts represent the force. The electricity capacity of homes, in terms of volts and amps, is described next.

Volts

In the past, homes were wired for 110 or 220 volts. Currently, homes are being wired for 120 or 240 volts. This increase in voltage is substantially due to the added electrical drawing appliances that are included in existing and new home construction, such as:

- Washers
- Dryers

- Dishwashers
- Central air-conditioning

Amps

A home may be designed to bring in 30, 60, 100, 150, 200, 300, or 400 amps of electricity. The standard for homes that do not have electric heat or central air-conditioning is 100 amps. In homes with electric heat, central air-conditioning, or a large number of appliances, service of 150 to 400 amps is needed. In smaller and older homes, 30- or 60-amp service may still be found.

COMMON CONSTRUCTION TERMS

As a real estate professional, you will need to be knowledgeable about a variety of types and styles of residential properties, as well as some of the basic principles of construction. In this section, you will learn several of the most common construction terms you will encounter.

Backfill

Backfill is the soil placed around the walls of a foundation to replace soil removed in the process of construction. Backfill is used to brace the foundation walls.

Bearing Wall

A bearing wall is a wall that bears the weight of the structure above the wall. It supports ceiling joists, an upper story, or the roof of the house. All exterior walls of a house are bearing walls, but only some walls within a house are bearing walls. If the wall serves only to divide the interior space into rooms and is not used to support the structure above it, the wall is *not* a bearing wall. If the wall supports the structure above it, it *is* a bearing wall.

Bearing walls are particularly important when considering remodeling. Nonbearing walls can usually be altered or removed without major effects on the overall structure. A bearing wall should not be altered or removed except by a qualified individual because changing or removing a bearing wall can result in severe damage to the structure.

Because of their importance, bearing walls are often constructed with stronger materials and techniques than nonbearing walls. Bearing walls are often difficult to identify in an existing house because there are no obvious signs that indicate that a wall is a bearing wall. Bearing walls can be constructed at any angle to other walls, doorways, etc.

Commercial Acre

A commercial acre is the area remaining after an acre of land has been deducted for the footage for streets, curbs, sidewalks, parks, etc. It is the area available for constructing any buildings on the property.

Coaching Tips: This term should not be confused with a builders acre. In many states, a builders acre is comprised of 40,000 square feet of area. You should know that for all arithmetic calculations, an acre consists of 43,560 square feet in area.

Conduit

A conduit is a metal pipe or covering used to protect electrical wiring in a building.

Deciduous

A deciduous tree loses its leaves in the fall or winter; the type of tree that does not lose its leaves is called an evergreen tree.

Drywall

Drywall is the wallboard used on interior walls. It is also called sheetrock. It is called drywall because it is dry when nailed to the wall studs. This is in contrast to another form of interior wall finish called lath and plaster, in which the plaster is applied in wet form to the lath.

Elevation Drawing

An elevation drawing shows the front and side views of the exterior of the house as it will appear when construction is completed. This drawing illustrates the exterior finish as well as the placement of windows, doors, vents, skylights, etc.

Energy Efficiency Ratio (EER)

The EER is a number (a ratio) used to represent the energy efficiency of appliances such as refrigerators, air conditioners, etc. The higher the EER is, the greater the energy efficiency is. (This means that as the EER goes up, the amount of energy used goes down.)

Flashing

Flashing is sheet metal used on the roof of a house to protect against water seeping through the roof. It is used in areas where the shingles do not completely cover or seal a junction between two elements of the roof. For example, it is used where the gables of a roof join the main roof and around chimneys and vent pipes.

Footing

A footing is a concrete base or support under a foundation wall. It is made by pouring the concrete into a trench dug into the ground. The trench is wider than the foundation wall so that the weight of the foundation is distributed over a larger area of ground. The foundation is then constructed on top of the footing.

Foundation

The foundation is the part of the building that supports the first floor of the building and is attached to the ground. A foundation is most often made of poured concrete but may also be made of a combination of poured concrete and concrete block. The entire foundation consists of several components and may include the footing, foundation walls, bearing posts, and/or piers, depending on the type of structure. The foundation plan is a drawing that shows each of these various elements as they are to be constructed.

Header

A header is a beam that runs across the top of a door or window opening in the frame of a house. A header is used because the door or window opening is wider than the distance between normal wall studs, and additional strength is needed across this width to support the roof above the door or window.

Joist

A joist is a supporting beam in the floor or ceiling. All joists are parallel to each other and are usually spaced 16 inches apart.

Percolation Test

A percolation test is conducted by an engineer to determine the extent to which the soil is able to absorb water. A percolation test should be completed before a septic tank is installed. As a means of remembering, think of a percolation test as you would of percolated coffee makers. In this type of coffee maker, water boils and rises up the hollow tube through its top opening into the coffee grinds. The grinds are able to absorb the boiling water to its saturation point. Coarse grounds will absorb more water than that of fine grounded coffee.

Plot Plan (Plot Map)

The plot plan is a map that shows the boundaries and dimensions of the property and the location of all improvements to the land, such as buildings, driveways, patios, walks, etc.

Potable Water

Potable water is drinkable water that is free of contamination.

R Value

The R value rates the effectiveness of insulation materials. The R stands for resistance to heat transmission. The higher the R value is for a particular insulation material, the better the insulation effect.

Rafter

Rafters are parallel boards that support the roof. The angle of these boards determines the steepness (or pitch) of the roof.

Ridgeboard

The ridgeboard runs across the length of the roof at its highest point. It is the highest structural point in a frame house or structure.

Roof

There are four basic types of roofs you should be familiar with:

1. **Gable**—A roof sloping on two sides.
2. **Hip**—A roof sloping on four sides.
3. **Gambrel**—A roof divided into two sections with different slopes for each section. Only two sides of the roof are sloped.
4. **Mansard**—A roof with two sections with different slopes (like the gambrel), but all four sides of the roof are sloped.

   All of the major roof styles are illustrated in Figure 16.2.
   You should also be familiar with what is called the *pitch* of a roof. The pitch is the angle of the slope of the roof. The steeper the slope is, the greater the pitch. A roof with a steeper pitch will normally last longer than a roof with a lower pitch.

Sheathing

Sheathing is the first layer of the exterior finish materials placed on the outside of the wall studs or roof rafters. Sheathing materials are usually boards, plywood, pressed board, or wallboard.

FIGURE 16.2

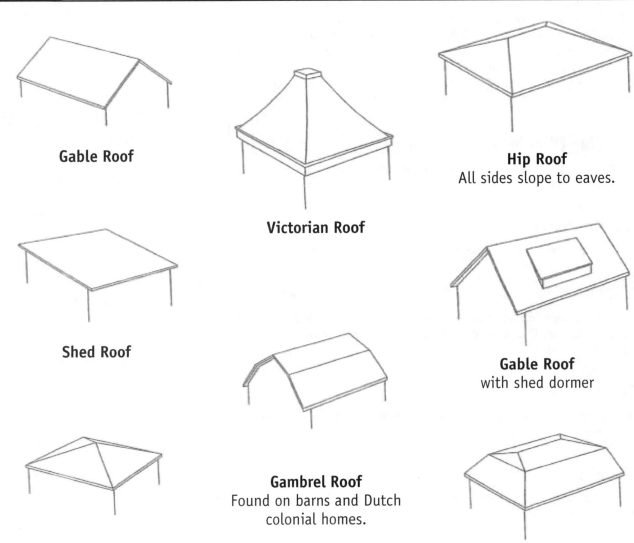

Gable Roof

Victorian Roof

Hip Roof
All sides slope to eaves.

Shed Roof

Gambrel Roof
Found on barns and Dutch
colonial homes.

Gable Roof
with shed dormer

Pyramid Roof
All sides slope from one point
(no ridge line).

Mansard Roof
(French style)

Coaching Tips: Solid sheathing means the boards forming the sheathing are butted next to each other so there are no gaps. The exterior finish materials of the walls and roof are applied on top of the sheathing.

Sill

The sill is the lowest structural member of the frame of a house that rests on the foundation.

Soil Pipe

A soil pipe carries sewage waste from the house to the main sewer line.

FIGURE 16.3

Additional Dictionary of Construction Terms at a Glance

- **Culvert:** A drain that runs under a road.
- **Flashing:** Metal strips used to prevent water seepage.
- **Footing:** A concrete base or support under a foundation wall. It is made by pouring the concrete into a trench dug into the ground.
- **Knob:** A component in an outdated electrical system.
- **Sash:** A frame that holds a pane of glass.
- **Shake:** Roofing material made of wood.
- **Shell:** The framework of a building.
- **Shingles:** *Not* considered sheathing. They make up one type of roof finishing material that is attached to the sheathing.
- **Slabs:** Flat pieces of concrete that rest on the ground or on footings that provide support.
- **Slate:** A type of hard rock.
- **The R in R value:** Stands for resistance to heat flow.
- **Trusses:** Framing units that are assembled at a factory and usually consist of several triangle-shaped sections.

Sole Plate

The sole plate is a horizontal member to which the wall studs are attached.

Stud

Studs are vertical boards (usually a 2 × 4) that make up the supporting elements of a wall or partition. The maximum legal distance between studs is 16 inches.

A list of additional construction terms is shown in Figure 16.3. Major architectural styles for residential homes are illustrated in Figures 16.4a and 16.4b.

RESIDENTIAL LOTS

A **lot** is defined as a portion of a subdivision. Subdivisions are larger parcels of real property that are subdivided into smaller parcels known as lots. Residences may be built on various types of lots. Some of the different types of lots include:

- Corner lots
- Interior lots
- T lots
- Cul-de-sac lots
- Key lots
- Flag lots

Corner Lots

A **corner lot** sits at the intersection of two streets. The lot has frontage along both streets. (Frontage refers to the length of the property that abuts the street.)

Coaching Tips: When dimensions of property are quoted, by practice, the first dimension is normally indicative of the frontage. For example, a lot with dimensions consisting of 50 × 100 would indicate a frontage of 50 feet and a depth of 100 feet.

FIGURE 16.4

New England Colonial
A box-shaped two-story house with a center entrance, wood siding, and shutters.

Georgian Colonial
A brick two-story house with a center entrance and a hip roof.

Southern Colonial
A two-story house with pillars and shutters.

Dutch Colonial
A two-story house with a gambrel roof.

California Bungalow
A small one-story house with a low-pitched roof.

California Ranch
A one-story house with a low-pitched roof and a sprawling floor plan.

Spanish
A house with a tile roof and arches.

Cape Cod
A house with a second story above the eaves, a high-pitched roof, wood siding, and a large chimney.

French Provincial
A formal house with a high-pitched slate hip roof, a stone or brick exterior, and shutters.

(a)

Victorian
A house with
ornate gables.

English Elizabethan
A house with a high-
pitched slate roof,
rough half-timbers,
and a plaster exterior.

Monterey
A two-story
house with a
front balcony.

French Norman
A house with a tower
as the main entrance
and a steep roof.

English Tudor
A house with a high-pitched
slate roof, a cathedral-
like entrance, and a
masonry exterior.

Mediterranean or Italian
A house with a tile roof,
a stucco exterior, and
rounded decorative work
above the windows.

Contemporary
A house of
modern design.

(b)

Interior Lots

An **interior lot** is surrounded by other lots on three sides (left, right, and rear). The interior lot has frontage on just one street.

T Lots

A **T lot** is a type of interior lot that is located at the end of a T intersection.

Cul-de-sac Lots

Cul-de-sac lots are located at the end of a cul-de-sac (a dead-end street with a circular turnaround). They are part of subdivisions. Because of the curved turnaround, these lots are often irregular in shape. That is, they are tapered with a smaller frontage but larger backyards.

Key Lots

A **key lot** is surrounded by many other lots. Often, a key lot is an extremely deep lot. The side yard abuts the rear of many different properties that are located on a street that runs perpendicular to the street where the key lot is located.

Flag Lots

A **flag lot** is shaped like a flag on a flagpole. Often, a flag lot is located behind another lot. The flagpole portion of the lot is the access road or driveway that runs along the front lot to the street. The flag portion of the lot is the square or rectangular lot that is located behind the front lot.

Coaching Tips: Lots at a Glance

- A corner lot sits at the intersection of two streets.
- An interior lot is surrounded by other lots on three sides (left, right, and rear).
- A T lot is a type of interior lot that is located at the end of a T intersection.
- A cul-de-sac lot is located at the end of a cul-de-sac.
- A key lot is surrounded by many other lots (often a deep lot that abuts the rear of many different properties along its side yards).
- A flag lot is shaped like a flag on a flagpole.

ENVIRONMENTAL HAZARDS

In recent years, there has been an increased concern about environmental protection. This concern has had an effect on the real estate profession. For example, a real estate licensee is liable if he fails to disclose defects in a property that could affect the health or safety of the occupants. Because environmental hazards affect health and safety, a licensee is obligated to disclose if such hazards exist on property involved in a real estate transaction. Some of the environmental hazards that affect real property include the following:

- Radon
- Formaldehyde gas
- Asbestos
- Lead
- Groundwater contamination

- Hazardous waste dumps
- Underground storage tanks

In the remainder of this chapter, we will look at each of these types of hazards and some guidelines to follow to avoid legal problems related to environmental hazards.

Radon

Radon is a colorless, odorless toxic gas that enters a building from the ground through openings around plumbing or through cracks in the foundation. It is derived from the natural decay of uranium. Because it enters a building from the ground, radon gas is not typically a problem in high-rise buildings or the upper floors of commercial facilities. However, it can be a problem in some homes and schools. Radon gas is hazardous because it can cause damage to the lungs.

To find out if a particular property may be affected by radon gas, you can:

- Contact a local, state, or federal environmental agency
- Ask the owners of nearby property if they know of any problems
- Recommend that the seller have the property tested for radon

Currently, it is not uncommon for a buyer to request a radon test before making an offer. Radon tests are easy to obtain, and if a problem is found, it is usually easy and inexpensive to correct. If a radon test is conducted, the results of the test must be disclosed to the seller and all potential buyers. There are publications available from the U.S. Environmental Protection Agency (EPA) for homeowners interested in obtaining information about radon gas. You may want to obtain copies of these publications to give to prospective buyers. You should also be aware that Florida state law requires that all licensees attach radon disclosure statements on all contracts.

Formaldehyde Gas

Formaldehyde gas is emitted by materials contained in the following household items:

- Furniture
- Draperies
- Carpet
- Plywood

Formaldehyde gas is also emitted by a thermal insulation called **urea-formaldehyde foam insulation**, which was used in many older homes. Formaldehyde gas may cause irritation to the eyes, nose, and throat. In addition, it may cause more serious problems such as cancer. However, the level of formaldehyde that typically occurs in a home is not sufficient to produce serious problems. If you suspect that a home contains urea-formaldehyde foam insulation, you should recommend that the seller do the following:

- Have the air inside the home tested for formaldehyde gas
- Consult a health authority

If a problem with formaldehyde gas exists, the material emitting the gas must be removed.

Asbestos

In the past, **asbestos** was used as insulation in many buildings because of its fire-retardant qualities. Asbestos fibers can cause serious lung diseases, including cancer. Although asbestos is typically found in older buildings with public occupancy, it also can be found in the ceilings, floors, and pipes in older homes. Some of the indicators of the presence of asbestos include:

- Ceilings or walls covered with a grainy plaster
- Ceilings or walls sprayed with a fluffy, stringy material
- Pipes or boilers wrapped with fibrous material or with a cement or felt-type insulation

A licensee handling older buildings should have these buildings inspected for asbestos or recommend that the owner contact an asbestos consultant.

In addition, the seller and potential buyers should be informed if the licensee knows or believes that a building contains asbestos. If asbestos is found, the removal is a complicated and expensive procedure.

Lead

Exposure to lead typically comes from lead plumbing and lead-based paints. Serious problems can occur if an individual:

- Drinks water containing lead particles from lead plumbing
- Ingests flakes of lead-based paint
- Inhales lead particles

For example, if lead particles are inhaled or ingested by an adult with high blood pressure, her condition may worsen. Also, if a child is exposed to lead, she may suffer from impaired physical and/or mental development. Young children and pregnant women are at greater risk.

As a real estate licensee, you should be aware of the following issues related to lead contamination:

- Department of Housing and Urban Development (HUD) housing must be in compliance with HUD regulations related to inspecting and testing for lead contamination.
- The use of lead plumbing in a system connected to a public water supply is prohibited by the EPA.
- If the level of lead in a residential plumbing system exceeds EPA standards, HUD and Veterans Affairs (VA) assistance is not available.
- Homes with peeling paint built in or before 1978 are those most likely to experience lead contamination.

In addition, to protect families from exposure to lead, Congress passed the Residential Lead-Based Paint Hazard Reduction Act of 1992 (also known as Title X). Section 1018 of this law requires the disclosure of known information on lead-based paint and lead-based paint hazards before the sale or lease of most housing built before 1978. The Residential Lead-Based Paint Hazard Reduction Act includes the following requirements:

- Sellers and lessors must disclose the presence of known lead-based paint and lead-based paint hazards and provide available reports to buyers or renters.
- Sellers and lessors must provide buyers and renters with a federally approved pamphlet titled *Protect Your Family from Lead in Your Home*.
- Sellers must give buyers a 10-day period to conduct a lead-based paint and lead-based hazard inspection (at the buyers' expense).
- Sales contracts and leases must include certain disclosures.
- Sellers, lessors, and real estate agents share the responsibility for ensuring compliance. Thus, as an agent, you are responsible for informing a seller or lessor of his obligations under the law and for ensuring that he makes the required disclosures.

Coaching Tips: The Residential Lead-Based Paint Hazard Reduction Act does *not* require the testing or removal of lead-based paint by sellers or lessors nor does it require either sellers or lessors to pay for a buyer or tenant to conduct a lead-based paint test.

Groundwater Contamination

Groundwater contamination occurs when a supply of drinking water is contaminated by any of the following:

- Pesticides and fertilizers used in farming
- Leaking **underground storage tanks**
- Hazardous waste dumps
- Mining
- Any other source of contamination

To determine if groundwater may be contaminated, a licensee may do any of the following:

- Contact the appropriate health authority for information about the quality of the water.
- Ask the owners of nearby property if they know of any problems with the water.
- Inspect the property for the presence of dumping, mining, or other sources of contamination.
- Keep up-to-date on reports of groundwater contamination that could affect property in the area.
- Inspect the property for patches of oil, areas where nothing will grow, and other signs of contamination.
- Determine how the property was used by previous owners.
- Inspect the property for signs of previous commercial use, such as the presence of asphalt and/or cement.
- Contact the appropriate agency to find out if any previous owners were cited for violating environmental protection laws.
- Ask the seller and/or the appropriate authority if there are any underground storage tanks on the property.
- Inspect the property for air vents sticking out of the ground, which may indicate the presence of an underground storage tank.
- Hire an expert to test the groundwater for contamination.

Most tests for common groundwater contaminants are relatively easy and inexpensive. These tests can be conducted by private laboratories. However, if the water needs to be tested for industrial contaminants, the procedures are more complex and expensive. When such tests are needed, you (or the seller) should contact the proper environmental authority. If you know or suspect that there is a problem with the groundwater, you should inform the seller and any prospective buyers. Also, if there is reason to believe that the source of contamination is a hazardous waste dump or an underground storage tank, you should strongly encourage the seller and buyer to contact the appropriate environmental protection agency and/or health authority.

For example, if you know that a property was previously used as a gas station or oil distributor, you should recommend that the seller and/or buyer consult the appropriate environmental agency.

Disclosure Statement

As explained previously, whenever you know or suspect that a property is affected by an environmental hazard, you must disclose this to the seller and any potential buyers. One way to make a disclosure to potential buyers is to have the seller complete an environmental disclosure statement. The environmental disclosure statement may be a checklist of environmental conditions. The seller would simply check off all of the conditions that apply to her property. The licensee would give a copy of the checklist to any prospective buyers. The licensee may also decide to give buyers copies of any relevant government publications related to certain environmental conditions. By using an environmental disclosure form, licensees may protect themselves and the sellers from liability related to disclosure of property defects.

Due Diligence Investigation

The Superfund Amendments and Reauthorization Act of 1986 permits a property owner to use an *innocent landowner* defense if environmental problems arise after the owner sells the property. In order to use the innocent landowner defense, the owner must prove that a due diligence investigation of the property was conducted before ownership was transferred. A due diligence investigation is a very thorough and time-consuming process. There is a set of minimum requirements for the investigation. The following information must be included in the investigation:

- A review of previous and current ownership and use of the property, including uses involving environmental hazards.
- A review of all previous inspections, investigations, litigation, etc., involving environmental hazards.
- An evaluation of adjacent properties and any associated hazards.
- A review of the drainage, sewer, and septic systems.

This list is *not* a complete list of the requirements. A property owner who wishes to use the innocent landowner defense needs to obtain a thorough list and complete each requirement.

SUMMARY

Because most licensees will be dealing with both new and existing properties, product knowledge becomes essential. The licensee should familiarize themselves with common construction terminology. Housing in Florida is generally constructed with foundations consisting of slab on slab. This is primarily because the water table is high. Therefore, basements and crawl spaces are not common. Platform framing is the most common framing while roof designs vary. Finishes would include improvements designed to protect against wind and other climate hazards. This would include storm screens and wind shading on windows and Florida rooms.

REVIEW QUESTIONS

1. A type of framing allows for open interiors without the interruption of many supporting walls would be:
   a. Platform.
   b. Post and beam.
   c. Balloon.
   d. Joist.

2. A double-hung window is a window that:
   a. Features insulated glass.
   b. Opens from the bottom.
   c. Swings out to open.
   d. Opens from either the bottom or top.

3. Air flow in a building:
   a. Prevents water condensation.
   b. Provides more comfortable interiors.
   c. Promotes the flow of heat.
   d. Reduces accumulation of odors and gas.

4. Insulation is rated by:
   a. Depth of material.
   b. The Department of Energy.
   c. Resistance to heat flow.
   d. Type of installation.

5. Sarah plans to build an expensive two-story home with a stucco exterior. To reduce the possibility of cracks in the stucco finish, she might consider:
   a. Platform framing.
   b. Balloon framing.
   c. A pier foundation with a crawl space.
   d. Fixed windows.

6. Today's homes have many electrical appliances that are used everyday. Most homes are wired for:
   a. 110 and 220 volts.
   b. 110 and 240 volts.
   c. 120 and 220 volts.
   d. 120 and 240 volts.

7. A type of roof that features two planes with an overhang on two sides of the building is a:
   a. Gable roof.
   b. Hip roof.
   c. Gambrel roof.
   d. Mansard roof.

8. The pitch of a roof measures the roof's:
   a. Height.
   b. Slope.
   c. Span.
   d. Run.

9. A long skinny lot is known as a:
   a. Key lot.
   b. Flag lot.
   c. Corner lot.
   d. Interior lot.

10. Once the roof trusses are hoisted into place, the next step of roof construction is installing the:
    a. Insulation.
    b. Shingles.
    c. Sheathing.
    d. Felt.

11. Which type of window opens by swinging outward?
    a. Jalousie
    b. Fixed
    c. Double-hung
    d. Casement

12. Julian wants to add a second story to his ranch-style home. A major concern is whether:
    a. The foundation is deep enough.
    b. A new roof system can be installed.
    c. The bearing walls are adequate.
    d. The design will be pleasing.

13. The force of the electrical flow along the transmission wires is measured in:
    a. Wattage.
    b. Amps.
    c. Current.
    d. Volts.

14. Brad is considering buying his neighbor's home that was built in the 1960s. The home is listed with ABC Realty. Before showing the house, ABC Realty:
    a. Must give Brad an EPA pamphlet that describes the danger of lead-based paint.
    b. Can have Brad sign a waiver of the inspection requirements.
    c. Will provide a seller's statement that the seller will pay for the property inspection.
    d. Will give a statement that Brad must pay for a required inspection.

15. All persons in Florida must be given a disclosure regarding the possibility of the presence of radon gas on the property at or before the time of entering into a sale and purchase or rental agreement. Which of these statements is true?
    a. Prospective buyers and lessees must sign the radon gas disclosure.
    b. All parties must execute the radon gas disclosure.
    c. No inspection or remedy regarding radon is required.
    d. The radon disclosure cannot be included as a portion of the contract.

16. Asbestos was commonly used as insulation and a fire retardant in the 1970s. When asbestos fibers become friable (airborne), their inhalation can cause serious respiratory diseases. Florida laws:
    a. Require the removal of asbestos material from buildings.
    b. Do not address the presence of asbestos in buildings. Federal laws prevail.
    c. Require that asbestos be encapsulated, a procedure safer than removal.
    d. Require a mandatory disclosure for buildings built before 1979 stating that asbestos material may be present.

17. Which statement is FALSE regarding subdivisions?
    a. Winding streets in subdivisions are aesthetically pleasing.
    b. Four-way stops are safer in subdivision intersections.
    c. Conformity of the homes in the subdivision raises the value of all the houses.
    d. T-intersection lots are the most desirable lots and command a larger price.

18. A rectangular lot reached by a long access road is a(n):
    a. Key lot.
    b. Interior lot.
    c. Cul-de-sac lot.
    d. Flag lot.

19. In Florida, building codes are mandated by:
    a. The state of Florida.
    b. Municipalities.
    c. Counties.
    d. The type of zoning district.

Chapter 17

KEY TERMS

appreciation	leverage
book value	liquidation analysis
bulk	liquidity
cash flow	return of investment
equity	return on investment
going concern value	tax shelter
goodwill	

LEARNING OBJECTIVES

After completing this lesson, you will be able to:

- Describe the goals of investing in real estate.
- Identify the advantages and disadvantages of investing in real estate.
- Explain the risks of investing in real estate.
- Point out the importance of an investment analysis.
- Distinguish between the different types of risk.
- Describe the characteristics of business brokerage and how it differs from real estate brokerage.
- Calculate problems involving value.
- Calculate problems involving commission.
- Calculate problems involving the determination of cost.
- Calculate problems involving the determination of price.

Investing in Real Estate and Business Brokerage

REAL ESTATE INVESTMENTS

An investor's goal is to seek out investments that will ultimately meet the investor's three primary objectives:

1. An annual return on the investor's invested capital (represents investor profit, **return on investment**)

2. Preservation and/or return of the principal investment (represents investor **return of investment**)

3. Increased values derived during the property-holding period

However, when discussing the investment of capital funds, it is important to note that investors are not buying the "bricks and mortar." It is not the real property nor the stocks, bonds, or purchase of a business that an investor seeks. Rather, it is primarily the **cash flow** associated with the investment and the yields to the investor that are desired. Investors primarily seek returns of and on their investments. Cash flow is what delivers these returns to the investor. Cash flow also refers to receipts less payments over a period of time. Therefore, real property, not unlike other investment types, is merely the investment vehicle that houses the cash flow that investors truly seek. In fact, regardless of the vehicle that houses the cash flow, the moment that vehicle does not produce the required returns, or other vehicles provide higher returns (profits) than the current investment vehicle, the investor will sell and move into a more aggressive investment vehicle.

Many investors gravitate toward real property as their investment vehicle of choice. This is primarily because, historically, investment in real property not only yields the investor profits during the holding period, but also tends to retain its overall value over time.

Investments and their vehicles always react in a cyclical manner. When times are good, they increase in value; when times are bad, they decrease in value. The property's value is a direct derivative of the income that is attributable to the property at any given time.

The Licensee Regarded as an Expert

Investors often seek the guidance of a real estate broker to locate a property for an investment opportunity, and to provide assistance in the analysis of the investment prior to purchase. Therefore, a licensee must have a thorough knowledge and clear understanding of the investment-analysis process. However, keep in mind that the unauthorized practice of law is a direct violation of licensee law. Strongly consider this before giving investment guidance and advice to an investor.

Property Types and Subtypes

Before we look at real estate as an investment, we should review the different types of real property:

- Residential
- Commercial
- Industrial
- Agricultural
- Mixed use

Residential Property

Under zoning definitions, residential property is any property intended for dwelling purposes. However, the term is expanded when discussing it in transactional terms. Within this context, transactional residential property is defined to include the following:

- Improved property containing one to four units intended for dwelling purposes.
- Unimproved property that, when and if improved, will consist of one to four units intended for dwelling purposes.
- Farm/agricultural land of ten or fewer acres.

Residential property as a basic property group takes on many forms. Residential property subtypes consist of:

- Single-family homes
- Multifamily dwellings
- Condominiums
- Cooperatives
- Condops (hybrid of condo/co-op formation)
- Rental units
- Agricultural land of ten or fewer acres (agricultural land with more than ten acres is considered nonresidential, agricultural property)

Because housing is a necessity for all people, it is in greater demand than other types of real property. Due to this demand, the residential housing market is the most active of the basic property group types.

All other property types that are not residential property are considered nonresidential property, including:

- Improved or unimproved property with greater than four dwelling units
- All investment property, regardless of its use

In essence, all nonresidential property types fall under the category of investment property, while only residential properties containing greater than four units are considered investment property. In fact, there are two types of property transactions:

- Residential transactions
- Commercial transactions

If you recall, residentional and commercial transactions was covered in Chapter 12. Investment property is not for dwelling purposes by its owner(s). Investment property is used to generate income for investment purposes.

Commercial Property

Commercial property is property that is used by business or operating enterprises. Commercial property includes:

- Offices
- Retail establishments
- Hotels/motels

Offices

Office buildings house businesses. Depending on their proximity within given marketplaces, office buildings are constructed in a variety of sizes. They can be low-rise, mid-rise, or high-rise. The location and zoning of a particular parcel of real estate will dictate the size and height of a building. Office buildings may be either single- or multitenant properties. The **bulk** (total building size in square footage) of any development is always determined by zoning allowances.

Retail Establishments

Retail property takes many shapes and forms. The size of a retail facility dictates what category of retail the property takes. For example, urban retail can be the neighborhood store on your block; however, with careful planning, larger projects can be created. The retail facility's success depends on the needs of the community surrounding it. Some of the different forms of retail property include the following:

- Regional shopping centers
- Shopping malls
- Strip centers
- Neighborhood shopping centers
- Factory outlet malls/centers

Hotels/Motels

Most people perceive hotel/motel properties as short-term and transient residences. However, a careful inspection of the public records concerning zoning categorization reveals that these properties are zoned as commercial (not residential).

In many cases, it would not be unusual for zoning to allow a "multi" use for hotels/motels. For example, a particular hotel may be a 400-room high-rise in a central urban location. It would not be unusual to split the property into two—in theory, a building inside another building. The lower portion may consist of short-term hotel accommodations, while the upper portion may consist of permanent housing such as cooperative or condominium housing. An example of this would be the world-renowned Plaza Hotel in New York City. That property is undergoing a transformation that will mirror the concept of the "building within the building." Lower floors will be for interim/transient short-term stay (hotel), while the upper floors—with their dramatic views of Central Park and the New York skyline—will be luxury condominiums. The Plaza Hotel will be considered a mixed-use property. Mixed-use properties will be covered in more detail later in this chapter.

Industrial Property

Industrial property consists of uses associated with manufacturing, including:

- Heavy manufacturing
- Light manufacturing

- Loft buildings
- Warehousing
- Assembly and distribution

Heavy and light manufacturing are usually associated with the conversion of raw materials into a finished product. This would be substantially different from a warehousing use. While heavy and light manufacturing spaces are used to create the finished product, the warehouse is used to store the finished product prior to its distribution to the marketplace (e.g., the neighborhood store).

Agricultural Property

Agricultural property refers to various types of farm lands over ten acres. In many cases, investors purchase agricultural property that is located in the path of future development with the idea that the value of the property will increase because of development or that the property will be rezoned in the future.

Mixed-Use Property

Since the mid-1980s, mixed-use property has been very popular. In some cases, municipal tax benefits are available on these types of properties. These tax benefits are offered when there is a need for housing and/or other property uses in an area. This property type can be a new development, or, more recently, conversion of a previous single-use property into a multiuse property. For example, developers have taken buildings that have experienced both functional and economic obsolescence problems and converted them into mixed-use property. These properties will incorporate two or more property use types. An example of this would be commercial uses on the lower portion of the property in question and residential uses on the upper portion. As previously discussed, commercial uses may vary from offices, to retail establishments, to hotels or motels.

Coaching Tips: **Property Descriptions at a Glance**

- **Residential property includes improved property containing one to four units intended for dwelling purposes or unimproved property that, when and if improved, will consist of one to four units intended for dwelling purposes.**
- **Commercial property includes offices, retail establishments, and hotels/motels.**
- **Industrial property includes manufacturing facilities and warehouses.**
- **Agricultural property refers to various types of farm lands over ten acres.**

Goals of Investments

We just looked at the types of real property that may be of interest to investors. As previously mentioned, some of the reasons for real property investment include:

- An annual return on the investor's invested capital (represents investor profit). This is also known as the return on the investment (ROI).
- Preservation and/or return of the principal investment. This is also known as the return of the investment.
- Increased values derived during the property holding period (that is, **appreciation**).

With these objectives in mind, let's look at the advantages and disadvantages of investing in real estate compared to other types of investment.

Advantages of Investing in Real Estate

Due to the scarcity of unimproved land within active real estate markets, investors gravitate to long-term investment in real property. Some of the advantages of real property investment include:

- A good rate of return
- A hedge against inflation
- Equity buildup
- The use of leveraging (borrowed funds) versus buyers outlay of cash within one investment
- Tax advantages

A Good Rate of Return

One of the objectives of investing is to achieve a good annual return on invested capital. In essence, the goal is to make a profit by putting money to use in an investment. Compared to other investment alternatives, real estate typically provides a higher rate of return. Real estate investment, like any other vehicle, is cyclical in nature. However, the long-term investor will achieve large benefits by investing in and holding real property.

A Hedge against Inflation

Because of the scarcity of strategically located property, over the years, real property investment has kept up with inflationary trends. Inflation refers to an increase in the supply of money in the economy without a corresponding increase in the production of goods and services. Inflation results in an increase in prices and a corresponding decrease in purchasing power (that is, a decrease in the value of a dollar). As the purchasing power of the dollar decreases, many investments lose value over time. However, this is not true with real estate because the value of real property typically increases faster than inflation. Inflation is generally considered a negative within the overall economy; however, inflation is embraced by the property owner. The result for the owner is an immediate increase in the overall value of the property. This equates to a value over and above the owner's initial investment cost. This increase in value occurs regardless of the income attributable to the property at that time. Appreciation normally would occur through the increase in rents attributable to that property. The unnatural increase in value due to inflation may result in the owner's ability to refinance the property at a higher property value than the rents would normally command for that property.

Equity Buildup

When real property increases in value, the result is equity buildup. **Equity** refers to the difference between the market value of a property and the unpaid balance of any loans on that property. Equity increases (builds up) as any loan is paid down and as the property appreciates. Appreciation refers to any increase in the value of property.

Leverage

Leverage refers to the use of borrowed funds with the anticipation of earning substantial profits not only on the investment, but also on the borrowed funds. For example, an investor may purchase a property by making a down payment equal to 25 percent of the value of the property and borrow the remaining 75 percent. The property may immediately begin generating a return for the investor on the full value of the property even though her own capital investment was only 25 percent of the property's value.

Leveraging can be advantageous when planned appropriately. Planning starts with establishing the effects of the debt on the cash flow. The cost of the annual debt service (amount paid for principal and interest on the loan) must be subtracted from net operating income attributable to the property. The difference will determine if earnings are sufficient to cover the debt placed on the property. (A positive value indicates that earnings are sufficient to cover the debt. A negative value indicates that earnings are not sufficient.)

Tax Advantages

Real estate investments have many tax advantages (although some of the advantages were limited or eliminated by the 1986 Tax Reform Act). Some of the advantages that still exist include tax deductions for interest payments, taxes, and depreciation on improvements. An investment that results in tax advantages is sometimes referred to as a **tax shelter**. Tax issues related to real property ownership are discussed in more detail in Chapter 18.

Disadvantages of Investing in Real Estate

Some of the disadvantages of real property investment include:

- Illiquidity
- Market conditions
- The need for property management
- Risk

Illiquidity

Liquidity refers to the ability to convert an asset into cash by selling it. An asset that can be readily sold and converted to cash is considered liquid. For example, stocks are considered liquid assets. An asset that *cannot* be readily sold and converted to cash is considered illiquid. Real property is considered illiquid because quick sales are not easily achieved. Therefore, one of the disadvantages of investing in real estate is illiquidity of the investment.

Market Conditions

A real estate investment may be adversely affected by the market. For example, a change or an erosion of market conditions can result in loss of property value. This would be a direct result of lower rents attributable to the property during these times.

Because land cannot be moved, the market for real estate is a local one, and real estate investors often have preferences for certain geographic areas.

Management

Another disadvantage of investing in real estate is management. Managing real property can be both time consuming and labor intensive. Depending on the property and the investor, the investor may choose to manage the property himself or be an absentee owner. If the investor chooses to be an absentee owner, a property manager would be hired. In addition to hiring a property manager, a real estate investor may also require the services of attorneys, financial consultants, and other professionals.

Risk

Real estate investors are exposed to risk. Risk refers to the chance of losing one's invested capital. When making a decision about investment property, an investor must analyze the risk.

There are various types of risk any investor must take into consideration prior to investing money. Risks associated with general business conditions must be assessed, such as:

- Business risk
- Financial risk
- Purchasing-power risk
- Interest-rate risk
- Risks that affect return
- Liquidity risk
- Safety risk

Risks Associated with General Business Conditions

Business risk is risk related to any variation between predicted income and expenses and actual income and expenses.

Financial risk is risk related to the ability of the investment to pay operating expenses from the various sources of funds, including income from operations, equity, and borrowed funds.

Purchasing-power risk is risk associated with inflation, which reduces the value of any yield from an investment. (As mentioned previously, inflation results in an increase in prices and a corresponding decrease in purchasing power; that is, a decrease in the value of a dollar.)

Interest-rate risk is the risk caused by a change in interest rates. For example, when there is a loan on a property, any increase in the interest rate by the lender can result in a decrease in the value of the property.

There are other risks that can affect the return on the investment as well as the return of the invested capital. These risks include the following:

- Liquidity risk—The risk associated with any loss that might result if the investment has to be sold quickly.
- Safety risk—The chance of losing one's invested capital (market risk) and/or expected earnings (risk of default).
- Market risk—The risk resulting from a decrease in the market value of the investment.
- Risk of default—The chance that the investor's actual earnings will be less than expected.

Coaching Tips: **Risk at a Glance**

- **Risk related to any variation between predicted income and expenses and actual income and expenses is business risk.**
- **Purchasing-power risk refers to risk associated with inflation, which reduces the value of any yield from an investment.**
- **Liquidity risk refers to risk associated with any loss that might result if the investment has to be sold quickly.**
- **Market risk refers to risk resulting from a decrease in the market value of the investment.**
- **Interest-rate risk refers to risk caused by a change in interest rates.**

Property Investment Analysis

Before purchasing nonresidential property, a complicated investment review process occurs. This review process requires an understanding of the terms and conditions within any lease on a property, as well as effect of these terms and conditions on the property income bottom line. Therefore, a licensee assisting an investor is required to have a keen awareness of lease clauses and their financial impact on the investor when reviewing leases.

For example, commercial leases tend to be modified gross leases. This means that the tenant/lessee will pay an amount that is established as the base rent to the landlord/lessor. However, it is prevalent today that commercial leases contain provisions that cover the owner against increased costs in operations due to real property tax increases or increased costs in delivering the services expected by the tenant that are called for in the lease. These clauses, called escalation clauses, entitle the owner to bill the tenant for cost increases.

Most commercial leases break down rents into two types of payments:

1. Base rent—The amount that the landlord and tenant have initially agreed upon.

2. Additional rent—Any amounts paid to the landlord for one or all of the following items:

   - Property tax increases
   - Operating expense increases
   - Utility costs paid by the landlord that are reimbursable by the tenant
   - Any service within the property performed by the landlord on the tenant's behalf that requires a reimbursement from the tenant

The licensee is required to look at a broad number of factors that affect value in the analysis. Some of the factors that require careful review include:

- External economic influences
- Locational considerations
- Financial analyses
- Risk analyses

External economic influences can exist on either a national or a local level. On a national level, upward or downward changes in interest rates affect the cost of borrowed funds to the investor. On a local level, zoning constraints affect a property's use or size in relation to investor requirements.

Because these influences are outside the property line, they are items and trends that are not in the control of the investor. However, the investor may be positively or negatively impacted by a change in national or local trends.

An investment analysis must also include an examination of locational considerations, which include:

- Zoning
- Site and environmental factors
- Time-distance relationships to amenities (The relationship of a property to amenities or supporting facilities, measured in both distance and time, is referred to as *linkage.*)

Another component of the investment analysis is a financial analysis, which should include:

- An income versus expense analysis (cash flow analysis)
- An examination of current leases
- The need for any future capital improvements
- Any present and future local law compliance issues
- Present and future market conditions

The investment analysis also includes a risk analysis, which includes an examination of the following:

- Any potential changes in interest rates (Any change in rates will affect the way an investor looks at acquisition value. As mentioned earlier, the higher the rate is for borrowed funds, the greater the cost of servicing the annual debt, thereby creating lower value.)
- Property income and its ability to cover:
  - Operating expenses
  - Debt service
  - A loss in property value

CALCULATING PRICE AND COMMISSIONS

The price or value of a property may be determined by the following equations:

$$\text{Price} = \frac{\text{Annual Net Income}}{\text{Capitalization Rate}}$$

$$\text{Price} = \frac{\text{Income}}{\text{Rate}}$$

$$\frac{\text{Income}}{\text{Rate}} = \text{Price} \quad \text{So in this case} \quad \frac{\$42,000}{.10} = \$420,000$$

$$\text{Price} = \frac{\text{Net Income}}{\text{Capitalization Rate}}$$

In order to better understand these equations, let's cover two basic types of math problems:

1. Those involving commissions on sales
2. Those involving investments and return on investments

Then we will cover two additional problem types:

1. Those involving estimates of value based on rates of return (capitalization problems)
2. Those involving loans

Before learning how to solve the following problems, you will first learn a name for each type of problem. A big part of learning how to solve these problems is learning how to recognize and name the type of problem you are solving. Once you are able to do this, the process of completing the necessary calculations is much simpler.

Commission Problems

Let's begin with the first type of problem—those involving commissions paid on the sale of real estate. We will call this type of problem a commission problem. While solving commission problems, you will be organizing information in a way that will be used in the first four types of problems. We will refer to this method of organization as the T-bar.

Before working on the first commission problem, let's define some basic terms:

- Commission (C)—The amount a broker receives for selling a property.
- Sales Price (P)—The amount the property sells for.
- Rate of Commission (R)—The commission expressed as a percentage of the sales price.

Problem: A property sells for $120,000. The listing broker will receive a commission of 6 percent for selling the property. How much is his commission?

We can express the relationship between these three numbers using the T-bar as follows:

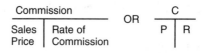

The best way to remember this formula is to remember CPR. This will be the code for commission problems. The T-bar is a simple way to remember the arithmetic steps needed to solve a problem like the one above. Let's stop and take a look at how it works before we come back to our commission problem. The position of the numbers in the T-bar is important because the position determines whether a number is to be multiplied or divided by another number.

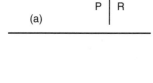

For example, the T-bar for commission problem is shown to the left (a). The first thing you should note is how the letters are placed in the T-bar. Whenever you learn a T-bar, you will be given a three-letter code to remember its contents. In this case, it is CPR. The first letter of the code *always* goes on top of the T-bar. The second letter *always* goes on the bottom left. The third letter *always* goes on the bottom right, as shown.

Now, let's look at how we use the T-bar to help solve problems. The first step to solve a problem is to block out one of the letters in the T-bar. *Always* block out the letter that is an unknown. The unknown is the number we are trying to find by solving the problem.

When we block out any one of the letters, we are left with two letters with a line between them. The direction of the line tells us whether to multiply or divide the numbers represented by the letters.

For example, if we block out the top letter as shown to the left (b), we are left with the P and R and a vertical line between them. (P and R are side-by-side.) The vertical line means that we multiply the two numbers.

If we block out the P as shown to the left (c), we are left with the C and R and a horizontal line between them. (C is above R.) The horizontal line means that we divide the top number by the bottom number.

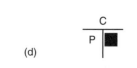

If we block out the R as shown to the left (d), we are left with the C and P and a horizontal line between them. (C is above P.) The horizontal line means that we divide the top number by the bottom number.

Let's go back and see how to use this T-bar to solve our commission problem.

Problem: A property sells for $120,000. The listing broker will receive a commission of 6 percent for selling the property. How much is his commission?

In this problem, we know the following:

Sales Price (P) = $120,000
Rate of Commission (R) = 6 percent

The one thing we don't know is the commission (C). But we can determine the commission by entering what we know into our T-bar, as shown next.

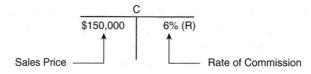

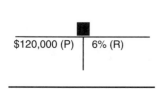

When we block out the unknown (C) as shown on the left, we are left with P and R separated by a vertical line. This means that we multiply $120,000 by 6 percent to get the value for C, as shown next:

$$\begin{array}{r} \$120,000 \\ \underline{0.06} \\ \$\ 7,200 \end{array}$$

This tells us that C (Commission) is $7,200, which is the listing broker's commission.

Once you know the commission T-bar (CPR), you can work any problem of this type by substituting the two known values from the problem into the formula. Let's look at a similar commission problem.

Problem: A salesperson will receive 45 percent of a 6 percent commission for selling a property listed by her broker. If she sells a property for $150,000, how much will she earn?

The only thing different about this problem is that the salesperson doesn't get the entire commission. First, let's use the commission T-bar to determine the amount of the *broker's* total commission.

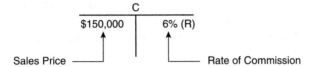

The broker's commission is $9,000:

$$\$150,000 \times 0.06 = \$9,000$$

The salesperson's commission is 45 percent of the total commission ($9,000), so the salesperson's commission is:

$$\$9,000 \times 0.45 = \$4,050$$

The salesperson will earn $4,050 for selling the property.

Now, let's look at how we can use the same T-bar to solve a problem that looks more difficult (but really isn't).

Problem: A broker lists and sells a property. As compensation, he receives a 5 percent commission that amounts to $7,800. What was the selling price of the property?

To solve the problem, enter the two things we know into the T-bar to find out what to multiply or divide.

$$
\begin{array}{c|c}
\$7,800 & \\
\hline
P & .05
\end{array}
\quad
\begin{array}{l}
\longleftarrow \quad C = \text{Commission Amount} \\
\longleftarrow \quad R = \text{Rate of Commission}
\end{array}
$$

When we block out the unknown (P), we are left with $7,800 over 0.05, which means to divide:

$$\$7,800 \div 0.05 = \$156,000$$

The house sold for $156,000.

Investment Problems

Now, let's look at investment problems. These problems can be worked using a T-bar similar to the one you just used. The T-bar is as follows:

$$
\begin{array}{c|c}
\multicolumn{2}{c}{\text{Profit}} \\
\hline
\text{Amount} & \text{Rate of} \\
\text{Invested} & \text{Return}
\end{array}
\quad \text{OR} \quad
\begin{array}{c|c}
\multicolumn{2}{c}{P} \\
\hline
A & R
\end{array}
$$

Note that the code for investment problems is PAR.

First, let's look at the elements in the investment T-bar:

- Profit—The amount of money made on an investment. It may also be called yield, income, or return.

Coaching Tips: Profit does not include and should not be confused with the original amount of money or the principal investment that the investor invested and got back. It is *only* the additional money earned *above* what the investor originally invested. Profit is usually the remaining income after the property's operational expenses have been paid.

- Amount Invested—The amount of money the investor spent initially in order to acquire the property (the selling price, *not* the down payment).
- Rate of Return—The percentage (rate) that the investor makes (or wants to make) on an investment. This amount ultimately equates the dollar profit amount found in the P of the T-bar. The rate of return is the percentage of the original investment needed as profit for parking one's money within an investment. The receipt of interest given by a bank on deposits is another form of rate of return.

Now, let's look at a problem using the investment T-bar.

Problem: An investor purchased two lots for $30,000 each. She later divided the land into three lots and sold them for $25,000 each. What was her rate of return?

Let's look at what we know and don't know:

- Amount Invested—The investor paid $30,000 for each of two lots, for a total investment of $60,000.
- Profit—The investor sold three lots for $25,000 each, for a total price of $75,000. The price ($75,000) less the cost ($60,000) gives the profit, which in this case is $15,000.
- Rate of Return—This is what we want to find.

Now, let's take what we know and enter it into the T-bar:

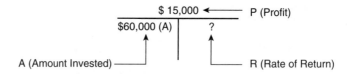

The investor's rate of return is 25 percent:

$$\$15,000 \div \$60,000 = 0.25$$

Now, let's look at a different type of problem using the same T-bar.

Problem: An investor wants to earn a return of $250 per month on an investment that has a rate of return of 8 percent. How much will the investor need to invest to do this?

Again, let's start with what we know and don't know:

- Profit—The amount that the investor wants to earn is $250 per month. For 12 months, this would be $250 × 12 = $3,000.
- Rate of Return—The investment yields a rate of return of 8 percent.
- Amount Invested—This is what we want to determine.

Now, let's take what we know and enter it in the T-bar.

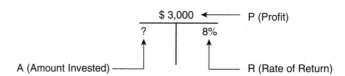

When we block out the unknown (A), we are left with $3,000 over 8 percent, which means to divide:

$$\$3,000 \div 0.08 = \$37,500$$

The investor must invest $37,500 to obtain the desired profit of $250 per month.

Now, let's look at an investment problem that looks very different from those you just worked, but is easy to work using the same T-bar.

Problem: A borrower borrows $6,000 and signs a note for it that must be paid off in 12 months, with interest at 10 percent. The lender then immediately sells the note to an investor for $5,000. What is the investor's rate of return?

First, let's look at what we know and don't know:

- Rate of Return—This is what we want to find. (It is *not* 10 percent.)
- Amount Invested—This is $5,000, the amount paid for the note.
- Profit—We must calculate the profit, as shown next.

At the end of the year, the note will have earned 10 percent of its face value of $6,000, or $600. When the note is paid off, the investor will have received a total of $6,600 (the original $6,000 principal plus $600 in interest).

The investor's profit is the total amount received less the amount she paid for the note:

$$\$6,600 - \$5,000 = \$1,600$$

Now, let's take what we know and enter it in the T-bar.

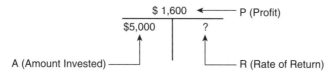

When we block out the unknown (R), we are left with $1,600 over $5,000, which means to divide:

$$\$1,600 \div \$5,000 = 0.32$$

The investor's rate of return is 32 percent.

Value Problems

Now, let's look at value problems. These problems can be solved using a T-bar similar to the ones you have just used:

$$\frac{\text{Income}}{\text{Rate of} \mid \text{Value of}} \quad \text{OR} \quad \frac{\text{I}}{\text{R} \mid \text{V}}$$
$$\text{Capitalization} \mid \text{Property}$$

Note that the code for value problems is IRV. The value T-bar is used to work problems based on the income method for appraising income-producing property. The income method uses the process of capitalization. *Capitalization is the process of determining the value of a property from how much net income it produces.* The capitalization rate is the percentage used for the rate of return that an investor obtains or desires to obtain by buying and owning the income-producing property.

First, let's look at the elements in the value T-bar (IRV):

- Income—The annual net operating income (NOI) that an income property produces. Note two important elements:
  - If the income is expressed as monthly or quarterly income, it must first be converted to annual income before using the T-bar.
  - If gross income is given, it must be converted to net income before using the T-bar.

- Rate of Capitalization—The rate of return that the investor receives or wants to receive.
- Value—The market value of the income-producing property.

Now, let's look at a problem using the value T-bar.

Problem: An investor is evaluating an income-producing property for possible purchase. The property produces a monthly net income of $3,200. If the investor wants to earn a 12 percent return, how much can she afford to pay for the property?

Again, let's start with what we know and don't know

- Income—The monthly net income is $3,200. Multiply this by 12 to get the annual net income, which is $38,400.
- Rate of Capitalization—The investor wants to earn 12 percent, which is the rate of capitalization.
- Value—The value of the property is what we want to determine.

Now, let's take what we know and enter it in the T-bar.

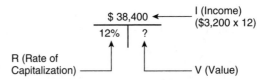

When we block out the unknown (V), we are left with $38,400 over 12 percent, which means we divide:

$$\$38,400 \div 0.12 = \$320,000$$

The value of the property is $320,000, which means the investor can pay $320,000 for the property and obtain a 12 percent return.

Now, let's look at a different kind of problem using the value T-bar.

Problem: An investor is considering an income-producing property that is valued at $560,000 using a capitalization rate of 8 percent. How much could the investor afford to pay for the property if a capitalization rate of 10 percent were used?

Before starting the problem, we need to look at our strategy. There are really two problems here:

1. The value of the property with an 8 percent rate.
2. The value of the property with a 10 percent rate.

The value we are interested in is the value with a 10 percent rate, but there is a problem. If we try to work the problem using a 10 percent capitalization rate, we'll find that there are *two* things we don't know (income and value) and only *one* thing we do know (the 10 percent capitalization rate). Because only one of the three items is known, we can't work the problem. The solution is to work the problem first using the 8 percent capitalization rate. This will determine the net income. Once this is done, we will have *two* known items (income and capitalization rate), which will allow us to work the problem with the 10 percent rate. Working the problem with the 10 percent rate will sove the problem.

First, let's look at what we know and don't know to work the problem using an 8 percent capitalization rate:

- Income—We don't know this yet, but we can find out what it is by using an 8 percent capitalization rate to solve the problem.
- Rate of Capitalization—In this case, it is 8 percent.
- Value—This is $560,000 when a 8 percent capitalization rate is used.

Now, let's take what we know and enter it in the T-bar.

$$? \longleftarrow \text{I (Income)}$$

R (Rate of Capitalization) $\longrightarrow$ 8% | $560,000 $\longleftarrow$ V (Value)

When we block out the unknown (I), we are left with 8 percent and $560,000 with a vertical line between them, which means we multiply:

$$0.08 \times \$560,000 = \$44,800$$

The annual net income for the property is $44,800.

Now that we know the annual net income for the property ($44,800), we can work the problem using a 10 percent capitalization rate to find out how much the investor could pay for the property valued at that rate of return. Let's look at what we know and don't know.

- Income—$44,800 (from the problem we just completed)
- Rate of Capitalization—10 percent
- Value—This is what we want to determine.

Now, let's enter these values in the T-bar (IRV).

$$\$44,800 \longleftarrow \text{I (Income)}$$

R (Rate of Capitalization) $\longrightarrow$ 10% | ? $\longleftarrow$ V (Value)

When we block out the unknown (V), we are left with $44,800 over 10 percent, so we divide:

$$\$44,800 \div 0.10 = \$448,000$$

The property's value is $448,000 at a 10 percent capitalization rate.

There is one remaining type of value problem we will cover.

Problem: An investor owns an apartment building that is near an airport. Because of the airport noise, the investor is losing $200 per month net income. Using a capitalization rate of 8 percent, how much has the property lost in value?

This is an interesting application of the value T-bar. In this case, we don't need to know the actual value of the property, just the amount of value that has been lost. Let's look at how this is done. First, let's look at what we know and don't know.

- Income—This is the key to this problem. We know the amount of net income *lost* each month. If we convert this to an annual loss, we can use this amount directly in the IRV T-bar to get the amount of *value* lost as well. (To convert to annual income loss, we multiply $200 × 12 to get $2,400, which we'll use in the T-bar.)
- Rate of Capitalization—8 percent.
- Value—In this case, we don't know the value. What we want to know is the *loss* in value. We can find it by using the *loss* in net income in our T-bar, as noted above.

Now, let's enter our values in the T-bar.

$$\$2,400 \longleftarrow \text{I (Income LOST)}$$

R (Rate of Capitalization) $\longrightarrow$ 8% | ? $\longleftarrow$ V (Value LOST)

When we block out the unknown (V), we are left with $2,400 over 8 percent, which means we divide:

$$\$2,400 \div 0.08 = \$30,000$$

The *loss* in value is $30,000.

Loan Problems

There is one last type of problem that uses a T-bar, called a loan problem. The T-bar for a loan problem is as follows:

Note that the code for loan problems is IRB. First, let's look at the elements in the loan T-bar.

- Interest—The money the borrower pays the lender for the use of the lender's money. When solving problems, the interest must be converted to interest earned in a year.
- Rate of Interest—The interest rate is the percentage of the loan paid as interest in a year.
- Balance—The amount owed on the loan at any point in time. It is also referred to as the principal on the loan.

Now, let's look at a problem using the loan T-bar.

Problem: A borrower obtained a straight note of $12,000 for 6 months. At the end of the term of the note, he made a payment for the entire principal and interest of $12,660. What was the interest rate on the note?

Let's first look at what we know and what we don't know.

- Interest—The interest for 6 months is the total amount paid less the principal, which is $12,660 less $12,000, or $660. To convert this to annual interest, multiply by 2 to get $1,320.
- Rate of Interest—This is what we want to determine.
- Balance on Loan—The balance on the loan for the entire period was $12,000 because no principal payments were made during the term of the loan.

Now, let's enter these values in the T-bar (IRB).

When we block out the unknown (R), we are left with $1,320 over $12,000, which means to divide:

$$\$1,320 \div \$12,000 = 0.11$$

The interest rate on the loan is 11 percent.

Let's look at a different type of problem that uses the loan T-bar (IRB).

Problem: A borrower obtains an amortized loan for $140,000 to be paid back over 30 years at an interest rate of 10.5 percent, with monthly payments of $1,280.64 including principal and interest. How much of the first month's payment is applied to the principal?

The key to this problem is to find the amount of the first payment that is applied to interest. Then you can subtract that amount from the monthly payment to determine how much of the first payment goes to the principal. To find the amount of interest in the first payment, we must first find the amount of interest paid per year. To find the amount of interest paid per year, we use the loan T-bar.

First, let's look at what we know and don't know.

- Interest—This is what we want to find. Once we know this, we can use it to find the interest in the first payment, then we can determine the principal in the first payment.

- Rate of Interest—10.5 percent.
- Balance on Loan—Because we are dealing with a new loan, the interest in the first month is based on a balance of $140,000.

Now, let's enter these values in the T-bar (IRB).

When we block out the unknown (I), we multiply 10.5 percent by $140,000. This gives us $14,700.

The interest for the first year of the loan is $14,700.

To get interest paid in the first month we divide by 12:

$$\$14,700 \div 12 = \$1,225$$

The first month's payment includes $1,225 for interest. Because we know from the problem that the monthly payment is $1,280.64, we can find the amount paid to principal by subtracting:

$$\$1,280.64 - \$1,225.00 = \$55.64$$

The first month's payment includes $55.64 paid to principal.

CALCULATING COST AND PRICE

Before learning how to solve the problems in this section, you will first learn a name for each type of problem. A big part of learning how to solve these problems is learning how to recognize and name the type of problem you are solving. Once you are able to do this, the process of completing the necessary calculations is much simpler.

The two types of problems presented in this section are very similar and are basically the reverse of each other. We will call these problems cost problems and price problems. Let's start with an example of a cost problem.

Cost Problems

Problem: The Adams family sold their home for $122,400. This price is a 20 percent increase over the price they paid for it when they bought it. What did they pay for the house originally?

First, this is called a cost problem because it asks you to determine the original cost of the house. Before working the problem, let's look at some general elements you will find in a cost problem:

- First, you will be given the price at which the property just sold.
- Second, you will be given a percentage by which the recent selling price exceeds the original price.
- Third, you will be asked to find the original price.

    Now, let's look at how we solve this type of problem.
    The solution is very simple and involves only three steps:

- **Step 1:** Add the percent that the price has increased to 100 percent.
- **Step 2:** Convert this percent to a decimal.
- **Step 3:** Divide the recent sales price by the answer from Step 2.

    Now, let's work the problem above using these three steps, and you will see how easy it is!

- **Step 1:** Add the percent that the price has increased to 100 percent:

$$100 \text{ percent} + 20 \text{ percent} = 120 \text{ percent}$$

- **Step 2:** Convert this percent to a decimal:

$$20 \text{ percent becomes } 1.20$$

- **Step 3:** Divide the recent sales price by the answer from Step 2:

$$\$122,400 \div 1.20 = \$102,000$$

$102,000 is the original price of the home.

Price Problems

Now, let's look at a similar type of problem—the price problem. Let's start with an example.

Problem: A seller plans to sell his home and wants to receive $152,000 after the broker's 5 percent commission is deducted. What should the sales price be?

First, this is called a price problem because it asks you to determine the sales price of the house. This problem is similar to the cost problem you just solved. Before working the problem, let's look at some general elements you will find in a price problem:

- First, you will be given a net amount that will be received or has been received.
- Next, you will be given a percentage by which the selling price exceeds the net amount.
- Third, you will be asked to find the selling price.

Now, let's look at how we solve this type of problem.

The solution to this type of problem is very simple and also involves only three steps:

- **Step 1:** Subtract the percent to be deducted from 100 percent.
- **Step 2:** Convert this percent to a decimal.
- **Step 3:** Divide the net to be received by the answer from Step 2.

Now, let's work the problem above using these three steps, and you will see how easy it is!

- **Step 1:** Subtract the percent to be deducted from 100 percent:

$$100 \text{ percent} - 5 \text{ percent} = 95 \text{ percent}$$

- **Step 2:** Convert this percent to a decimal:

$$95 \text{ percent becomes } 0.95$$

- **Step 3:** Divide the net to be received by the answer from Step 2:

$$\$152,000 \div 0.95 = \$160,000$$

The sales price should be $160,000.

Before we continue, let's stop and compare the cost and price problems you just solved. The table below shows a condensed comparison of the steps in each problem.

Cost	Price
1. Add a percent to 100 percent.	1. Subtract a percent from 100 percent.
2. Convert to a decimal.	2. Convert to a decimal.
3. Divide the decimal into a number.	3. Divide the decimal into a number.

As you can see above, the only difference in the way you solve the problems is the first step. If you remember whether to add or subtract in the first step, the rest is easy.

Let's look at a simple way to remember the correct first step.

The best way to remember whether to add or subtract a percent to 100 percent is remember the mnemonic **CAPS:**

- *C*ost problem
- *A*dd a percent to 100 percent
- *P*rice problem
- *S*ubtract a percent from 100 percent

Now, let's continue with another variation of the price problem.

Problem: The Greens sold their home after paying off their mortgage. From the sales price paid by the buyer, the escrow company deducted expenses totaling $612 and the broker's 6 percent commission. The Greens received a check from the escrow company for $65,188. What was the sales price of the house?

The only difference between this problem and the previous price problem is the net amount is affected by two things—the expenses totaling $612 and the broker's 6 percent commission. The first step in this situation is to add the expenses of $612 to the amount of the check received from the escrow company. (Think of this as a preliminary step you take before solving the problem as you did in the previous price problem.) We can then follow the steps we just covered to work the problem:

- **Preliminary Step:** Add the deductions ($612) to check amount ($65,188). This equals a value of $65,800, which we will use as the net received.

- **Step 1:** Subtract the broker's commission from 100 percent:

$$100 \text{ percent} - 6 \text{ percent} = 94 \text{ percent}$$

- **Step 2:** Convert this percent to a decimal:

$$94 \text{ percent becomes } 0.94$$

- **Step 3:** Divide the net received amount by the answer from Step 2:

$$\$65,800 \div 0.94 = \$70,000$$

The sales price of the house was $70,000.

There is another variation of this problem that you may encounter.

Problem: An investor purchased a second mortgage at a 15 percent discount and paid $15,640 for the note. What was the original face value of the note?

The solution to this type of problem involves the three steps used in the first price problem:

- **Step 1:** Subtract the percent of discount from 100 percent.
- **Step 2:** Convert this percent to a decimal.
- **Step 3:** Divide the amount paid to the seller for the note by the answer from Step 2.

Now, let's work the problem above using these three steps and again, you will see how easy it is!

- **Step 1:** Subtract the percent of discount from 100 percent:

$$100 \text{ percent} - 15 \text{ percent} = 85 \text{ percent}$$

- **Step 2:** Convert this percent to a decimal:

$$85 \text{ percent becomes } 0.85$$

- **Step 3:** Divide the amount paid for the note by the answer from Step 2:

$$\$15,640 \div 0.85 = \$18,400$$

$18,400 is the original face value of the note.

Now, let's look at one final variation of a price problem.

Problem: Ms. Jones just bought a house for $136,500. How much would it have to increase in value for Ms. Jones to resell it and pay a 5 percent commission without taking a loss?

To solve this problem, we use the same three steps as in the previous price problems:

- **Step 1:** Subtract the 5 percent commission from 100 percent:

$$100 \text{ percent} - 5 \text{ percent} = 95 \text{ percent}$$

- **Step 2:** Convert this percent to a decimal:

$$95 \text{ percent becomes } 0.95$$

- **Step 3:** Divide the amount paid for the property by the answer from Step 2:

$$\$136{,}500 \div 0.95 = \$143{,}684$$

At this point, we know that the house must sell for $143,684, but that's not what we are looking for. The problem asks how much the house must *increase* in value. The last step is to subtract the amount Ms. Jones paid for the house from $143,684:

$$\$143{,}684 - \$136{,}500 = \$7{,}184$$

The house must *increase* in value by $7,184 for Ms. Jones to avoid taking a loss.

BUSINESS BROKERAGE

Previously, we looked at the issues involved in investing in real estate. Another area of investment is business brokerage, which is the buying, selling, or leasing of a business. Business brokerage presents many great opportunities for investors.

Comparison to Real Estate Brokerage

Business brokerage is similar to real estate brokerage because it almost always involves the sale of real property or the assignment of a lease. Also, individuals engaged in the purchase or sale of a business for a fee must hold a Florida real estate license.

However, you should be aware of some important differences between business brokerage and real estate brokerage. One difference is business brokerage may involve the transfer of assets other than real estate, such as personal property, corporate stock (of a corporation), and **goodwill**. Goodwill refers to an intangible asset that usually reflects the following:

- The business's name recognition
- The business's customer base
- The business's employees

Additionally, the value of a business does not necessarily equal the value of the real estate. The value of a business as an operating entity is called the **going concern value**. This value is not just the value of the tangible property. Rather, it also includes intangible assets, such as goodwill, trademarks, patents, copyrights, etc.

Another difference is purchasers of businesses tend to consider a larger geographic area than the typical home buyer.

Expertise

Because business brokerage differs from real estate brokerage, business brokerage requires special expertise in other areas. For example, a licensee engaged in business brokerage must have a clear understanding of the following:

- Tax laws
- Accounting
- Finance
- Business entity formation, including:
  - Corporations, whose value lies in stock value
  - Partnerships
  - Limited liability partnerships
  - Limited liability companies
  - Trusts

Coaching Tips: **Business Brokerage at a Glance**

- **Business brokerage is similar to real estate brokerage in that business brokerage almost always involves the sale of real property or the assignment of a lease.**

- **Business brokerage may involve the transfer of assets other than real estate, such as personal property, corporate stock (of a corporation), and goodwill.**

- **A Florida real estate license is required for both real estate brokerage and business brokerage.**

- **The value of a business as an operating entity is called the going concern value.**

- **Purchasers of businesses tend to consider a larger geographic area than the typical home buyer.**

Sale of a Business

The following are some of the steps that would take place during the sale of a business:

1. The business is listed.
2. The business assets are determined.
3. An estimated value for the business is determined. This is achieved by a review of the business financial statements.
4. The value of all liabilities is subtracted from the estimated value of the business.
5. If the business is a corporation, the value of the business is divided by the total number of shares of stock to determine the value per share. The value per share is multiplied by the number of shares to be sold.
6. Compliance with applicable laws must be verified.
7. The business is marketed.
8. A buyer is located.
9. Closing takes place.

Valuation of a Business

As just mentioned, one of the steps in the sale of a business is estimating the value of the business. The methods of appraising a business are similar to the methods of appraising real property. These methods are listed below:

- Comparable sales analysis—The process of comparing the business being appraised to similar businesses that have sold recently.

- Cost approach—The process of estimating value based on the current cost to reproduce or replace the improvements.
- Income capitalization analysis—The process of estimating the income a business can be expected to produce and converting that into an estimated value using a capitalization rate.
- **Liquidation analysis**—The process of estimating the assets, liabilities, and amount the business could be sold for in the event the business is terminated or goes bankrupt.

It is important to note that lenders are primarily interested in the liquidation value of a business than any other type of value analysis. Another term for liquidation value for businesses is the **book value**.

Coaching Tips: Valuation Analysis at a Glance

- Comparable sales analysis involves comparing the business being appraised to similar businesses that have sold recently.
- The cost approach involves estimating value based on the current cost to reproduce or replace the improvements.
- Income capitalization analysis involves estimating the income a business can be expected to produce and converting that into an estimated value using a capitalization rate.
- Liquidation analysis involves estimating the assets, liabilities, and amount the business could be sold for in the event the business is terminated or goes bankrupt. It is also called book value

---

SUMMARY

Investors park money in investments to achieve returns on those investments by their cash flows. Real property is a popular vehicle that houses investments. Prior to purchasing real property, investors are cautioned to analyze a variety of issues that directly affect the investment potential of the acquisition. Carelessness and complicity generally will lead to loss of invested capital. Licensees are advised to seek more education in this arena. Knowledge and use of the T-Bar aids both investor and licensee to evaluate cash flow activities. A thorough understanding of cash flows becomes essential to successful investment.

Business brokerage creates opportunities for licensees to earn money. This field entails the purchase and sale of businesses and their respective assets. In Florida, anyone that engages in this practice for a fee must hold a real estate license. Knowledge is required in evaluating financial statements. This is required in order to derive the appropriate value of the business. Valuation of a business is derived in a similar manner to that of property valuation. The value is achieved through the application of the sales comparison approach, the cost approach, the income approach or the liquidation approach to appraisal.

REVIEW QUESTIONS

1. There are many advantages available for investors to invest in real property. Which of the following would NOT be considered an advantage to investing in real property?
   a. A good rate of return
   b. A hedge against inflation
   c. Illiquidity
   d. Equity buildup

2. Risk is the possibility of losing some portion, or possibly all, of your investment. One type of risk associated with property investment is the possibility that the property will not generate enough money to cover the operating costs of the property. This type of risk is known as:
   a. Business risk.
   b. Financial risk.
   c. Purchasing power risk.
   d. Safety risk.

3. Investors may believe the greatest advantage of investing in property is leverage. Leverage is defined as:
   a. Your property pays all its own bills, such as the insurance, taxes, and all maintenance costs.
   b. Your property is paying back the money you borrowed in order to make the purchase.
   c. The tax advantages you gained allow you to shelter income from the property from tax payments.
   d. The use of borrowed funds to purchase the property.

4. A lease whereby the lessee pays a fixed sum of money to the lessor and the lessor is charged with paying for all expenses associated with property can be best described as a:
   a. Gross lease.
   b. Net lease.
   c. Variable lease.
   d. Graduated lease.

5. Which of the following makes real property investment unique?
   a. The influence of the national economy
   b. Fluctuations in the cost of money
   c. Changes in the tax codes that may reduce after tax cash flow
   d. The local nature of property markets

6. Which of the following would be considered the most active type of real property purchase?
   a. Shopping centers
   b. Office buildings
   c. Residential property
   d. Industrial property

7. Limiting the uses allowed for land in any community is governed by:
   a. Federal land-use laws.
   b. The rights of individual states.
   c. Municipal zoning requirements.
   d. Overall county ordinances.

8. Christian borrowed the bulk of the money he used to purchase an apartment complex. He anticipates that income activities derived from the property will not only pay all the expenses associated with his ownership, but will also yield additional funds to invest in another property. The additional funds he hopes to use can best be classified in business terms as:
   a. Return on investment.
   b. Return of investment.
   c. Before tax cash flow.
   d. Equity buildup.

9. Darla is looking at a small apartment to buy as an investment. The annual net operating income is $24,000. The monthly mortgage payment on the property would be $4,666. Darla wants to achieve a return of 11 percent. What is the value of the property? Round to the nearest dollar.
   a. $263,636
   b. $260,600
   c. $218,182
   d. $175,764

10. Paul signed a contract with his registered broker to collect 40 percent of any commission his broker receives when Paul sells a property. Paul sold a condominium and his broker received a 6 percent commission of $3,510. What was the price paid for the condo?
    a. $47,640
    b. $58,500
    c. $60,000
    d. $87,750

11. Using the figures in Question 10, what was the size of Paul's check?
    a. $1,404
    b. $2,106
    c. $2,340
    d. $3,510

12. An apartment complex has 28 units and each unit rents for $775 per month. The apartment complex has a 5 percent vacancy rate, expenses of $82,460, and a net operating income of $164,920. If an investor wants a return of 9.5 percent, what is the price of the property?
    a. $868,000
    b. $1,736,000
    c. $1,873,100
    d. $2,741,100

13. An industrial property produces a monthly net operating income of $5,715. How much would you pay for the property if you require a 12 percent return on your investment?
    a. $768,096
    b. $665,800
    c. $571,500
    d. $489,857

14. You purchased a small building for $209,000. Your annual net operating income is $25,080. With a vacancy rate of 5 percent, and expenses of $12,292, what is the capitalization rate for the property?
    a. 6.1 percent
    b. 12 percent
    c. 12.8 percent
    d. 17.8 percent

15. When Bettie sold her house, she got a check at closing for $121,600. Her expenses on the transaction were a first mortgage payoff of $135,700, a 7 percent commission to ABC Realty, and $31,000 in other closing costs. What did her house sell for?
    a. $288,300
    b. $308,500
    c. $310,000
    d. $339,781

16. Jamie bought a rental property for $200,000 and she is pleased with her 11 percent return. If the operating expenses on her property represent a sum of $1,000 per month, what is the net operating income on the rental?
    a. $10,000
    b. $21,000
    c. $22,000
    d. $34,000

17. Phillip bought three lots on the water at $100,000 each. He subdivided the property into six lots that he sold for $62,500 each. What was Phillip's percent of profit?
    a. 10 percent
    b. 15 percent
    c. 20 percent
    d. 25 percent

18. Randall owned 3/8 of a small farm. When the farm was sold, Randall received $45,000. What was the price of the farm?
    a. $168,750
    b. $120,000
    c. $90,000
    d. $72,000

19. When appraising real property, an appraiser must use all three approaches to appraisal. In addition to these three approaches, which of the following approaches to value would be used when performing a business appraisal?
    a. Insurance valuation
    b. Replacement cost
    c. Liquidation analysis
    d. Assessed valuation

20. 5 years ago, you purchased a lot for $15,000. In the area where the lot is located, property has increased in value at 3.5 percent per year. What is your lot worth today?
    a. $20,250
    b. $17,625
    c. $15,263
    d. $15,525

Chapter 18

LEARNING OBJECTIVES

After completing this lesson, you will be able to:

- Identify the two major types of real property taxes.
- Recognize which types of properties are immune or exempt from taxation.
- Explain how ad valorem taxes are assessed and computed.
- Describe the purpose of special assessment taxes.
- Explain the method for collecting special assessment taxes.
- Identify the expenses related to real property that can be deducted from income for tax purposes.
- Know the conditions under which income tax is charged on the sale of real property.
- Know the formulas that will be used to calculate tax liability for various types of ownership.

Taxes Affecting Real Estate

TAXATION

Real property taxation is a primary source of revenue for both state and local governments. The federal government does not have the authority to tax real property directly; however, it does have the authority to tax the *sale* of real property.

There are two categories of taxes on real property:

1. Ad valorem taxes
2. Special assessment taxes

Ad Valorem Taxes

Ad valorem taxes are based on the value of land and the improvements to the land. **Ad valorem** is a Latin term that means "according to valuation." Ad valorem taxes are assessed on real property on a regular basis (usually annually) and are used by the government as a primary source of revenue to fund the government's operations.

The **assessed value** of property is the value established for the purpose of determining taxes. Florida law has established that assessed value is based on **just value**, or the fair market value of the property. It should be noted that assessed value may not always reflect the property's market value. In addition, there may be times where assessed value is greater than market value; however, for the most part, the market value is greater than the assessed value. In some other states, assessed value is a percentage of the market value. In Florida, assessed values are established annually. The county property appraiser is given the task of establishing the assessed value through an appraisal. For most parcels, this involves the following:

- A careful review of the property characteristics
- An analysis of highest and best use
- The application of the three approaches to value (sales comparison, cost, and income—see Chapter 15)

When the county property tax appraiser is reviewing an income-producing property, the income capitalization approach will most likely be used to determine the assessed value. In many states, the taxing authority relies on income and expense statements that must be submitted to the assessor. This enables the assessor to appropriately capitalize the net operating income attributable to that property to arrive at a value conclusion.

Some of the information that would be included and reviewed to determine the assessed value of an income-producing property would be:

- Occupancy
- Vacancy information
- Rents received
- Leasing incentives (such as rent abatement)
- Expenses being paid

Grievance Process for Contesting Property Tax Assessments

Most of any county's revenue is derived from property taxes. Therefore, as mentioned previously, the job of the county appraiser is to assess the value of property for the purpose of taxation to fund the operations of government.

On occasion, the county property appraiser may establish an assessed value that the owner does not consider fair and accurate. Under the law, the property owner has the right to contest the assessment derived by the county property appraiser by taking the following steps:

- **Step 1:** In Florida, a property owner is given an opportunity to contest the findings of the county property appraiser within 25 days after the notice of assessment is mailed. The owner or her representative will go before the county property appraiser's office to obtain a reduction determination. The property owner is then given a chance to argue and present the facts as to why a property assessment reduction is appropriate. During this process, the property owner may appear on her own behalf or have a representative appear for her. Representatives may include, but are not limited to, another appraiser hired by the property owner, a lawyer, or a property tax reduction service representative.
- **Step 2:** In the event that the county property appraiser's office rejects the request for reduction, the property owner has the right to appeal the findings of the county property appraiser's office by going before the Value Adjustment Board. The board itself is comprised of five elected members.
- **Step 3:** The board will determine whether or not the appeal should be granted or denied. If granted, the board has the power to adjust the assessment accordingly. If denied, the property owner is left with only one final alternative—litigation. A certiorari proceeding occurs in court, which is a formal litigation appeal process and the final relief that is available to a taxpayer. The court will either uphold previous determinations or will order a reassessment of the property, which may or may not yield net tax relief to the taxpayer.

Coaching Tips: Property Tax Grievance Process at a Glance

There are three ways an owner can contest a property tax assessment:

1. Within 25 days after the notice of assessment is mailed, the owner or the owner's representative can go before the county property appraiser's office to obtain a reduction determination.
2. If the request for reduction is rejected, the owner can appeal the findings of the county property appraiser's office by going before the Value Adjustment Board.
3. If the appeal is rejected by the board, the owner has another alternative—litigation by way of a certiorari proceeding.

Immune and Exempt Properties

Certain properties are immune from taxation, including:

- Government-owned buildings
- Other property designated as immune include properties such as municipal airports and military bases

Immune properties are not subject to taxation.

Other properties are exempt (or partially exempt) from taxation. **Exempt properties** are subject to taxation, but the owner is not obligated to pay all (or part) of the taxes. Examples of exempt properties include:

- Property owned by churches and charitable organizations (as long as it is used for a religious or charitable purpose)
- Homesteads
- Property owned by widows or widowers, individuals who are blind, or individuals with other disabilities

Let's look at some of the types of exempt properties.

Homestead Exemption

An owner of real property in Florida is entitled to claim his primary residence as a homestead. A $25,000 real property tax exemption is available for anyone who qualifies for the exemption. This $25,000 exemption is applied *only* against the assessed valuation of the home. Although a property owner may own more than one home in Florida, only one property may be eligible for the homestead exemption.

To qualify, the property owner must have owned the property as of January 1 and must show proof of ownership to the county property appraiser's office no later than March 1. Let's look at how the homestead exemption works. Here is the formula for calculating property tax that includes a homestead:

$$\begin{array}{l} \text{Assessed Property Value} \\ - \text{ Granted Homestead Exemption} \\ \hline = \text{Property Value Subject to Taxation} \\ \times \text{ Mill Rate (Tax Rate)} \\ \hline \text{Annual Tax} \end{array}$$

Example

Assume a property has an assessed value of $100,000, and the owner qualifies for the homestead exemption. The **taxable value** of the property is calculated by subtracting the exemption from the assessed value:

$$\begin{array}{l} \$100,000 \text{ Assessed Value} \\ -\$\ 25,000 \text{ Homestead Exemption} \\ \hline \$\ 75,000 \text{ Taxable Value} \end{array}$$

Thus, the amount of the property tax will be based on the taxable value, not the assessed value.

Blind Individuals Exemption

Persons who are legally blind are entitled to a $500 property tax exemption. This exemption is in addition to the $25,000 homestead exemption. Thus, if an individual is legally blind and qualifies for a homestead exemption, the total property tax exemption is $25,500.

Surviving Spouse Exemption

A spouse of a deceased individual is entitled to an additional $500 property tax exemption. However, the exemption ceases if that person remarries.

Disability Exemption

A person who is considered 10 percent or more disabled as a result of a disability incurred while in military service is entitled to an additional $5,000 property tax exemption. Persons who are totally and permanently disabled due to disabilities incurred in military service are entitled to a total exemption from property taxes. Certain totally and permanently disabled nonveterans may also qualify for total exemption from property taxes (such as a quadriplegic). Upon the death of the disabled veteran, this benefit may extend to the widow or widower's spouse.

It should be noted that in 2001, Florida legislature provided the right, but, not the obligation, to grant additional exemptions on homestead taxes to persons 65 years of age or older that reside within a low-income household.

Coaching Tips: Property Tax at a Glance

- Immune properties are not subject to taxation.
- Exempt properties are subject to taxation, but the owner is not obligated to pay all (or part) of the taxes.
- Homestead exemption available to Florida resident(s) on their primary residence.
  - The amount of a full homestead exemption is $25,000.
  - The exemption is $500 for individuals who are blind, widows or widowers. Individuals who are 10 percent or more disabled due to a service-related disability are entitled to an additional $5,000 property tax exemption.

Save Our Home

In Florida, assessed values are updated annually. The Save Our Home amendment to the state constitution restricts the amount the assessed value of homestead property can increase. The increase in assessed value of a homestead is limited to *the lesser of:*

- 3 percent over the preceding year's assessed value
- The percentage change in the Consumer Price Index

When the property is transferred, these limits are lifted and the property is assessed at its just value. Thus, in some cases, the assessed value may rise significantly when property is sold or otherwise transferred (if the property value had increased significantly during the seller's ownership). *As of calendar year 2005, sellers of residential property (as defined by 475, F.S.) in Florida are required to provide a buyer with a property tax disclosure.* This disclosure primarily is intended to inform the buyer of the following important information:

- The property tax amount at the time of sale may not be the same amount in the subsequent year following the sale.
- A reassessment may occur as a result of the sale.

Green Belt Law Exemption

Florida has a law known as the **Green Belt Law**. This law provides favorable tax treatment for agricultural properties. Under this law, the assessed value must be based on the property's current agricultural use, and not the highest and best use of the property. In some cases, agricultural land may be located in an area where the property would have a much higher value if it were converted to another use (such as commercial). Thus, the law provides benefits for farmers by reducing their potential tax bills. Any change in how the property is classified must be filed prior to March 1 of any year. In the event the classification change is denied, the property owner may seek relief through the property tax grievance process.

Calculation of Real Property Tax

State and local governments are funded by many sources of revenue, including sales tax, income tax, public utility revenues, and real property taxes. In most places throughout the country, real property taxes act as the largest revenue source to fund the government. In Florida, where there is no individual state income tax, property taxes become essential toward funding the government. The following districts rely on taxes for funding:

- County
- City
- Special districts
- Schools

Each of these districts submits its request for annual budgeting. Each taxing unit uses separate tax rates that relate to its financial operational needs. The sum total of all the budgets, once approved, becomes the annual fiscal budget. Revenues must be collected to fund the budget. Real property taxes come from the district's **tax base**, which is the total taxable value of all real property in the district. The end result of the aggregate of each taxing unit is the property tax bill.

The mill rate (or millage rate) is the rate of taxation on the taxable value. The mill rate is expressed as thousandths of a dollar. One **mill** equals 1/1,000 of one dollar. (One mill also equals 1/10 of one cent.)

To convert the mill rate to dollars, divide the number of mills by 1,000. For example, 40 mills equals 0.04 dollars:

$$40 \div 1,000 = 0.04$$

Conversely, to convert dollars to mills, multiply the dollars by 1,000. For example, 0.008 dollars equal 8 mills:

$$0.008 \times 1,000 = 8$$

The millage rate is set by the local government entity by dividing the amount of revenue needed from property taxes by the total taxable value of all real property in the district. The total amount of revenue needed from real property is equal to the annual fiscal budget less any nonproperty tax revenue. This is shown in the following formula:

$$\frac{\text{Annual Fiscal Budget} - \text{Nonproperty Tax Revenue}}{\text{Total Taxable Value}}$$

Let's look at an example.

Assume the annual budget for the county is $16,500,000 and revenues from sources other than real property taxes equal $500,000. If the taxable value of real property in the county equals $2,000,000,000, then the tax rate is calculated using the following formula:

$$\frac{\$16,500,000 - \$500,000}{\$2,000,000,000}$$

The tax rate in this case is 0.008 per dollar of taxable value, or 8 mills.

Once the property is assessed and the mill rate is set, taxes can be computed for a given property using the following formula:

$$\begin{array}{rl} & \text{Assessed Value} \\ - & \text{Exemption, if any} \\ \hline = & \text{Taxable Value} \\ & \text{Mill Rate} \\ \hline = & \text{Taxes To Be Paid} \end{array}$$

Let's look at an example.

Assume that the owner of a property qualifies for a homestead exemption and the assessed value is $100,000. If the mill rate is 8 mills, the taxes for the property are computed as follows:

$100,000	Assessed Value
−$ 25,000	Exemption
$ 75,000	Taxable Value
×0.008	Mill Rate (8 mills)
$ 600	Taxes To Be Paid

The above mill rate (8 mills) is given as an example only. The actual rate may vary from area to area.

Truth-in-Millage (TRIM)

Tax laws require the county tax offices to mail the assessed value and the millage rates for the county, municipality, and school board prior to the actual rendering of the tax bills. This is done to give the property owner time to determine whether or not over-assessment has occurred as well as to file a grievance. This notice is referred to as the **truth-in-millage (TRIM) notice**.

Ad valorem taxes in Florida are levied on a calendar-year basis. The tax year begins on January 1 and ends on December 31. Ad valorem taxes are paid in **arrears**, which means they are paid at the end of the tax year. Thus, although taxes are levied on January 1 and a lien is placed on the property on that date, the taxes can be paid anytime during the tax year without penalty or late fee. Ad valorem tax liens have priority over all other property tax liens.

Taxes can be paid in a variety of ways, such as in one payment or in four installments. If a taxpayer pays the taxes promptly, the municipality may make a discount available. Taxes are delinquent if they are not paid by April 1 of the following year. If property taxes are not paid when due, the property may be sold to pay for the taxes.

Special Assessment Taxes

Special assessment taxes are usually levied to fund a specific project that benefits only some of the citizens in a government jurisdiction. Examples of uses for special assessment taxes might include:

• Street paving in a neighborhood

• Water and sewer installation

• Street lights for a street or neighborhood

The amount of the tax is based on the benefits received, not necessarily on the value of the property owned. Special assessment taxes are usually collected in a series of payments spread over a period of years and assessed on the basis of the front footage (on the road) of the property.

When the assessments have been paid off, the special assessment district is dissolved and the tax is terminated. Special assessment tax liens take priority over all liens except ad valorem tax liens.

Coaching Tips:

• **Property tax means both ad valorem and special assessment.**

• **Special assessment taxes are used for specific projects.**

• **Size and front footage are only some of the factors that affect value.**

- Cost may or may not be related to current value.
- Improvements attached to land are also real property.
- The value established for the purpose of determining taxes is called assessed value.
- The county property appraiser is given the task of establishing the assessed value through an appraisal.

FEDERAL INCOME TAX

The federal government has the authority to tax income. There are basically three types of income that a taxpayer may earn during the course of a tax year:

1. Active income
2. Passive income
3. Portfolio income

Exempt income is income that is not subject to taxation.

Coaching Tips: **This chapter provides a brief overview of the federal tax issues related to real property. In many real situations, the necessary calculations will be much more complex than those covered in this chapter. In any particular situation, a taxpayer may need to contact a professional tax advisor.**

Active Income

Active income includes compensation derived directly from employment activities, such as:

- Salary/wages
- Commissions
- Gratuities

Passive Income

Passive income encompasses income from a business activity or investment where the individual is passive and not actively in charge of the day-to-day management of that activity or investment. Examples include:

- Limited partnerships
- Income from income-producing real property investments where the individual receives profits but is not actively engaged in the real estate business
- Profits from the sale of stocks
- Any other investment where the taxpayer is not participating in an active role

Portfolio Income

Portfolio income includes any income derived from such items as:

- Stock dividends
- Interest earned on deposits or loans
- Royalties earned on intellectual property
- Annuities

Coaching Tips: Categories of Federal Taxable Income at a Glance

- Active income refers to compensation derived from employment, such as wages/salary, commissions, and/or gratuities.

- Passive income is income from a business activity or investment where the individual is passive and not actively in charge of the day-to-day management of that activity or investment.

- Portfolio income is income derived from stock dividends, interest, royalties, and annuities.

- Exempt income refers to income not subject to taxation.

FEDERAL INCOME TAX AND REAL PROPERTY

There are two major issues involving federal income tax and real property:

1. Whether or not certain items may be deducted when calculating income tax due

2. How income tax is calculated when real estate is sold

How these issues are handled depends on whether you are an individual who owns a home or a business or investor who owns property.

Deductions

Expenses related to real estate ownership may be deducted from income when calculating income taxes. The list of items that can be deducted depends on whether you are an owner/occupant of a home or the owner of a business or investment property (see Figure 18.1). Let's compare these by looking at a list of what is deductible in the two situations.

An individual who owns a home may deduct the following items from his income to determine his **taxable income**:

- Property taxes
- Mortgage interest, including:
  - Origination fees to obtain a mortgage (i.e., points). When loans require the borrower to pay upfront charges (origination fees), these charges are deductible in the year that they are incurred. These origination fees are paid to the lender and act as a form of pre-paid interest. These fees enhance the yield to the lender. However, this does not apply to refinanced loans. In this situation, the borrower is required to recover or amortize the same over the life of the loan. He may only deduct that portion as it relates to the term of the loan (i.e. 5 year loan, deduct 20% per year) In essence, the points are amortized over the remaining term or life of the loan.
  - Interest on home equity mortgages up to $100,000. Interest on loans exceeding $100,000 is not eligible as a deduction.

A business or investor who owns property may deduct the following:

- Property taxes
- Mortgage interest

Note also that there are three additional items that may be deducted by a business or investor who owns property:

1. Expenses of operation

2. Depreciation

3. Operational losses

These items are deductible on business/investment property but not on a personal residence.

FIGURE 18.1

REAL ESTATE ASPECTS OF THE TAX REFORM ACT 1986, TAX REVENUE ACT 1987, TAXPAYER RELIEF ACT OF 1997, AND OTHER RECENT REVISIONS

Summary of Rules for Homeowners

1. Mortgage interest deductions are allowed for acquisition debt (purchase money loan) up to a maximum loan of $1 million on all combined mortgages on a first and second residence. If you borrow more than $1 million, the interest paid on the excess over $1 million is not deductible. No interest deduction is allowed for three or more personal-use homes.

2. For the refinance of an existing home, the remaining loan balance on acquisitions loan(s) plus $100,000 will be the maximum refinance loan allowed if the homeowner wishes to deduct all the interest as a qualified home loan. However, if a refinance loan exceeds the home's value, a portion of the interest paid is not deductible.

3. The $250,000 for singles and $500,000 for joint-filing married couples exemption noted on previous pages are still valid.

4. Installment sale treatment is still allowed for homeowners.

Summary of Rules for Income Property Owners

1. Depreciation (cost recovery) on buildings and improvements is 27½ years for residential rental and longer periods for nonresidential rental. The straight-line method must be used.

2. Rental property mortgage interest is fully deductible against rental income, with no dollar loan limits such as the $1 million cap placed on homeowners. However, any tax loss created by interest and depreciation deductions fall under the passive tax loss rules listed herein.

3. Real estate rentals are considered "passive" investments and produce either passive income or passive loss, depending on the property's cash flow. The general rule is that a passive real estate loss can only be used to offset other passive income, NOT active or portfolio income such as salaries, commissions, profits, interest, and dividends. Prior to tax law changes, real estate losses could be used to offset active or portfolio income.

4. Special $25,000 exception to the passive loss rules if a person meets the following test:

   a. Is an individual owner of 10 percent or more interest in rental real estate

   b. Is actively involved in the management (owner can use property managers but he or she must make the key decisions)

   c. Has a modified adjusted gross income of $100,000 or less

   If the owner of rental real estate meets this test, he or she can use up to $25,000 in passive losses from real estate to offset active or portfolio income, such as salaries and interest, after first offsetting passive income.

5. If the rental property owner's modified adjusted gross income exceeds $100,000, the $25,000 amount is reduced $1 for every $2 above the $100,000. Any unused passive losses from rental real estate can be carried forward to reduce future passive income and gain upon sale of the property. The passive loss rules do not eliminate the investor's right to use real estate losses. However, the law's changes will, in some cases, delay the right to use the loss until a later date, such as the date of resale.

6. The right for a real estate investor to do a 1031 tax-deferred exchange remains the same; recent tax law changes have not eliminated this technique.

7. Installment sales treatment for real estate investors is still allowed. Installment sale treatment for real estate dealers has been abolished.

There are many other tax law changes, but these are the items that have a major impact on real estate. The preceding is listed for information purposes and should not be considered tax advice. For tax advice, a person should seek competent tax advisers.

Deductions on Residential Property

Interest on Mortgage

With residential property, the interest paid during a year on all mortgages on first and second homes is deductible from income. Delinquent or late payments that are accrued by December 31 of each year are not deductible for that year. Extensive prepayment of interest is not allowed. Only interest due and payable by the end of the year plus 1 month can be claimed as a current deduction.

In addition, discount points charged on mortgage loans are considered prepaid interest. Therefore, discount points are deductible in the year that they are paid.

Local Property Taxes

Any property taxes paid on residential property are deductible in the year they are paid.

Uninsured Casualty Losses

Casualty losses occur by fire, theft, weather, earthquakes, floods, and other natural causes. Casualty losses that are not covered by insurance may be deductible from income in the year that they occur. An uninsured casualty loss is only deductible if it exceeds a $100 IRS deductible plus 10 percent of the taxpayer's adjusted gross income. For example, if a chandelier is stolen and it is not covered by insurance, the loss would be deductible in that year if the uninsured amount exceeds $100 plus 10 percent of the owner's adjusted gross income.

Deductions on Business/Investment Property

With business or investment property, mortgage interest, local property taxes, and uninsured casualty losses are deductible in the year they are paid. The rules for some of these are different than for a personal residence, but the differences are beyond the scope of this course. There are also some items that can be deducted with business/investment property but not with personal residences. Let's look at two of these deductions:

1. Expenses of operation
2. Depreciation

Expenses of Operation

With business or investment property, certain expenses of operation are deductible in the year they are paid, including:

- Repairs to the property
- Maintenance costs, such as for repair of appliances
- Insurance
- Management fees
- Utilities

Note that the list does not include vacancy losses, which are not deductible.

Depreciation

Depreciation is a deduction for business/investment property but not deducted for a personal residence. In the investment world, depreciation is also commonly referred to as cost recovery. Depreciation is a loss due to three events:

1. Physical deterioration
2. Functional obsolescence
3. External obsolescence

Depreciation is a tax deduction that is based on the concept that all property loses its value over time because the property ages and must be replaced. Consequently, the tax law allows a business or investor to deduct the cost of the property over a period of years. Remember, this deduction cannot be taken on a personal residence.

Note that depreciation is a tax issue and does not mean the property will actually lose its value or require replacement at the end of the depreciation period. In fact, the property will usually appreciate (increase in value) rather than depreciate (decrease in value) over the period the property is depreciated for tax purposes. Nevertheless, the owner is allowed to deduct an amount for depreciation when computing taxes. For tax purposes, depreciation can be thought of as the deduction of a certain percentage of the cost of any improvements to land over a period of years set by the tax law. (An example of an improvement is a building.)

Note that depreciation is based *only* on the cost of improvements to real estate, not the land itself. *Land is never depreciated.*

Depreciation is allowed on all improvements, including fruit and nut trees, as well as more familiar improvements, like buildings. A good way to separate the value of improvements from the value of the land itself is by using the property tax assessment. The tax assessment is broken down into two categories—the value of the land itself and the value of any improvements to the land. When a property is assessed for tax purposes when it is sold, these values will reveal the original cost of the land and improvements. Now let's look at an example.

A residential rental property was purchased for $100,000. The value of the land included in this purchase price was $20,000.

In this situation, the land value is 20 percent of the total value of the property ($20,000 ÷ $100,000 = 0.20 or 20 percent). Thus, the value of the improvements amounts to 80 percent of the total value of the property.

In addition to the $100,000 purchase price, there are other costs associated with acquiring the property, including attorney fees, appraisals, surveys, etc.

Collectively, these costs are referred to as the cost of acquisition. Assume the following cost of acquisition for our example:

$ 6,000	Commissions
$ 4,000	Legal Fees
$ 1,500	Appraisal
+$ 900	Survey
$12,400	Cost of Acquisition

The total cost to acquire the property is equal to the purchase price plus the cost of acquisition:

$100,000	Purchase Price
+$ 12,400	Cost of Acquisition
$112,400	Total Cost to Acquire Property

Because depreciation is based on the improvements only (and not the land), we must determine how much of this total cost is attributed to the improvements.

As mentioned earlier, the improvement portion of the property is 80 percent. Therefore:

$112,400	Total Cost to Acquire Property
× 0.80	80 Percent Improvement Portion
$ 89,920	Total Cost Attributed To Improvements

This amount is used to calculate depreciation and is referred to as the depreciable basis.

For residential rental property, the law allows the improvements to be depreciated over a period of 27.5 years.

The amount to be depreciated, $89,920, divided by 27.5 years gives an annual depreciation amount of $3,270. This amount may be deducted each year for depreciation.

There are different mathematical formulas for computing the amount of depreciation. The previous example used the simplest formula, called the straight-line method of depreciation, in which the amount of depreciation is the same each year. The straight-line method using the 27.5-year recovery period is used for residential rental property put into use after December 31, 1986. The straight-line method of depreciation is also used for some nonresidential (commercial) real property. However, the 27.5-year recovery period used for residential rental property is not used for nonresidential real property. The recovery period used for nonresidential real property depends on when the property was put into use. For nonresidential property put into use after May 13, 1993, the recovery period is 39 years.

Another method of calculating depreciation, called the accelerated method, can be used on some real property put into use before December 31, 1986. The primary difference is that this method results in greater values for depreciation in the early years and less depreciation in later years.

In this chapter, we looked a few of the methods used to calculate depreciation. The remaining methods of calculating depreciation are beyond the scope of this course. The method that must be used for a particular property depends on the type of property (nonresidential versus residential rental property) and the date when the property was put into use. To determine which method applies to a particular property, an owner may need to consult a professional tax advisor.

Tax on Sale of Property

We just looked at the different real estate–related expenses that may be deducted from income for tax purposes. The second major issue relating to real estate and income taxes is the payment of taxes on any profits made when real estate is sold.

When real property is sold, the profits that are made are called *gains*. Generally, gains from the sale of real property are capital gains, which are taxed. These taxes are called capital gains taxes. Later, we will look at the tax rate for capital gains. However, let's look first at how the amount of capital gain is determined when real property is sold. The procedure is slightly different for residential and business or investment property, so we will begin with residential property.

Capital gain is the difference between the *amount realized* on the sale of the property and the *adjusted basis* of the property:

Amount Realized
− Adjust Basis
Capital Gain

Let's look at each of the terms in the formula for calculating capital gains in more detail.

The sales price of the home is obviously the price at which the home was sold. For tax purposes, however, certain expenses of the sale may be deducted from the sales price for determining profit. The result of these deductions is the amount realized.

The amount realized is the actual selling price of the property *less* the costs of the sale, including:

• Real estate commissions
• Any closing costs or points paid by the seller
• Attorney fees
• Survey costs

By subtracting these items from the sales price, the amount of profit for tax purposes is *reduced* by the amount of these expenses, which lowers the amount of tax that must be paid.

Coaching Tips: **The costs of a sale are not deductible from the seller's income in the year they are paid unless the costs are interest expenses. One deductible interest expense is an interest prepayment penalty charged by a lender when the seller's mortgage is paid off after the home is sold.**

The second item in the formula is the adjusted basis. The basis is simply the original cost of the home, including the cost of acquisition such as attorney fees, appraisal reports, etc. For tax purposes, this basis is adjusted for certain other expenses.

The adjusted basis equals the basis (purchase price and cost of acquisition) *plus* the cost of any capital improvements to the property, such as the addition of a room, swimming pool, patio, etc., or remodeling of a kitchen or bathroom. By adding these items to the basis, the amount of profit for tax purposes is *reduced* by the amount of these expenses, which lowers the amount of tax that must be paid.

By treating major improvements to the property as capital improvements, the costs of these items are not deductible from income in the year they are paid. In addition, the costs of these items increase the amount that is subject to depreciation, so their cost is depreciated over the life of the ownership.

Earlier, we pointed out that the computation for capital gains from the sale of real property differs for residential and business or investment property. Let's take a look at how the tax calculation differs in these two situations.

As you just learned, the amount of profit on residential property that is subject to taxation is calculated by the following formula:

Amount Realized
 − Adjust Basis
_____
Capital Gain

There is only one difference in this formula when business or investment property is sold—how the adjusted basis is calculated.

As you learned earlier, the owner of a business or investment property is allowed to deduct from income an amount for depreciation each year the property is owned. In order to avoid double benefits for depreciation (which is taking deductions during the holding period and maintaining the same adjusted basis at time of sale), the formula for the adjusted basis must be modified. This modification entails subtracting the total amount of depreciation deducted during the ownership of the property from the adjusted basis. The modified formula is shown next along with the formula for residential property.

Residential Property	Business/Investment Property
Purchase Price	Purchase Price
+ Cost of Acquisition	+ Cost of Acquisition
+ Capital Improvements	+ Capital Improvements
Adjusted Basis	− Accumulated Depreciation
	Adjusted Basis

There are four more situations we will cover regarding income taxes:

1. Exclusion of capital gains from the sale of a home
2. Capital gains tax rates
3. Installment sales
4. Real estate exchanges

Exclusion of Capital Gains

Under the current tax law, some homeowners can exclude from their taxable income some or all of the gain they earn when they sell a home. Homeowners can exclude gain up to a maximum of $250,000 (or $500,000 if married filing a joint return). Because home prices have risen substantially over the past three decades, the $250,000/$500,000 exclusion of gain is an important tax break for many homeowners. In the next section of this chapter, we will look at this exclusion in more detail.

Qualifying Rules

To qualify for this exclusion, a homeowner must meet an ownership test and a use test.

Ownership Test

A homeowner must have *owned* the home for at least 2 years during the previous 5-year period ending on the date of sale.

Use Test

A homeowner must have *lived in* the home as her principal residence for a period totaling two of the previous 5 years ending on the date of sale. This 2-year period may be continuous or interrupted and the homeowner does not have to occupy the property as a principal residence on the date of sale. Temporary absences for vacations, hospital confinements, etc., count as periods of use even though the home may be rented out or occupied by others during such absences.

Amount of Exclusion

If a homeowner sells a personal residence, the homeowner may be permitted to exclude gain on the sale up to one of the following:

- $250,000
- $500,000 if all of the following conditions are true:
  - The homeowner is married and files a joint tax return for the year of the sale.
  - Either spouse meets the ownership test.
  - Both spouses meet the use test. (However, if only one spouse meets the use test, that spouse can exclude up to $250,000 of gain on a separate or joint return.)
  - Neither spouse is excluding gain from the sale of another home during the year. (However, if each spouse sells a home during the same year, they can each exclude up to $250,000 of gain.)

Exercising the Exclusion

Typically, homeowners are only allowed to take the $250,000/$500,000 exclusion of gain once every 2 years. That is, a homeowner cannot exclude gain on the sale of a home if during the previous 2-year period, the homeowner sold another home and excluded all or part of the gain from the previous sale. Gain from the recent sale must be included in the homeowner's taxable income. However, the homeowner may be allowed to claim a reduced exclusion if the home was sold because of a change in health or place of employment. To learn more about claiming a reduced exclusion, taxpayers should consult the relevant IRS publications or an experienced tax advisor.

Prior to the enactment of the Taxpayer Fairness Act of 1997, homeowners 55 years of age or older enjoyed a once-in-a-lifetime tax exclusion on gain from the sale of their residences of up to $125,000. Even if this privilege was exercised, exclusion of gain under the current law is available to these homeowners. The $250,000/$500,000 exclusion is not a once-in-a-lifetime exclusion. If certain conditions are met, a homeowner can exercise this exclusion each time he/she sells a home.

Capital Gains Tax Rates

If a homeowner sells a home and does not qualify for the exclusion, capital gain from the sale is taxable. Previously, the maximum **tax rate** on a capital gain was 28 percent. Under the current tax law, the maximum tax rate may be 8 percent, 10 percent, 15 percent, 25 percent, or 28 percent. The maximum capital gains tax rate that applies to a specific transaction depends on two factors:

1. The type of property sold
2. How long the property was held before the sale. (For example, gains from the sale of property owned for more than 1 year are categorized as long-term gains and are taxed at a maximum rate of 15 percent. Gains from the sale of property owned 1 year or less are categorized as short-term gains and are taxed at the taxpayer's ordinary income tax rate, which may be 28 percent, 33 percent, or 36 percent.)

This course will not cover how to determine the capital gains tax rate for specific situations.

Installment Sales

In an **installment sale**, the seller receives payment for the property over a period of years. In this situation, the seller can avoid paying the entire amount of taxes on any gain from the sale in the year the sale took place. Rather, the seller can postpone the payment of taxes to future years, when the installment payments are actually received.

Real Estate Exchanges

Real estate exchanges may defer taxes that would otherwise be due if a property were sold. Exchanges of real property are often referred to as tax-free exchanges, but they are not really tax-free; the tax payments are postponed. The correct term for exchanges is tax-deferred. The only properties eligible for tax-deferred exchanges include real property held for investment, income, trade, or business. Personal residences are not eligible. (Residential investment property, such as an apartment complex, is eligible because is it considered investment property.) If properties are exchanged on a tax-deferred basis, both properties must be one of these eligible types of property. (This is referred to as a **like-for-like trade** because the two properties traded are both eligible.) Any eligible type of property may be traded for any other eligible type of property. For example, a vacant lot owned by an investor may be traded for a duplex or an office building because both properties would be eligible.

There are two possible trade situations—a trade in which the values of two properties are the same and a trade in which they are different. When the values of two properties are the same, neither party is required to pay income tax resulting from the exchange. In this situation, the cost basis for tax purposes is the same for the two properties, and no tax is due because there is no gain or loss for either party. When the values of the two properties are not the same, the party trading the lower-valued property usually gives the other party money or an item of value in addition to the real property exchanged. This money or item is called **boot**.

In this situation, the party who trades a lower-valued property for a higher-valued one (trades up) will not pay taxes resulting from the exchange. The party who trades a higher-valued property for a lower-valued one (trades down) will pay taxes resulting from the exchange. This occurs for one of the following reasons:

• The payment of boot
• The exchange of mortgages with different balances

Let's look at each of these.

When a boot is paid along with an exchange of real property, the person who receives the boot is liable for taxes on the amount (or monetary value) of the boot. A tax liability also occurs when two properties are exchanged that have two different mortgage balances, even if no boot is paid. If a taxpayer receives a smaller mortgage balance in exchange for a larger one, the difference in the balances is considered income to that taxpayer and is called *mortgage relief.* The amount of the mortgage relief (reduction in mortgage balance) is taxable.

SUMMARY

Federal state and local taxation affects both individuals and businesses engaged in real property ownership. On state and local levels, property taxes are levied on real property. On a Federal level, income derived from income producing activities is taxed. Both individuals and businesses engaged in real property ownership need to familiarize themselves with the impact of taxation. Tax knowledge is essential when making buying or selling considerations and/or decisions. Licensees should familiarize themselves with the impact of taxation on real property purchases and sales. Although licensees are cautioned against giving any type of tax advice, licensees should have knowledge of this subject.

REVIEW QUESTIONS

1. In Florida, taxes on real property are calculated:
   a. On a quarterly basis.
   b. Biannually.
   c. On a fiscal year basis.
   d. For each calendar year.

2. Property taxes become a lien on real property in Florida on:
   a. January 1.
   b. April 1.
   c. November 1.
   d. December 31.

3. In Florida, unpaid property taxes from the previous year become delinquent on:
   a. December 31 of the following year.
   b. November 1 of the following year.
   c. April 1 of the following year.
   d. January 1 of the following year.

4. John was shocked when he received his TRIM notice, and he wants the assessed value of his property lowered. What is the first thing John must do?
   a. File a suit against the taxing authority.
   b. Go to the county property appraiser's office to contest the assessed value.
   c. Contact the county tax collector or a representative.
   d. Make an appointment with the Value Adjustment Board.

5. The notice of John's assessed property value and the current millage rate for the county, school board, and city was mailed on August 5. John wants to file a protest regarding the assessed value. How long does he have to protest?
   a. John must file a protest on or before August 15.
   b. John has until August 30 to file a protest.
   c. John's protest must be filed by September 1.
   d. John must register his protest before October 15.

6. John went to the county property appraiser's office to protest the assessed value of his property, but received no satisfaction. If John wants to continue his quest for a lower assessed value, what is the next step?
   a. John can go to the Value Adjustment Board.
   b. Contact the county tax collector or a representative.
   c. Register his protest in writing with the county appraiser.
   d. Litigate.

7. Governments do not pay property taxes to each other in Florida, so government-owned property is not assessed for property tax purposes. Thus, government-owned property is:
   a. Partially exempt from taxation.
   b. Exempt from taxation.
   c. Immune from taxes.
   d. Disallowed from taxes.

8. Harry was granted a homestead tax exemption. His home has a market value of $275,000. The assessed value of the home is $213,000. What is the taxable value?
   a. $275,000
   b. $213,000
   c. $250,000
   d. $188,000

9. Harry's property is subject to a tax rate of 24 mills. Use the figures in Question 8 to calculate Harry's property taxes.
   a. $6,600
   b. $5,112
   c. $6,000
   d. $4,512

10. Gary was wounded in the Vietnam War and the VA has rated Gary's disability at 30 percent. Gary has declared a homestead on his residence in Florida and has been granted a homestead exemption. Last year, Gary's wife died. What is Gary's homestead exemption?
    a. $31,000
    b. $30,500
    c. $26,000
    d. $25,500

11. Sue is a widow who lives in Plantation in Broward County. County taxes are 9.4 mills. City taxes are 9.6 mills. School board taxes are 6 mills. Sue has a homestead exemption. How much will Sue save in taxes because of her exemption?
    a. $705.00
    b. $697.50
    c. $637.50
    d. $625.00

12. The tax rate for a particular local government is the result of:
    a. The Florida State Legislature.
    b. Registered voters of the state.
    c. Majority vote of voters in each tax district.
    d. How much money each department of the local government needs.

13. Charles is widowed and legally blind. He has qualified for a homestead exemption. The market value of his home is $175,000 and the assessed value is $93,000. The city tax rate is 9.1 mills, the school board tax is 7.8 mills, and the county tax rate is 8.4 mills. Calculate the county taxes Charles must pay.
    a. $1,720.40
    b. $1,707.75
    c. $1,695.10
    d. $562.80

14. The law that caps the assessed value for homestead property is the:
    a. Value Adjustment Law.
    b. Save Our Home.
    c. The Seventh Amendment.
    d. The Green Belt Law.

15. Florida's Green Belt Law was passed:
    a. To provide green space within city development.
    b. In order to protect the environment.
    c. To provide clean air and drinking water for Floridians.
    d. To protect farmers.

16. When assessing the value of agricultural land, tax assessors:
    a. Must use a constant value on all land used for farming.
    b. Can never value farmland at its highest and best use.
    c. Are not required to perform a full appraisal.
    d. Must factor in the highest and best use of the land.

17. John and Mary are married. They sold the home they lived in for 5 years and realized a profit of $617,000. What is the result?
    a. They will be exempt from taxes on the profit if one of them is over 55 years of age.
    b. There will be no taxes due on the profit if they purchase a home of equal or more value within 18 months of the sale.
    c. The profit over $500,000 will be taxed as a capital gain.
    d. The profit over $500,000 will be subject to ordinary income taxes.

18. An industrial property sold for $125,000. Land was 20 percent of the value. Calculate the annual depreciation. Round to the nearest dollar.
    a. $4,545
    b. $4,364
    c. $3,584
    d. $2,564

19. One advantage of home ownership is the:
    a. Deduction of mortgage payments on a first and second residence.
    b. Deduction of taxes on a first home only.
    c. Deduction of taxes on a first and a second residence.
    d. Deduction of mortgage payments on a first home only.

20. When a lender charges points for a loan involving a principle residence:
    a. All points can be deducted for income tax purposes in the year they were paid.
    b. Points are deductible only when they are amortized out over the life of the loan.
    c. Points on loans are only deductible as an expense for income property.
    d. Points are not deductible in the year paid if the loan was a refinance.

21. Homeowners would NOT be allowed to deduct which of the following expenses for IRS tax purposes?
    a. Ad valorem taxes
    b. Depreciation
    c. Mortgage interest
    d. Up to $500,000 profit when selling the home

22. Investment property owners would NOT be allowed to deduct which of the following expenses for IRS tax purposes?
    a. Depreciation
    b. Hazard insurance
    c. Reserves for replacements
    d. Ad valorem taxes

Chapter 19

KEY TERMS

buyer's market   seller's market
demand   supply
household   vacancy rates

LEARNING OBJECTIVES

After completing this lesson, you will be able to:

- Describe the physical characteristics of real estate.
- Understand the economic characteristics of real estate.
- Know the factors that influence supply and demand.
- Recognize the different market indicators.

The Real Estate Market

PHYSICAL CHARACTERISTICS OF REAL ESTATE

There are five primary characteristics or real estate:

1. Immobility—The location of property is fixed and not mobile. A property's location is what determines its value to an owner or buyer.

2. Markets are slow to respond to change in supply and demand—When demand increases, the creation of new product is required to meet that demand. The problem, however, is creating the product. Once a residential single-family construction project begins, it can take as little as 6 months to as much as 12 months before construction is complete. The time period to construct multifamily housing is even longer—from 12 to 18 months. Therefore, supply of housing moves at a slow pace in response to a change in market conditions.

3. Indestructibility of land—Land cannot be made or destroyed. Physically, land is permanent. Therefore, improvements are ultimately added to the land. In some cases, added improvements are for owner/occupant purposes. In other cases, they are for income-producing purposes. In either case, the creation of these improvements is always governed by local laws. Ownership in real property is not considered to be a liquid investment. Therefore, anyone investing in real property is considered a long-term investor. This is due to the indestructibility of the land as well as the large initial investment required at the time the property is acquired. Additionally, real property is considered a long-term investment because of the property's ability to provide returns on invested capital. Furthermore, where improvements made to real property experience depreciation, land is not depreciable.

Coaching Tips: **Only improvements made or added to the land are insurable, land is not.**

---

4. Heterogeneous—No two parcels of property are the same. Therefore, each parcel is said to be heterogeneous or unique. Lots contained on the same street within a subdivision are different. A corner lot differs from the lot next to it merely by its location.

5. Governmental controls influence the market through zoning, building codes, taxes, and other influences—While the federal government controls our money supply, local laws such as zoning, building codes, and property/income taxes govern and influence development. Areas with low property taxation are more likely to experience growth than those with high property tax bases.

ECONOMIC CHARACTERISTICS OF REAL PROPERTY

As discussed in Chapter 15, there are various principles or elements that constitute a property's value. Timing is an essential element. Let's examine how the principle of demand and supply interact with market conditions.

Demand

Demand for property means that someone has a desire to own or use the property. If demand is to have an effect on the value of property, it must be accompanied by purchasing power. If someone desires a property but doesn't have the financial ability to act on that desire, there is no effective demand for the property. When someone has a desire for property and the purchasing power to act on that desire, the resulting demand for the property contributes to the property's value.

Price of Real Estate

When there is a high demand for property, prices rise. Conversely, when there is a greater availability of property, prices fall. Therefore, as a buyer, seller, or licensee, one must understand the scale of economies to succeed in the real estate marketplace.

For example, economic growth is stimulated when the marketplace sees the demand as exceeding the available supplies. This is the reason supply is created. Supply is created to meet demand. Let's look at the stimulating factors that create demand.

Population and Households

When looking at population and household trends, it is easy to see that our overall population has grown considerably. A **household** is defined by the U.S. Census Bureau as a space designed for dwelling purposes occupied by one or more persons. Although each person in the population does not represent a household, one can make determinations as to the minimum amount of product required to meet the demand within a geographical area. A careful look at previous statistics concerning an area's inventory and sales output will help determine a market's absorption rate.

In previous years, careful study has revealed that real estate markets, particularly those in the sunshine states like Arizona and New Mexico, have seen and experienced the greatest growth margins. This is certainly evident in the Florida housing market. The housing arena is the most active marketplace. Everyone needs a roof over their heads. This is the primary factor that drives the demand for housing. Population increase fuels the need for additional housing and other real property types, such as:

- Schools designed to meet the needs of a growing community
- Hospitals designed to meet the needs of the aging and sick
- Office space
- Government buildings
- Recreational facilities
  - Parks
  - Playgrounds
  - Community facilities

Consumer Income

Income trends can make or break real estate markets. For example, high rates of unemployment could reduce the demand for purchased property. This event can lead to a decline in property values as well as diminish the areas desirability to a buyer. Population will gravitate to areas that offer the best employment opportunities. Lifestyles may become secondary to employment opportunities.

On the other hand, it should be noted that lower property tax rates tend to increase one's disposable income and thereby can result in an increase in demand.

Availability of Mortgage Funds

Demand is dependant on the availability of borrowed funds. When interest rates are low, property values increase to reflect the availability of money within the credit system. However, when interest rates are high, property values drop. This is due to the increased cost for debt service, which occurs when the Federal Reserve tightens the available money supply. In recent years, interest rates have been at historic lows.

Currently, however, mortgage rates are steadily increasing and ultimately pricing certain sections of the buying population out of the market. This is a contributing factor toward the cooling of the nationwide real estate/housing economy.

The following is an illustration of the significance of rising or falling interest rates to the consumer.

Example 1
Assume the following loan information:
    Loan amount: $500,000 fully amortized over maturity
    Interest rate: 10 percent
    Maturity/term of loan: 25 years
    Monthly payment: $4,543.50

Example 2
Assume the following loan information:
    Loan amount: $500,000 fully amortized over maturity
    Interest rate: 9 percent
    Maturity/term of loan: 25 years
    Monthly payment: $4,195.98

As you can see by Examples 1 and 2, a 1 percent (or 100 basis points) change in the rate equates to a monthly payment differential of $347.52. When annualized, the difference between a 9 percent loan versus a 10 percent loan is approximately $4,170.22. This can be a significant difference to a borrower.

Consumer Preferences

Consumers are also an important factor regarding demand. When shopping for housing, one consumer may seek new construction while another may seek older housing. Different consumer preferences at any given time and place will dictate demand. Examples of consumer preferences include:

- Architectural styles:
  - Cape Cod
  - Ranch
  - Split-level
- Single-family detached housing
- Townhouse
- Cooperative high-rise
- Condominium high-rise

For example, the aging population may be considering downsizing from large homes to something smaller, such as apartments.

To keep up with the demands of consumers, developers and property owners must recognize the needs of their constituency and must keep up with changes that occur in housing preferences.

Coaching Tips: **Demand Factors at a Glance**

- Price
- Population and households
- Consumer income
- Availability of mortgage funds
- Tastes or preferences

Supply

Supply (as it pertains to real property) can be defined as the amount of housing stock of properties available for sale or for lease. Let's examine some of the factors that make up and play an integral role in the supply of housing.

Availability of Skilled Labor

The creation of supply results from the work of craftsmen who practice various construction trades. In residential construction, this includes the following:

- Electricians
- Plumbers
- Carpenters
- Roofers
- Masons

In commercial construction, many of these craftsmen will be utilized as well as:

- Steel workers
- Heating and air-conditioning contractors
- Sheet-rock contractors

Any area of the country that experiences growth must also have available skilled labor. Growth is one of many economic cycles. The growth cycle occurs when the need to grow the supply side of the economy arises. As you will see, the growth cycle generally is sparked during times when inventories are low. This theory holds true for any product in demand by the consumer. Therefore, availability of skilled labor becomes imperative to the supplier.

Availability of Construction Loans and Financing

The construction industry is dependant on the availability of construction financing, including:

- Short-term (interim) construction financing—Short-term loans are used to construct improvements. These loans are short-term in maturity (generally 12 to 18 months) and due to the nature of their risk, they usually bear higher rates of interest than that of other types of loans.
- Long-term (takeout) loans—These loans pay for the construction loan and act as the property's permanent financing.

As interest rates on these types of loans rise, less supply is generated. When rates begin to fall or are steady, supply increases.

Availability of Land

In many cities throughout the country, prime land availability has dwindled. Where there may appear to be abundant amount of land available, other factors may affect the desirability of that land to subdividers and developers. Zoning and local building codes can create major constraints within any development consideration. This is particularly true when dealing with large tracts of land.

Cities with vast land availability will always experience new speculative construction. However, due to the continuous availability of land in these areas, resale market values tend to be nonexistent because they cannot keep up with the value of newer construction.

Availability of Materials

As previously discussed, when we enter an economic growth economy, supply usually increases. In order to provide additional supply to the marketplace, the availability of materials used in real property construction must be available. In the absence of construction material supply, the cost of constructing the improvement increases. From a project feasibility point of view, the increased cost will probably impede the development of the project.

INTERPRETING MARKET CONDITIONS

Whenever the economic climate changes, real estate markets are directly affected. The effect can be on a national or local level. There are generally three types of markets that buyers or sellers experience:

1. **Seller's market**—This occurs when there are more buyers than there are sellers or available product

2. **Buyer's market**—This occurs when there are more sellers than there are buyers.

3. Transitioning market—This occurs at the end of a buyer's or seller's market. In this type of market, conditions tend to resemble a tug-of-war between the buyer and seller. At the end of a seller's market, a seller may not recognize the changing market conditions fast enough to capture a sale. Sellers who do not react to the shift away from a seller's market will lose out on oppurtunities to sell because they won't be flexible when pricing their homes

   At the end of a buyer's market, a buyer may not grasp the need to pay more for a property. Therefore, a buyer may lose deals to other buyers who recognize the changing environment. Ultimately, that buyer will end up paying more for a property that he could have bought for less. Irrespective of market conditions, everyday is a day to buy because prices usually go up.

Price Levels

Property price levels change frequently. There are various ways of recognizing when this happens:

- Issuance of new construction building permits indicates the amount of new housing supply.
- Increase or decrease in vacancies of rental property.
  - When vacancies are on the rise, it is cheaper to buy than it is to lease.
  - When the supply of housing for sale increases beyond demand, it is cheaper to rent than it is to buy.

- Population increase within a community or region will always spur creation of new supply to meet the anticipated demand.

Coaching Tips: Watching the retail sector is a wonderful indication of consumer trends. When retail stores experience high vacancy rates, this is an indication that consumers are not spending as much money to support retail sales. The result is vacancies. Conversely, when the vacancy rate for retail stores in a marketplace is low, this is an indication that consumers have resumed spending trends, thereby, increasing retail leasing of space.

Vacancy Rates

As previously discussed above, **vacancy rates** are always an indication of market trends. Vacancy rates are generally quoted as percentages as opposed to numbers representing available product. Rising vacancy rates indicate a buyer's market while lower rates indicate a seller's market.

Sales Volume

The current market condition can be determined by examining the homes that have recently sold. Consumers today are in a much better position to gather information about pricing on previous sales because of the Internet. Today, there are various types of reports that are available and are published by real estate firms. This information is usually provided by real estate companies as a means of branding and marketing. Information contained within these reports may include:

- Quarterly or semiannual sales information broken down by:
  - Property type
    - Single-family housing
    - Cooperatives
    - Condominiums
    - Townhouses
  - Neighborhood
  - Percentage of increase or decrease in the sales pricing information from previously reported periods
- Cost per square foot for the purchase of a property
- Time on the market prior to a property's sale

Note that these reports are only as good or as accurate as the companies that compile them. Therefore, any information presented in these reports should be confirmed.

SUMMARY

Changes within the economic environment dictate whether or not to create supply or consolidate it. When conditions suggest an oversupply, new supply development comes to a halt and consolidation of existing supply inventory occurs. Generally speaking, the amount of time that a market rises is probably the amount of time required to absorb any existing product. The real estate housing market can sometimes seem immune and contrary to that of a deteriorating business climate. In order to capitalize on the times, buyers, sellers, and licensees must be able to recognize the cause for change in the real estate environment.

REVIEW QUESTIONS

1. A factor that makes the real estate market different from other markets is:
   a. The real estate market is centralized.
   b. Information about individual real estate markets is readily available.
   c. The real estate market is quick to respond to changes in supply and demand.
   d. Real property is not homogeneous.

2. Another characteristic of the real estate market that contributes to its uniqueness is:
   a. Real estate markets tend to be local.
   b. Land is depreciable.
   c. Property insurance can cover all losses.
   d. The value of each property stands alone.

3. Highest and best use of land:
   a. Is unconditionally set by zoning.
   b. Is determined by examining any allowable alternative uses.
   c. Will not change with time.
   d. Is not influenced by surrounding areas.

4. Unlike the markets for stocks, bonds, commodities, and hard goods, the real estate market:
   a. Is subject to government controls at all levels of government.
   b. Is independent of decisions by the Federal Reserve.
   c. Is only dependent on interest rates.
   d. Is quick to respond to changes in supply and demand.

5. The U.S. Census Bureau has defined a person or group of persons who occupy a separate housing space as a:
   a. Housing unit.
   b. Household.
   c. Home.
   d. Family unit.

6. Which statement does NOT describe the real estate market?
   a. Property is unique to its location.
   b. Land is indestructible.
   c. Real property construction has become standardized.
   d. Federal Reserve decisions influence the market.

7. Government controls are a large influence on the market for real property. An example of a direct control on the real estate market would be:
   a. Monetary policy.
   b. Changes in the discount rate.
   c. Changes in the reserve requirement.
   d. Statewide building codes.

8. An example of an indirect control on the real estate market would be:
   a. Building codes.
   b. Zoning ordinances.
   c. Building moratoriums.
   d. Open-market operations.

9. Which of the following variables influences the demand for real property?
   a. Land is available.
   b. Skilled labor is readily available.
   c. Construction materials can be readily obtained.
   d. The price for housing is attractive.

10. Which of the following variables influence the supply of real property?
    a. The price of properties is within reach.
    b. People want homes and have the money to buy.
    c. The price of money is reasonable.
    d. Land for homes is readily available.

11. When trying to predict the revival of a real estate market, people look to:
    a. The price of money.
    b. Decisions by the Federal Reserve.
    c. The availability of skilled labor.
    d. Vacancy rates of exiting properties.

12. In recent years in the Florida housing market, buyers had to compete for desirable homes. This was an indication of:
    a. Builder activity.
    b. An increase in supply.
    c. A seller's market.
    d. A buyer's market.

13. One of the leading indicators that the federal government looks to when predicting the economy is the construction industry. In terms of a local property market, an increase in the issuance of building permits would be a factor of:
    a. A buyer's market.
    b. A seller's market.
    c. An influence on the prices for property.
    d. A downturn in the market.

14. While driving around your community, you notice a surprising number of "For Rent" signs. You might conclude that:
    a. The market is about to explode.
    b. A seller's market is in effect.
    c. Rental signs may reflect a buyer's market.
    d. More people have invested in property. An investor's market prevails.

15. One of the influences on the supply of property is:
    a. Price of properties.
    b. Household composition.
    c. Consumer desires.
    d. Availability of construction loans.

16. Which statement does NOT describe the real estate market?
    a. An increase in price indicates a seller's market.
    b. Real estate is heterogeneous.
    c. Real estate is immobile.
    d. Demand rises as prices increase.

17. Which of the following has the greatest affect on the real estate market:
    a. Actions by the Federal Reserve.
    b. Consumers.
    c. Large manufacturers and builders.
    d. Producers of goods.

18. Fannie Mae's definition of market value assumes the market is in equilibrium. When supply exceeds demand, an appraiser will make adjustments to comparable properties to indicate that:
    a. Because buyers have an advantage, a downward adjustment will be made to comparable properties.
    b. Because sellers have an advantage, a downward adjustment will be made to the comparable properties.
    c. Because buyers have an advantage, an upward adjustment will be made to the comparable properties.
    d. Because sellers have an advantage, an upward adjustment will be made to the comparable properties.

19. One indicator of the demand for housing in any particular housing market would be:
    a. A local increase in the occupancy rate that cannot be tied to reduced rents or other rental promotions.
    b. The number of commercial building starts.
    c. A projected increase in population numbers.
    d. National housing trends.

20. If the only change in the economy is a small increase in long-term interest rates:
    a. The real estate market will not be affected.
    b. People will continue to buy homes.
    c. The demand for homes may rise.
    d. The housing market may fall.

Chapter 20

KEY TERMS

buffer zone
building codes
building inspections
building permits
concurrency
condemnation
eminent domain

environmental impact statement
escheat
health ordinances
service industry
special exception
variance
zoning ordinances

LEARNING OBJECTIVES

After completing this lesson, you will be able to:

- Explain the purpose of land-use controls.
- Understand land-use planning background studies.
- Describe the role of zoning ordinances in land-use control.
- Differentiate between a nonconforming use, a variance, and a special exception.
- Identify the features of the National Flood Insurance Program.
- Describe how private restrictions are used on land-use control.

Planning and Zoning

THE HISTORY OF URBAN PLANNING AND ZONING

Prior to the implementation of zoning regulations, restrictions were put into place by the early urban planners of our nation. These restrictions included prohibiting or limiting certain uses of property in areas when those uses were in conflict with the remainder of the community's land use. However, due to the industrial revolution and prior to the implementation of zoning regulations, most of the country was experiencing a laissez-faire (French for let proceed) approach to land use regulations.

In addition, prior to the invention of the elevator and its implementation in high-rise construction, most properties were low-rise in height. This ensured that all properties in some manner conformed to the surrounding properties. Therefore, each property was able to enjoy unlimited open air and light.

For example, in New York City, the use of the elevator in commercial construction gave birth to high-rise properties. In the early 1920s, the construction of the Equitable Building in lower Manhattan created problems for the neighboring properties. Properties neighboring the Equitable Building high-rise were now deprived of the air and light that they enjoyed before the Equitable Building was built. These properties experienced (as the day went on) loss of light directly resulting from the height of the property. The building's height cast a six-acre shadow over the neighboring properties, which infuriated the neighboring property owners. As a direct result of this event and the birth of high-rise construction, New York City's first zoning resolution was born. Many other municipalities probably experienced similar urban planning issues that required the creation and adaptation of zoning resolutions.

Certainly, the decisions that were made in those days affected the future of how land use would evolve. Urban planners were now charged with the municipality's future growth and land uses. Some of the areas of concern were:

- Air and light
- Creation of zoning districts with the intent of creating conformity within those zones
- Height restrictions
- Density issues
- Health, safety, and welfare of the constituency

Note that the concerns were different from city to ciy. For example, in cities that were financial or business capitals, early development trended vertically. In less populated areas, development trended horizontally. Therefore, local planning agencies were

394 Chapter 20 • Planning and Zoning

created. Florida's Growth Management Act of 1985 mandated the creation of additional infrastructure to account for the expansion of development to satisfy the growth in population. Prior to the commencement of any new development, the act called for the creation of infrastructure to include consideration in areas such as:

- Water and wastewater treatment facilities
- The creation of new sewer systems
- The building of roadways

As a result of the Growth Management Act of 1985, the Department of Community Affairs was given the responsibility under Chapter 163, F.S., to regulate city, county, and regional plans. This would also play the major role in the guiding and controlling of future growth throughout the state.

PUBLIC LAND-USE CONTROL

Public land-use controls are enacted to ensure an orderly pattern of growth in a community and to preserve property values.

These controls are established under a government's police power, primarily at the county and city level, through enabling legislation. These powers are also designed to protect the public in areas such as:

- Health issues through state and local **health ordinances**
- Safety issues through state and local building codes

Zoning Ordinances

The principal mechanism of public land-use control is through **zoning ordinances**. Through zoning ordinances, the government and local municipalities can regulate such things as:

- Permitted uses for land
- Type, size, and height of structures built on the land
- Open-air requirements in relation to site improvement
- Density factors that will dictate the project size and occupancy of the land
- Location of structures on the land such as setback requirements, including:
  - Rear yard
  - Side yard
  - Frontage setbacks, when necessary

  There are several zoning classifications:

- Residential use for dwelling purposes only. This type of zoning regulates lot size, setbacks, and density, which is the maximum number of homes allowed to be built per acre of land.
- Commercial use for commerce and business purposes, including offices, retail space, hotels/motels, and other business district uses. This type of zoning regulates the intensity of use, parking requirements, as well as height and size limitations.
- Industrial manufacturing uses such as heavy manufacturing, light manufacturing, warehousing, and loft space. This type of zoning controls emissions, effluents, noise, odor, smoke, and chemicals.
- Agricultural for farmland.
- Special use, which includes property owned by the government such as post offices and schools.
- Mixed use, which is a hybrid of two allowed uses within one parcel of property. This could include:

- Upper floors of a building used as residential units
- Lower floors of the same building used for commercial uses such as:
  - Medical space
  - Retail space
  - Office space

Wherever two different zones border each other, zoning will usually require the creation of a **buffer zone**, which is a strip of land that varies in size from community to community and acts as a separator between two zones. Buffer zones are of importance wherever residential zones border and abut commercial or industrial zones.

Nonconforming Use

When zoning for a particular property is changed or implemented after a property is built, a nonconforming use results if the property does not conform to the new zoning ordinances. New or revised ordinances usually contain a grandfather clause that allows the nonconforming property already in existence to remain in use. However, the grandfather clause usually will not allow the property to be remodeled or expanded.

Variance

When a zoning ordinance is already in effect, any new structure or modifications to existing structures must conform to the ordinance. Permission for an exemption to some of the specific requirements within a zoning classification may sometimes be granted through a zoning **variance**. Variances can only be issued *within* a zoning classification and cannot be used to change the zoning classification for a given property. To obtain a variance, the property owner must demonstrate that a hardship exists or that complying with the zoning would create a hardship.

There are two types of variances:

1. Area
2. Use

Area Variance

Area variances grant the property owner permission to utilize land in a way that is in conflict with current zoning *area* requirements because the property owner cannot satisfy one of the following:

- Physical requirements of zoning
- Dimensional requirements of zoning

For example, a zoning ordinance may require that houses are built at least 30 feet back from the road. If the topography of a particular parcel of land does not allow a structure to be built that far back from the road (e.g., because of the slope of the land, or location of a body of water, etc.), the owner may be granted a variance allowing the house to be built closer to the road.

Use Variance

Use variances grant the property owner permission to *utilize* land in a way that is prohibited under the current zoning. In order to be eligible to obtain a use variance, a property owner will have to demonstrate some of the following criteria:

- The property owner is experiencing hardship.
- The property owner hardship is exclusive to that owner's property versus the entire neighborhood or area.

- As a result of the hardship, the property owner is unable to capture the economic benefits inherent to property ownership.
- If the variance is granted, the general character of the neighborhood will not be altered.
- The hardship is not self-created.

  Note that variances are generally not granted without public hearings

Special Exception

A property owner may also be granted a **special exception**, which allows a specific use for a specific property. Usually, a special exception is permitted when the use of the property would be in the public interest. For example, a property owner may be issued a special exception allowing a hospital to be built on land that is zoned for residential use if the local area is in need of a hospital.

A special exception is different than a variance. A variance is only issued when an owner is able to show that complying with the zoning would create a hardship. A special exception is issued when the public would be best served by a land use that differs from the existing zoning.

Master Plan

Zoning ordinances are usually tied to a long-range master or comprehensive plan for future growth in the community. Under the Florida Growth Management Act of 1985, all levels of government (city and county) are required to establish comprehensive plans for future growth. A comprehensive plan must contain certain elements that are coordinated with the comprehensive plans of surrounding areas. A comprehensive plan must address:

- Future land use
- Traffic circulation
- Sanitary sewer, solid waste, drainage, and water
- Conservation and protection of natural resources
- Recreation areas
- Housing
- Coastal area management and protection, if applicable
- Intergovernmental coordination

The Florida Growth Management Act of 1985 also has a **concurrency** provision. According to this provision, sufficient infrastructure (sewer, water, and transportation systems) must exist before new development is permitted.

Local Planning Agency

Each local government must establish a local planning agency (or local planning commission). The local planning agency is responsible for developing the comprehensive plan. The local planning agency must ensure that development in the community is consistent with the comprehensive plan. The local planning agency is responsible for:

- Subdivision plat approval
- Site plan approval
- Sign control

Subdivision Plat Approval

Before a subdivision can be developed, the developer must submit a subdivision plat to the local planning agency for approval. The subdivision plat is a visual map of the subdivided land. It is an architectural rendering of the subdivided parcels that will indicate:

- Egress (exit) from the subdivision
- Ingress (entry) into the subdivision
- Sidewalks where applicable

Note that prior to the approval and recording of the plat map of subdivision by the necessary authorities, the subdivider may not sell and/or transfer subdivided lots to the public.

Site Plan Approval

For large developments (other than subdivisions), the developer must submit a site plan to the local planning agency for approval. The site plan is a detailed description of the project.

Signage Control

The local planning agency is also responsible for signage control. The purpose of signage control is to ensure that signs do not distract drivers or otherwise create dangerous conditions. It is also designed to control the use and installation of unsightly or unusual signage that may not conform to a neighborhood's standards.

Composition

The local planning agency is composed of members of the public who are typically appointed by the city or county commission. These members are typically volunteers, not paid employees. The members of the planning agency are not trained as city or county planners. Rather, they come from a variety of professions and make recommendations based on what they believe is in the best interest of the residents of the community. Members on planning boards are not elected; they are appointed. It is for this reason that members serving on a planning board are not compensated. Serving is voluntary. However, the planning agency does have a support staff made up of individuals who are paid employees and trained planners. The size of planning boards varies depending on a municipality's size and need for area coverage.

The Process of Planning

The process of planning includes reviewing various types of studies that indicate the following:

- Past trends
- Current trends
- Projected trends

One primary area of study that is important to note is the business environment, which creates employment. There are two types of business industries to study:

1. Base industry—Local businesses that attract people and money from other parts of the nation such as resort and recreation industries.
2. **Service industry**—Services the local constituency through various trades such as convenience stores and local retailers.

Developments of Regional Impact

Any development in Florida that will affect residents in more than one county is referred to as a development of regional impact. An **environmental impact statement** must be prepared to address the impact that the project may or will have on the environment and its neighboring communities.

Building Codes

Building codes are often confused with zoning ordinances. Building codes set the allowable minimum standards for construction of improvements on real property. They are established under the government's police powers, but they are *not* part of the zoning process. Enforcement of the Florida Building Code is accomplished through the issuance of:

- **Building permits** grant permission to construct improvements and are issued by local government
- **Building inspections** are inspections conducted by representatives of local building departments to establish construction conformance with filed plans and specifications on new construction as well as code compliance on existing construction.
- Certificates of occupancy are issued to a property owner by the local building department and state that the property conforms to building codes and may be occupied.

The police power of **condemnation** is used to take possession of property that belongs to the private sector. **Eminent domain** is the power that allows the government to take private property if the taking is necessary to benefit the general public in areas such as new public transportation, new highways, and various other public uses.

PRIVATE LAND-USE CONTROLS

Private land-use controls can be initiated by deed restrictions (also known as restrictive covenants). These restrictions are usually placed on property by the subdivider or developer of the property. They are appurtenances and as such run with the property from owner to owner. Restrictions are recorded along with the master plan of the subdivision when it is recorded in the public records. These covenants or restrictions may *not* do any of the following:

- Violate existing public ordinances
- Prevent the owner from selling or conveying the property
- Break any laws

Otherwise, a property may have any reasonable restriction.

Deed restrictions may be removed or terminated if they are not enforced. Laches (doctrine of laches) is a term used to describe unenforced rights or restrictions. If rights or restrictions are not enforced, they terminate after the passing of a statutory time period. In essence, "use them or lose them."

Deed restrictions tend to be more restrictive than limitations imposed by zoning ordinances. They may include such requirements as:

- The style and size of homes
- The location, style, and materials used in fences
- Limitations on the erection and/or placement of outbuildings such as tool sheds
- Bans on parking of trucks, recreational vehicles, or boats in residential neighborhoods

The most common restriction might be minimum setback requirements from neighboring properties. Another example of a common restriction would be a minimum square foot size of any home constructed within a subdivision. These restrictions maintain land values and therefore protect the subdivider as well as the landowner who purchases a lot from the subdivider.

However, from time to time, contradictions between private deed restrictions and zoning ordinances may occur. In these situations, the *more* restrictive restriction will always prevail. The theory behind this is that the more restrictive issue has probably covered the concerns implied by the less restrictive issue. For example, if zoning limits building heights to 40 feet and a deed restriction limits height to 30 feet, the deed restriction limit of 30 feet would apply. The deed restriction not only addresses the concern of zoning but is, in fact, even more restrictive and will therefore prevail.

Enforcement

Deed restrictions are enforced by property owners in a subdivision, usually through a neighborhood association. If an owner violates a restriction, another owner or the owners' association may file a civil suit in court to block the action. Usually, neighboring property owners bring suit in court.

Deed restrictions and other private land-use restrictions *run with the land* and are binding on all future owners. Conceivably, the restrictions could last forever; however, if the restrictions are outdated, they can be invalidated by court action. Private restrictions may not be used to discriminate on the basis of race, color, sex, religion, or national origin. Any such restrictions are unenforceable.

Coaching Tips: Land-Use Controls at a Glance

- Public land-use controls regulate, not limit, growth.
- A grandfather clause allows a nonconforming use to remain.
  - A grandfather clause is used when a new ordinance is passed.
  - A nonconforming use occurs when a new ordinance is passed.
- A variance is an exemption from an existing or preexisting zoning ordinance.
  - Variances never change the zoning classification.
  - Variances are often granted for expansion.
  - Variances are granted either for use or for area.
- A buffer zone is a strip of land that varies in size from community to community and acts as a separator between two zones.
- Eminent domain allows the state to take property under certain conditions.
- Condemnation is used as the vehicle to take property under eminent domain.
- Escheat occurs when someone dies with no will and no heirs.
- Deed restrictions are imposed by private individuals.
  - They may be more or less restrictive than zoning regulations.
  - Deed restrictions may deal with aesthetic qualities.
- Both deed restrictions and zoning regulations deal with how land is used.
  - Zoning ordinances take precedence only if more restrictive.
  - Deed restrictions take precedence only if more restrictive.
- Laches describes unenforced rights or restrictions.
  - Unenforced rights or restrictions terminate after the passing of a statutory time period.

SUMMARY

Decisions we make today affect how development will occur tomorrow. Social acceptance of development projects becomes essential to ensure success. Urban planning is instituted to regulate the progress of growth while preserving elements such as air and light. Building codes exist to protect the public's health, safety, and welfare. Zoning ordinances control project bulk (size) while preserving the environment. Zoning ordinances can be appealed when a property owner faces financial undue hardships as a result of zoning. Whenever a project affects the residents of more than one county in Florida, development of regional impact studies are performed. The intent of this study is environmental preservation.

REVIEW QUESTIONS

1. During the Industrial Revolution and prior to the creation of zoning laws, the lack of emphasis on city planning was generally due to:
   a. The movement of disaffected persons to the West.
   b. An increase in the number of family farms.
   c. The philosophy of *laissez-faire*.
   d. The movement from farms to the city.

2. The requirement of Florida's Growth Management Act that electricity, drinking water, roads, parks, sewers, etc., must be present before new building permits can be issued is the:
   a. Services provision.
   b. Concurrency provision.
   c. Infrastructure requirement.
   d. Environmental provision.

3. Another requirement of the Growth Management Act is that all communities must have a plan of how the community will expand in the future, and this plan must be designed to curb urban sprawl. This plan is referred to in the law as the:
   a. Comprehensive plan.
   b. Environmental impact statement.
   c. Services plan.
   d. Growth management plan.

4. The requirement for all communities to have in place a comprehensive plan gave rise to local planning commissions. Local planning commission members are:
   a. Elected by the local community.
   b. Appointed, unpaid members who advise city officials.
   c. The final decision makers on city expansion.
   d. Are community board volunteers.

5. The comprehensive plan:
   a. Cannot be altered.
   b. Must be updated on an annual basis.
   c. Must be revised every 5 years.
   d. Must be revised every 10 years.

6. While local planning commissions usually act in an advisory capacity, they often have the final authority in several local matters. Final authority of planning commissions would NOT include:
   a. Site plan approval.
   b. Subdivision approval.
   c. Zoning ordinances.
   d. Sign control.

7. Florida's comprehensive requirements state a city's comprehensive plan must:
   a. Control lot size in subdivisions.
   b. Set building height and size limitations.
   c. Address traffic circulation.
   d. Control emission and effluents.

8. The comprehensive plan allows:
   a. Control of density.
   b. Control of intensity of use.
   c. Issuance of building permits.
   d. Land-use control ordinances.

9. The right to pass zoning ordinances originates from:
   a. Police powers.
   b. State constitutions.
   c. Public policy.
   d. Voters' consent.

10. Sarah wants permission to exceed the setback requirements on her lot. In order to do so, she:
    a. Can appeal to the planning commission.
    b. Ask for a variance.
    c. Go before the Value Adjustment Board.
    d. Must litigate.

11. State building codes are:
    a. Enforced by the state.
    b. Enforced by local governments.
    c. Enforced by county regulations.
    d. Based on population density.

12. Residential zoning is designed to regulate:
    a. Density.
    b. Intensity.
    c. Traffic.
    d. Social services.

13. Commercial zoning is designed to regulate:
    a. Density.
    b. Intensity.
    c. Easements.
    d. Air quality.

14. A strip of land that separates one land use from another is a(n):
    a. Easement.
    b. Buffer zone.
    c. Green space.
    d. Variance.

15. Arthur needs a variance in order to build a pool in his backyard. In order to have a variance granted, Arthur must prove:
    a. A hardship regarding the use of the land exists.
    b. The lack of a pool will cause an economic hardship when he sells.
    c. Other homes in the neighborhood have pools like this.
    d. He needs a pool to meet his wife's medical requirements for recovery.

16. A mobile home park is zoned residential and is populated by persons over the age of 62. The city decided to allow doctors' offices on a nearby street, although that area is also zoned residential. This is an example of a:
    a. Nonconforming use.
    b. Special exception.
    c. Change in zoning.
    d. Special use.

17. Jack followed the zoning requirements when he built a small convenience store on his corner lot. Later, the city changed the zoning to multifamily use. In this situation:
    a. Jack's store is legal.
    b. Jack will have to close his business.
    c. Jack must ask for a variance.
    d. Jack must go to court.

18. A local developer has acquired a parcel of land that is large enough to divide into 25 home sites after allowing for sidewalks, streets, and green space. Before the developer can develop the land, he must submit the subdivision plat to the:
    a. City Building Code Enforcement.
    b. Local planning commission.
    c. Enforcement of Florida Building Codes.
    d. Department of Housing and Urban Development.

19. An example of a base industry is a:
    a. Paper mill.
    b. Branch bank.
    c. Grocery store.
    d. Movie theater.

20. The broadest restrictions on the use of property from the private sector come from:
    a. Police power.
    b. Eminent domain.
    c. Deed restrictions.
    d. Zoning ordinances.

Math Busters Guide to Real Estate Math

This appendix summarizes mathematical formulas commonly used by real estate professionals. By studying and memorizing these formulas, you will have a basic understanding of the key formulas needed to succeed in this course.

KEY FORMULAS

1. Calculating Commissions:

Sales Price × Commission Rate = **Commission Amount**

2. Calculating Commission Rate:

Net Sales Price (after Commissions but before Expenses) ÷ Commission Amount = **Commission Rate**

3. Calculating Purchase Price:

Sales Price ÷ Commission Rate = **Purchase Price**

4. Calculating Simple Interest:

Outstanding Loan Balance × Interest Rate = **Annual Interest**

5. Calculating Total Interest:

Principal × Rate × Time = **Total Interest**

6. Calculating Dollar Amount of Discount Points(s):

Loan Amount × Number of Points (in decimal form) = Dollar Amount of Points

7. Calculating Area:

Triangle: Base × Height × 0.50 = Area of a Triangle
Square: Side × Side = Area of a Square
Rectangle: Length × Width = Area of a Rectangle

8. Calculating Prorations (365/360 day method):

Monthly Prorations using a 365 day year

Step 1:

Amount ÷ Actual Number of Days in Month = Daily Rate

Step 2:

Daily Rate × Number of Days Attributable = Proration

Monthly Prorations using a 360 day year
Step 1:

Amount ÷ 30 Days in Month = Daily Rate

Step 2:

Daily Rate × Number of Days Attributable = Proration

Annual Prorations
Step 1:

Amount ÷ 360 Days or 365 Days (as case may be) = Daily Rate

Step 2:

Daily Rate × Number of Days Attributable = Proration

9. Calculating State Transfer Taxes:

State Documentary Stamps on a Deed
Step 1:

Sale Price ÷ $100 (or any fraction thereof, round up) = Taxable Units of $100

Step 2:

Taxable Units of $100 × $0.70 (tax rate) = Deed Transfer Tax

Note: In Dade County, the tax rate on deeds is $0.60.

State Documentary Stamps on Notes
Step 1:

Note Amount ÷ $100 (or any fraction thereof, round up) = Taxable Units of $100

Step 2:

Taxable Units of $100 × $0.35 (tax rate) = Deed Transfer Tax

Note: This tax is applicable to new and assumed notes, but is not applied when the property is purchased subject to the mortgage.

Intangible Tax on Mortgage

New Mortgage Amount × 0.002 (2 mills tax rate) = Intangible Tax

Note: This tax is only applied against new money introduced to the transaction and does not apply to assumed or to subject to the mortgage amounts.

10. Calculating Real Property Taxes:
Step 1:

Assessed Valuation − Homestead and/or Other Deduction = Adjusted Assessed Valuation

Step 2:

Adjusted Assessed Valuation × Tax or Mill Rate = Annual Property Tax

11. Calculating Capitalization:

IRV

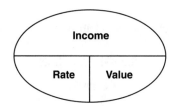

Income = Rate × Value
Rate   = Income ÷ Value
Value = Income ÷ Rate

12. Calculating Accrued Depreciation:

Lump-Sum Age-Life Method

    Effective Age
÷ Economic Life
× Reproduction/Replacement Cost (new)
= Accrued Depreciation

13. Analysis of Cash Flow:

Cash World and Tax World

CASH WORLD	TAX WORLD
Potential Gross Income (PGI)	Net Operating Income (NOI)
− Vacancy & Collection Losses (V&C)	+ Reserve for Replacements (R&R)
+ Other Income (OI)	= Adjusted Net Operating Income (ANOI)
= Effective Gross Income (EGI)	− Mortgage Interest (MI)
− Operating Expenses (OE)	− Annual Depreciation Allowance (ADA)
= Net Operating Income (NOI)	− Suspended/Carryover Loss (SCL)
− Annual Debt Service (ADS)	= Taxable Income (TI)
= Before Tax Cash Flow	× Marginal Tax Rate (MTR)
− Income Tax (IT)	= Income Tax (IT)
= After Tax Cash Flow (ATCF)	

Rent Per Square Foot

Annual Dollars ÷ Number of Square Feet = Dollars Per Square Foot

Operating Expenses Per Square Foot

Annual Operating Expenses ÷ Total Building Square Footage = Operating Expenses in Dollars Per Square Foot

Loan to Value Ratio (LVR)

Represents the lenders investment in the property (loan) as compared with the lesser of the purchase price or appraised value (value).

$$LVR = \frac{Loan\ Amount}{Value}$$

Example:

$$LVR = \frac{378,000}{472,500} = 0.80\ or\ 80\ percent$$

Debt Service Coverage Ratio (DSCR)

Represents the amount by which the NOI exceeds the annual debt service. Higher ratios are preferred as a hedge against:

- Loss of value
- Lower NOI
- Vacancies

$$DSCR = \frac{NOI\ (Net\ Operating\ Income)}{ADS\ (Annual\ Debt\ Service)}$$

Example:

If the net operating income is $75,600 and annual debt service is $56,100

$$DSCR = \frac{\$75,600}{\$56,100} = 1.347\ or\ rounded\ off\ 1.35$$

Operating Expense Ratio (OER)

Represents the amount of the effective gross income that will be used to pay operating expenses.

$$OER = \frac{Operating\ Expenses}{Effective\ Gross\ Income}$$

Example:

If annual operating expenses are $82,900 and Effective Gross Income is $158,500:

$$\frac{82,900}{158,500} = 0.523\ or\ 52.3\ percent$$

Cash Break-Even Ratio (CBR)

Represents the potential gross income that is absorbed by cash charges.

Formula:

$$CBR = \frac{Operating\ Expenses + Debt\ Service - Reserves\ for\ Replacements}{Potential\ Gross\ Income}$$

Example:

If reserves for replacements are $12,500 and potential gross income is $172,300:

$$\frac{\$82,900 + 56,100 - 12,500}{172,300} = 0.734\ or\ 73.4\ percent$$

Margin of Safety

Represents the difference between cash receipts/cash disbursements and is the difference between 1.00 and the cash break-even ratio.

$$Margin\ of\ Safety = 1.00 - 0.734 = 0.266\ or\ 26.6\ percent$$

Equity Dividend Rate (EDR)

Represents the rate of return to an investor on his equity from an income-producing property. It is computed by dividing before tax cash flow (BTCF) by the equity. EDR is referred to as cash-on-cash return.

$$EDR = \frac{\text{Before Tax Cash Flow}}{\text{Equity}}$$

Example:
If before tax cash flow is $15,000 and equity is $94,500:

$$EDR = \frac{15,000}{94,500} = 0.1587 \text{ or } 15.87 \text{ percent}$$

14. Mortgage Loans: Conventional:
Many lenders will use either or both of the following two ratios:

Monthly Housing Expense Ratio:

PITI = Principal, Interest, Taxes, and Insurance
PITI ÷ Monthly Gross Income = 28 percent or less

Total (Monthly) Fixed Obligations Ratio:

PITI + Total Monthly Obligations ÷ Monthly Gross Income = 36 percent or less

15. Mortgage Loans: Nonconventional/FHA Insured:
Buyer must meet the following two ratios

Monthly Housing Expense Ratio:

PITI ÷ Monthly Gross Income = 31 percent or less

Total (Monthly) Fixed Obligations Ratio:

PITI + Total Monthly Obligations ÷ Monthly Gross Income = 43 percent or less

16. Yield Calculation:
Loan Discount or Points:
The purpose is to increase the lender's yield on the money loaned through prepaid interest. Discount points may also be used to buydown the interest rate using the following rule of thumb: 1 point = 1/8 percent of loan amount on a 25–30 year loan.

17. Measures and Definitions:

Check: A square parcel of land consisting of 24 miles on each side. It is used as a correction for the earth's curvature. A check contains 576 square miles that includes:

- 16 townships
- 576 sections
- 368,640 acres

Township: A square tract of land whose sides measure 6 miles each; and contain 36 sections of land each being one square mile.

Section: A square tract of land whose sides measure 1 mile each.

Acres in a section: 640 acres of land

Acres in a ¼ section: 160 acres of land

Acres in a ¼ of a ¼ section: 40 acres of land

Acres in a ¼ of a ¼ of a ¼ section: 10 acres of land

Acres in a ¼ of a ¼ of a ¼ of a ¼ section: 2.5 acres of land

Acre: 43,560 square feet.

Mile: 5,280 linear feet.

Leverage: Is the use of borrowed funds.

Loan Constant: Is the percentage of the initial loan that is repaid in equal monthly or annual installments. The two components that comprise the loan constant include:

1. Interest (discount rate)

2. Principal reduction (sinking fund factor)

The sinking fund factor provides the lender with a return of a portion of the principal amount originally loaned. Compound interest tables will contain a column entitled "Installment to Amortize $1.00." The numbers contained in this column are:

- Loan constants for different loan terms
- The sum of the discount rate and the sinking fund factor

Before Tax Cash Flow (BTCF): Is the cash return after making annual debt service. The BTCF is expressed in a dollar amount. It is also the cash throw-off or gross spendable income after deducting debt service but before making any income tax payment.

Before Tax Cash Flow = Net Operating Income − Annual Debt Service

Equity Dividend Rate (EDR): Is the ratio of the cash return (BTCF) divided by the investor equity. Equity dividend rate is also expressed in percentage terms.

Answers to Chapter Review Questions

Chapter 1

1. C.	2. D.	3. D.	4. A.	5. C.
6. D.	7. B.	8. A.	9. C.	10. B.
11. C.	12. D.	13. A.	14. D.	15. A.
16. C.	17. D.	18. B.	19. A.	20. D.

Chapter 2

1. C.	2. A.	3. C.	4. D.	5. C.
6. B.	7. D.	8. D.	9. B.	10. C.
11. D.	12. A.	13. A.	14. B.	15. D.
16. C.	17. B.	18. A.	19. B.	20. D.

Chapter 3

1. A.	2. C.	3. A.	4. D.	5. B.
6. D.	7. D.	8. B.	9. A.	10. C.
11. D.	12. A.	13. A.	14. C.	15. D.
16. A.	17. B.	18. D.	19. C.	20. A.

Chapter 4

1. D.	2. B.	3. C.	4. A.	5. B.
6. D.	7. B.	8. C.	9. D.	10. A.
11. C.	12. C.	13. D.	14. B.	15. D.
16. C.	17. D.	18. B.	19. B.	20. B.

Chapter 5

1. B.	2. A.	3. D.	4. C.	5. C.
6. C.	7. C.	8. B.	9. D.	10. A.
11. B.	12. A.	13. D.	14. D.	15. C.
16. D.	17. B.	18. C.	19. A.	20. C.
21. B.				

Chapter 6

1. D.	2. B.	3. C.	4. C.	5. C.
6. C.	7. D.	8. B.	9. D.	10. B.
11. D.	12. C.	13. A.	14. C.	15. B.
16. D.	17. D.	18. B.	19. D.	

Chapter 7

1. C.	2. D.	3. A.	4. D.	5. C.
6. A.	7. C.	8. B.	9. D.	10. C.
11. B.	12. A.	13. B.	14. A.	15. C.
16. B.	17. D.	18. D.	19. B.	20. D.
21. A.				

Chapter 8

1. C.	2. D.	3. C.	4. B.	5. C.
6. A.	7. A.	8. C.	9. A.	10. B.
11. D.	12. C.	13. A.	14. D.	15. B.
16. D.	17. C.	18. D.		

Chapter 9

1. C.	2. C.	3. C.	4. A.	5. D.
6. B.	7. D.	8. A.	9. B.	10. A.
11. D.	12. B.	13. B.	14. C.	15. A.
16. A.	17. C.	18. C.	19. A.	20. A.

Chapter 10

1. A.	2. B.	3. D.	4. B.	5. D.
6. A.	7. C.	8. C.	9. C.	10. A.
11. D.	12. C.	13. D.	14. C.	15. D.
16. C.	17. B.	18. A.	19. C.	20. A.

Chapter 11

1. D.	2. A.	3. C.	4. D.	5. C.
6. B.	7. D.	8. A.	9. D.	10. D.
11. B.	12. A.	13. C.	14. D.	15. A.
16. D.	17. C.	18. A.	19. D.	20. B.
21. D.				

Chapter 12

1. C.	2. B.	3. A.	4. D.	5. C.
6. B.	7. B.	8. A.	9. D.	10. A.
11. C.	12. C.	13. B.	14. D.	15. A.
16. C.	17. B.	18. D.	19. C.	20. A.

Chapter 13

1. B.	2. B.	3. B.	4. B.	5. C.
6. A.	7. C.	8. C.	9. A.	10. B.
11. C.	12. B.	13. C.	14. A.	15. D.
16. D.	17. B.	18. A.		

Chapter 14

1. D.	2. C.	3. A.	4. A.	5. B.
6. C.	7. A.	8. A.	9. C.	10. D.
11. C.	12. C.	13. D.	14. D.	15. D.
16. D.	17. B.	18. B.	19. C.	20. D.

Chapter 15

1. C.	2. C.	3. D.	4. B.	5. D.
6. A.	7. D.	8. C.	9. B.	10. B.
11. A.	12. D.	13. C.	14. C.	15. B.
16. B.	17. C.	18. D.	19. D.	

Chapter 16

1. B.	2. D.	3. A.	4. C.	5. B.
6. D.	7. A.	8. B.	9. A.	10. C.
11. D.	12. C.	13. D.	14. A.	15. C.
16. B.	17. D.	18. D.	19. A.	

Chapter 17

1. C.	2. B.	3. D.	4. A.	5. D.
6. C.	7. C.	8. A.	9. C.	10. B.
11. A.	12. B.	13. C.	14. B.	15. C.
16. C.	17. D.	18. B.	19. C.	20. B.

Chapter 18

1. D.	2. A.	3. C.	4. B.	5. B.
6. A.	7. C.	8. D.	9. D.	10. B.
11. C.	12. D.	13. D.	14. B.	15. D.
16. B.	17. C.	18. D.	19. C.	20. D.
21. B.	22. C.			

Chapter 19

1. D.	2. A.	3. B.	4. A.	5. B.
6. C.	7. D.	8. D.	9. D.	10. D.
11. D.	12. C.	13. B.	14. C.	15. D.
16. D.	17. B.	18. A.	19. A.	20. D.

Chapter 20

1. C.	2. B.	3. A.	4. B.	5. C.
6. C.	7. C.	8. D.	9. A.	10. B.
11. B.	12. A.	13. B.	14. B.	15. A.
16. B.	17. A.	18. B.	19. A.	20. C.

Practice End-of-Course Exam

The following practice exam includes 100 multiple-choice questions that cover key topics from chapters in this textbook. After reading each question, select the most accurate response. You may use the answer sheet provided at the end of this exam to indicate your answers.

QUESTIONS

1. The Neighbors listed their home with Acme Realty and were given a single agent brokerage notice. Paul Neighbor doesn't want people knocking on his door unannounced and asked that no company yard sign be placed in the front yard. In this situation:

   A. A listing gives the company a legal right to install the sign, so the sign can be placed in the yard.

   B. The agent should explain the importance of the yard sign to Paul, and then install it.

   C. The agent should talk to Paul about the sign. If Paul won't change his mind, the company must obey or withdraw from the listing.

   D. Acme Realty must give Paul the no brokerage relationship notice and continue with the listing procedures.

2. Millie qualified for homestead on her residence in Clearwater, Florida. Millie is 78 years of age and is permanently disabled. Her husband, Gary, is deceased. What is Millie's cumulative tax exemption on her residence?

   A. $25,000

   B. $25,500

   C. $26,000

   D. $30,500

3. Linda, the only broker for her firm, had her license temporarily suspended. What will happen to the licenses of the associates who are registered to work under Linda?

   A. The licenses will be cancelled.

   B. The licenses will be placed in involuntary inactive status.

   C. The licenses of the associates will not be affected.

   D. The licenses will be temporarily suspended with Linda's.

4. When Linda's real estate license is suspended, according to Florida law, her license becomes:

   A. Ineffective.

   B. Cancelled.

   C. Involuntary inactive.

   D. Null and void.

5. Broker George prepared a comparative market analysis for a neighbor and charged the neighbor for the service.

   A. It is illegal to charge for a CMA.

   B. George must have an appraisal license.

   C. This was legal if the CMA followed the Uniform Standards of Professional Appraisal Practice.

   D. George's action was legal.

6. Susan asked her friend, Nell, to appraise her home. Nell works as a sales associate for Broker Jones.

   A. Nell must follow the Uniform Standards of Professional Appraisal Practice (USPAP).

   B. Only brokers can perform appraisals without an appraisal license.

   C. Nell can't do this unless she is a licensed appraiser.

   D. Nell can complete the appraisal, but cannot charge for the service.

7. A licensed attorney who lives in Alabama sent a client to a broker in Pensacola when the client wanted to purchase a Florida home. The broker was appreciative of the referral and sent the attorney a very nice gift.

   A. The broker didn't share the commission, so this is legal.

   B. This is legal because the gift went to an attorney.

   C. The broker violated Florida real estate laws.

   D. It would have been legal if the attorney practiced in Florida.

8. A developer gave some land in the subdivision to the city for use as a children's playground. This action was a(n):

   A. Dedication.

   B. Accommodation.

   C. Follow-up.

   D. Legal requirement.

9. In order to apply for a real estate license in Florida, an applicant:

   A. Must declare residency in Florida.

   B. Has to be a U.S. citizen.

   C. Cannot have an active license in another state.

   D. Must disclose any juvenile encounter with the law.

10. Luann owns two time-shares that she seldom uses, so she advertised them in the classified ads in the *Miami Herald*.

   A. Time-shares are not real property, so no license is required.

   B. Luann doesn't need a license to do this.

   C. The time-shares must be sold through a real estate company.

   D. Time-shares are real property, so a license is required.

11. Cletus qualified for his sales associate license last year. Now he wants to open a real estate company. This requires a broker license. Which of the following statements is true?

   A. Cletus cannot apply to be a broker until his initial license has been renewed.

   B. Cletus must successfully complete the 45-hour post license course before he can apply to be a broker.

   C. Anyone can apply to be a broker at any time.

   D. When Cletus completes a minimum number of transactions, his application will be considered.

12. Buzz let his third real estate license expire 14 months ago, and now Buzz regrets letting the license expire. How can he remedy this?

    A. Buzz must take FREC Course I.

    B. Buzz can pay a late fee and a renewal fee to regain his license.

    C. If Buzz takes a 14-hour continuing education class, he can renew the license.

    D. After he completes a 28-hour FREC-approved course, Buzz can reactivate the license.

13. A transaction broker must provide which of the following duties?

    A. Loyalty

    B. Limited confidentiality

    C. Full disclosure

    D. Obedience to all lawful instructions

14. A buyer received a no brokerage relationship notice from a firm. What duties are owed to the buyer?

    A. Skill care and diligence

    B. Limited confidentiality

    C. Disclosure of all material facts

    D. Obedience

15. Recently, the Florida Real Estate Commission changed two of the administrative rules. Their power to do this comes from their:

    A. Executive powers.

    B. Quasi-legislative duties.

    C. Quasi-judicial powers.

    D. Composite powers.

16. Mary changed her residence from Kenneth City to Largo, but she still works out of her employing broker's office in Pinellas Park.

    A. There is no paperwork required in this situation.

    B. Mary has 60 days to sign the irrevocable consent to service.

    C. The DBPR must be notified of address changes before 10 days pass.

    D. Mary must reregister her employing broker with her new address.

17. The seven persons who serve on the Florida Real Estate Commission:

    A. Are employed by the Division of Real Estate.

    B. Receive $50 per day when on Commission business.

    C. Are appointed by the secretary of the DBPR.

    D. Must have brokers' licenses.

18. Frank serves as the broker of record for two different real estate companies. Frank:

    A. Has multiple licenses.

    B. Has a group license.

    C. Has violated F.S. 475.

    D. Can operate only one business in Florida.

19. Shirley operates her brokerage business out of her home.

    A. An office sign is not required for a home office.

    B. An exterior office sign is required.

    C. Shirley's name must be on an office sign.

    D. Shirley can't operate a business out of her home.

20. Broker associate Jeremy received a check from a buyer after 2 p.m. on Friday as a deposit to be included with an offer. The broker's normal banking day is Monday, but Monday is a legal holiday. However, banks will be open until noon on Saturday. What is true about the deposit?

   A. Jeremy must deposit the check on Saturday before the banks close.

   B. Jeremy must give the check to the broker before the end of Monday.

   C. The deposit must be turned over to the broker and out of Jeremy's hands before the end of Tuesday.

   D. Jeremy has until Wednesday to hand over the check to the broker.

21. The broker places all escrow deposits in an interest-bearing account, and transfers the earned interest into his operating account every 2 weeks. What is true about this situation?

   A. Any interest from an escrow account must be distributed to the buyer and seller.

   B. The broker's action is legal if the buyer and seller agreed in writing.

   C. Escrow accounts cannot be interest-bearing accounts.

   D. Only the seller can receive the interest from an escrow account.

22. The broker for Homes Realty Company keeps around $2,000 in the escrow account to pay for the bank charges on the account.

   A. This is legal if the escrow records are current and accurate.

   B. Only the broker can sign checks on the account.

   C. Escrow records must be kept for 4 years.

   D. The broker is guilty of commingling.

23. A broker gives all binder deposits to a Florida attorney to hold. On a recent transaction, the buyer and seller are not going to close and both parties are claiming the buyer's deposit.

   A. The escrow dispute makes no legal demands on the broker.

   B. The broker must notify FREC of the dispute before 30 business days pass.

   C. The broker must notify FREC of the dispute before 15 business days pass.

   D. The broker can return the money to the buyer.

24. One of the settlement procedures available to a broker in an escrow dispute would be hiring a third party to recommend a solution. This procedure is called:

   A. Arbitration.

   B. Mediation.

   C. An escrow disbursement order.

   D. Litigation.

25. Which of these activities requires a real estate license?

   A. Joe works for a motel and receives 10 percent of the room rent for every room he rents after 9 p.m.

   B. Sarah is paid a salary by the condo association for renting vacant condos to vacationers for up to 6-month periods.

   C. Ben leases interests in local businesses to out-of-state investors.

   D. Steele was paid handsomely for helping sell a radio station.

26. Jill purchased a list of rentals, but immediately decided to live with her cousin instead. She asked for a refund, but the realty company that sold her the list refused because the no-refund policy was clearly stated.

   A. Jill has no legal recourse. She should have read the company policy.

   B. The company must refund 100 percent of the fee charged to Jill.

    C. Refusing to refund the fee is a second-degree misdemeanor.

    D. The realty company can be subject to civil and criminal actions and can be punished administratively by FREC.

27. In a real estate partnership, the only partner with a broker license died. In this circumstance:

    A. The partnership must appoint a new broker before 14 calendar days pass.

    B. The partnership is dissolved and must be reformed.

    C. The partnership's registration is automatically cancelled.

    D. There's no legal requirement for a general partner to be an active broker.

28. Broker June is going to open a new real estate business as a sole proprietorship. She's chosen the name Good Deal Realty as the business name. June:

    A. Must advertise that she is doing business as Good Deal Realty.

    B. Must register the business name with FREC.

    C. Must file her business plan with the Florida Department of State.

    D. Cannot use a trade name for a sole proprietorship.

29. A seller is refusing to pay a broker a legally owed commission. The broker can:

    A. Ask for an escrow disbursement order.

    B. Place a lien on the seller's property.

    C. Withhold the escrow deposit until the seller pays the commission.

    D. File a lawsuit in a civil court.

30. One difference between a general partnership and a limited partnership is:

    A. A limited partnership can't be a real estate business.

    B. Limited partners can participate in the business.

    C. Limited partners cannot hold a real estate license.

    D. Limited partners can be associates.

31. Following a formal complaint, an agreement reciting the punishment is entered into between a licensee and DRE attorneys. This agreement is called a:

    A. Final order.

    B. Stipulation.

    C. Probable cause determination.

    D. Writ of supersedeas.

32. In the seven-step complaint process, the person who issues a summary suspension is the:

    A. Florida real estate chair.

    B. Administrative law judge.

    C. Secretary of the DBPR.

    D. Appeals court judge.

33. A complaint filed against a licensee must:

    A. Be in writing.

    B. Not be anonymous.

    C. Involve Florida real estate laws.

    D. Have occurred in Florida.

34. As a result of a visit from a Division of Real Estate auditor, Sure Fire Realty received a citation. The broker is sure the citation is an error. How can she remedy this?

    A. She has 30 days to request an informal hearing.

    B. The citation must be paid, and then can be disputed.

    C. She has 30 days to report the error to the DBPR.

    D. She must dispute the citation in writing within 30 days.

35. A broker followed an escrow disbursement order and gave the escrow funds to the seller as ordered. The buyer then successfully sued the broker in a civil court and was granted a monetary judgment. Because of the legal entanglement, and a judgment against the broker, what will happen to the broker's license?

    A. The license will be automatically suspended.

    B. The license may be revoked.

    C. No action will be taken against the broker.

    D. The DBPR will initiate an investigation.

36. Five people were damaged in a land investment scam. The broker who was responsible for the damages had an active license at the time. Each of the five was awarded $100,000 by the courts, but the broker can't pay the judgments. How much can these persons collect from the Real Estate Recovery Fund?

    A. FREC will not award any payments in this case.

    B. Each person can collect $50,000 from the Real Estate Recovery Fund.

    C. They will have to split $50,000.

    D. The payout from the fund will be limited to $150,000.

37. The money held in the Real Estate Recovery Fund originates from:

    A. Administrative fines collected from licensees.

    B. A trust that is funded by the legislature.

    C. Money set aside from the DRE's budget.

    D. Fees added to the issuing of licenses.

38. Which of the following is a protected class under the federal Fair Housing Act?

    A. Age

    B. Religion

    C. Marital status

    D. Receipt of income from public-assistance programs

39. When a prospective buyer applies for a loan with a lender for the purchase of a new home, the law that states lenders must give the borrower a good faith estimate of closing costs is the:

    A. Real Estate Settlement Procedures Act.

    B. Consumer Credit Protection Act (Truth in Lending).

    C. Equal Credit Opportunity Act.

    D. Sherman and Clayton Fair Trade Acts.

40. A small portion of a lot fell into a bordering stream and was carried away by the rising waters. The loss of the land is termed:

    A. Accretion.

    B. Alluvion.

    C. Erosion.

    D. Reliction.

41. The officers and directors of a real estate corporation who are active in the real estate business become licensed:

A. By filing the appropriate paperwork with the Florida Department of State.

B. In the same manner as other real estate licensee applicants.

C. Automatically through the licensing and registration of the corporation.

D. By being appointed or elected to the corporation's board of directors.

42. Ann left her farm to her cousin for as long as her uncle lives; when the uncle dies, Ann's son will own it. Ann's son now has a:

A. Reversionary estate.

B. Remainder estate.

C. Life estate.

D. Joint estate.

43. The seller removed a corner bookcase before the closing papers were signed. The wall is damaged where the bookcase was removed, and the floor is a different color where the bookcase stood. Courts would likely rule the bookcase:

A. Was personal property and belonged to the seller.

B. Could be removed because it wasn't mentioned in the contract.

C. Was a fixture because it was adapted to fit in a corner.

D. Was a fixture because it left damage when it was moved.

44. Dan and Jack combined their assets to buy some property together. Dan put up less money and only has a one-third share. According to these facts, the property is owned as a:

A. Joint tenancy.

B. Tenancy by the entirety.

C. Tenancy in common.

D. Holdover estate.

45. Cooperatives, a form of residential ownership organized as a corporation, are regulated by the:

A. Florida Real Estate Commission.

B. Division of Florida Land Sales, Condominiums, and Mobile Homes.

C. Division of Real Estate.

D. Department of Housing and Urban Development.

46. Minnie is married to Ralph and they live in Minnie's homestead. Minnie has children from a previous marriage, but she has no children with Ralph. If Minnie dies intestate:

A. Her husband, Ralph, will own the homestead.

B. Minnie's children will own the home by descent.

C. Ralph will receive a life estate; the children are vested remaindermen.

D. Minnie's children and Ralph will be tenants in common.

47. Dave signed a contract to purchase a condominium in downtown Tampa from a developer. Unfortunately, Dave immediately regretted the purchase. Which of the following best applies to Dave's situation:

A. Dave has 15 days to cancel the purchase in writing.

B. Dave must cancel the purchase before three business days pass.

C. A signed contract is legally binding.

D. Dave can cancel, but must forfeit his binder deposit.

48. What governmental power is used to take private property when it is needed for a public purpose?

    A. Police power

    B. Eminent domain

    C. Adverse possession

    D. Constructive notice

49. Bobby's land is being taken for a new extension to the highway and he doesn't want to give the land up. Bobby:

    A. Can go to court to sue over the taking.

    B. Can file an injunction to stop the taking.

    C. Has no recourse or options available.

    D. Can sue in court over the price he is being paid.

50. A valid deed:

    A. Must be signed by a competent grantee and grantor.

    B. Is signed by a competent grantor and two witnesses.

    C. Must be recorded to be legal.

    D. Must be notarized.

51. A deed that contains no warranties whatsoever, not even a claim of ownership, is a:

    A. Quitclaim deed.

    B. Bargain and sale deed.

    C. Special warranty deed.

    D. General warranty deed.

52. Which section is due east of Section 14, T2N, R3W?

    A. Section 13

    B. Section 15

    C. Section 16

    D. Section 11

53. Which legal description contains 2.5 acres?

    A. The SW ¼ of the SE ½ and the NE ¼ of the NW ¼ of Section 8

    B. The SW ¼ of the SE ¼ of the NE ¼ of the NW ¼ of Section 6

    C. The SW ¼ of the SW ¼ of the SW ¼ of Section 36

    D. The N ½ of the SW ¼ of the SW ¼ of the NE ¼ of Section 4

54. What is the most critical feature of a metes and bounds legal description?

    A. The accurate description of a corner monument

    B. Accuracy of the "calls"

    C. An accurate point of beginning

    D. Understanding compass directions

55. The law that requires any contract that conveys a part or whole interest in real property to be considered enforceable must be in writing is the:

    A. Statute of Frauds.

    B. Statute of Limitations.

    C. Florida Statute 475.

    D. Chapter 61J2, FAC.

56. Which of these contracts is an exception to the statute of frauds?

    A. A listing agreement for more than one year

    B. An option contract

    C. A sale contract

    D. A listing agreement for one year or less

57. The statute of limitations for a parol contract is:

    A. 3 years.

    B. 4 years.

    C. 5 years.

    D. 10 years.

58. Once a seller has signed a listing contract, law requires:

    A. The listing must be placed in the multiple-listing service before five business days pass.

    B. The seller must be given a copy of the listing before 24 hours pass.

    C. The broker is due a commission regardless of who sells the property.

    D. The broker must accept any offer that conforms to the listing agreement.

59. Four real estate companies have a listing from the seller. This listing is a(n):

    A. Exclusive agency listing.

    B. Exclusive right of sale listing.

    C. Open listing.

    D. Net listing.

60. Before the showing of a home that was built in the 1960s, the prospective buyers:

    A. Must sign the lead-based paint disclosure.

    B. Must have the property inspected for lead-based paint.

    C. Must receive an EPA pamphlet describing the dangers of lead in paint.

    D. Must receive the required inspection report from the sellers.

61. Which of the following is a requirement for a legal contract?

    A. Signatures of both parties

    B. Mutual assent

    C. Receipt of a binder deposit

    D. Acknowledgment

62. In a lien theory state:

    A. The mortgagor holds title while the mortgagee holds a lien.

    B. The mortgagee holds the title.

    C. The mortgage is the legal evidence of the debt.

    D. The mortgage creates a contract for deed.

63. In an adjustable-rate mortgage, the portion of the interest rate that represents the lender's expenses and profit is termed:

    A. The index.

    B. The rate cap.

    C. The annual percentage rate (APR).

    D. The margin.

64. In a level-payment fixed-rate mortgage:

   A. The portion of the payment that pays interest never changes.

   B. The portion of the payment that amortizes the loan gradually decreases with each payment.

   C. The portion of the payment that pays principal gradually increases with each payment.

   D. The portion of the payment that pays interest gradually increases with each payment.

65. According to the Department of Veteran Affairs, a VA loan:

   A. Is not a government-insured loan.

   B. Requires a minimum 3 percent cash investment.

   C. Can be a direct loan from the VA.

   D. Is only available for veterans.

66. In order to qualify for an FHA loan:

   A. The housing expense ratio cannot exceed 29 percent.

   B. The interest rate cannot exceed 7 percent.

   C. The borrower must obtain a certificate of eligibility.

   D. The borrower must pay a one-time upfront insurance premium.

67. The action by the Federal Reserve System to influence the cost of money in the economy and the amount of money available is the:

   A. Open-market operations.

   B. Discount rate.

   C. Monetary policy.

   D. Discount rate.

68. When the Federal Reserve purchases U.S. Treasury securities:

   A. The supply of money increases.

   B. The supply of money decreases.

   C. Interest rates increase.

   D. The cost of money is unchanged.

69. When a title company prepares a HUD-1 Uniform Settlement Statement, the unpaid property taxes:

   A. Are charged to the seller only.

   B. Appear as a credit to the seller and a debit to the buyer.

   C. Appear as a debit to the seller and a credit to the buyer.

   D. Are charged to the buyer only.

70. How is the binder deposit entered on the closing statement?

   A. Debit the seller and the credit buyer

   B. Credit the seller and debit the buyer

   C. Debit to the buyer only

   D. Credit to the buyer only

71. In any exchange of property ownership in Florida, the documentary stamp tax on the deed:

   A. Is paid annually to the state.

   B. Is based on the entire purchase price.

   C. Is always charged to the buyer.

   D. Depends on the financing terms.

72. A buyer paid $200,000 for a house. The $200,000 is the property's:

   A. Cost.

   B. Price.

   C. Value.

   D. Assessment.

73. The majority of savings associations and thrift institutions are regulated by:

   A. The Federal Reserve System.

   B. The Office of Thrift Supervision.

   C. Individual states.

   D. The Government National Mortgage Association.

74. A lender charged 6.5 percent interest plus 6 points for a conventional 30 year loan. What is the approximate yield on the loan?

   A. 6.75 percent

   B. 7 percent

   C. 7.25 percent

   D. 7.50 percent

75. All three approaches to estimating value of real property utilize:

   A. Assemblage.

   B. The principle of substitution.

   C. The principle of conformity.

   D. The law of diminishing returns.

76. Which of the following variables below is subtracted to derive the net operating income?

   A. Other income

   B. Property tax

   C. Mortgage payment

   D. IRS tax

77. An appraiser estimated that the pool Jude paid $40,000 to install increased the value to Jude's home by approximately $25,000. This is an example of:

   A. External obsolescence.

   B. An over-improvement.

   C. Functional obsolescence.

   D. Straight-line depreciation.

78. When estimating the value of property, the cost depreciation approach to value:

   A. Uses the law of increasing and diminishing returns.

   B. Relies on the principle of anticipation.

   C. Never depreciates land.

   D. Adjustments are made to the comparable properties.

79. The approach to value most relevant to estimating the value of a vacant lot in a subdivision is usually the:

   A. Sales comparison approach.

   B. Cost depreciation approach.

   C. Income capitalization approach.

   D. Straight-line approach.

80. You live in a semitropical climate zone and you read that adding insulation to the attic will reduce the electric bill. What part of the government would you look to when deciding the insulation R values recommended for your locale?

    A. Florida Department of Agriculture and Consumer Services

    B. The Department of Energy

    C. Local Code Enforcement Agency

    D. Environmental Protection Agency

81. A window type that swings out to open is a:

    A. Fixed window.

    B. Jalousie window.

    C. Hopper window.

    D. Casement window.

82. Which expense can a homeowner deduct when calculating taxable income?

    A. Maintenance costs for the home

    B. Repairs to the roof

    C. Mortgage interest paid on a second home

    D. Property insurance on a principal residence

83. Joseph has experienced a hardship due to zoning requirements on his residential lot. He can go to the zoning board of adjustment and request a:

    A. Special exception.

    B. Variance.

    C. Zoning change for his lot.

    D. Permit for a nonconforming use.

84. An appraiser adjusts the value of a property because of traffic noise from a nearby street. This is an example of:

    A. Physical deterioration.

    B. Functional obsolescence.

    C. The principle of anticipation.

    D. External obsolescence.

85. Which of the following is an advantage of investing in real property?

    A. A local market

    B. Liquidity

    C. Leverage

    D. Risk

86. A type of investment in real property that is organized like a mutual fund and offers liquidity to the investor is a(n):

    A. Ostensible partnership.

    B. Joint venture.

    C. Limited liability partnership.

    D. Real estate investment trust.

87. When examining an economic base study, an example of an area service industry would be a:

    A. Citrus sorting facility.

    B. Branch bank.

    C. Film project.

    D. Tomato packing plant.

88. A corner grocery store was the legal use of a lot. The city changed the zoning to residential. What is true in this situation?

   A. The lot's use must be changed.

   B. The store's owner can ask for a variance.

   C. The grocery store is a nonconforming use.

   D. The store's owner must be compensated.

89. The portion of Florida's Growth Management Act that requires that electricity and drinking water must be available before a building permit can be issued is the:

   A. Concurrency provision.

   B. Infrastructure provision.

   C. Comprehensive plan.

   D. Zoning requirement.

90. Members of the local planning commission generally:

   A. Are elected by the local communities.

   B. Serve for a term of 4 years.

   C. Cannot serve more than two consecutive terms.

   D. Are appointed, unpaid community members.

91. The Smiths signed a contract to purchase a home for $72,500. They gave the broker a $7,500 deposit that the broker is holding in escrow. They are assuming a mortgage for $59,760. The sellers will take back a new second mortgage for $3,640. Calculate the taxes to the state on this transaction.

   A. $733.53

   B. $736.33

   C. $736.68

   D. $737.03

92. An investor is analyzing a property with an effective gross income of $850,000 and the operating expenses, including reserves for replacements of $112,000, add up to $530,000. Capitalization rates for competing similar properties are 12 percent. What should the investor pay for the property?

   A. $1,733,334

   B. $2,666,667

   C. $4,416,667

   D. $7,416,667

93. A duplex is scheduled to close on April 12. The seller collected the rent for April on the first of the month amounting to $525 per unit. According to the sale contract, the buyer is due the rental income for the day of closing. Calculate the proration.

   A. $385 debit to the seller; $385 credit to the buyer.

   B. $665 debit to the seller; $665 credit to the buyer.

   C. $385 credit to the seller, $385 debit to the buyer.

   D. $665 credit to the seller, $665 debit to the buyer.

94. The owners sold their home for $234,300, which gave them a 10 percent profit over their original cost. What did they originally pay for the home?

   A. $195,250

   B. $208,527

   C. $210,870

   D. $213,000

95. An investor purchased an apartment complex for $320,000. There are ten units that rent for $750 monthly. Land represents 20 percent of the value. Calculate the annual depreciation. Round to the nearest dollar.

    A. $90,000

    B. $11,635

    C. $9,309

    D. $6,564

96. The seller agreed to pay a 6 percent commission to the listing broker. The broker will split the commission at 50 percent with a cooperating broker. The listing sales associate gets 70 percent of her broker's share; the selling sales associate gets 30 percent of her broker's share. What was the size of the check of the sales associate who sold the property for $146,000?

    A. $1,314

    B. $2,628

    C. $3,066

    D. $8,760

97. A building purchased 5 years ago was valued at $270,000. The useful economic life of the building is 25 years. Use the straight-line method of depreciation to calculate the building's current depreciated value.

    A. $54,000

    B. $67,500

    C. $202,500

    D. $216,000

98. Van has qualified for a homestead exemption. The city tax rate is 9.6 mills; the county tax rate is 8.5 mills; the school board tax rate is 8.4 mills. The assessed value of Van's home is $285,500. How much will Van save as a result of declaring homestead?

    A. $7,565.75

    B. $1,250.25

    C. $662.50

    D. $65.00

99. A developer purchased four 120-foot lots for $48,000 each and divided them into six lots of equal front footage. The developer sold the lots for $500 per front foot. Calculate the developer's percent of profit.

    A. 9 percent

    B. 10.2 percent

    C. 15.5 percent

    D. 25 percent

100. In order to obtain a new mortgage loan of $62,000, a buyer agreed to pay all of the state transfer taxes on the new loan. Calculate the tax owed to the state.

    A. $124

    B. $216

    C. $341

    D. $434

PRACTICE EXAM

Score: _____

Wrong Ways to mark answers:

RIGHT WAY to mark answers:
●

1 Ⓐ Ⓑ Ⓒ Ⓓ   21 Ⓐ Ⓑ Ⓒ Ⓓ   41 Ⓐ Ⓑ Ⓒ Ⓓ   61 Ⓐ Ⓑ Ⓒ Ⓓ   81 Ⓐ Ⓑ Ⓒ Ⓓ

2 Ⓐ Ⓑ Ⓒ Ⓓ   22 Ⓐ Ⓑ Ⓒ Ⓓ   42 Ⓐ Ⓑ Ⓒ Ⓓ   62 Ⓐ Ⓑ Ⓒ Ⓓ   82 Ⓐ Ⓑ Ⓒ Ⓓ

3 Ⓐ Ⓑ Ⓒ Ⓓ   23 Ⓐ Ⓑ Ⓒ Ⓓ   43 Ⓐ Ⓑ Ⓒ Ⓓ   63 Ⓐ Ⓑ Ⓒ Ⓓ   83 Ⓐ Ⓑ Ⓒ Ⓓ

4 Ⓐ Ⓑ Ⓒ Ⓓ   24 Ⓐ Ⓑ Ⓒ Ⓓ   44 Ⓐ Ⓑ Ⓒ Ⓓ   64 Ⓐ Ⓑ Ⓒ Ⓓ   84 Ⓐ Ⓑ Ⓒ Ⓓ

5 Ⓐ Ⓑ Ⓒ Ⓓ   25 Ⓐ Ⓑ Ⓒ Ⓓ   45 Ⓐ Ⓑ Ⓒ Ⓓ   65 Ⓐ Ⓑ Ⓒ Ⓓ   85 Ⓐ Ⓑ Ⓒ Ⓓ

6 Ⓐ Ⓑ Ⓒ Ⓓ   26 Ⓐ Ⓑ Ⓒ Ⓓ   46 Ⓐ Ⓑ Ⓒ Ⓓ   66 Ⓐ Ⓑ Ⓒ Ⓓ   86 Ⓐ Ⓑ Ⓒ Ⓓ

7 Ⓐ Ⓑ Ⓒ Ⓓ   27 Ⓐ Ⓑ Ⓒ Ⓓ   47 Ⓐ Ⓑ Ⓒ Ⓓ   67 Ⓐ Ⓑ Ⓒ Ⓓ   87 Ⓐ Ⓑ Ⓒ Ⓓ

8 Ⓐ Ⓑ Ⓒ Ⓓ   28 Ⓐ Ⓑ Ⓒ Ⓓ   48 Ⓐ Ⓑ Ⓒ Ⓓ   68 Ⓐ Ⓑ Ⓒ Ⓓ   88 Ⓐ Ⓑ Ⓒ Ⓓ

9 Ⓐ Ⓑ Ⓒ Ⓓ   29 Ⓐ Ⓑ Ⓒ Ⓓ   49 Ⓐ Ⓑ Ⓒ Ⓓ   69 Ⓐ Ⓑ Ⓒ Ⓓ   89 Ⓐ Ⓑ Ⓒ Ⓓ

10 Ⓐ Ⓑ Ⓒ Ⓓ   30 Ⓐ Ⓑ Ⓒ Ⓓ   50 Ⓐ Ⓑ Ⓒ Ⓓ   70 Ⓐ Ⓑ Ⓒ Ⓓ   90 Ⓐ Ⓑ Ⓒ Ⓓ

11 Ⓐ Ⓑ Ⓒ Ⓓ   31 Ⓐ Ⓑ Ⓒ Ⓓ   51 Ⓐ Ⓑ Ⓒ Ⓓ   71 Ⓐ Ⓑ Ⓒ Ⓓ   91 Ⓐ Ⓑ Ⓒ Ⓓ

12 Ⓐ Ⓑ Ⓒ Ⓓ   32 Ⓐ Ⓑ Ⓒ Ⓓ   52 Ⓐ Ⓑ Ⓒ Ⓓ   72 Ⓐ Ⓑ Ⓒ Ⓓ   92 Ⓐ Ⓑ Ⓒ Ⓓ

13 Ⓐ Ⓑ Ⓒ Ⓓ   33 Ⓐ Ⓑ Ⓒ Ⓓ   53 Ⓐ Ⓑ Ⓒ Ⓓ   73 Ⓐ Ⓑ Ⓒ Ⓓ   93 Ⓐ Ⓑ Ⓒ Ⓓ

14 Ⓐ Ⓑ Ⓒ Ⓓ   34 Ⓐ Ⓑ Ⓒ Ⓓ   54 Ⓐ Ⓑ Ⓒ Ⓓ   74 Ⓐ Ⓑ Ⓒ Ⓓ   94 Ⓐ Ⓑ Ⓒ Ⓓ

15 Ⓐ Ⓑ Ⓒ Ⓓ   35 Ⓐ Ⓑ Ⓒ Ⓓ   55 Ⓐ Ⓑ Ⓒ Ⓓ   75 Ⓐ Ⓑ Ⓒ Ⓓ   95 Ⓐ Ⓑ Ⓒ Ⓓ

16 Ⓐ Ⓑ Ⓒ Ⓓ   36 Ⓐ Ⓑ Ⓒ Ⓓ   56 Ⓐ Ⓑ Ⓒ Ⓓ   76 Ⓐ Ⓑ Ⓒ Ⓓ   96 Ⓐ Ⓑ Ⓒ Ⓓ

17 Ⓐ Ⓑ Ⓒ Ⓓ   37 Ⓐ Ⓑ Ⓒ Ⓓ   57 Ⓐ Ⓑ Ⓒ Ⓓ   77 Ⓐ Ⓑ Ⓒ Ⓓ   97 Ⓐ Ⓑ Ⓒ Ⓓ

18 Ⓐ Ⓑ Ⓒ Ⓓ   38 Ⓐ Ⓑ Ⓒ Ⓓ   58 Ⓐ Ⓑ Ⓒ Ⓓ   78 Ⓐ Ⓑ Ⓒ Ⓓ   98 Ⓐ Ⓑ Ⓒ Ⓓ

19 Ⓐ Ⓑ Ⓒ Ⓓ   39 Ⓐ Ⓑ Ⓒ Ⓓ   59 Ⓐ Ⓑ Ⓒ Ⓓ   79 Ⓐ Ⓑ Ⓒ Ⓓ   99 Ⓐ Ⓑ Ⓒ Ⓓ

20 Ⓐ Ⓑ Ⓒ Ⓓ   40 Ⓐ Ⓑ Ⓒ Ⓓ   60 Ⓐ Ⓑ Ⓒ Ⓓ   80 Ⓐ Ⓑ Ⓒ Ⓓ   100 Ⓐ Ⓑ Ⓒ Ⓓ

Answers to End-of-Course Exam

1. C. A principal's legal instructions must be obeyed. Acme must explain the consequences of having no sign and if Paul won't change the instructions, Acme must obey or withdraw from the listing.

2. C. Add $500 for widow and $500 for nonveteran permanent disability to $25,000. Age doesn't qualify for an exemption unless Millie lives in a low-income household and the city or/and the county has granted additional exemptions for those circumstances.

3. B. When the license of the only broker for a firm is no longer active, the licenses of the associates registered as the broker's employees will be involuntarily inactive.

4. A. A suspended license will become effective after the suspension expires; therefore, a suspended license is ineffective.

5. D. There is nothing in Florida statutes that prevents charging for CMAs.

6. A. Real estate licensees can perform appraisals without an appraisal license, but must know and follow USPAP.

7. C. A licensee cannot compensate any unlicensed person for a referral.

8. A. A gift of land by a private individual to a local government when the land will serve a public purpose is dedication.

9. D. Statements A, B, and C are false. Only the last statement is true. When filling out an application for a real estate license, the applicant must disclose within the application any encounter(s) with the law.

10. B. Time-shares are real property; however a license is not required to sell your own property.

11. B. No sales associate can apply for a broker license unless the 45-hour postlicense class has been completed.

12. D. Any person holding a valid license that has been expired for more than 12 months but less than 24 months can complete a required 28-hour course and reactivate the license.

13. B. Only a transaction broker owes customers limited confidentiality. A single agent broker owes principals the other duties listed.

14. C. From this list, only disclosure of all material facts is owed to customers who have received the no brokerage disclosure notice.

15. B. FREC's power to write rules that become part of Florida statutes (Chapter 61J2) are quasi-legislative powers.

16. C. The DBPR must be informed of any change in a mailing address before 10 days pass.

17. B. Commissioners are appointees, not employees, and receive no salary; they are paid $50 per day plus expenses when on Commission business.

18. A. A broker who serves as the broker for more than one real estate business in Florida holds multiple Florida broker licenses.

19. C. A realty business from your home is legal if the zoning permits this. All offices must display the office sign. It can be an exterior or an interior sign. The sign must include the name of a broker of record for the firm.

20. C. A binder deposit must be out of an associate's hands before the end of the next business day, which would be Tuesday.

21. B. The escrow account can be interest bearing and the broker can keep the interest if the buyer and seller agreed to these actions in writing.

22. D. A broker can place up to $1,000 of personal or other funds in an escrow account to pay for the bank charges. More than $1,000 makes the broker guilty of commingling.

23. A. When a broker gives the escrow deposit to a Florida attorney or a Florida title company to hold, the broker is relieved of any further actions regarding the deposits.

24. B. The procedure described is mediation.

25. C. Joe works for a transient occupancy facility and doesn't need a license. Sarah's salary and the short rental periods are license exemptions. The sales of radio and television stations are exempted from license requirements. Out of this list, only Ben must have a real estate license.

26. D. Violating the laws regarding the selling of rental lists is a first-degree misdemeanor. The required refund was 75 percent of the fee. The action made the company subject to civil, criminal, and administrative punishment.

27. A. When the active broker in a real estate partnership dies, resigns or is terminated, in order to maintain the registration of that partnership they have 14 calendar days to substitute the old party with a new a party possessing an active brokers license.

28. B. Brokers only have to register the trade name with FREC.

29. D. The only option open to a broker in this situation is to sue the seller.

30. D. A limited partnership can be a real estate business in Florida. Limited partners cannot participate in the business, and only contribute money or property. Because of this requirement, associates can be limited partners.

31. B. The question refers to a stipulation— after a formal complaint was issued in the complaint process this is one of the three possible elections available to the licensee.

32. C. A summary, or emergency, suspension is issued by the secretary of the DBPR.

33. A. Anonymous complaints are considered; the complaint need not involve real estate and does not have to be located in Florida. However, the DRE will only consider written complaints.

34. D. A citation can be disputed in writing within 30 days of receipt.

35. C. The broker followed legal procedures, and there will be no action against the license.

36. C. The maximum amount that will be paid from the Real Estate Recovery Fund for one transaction is $50,000.

37. D. The Real Estate Recovery Fund is funded from fees added to the issuing of new and renewed licenses.

38. B. In this list, only religion is a protected status in housing.

39. A. It is the Real Estate Settlement Procedures Act (RESPA).

40. C. A loss of the land mass due to the action of water is termed erosion.

41. C. Everybody must qualify for a license by demonstrating knowledge of real estate laws and fulfilling all application requirements.

42. B. The son is the remainderman and has a remainder estate until the uncle dies, at which time the son will own the farm fee simple.

43. D. Courts have ruled that if damage occurred when an item was removed, the item was a fixture and part of the real property.

44. C. If there are unequal interests in the property, the estate must be a tenancy in common.

45. B. The Division of Florida Land Sales, Condominiums, and Mobile Homes regulates all multiple ownership properties, such as cooperatives.

46. C. Florida law will give a surviving spouse whose name is not on the deed of a homestead a life estate in the property. Any children of Minnie's, whether by Ralph or not, will be vested remaindermen who will own the home when Ralph dies.

47. A. A buyer has 15 days to cancel the purchase of a condo from a developer. The cancellation must be in writing. The law states the buyer's money must be returned.

48. B. Eminent domain gives the government the right to take land from a private owner as long as the land is taken for a public purpose.

49. D. While Bobby can't stop the taking, he can ask for a condemnation hearing to protest the price the government is paying.

50. B. Florida law does not require a deed to be recorded to be legal. Courts have ruled actual notice and constructive notice are equal under the law. Notarization is not a deed requirement; it is a requirement for instruments that are placed in the public records. The grantee never signs. However, the grantor must be competent and two witnesses to the grantor's signature must sign as well.

51. A. The quitclaim deed is the simplest deed and contains no warranties at all.

52. A. When numbering the sections in a township, east is to the right. Section 13 is due east of Section 14.

53. B. A ¼ of a ¼ of a ¼ of a ¼ of a section contains 2.5 acres.

54. C. An accurate point of beginning (POB) is the most critical feature of a metes and bounds legal description. If you don't start in the right place, you will not describe the boundaries.

55. A. The statute of frauds states that in order for a contract that conveys an interest in real property to be enforceable, the contract must be in writing. Of course, there are three exceptions to the statute of frauds.

56. D. One of the three exceptions to the statute of frauds (oral contracts that Florida courts will enforce) is an oral listing agreement for 1 year or less.

57. B. The statute of limitations states that any oral (parol) contract that has not been completed before 4 years pass is null and void.

58. B. Sellers who sign written listings must receive a copy of the listing within 24 hours of the signing.

59. C. When several companies have the listing and the seller has reserved the right to sell the property without paying a commission, this describes an open listing.

60. C. No inspection is required for the presence of lead-based paint in residential sales and leases for properties built before 1978. However, before being shown such a property for sale or lease, prospective buyers or lessees must receive the EPA pamphlet regarding the dangers of lead in paint. The lead-based paint disclosure isn't signed unless the buyers are going to make an offer.

61. B. Only the seller signs option contracts, not both parties; consideration for a contract can be good rather than valuable; acknowledgment (notarization) is not required; but there must be an offer and an acceptance, which is mutual assent.

62. A. The note is the legal evidence of the debt. In a lien theory state such as Florida, the buyer (mortgagor) owns the property and the lender (mortgagee) holds a lien.

63. D. The margin or spread is the percentage added to the index to cover the lender's expenses and any profit on the loan.

64. C. The part of the payment that pays back (amortizes) the loan gradually increases with each payment.

65. C. The VA has the power to make direct loans where lenders for VA loans are not available otherwise. The other statements are false.

66. D. The current housing expense ratio for an FHA loan is 31 percent. The FHA doesn't set interest rates. The FHA loan is a government-insured loan and the borrower must pay an upfront mortgage insurance premium (MIP).

67. C. The Fed's obligation to influence the money supply and the cost of funds is the monetary policy.

68. A. When the Fed buys U.S. Treasury securities, money is released into the economy.

69. C. Unpaid property taxes are entered on the closing statement as a debit to the seller and a credit to the buyer.

70. D. On the closing statement, the binder deposit appears as a credit to the buyer only.

71. B. The documentary stamp tax on the deed is a one-time charge to the state based on the entire purchase price and by custom is charged to the seller.

72. B. The $200,000 is the price paid. Assessment is the value for tax purposes. Cost is how much money it took to create the property. From this information, we can't know what the value is.

73. B. Most savings associations and thrift institutions belong to the Federal Home Loan Bank System and are regulated by the Office of Thrift Supervision.

74. C. Six points will increase the yield to the lender by approximately 6/8 of 1 percent. The fraction 6/8 equals 0.75. Add 0.75 to 6.5 to result in 7.25 percent.

75. B. The principle of substitution is the basis of all three approaches to estimating the value of real property.

76. B. Other income is *added* in the calculation. Mortgage payments and IRS taxes are subtracted after the NOI is calculated. Only the property tax, a part of the operating expenses, is subtracted when calculating the NOI.

77. B. The cost of the pool is $40,000; the value of the pool is $25,000. When an improvement adds less value to the property than the improvement's cost, the result is an over-improvement.

78. C. The cost depreciation approach to value never depreciates the land.

79. A. The vacant lot in a subdivision is a residential property. The sales comparison approach to value is preferred in estimating the value of residential properties.

80. B. The Department of Energy recommends insulation R values for different parts of the country.

81. D. A casement window swings out.

82. C. Out of this list, only the interest portion of mortgage payments on a second home is tax deductible.

83. B. When zoning creates a hardship for an individual landowner, the owner can ask for a variance.

84. D. A decrease in value due to conditions outside the property line is external obsolescence.

85. C. Leverage, the use of borrowed funds to capture a stream of income, is an advantage of property investment.

86. D. The statement describes a real estate investment trust (REIT).

87. B. A service industry is where the local people go for some service.

88. C. A use that was legal before the zoning was changed is a legally nonconforming use and can continue.

89. A. The concurrency provision of the Growth Management Act requires all infrastructure must be in place before new building can occur.

90. D. Planning commissioners are generally appointed, unpaid members who are serving to benefit their community.

91. D. Deed: $72,500 ÷ 100 × $0.70 = $507.50. Note: $59,760 ÷ 100 = 597.6 = 598 × $0.35 = $209.30. Note: $3,640 ÷ 100 = 36.4 = 37 × $0.35 = $12.95. New mortgage: $3,640 × $0.002 = $7.28. Total = $737.03. (Documentary stamp taxes are calculated for every unit of $100; plus any portion of $100, no matter how small counts for another $100 unit.)

92. B. EGI $850,000 − OE $530,000 = $320,000 NOI. Price = NOI ÷ Capitalization Rate. $530,000 ÷ 0.12 = $2,666,667.

93. B. Total rent is $1,050. Buyer gets 19 days of the rent. $1,050 ÷ 30 days = $35 per day × 19 days = $665 rent due to buyer.

94. D. The sale price received represents 110 percent of the purchase price. $234,300 ÷ 1.10 = $213,000.

95. C. Improvements are 80 percent of the value. Depreciation of residential investment properties is based on 27.5 years. $320,000 × 0.80 = $256,000. $256,000 ÷ 27.5 years = $9,309.

96. A. $146,000 × 0.06 = $8,760. $8,760 × 0.50 = $4,380. $4,380 × 0.30 = $1,314.

97. D. $270,000 ÷ 25 years = $10,800 depreciation per year. $10,800 × 5 years = $54,000. $270,000 − $54,000 = $216,000.

98. C. Add the mills: 9.6 + 8.5 + 8.4 = 26.5 mills = $0.0265. $25,000 × 0.0265 = $662.50.

99. D. $48,000 × 4 lots = $192,000 paid. 4 lots × 120 feet = 480 feet × $500 = $240,000 sale price. $240,000 − $192,000 = $48,000 profit. $48,000 ÷ $192,000 = 0.25.25 percent profit.

100. C. A new mortgage has two instruments—the mortgage and the note—that are subject to the state transfer tax. Note: $62,000 ÷ 100 = 620 × $0.35 = $217.00. New mortgage $62,000 × $0.002 = $124 intangible tax. $217 + $124 = $341.

Example Real Estate Forms

DISCLOSURE FORMS

IMPORTANT NOTICE

FLORIDA LAW REQUIRES THAT REAL ESTATE LICENSEES PROVIDE THIS NOTICE TO POTENTIAL SELLERS AND BUYERS OF REAL ESTATE.

You should not assume that any real estate broker or salesperson represents you unless you agree to engage a real estate licensee in an authorized brokerage relationship, either as a single agent or as a transaction broker. You are advised not to disclose any information you want to be held in confidence until you make a decision on representation.

TRANSACTION BROKER NOTICE

FLORIDA LAW REQUIRES THAT REAL ESTATE LICENSEES OPERATING AS TRANSACTION BROKERS DISCLOSE TO BUYERS AND SELLERS THEIR ROLES AND DUTIES IN PROVIDING A LIMITED FORM OF REPRESENTATION.

As a transaction broker, (insert name of Real Estate Firm and its Associates) provides to you a limited form of representation that includes the following duties:

1. Dealing honestly and fairly;
2. Accounting for all funds;
3. Using skill, care, and diligence in the transaction;
4. Disclosing all known facts that materially affect the value of residential real property and are not readily observable to the buyer;
5. Presenting all offers and counteroffers in a timely manner, unless a party has previously directed the licensee otherwise in writing;
6. Limited confidentiality, unless waived by a party. This limited confidentiality will prevent disclosure that the seller will accept a price less than the asking or listed price, that the buyer will pay a price greater than the price submitted in a written offer, of the motivation of any party for selling or buying property, that a seller or buyer will agree to financing terms other than those offered, or of any other information requested by a party to remain confidential; and
7. Any additional duties that are entered into by this or by separate written agreement.

Limited representation means that a buyer or seller is not responsible for the acts of the licensee. Additionally, parties are giving up their rights to the undivided loyalty of the licensee. This aspect of limited representation allows a licensee to facilitate a real estate transaction by assisting both the buyer and the seller, but a licensee will not work to represent one party to the detriment of the other party when acting as a transaction broker to both parties.

Seller or (buyer)

_____   _____
Signature   Date

_____   _____
Signature   Date

IMPORTANT NOTICE

FLORIDA LAW REQUIRES THAT REAL ESTATE LICENSEES PROVIDE THIS NOTICE TO POTENTIAL SELLERS AND BUYERS OF REAL ESTATE.

You should not assume that any real estate broker or salesperson represents you unless you agree to engage a real estate licensee in an authorized brokerage relationship, either as a single agent or as a transaction broker. You are advised not to disclose any information you want to be held in confidence until you make a decision on representation.

SINGLE AGENT NOTICE

FLORIDA LAW REQUIRES THAT REAL ESTATE LICENSEES OPERATING AS SINGLE AGENTS DISCLOSE TO BUYERS AND SELLERS THEIR DUTIES.

As a single agent, (insert name of Real Estate Entity and its Associates) owe to you the following duties:

1. Dealing honestly and fairly;
2. Loyalty;
3. Confidentiality;
4. Obedience;
5. Full disclosure;
6. Accounting for all funds;
7. Skill, care, and diligence in the transaction;
8. Presenting all offers and counteroffers in a timely manner, unless a party has previously directed the licensee otherwise in writing; and
9. Disclosing all known facts that materially affect the value of residential real property and are not readily observable.

Seller or (buyer)

_____   _____
Signature   Date

_____   _____
Signature   Date

IMPORTANT NOTICE

FLORIDA LAW REQUIRES THAT REAL ESTATE LICENSEES PROVIDE THIS NOTICE TO POTENTIAL SELLERS AND BUYERS OF REAL ESTATE.

You should not assume that any real estate broker or salesperson represents you unless you agree to engage a real estate licensee in an authorized brokerage relationship, either as a single agent or as a transaction broker. You are advised not to disclose any information you want to be held in confidence until you make a decision on representation.

NO BROKERAGE RELATIONSHIP NOTICE

FLORIDA LAW REQUIRES THAT REAL ESTATE LICENSEES WHO HAVE NO BROKERAGE RELATIONSHIP WITH A POTENTIAL SELLER OR BUYER DISCLOSE THEIR DUTIES TO SELLERS AND BUYERS.

As a real estate licensee who has no brokerage relationship with you, (insert name of Real Estate Entity and its Associates) owe to you the following duties:

1. Dealing honestly and fairly;
2. Disclosing all known facts that materially affect the value of residential real property which are not readily observable to the buyer; and
3. Accounting for all funds entrusted to the licensee.

Seller or (buyer)
_____   _____
Signature   Date

_____   _____
Signature   Date

FLORIDA LAW ALLOWS REAL ESTATE LICENSEES WHO REPRESENT A BUYER OR SELLER AS A SINGLE AGENT TO CHANGE FROM A SINGLE AGENT RELATIONSHIP TO A TRANSACTION BROKERAGE RELATIONSHIP IN ORDER FOR THE LICENSEE TO ASSIST BOTH PARTIES IN A REAL ESTATE TRANSACTION BY PROVIDING A LIMITED FORM OF REPRESENTATION TO BOTH THE BUYER AND THE SELLER. THIS CHANGE IN RELATIONSHIP CANNOT OCCUR WITHOUT YOUR PRIOR WRITTEN CONSENT.

As a transaction border,:_____ (insert name of Real Estate Firm and its Associates) provides to you a limited form of representation that includes the following duties:

1. Dealing honestly and fairly;
2. Accounting for all funds;
3. Using skill, care, and diligence in the transaction;
4. Disclosing all known facts that materially affect the value of residential real property and are not readily observable to the buyer;
5. Presenting all offers and counteroffers in a timely manner, unless a party has previously directed the licensee otherwise in writing;
6. Limited confidentiality, unless waived by a party. This limited confidentiality will prevent disclosure that the seller will accept a price less than the asking or listed price, that the buyer will pay a price greater than the price submitted in a written offer, of the motivation of any party for selling or buying property, that a seller or buyer will agree to financing terms other than those offered, or of any other information requested by a party to remain confidential; and
7. Any additional duties that are entered into by this or by separate written agreement.

Limited representation means that a buyer or seller is not responsible for the acts of the licensee. Additionally, parties are giving up their rights to the undivided loyalty of the licensee. This aspect of limited representation allows a licensee to facilitate a real estate transaction by assisting both the buyer and the seller, but a licensee will not work to represent one party to the detriment of the other party when acting as a transaction broker to both parties.

_____ I agree that my agent may assume the role and duties of a transaction broker. [must be initialed or signed]

DISCLOSURE OF INFORMATION ON LEAD-BASED PAINT AND/OR LEAD-BASED PAINT HAZARDS

Disclosure of Information on Lead-Based Paint and/or Lead-Based Paint Hazards

Lead Warning Statement

Every purchaser of any interest in residential real property on which a residential dwelling was built prior to 1978 is notified that such property may present exposure to lead from lead-based paint that may place young children at risk of developing lead poisoning. Lead poisoning in young children may produce permanent neurological damage, including learning disabilities, reduced intelligence quotient, behavioral problems, and impaired memory. Lead poisoning also poses a particular risk to pregnant women. The seller of any interest in residential real property is required to provide the buyer with any information on lead-based paint hazards from risk assessments or inspections in the seller's possession and notify the buyer of any known lead-based paint hazards. A risk assessment or inspection for possible lead-based paint hazards is recommended prior to purchase.

Seller's Disclosure

(a) Presence of lead-based paint and/or lead-based paint hazards (check (i) or (ii) below):

(i)—— Known lead-based paint and/or lead-based paint hazards are present in the housing (explain).

_____

(ii)——Seller has no knowledge of lead-based paint and/or lead-based paint hazards in the housing.

(b) Records and reports available to the seller (check (i) or (ii) below):

(i)——Seller has provided the purchaser with all available records and reports pertaining to lead-based paint and/or lead-based paint hazards in the housing (list documents below).

_____

(ii)—— Seller has no reports or records pertaining to lead-based paint and/or lead-based paint hazards in the housing.

Purchaser's Acknowledgment (initial)

(c)——Purchaser has received copies of all information listed above.

(d)——Purchaser has received the pamphlet *Protect Your Family from Lead in Your Home.*

(e)——Purchaser has (check (i) or (ii) below):

(i)—— received a 10-day opportunity (or mutually agreed upon period) to conduct a risk assessment or inspection for the presence of lead-based paint and/or lead-based paint hazards; or

(ii)—— waived the opportunity to conduct a risk assessment or inspection for the presence of lead-based paint and/or lead-based paint hazards.

Agent's Acknowledgment (initial)

(f)——Agent has informed the seller of the seller's obligations under 42 U.S.C. 4852d and is aware of his/her responsibility to ensure compliance.

Certification of Accuracy

The following parties have reviewed the information above and certify, to the best of their knowledge, that the information they have provided is true and accurate.

Seller	Date	Seller	Date
Purchaser	Date	Purchaser	Date
Agent	Date	Agent	Date

Disclosure of Information on Lead-Based Paint and/or Lead-Based Paint Hazards

Lead Warning Statement
Housing built before 1978 may contain lead-based paint. Lead from paint, paint chips, and dust can pose health hazards if not managed properly. Lead exposure is especially harmful to young children and pregnant women. Before renting pre-1978 housing, lessors must disclose the presence of known lead-based paint and/or lead-based paint hazards in the dwelling. Lessees must also receive a federally approved pamphlet on lead poisoning prevention.

Lessor's Disclosure
(a) Presence of lead-based paint and/or lead-based paint hazards (Check (i) or (ii) below):
   (i)—— Known lead-based paint and/or lead-based paint hazards are present in the housing (explain).

_____

   (ii)——Lessor has no knowledge of lead-based paint and/or lead-based paint hazards in the housing.
(b) Records and reports available to the lessor (Check (i) or (ii) below):
   (i)—— Lessor has provided the lessee with all available records and reports pertaining to lead-based paint and/or lead-based paint hazards in the housing (list documents below).

_____

   (ii)——Lessor has no reports or records pertaining to lead-based paint and/or lead-based paint hazards in the housing.

Lessee's Acknowledgment (initial)
(c)——Lessee has received copies of all information listed above.
(d)——Lessee has received the pamphlet *Protect Your Family from Lead in Your Home.*

Agent's Acknowledgment (initial)
(e)—— Agent has informed the lessor of the lessor's obligations under 42 U.S.C. 4852d and is aware of his/her responsibility to ensure compliance.

Certification of Accuracy
The following parties have reviewed the information above and certify, to the best of their knowledge, that the information they have provided is true and accurate.

_____	_____	_____	_____
Lessor	Date	Lessor	Date
_____	_____	_____	_____
Lessee	Date	Lessee	Date
_____	_____	_____	_____
Agent	Date	Agent	Date

Source: Federal Register/Vol. 61, No. 45/Wednesday, March 6, 1996/Rules and Regulations.

IRREVOCABLE CONSENT TO SERVICE FORM

Charlie Crist, Governor
Holly Benson, Secretary

Department of Business & Professional Regulation

Division of Real Estate
Thomas O'Bryant, Director
400 West Robinson Street, N801
Orlando, Florida 32801-1757

Phone: 407.481.5662
Fax: 407.317.7245
www.MyFlorida.com/dbpr
www.MyFloridaLicense.com

IRREVOCABLE CONSENT TO SERVICE

I agree, as the holder of a Florida Real Estate license, to submit to the jurisdiction of the Department of Business and Professional Regulation and the Division of Administrative Hearings, which agreement is irrevocable.

I agree, as the holder of a Florida Real Estate license, that the Director of the Division of Real Estate and his/her successors in office shall receive service of all legal process issued against me in any administrative or civil action or proceeding in this state, and process so served shall be valid and binding, which agreement is irrevocable. I further agree to file with the Division of Real Estate an address (shown below) where a copy of the process served upon the Division Director is to be sent by registered mail, and that I will keep said address current.

Name (Please Print) _____ License # _____

Number   Street Address   City   State   Zip

_____ (Signature)

STATE OF _____

COUNTY OF _____

The foregoing instrument was acknowledged before me this _____ day of _____, 20____,

_____
by: Signature of Notary Public--State of Florida (Out of State Notary Acceptable)

_____
(Print, Type, or Stamp Commissioned Name of Notary Public)

Personally Known _____ Or Produced Identification _____

Type of Identification Produced _____

Forward Form to:
Florida Department of Business and Professional Regulation
1940 North Monroe Street
Tallahassee, Florida 32399

Source: Florida Department of Business and Professional Regulation (http://www.myflorida.com/dbpr/re/index.html).

EXCLUSIVE RIGHT-OF-SALE LISTING AGREEMENT–COOP

Date:_____

Re: Any Property, Florida (the "Unit")

To:

In consideration for the work you are presently doing and are going to do in the future on our behalf, we hereby appoint and grant _____ ("Broker") the sole "exclusive right-to-sell" the proprietary lease and shares of stock allocated to the above referenced apartment/unit. This shall include but not be limited to (i) the outright sale of the Unit; (ii) by sale of the Corporation/Entity that is the registered owner of the shares and proprietary lease or by any other disposition method.

We understand and you have fully disclosed that an "exclusive right-to-sell" means that if we the owner find a buyer, you the Broker find a buyer or another outside broker not within your employ finds a buyer and/or any other person finds a buyer, the agreed commission will be due to you the Broker in either of the cases above.

The terms of this agreement are as follows:

1.   This agreement shall be effective as of _____("Effective Date").
         It shall continue in full force and effect for the earlier of one (1) year from the Effective Date or closing of sale.

2.   Broker is authorized to offer the _____ shares for sale at a price of $_____ and to represent that the monthly maintenance charge is $_____.

3.   If the shares and the proprietary lease are sold pursuant to this agreement, Seller agrees to pay Broker and Broker agrees to accept a commission equal to six (6%) percent of the total sales price and/or any other valuable consideration received by us. This commission will be due and payable by certified check or attorney's escrow check, at closing, in full and without setoff of any kind.

4.   Broker will offer the Unit through your own organization and direct as well as oversee its sale. Seller shall receive from Broker a monthly report of all pertinent developments.

5.   Seller hereby authorizes Broker to solicit the cooperation of other licensed real estate brokers who will act as agents for the prospective buyers, and to work with them on a cooperating basis. In the event another licensed real estate broker is involved in the transaction, you will share the commission with such broker and in no event will the commission paid by Seller exceed six (6%) per cent of the sale price as outlined in paragraph #3 herein.

6.   Seller agrees that during the life of this agreement, Seller will refer all inquiries, including but not limited to the Cooperative, concerning the sale of the Unit to Broker.

7.   Within ten (10) days after the expiration of this listing, Broker shall deliver to Seller a list of names of persons who inspected the premises during athe listing term. If within one (1) year after the expiration of the listing term a contract is signed to sell the premises to a person contained on the list, Broker shall be entitled to a commission provided for in paragraph #3 herein.

8.   This agreement shall bind and benefit the personal representatives, successors, assigns of the parties. This agreement may not be changed, rescinded or modified except in writing, signed by both parties.

9.   In the event Seller becomes legally entitled to retain any deposit paid to Seller pursuant to a signed contract of sale, by a person introduced during the term of this agreement, Seller agrees to pay Broker six (6%) per cent of that amount to Broker. This payment shall be non-refundable.

10.   Seller warrants and represents to Broker that Seller is in fact the owner of the shares and proprietary lease covering the Unit and that Seller has marketable title to the Unit.

         If the above is in accordance with your understanding, please indicate your acceptance on the signature line provided below.

         Sincerely,

         _____
         Broker:

         Agreed & Accepted:

         _____
         Seller:

Source: Parker Madison Partners, Inc., New York, New York. Reprinted with permission.

RESIDENTIAL SALE AND PURCHASE
CONTRACT: CONDOMINIUMS

Residential Sale and Purchase Contract: Comprehensive Addendum
FLORIDA ASSOCIATION OF REALTORS®

1* The clauses below will be incorporated into the Contract between _____ (Seller)
2* and _____ (Buyer) concerning the Property described as _____
3* _____ only if initialed by all parties:

4   ASSOCIATION DISCLOSURES

5* (_____) (_____) - (_____)(_____) A. Condominium Association: The Property is a condominium which is subject to the rules
6   and regulations of a condominium association ("Association"). Seller's warranty under Paragraph 8 of the Contract or
7   Paragraph H of the Comprehensive Addendum (if applicable) extend to the unit and limited common elements appurtenant to
8   the Property and not to any common elements or any other property.
9   (1) Documents: Seller will, at Seller's expense, deliver to Buyer the condominium documents referenced in subparagraph (8) below no
10* later than 3 days from Effective Date (if Buyer has already received the required documents, indicate receipt by initialing here (_____)
11* (_____) Date received _____, _____). If this Contract does not close, Buyer will immediately return the documents to
12* Seller, failing which Buyer authorizes Escrow Agent to reimburse Seller $_____ from the deposit for the cost of the documents.
13 (2) Association Approval: If the condominium declaration or bylaws give the Association the right to approve Buyer as a
14* purchaser, this Contract is contingent on such approval by the Association. Buyer will apply for approval within _____ days from
15 Effective Date and use diligent effort to obtain approval, including making personal appearances and paying related fees if
16 required. Buyer and Seller will sign and deliver any documents required by the Association to complete the transfer. If Buyer is
17 not approved, this Contract will terminate and Seller will return Buyer's deposit unless this Contract provides otherwise.
18 (3) Right of First Refusal: If the Association has a right of first refusal to buy the Property, this Contract is contingent on the Association
19 deciding not to exercise such right. Seller will, within 3 days from receipt of the Association's decision, give Buyer written notice of the
20 decision. If the Association exercises its right of first refusal, this Contract will terminate, Buyer's deposit will be refunded unless this
21 Contract provides otherwise and Seller will pay Broker's full commission at closing in recognition that Broker procured the sale.
22 (4) Application/Transfer Fees: Buyer will pay any application and/or transfer fees charged by the Association.
23* (5) Parking: Seller will assign to Buyer at closing parking space(s) _____.
24 (6) Fees: Seller will pay all fines imposed against the Unit as of Closing Date and any fees the Association charges to provide information
25 about its fees or the Property, and will bring maintenance and similar periodic fees and rents on any recreational areas current as of
26 Closing Date. If, after the Effective Date, the Association imposes a special assessment for improvements, work or services, Seller will
27 pay all amounts due before Closing Date and Buyer will pay all amounts due after Closing Date. Seller represents that he/she is not
28* aware of any pending special or other assessment that the Association is considering except as follows:_____
29* _____
30* Seller represents that he/she is not aware of pending or anticipated litigation affecting the Property or the common elements,
31* if any, except as follows:_____
32* _____
33 Seller represents that the current maintenance fee is:
34* $_____ per _____ to _____
35* $_____ per _____ to _____
36* $_____ per _____ to _____
37* and that there ☐ is ☐ is not a recreation or land lease with the Property. If there is a recreation or land lease, the current
38* payment is $_____ per month.
39 (7) Sprinkler System: IF THE UNIT OWNERS VOTED TO FOREGO RETROFITTING EACH UNIT WITH A FIRE
40 SPRINKLER OR OTHER ENGINEERED LIFE SAFETY SYSTEM, SELLER SHALL PROVIDE THE BUYER, BEFORE
41 CLOSING, A COPY OF THE CONDOMINIUM ASSOCIATION'S NOTICE OF THE VOTE TO FOREGO RETROFITTING.
42 (8) Buyer Acknowledgement / Seller Disclosure: (Check whichever applies)
43* ☐ THE BUYER HEREBY ACKNOWLEDGES THAT BUYER HAS BEEN PROVIDED A CURRENT COPY OF THE DECLARATION OF
44 CONDOMINIUM, ARTICLES OF INCORPORATION OF THE ASSOCIATION, BYLAWS AND RULES OF THE ASSOCIATION, AND A COPY
45 OF THE MOST RECENT YEAR-END FINANCIAL INFORMATION AND FREQUENTLY ASKED QUESTIONS AND ANSWERS DOCUMENT
46 MORE THAN 3 DAYS, EXCLUDING SATURDAYS, SUNDAYS, AND LEGAL HOLIDAYS, PRIOR TO EXECUTION OF THIS CONTRACT.
47* ☐ THIS AGREEMENT IS VOIDABLE BY BUYER BY DELIVERING WRITTEN NOTICE OF THE BUYER'S INTENTION TO CANCEL
48 WITHIN 3 DAYS, EXCLUDING SATURDAYS, SUNDAYS, AND LEGAL HOLIDAYS, AFTER THE DATE OF EXECUTION OF THIS
49 AGREEMENT BY THE BUYER AND RECEIPT BY BUYER OF A CURRENT COPY OF THE DECLARATION OF CONDOMINIUM,
50 ARTICLES OF INCORPORATION, BYLAWS AND RULES OF THE ASSOCIATION, AND A COPY OF THE MOST RECENT YEAR-END
51 FINANCIAL INFORMATION AND FREQUENTLY ASKED QUESTIONS AND ANSWERS DOCUMENT IF SO REQUESTED IN WRITING.
52 ANY PURPORTED WAIVER OF THESE VOIDABILITY RIGHTS SHALL BE OF NO EFFECT. BUYER MAY EXTEND THE TIME FOR
53 CLOSING FOR A PERIOD OF NOT MORE THAN 3 DAYS, EXCLUDING SATURDAYS, SUNDAYS, AND LEGAL HOLIDAYS, AFTER
54 THE BUYER RECEIVES THE DECLARATION, ARTICLES OF INCORPORATION, BYLAWS AND RULES OF THE ASSOCIATION, AND
55 A COPY OF THE MOST RECENT YEAR-END FINANCIAL INFORMATION AND FREQUENTLY ASKED QUESTIONS AND ANSWERS
56 DOCUMENT IF REQUESTED IN WRITING. BUYER'S RIGHT TO VOID THIS AGREEMENT SHALL TERMINATE AT CLOSING.
57* FARA-8   Rev. 10/04   © 2004 Florida Association of Realtors®   All Rights Reserved   Page _____ of Addendum No. _____

1° The clauses below will be incorporated into the Contract between _____ (Seller)
2° and _____ (Buyer) concerning the Property described as _____
3° _____ only if initialed by all parties:

4° (____)(____) - (____)(____) B. Homeowners' Association: The Property is located in a community with a ☐ voluntary
5° ☐ mandatory (see the disclosure summary below) homeowners' association ("Association"). Seller's warranty under
6° Paragraph 8 of the Contract or Paragraph H of the Comprehensive Addendum (if applicable) extend only to the Property and
7° does not extend to common areas or facilities described below.
8° Notice: Association documents may be obtained from the county record office or, if not public record, from the developer or
9° Association manager. The Property may be subject to recorded restrictive covenants governing the use and occupancy of
10° properties in the community and may be subject to special assessments.
11° (1) Association Approval: If the Association documents give the Association the right to approve Buyer as a purchaser, this
12° Contract is contingent on such approval by the Association. Buyer will apply for approval within _____ days from Effective
13° Date (5 days if left blank) and use diligent effort to obtain approval, including making personal appearances and paying
14° related fees if required. Buyer and Seller will sign and deliver any documents required by the Association to complete the
15° transfer. If Buyer is not approved, this Contract will terminate and Seller will return Buyer's deposit unless this Contract
16° provides otherwise.
17° (2) Right of First Refusal: If the Association has a right of first refusal to buy the Property, this Contract is contingent on the
18° Association deciding not to exercise such right. Seller will, within 3 days from receipt of the Association's decision, give
19° Buyer written notice of the decision. If the Association exercises its right of first refusal, this Contract will terminate, Buyer's
20° deposit will be refunded unless this Contract provides otherwise and Seller will pay Broker's full commission at closing in
21° recognition that Broker procured the sale.
22° (3) Fees: Buyer will pay any application, transfer and initial membership fees charged by the Association. Seller will pay all
23° fines imposed against the Property as of Closing Date and any fees the Association charges to provide information about its
24° fees or the Property, and will bring maintenance and similar periodic fees and rents on any recreational areas current as of
25° Closing Date. If, after the Effective Date, the Association imposes a special or other assessment for improvements, work or
26° services, Seller will pay all amounts due before Closing Date and Buyer will pay all amounts due after Closing Date. Seller
27° represents that he/she is not aware of any pending special or other assessment that the Association is considering except as
28° follows:

29° $_____ per _____ to _____
30° The following dues/maintenance fees are currently charged by the homeowners' association:
31° $_____ per _____ to _____
32° $_____ per _____ to _____
33° $_____ per _____ to _____

34° (4) Disclosure Summary for Mandatory Associations: IF THE DISCLOSURE SUMMARY REQUIRED BY SECTION 720.401,
35° FLORIDA STATUTES, HAS NOT BEEN PROVIDED TO THE PROSPECTIVE PURCHASER BEFORE EXECUTING THIS
36° CONTRACT FOR SALE, THIS CONTRACT IS VOIDABLE BY BUYER BY DELIVERING TO SELLER OR SELLER'S AGENT OR
37° REPRESENTATIVE WRITTEN NOTICE OF THE BUYER'S INTENTION TO CANCEL WITHIN 3 DAYS AFTER RECEIPT OF THE
38° DISCLOSURE SUMMARY OR PRIOR TO CLOSING, WHICHEVER OCCURS FIRST. ANY PURPORTED WAIVER OF THIS
39° VOIDABILITY RIGHT HAS NO EFFECT. BUYER'S RIGHT TO VOID THIS CONTRACT SHALL TERMINATE AT CLOSING.

40° Disclosure Summary For (Name of Community) _____:
41° (1) AS A PURCHASER OF PROPERTY IN THIS COMMUNITY, YOU WILL BE OBLIGATED TO BE A MEMBER OF A
42° HOMEOWNERS' ASSOCIATION.
43° (2) THERE HAVE BEEN OR WILL BE RECORDED RESTRICTIVE COVENANTS GOVERNING THE USE
44° AND OCCUPANCY OF PROPERTIES IN THIS COMMUNITY.
45° (3) YOU WILL BE OBLIGATED TO PAY ASSESSMENTS TO THE ASSOCIATION. ASSESSMENTS MAY BE SUBJECT TO
46° PERIODIC CHANGE. IF APPLICABLE, THE CURRENT AMOUNT IS $_____ PER _____.
47° YOU WILL ALSO BE OBLIGATED TO PAY ANY SPECIAL ASSESSMENTS IMPOSED BY THE ASSOCIATION. SUCH
48° SPECIAL ASSESSMENTS MAY BE SUBJECT TO CHANGE. IF APPLICABLE, THE CURRENT AMOUNT IS
49° $_____ PER _____.
50° (4) YOU MAY BE OBLIGATED TO PAY SPECIAL ASSESSMENTS TO THE RESPECTIVE MUNICIPALITY, COUNTY, OR
51° SPECIAL DISTRICT. ALL ASSESSMENTS ARE SUBJECT TO PERIODIC CHANGE.
52° (5) YOUR FAILURE TO PAY SPECIAL ASSESSMENTS OR ASSESSMENTS LEVIED BY A MANDATORY HOMEOWNERS'
53° ASSOCIATION COULD RESULT IN A LIEN ON YOUR PROPERTY.

(See Continuation)

54° FARA-8 Rev. 10/04 © 2004 Florida Association of Realtors® All Rights Reserved   Page _____ of Addendum No. _____

55* (___)(___) - (___)(___) B. Homeowners' Association (CONTINUATION)

56 (6) THERE MAY BE AN OBLIGATION TO PAY RENT OR LAND USE FEES FOR RECREATIONAL OR OTHER COMMONLY
57 USED FACILITIES AS AN OBLIGATION OF MEMBERSHIP IN THE HOMEOWNERS' ASSOCIATION. IF APPLICABLE, THE
58* CURRENT AMOUNT IS $_____ PER _____.
59 (7) THE DEVELOPER MAY HAVE THE RIGHT TO AMEND THE RESTRICTIVE COVENANTS WITHOUT THE APPROVAL
60 OF THE ASSOCIATION MEMBERSHIP OR THE APPROVAL OF THE PARCEL OWNERS.
61 (8) THE STATEMENTS CONTAINED IN THIS DISCLOSURE FORM ARE ONLY SUMMARY IN NATURE, AND, AS A
62 PROSPECTIVE PURCHASER, YOU SHOULD REFER TO THE COVENANTS AND THE ASSOCIATION GOVERNING
63 DOCUMENTS BEFORE PURCHASING PROPERTY.
64 (9) THESE DOCUMENTS ARE EITHER MATTERS OF PUBLIC RECORD AND CAN BE OBTAINED FROM THE RECORD
65 OFFICE IN THE COUNTY WHERE THE PROPERTY IS LOCATED, OR ARE NOT RECORDED AND CAN BE OBTAINED
66 FROM THE DEVELOPER.

67 Buyer acknowledges receipt of this summary before signing this Contract.

68* _____ _____   _____ _____
69 Buyer   Date   Buyer   Date

1ˢ The clauses below will be incorporated into the Contract between _____ (Seller)
2ˢ and _____ (Buyer) concerning the Property described as _____
3ˢ _____ only if initialed by all parties:

4 <center>FINANCING</center>

5ˢ (____)(____) - (____)(____) C. Seller Financing: Buyer will execute a purchase money note and mortgage to Seller that
6ˢ ☐ is ☐ is not subordinate to any third party financing in the amount of $_____, bearing annual interest
7ˢ at _____% and payable as follows: _____
8ˢ _____
9 The mortgage, note, and any security agreement will be in a form acceptable to Seller and following forms generally accepted in
10 the county where the Property is located; will provide for a late payment fee and acceleration at the mortgagee's option if Buyer
11 defaults; will give Buyer the right to prepay without penalty all or part of the principal at any time(s) with interest only to date of
12 payment; will be due on conveyance or sale; and will require Buyer to keep Property insured, with Seller as additional named
13 insured, against loss by fire (and flood, if Property is in a flood zone) with extended coverage in an amount not less than the
14 greater of the amount of the purchase money mortgage and note or full replacement value for the real property. Buyer will
15 provide Seller by March 1 each year with written evidence that the real property taxes have been paid in full for the previous
16 year. Buyer authorizes Seller to obtain credit, employment and other necessary information to determine creditworthiness for
17 the financing. Seller will provide written notice to Buyer within 10 days from Effective Date if Seller will not make the loan. If no
18 notice is provided, Seller will provide the requested Seller financing.

19ˢ (____)(____) - (____)(____) D. Mortgage Assumption: Buyer will take subject to and assume and pay existing first mortgage
20ˢ to _____ LN# _____ in the approximate amount of
21ˢ $_____ currently payable at $_____ per month including principal, interest, ☐ taxes and insurance
22ˢ and having a ☐ fixed ☐ other (describe) _____ interest rate of
23ˢ _____% which ☐ will ☐ will not escalate upon assumption. Any variance in the mortgage will be adjusted in the balance due at
24 closing with no adjustment to purchase price. Buyer will pay assumption/transfer fee and purchase Seller's escrow account dollar for
25ˢ dollar. If the lender disapproves Buyer, or the interest rate upon transfer exceeds _____% or the assumption/transfer fee exceeds
26ˢ $_____, this agreement will terminate and Buyer's deposit(s) will be returned unless either party elects to pay the excess.

27ˢ (____)(____) - (____)(____) E. FHA Financing: (Buyer will be referred to as "purchaser" in the following statement) "It is
28 expressly agreed that notwithstanding any other provisions of this contract, the purchaser shall not be obligated to complete
29 the purchase of the property described herein or to incur any penalty by forfeiture of earnest money deposits or otherwise
30 unless the purchaser has been given in accordance with HUD/FHA or VA requirements a written statement by the Federal
31 Housing Commissioner, Department of Veterans Affairs, or a Direct Endorsement lender setting forth the appraised value of
32 property of not less than $_____ The purchaser shall have the privilege and option of proceeding with
33 consummation of the contract without regard to the amount of the appraised valuation. The appraised valuation is arrived at to
34 determine the maximum mortgage the Department of Housing and Urban Development will insure. HUD does not warrant the
35 value nor the condition of the property. The purchaser should satisfy himself/herself that the price and condition of the property
36 are acceptable." If Buyer elects to proceed with the Contract without regard to the amount of reasonable value established by
37 the Federal Housing Commissioner, U.S. Department of Veterans Affairs, or Direct Endorsement lender, such election must be
38 made within 3 days from Buyer's receipt of the appraisal.
39 (1) Fees, Prepayments: Seller will pay tax service, underwriting and document preparation fees required by the lender;
40ˢ recording fees for assigning Buyer's mortgage and _____
41ˢ up to a maximum cost of $_____ ($250.00 if left blank), Buyer will pay all prepayments and escrows for taxes,
42 hazard insurance, FHA insurance, and flood insurance, when applicable.
43 (2) Repairs: In the event a lender, as a result of the FHA appraisal, requires repairs to items not covered by Seller's
44 warranty in Paragraph 8 of the Contract or Paragraph H of the Comprehensive Addendum (if applicable), Seller will make
45ˢ required repairs up to a maximum cost to Seller of _____ ($250.00 if left blank). Required repairs to
46 warranted items are subject to the Repair Limit defined in the Contract. If the cost of repairs to warranted or unwarranted
47 items exceeds the respective limit, Seller will, within 3 days after receiving notice of the excess cost, deliver to Buyer
48 written notice of Seller's intent to pay some, all, or none of the excess amount. If Seller pays less than the full amount of the
49 excess cost, Buyer may pay the balance or cancel the Contract. Buyer's election must be in writing and provided to Seller
50 within 3 days after receipt of Seller's notice.
51 (3) Home Inspection: Buyer has received and signed the "For Your Protection: Get a Home Inspection" notice.
52 (4) FHA Certification: Buyer and Seller are signatories to the Contract. The selling real estate agent or broker involved in
53 this transaction states: I certify that the terms of this Contract for Sale and Purchase are true and correct to the best of my
54 knowledge and belief and that any other agreements entered into by any of these parties in connection with this
55 transaction are part of, or attached to, the Contract.

56ˢ _____   _____
57 *Selling Sales Associate or Broker*   *Date*   *Listing Sales Associate or Broker*   *Date*

58ˢ FARA-8   Rev. 10/04   © 2004   Florida Association of REALTORS®   All Rights Reserved   Page _____ of Addendum No._____

¹ The clauses below will be incorporated into the Contract between _____ (Seller)
² and _____ (Buyer) concerning the Property described as _____
³ _____ only if initialed by all parties:

⁴ (____) (____) - (____)(____) F. VA Financing: "It is expressly agreed that, notwithstanding any other provision of this
⁵ Contract, the Buyer will not incur any penalty by forfeiture of earnest money or otherwise be obligated to complete the
⁶ purchase of the property described herein, if the Contract purchase price or cost exceeds the reasonable value of the
⁷ property as established by the U.S. Department of Veterans Affairs. The Buyer will, however, have the privilege and option of
⁸ proceeding with the consummation of this Contract without regard to the amount of reasonable value established by the U.S.
⁹ Department of Veterans Affairs." If Buyer elects to proceed with the Contract without regard to the amount of reasonable
¹⁰ value established by the U.S. Department of Veterans Affairs, such election must be made within 3 days from Buyer's receipt
¹¹ of the appraisal.

¹² Seller will pay up to $_____ ($250.00 if left blank) toward Buyer's loan and closing costs. In the event a lender,
¹³ as a result of the VA appraisal, requires repairs to items not covered by Seller's warranty in Paragraph 8 of the Contract or
¹⁴ Paragraph H of the Comprehensive Addendum (if applicable), Seller will make required repairs up to a maximum cost to
¹⁵ Seller of $_____ ($250.00 if left blank). Required repairs to warranted items are subject to the Repair Limit
¹⁶ defined in the Contract. If the cost of repairs to warranted or unwarranted items exceeds the respective repair limit, Seller
¹⁷ will, within 3 days from receipt of notice of the excess cost, deliver to Buyer written notice of Seller's intent to pay the excess
¹⁸ cost or cancel the Contract.

¹⁹ (____) (____) - (____)(____) G. New Mortgage Rates: Buyer will not be obligated to complete the purchase unless
²⁰ Buyer is able to obtain the financing at a fixed interest rate not exceeding _____% or a variable/adjustable interest rate not
²¹ exceeding _____% at origination, with no more than _____ discount points charged. Buyer ☐ will ☐ will not accept a
²² balloon mortgage.

²³ FARA-8   Rev. 10/04   © 2004   Florida Association of Realtors®   All Rights Reserved   Page ____ of Addendum No. ____

1° The clauses below will be incorporated into the Contract between _____ (Seller)

2° and _____ (Buyer) concerning the Property described as _____

3° _____ only if initialed by all parties:

4 PROPERTY

5° (_____) (_____) - (_____)(_____) H. As Is With Right to Inspect: This clause replaces Paragraphs 6 and 8 of the Contract but

6 does not modify or replace Paragraph 9. Paragraph 5(a) Repair and Termite Repair Limits are 0%. Seller makes no warranties

7 other than marketability of title. Seller will keep the Property in the same condition from Effective Date until closing, except for

8 normal wear and tear ("maintenance requirement"), and will convey the Property in its "as is" condition with no obligation to

9 make any repairs. Buyer may, at Buyer's expense, conduct professional and walk-through inspections as described below. If

10 Buyer fails to timely conduct any inspection which Buyer is entitled to make under this paragraph, Buyer waives the right to the

11 inspection and accepts the Property "as is." Seller will provide access and utilities for Buyer's inspections. Buyer will repair all

12 damages to the Property resulting from the inspections and return the Property to its pre-inspection condition. Buyer may, by

13° _____, _____ ("Inspection Period") (within 10 days from Effective Date if left blank) make any and all

14 inspections of the Property. The inspection(s) will be by a person who specializes in and holds an occupational license (if required

15 by law) to conduct home inspections or who holds a Florida license to repair and maintain the items inspected. Buyer may

16° cancel this Contract by written notice to Seller within ____ days (within 5 days if left blank) from the end of the Inspection Period if

17° the estimated cost of treatment and repairs determined to be necessary by Buyer is greater than $_____. For the

18 cancellation to be effective, Buyer must include in the written notice a copy of the inspector's written report, if any, and treatment

19 and repair estimates from the inspector or person(s) holding an appropriate Florida license to repair the items inspected. Any

20 conditions not reported in a timely manner will be deemed acceptable to Buyer. Buyer may, on the day before Closing Date or

21 any other time agreeable to the parties, walk through the Property solely to verify that Seller has fulfilled the contractual

22 obligations. No other issues may be raised as a result of the walk-through inspection.

23° (_____) (_____) - (_____)(_____) I. Inspections (check as applicable)

24° ☐ (1) Self-Inspection: Buyer and Seller agree that unlicensed persons, including the parties themselves, may conduct

25 the inspections (except for Buyer's wood-destroying organism inspection) permitted in Paragraph 8 of the Contract or

26 Paragraph H of this Addendum. However, if the inspection findings differ and the parties cannot resolve the differences,

27 Buyer and Seller together will choose, and will equally split the cost of, a professional inspector as defined in Paragraph 8

28 of the Contract whose report will be binding on the parties.

29° ☐ (2) Right to Cancel Based on Inspection Results: Within the Inspection Period provided in Paragraph 6 of the

30 Contract, Buyer will, at Buyer's sole expense, complete any desired inspections of the Property in addition to those

31 referenced in Paragraphs 7 and 8(a)(2). If Buyer is for any reason unhappy with a condition of the Property noted in during

32 the inspection results, Buyer may cancel the Contract by delivering written notice to Seller along with a copy of the

33 inspection results within 2 days from the end of the Inspection Period, and Buyer will, at Buyer's sole expense,

34 immediately repair all damage resulting from Buyer's inspections and restore the Property to its pre-inspection condition;

35 this obligation will survive termination of the Contract. If the Contract is not canceled, the parties' obligations remain as

36 specified in the Contract. This Paragraph does not modify or replace the rights and obligations of the parties under

37 Paragraph 9 of the Contract.

38° (_____) (_____) - (_____)(_____) J. Insulation Disclosure (New Homes Only): Insulation has been or will be installed in the new

39 residence as follows:

40 Location	Type	Thickness	Manufacturer R-Value
41° Interior Walls			
42° Flat Ceiling Area			
43° Sloped Ceiling Area			
44° Common Walls Between House & Garage			
45° Exterior Walls			
46° Other _____			

1" The clauses below will be incorporated into the Contract between _____ (Seller)
2" and _____ (Buyer) concerning the Property described as _____
3" _____ only if initialed by all parties:

4" (____) (____) - (____)(____) K. Pre-1978 Housing Lead-Based Paint Warning Statement: "Every purchaser of any interest
5" in residential real property on which a residential dwelling was built prior to 1978 is notified that such property may present
6" exposure to lead from lead-based paint that may place young children at risk of developing lead poisoning. Lead poisoning in
7" young children may produce permanent neurological damage, including learning disabilities, reduced intelligence quotient,
8" behavioral problems, and impaired memory. Lead poisoning also poses a particular risk to pregnant women. The seller of any
9" interest in residential real property is required to provide the buyer with any information on lead-based paint hazards from risk
10" assessments or inspections in the seller's possession and notify the buyer of any known lead-based paint hazards. A risk
11" assessment or inspection for possible lead-based paint hazards is recommended prior to purchase." For purposes of this
12" addendum, lead-based paint will be referred to as "LBP" and lead-based paint hazards will be referred to as "LBPH."
13" (1) LBP/LBPH in Housing: Seller has no knowledge of LBP/LBPH in the housing and no available LBP/LBPH records or
14" reports, except as indicated: (describe all known LBP/LBPH information, list all available documents pertaining to
15" LBP/LBPH and provide documents to Buyer before accepting Buyer's offer) _____
16" _____
17" _____
18" _____
19" (2) Lead-Based Paint Hazards Inspection: Buyer waives the opportunity to conduct a risk assessment or inspection for
20" the presence of LBP/LBPH unless this box is checked (❏ Buyer may, within the Inspection Period, conduct a risk
21" assessment or inspection for the presence of LBP/LBPH in accordance with the provisions of paragraph 8(a) or H.
22" LBP/LBPH conditions that are unsatisfactory to Buyer will be treated as "warranted items" for purposes of paragraphs
23" 8(a)(2) and (3) only).
24" (3) Certification of Accuracy: Buyer has received the pamphlet entitled "Protect Your Family From Lead in Your Home" and
25" all of the information specified in paragraph (1) above. Licensee has notified Seller of Seller's obligations to provide and
26" disclose information regarding lead-based paint and lead-based paint hazards in the property as required by federal law
27" (42 U.S.C. 4852d) and is aware of his or her obligation to ensure compliance with federal lead-based paint law. Buyer,
28" Seller and each licensee has reviewed the information above and certifies, to the best of his or her knowledge, that the
29" information he or she has provided is true and accurate.

30" _____ _____ _____ _____
31" Buyer   Date   Seller   Date
32"
33" _____ _____ _____ _____
33" Buyer   Date   Seller   Date
34"
35" _____ _____ _____ _____
35" Selling Licensee   Date   Listing Licensee   Date

36" (____) (____) - (____)(____) L. Insurance: (check whichever applies)
37" ❏ (1) Homeowners Insurance: If Buyer is unable to obtain basic Homeowner or Fire and Hazard Coverage from
38" a standard carrier or the Citizen's Property Insurance Corporation at a first year annual premium not to
39" exceed $_____ or _____% of the purchase price and/or flood insurance through the National Flood
40" Insurance Program at a first year premium not to exceed $_____ or _____% of the purchase price by
41" _____, _____ (no later than 5 days prior to Closing Date if left blank), Buyer may cancel the Contract by
42" delivering written notice to the Seller.

43" ❏ (2) Flood Insurance: Buyer is notified that the Property is located in an area that: ❏ is a defined floodable area and
44" flood insurance is required. ❏ was declared a flood disaster area after September 23, 1994 and received federal disaster
45" relief assistance on the condition that flood insurance be obtained in accordance with applicable federal law. Buyer is
46" required to obtain such flood insurance if the Property is not so insured as of the date of transfer and will be required to
47" maintain flood insurance in accordance with applicable federal law with respect to the Property.

48" (____) (____) - (____)(____) M. Housing for Older Persons: Buyer acknowledges that the owners' association, developer
49" or other housing provider intends the Property to provide housing for older persons as defined by federal law. While Seller
50" and Broker make no representation that the Property actually qualifies as housing for older persons, the housing provider has
51" stated that it provides housing for persons who are ❏ 62 years of age and older. ❏ 55 years of age and older.

52" FARA-6   Rev. 10/04   © 2004   Florida Association of Realtors®   All Rights Reserved   Page____of Addendum No.____

1° The clauses below will be incorporated into the Contract between _____ (Seller)
2° and _____ (Buyer) concerning the Property described as _____
3° _____ only if initialed by all parties:

4   MISCELLANEOUS CLAUSES

5° (____) (____) - (____)(____) N. Unimproved and/or Agricultural Property: If the Property is an unimproved parcel of land
6° and is intended to be improved for residential or other purposes, Buyer has _____ days, through consultation with
7   appropriate public authorities or otherwise, to be satisfied that either public sewerage and water are available to the Property
8   or that the Property will be approved for the installation of a well and/or private sewerage disposal system and that existing
9   zoning and other pertinent regulations, including concurrency, allow Buyer's intended use of the Property.

10° (____) (____) - (____)(____) O. Interest-Bearing Escrow Account: All deposits will be held in an interest bearing escrow
11° account with all accrued interest to be paid to _____ at
12 closing. Deposits will accrue interest only from the date the bank receives and credits them through the date Escrow Agent is
13 notified that the transaction is scheduled for closing and the funds are transferred. Escrow Agent is authorized to deduct a
14° $_____ service charge from the earned interest before disbursing the funds.

15° (____) (____) - (____)(____) P. Back-up Contract: (Check whichever applies)
16°   ☐ (1) This back-up Contract is subject to the termination of a prior executed contract between Seller and a third party for
17   the sale of the Property. If the prior executed contract is terminated and Seller delivers written notice of the termination to
18°   Buyer before 5:00 p.m. on _____, _____, this contingency will be removed and this back-up
19   Contract will move into first position. If Buyer does not receive notice of the prior contract's termination by the above
20   deadline, Buyer may cancel this back-up Contract at any time and Buyer's deposit will be refunded.
21°   ☐ (2) Seller will have the right to continue to show the Property and solicit and enter into bona fide back-up purchase
22   contracts with third parties that are subject to the termination of this primary Contract. Upon entering into a back-up
23   contract, Seller will give Buyer a copy of the back-up contract with the third parties' identification and purchase price
24°   information obliterated. To continue with this primary Contract, Buyer must make an additional deposit of $_____
25   within 72 hours (to be computed as consecutive hours, not business days) from receipt of the back-up contract. By giving
26   the additional deposit to Escrow Agent within the 72 hour period, Buyer waives all contingencies for financing and sale of
27   Buyer's property and the parties will close on Closing Date. The additional deposit will be credited to Buyer at closing. If
28   Buyer fails to timely make the additional deposit, this primary Contract will terminate and Buyer's deposit will be refunded.

29° (____) (____) - (____)(____) Q. Broker - Personal Interest in Property: _____ has an active or
30 inactive real estate license and has a personal interest in the property: (specify if licensee is related to a party, is acting as Buyer
31° or Seller, etc.) _____

32° (____) (____) - (____)(____) R. Rentals:(check whichever applies)
33°   ☐ (1) Pre-Occupancy Agreement: If Buyer occupies the Property before closing, Buyer will accept the Property in its
34   existing condition on the date of occupancy, relieving Seller of any additional repair or treatment obligations, and will maintain
35   the Property and assume all liability for and risk of loss to it from the date of occupancy. Effective on the date of occupancy,
36   this clause replaces Paragraph 9 of the Contract. Buyer and Seller will sign and deliver a written lease containing mutually
37   agreeable terms concerning Buyer's pre-closing occupancy of the Property and prepared at Buyer's expense.
38°   ☐ (2) Post-Occupancy Agreement: Buyer and Seller will sign and deliver a written lease, containing mutually agreeable
39   terms concerning Seller's occupancy of the Property after Closing Date and prepared at Seller's expense.
40°   ☐ (3) Existing Tenant: The Property is currently used as a rental property and Buyer's rights will be subject to those of
41°   existing tenants. Seller will, within _____ days from Effective Date and at Seller's expense, deliver to Buyer current copies
42°   of the rent roll; leases; income and expense statements for the period January 1, _____ through December 31, _____,
43°   as evidence that the Property generated income of $_____ against expenses of $_____;
44   and agreements with third parties that will remain in effect after closing. Buyer may terminate this Contract by written
45°   notice to Seller within _____ days from Effective Date if the statements differ materially from Seller's representations. If
46   Buyer fails to provide timely written notice, Buyer will be deemed to waive this contingency. Seller will assign leases and
47   rental agreements, and transfer deposits and advance rents, to Buyer at closing.
48°   ☐ (4) Vacating Tenant: The Property is currently used as a rental property. Seller will ensure that the existing tenant vacates
49   the Property prior to the time agreed upon for the Walk-Through Inspection.

50° (____) (____) - (____)(____) S. Sale/Lease of Buyer's Property: This Contract is contingent on the lease or closing of
51° Buyer's property located at _____. If
52° Buyer's property is not closed or subject to a signed lease acceptable to Buyer's lender by _____,
53° _____, ("Deadline"), Buyer will, within 3 days from Deadline, provide Seller with written notice canceling this Contract, and
54 Seller will refund Buyer's deposit. If Buyer does not timely provide written notice of cancellation, this contingency will be
55 deemed removed.

56° FARA-8   Rev. 10/04   © 2004   Florida Association of Realtors®   All Rights Reserved   Page _____ of Addendum No. _____

1* The clauses below will be incorporated into the Contract between _____ (Seller)
2* and _____ (Buyer) concerning the Property described as _____
3* _____. only if initialed by all parties:

4* (_____) (_____) - (_____)(_____) T. Rezoning: Buyer will have until _____, _____ to obtain the following
5* zoning for the Property from the appropriate government agency: Zoning _____ for use of the Property as
6* _____. Seller will sign all forms
7 required by the government agency. Buyer will pay all costs associated with the rezoning application and proceedings. If
8 rezoning is not obtained, this Contract will terminate and Buyer's deposit will be refunded.

9* (_____) (_____) - (_____)(_____) U. Assignment: Seller agrees that Buyer may assign this Contract to _____
10* _____
11* Buyer will deliver a copy of the assignment to Seller and ☐ will ☐ will not be released from the duty to perform this Contract.

12* (_____) (_____) - (_____)(_____) V. Property Disclosure Statement: This offer is contingent on Seller completing, signing and
13 delivering to Buyer a written real property disclosure statement within 3 days from Effective Date. If the statement discloses any
14 material information about the Property that is unacceptable to Buyer, Buyer may cancel this Contract by written notice to
15 Seller within 3 days from receipt of Seller's written statement.

16* (_____) (_____) - (_____)(_____) W. Foreign Investment in Real Property Tax Act ("FIRPTA"): If a Seller is a "foreign person" as
17 defined by FIRPTA, Section 1445 of the Internal Revenue Code requires Buyer to withhold 10% of the amount realized by the
18 Seller on the transfer and remit the withheld amount to the Internal Revenue Service (IRS) unless an exemption applies. The
19 primary exemptions are (1) Seller provides Buyer with an affidavit that Seller is not a "foreign person", (2) Seller provides
20 Buyer with a Withholding Certificate providing for reduced or eliminated withholding, or (3) the gross sales price is $300,000 or
21 less, Buyer is an individual who purchases the Property to use as a residence, and Buyer or a member of Buyer's family has
22 definite plans to reside at the Property for at least 50% of the number of days the Property is in use during each of the first two
23 12 month periods after transfer. The IRS requires Buyer and Seller to have a U.S. federal taxpayer identification number
24 ("TIN"). Buyer and Seller agree to execute and deliver as directed any instrument, affidavit or statement reasonably necessary
25 to comply with FIRPTA requirements including applying for a TIN within 3 days from Effective Date and delivering their
26 respective TIN or Social Security numbers to the Closing Agent. If Seller applies for a withholding certificate but the application
27 is still pending as of closing, Buyer will place the 10% tax in escrow at Seller's expense to be disbursed in accordance with
28 the final determination of the IRS, provided Seller so requests and gives Buyer notice of the pending application in accordance
29 with Section 1445. If Buyer does not pay sufficient cash at closing to meet the withholding requirement, Seller will deliver to
30 Buyer at closing the additional cash necessary to satisfy the requirement. Buyer will timely disburse the funds to the IRS and
31 provide Seller with copies of the tax forms and receipts.

32* (_____) (_____) - (_____)(_____) X. 1031 Exchange: If either Seller or Buyer wishes to enter into a like-kind exchange (either
33 simultaneously with closing or after) under Section 1031 of the Internal Revenue Code ("Exchange"), the other party will
34 cooperate in all reasonable respects to effectuate the Exchange including executing documents; provided, however, that the
35 cooperating party will incur no liability or cost related to the Exchange and that the closing shall not be contingent upon,
36 extended or delayed by the Exchange.

37* (_____) (_____) - (_____)(_____) Y. Additional Clauses _____
38* _____
39* _____
40* _____
41* _____
42* _____
43* _____
44* _____
45* _____
46* _____
47* _____
48* _____
49* _____
50* _____
51* _____
52* _____
53* _____
54* _____
55* _____
56* _____
57* _____
58* FARA-8   Rev. 10/04   © 2004   Florida Association of REALTORS®   All Rights Reserved   Page _____ of Addendum No. _____

Source: Florida Association of REALTORS©. Reprinted with permission.

RESIDENTIAL SALE AND PURCHASE CONTRACT

Residential Sale and Purchase Contract
FLORIDA ASSOCIATION OF REALTORS®

1* **1. SALE AND PURCHASE:** _____ ("Seller")
2* and _____ ("Buyer")
3 agree to sell and buy on the terms and conditions specified below the property described as:
4* Address: _____
5* _____ County: _____
6* Legal Description: _____
7* _____ Tax ID No: _____
8 together with all improvements and attached items, including fixtures, built-in furnishings, built-in appliances, ceiling fans, light
9 fixtures, attached wall-to-wall carpeting, rods, draperies and other window coverings. The only other items included in the
10* purchase are: _____
11* _____
12* _____
13* The following attached items are excluded from the purchase: _____
14* _____
15 The real and personal property described above as included in the purchase is referred to as the "Property." Personal property listed
16 in this Contract is included in the purchase price, has no contributory value and is being left for Seller's convenience.

17   **PRICE AND FINANCING**
18* **2. PURCHASE PRICE:** $_____ payable by Buyer in U.S. currency as follows:
19*   (a) $_____   Deposit received (checks are subject to clearance) _____, _____ by
20*   _____ for _____ ("Escrow Agent")
21   *Signature*   *Name of Company*
22*   (b) $_____   Additional deposit to be delivered to Escrow Agent by _____,
23*   _____ or _____ days from Effective Date. (10 days if left blank)
24*   (c) _____   Total financing (see Paragraph 3 below) (express as a dollar amount or percentage)
25*   (d) $_____   Other: _____
26*   (e) $_____   Balance to close (not including Buyer's closing costs, prepaid items and prorations). All funds paid
27   at closing must be paid by locally drawn cashier's check, official bank check, or wired funds.
28* **3. FINANCING: (Check as applicable)** ☐ (a) Buyer will pay cash for the Property with no financing contingency.
29*   ☐ (b) Buyer will apply for the financing specified in paragraph 2(c) at the prevailing interest rate and loan costs based on
30*   Buyer's creditworthiness (the "Financing") within _____ days from Effective Date (5 days if left blank) and provide Seller with a
31*   written Financing commitment or approval letter ("Commitment") within _____ days from Effective Date (30 days if left blank)
32   ("Commitment Period"). Buyer will keep Seller and Broker fully informed about loan application status, progress and
33   Commitment issues and authorizes the mortgage broker and lender to disclose all such information to Seller and Broker. Once
34   Buyer provides the Commitment to Seller, the financing contingency is waived and Seller will be entitled to retain the deposits
35   if the transaction does not close by the Closing Date unless (1) the Property appraises below the purchase price and either the
36   parties cannot agree on a new purchase price or Buyer elects not to proceed, or (2) another provision of this Contract requires
37   the deposits to be returned. If Buyer, using diligence and good faith, cannot provide the Commitment within the Commitment
38   Period, this Contract will be terminated and Buyer's deposits refunded.

39   **CLOSING**
40 **4. CLOSING DATE; OCCUPANCY:** Unless extended by other provisions of this Contract, this Contract will be closed on
41* _____, _____ ("Closing Date") at the time established by the closing agent, by which time Seller will (a) have removed all
42 personal items and trash from the Property and swept the Property clean and (b) deliver the deed, occupancy and possession, along with
43 all keys, garage door openers and access codes, to Buyer. If on Closing Date insurance underwriting is suspended, Buyer may
44 postpone closing up to 5 days after the insurance suspension is lifted. If this transaction does not close for any reason, Buyer will
45 immediately return all Seller-provided title evidence, surveys, association documents and other items.

46 **5. CLOSING PROCEDURE; COSTS:** Closing will take place in the county where the Property is located and may be conducted by
47 mail or electronic means. If title insurance insures Buyer for title defects arising between the title binder effective date and recording
48 of Buyer's deed, closing agent will disburse at closing the net sale proceeds to Seller and brokerage fees to Broker as per
49 Paragraph 19. In addition to other expenses provided in this Contract, Seller and Buyer will pay the costs indicated below.
50   (a) Seller Costs: Seller will pay taxes and surtaxes on the deed and recording fees for documents needed to cure title; up to
51* $_____ or _____% (1.5% if left blank) of the purchase price for repairs to warranted items ("Repair Limit");

52* Buyer (____)(____) and Seller (____)(____) acknowledge receipt of a copy of this page, which is Page 1 of 7 Pages.
53 FAR-8   Rev. 10/04   © 2004   Florida Association of REALTORS®   All Rights Reserved

54" and up to $_____ or _____% (1.5% if left blank) of the purchase price for wood-destroying organism
55" treatment and repairs ("WDO Repair Limit"); Other: _____
56" (b) Buyer Costs: Buyer will pay taxes and recording fees on notes and mortgages; recording fees on the deed and financing
57" statements; loan expenses; lender's title policy; inspections; survey; flood insurance; Other: _____
58" (c) Title Evidence and Insurance: Check (1) or (2):
59" ☐ (1) The title evidence will be a Paragraph 10(a)(1) owner's title insurance commitment. ☐ Seller ☐ Buyer will select the title
60" agent. ☐ Seller ☐ Buyer will pay for the owner's title policy, search, examination and related charges. Each party will
61 pay its own closing fees.
62" ☐ (2) Seller will provide an abstract as specified in Paragraph 10(a)(2) as title evidence. ☐ Seller ☐ Buyer will pay for
63 the owner's title policy and select the title agent. Seller will pay fees for title searches prior to closing, including tax
64 search and lien search fees, and Buyer will pay fees for title searches after closing (if any), title examination fees and
65 closing fees.
66" (d) Prorations: The following items will be made current (if applicable) and prorated as of the day before Closing Date: real
67 estate taxes, interest, bonds, assessments, association fees, insurance, rents and other current expenses and revenues of
68 the Property. If taxes and assessments for the current year cannot be determined, the previous year's rates will be used with
69 adjustment for exemptions and improvements. Buyer is responsible for property tax increases due to change in ownership.
70" (e) Special Assessment by Public Body: Regarding special assessments imposed by a public body, Seller will pay (i) the full
71 amount of liens that are certified, confirmed and ratified before closing and (ii) the amount of the last estimate of the assessment if
72 an improvement is substantially completed as of Effective Date but has not resulted in a lien before closing, and Buyer will pay all
73 other amounts.
74" (f) Tax Withholding: Buyer and Seller will comply with the Foreign Investment in Real Property Tax Act, which may require
75 Seller to provide additional cash at closing if Seller is a "foreign person" as defined by federal law.
76" (g) Home Warranty: ☐ Buyer ☐ Seller ☐ N/A will pay for a home warranty plan issued by _____ at a
77" cost not to exceed $_____. A home warranty plan provides for repair or replacement of many of a home's mechanical
78 systems and major built-in appliances in the event of breakdown due to normal wear and tear during the agreement period.

79 **PROPERTY CONDITION**
80" **6. INSPECTION PERIODS:** Buyer will complete the inspections referenced in Paragraphs 7 and 8(a)(2) by _____,
81" _____ (within 10 days from Effective Date if left blank) ("Inspection Period"); the wood-destroying organism inspection
82" by _____, _____ (at least 5 days prior to closing, if left blank); and the walk-through inspection on the
83 day before Closing Date or any other time agreeable to the parties; and the survey referenced in Paragraph 10(c) by
84" _____, _____ (at least 5 days prior to closing if left blank).

85 **7. REAL PROPERTY DISCLOSURES:** Seller represents that Seller does not know of any facts that materially affect the value
86 of the Property, including but not limited to violations of governmental laws, rules and regulations, other than those that Buyer
87 can readily observe or that are known by or have been disclosed to Buyer. Seller will have all open permits (if any) closed out,
88 with final inspections completed, no later than 5 days prior to closing.
89 (a) Energy Efficiency: Buyer acknowledges receipt of the energy-efficiency information brochure required by Section 553.996,
90 *Florida Statutes.*
91 (b) Radon Gas: Radon is a naturally occurring radioactive gas that, when it has accumulated in a building in sufficient
92 quantities, may present health risks to persons who are exposed to it over time. Levels of radon that exceed federal and
93 state guidelines have been found in buildings in Florida. Additional information regarding radon and radon testing may be
94 obtained from your county public health unit. Buyer may, within the Inspection Period, have an appropriately licensed person
95 test the Property for radon. If the radon level exceeds acceptable EPA standards, Seller may choose to reduce the radon
96 level to an acceptable EPA level, failing which either party may cancel this Contract.
97 (c) Flood Zone: Buyer is advised to verify by survey, with the lender and with appropriate government agencies which flood
98 zone the Property is in, whether flood insurance is required and what restrictions apply to improving the Property and rebuilding
99 in the event of casualty. If the Property is in a Special Flood Hazard Area or Coastal High Hazard Area and the buildings are built
100 below the minimum flood elevation, Buyer may cancel this Contract by delivering written notice to Seller within 20 days from
101 Effective Date, failing which Buyer accepts the existing elevation of the buildings and zone designation of the Property.
102 (d) Homeowners' Association: If membership in a homeowners' association is mandatory, an association disclosure
103 summary is attached and incorporated into this Contract. BUYER SHOULD NOT SIGN THIS CONTRACT UNTIL
104 BUYER HAS RECEIVED AND READ THE DISCLOSURE SUMMARY.
105 (e) PROPERTY TAX DISCLOSURE SUMMARY: BUYER SHOULD NOT RELY ON THE SELLER'S CURRENT PROPERTY
106 TAXES AS THE AMOUNT OF PROPERTY TAXES THAT BUYER MAY BE OBLIGATED TO PAY IN THE YEAR SUBSEQUENT
107 TO PURCHASE. A CHANGE OF OWNERSHIP OR PROPERTY IMPROVEMENTS TRIGGERS REASSESSMENTS OF THE
108 PROPERTY THAT COULD RESULT IN HIGHER PROPERTY TAXES. IF YOU HAVE ANY QUESTIONS CONCERNING
109 VALUATION, CONTACT THE COUNTY PROPERTY APPRAISER'S OFFICE FOR FURTHER INFORMATION.
110 (f) Mold: Mold is part of the natural environment that, when accumulated in sufficient quantities, may present health risks to
111 susceptible persons. For more information, contact the county indoor air quality specialist or other appropriate professional.

112" Buyer (____) (____) and Seller (____) (____) acknowledge receipt of a copy of this page, which is Page 2 of 7 Pages.
FAR-8   Rev. 10/04   © 2004   Florida Association of Realtors®   All Rights Reserved

113 **8. MAINTENANCE, INSPECTIONS AND REPAIR:** Seller will keep the Property in the same condition from Effective Date until
114 closing, except for normal wear and tear ("maintenance requirement") and repairs required by this Contract. Seller will provide
115 access and utilities for Buyer's inspections. Buyer will repair all damages to the Property resulting from the inspections,
116 return the Property to its pre-inspection condition and provide Seller with paid receipts for all work done on Property upon its
117 completion. If Seller, using best efforts, is unable to complete required repairs or treatments prior to closing, Seller will give
118 Buyer a credit at closing for the cost of the repairs Seller was obligated to make. At closing, Seller will assign all assignable repair
119 and treatment contracts to Buyer and provide Buyer with paid receipts for all work done on the Property pursuant to the
120 terms of this Contract.
121   (a) Warranty, Inspections and Repair:
122   (1) Warranty: Seller warrants that non-leased major appliances and heating, cooling, mechanical, electrical, security,
123   sprinkler, septic and plumbing systems, seawall, dock and pool equipment, if any, are and will be maintained in working
124   condition until closing; that the structures (including roofs) and pool, if any, are structurally sound and watertight; and
125   that torn or missing pool cage and screen room screens and missing roof tiles will be replaced. Seller does not warrant
126   and is not required to repair cosmetic conditions, unless the cosmetic condition resulted from a defect in a warranted
127   item. Seller is not obligated to bring any item into compliance with existing building code regulations unless necessary
128   to repair a warranted item. "Working condition" means operating in the manner in which the item was designed to
129   operate and "cosmetic conditions" means aesthetic imperfections that do not affect the working condition of the item,
130   including pitted marcite; missing or torn window screens; fogged windows; tears, worn spots and discoloration of floor
131   coverings/wallpapers/window treatments; nail holes, scratches, dents, scrapes, chips and caulking in bathroom
132   ceiling/walls/flooring/tile/fixtures/mirrors; cracked roof tiles; curling or worn shingles; and minor cracks in floor
133   tiles/windows/driveways/sidewalks/pool decks/garage and patio floors.
134   (2) Professional Inspection: Buyer may, at Buyer's expense, have warranted items inspected by a person who
135   specializes in and holds an occupational license (if required by law) to conduct home inspections or who holds a Florida
136   license to repair and maintain the items inspected ("professional inspector"). Buyer must, within 5 days from the end of the
137   Inspection Period, deliver written notice of any items that are not in the condition warranted and a copy of the inspector's
138   written report, if any, to Seller. If Buyer fails to deliver timely written notice, Buyer waives Seller's warranty and accepts
139   the items listed in subparagraph (a) in their "as is" conditions, except that Seller must meet the maintenance requirement.
140   (3) Repair: Seller will obtain repair estimates and is obligated only to make repairs necessary to bring warranted items
141   into the condition warranted, up to the Repair Limit. Seller may, within 5 days from receipt of Buyer's notice of items
142   that are not in the condition warranted, have a second inspection made by a professional inspector and will report
143   repair estimates to Buyer. If the first and second inspection reports differ and the parties cannot resolve the differences,
144   Buyer and Seller together will choose, and equally split the cost of, a third inspector, whose written report will be
145   binding on the parties. If the cost to repair warranted items equals or is less than the Repair Limit, Seller will have the
146   repairs made in a workmanlike manner by an appropriately licensed person. If the cost to repair warranted items
147   exceeds the Repair Limit, either party may cancel this Contract unless either party pays the excess or Buyer
148   designates which repairs to make at a total cost to Seller not exceeding the Repair Limit and accepts the balance of
149   the Property in its "as is" condition.
150   (b) Wood-Destroying Organisms: "Wood-destroying organism" means arthropod or plant life, including termites, powder-post
151 beetles, oldhouse borers and wood-decaying fungi, that damages or infests seasoned wood in a structure, excluding fences.
152 Buyer may, at Buyer's expense and prior to closing, have the Property inspected by a Florida-licensed pest control business to
153 determine the existence of past or present wood-destroying organism infestation and damage caused by infestation. If the
154 inspector finds evidence of infestation or damage, Buyer will deliver a copy of the inspector's written report to Seller within 5
155 days from the date of the inspection. If Seller previously treated the Property for wood-destroying organisms, Seller does not
156 have to treat the Property again if (i) there is no visible live infestation, and (ii) Seller transfers a current full treatment warranty to
157 Buyer at closing. Otherwise, Seller will have 5 days from receipt of the inspector's report to have reported damage estimated by
158 a licensed building or general contractor and corrective treatment estimated by a licensed pest control business. Seller will have
159 treatments and repairs made by an appropriately licensed person at Seller's expense up to the WDO Repair Limit. If the cost to
160 treat and repair the Property exceeds the WDO Repair Limit, either party may pay the excess, failing which either party may
161 cancel this Contract by written notice to the other. If Buyer fails to timely deliver the inspector's written report, Buyer accepts the
162 Property "as is" with regard to wood-destroying organism infestation and damage, subject to the maintenance requirement.
163   (c) Walk-through Inspection: Buyer may walk through the Property solely to verify that Seller has made repairs required
164 by this Contract and has met contractual obligations. No other issues may be raised as a result of the walk-through
165 inspection. If Buyer fails to conduct this inspection, Seller's repair and maintenance obligations will be deemed fulfilled.

166 **9. RISK OF LOSS:** If any portion of the Property is damaged by fire or other casualty before closing and can be restored within
167 45 days from the Closing Date to substantially the same condition as it was on Effective Date, Seller will, at Seller's expense,
168 restore the Property and the Closing Date will be extended accordingly. Seller will not be obligated to replace trees. If the
169 restoration cannot be completed in time, Buyer may accept the Property "as is", in which case with Seller will credit the
170 deductible and assign the insurance proceeds, if any, to Buyer at closing in such amounts as are (i) attributable to the Property
171 and (ii) not yet expended in making repairs, failing which either party may cancel this Contract. If the Property is a
172 condominium, this paragraph applies only to the unit and limited common elements appurtenant to the unit; if the Property is in
173 a homeowners' association, this paragraph will not apply to common elements or recreation or other facilities.

174* Buyer (____)(____) and Seller (____)(____) acknowledge receipt of a copy of this page, which is Page 3 of 7 Pages.
FAR-8   Rev. 10/04   © 2004   Florida Association of REALTORS®   All Rights Reserved

TITLE

175
176 **10. TITLE:** Seller will convey marketable title to the Property by statutory warranty deed or trustee, personal representative or
177 guardian deed as appropriate to Seller's status.
178   (a) **Title Evidence:** Title evidence will show legal access to the Property and marketable title of record in Seller in accordance with
179   current title standards adopted by the Florida Bar, subject only to the following title exceptions, none of which prevent residential
180   use of the Property: covenants, easements and restrictions of record; matters of plat; existing zoning and government regulations;
181   oil, gas and mineral rights of record if there is no right of entry; current taxes; mortgages that Buyer will assume; and
182   encumbrances that Seller will discharge at or before closing. Seller will, at least 2 days prior to closing, deliver to Buyer Seller's
183   choice of one of the following types of title evidence, which must be generally accepted in the county where the Property is located
184   (specify in Paragraph 5(c) the selected type). Seller will use option (1) in Palm Beach County and option (2) in Miami-Dade County.
185   (1) A title insurance commitment issued by a Florida-licensed title insurer in the amount of the purchase price and
186   subject only to title exceptions set forth in this Contract.
187   (2) An existing abstract of title from a reputable and existing abstract firm (if firm is not existing, then abstract must be
188   certified as correct by an existing firm) purporting to be an accurate synopsis of the instruments affecting title to the
189   Property recorded in the public records of the county where the Property is located and certified to Effective Date.
190   However, if such an abstract is not available to Seller, then a prior owner's title policy acceptable to the proposed
191   insurer as a base for reissuance of coverage. Seller will pay for copies of all policy exceptions and an update in a format
192   acceptable to Buyer's closing agent from the policy effective date and certified to Buyer or Buyer's closing agent,
193   together with copies of all documents recited in the prior policy and in the update. If a prior policy is not available to
194   Seller then (1) above will be the title evidence. Title evidence will be delivered no later than 10 days before Closing Date.
195   (b) **Title Examination:** Buyer will examine the title evidence and deliver written notice to Seller, within 5 days from receipt of
196   title evidence but no later than closing, of any defects that make the title unmarketable. Seller will have 30 days from
197   receipt of Buyer's notice of defects ("Curative Period") to cure the defects at Seller's expense. If Seller cures the defects
198   within the Curative Period, Seller will deliver written notice to Buyer and the parties will close the transaction on Closing
199   Date or within 10 days from Buyer's receipt of Seller's notice if Closing Date has passed. If Seller is unable to cure the
200   defects within the Curative Period, Seller will deliver written notice to Buyer and Buyer will, within 10 days from receipt of
201   Seller's notice, either cancel this Contract or accept title with existing defects and close the transaction.
202   (c) **Survey:** Buyer may, at Buyer's expense, have the Property surveyed and deliver written notice to Seller, within 5 days from
203   receipt of survey but no later than closing, of any encroachments on the Property, encroachments by the Property's improvements
204   on other lands or deed restriction or zoning violations. Any such encroachment or violation will be treated in the same manner as a
205   title defect and Buyer's and Seller's obligations will be determined in accordance with subparagraph (b) above. If any part of the
206   Property lies seaward of the coastal construction control line, Seller will provide Buyer with an affidavit or survey as required by law
207   delineating the line's location on the property, unless Buyer waives this requirement in writing.

208   MISCELLANEOUS
209 **11. EFFECTIVE DATE; TIME:** The "Effective Date" of this Contract is the date on which the last of the parties initials or signs the
210 latest offer. Time is of the essence for all provisions of this Contract. All time periods will be computed in business days (a
211 "business day" is every calendar day except Saturday, Sunday and national legal holidays). If any deadline falls on a Saturday,
212 Sunday or national legal holiday, performance will be due the next business day. All time periods will end at 5:00 p.m. local
213 time (meaning in the county where the Property is located) of the appropriate day.

214 **12. NOTICES:** All notices will be made to the parties and Broker by mail, personal delivery or electronic media. Buyer's failure
215 to deliver timely written notice to Seller, when such notice is required by this Contract, regarding any contingencies will
216 render that contingency null and void and the Contract will be construed as if the contingency did not exist. Any notice,
217 document or item given to or received by an attorney or Broker (including a transaction broker) representing a party will
218 be as effective as if given to or by that party.

219 **13. COMPLETE AGREEMENT:** This Contract is the entire agreement between Buyer and Seller. Except for brokerage
220 agreements, no prior or present agreements will bind Buyer, Seller or Broker unless incorporated into this Contract.
221 Modifications of this Contract will not be binding unless in writing, signed or initialed and delivered by the party to be bound.
222 Signatures, initials, documents referenced in this Contract, counterparts and written modifications communicated electronically
223 or on paper will be acceptable for all purposes, including delivery, and will be binding. Handwritten or typewritten terms
224 inserted in or attached to this Contract prevail over preprinted terms. If any provision of this Contract is or becomes invalid or
225 unenforceable, all remaining provisions will continue to be fully effective. Buyer and Seller will use diligence and good faith in
226 performing all obligations under this Agreement. This Contract will not be recorded in any public records.

227 **14. ASSIGNABILITY; PERSONS BOUND:** Buyer may not assign this Contract without Seller's written consent. The terms
228 "Buyer," "Seller," and "Broker" may be singular or plural. This Contract is binding on the heirs, administrators, executors,
229 personal representatives and assigns (if permitted) of Buyer, Seller and Broker.

230   DEFAULT AND DISPUTE RESOLUTION
231 **15. DEFAULT:** (a) **Seller Default:** If for any reason other than failure of Seller to make Seller's title marketable after diligent effort, Seller
232 fails, refuses or neglects to perform this Contract, Buyer may choose to receive a return of Buyer's deposit without waiving the right to
233 seek damages or to seek specific performance as per Paragraph 16. Seller will also be liable to Broker for the full amount of the
234* Buyer (_____)(_____) and Seller (_____)(_____) acknowledge receipt of a copy of this page, which is Page 4 of 7 Pages.
FAR-8   Rev. 10/04   © 2004   Florida Association of Realtors®   All Rights Reserved

235 brokerage fee. (b) Buyer Default: If Buyer fails to perform this Contract within the time specified, including timely payment of all deposits,
236 Seller may choose to retain and collect all deposits paid and agreed to be paid as liquidated damages or to seek specific performance as
237 per Paragraph 16; and Broker will, upon demand, receive 50% of all deposits paid and agreed to be paid (to be split equally among
238 cooperating brokers except when closing does not occur due to Buyer not being able to secure Financing after providing a Commitment,
239 in which case Broker's portion of the deposits will go solely to the listing broker) up to the full amount of the brokerage fee.

240 **16. DISPUTE RESOLUTION:** This Contract will be construed under Florida law. All controversies, claims and other matters in
241 question arising out of or relating to this transaction or this Contract or its breach will be settled as follows:
242   (a) Disputes concerning entitlement to deposits made and agreed to be made: Buyer and Seller will have 30 days from the
243   date conflicting demands are made to attempt to resolve the dispute through mediation. If that fails, Escrow Agent will
244   submit the dispute, if so required by Florida law, to Escrow Agent's choice of arbitration, a Florida court or the Florida Real
245   Estate Commission. Buyer and Seller will be bound by any resulting award, judgment or order.
246   (b) All other disputes: Buyer and Seller will have 30 days from the date a dispute arises between them to attempt to
247   resolve the matter through mediation, failing which the parties will resolve the dispute through neutral binding arbitration
248   in the county where the Property is located. The arbitrator may not alter the Contract terms or award any remedy not
249   provided for in this Contract. The award will be based on the greater weight of the evidence and will state findings of fact
250   and the contractual authority on which it is based. If the parties agree to use discovery, it will be in accordance with the
251   Florida Rules of Civil Procedure and the arbitrator will resolve all discovery-related disputes. Any disputes with a real
252   estate licensee or firm named in Paragraph 19 will be submitted to arbitration only if the licensee's broker consents in
253   writing to become a party to the proceeding. This clause will survive closing.
254   (c) Mediation and Arbitration; Expenses: "Mediation" is a process in which parties attempt to resolve a dispute by
255   submitting it to an impartial mediator who facilitates the resolution of the dispute but who is not empowered to impose a
256   settlement on the parties. Mediation will be in accordance with the rules of the American Arbitration Association ("AAA") or
257   other mediator agreed on by the parties. The parties will equally divide the mediation fee, if any. "Arbitration" is a process in
258   which the parties resolve a dispute by a hearing before a neutral person who decides the matter and whose decision is
259   binding on the parties. Arbitration will be in accordance with the rules of the AAA or other arbitrator agreed on by the
260   parties. Each party to any arbitration will pay its own fees, costs and expenses, including attorneys' fees, and will equally
261   split the arbitrators' fees and administrative fees of arbitration.

262   **ESCROW AGENT AND BROKER**
263 **17. ESCROW AGENT:** Buyer and Seller authorize Escrow Agent to receive, deposit and hold funds and other items in escrow and,
264 subject to clearance, disburse them upon proper authorization and in accordance with Florida law and the terms of this Contract,
265 including disbursing brokerage fees. The parties agree that Escrow Agent will not be liable to any person for misdelivery of escrowed
266 items to Buyer or Seller, unless the misdelivery is due to Escrow Agent's willful breach of this Contract or gross negligence. If Escrow
267 Agent interpleads the subject matter of the escrow, Escrow Agent will pay the filing fees and costs from the deposit and will recover
268 reasonable attorneys' fees and costs to be paid from the escrowed funds or equivalent and charged and awarded as court costs in
269 favor of the prevailing party. All claims against Escrow Agent will be arbitrated, so long as Escrow Agent consents to arbitrate.

270 **18. PROFESSIONAL ADVICE; BROKER LIABILITY:** Broker advises Buyer and Seller to verify all facts and representations that are
271 important to them and to consult an appropriate professional for legal advice (for example, interpreting contracts, determining the
272 effect of laws on the Property and transaction, status of title, foreign investor reporting requirements, etc.) and for tax, property
273 condition, environmental and other specialized advice. Buyer acknowledges that Broker does not reside in the Property and that all
274 representations (oral, written or otherwise) by Broker are based on Seller representations or public records. Buyer agrees to rely
275 solely on Seller, professional inspectors and governmental agencies for verification of the Property condition, square footage
276 and facts that materially affect Property value. Buyer and Seller respectively will pay all costs and expenses, including reasonable
277 attorneys' fees at all levels, incurred by Broker and Broker's officers, directors, agents and employees in connection with or arising
278 from Buyer's or Seller's misstatement or failure to perform contractual obligations. Buyer and Seller hold harmless and release
279 Broker and Broker's officers, directors, agents and employees from all liability for loss or damage based on (1) Buyer's or Seller's
280 misstatement or failure to perform contractual obligations; (2) Broker's performance, at Buyer's and/or Seller's request, of any task
281 beyond the scope of services regulated by Chapter 475, F.S., as amended, including Broker's referral, recommendation or retention
282 of any vendor; (3) products or services provided by any vendor; and (4) expenses incurred by any vendor. Buyer and Seller each
283 assume full responsibility for selecting and compensating their respective vendors. This paragraph will not relieve Broker of statutory
284 obligations. For purposes of this paragraph, Broker will be treated as a party to this Contract. This paragraph will survive closing.

285 **19. BROKERS:** The licensee(s) and brokerage(s) named below are collectively referred to as "Broker." Instruction to Closing
286 Agent: Seller and Buyer direct closing agent to disburse at closing the full amount of the brokerage fees as specified in separate
287 brokerage agreements with the parties and cooperative agreements between the brokers, except to the extent Broker has
288 retained such fees from the escrowed funds. In the absence of such brokerage agreements, closing agent will disburse
289 brokerage fees as indicated below. This paragraph will not be used to modify any MLS or other offer of compensation made by
290 Seller or listing broker to cooperating brokers.

291* Buyer (_____) (_____) and Seller (_____) (_____) acknowledge receipt of a copy of this page, which is Page 5 of 7 Pages.
FAR-8   Rev. 10/04   © 2004   Florida Association of REALTORS®   All Rights Reserved

292*
293* *Selling Sales Associate/License No.* _____　　*Selling Firm/Brokerage Fee: ($ or % of Purchase Price)* _____

294*
295* *Listing Sales Associate/License No.* _____　　*Listing Firm/Brokerage fee: ($ or % of Purchase Price)* _____

296

ADDENDA AND ADDITIONAL TERMS

297　20. ADDENDA: The following additional terms are included in addenda and incorporated into this Contract (check if applicable):

298* ☐ A. Condo. Assn.	☐ H. As Is w/Right to Inspect	☐ O. Interest-Bearing Account	☐ V. Prop. Disclosure Stmt.
299* ☐ B. Homeowners' Assn.	☐ I. Inspections	☐ P. Back-up Contract	☐ W. FIRPTA
300* ☐ C. Seller Financing	☐ J. Insulation Disclosure	☐ Q. Broker - Pers. Int. in Prop.	☐ X. 1031 Exchange
301* ☐ D. Mort. Assumption	☐ K. Pre-1978 Housing Stmt. (LBP)	☐ R. Rentals	☐ Y. Additional Clauses
302* ☐ E. FHA Financing	☐ L. Insurance	☐ S. Sale/Lease of Buyer's Property	☐ Other_____
303* ☐ F. VA Financing	☐ M. Housing Older Persons	☐ T. Rezoning	☐ Other_____
304* ☐ G. New Mort. Rates	☐ N. Unimproved/Ag. Prop.	☐ U. Assignment	☐ Other_____

305* **21. ADDITIONAL TERMS:** _____

306* _____
307* _____
308* _____
309* _____
310* _____
311* _____
312* _____
313* _____
314* _____
315* _____
316* _____
317* _____
318* _____
319* _____
320* _____
321* _____
322* _____
323* _____
324* _____
325* _____
326* _____
327* _____
328* _____
329* _____
330* _____
331* _____
332* _____
333* _____
334* _____
335* _____
336* _____
337* _____
338* _____
339* _____
340* _____
341* _____
342* _____
343* _____
344* _____
345* _____
346* _____
347* _____

348* Buyer (____)(____) and Seller (____)(____) acknowledge receipt of a copy of this page, which is Page 6 of 7 Pages.

FAR-8　Rev. 10/04　© 2004　Florida Association of REALTORS®　All Rights Reserved

349   This is intended to be a legally binding contract. If not fully understood, seek the advice of an attorney prior to signing.

350   OFFER AND ACCEPTANCE
351* (Check if applicable: ☐ Buyer received a written real property disclosure statement from Seller before making this Offer.)
352   Buyer offers to purchase the Property on the above terms and conditions. Unless this Contract is signed by Seller and a copy
353* delivered to Buyer no later than _____ ☐ a.m.☐ p.m. on _____, _____, this offer will be revoked
354   and Buyer's deposit refunded subject to clearance of funds.

355* Date: _____   Buyer: _____
356*   Print name: _____

357* Date: _____   Buyer: _____
358* Phone: _____   Print name: _____
359* Fax: _____   Address: _____
360* E-mail: _____

361* Date: _____   Seller: _____
362*   Print name: _____

363* Date: _____   Seller: _____
364* Phone: _____   Print name: _____
365* Fax: _____   Address: _____
366* E-mail: _____   _____

367   COUNTER OFFER/REJECTION
368* ☐ Seller counters Buyer's offer (to accept the counter offer, Buyer must sign or initial the counter offered terms and deliver a copy
369* of the acceptance to Seller by 5:00 p.m. on _____, _____). ☐ Seller rejects Buyer's offer.

370* | Effective Date: _____ (The date on which the last party signed or initialed acceptance of the final offer.) |

371* Buyer (____) (____) and Seller (____) (____) acknowledge receipt of a copy of this page, which is Page 7 of 7 Pages.

Source: Florida Association of REALTORS©. Reprinted with permission.

Glossary

Chapter 1

absentee owner—Investors who own income-producing properties who do not have the time or the expertise to devote to a project.

agricultural/farm area—Chapter 475, F.S., defines agricultural property as any property consisting of greater than ten acres.

appraisal—an opinion of value that is based upon certain facts as of a given date.

brokerage—is the business of bringing together buyers and sellers or landlords and tenants for a fee.

commercial transaction—any transaction for the sale or lease of real property containing greater than four units or more than ten acres of agricultural property.

comparative market analysis (CMA)—an opinion of value by examining recently sold properties, listings of properties currently on the market, and previous expired-listing information. It is never referred to as an appraisal.

dedication—private property given by an owner for the public's use.

plat map of subdivision—a visual rendering of the proposed development. Streets, building lots, water, sewer, and public utilities are often the subject of the rendering.

property management—the real estate sector whose business is dealing with the management of real property.

real estate brokerage—the business of matching buyers with sellers and tenants with landlords.

residential transaction—any transaction involving the sale or leasing of a property that contains four (4) or fewer units intended for dwelling purposes. This definition is expanded to include ten (10) acres or less of agricultural property.

restrictive covenants—covenants designed to create a means of conformity within a particular subdivision. Examples include setback requirements, size minimum square footage requirements, property use(s), and in most cases the architectural design of the improvement.

Uniform Standards of Professional Appraisal Practice (USPAP)—dictates how appraisers must accomplish their assignments.

Chapter 2

broker—any person, corporation, partnership, limited liability partnership, or limited liability company who performs a real estate act for another, in exchange for or in anticipation of compensation or other valuable consideration.

broker associate—a person who is licensed and is otherwise qualified as a real estate broker but, rather than forming his own business, chooses to work under the name and supervision of another broker.

caveat emptor—the Latin term for "let the buyer beware,"

compensation—a payment or something given of value.

deficiency letter—informs the licensee that she has not completed the required continuing education prior to license renewal.

Florida residency—Rule 61J2-26.002 defines a Florida resident as anyone who has resided in Florida continuously for four calendar months or more within a calendar year. This definition would also include ones intent to reside for four calendar months or more within a calendar year.

irrevocable consent to service—*is a* form that a nonresident applicant signs designating the director of the Florida Division of Real Estate as the recipient of any legal notices against and on the nonresident's behalf.

license—state permission to operate as a real estate agent.

mutual recognition agreement—under such an agreement, Florida will mutually recognize the education and experience that a licensee has obtained by holding a real estate license in another state toward a license in the subject state.

nolo contendere—means the person does not dispute the charges but does not admit any guilt.

registration—the official placement of a real estate brokerage business or practice within the records of the Florida Department of Business Regulation (DBPR).

Rule 61J2-26.002—states that one is a Florida resident after residing in Florida continuously for four calendar months or more within a calendar year.

sales associate—a person associated with a licensed real estate broker who assists in performing services offered by the broker. A sales associate is licensed to work for, and act as a representative of, the broker.

Chapter 3

active license—is where the licensee is free to be actively engaged in real estate activities as defined by FREC.

canceled—a license that is canceled is considered void.

cease to be in force—licenses that are issued but cease to be in force when notification has not been received by FREC as a result of a change of address or a change of the licensee's association occurs.

Department of Business and Professional Regulation (DBPR)—is charged with regulating licensed professions and professionals within the state of Florida.

Division of Real Estate (DRE)—performs ministerial, administrative and all functions concerning the regulation of the real estate industry.

Florida Real Estate Commission (FREC)—the regulatory body whose purpose is to protect the general public by regulating real estate brokers, broker associates, sales associates, real estate schools and instructors.

group license—an owner-developer who owns property in the name of several entities may submit proof that such entities are so connected or affiliated that ownership is essentially held by the same individual(s). Any sales associate or broker associate working for the owner-developer may be issued a group license. The licensee is considered to hold one license and to be working for one employer.

inactive license—is where the licensee is not actively engaged in real estate activities.

ineffective—a license that is issued to an individual, however, predicated on the circumstances specific to that individual, the licensee may not use it.

involuntarily inactive—involuntary inactive status occurs automatically when a licensee fails to renew his license in a timely manner.

multiple licenses—any broker that holds more than one broker license at one time is termed as a holder licenses.

prima facie—on face value evidence.

void—having no legal effect.

voluntarily inactive—is when a licensee holds a valid real estate license but chooses not to engage actively in the practice of real estate.

Chapter 4

agency—is the name for the relationship created between the agent and the principal. An agency relationship is created by employing the agent under a contract.

agency coupled with an interest—this type of relationship exists when an agent has some form of interest within the property in question.

agent—any person who transacts business activities on behalf of another (usually for a fee).

caveat emptor—Latin for "let the buyer beware."

consent to transition—gives rise to the need for a licensee to change his relationship with a principal; therefore, the consent to transition form is used to apprise a principal of the agent's need to transition to another authorized form of agency relationship. Prior to any transition on the part of a licensee, the written consent of the principal is required.

customer—the third party in a transaction who is owed fair and honest dealing.

designated sales associate—the broker may designate one sales associate to act as a single agent for the buyer and a different sales associate to act as a single agent for the seller. Both buyer and seller must have assets of $1 million or more and must execute documents evidencing same.

dual agency—a relationship in which the agent represents both the buyer (or lessee) and the seller (or lessor) within the same transaction. In Florida this relationship is illegal.

fiduciary—any agent under an agency relationship who is granted a position of the highest form of trust and owes a party fiduciary responsibilities.

general agency—a general agent is authorized to act for the principal in a specific business or trade (i.e. management company under a property management agreement with the owner).

limited confidentiality—the licensee's duty of confidentiality is limited. The licensee may not disclose to one party what she knows about the other.

limited representation—the broker does not represent either party in a fiduciary capacity as a single agent. Rather, the broker provides a limited form of nonfiduciary representation to the buyer, seller, or both.

nonrepresentation—the broker is not obligated to provide the fiduciary duties that a broker owes to a principal under a single agency relationship. The broker must provide fair and honest dealing.

principal (client)—the person who hires or appoints an agent to act on her behalf is called the principal or the client.

residential sale—the sale of improved land used as one- to four-family dwelling units, the sale of unimproved land intended for use as one- to four-family dwelling units and/or the sale of farm/agricultural land of up to ten acres.

single agent—a licensee represents either a buyer or a seller but never both within the same transaction.

special agent—the agency relationship authorizing the agent to perform a narrow and specific range of duties concerning an act or transaction (i.e. a broker under a listing agreement with the principal).

transaction broker—a broker who provides limited non-fiduciary representation to one or both parties to the transaction.

universal agency—in a universal agency, the agent is given the legal authority to transact matters of all types for the principal. This relationship provides the broadest scope of powers.

Chapter 5

arbitration—when parties who are unable to agree among themselves seek the assistance of a third party (one or more arbitrators) who formulates a decision that is binding on all the parties involved.

blind ad—any advertisement that does not include the brokerage firm name is called a blind ad.

commingle—the mixing of funds belonging to others with the broker's personal funds or business funds.

conflicting demands—demands made upon the escrowed funds when two parties (such as a buyer and a seller) do not agree as to how the funds should be disbursed.

conversion—is when the broker unlawfully takes funds belonging to others for her own personal use.

corporation—is defined as a legal person/entity organized under the laws of Florida or another state. A corporation may include one or more people.

deposit—money or other valuable consideration belonging to others placed with an escrow agent.

double taxation—money that is taxed once on the profits of the corporation and once on the dividends paid to its shareholders.

earnest money—is a deposit paid by a prospective buyer to show his intention to go through with the sale.

escrow (trust) account—is established to hold the funds of others that have been entrusted to the broker.

escrow disbursement order (EDO)—is the instructions given by FREC to the licensee to distribute the funds to one party or the other. FREC may or may not issue an EDO.

general partnership—is formed when two or more partners comprise the business entity.

good-faith doubt—when the broker questions or doubts the parties willingness and desire to transact business.

interpleader—is when the broker deposits the escrowed funds with the courts and petitions the courts to decide on the appropriate disbursement.

limited liability company—are basically hybrids of corporations and partnerships. A limited liability company has full liability protection to the same degree as a corporation and profit that is not subject to double taxation. Rather, like partnerships, limited liability companies enjoy profit that is taxed once.

limited liability partnership—a partner is not liable for negligent acts committed by another partner. A partner is, however, liable for his own negligent acts.

limited partnership—is created with one or more general partners and one or more limited partners.

mediation—when parties who are unable to agree among themselves seek the assistance of a third party (a mediator) for the purpose of providing a recommended nonbinding solution.

ostensible partnership—an entity that appears to be a partnership but is not a real partnership. The parties act like a partnership exists, when in fact, one does not. Because ostensible partnerships are deceitful, such entities are prohibited.

point of contact information—is the method by which the brokerage firm or licensee may be contacted such as, e-mail address, mailing address, street address, phone number and/or fax number.

sole proprietor—is a business where the sole owner is the individual licensee.

trade name—a fictitious name other than one's own name used to conduct one's business.

Chapter 6

citation—identifies a violation and the penalty required.

complaint—an allegation to a violation of a rule or law.

formal complaint—lists the charges set forth against the respondent licensee. The licensee then has a prescribed period of time to either accept or reject the charges set forth within the complaint.

legally sufficient—a complaint containing facts concerning allegations that if they were true, a rule, regulation, or statute has been violated.

letter of guidance—a letter that suggests action or actions to be taken concerning the subject.

notice of noncompliance—identifies the violation of law and describes steps the licensee must take to comply with the law. If the licensee fails to comply, disciplinary procedures may proceed.

probable cause—defined as reasonable grounds for charging and prosecuting a licensee.

probable cause panel—a panel consisting of two appointed members of FREC who are appointed by the Commission Chair whose sole purpose is to establish whether or not probable cause exists.

recommended order—at the conclusion of a formal hearing, the Administrative Law Judge will issue a recommended order to FREC. The recommended order includes, case findings, a conclusion and the recommended penalty.

revocation—a permanent removal from the real estate practice.

summary (emergency) suspension—emergency action taken against a license to protect the public against future repeated offenses while determination is made as to charges and penalties.

Chapter 7

actual eviction—refers to the legal removal of the tenant from the leased property because she violates some provision of the lease.

blockbusting—also referred to as panic selling, is the illegal practice of inducing owners to sell their properties by using information about changes or expected changes in the makeup of the neighborhood.

constructive eviction—is when the landlord causes or permits a situation to occur that makes it impossible for the tenant to enjoy the premises under the terms of the lease.

Division of Land Sales, Condominiums, and Mobile Homes—the agency responsible for regulating the sale of land contained within a subdivision in Florida is the Division of Land Sales, Condominiums, and Mobile Homes. This division is a part of the Department of Business and Professional Regulation (DBPR).

familial status—families with children under the age of 18 and pregnant women.

places of public accommodation—are privately owned businesses and nonprofit organizations open to the public.

property report—requires that certain disclosures be made to potential buyers and that each buyer be given a period during which he may cancel the sales contract and receive a full refund. The disclosure document that must be provided to purchasers is referred to as a property report.

Real Estate Settlement Procedures Act (RESPA)—was passed by Congress in 1974 and later revised in 1996 with the purpose to regulate financial institutions that originate loans secured by mortgages for housing transactions. RESPA applies to federally financed residential property transactions.

redlining—is the practice of discriminating when making loans in a neighborhood because of the makeup of the neighborhood in terms of race, color, religion, national origin, or sex.

seven-business day right of rescission—is when the buyer is permitted to cancel a sales contract within 7 days of signing it. This right of rescision does not apply to anyone (a builder) who is in the business of purchasing subdivided land for the sole purpose of building on the lots.

steering—refers to the practice of influencing potential buyers to buy only in certain areas or neighborhoods on the basis of race, color, religion, sex, or national origin.

Chapter 8

bundle of rights—aside from the title aspect to ownership in real property, ownership comes with other legal rights. These legal rights are termed as the bundle of rights.

chattel—personal property is also known as chattel or personalty.

common property—separate property consists of the individual dwelling units. Technically, a dwelling unit consists of only the four walls. This includes space between the walls, floor, and ceiling of the building. Common property is everything else.

concurrent ownership—any ownership held by two or more persons in property is called concurrent ownership.

condominium—is a form of individual fee ownership of a unit within a multifamily development property.

cond-op—a hybrid of condominiums and cooperatives.

cooperative—form of community ownership. Title to the land, building, and all other improvements to the property are held by the cooperative. The cooperative is organized as a not-for-profit corporation.

declaration of condominium—the instrument used to create the condominium.

elective share—the rights of a surviving spouse that has been excluded from the deceased spouse's will.

By law, the surviving spouse is entitled to a share of the decedent's estate.

estate at will (tenancy at will)—also referred to as a tenancy at will or, in Florida, a tenancy without a specified term. It may be terminated by either lessor or lessee at any time (at will). Otherwise, it is a normal landlord-tenant relationship.

estate for years—is a lease that has a specified starting and ending date. In spite of its name, it does not necessarily have to be for more than 1 year. It can be for any duration—as little as 1 day to many years.

estate in land—is the degree, quantity, nature, and extent of one's interest in the land. The term estate in land refers to an individual's interest in the land and not to the land itself or the physical properties of the land. Therefore, an estate in land is the interest held in land (real property or real estate).

estate in severalty—sole ownership or ownership in property by one person is called an estate in severalty.

exempt property—personal property that a spouse is automatically entitled to when the other spouse dies.

fee—represents the direct ownership within the land.

fee simple absolute—is the most preferred, common, and desirable form of ownership, the most complete form of ownership and the type that most property owners possess. It is not a defeasible estate.

fee simple defeasible—ownership bears conditions or is conditional on whether or not certain or specific events occur.

fee simple estate—is the most comprehensive and simplest form of property ownership; it is ownership in land itself.

fixture—when permanently attached to the real property, a fixture becomes a part of the real property via utility and permanence of the object to the property.

freehold estate—is commonly known as ownership interest in land (the fee).

holdover tenant—is when a tenant remains in possession beyond her legal tenancy without the consent of the landlord/lessor. The tenant/lessee is referred to as a holdover tenant or a tenant at sufferance.

homestead—is to ensure that families with unsecured debts cannot be removed from their homestead as a result of a forced sale of the property. It is also a tax exemption to an owner of a primary residence.

joint tenancy—two or more persons who hold title as joint tenants. The primary distinguishing characteristic of joint tenancy is the fact that it carries the rights of survivorship.

land—the ground and all permanent attachments.

leased property—a possessory right in the property but not ownership in the land.

leasehold—represents the possessory right to the land and improvement(s).

leasehold estate—nonfreehold estates or estates less than freehold are also called leasehold estates. This applies to any property that is leased by a tenant.

life estate—estates that are held for a lifetime (but not longer) are not inheritable and therefore may not be willed to heirs.

life estate pur autre vie—is based on the lifetime of a third party and it is inheritable only if the life tenant dies prior to the named third party whose life the life estate was predicated on.

monthly maintenance—the monthly payment by a shareholder in a cooperative that is not made in the form of rent; it is made and referred to as monthly maintenance.

owners association—ownership and community living arrangement whereby some form of governing authority within the development is required and is achieved through the creation of an owners association.

partition—is the dividing of common interests into separate interests owned in severalty.

personal property—includes all other property other than real property. Personal property is also known as chattel or personalty. If it is moveable, it is personal property.

personalty—personal property is also known as chattel or personalty.

property—the term property refers to the rights of ownership.

proprietary lease—an occupancy agreement granted to a shareholder in a cooperative that conveys rights of occupancy to the respective unit.

real property (real estate)—is land and all things attached to and affixed to it.

remainderman—the third party named to receive the fee simple estate is called the remainderman.

reversionary interest—the right to reclaim and regain legal possession of the property by the landlord at the end of the lease term.

right of survivorship—the right of a surviving party to the property of a deceased party.

separate property—the condominium unit owner receives a deed for the property. The individual units are called separate property.

statutory life estates —some life estates are created not by voluntary action, but by law. This type of life estate is called statutory life estates.

tenancy at sufferance —an estate at sufferance or tenancy at sufferance occurs when a tenant remains in possession beyond her legal tenancy without the consent of the landlord/lessor.

tenancy by the entirety —can be compared with joint tenancy. The primary difference lies with the relationship of the parties. Tenancy by the entirety is solely reserved for husband and wife relationships.

tenant in common —any two or more persons who hold title to property where the unity of possession is required, unlike joint tenancy, each tenant holds a separate title to his undivided interest within that subject property.

time-share —is a method of dividing up and selling a living unit for a specified period each year. Time-shares are almost exclusively resort-type properties, such as hotels, condominiums, townhouses, villas, recreational vehicles parks, and campgrounds.

Chapter 9

abstract of title —is a full summary of all instruments affecting the title to a property, such as deeds, wills, grants and a statement of all liens and encumbrances affecting the property and their present status.

acceptance —is the voluntary receipt and approval of an offer or in a property transfer, is presumed to have occurred if a grantee retains the deed when delivered, records the deed, encumbers the title or performs any other act of ownership.

acknowledgment —in a sale, acknowledgment is when the grantor (seller) must acknowledge his signature to the grantee (buyer). This is achieved by the grantor signing the deed before a notary public.

actual notice —is specific knowledge based on what you have actually seen, heard, read, or observed.

adverse possession —a lawful taking of another's property based on specific conditions and requirements; usually a private taking.

assignment —is the transfer of all rights that in a lease, the tenant (assignor) holds in the property and gives to another (assignee).

chain of title —allows interested parties to research the public records for the purposes of identifying the correct owner of record.

condemnation —a municipality's process that takes private property.

constructive notice —gives notice to the world as to the owner of a property by public recording and occupancy. It is presumed that anyone interested in the property has inspected both the records and the property itself to determine ownership.

covenant of further assistance —a clause in a deed that obligates the grantor to perform any acts necessary to protect the title being conveyed to the grantee. The covenant of further assistance is also called the covenant of further assurance.

covenant of seisin —is a clause in a deed whereby the grantor warrants that he is the owner of the property and that he has the right to convey the property.

covenant of warranty of title (covenant of warranty forever) —this ensures that the grantor will bear the expense of defending the title against the claims of others. There is no time limit on a covenant of warranty of title. It is sometimes called the covenant of warranty forever.

deed —is an instrument that is used to convey and transfer the ownership interest in real property from one or more parties to another. A deed is used to convey any fee estate, any life estate, or certain easements.

deed restriction —are enforceable restrictions on the ownership of private property that are contained in deeds.

delivery —to be valid, a deed must be delivered by the grantor to the grantee and accepted by the grantee. Delivery does not have to be a physical act of "handing over" the deed. If the grantor indicates by her actions that she intends for the grantee to own the property, then delivery has occurred.

doctrine of laches —the use and enforcement of one's rights or loss of same resulting from lack of enforcement and assertion of those rights.

easement —also known as a right of way is the right to use or occupy the property of another in a limited way.

eminent domain —a public taking of private property through the process known as condemnation.

encroachment —is an unauthorized intrusion of a building, fixture, or other improvement on the land of another.

escheat —when no existence of a valid will or remaining heirs to accept the property of a decedent, the property goes to the state.

fee —the land, also referred to as the fee.

general lien —is a lien that attaches to all property owned by the lienee (party being liened).

general warranty deed —also called the full covenant and warranty deed, is the most common form of deed. It provides the greatest guarantee about the title being conveyed.

graduated lease—the tenant pays a fixed rent for an initial period but the rent increases at specific intervals thereafter.

grant—the actual act of conveying ownership of real property is called a grant.

grantee—the buyer or recipient of a grant.

granting clause—the words grant and convey, either alone or in combination, are commonly used in the conveyance. Another name for the words of conveyance is the granting clause.

grantor—the seller or the giver of the grant.

gross lease—is where the tenant pays a fixed monthly or annual rent only and the property owner is responsible for all costs associated with running of the property.

ground lease—is a long-term lease of land. It is usually the subject of development.

habendum clause—found in most deeds, but not required, it is the clause that contains the type of estate being granted. The habendum clause describes the extent of interest being transferred.

index lease—also known as a modified gross lease, contains a provision for future rent increases based on increased operating costs to the landlord (for taxes, insurance, utilities, janitorial services, etc.).

leasehold—the improvement affixed to the fee (the land), referred to as the leasehold.

lien—a legal claim or charge for the repayment of debt/owing that one person has upon the property of another. It is used as security for repayment of a debt.

lis pendens—is a legal recorded notice of pending litigation concerning a subject property.

marketable title—Marketable title is one that is free of reasonable doubt as to ownership.

net lease—the tenant pays a fixed monthly rent, plus some or all of the expenses associated with the property, such as taxes, insurance, utilities, etc. The landlord pays only those expenses not paid by the tenant.

percentage lease—are leases commonly used for retail establishments in shopping malls. The landlord receives a percentage of the gross sales of the business as part or all of the rent.

quiet enjoyment—deals with the issue of title and/or rights associated with the granted estate.

quitclaim deed—is a deed that contains no warranties to title, either expressed or implied. It can be defined to be an instrument of release (as it may apply to any claim).

recourse loans—those where the borrower personally guarantees the repayment of the borrowed amount.

sandwich lease—occurs when a leased property is subleased.

special warranty deed—when the grantor is unable or unwilling to include all the covenants in a warranty deed. It includes only one covenant, the covenant against encumbrances.

specific lien—is a lien that attaches only to a specific property identified in the lien.

sublease—a further letting of space where the original tenant becomes the sub-landlord in relationship to the subsequent tenant known as the sub-tenant.

title—the sum of all facts or evidence of ownership.

title opinion—one method of determining marketable title and the opinion is normally made and given by attorneys. In essence, the attorney scrutinizes in a careful manner the abstract of title. The opinion letter or certificate of title opinion, as it is more commonly known, will indicate any encumbrances, liens, or easements that affect the property.

Torrens system—is a system of registered land titles, called Torrens land titles.

Chapter 10

base line—under the Government Rectangular System east/west lines are intersected by principal meridians (north/south lines) thus creating townships.

benchmark—permanent reference markers are also referred to as benchmarks.

block—is the largest unit within a subdivision. Each block is subdivided into individual lots that houses are built on.

check—is the 24-mile square that is achieved through the intersecting guide meridians.

correction lines—are lines that are made up of east/west lines situated every 24 miles to the north and south of the base line used to correct for the curvature of the earth.

government rectangular survey system—a method of legal property description established by Congress in the mid to late 1780s.

legal description—a description of property that is used for the purpose of transferring title is called a legal description.

lot—a block is the largest unit within a subdivision. Each block is subdivided into individual lots that houses are built on.

metes and bounds—metes means distance and bounds means direction. The metes and bounds method is the oldest method of legal description.

monument—is an object that is used to define a corner of a parcel of property.

point of beginning (POB)—a term used in a metes and bounds description that must always begin at a point of beginning. The point of beginning is identified as the POB on the plat and is usually marked by an iron pin placed by the surveyor.

principal meridian—each principal meridian (north/south lines) is intersected by only one base line. Throughout the United States, there are 36 different intersecting principal meridians and base lines.

range—a range runs north and south.

section—one of 36 units contained within a township. Each section measures 1 mile square. Each section within a township is represented by a number from 1–36.

tier (township)—a tier runs east and west.

township line—lines that are drawn every 6 miles north and south of a base line thereby forming east and west parcels of land.

Chapter 11

assignment—is the transfer of one's interest in a executory contract to another person.

attorney-in-fact—is someone who has been granted power of attorney limited to a specific transaction named in a document. A contract entered into by an attorney-in-fact is valid when the power of attorney has been properly granted. The party need not be an attorney.

bilateral contract—is one in which both parties promise to give up something or to perform in such a manner as required by the agreement. A promise is exchanged for a promise.

competent—a requirement for a valid contract that the parties to the contract be legally competent. There are three categories of people who are not legally competent; minors, intoxicated persons, and insane persons

contract—is an agreement between two parties to do something (legal object), or not to do something (legal object).

executed contract—is one where all requirements of the contract have been fulfilled and the parties have done what they agreed to do in the contract. In essence, all interested parties to the transaction have fully performed.

exclusive right to buy—an option contract gives an exclusive right to buy. This means that no one other than the person holding the option (the optionee) can buy the property during the option period.

executory contract—is one in which some or all requirements have not yet been completed.

expressed contract—is one in which the intent of the parties is stated (expressed) in the contract itself. An expressed contract can be either written or oral. The majority of real estate contracts are expressed agreements.

implied contract—is one where the intent of the parties is not stated but is indicated by their actions.

liquidated damages—sales contracts may include a statement that if the buyer breaches the contract, the seller may demand forfeiture of the earnest money deposit as liquidated damages.

meeting of the minds—a requirement of a valid contract is mutual agreement or mutuality. This is sometimes called a meeting of the minds or offer and acceptance. This means that there must be a mutual agreement on the provisions of the contract.

novation—is a substitution of a new contract for an old contract or substitution of a new party for an old party under an existing contract. Novation is also a means of general release from previous contractual obligations.

option contract—a unilateral contract in real estate that gives someone the right but not the obligation to buy a property.

rescision of a contract—voiding or canceling the contract, whereby, the parties to the contract are placed back in their original positions prior to the creation of the contract.

Statute of Frauds—requires that all contracts involving either the purchase of or sale of any parcel of real property must be in writing to be deemed enforceable.

Statute of Limitations—a specific time period for an innocent party to take action to remedy the breach of contract.

unenforceable—a contract that cannot be enforced in a court of law. An unenforceable contract is valid until challenged in court.

unilateral contract—is one which only one party promises to give up something. A promise is exchanged for some act or performance by the other party

valid contract—is one that is legally sufficient and meets all the essential requirements of the law to create a contract between two or more persons.

void contract—is one that is not recognized legally and has no legal effect. From its inception, the agreement lacks one or more of the necessary essential requirements for the creation of a valid and enforceable contract.

voidable contract—is one that is capable of being voided by one of the parties to the contract. It is binding on one party to the contract only and is valid until action is taken by one party to make it void.

Chapter 12

acceleration clause—a clause in the mortgage agreement that allows the lender to demand full and immediate payment (accelerate the payment) if the borrower fails to meet all terms of the promissory note.

amortized loan—is a payment plan concerning a loan whereby principal and interest are paid by equal periodic payments during the term of the loan. Payments are the same throughout the term of the loan.

assumption—when a new borrower assumes the obligation under an existing loan.

balloon payment—is the single large principal payment necessary to retire the loan at the end of the loan's term. This is known as a balloon payment.

certificate of estoppel—is a document that is completed by a borrower to acknowledge the full amount of the debt that the borrower owes. It is usually used when a lender is about to sell the mortgage note and the purchaser wants to verify the amount and terms of the note as well as the borrower's acknowledgment of the debt. Also used in financing and refinancing transactions and sales of income producing properties.

deed in lieu of foreclosure—commonly referred to as a friendly foreclosure where the borrower avoids foreclosure by signing the property over to the lender. This is done using a document called a deed in lieu of foreclosure.

deferred interest—a shared equity loan (also known as a shared appreciation loan), where the buyer receives favorable loan terms from the lender in exchange for the lender receiving a portion of the appreciation from the property, usually when the property is sold or refinanced, or in the case of income-producing properties, the lender shares in the net operating income as a dividend. The end payment to the lender is referred to as deferred interest.

deficiency judgment—when a foreclosure sale recovers less than the outstanding balance amount, the lender seeks a deficiency judgment from the courts to enforce a deficiency clause. When obtained, the lender may seek recovery of the differential from the original borrower. The amount of the deficiency judgment is limited to the amount of the outstanding debt that is not recovered.

due on sale clause—commonly referred to as the alienation clause that permits the mortgagee to call in the note if the mortgagor transfers the property either through sale or gift. It is used to prohibit the assumption of the mortgage loan by a buyer or the use of a wraparound mortgage.

equity—the difference between the market value of a property and the principal balance on any loans against it. At the time of purchase, equity is equal to the down payment.

home equity loan—usually a second mortgage (can be a first when no other prior lien exists) that is secured by the property.

hypothecation—a mortgage provides security for a note through a process called hypothecation. Hypothecation means that the real property is put up as security for a loan without surrendering possession of the property.

index plus a margin—the interest rate on an adjustable rate mortgage (ARM) loan is equal to the index plus a margin, which is a fixed number of percentage points (usually 1–3 percent, which is also expressed as 100–300 basis points).

interest—the money paid for the privilege of using the lender's principal (payment of rent for the use of another's money).

lien theory—in a lien theory state, the legal title remains in the possession of the borrower while the mortgage held by the lender creates a lien on the title in favor of the lender.

line of credit—a lender issues to a borrower a line of credit that can be borrowed, all or in part, at the demand of the borrower.

lis pendens—a notice of lis pendens is filed that informs the public that there is a legal action pending.

mortgage—is the instrument that places the property (by the borrower) as collateral for securing the repayment of the loan.

mortgagee—the lender is called the mortgagee because the lender is the one to whom the mortgage (collateral or security) is given/conveyed.

mortgagor—the borrower is called the mortgagor because the borrower gives/conveys the mortgage (collateral or security) to the lender.

negative amortization—is when the loan's principal balance increases with each installment payment rather than decreasing with each installment payment.

PITI—monthly payments made for *P*rincipal, *I*nterest, *T*axes and *I*nsurance.

power-of-sale clause—provides for nonjudicial foreclosure. It allows the property to be sold at public auction in the event of default by the borrower without going to court.

prepayment clause—is contained within the mortgage and will provide the borrower with the ability to prepay the outstanding principal balance (in part or in whole), either with or without a penalty.

prepayment penalty—is when the borrower prepays the outstanding principal balance in part or in whole at any time; however, with a pre-prescribed penalty for prepayment.

promissory note—is the instrument that evidences the borrowing and includes the borrower's promises to repay money borrowed from the lender.

reconveyance clause—a clause contained in a trust deed that requires the trustee (3rd neutral party holding the naked title) to reconvey title to the trustor (the borrower) when the loan has been paid in full.

statutory redemption—a period of time given to a borrower after foreclosure to repay the debt and take back ownership of the property.

subject to the mortgage—is the direct opposite of assumption. In a subject to the mortgage transaction, the buyer is not assuming the loan, the buyer is merely making the payments associated with that loan. In order for this arrangement to occur, the existing loan must not contain a due on sale clause.

subordination clause—the clause within a lease that states that the rights of the leasehold interest are secondary to that of a previous or subsequent lien or interest in the real property. A subordination clause is a major requirement by all lenders on income-producing property.

takeout loan—the construction loan is paid off when permanent financing is obtained on the property. The permanent financing is commonly referred to as the takeout loan.

term loan (straight loan)—are also called straight loans. They are interest only loans. The principal is paid in full at the end of the term of the loan. This is known as a balloon payment.

title theory—a financing theory involving a three party two instrument loan transaction secured by real property. The parties are referred to as, trustor (property owner/borrower), trustee (neutral third party appointed by both the borrower and the lender to hold the naked title) and the beneficiary (lender). The instruments are referred to as the note and trust deed or deed of trust.

wraparound loan—normally a second loan that is larger than the first and can only be used when there is no alienation (due on sale) clause on an existing loan. It is therefore an assumable mortgage.

Chapter 13

closing costs—charges that are incurred when a buyer takes out a loan for real property. The term closing costs includes a number of different loan charges that vary from lender to lender. There are two types of closing costs: variable costs and fixed costs.

conforming loan—for loans sold to Fannie Mae (Federal National Mortgage Association [FNMA]) or Freddie Mac, the guidelines developed by Freddie Mac must be used in making a conventional loan. These guidelines are often called the FNMA/FHLMC guidelines, because they are used by Fannie Mae as well. Any loan approved under these guidelines is called a conforming loan.

discount points—are prepaid interest paid at closing. The lender is able to increase its yield (or earnings) on the loan, while still being able to sell the loan in the secondary market at a discount. A lender is said to discount the loan when it charges discount points. Each discount point is equal to 1 percent of the loan amount.

discount rate—the interest rate the Fed charges to its member banks for borrowing funds.

disintermediation—occurs when depositors withdraw their savings in order to achieve higher yielding returns on invested capital within alternative investment vehicles. Disintermediation results in a scarcity of money available for mortgages.

entitlement—a veteran's entitlement is the amount of guarantee she is eligible to receive on a guaranteed loan.

intermediation—occurs when thrift institutions (commercial banks and savings associations) receive inflows of money into savings accounts. The purpose on the part of the depositor is to achieve high-yielding returns on the investment. These savings in turn are used to invest in larger investment projects. Intermediation results in funds being available for mortgages.

loan-to-value ratio (LTV)—is used to set a limit on how much money can be loaned on a particular property. It is expressed as a percentage and is computed in either of two ways: (1) The amount of the loan is divided by either the sales price, or (2) the amount of the loan is divided by the appraised value of the property, whichever is smaller.

mortgage bankers—a company or an individual that originates loans to others with their own funds and with the intent on selling those loans to investors.

mortgage brokers—bring together borrowers and lenders for a fee, usually based on a percentage of the loan. The lender then makes the loan directly to the borrower, and the mortgage broker has no further role.

mortgage company—also called a mortgage banker mortgage banker makes loans, using its own money, and then sells the loans to long-term investors. Once the loans have been sold, the mortgage company often retains the servicing of the loan (collects payments, keeps records, etc.) in return for a fee, such as 0.25 of 1 percent of the outstanding loan balance.

Office of Thrift Supervision—savings association members are chartered through and regulated by the Office of Thrift Supervision.

open-market operations—is a method to control the money supply by the Fed. This is where the Fed buys and sells securities.

origination fee—a type of variable closing cost, the origination fee is charged by the lender for processing the loan. It covers primarily the administrative costs to do the paperwork on the loan such as filling out forms and reviewing credit reports and appraisals. Origination fees are usually a percentage of the loan amount.

primary mortgage market—is the part of the market where lenders originate loans.

private mortgage insurance (PMI)—is usually required by a lender if the loan-to-value ratio exceeds 80 percent. The borrower pays an insurance premium for PMI, usually 1 percent or less at the origination of the loan, and less than 1 percent annually. Once the LTV is reduced below 80 percent, the PMI can usually be dropped.

purchase money mortgage (PMM)—is commonly referred to as seller financing.

reserve requirements—set forth the amounts of funds that Federal Reserve member banks must maintain on deposit at any one time. The Fed uses reserve requirements to control the country's money supply.

secondary mortgage market—provides an outlet where those who originate loans may sell their loans in order to secure capital to make more loans.

Chapter 14

arrears—periodic payments that are paid at the end of the payment period rather than before.

credit—is money that is received by someone from someone else.

debit—is a payment by someone to someone else.

prorate—in real property closings, it is the process of determining the cost to the appropriate party of an item that will be paid or received by the buyer or by the seller. It is always based on how long each party will own the property.

Chapter 15

appraisal—is a formal estimation of the value of real property as of a given date.

assemblage—refers to the process of combining two or more adjacent properties into one larger tract of land.

capitalization—is the present worth of the property based upon the income produced by that property.

comparables—are similar properties that have sold recently in the same neighborhood or area as the subject property. These similar properties are called comparables (comps).

comparative market analysis (CMA)—is a broker's opinion of value and is not an appraisal. It is used when a real estate licensee is asked to assist a seller in determining a suitable price for a property or to assist a buyer in evaluating a price offered by a seller.

cost—is usually synonymous with production, or the cost to produce an improvement. Cost may or may not equal market price or market value.

curable—is when remediation of a defect results in equal or greater value to the overall property through its utility as opposed to the cost of making the correction. A defect is considered curable if it is economically feasible to correct the problem.

depreciation—is a loss of value of any kind resulting from functional obsolescence (outdated layout, lighting, columns, etc.), physical deterioration (usually representative of poor maintenance and preventative maintenance programs) and/or economic/external obsolescence (declining neighborhoods, adverse zoning changes, interest rates, etc.).

effective gross income—is income found on a reconstructed income/expense statement. It is determined by subtracting from the potential gross income of a property the vacancy and collection loss while adding in any other income attributable to the property.

fair market value (market value)—is the price that an informed, willing seller would accept, and an informed, willing buyer would pay if the buyer or seller is not under any pressure to buy or sell, a reasonable amount of time is allowed for market exposure and the transaction is an arm's length transaction, meaning that neither the buyer nor the seller bears relation to the other and that each party is dealing from equal bargaining positions. Fair market value is often the subject of determining future rents when tenants receive options to renew their lease.

federally related transaction—is any transaction that includes or involves a financial institution insured or regulated by the federal government.

gross rent multiplier (GRM)—it is another form of analysis within the income approach used informally in selected applications involving income-producing property. Its primary use is for an investor who is evaluating several properties and wants a simple and quick way to eliminate some properties from consideration before doing formal price determinations.

highest and best use—is the legal and feasible use that generates the highest possible land value attributable to that use.

incurable—is when remediation of a defect results in lesser value to the overall property through its utility as opposed to the cost of making the correction. A defect is considered incurable if it is not economically feasible to correct the problem.

over-improvement—is the cost to upgrade a property whereby the upgrade does not produce a corresponding increase in the overall property value.

plottage—refers to any increase in value for a tract of land formed by combining two or more parcels.

principle of substitution—is the premise for all three approaches to appraisals. It suggests that a smart investor would not pay more for a property with equal utility that they could purchase for less.

progression—states that the value of a lower-valued property is increased if it is located among properties of higher value.

reconciliation—in every appraisal that is conducted, the three approaches to valuation are applied. It is only within the reconciliation step of the appraisal process that one of the three approaches is given weight over the other two to determine the appraiser's final estimate of value.

regression—is a principle of appraisal that states that the value of a higher valued property is decreased if it is located among properties of lower value.

replacement cost—is the cost to replace the improvements of the subject property with another building that performs the same function and utility but is not an exact replica of the subject property. It is used in the cost approach to appraisal.

reproduction cost—is the cost to produce an exact replica of the original subject property, using the same materials and construction techniques as the original. It is used in the cost approach to appraisal.

sales comparison approach—also referred to as the market data approach, it is based on a comparison of the subject property (the property being appraised) to similar properties that have recently sold. As with other approaches to appraisal, it assumes the basic principle of substitution in the purchase of real property.

situs—people have preferences for certain areas, and these preferences determine the value of land. A preference for certain areas is referred to as situs.

subject property—is the property being appraised.

Uniform Standards of Professional Appraisal Practice (USPAP)—identifies the procedures an appraiser must follow while performing appraisal services. Appraisers must always conform to the Uniform Standards of Professional Appraisal Practice (USPAP).

valuation—is an impartial estimate or opinion of the value of a parcel of property. It is based on specific data that can be used to support and defend the estimate or opinion of value.

Chapter 16

asbestos—a fibrous mineral found in soil and rocks.

casement window—a hinged sash that can be opened by swinging the sash outward.

corner lot—sits at the intersection of two streets. The lot has frontage along both streets. (Frontage refers to the length of the property that abuts the street.)

cul de sac lot—located at the end of a cul-de-sac (a dead-end street with a circular turnaround). They are part of subdivisions. Because of the curved turnaround, these lots are often irregular in shape. That is, they are tapered with a smaller frontage but larger backyards.

double-hung window—consists of two sashes, both of which slide vertically allowing the window to be opened at the top and bottom.

fixed window—consists of a sash that cannot be opened.

flag lot—is shaped like a flag on a flagpole. Often, a flag lot is located behind another lot. The flagpole portion of the lot is the access road or driveway that runs along the front lot to the street. The flag portion of the lot is the square or rectangular lot that is located behind the front lot.

gable—a roof sloping on two sides.

gambrel—a roof divided into two sections with different slopes for each section. Only two sides of the roof are sloped.

hip—a roof sloping on four sides.

horizontal sliding window—consists of sashes that slide horizontally to open or close the window.

insulation—materials used for the purpose of keeping the heat out of the home as it is in cold climates to keep the heat in the home.

interior lot—is surrounded by other lots on three sides (left, right, and rear). The interior lot has frontage on just one street.

key lot—is surrounded by many other lots. Often, a key lot is an extremely deep lot. The side yard abuts the rear of many different properties that are located on a street that runs perpendicular to the street where the key lot is located.

lot—is defined as a portion of a subdivision.

mansard—is a roof with two sections with different slopes (like the gambrel), but all four sides of the roof are sloped.

R value—the standard method to rate the effectiveness of insulation materials is the R value. The R stands for resistance to heat flow. The higher the R value for a particular insulation material, the better the insulation effect.

T lot—a type of interior lot that is located at the end of a T intersection.

underground storage tanks—used to store chemicals, gasoline or other petroleum products.

urea-formaldehyde foam insulation—foam insulation which emitted formaldehyde gas when it was previously used in many older homes before its usage was sharply curtailed by HUD.

Chapter 17

appreciation—increased values derived during the property holding period (that is, appreciation).

book value—is the liquidation value of a business. Another term for liquidation value for businesses is the book value.

bulk—is the total building size in square footage terms of any development as determined by zoning allowances.

cash flow—is receipts less payments from income activities over a period of time.

equity—is the difference between the market value of a property and the unpaid balance of any loans on that property. Equity increases (builds up) as any loan is paid down and as the property appreciates.

going concern value—is the value of a business that is expected to continue as an operating entity is called the going concern value.

goodwill—refers to an intangible asset that usually reflects the business's name recognition, the business's customer base, and the business's employees.

leverage—the use of borrowed funds with the anticipation of earning substantial profits not only on the investment, but also on the borrowed funds.

liquidation analysis—the process of estimating the assets, liabilities, and amount the business could be sold for in the event the business is terminated or goes bankrupt.

liquidity—is the ability to convert an asset into cash by selling it. An asset that can be readily sold and converted to cash is considered liquid. For example, stocks are considered liquid assets. Real property is not considered liquid.

return of investment—is the return of the principal investment (represents investor return of investment).

return on investment—is the profit on the investor's invested capital (represents investor profit, return on investment).

tax shelter—an investment that results in tax advantages is sometimes referred to as a tax shelter.

Chapter 18

active income—includes compensation derived directly from employment activities, such as salary/wages, commissions, gratuities.

ad valorem—is a Latin term that means "according to valuation."

arrears—payments that are made at the end of the payment period rather than at the beginning. Arrears is also used in the context of past due amounts when payment is due in advance and same has not been tendered.

assessed value—the value of a property established for the purpose of determining taxes.

boot—the unlike-kind portion in a 1031 exchange. It represents the taxable realized gain in the transaction. When the values of the two properties are not the same, the party trading the lower-valued property usually gives the other party money or an item of value in addition to the real property exchanged. This money or item is called boot.

exempt income—income that is not subject to taxation.

exempt property—are subject to taxation, but the owner is not obligated to pay all (or part) of the taxes.

Green Belt Law—provides favorable tax treatment for agricultural properties. Under this law, the assessed value must be based on the property's current agricultural use, and not the highest and best use of the property.

immune property—are not subject to taxation.

installment sale—is a means of financing where the seller receives payment for the property over a period of years. In this situation, the seller can avoid paying the entire amount of taxes on any gain from the sale in the year the sale took place. Rather, the seller can postpone the payment of taxes to future years, when the installment payments are actually received.

just value—the fair market value of the property.

like-for-like trade—if properties are exchanged on a tax-deferred basis, both properties must be one of these eligible types of property. (This is referred to as a like-for-like trade because the two properties traded are both eligible.)

mill—one mill equals 1/1,000 of one dollar. (One mill also equals 1/10 of one cent.)

passive income—is any income from a business activity or investment where the individual is passive and not actively in charge of the day-to-day management of that activity or investment.

portfolio income—is any income derived from stock dividends, interest earned on deposits or loans, and royalties earned on intellectual property and annuities.

special assessment taxes—are taxes levied to fund a specific project that benefits only some of the citizens in a government jurisdiction.

tax base—is the total taxable value of all real property in the district.

tax rate—the rate that a taxpayer's income tax payment or property tax payment is predicated on.

taxable income—the net income that is subject to taxation.

taxable value—the taxable value of the property is calculated by subtracting the exemption from the assessed value.

Truth in Millage (TRIM) notice—tax laws require the county tax offices to mail the assessed value and the millage rates for the county, municipality, and school board prior to the actual rendering of the tax bills. This is done to give the property owner time to determine whether or not over-assessment has occurred as well as to file a grievance. This notice is referred to as the Truth in Millage (TRIM) notice.

Chapter 19

buyer's market—occurs when there are more sellers than there are buyers.

demand—means that someone has a desire to own or use the property.

household—is defined by the U.S. Census Bureau as a space designed for dwelling purposes occupied by one or more persons.

seller's market—occurs when there are more buyers than there are sellers or available product.

supply—(as it pertains to real property) is the amount of housing stock of properties available for sale or for lease.

vacancy rate—is generally quoted as a percentage figure as opposed to numbers representing available product. Rising vacancy rates indicate a buyer's market while lower rates indicate a seller's market.

Chapter 20

buffer zone—a strip of land that varies in size from community to community and acts as a separator between two zones.

building codes—set the allowable minimum standards for construction of improvements on real property. They are established under the government's police powers.

building inspection—conducted by representatives of local building departments to establish construction conformance with filed plans and specifications on new construction as well as code compliance on existing construction.

building permits—grant permission to construct improvements and are issued by local government.

concurrency—the Florida Growth Management Act of 1985 also has a concurrency provision. According to this provision, sufficient infrastructure (sewer, water, and transportation systems) must exist before new development is permitted.

condemnation—the police power of condemnation is used to take possession of property that belongs to the private sector.

eminent domain—is the power that allows the government to take private property if the taking is necessary to benefit the general public in areas such as new public transportation, new highways, and various other public uses.

environmental impact statement—any development in Florida that will affect residents in more than one county is referred to as a development of regional impact. An environmental impact statement must be prepared to address the impact that the project may or will have on the environment and its neighboring communities.

escheat—occurs when someone dies with no will and no heirs. The decedent's remaining property is turned over to the state.

health ordinance—local codes designed to address and regulate the maintenance and sanitation of public areas.

service industry—services the local constituency through various trades such as convenience stores and local retailers.

special exception—a property owner may also be granted a special exception, which allows a specific use for a specific property.

special flood hazard area—an area designated as having susceptibility to flooding.

variance—permission for an exemption to some of the specific requirements within a zoning classification. Variances when granted allow for a deviation from the allowed zoning.

zoning ordinance—the principal mechanism of public land-use control. Through zoning ordinances, the government and local municipalities can regulate, permitted uses for land, type, size, and height of structures built on the land, open-air requirements in relation to site improvement, density factors that will dictate the project size and occupancy of the land, and location of structures on the land such as setback requirements.

Index

A

absentee owners, 8, 438
abstracts of title, 139, 443
acceleration clause, 198, 446
acceptance
  contracts of sale, 189
  defined, 443
  when presumed to have occurred, 136
accountability, 46
accrued depreciation, 404
acknowledgement, 443
active income, 369, 450
active licenses
  defined, 439
  versus inactive licenses, 36–37
  requirements for, 18–22
acts of law, 58–59
acts of the parties, 58
actual eviction, 102, 441
actual notice, 140, 443
ad valorem
  defined, 450
  taxes
    calculation of, 367–368
    contesting assessments, 364
    Green Belt Law exemption, 366
    immune/exempt properties,
      365–366
    liens, 153–154
    real property, 367–368
    Save Our Home amendment, 366
    truth-in-millage (TRIM), 368
ADA (Americans with Disabilities Act), 64
address requirements, 35
adjudication withheld, 16
adjustable rate mortgages (ARMs),
  207–208, 210
administrative law judges (ALJs), 81–82
administrative penalties, 32–33, 84–85
adverse possession, 134, 443
advertising, 64–65, 96
agency
  coupled with an interest, 49, 439
  defined, 439
  designated sales associates, 57
  law of, 43–44
  maintaining records, 57
  relationships
    Florida Brokerage Relationship Disclosure Act, 50
    overview, 44
    responsibilities to customer,
      47–48
    responsibilities to principal,
      44–46
    transitioning, 56
    types of, 50–56
  termination of, 58–59

  types of, 48–50
agents, 43, 439
agreements
  compensation, 51
  mutual
    innocent (unintentional) misrepresentation, 178
    intentional misrepresentation, 178
    mistakes, 179
    overview, 177–178
  mutual recognition, 20–21, 438
agricultural property, 6, 340, 438
air rights, 111
air-conditioning, 319
alienation clause, 200
ALJs (administrative law judges),
  81–82
alternative documentation, 242–243
Americans with Disabilities Act (ADA), 64
amortized loans
  defined, 446
  history of, 220
  versus other loans, 210
  overview, 205–206
amperages, 321
answers
  to chapter review questions, 408–411
  to practice end-of-course exam,
    428–432
anticipation principle, 282
appeals process, 83
applications
  license, 19
  loan, 245, 272
appraisal
  defined, 9, 438, 448
  versus pricing, 277–278
  process of, 285
  requirement of, 243
  Section 203(b) loan program,
    230–231
  after signing sales contract, 271
  VA loans, 234–235
Appraisal Qualifications Board (AQB), 278
appraisers, 9, 287
appreciation, 340, 450
appurtenant, easements, 142–143
AQB (Appraisal Qualifications Board), 278
arbitration, 67, 440
architects, 4
area
  calculating, 402
  variances, 395
ARMs (adjustable rate mortgages),
  207–208, 210
arrears
  ad valorem taxes, 368
  defined, 448, 450
  property taxes, 263

articles of incorporation, 71
asbestos, 329–330, 449
assemblage, 284–285, 448
assessed value, 363, 450
assets, buyers', 241
assignment
    defined, 443, 445
    discharging contracts, 180–181
    overview, 152
assignors, 181
associations, 73
assumption
    advantages/disadvantages, 238–239
    closing requirements, 238
    defined, 446
    overview, 235
    taking subject, 235–237
    when to use, 237–238
Astor, John J., 10
attorneys, 3
attorneys-in-fact, 180, 445

B

backfill, 321
back-up contracts, 189
balconies, 127
balloon framing, 314
balloon payments, 205, 210, 446
banks, commercial, 217
bargain and sale deeds, 138
base industries, 397
base lines, 163, 444
bearing walls, 321
before tax cash flow (BTCF), 406–407
benchmarks, 162, 444
bilateral contracts, 174–176, 445
binders, 189
blanket loans, 207, 210
blind ads, 65, 440
blind individuals exemption, 365
blockbusting
    defined, 92, 441
    housing violations, 94–95
blocks, 161, 444
book value, 356, 450
boot, 377, 450
branch offices, 64
breach of contracts, 185–186
bridge loans, 217
broker associates
    defined, 438
    escrow (trust) accounts, 66
    licensure, 16, 24
    postlicense education, 18–19
brokerage
    business, 6, 356–358
    defined, 4, 438
    real estate, 6–7
    types of, 5
brokers
    defined, 438

licensure
    activities that require, 23–24
    application, 19
    continuing education, 21–22
    examination, 19–20
    exemptions, 24–26
    nonresident, 20
    versus registration, 23
    renewal, 21
    requirements, 18–19
    state laws, 22–23
    via mutual recognition, 20–21
mortgage, 217
offices
    advertising, 64–65
    branch offices, 64
    change of address, 63
    change of employing broker, 63
    disposition of funds, 67–68
    disputes, 67–68
    escrow (trust) accounts, 65–66
    registration, 69–73
    rentals, 68
    signage, 64
BTCF (before tax cash flow), 406–407
budget loans, 206
buffer zones, 395, 451
building codes, 398, 451
building inspection, 398, 451
building permits, 398, 451
bulk, 339, 450
bundle of rights, 110, 441
business brokerage
    expertise required, 357
    overview, 6
    versus real estate, 356
    sale of businesses, 357
    valuation of businesses, 357–358
business entities, 69
buydown loans, 208, 210
buyers
    contracts contingent on sale of present home, 271
    poor treatment of minority, 96–97
    qualifying/underwriting
        appraisal, 243
        credit history, 242
        documentation, 242–243
        FHA guidelines, 241
        Freddie Mac guidelines, 239–240
        maximum loan amount, 243
        VA guidelines, 241–242
buyer's market, 387, 451

C

calculating
    accrued depreciation, 404
    area, 402
    capitalization, 404
    cash flow analysis, 404–406
    commissions, 402
    cost problems, 353–354

calculating (*Continued*)
  discount points, 402
  down payments, 224–225
  interest, 402
  mortgage loans, 406
  price and commissions, 345–353
  prorations, 402–403
  purchase price, 402
  real property taxes, 263–265, 403–404
  state transfer taxes, 403
  yield, 406
CAM (common area maintenance), 124
canceled licenses, 38, 84, 439
canvassing, 7
capital gains tax, 375–377
capitalization
  calculating, 404
  defined, 349, 448
  overview, 291–295
CAPS mnemonic, 355
carry back financing, 206
casement windows, 315–316, 449
cash flow, 337, 450
cash investment requirement, 229
cash to control situation, 202, 237
caveat emptor, 15, 47, 438–439
ceasing to be in force, licenses, 38, 439
central air-conditioning, 319
certificates of estoppel, 202, 446
certificates of reasonable value (CRV), 234
certified public accountants (CPAs), 4
chain of title, 136, 443
chattel, 109, 441
checks (24-mile squares), 164, 444
citations, 85, 440
civil penalties, 86
Civil Rights Act of 1866, 91
Civil Rights Act of 1968
  blockbusting, 92
  enforcement of, 93
  exemptions, 93
  overview, 91–92
  properties covered by, 92–93
  steering, 92
clients, 44
clients (principals), 44–46, 439
closing costs
  defined, 447
  overview, 243–245
  Section 203(b) loan program, 230
  VA loans, 233
closing day, 261
closing statements, 249–261
CMA. *See* comparative market analysis
commercial acres, 321
commercial banks, 217
commercial properties, 5, 339–340
commercial sales transactions
  defined, 438
  designated sales associates, 57
  example, 5
commingling, 66, 100, 440

commissions, 345–347, 402
common area maintenance (CAM), 124
common charges, 125
common law, 43–44
common property, 124, 441
community ownership
  condominiums, 124–126
  cooperatives, 126–128
  overview, 123–124
  planned-unit development (PUD), 128–129
  resort time-share developments, 129
community property, 122–123
comparable property, 303
comparables, 286, 448
comparative market analysis (CMA)
  defined, 438, 448
  overview, 9, 277–278
compensation
  agreements, 51
  defined, 438
  license law and, 15
competency
  contractual validity, 174, 179–180
  deeds, 135
  defined, 445
  leasing, 99, 151
  licensure, 15
  termination of agency, 58
competition principle, 283
complaints
  appealing, 83
  defined, 440
  final orders, 82–83
  formal, 81–82
  hearings, 81–82
  investigation of, 80
  probable cause panels, 80–81
concurrency provision, 396, 451
concurrent ownership
  community property, 122
  defined, 441
  joint tenancy, 120
  overview, 119–120
  tenancy by the entirety, 121
  tenancy in common, 120–121
condemnation, 398, 443, 451
conditional commitments, 230
condominiums
  defined, 441
  disclosure, 188
  overview, 124–126
cond-ops, 128, 441
conduits, 321
confidentiality, 46
conflicting demands, 67, 440
conforming loans, 239, 447
conformity principle, 284
consent to transition, 51, 439
Consent to Transition to Transaction Broker disclosure
        form, 56
consideration, 177
construction

environmental hazards
  asbestos, 329–330
  disclosure statements, 332
  due diligence investigation, 332
  formaldehyde gas, 329
  groundwater contamination, 331
  lead, 330–331
  radon, 329
exterior
  footings/foundations, 313
  framing, 313–314
  insulation, 314
  roofs, 316–317
  ventilation, 315
  wall covering, 315
  windows, 315–316
lots
  corner, 325–327
  cul-de-sac, 328
  flag, 328
  interior, 328
  key, 328
  T lots, 328
mechanical systems/equipment
  cooling systems, 319
  electrical system, 320–321
  heating systems, 318
  hot water systems, 320
  overview, 317
  plumbing systems, 319–320
  sewers/septic tanks, 320
  types of fuel, 318–319
types of, 10
construction loans, 208–209, 386
constructive eviction, 102, 441
constructive notice, 140, 443
consumer price index (CPI), 147
continuing education requirements,
    17–19, 21–22, 36
contract rent, 150
contracts
  back-up, 189
  bilateral, 174–175
  breach of, 185–186
  defined, 173, 445
  discharging methods
    assignment, 180–181
    novation, 181
    termination, 181–182
  executed, 176
  executory, 176
  expressed, 173
  implied, 173–174
  installment sales, 190
  legally competent parties, 179–180
  listing, 186–187
  option, 184–185
  of sale, 187–190
  after signing, 269–271
  Statute of Frauds, 183
  unilateral, 175–176
  valid, 174

validity and enforcement requirements
  competency, 179–180
  consideration, 177
  legal objective, 179
  mutual agreement, 177–179
  overview, 176
void, 174
voidable, 174
conventional loans
  down payments, 224–225
  math formulas for, 406
  overview, 223
  private mortgage insurance (PMI), 225–227
  types of, 224
conversion, 66, 440
cooling systems, 319
Cooperative Act, 127
cooperatives, 126–128, 441
corner lots, 325–327, 449
corporate tax liens, 154
corporation soles, 73
corporations, 71–72, 440
correction lines, 164, 444
cost, 280, 448
cost approach to pricing
  depreciation, 290–291
  overview, 287–289
  quantity survey method, 289–290
  reproduction versus replacement, 304–305
  square foot method, 289
  unit-in-place method, 289
covenant against encumbrances, 137
covenant of further assistance, 138, 443
covenant of quiet enjoyment, 138
covenant of seisin, 137, 443
covenant of warranty of title (covenant of warranty forever),
    138, 443
covenants
  mortgage, 199–200
  restrictive, 10, 438
CPAs (certified public accountants), 4
CPI (consumer price index), 147
credit, 255, 448
criminal penalties, 85–86
CRV (certificates of reasonable value), 234
cul-de-sac lots, 328, 449
culverts, 325
curable defects, 291, 448
custom homes, 10
customers
  defined, 439
  relationships, 44
  responsibilities to, 47–48

D

DBPR. *See* Department of Business and Professional
    Regulation
debit, 255, 448
deciduous trees, 322
declarations of condominium, 126, 441
dedication, 10, 438

deductions, federal income tax
   business/investment property, 372–374
   overview, 370–371
   residential property, 372
deed restrictions, 134, 443
deeds
   bargain and sale, 138
   defined, 443
   elements of, 135–137
   general warranty, 137–138,
      443–444
   overview, 134–135
   preparation of, 139
   quitclaim, 138–139, 444
   special warranty, 138, 444
deeds in lieu of foreclosure document, 204–205, 446
defeasance clause, 199
deferred interest, 209, 446
deficiency judgments, 155, 204, 446
deficiency letters, 22, 438
delivery, 136, 443
demand, 280–281, 451. *See also* supply and demand
      principle
Department of Business and Professional Regulation
      (DBPR), 23
   defined, 439
   disciplining licensees, 79
   divisions of, 31, 98
   escrow (trust) accounts, 66
Department of Housing and Urban Development
      (HUD), 11, 93, 219, 330
Department of Veterans Affairs (VA) loans
   appraisal, 234–235
   assumptions, 238, 270
   changes in, 201
   closing costs, 233
   discount points, 222, 233, 245
   down payments, 232
   eligible properties, 235
   escrow (trust) accounts, 233–234
   funding fee, 233
   interest rate, 233
   lead levels, 330
   liability, 234
   market analysis, 301
   maximum loan amount, 232
   origination fee, 244
   secondary mortgage market, 219–220
   term, 233
   termite inspection, 271
   underwriting, 240–242
deposits, 65, 440
depreciation
   calculating, 404
   defined, 448
   economic obsolescence, 291, 308
   functional obsolescence, 290–291, 307
   overview, 280, 372–374
   physical deterioration, 290, 307
designated sales associates, 57, 439
development, 10
diminishing and increasing returns principle, 284

disability exemption, 366
discharging contracts, 180–181
disclosures
   agency relationship, 46
   Consent to Transition to Transaction Broker disclosure
      form, 56
   contract of sale, 187–189
   environmental hazard, 332
   Florida Brokerage Relationship Disclosure Act, 43, 50
   Interstate Land Sales Full Disclosure Act, 99
   nonrepresentation relationship, 52–53
discount points
   calculating dollar amount of, 402
   defined, 447
   overview, 245
   Section 203(b) loan program, 230
   VA loans, 222, 233
discount rate, 215, 447
discounting loans, 221–223
disintermediation, 216, 447
Division of Land Sales, Condominiums, and Mobile
      Homes, 98, 441
Division of Professions and Regulation, 31
Division of Real Estate (DRE)
   defined, 439
   disciplining licensees, 79
   fingerprint card, 19
   functions of, 32
   overview, 31, 35
   registration, 63
Division of Service Operations and Licensure, 31
Division of Technology, 31
DOAH (Florida Division of Administrative Hearings), 81
doctrine of laches, 101, 135, 398, 443
doctrine of prior appropriation, 111
documentation, underwriting, 242–243
domestic corporations, 71
dominant estates, 142–143
double net, 148
double taxation, 71, 440
double-hung windows, 315–316, 449
down payments
   calculating, 224–225
   FHA loans, 241
   VA loans, 232
DRE. *See* Division of Real Estate
drywall, 322
dual agency, 51, 439
due diligence investigations, 332
due on sale clause, 200, 446

E

earnest money deposits, 66, 189, 440
easements
   appurtenant, 142–143
   creation of, 144–145
   defined, 443
   in gross, 143
   versus licenses, 143–144
   party wall, 143
   termination of, 145

economic (external) obsolescence, 291, 308

economic rent, 150

economy, national, 4–5

EDOs. *See* escrow disbursement orders

education, postlicense, 17–19, 21–22, 36

EER (energy efficiency ratio), 322

effective gross income, 294, 448

elective share, 122, 441–442

electrical systems, 320–321

electricity heating systems, 318

elevation drawings, 322

eligible properties (VA loans), 235

emergency (summary) suspension, 82, 441

eminent domain, 134, 398, 443, 451

encroachments, 145–146, 443

end-of-course exam, practice, 412–426

energy efficiency ratio (EER), 322

energy-efficiency disclosures, 188

engineers, 4

entitlements, 232, 447

environmental hazards

    asbestos, 329–330

    disclosure statements, 332

    due diligence investigations, 332

    formaldehyde gas, 329

    groundwater contamination, 331

    lead, 330–331

    overview, 328–329

    radon, 329

environmental impact statements, 398, 451–452

Environmental Protection Agency (EPA), 329

equity

    assumptions, 235–237

    buildup, 341

    defined, 446, 450

    loans types and, 208–210

escheat, 134, 443, 452

escrow (trust) accounts

    defined, 440

    disposition of funds, 67–68

    disputes, 67–68

    good-faith doubt, 68

    overview, 65–66

    Section 203(b) loan program, 230

    VA loans, 233–234

escrow disbursement orders (EDOs)

    defined, 440

    overview, 67–68

    Real Estate Recovery Fund, 86

estate/inheritance tax liens, 154

estates

    freehold, 114–117

    nonfreehold, 117–119

estates at sufferance, 118–119

estates at will (tenancy at will), 118, 442

estates for years, 118, 442

estates in land, 108

    defined, 442

    overview, 108–109

    types of, 114–117

estates in severalty, 119, 442

examinations

licensure, 19–20

    practice end-of-course, 412–426

excess from sale, 204

exclusive right to buy, 184, 445

executed/executory contracts, 176, 445

executive powers, 32

exempt income, 368, 450

exempt property right, 122, 442, 450

exemptions

    ad valorem tax, 365–366

    licensure, 24–26, 36

expressed contracts, 173–174, 445

exterior construction

    footings/foundations, 313

    framing, 313–314

    insulation, 314

    roofs, 316–317

    ventilation, 315

    wall covering, 315

    windows, 315–316

external (economic) obsolescence, 291, 308

external obsolescence, 291, 308

F

facilitators, 55

Fair Housing Act, 91

fair market value, 279, 448–449

familial status, 91, 441

Fannie Mae (Federal National Mortgage Association [FNMA]), 219–221, 239

FAR (Florida Association of Realtors), 11

farm property, 6, 340, 438

Federal Deposit Insurance Corporation (FDIC), 216

federal government, role in real estate business, 10–11

Federal Home Loan Bank System (FHLB), 215

Federal Home Loan Mortgage Corporation (FHLMC) (Freddie Mac), 220, 239–241

Federal Housing Administration (FHA)

    calculating mortgages, 406

    changes, 200–201

    loan insurance programs, 227–231

    overview, 221

    underwriting guidelines, 241

federal income tax

    active income, 369

    liens, 154

    passive income, 369

    portfolio income, 369–370

Federal Institutions Reform Recovery and Enforcement Act of 1989 (FIRREA), 9

Federal National Mortgage Association (FNMA) (Fannie Mae), 219–221, 239

Federal Reserve System, 215

federally related transactions, 278, 449

fee simple absolute, 115–116, 442

fee simple defeasible, 116, 442

fee simple estate, 115–116, 442

fees, 147, 442–443

    funding, 233

    origination, 244, 448

    sales associate, 17

FHA. *See* Federal Housing Administration
FHLB (Federal Home Loan Bank System), 215
FHLMC (Federal Home Loan Mortgage Corporation), 220
fiduciaries, 44–45, 48, 439
final orders, 82–83
finance
    foreclosure, 203–205
    hypothecation, 195
    lending practices, 209–210
    lien theory, 197–202
    loans
        priority of, 203
        types of, 205–209
    mortgages, 195
    title theory, 195–197
    underwriting risk, 209–210
financial reporting, 8
FIRREA (Federal Institutions Reform Recovery and
    Enforcement Act of 1989), 9
first mortgages, 203
fixed costs, 244–245
fixed windows, 316, 449
fixtures
    defined, 111–112, 442
    legal determination of, 112–113
    plants, trees, and crops, 112
    trade, 113–114
flag lots, 328, 449
flashing, 322, 325
Florida Association of Realtors (FAR), 11
Florida Bar, 26
Florida Brokerage Relationship Disclosure Act, 43, 50
Florida Building Energy-Efficiency Rating Act, 188
Florida Division of Administrative Hearings (DOAH), 81
Florida Real Estate Appraisal Board, 9
Florida Real Estate Commission (FREC)
    complaints, 80
    defined, 439
    escrow disputes, 67
    functions of, 32–34
    history of, 15
    licensure, 16–22
    misrepresentation, 178
    overview, 31, 34
    valuation, 279
Florida Real Estate Commission Education and Research
    Foundation, 34
Florida residency, 20, 438
Florida Residential Landlord and Tenant Act, 99–101
Florida Time-Share Act, 129
Florida Uniform Land Sales Practices Act, 98–99
FNMA (Federal National Mortgage Association) (Fannie
    Mae), 219–221, 239
footings, 313, 322, 325
foreclosure
    deeds in lieu of, 204–205, 446
    deficiency judgments, 204
    excess from sale, 204
    judicial, 203–204
    statutory redemption, 204
foreign corporations, 71
formal complaints, 81–82, 440

formaldehyde gas, 329
foundations, 313, 322
framing
    balloon, 314
    platform, 313
    post-and-beam, 314
FREC. *See* Florida Real Estate Commission
Freddie Mac (Federal Home Loan Mortgage Corporation
    [FHLMC]), 220, 239–241
freehold estates
    defined, 114, 442
    fee simple estates, 115–116
    statutory life estates, 117
    voluntary life estates, 116–117
friendly foreclosure, 204
functional obsolescence, 290–291, 307
funding fees, 233

G

gable roofs, 323, 449
gains, 374
gambrel roofs, 323, 449
general agency, 49, 439
general liens, 156, 443
general partnerships, 70, 440
general warranty deeds
    covenant against encumbrances, 137
    covenant of further assistance, 138
    covenant of quiet enjoyment, 138
    covenant of seisin, 137
    covenant of warranty of title, 138
    defined, 443–444
Ginnie Mae (Government National Mortgage Association
    [GNMA]), 219–220
going concern value, 356, 450
good-faith doubt, 68, 440
goodwill, 356, 450
Government National Mortgage Association [GNMA]
    (Ginnie Mae), 219–220
government rectangular survey system, 163–166, 444
graduated leases, 149–150, 444
graduated payment loans, 207, 228
grantees, 135, 444
granting, 135, 444
granting clause, 136, 199, 444
grantors, 135, 444
Green Belt Law exemption, 366, 451
GRM (gross rent multiplier), 295, 449
gross leases, 148, 444
gross rent multiplier (GRM), 295, 449
ground leases, 149, 444
groundwater contamination, 331
group licenses, 36, 439
Growth Management Act of 1985, 394
guide meridians, 164

H

habendum clause, 137, 444
headers, 322
health ordinances, 394, 452

hearing officer, 82
hearings, complaint, 81–82
heat pumps, 319
heating systems, 318
highest and best use
  analysis, 286
  defined, 449
  principle of, 283
hip roofs, 323, 450
holdover tenancy, 118, 442
home equity loans, 207, 446
homeowner association disclosure, 188
homeowner's insurance, 272–273
homestead
  defined, 442
  exemption, 365
  status, 122–123
honesty, 16–17
horizontal sliding windows, 315, 450
hot water systems, 320
hotels, 339
households, 283, 384, 451
housing law
  federal laws
    Civil Rights Act of 1866, 91
    Civil Rights Act of 1968, 91–93
    Real Estate Settlement Procedures Act (RESPA),
      97–98
  Florida laws
    versus federal, 93
    Florida Residential Landlord and Tenant Act,
      99–101
    Florida Uniform Land Sales Practices Act, 98–99
    leases covering residential dwelling units, 99–102
  violations
    advertising, 96
    blockbusting, 94–95
    improper listings, 95
    overview, 93–94
    redlining, 97
    steering, 96
    treatment of minorities, 95–97
HUD (Department of Housing and Urban Development),
  11, 93, 219, 330
hypothecation, 195, 446

I

illiquidity, 342
immune properties, 365, 451
implied contracts, 173–174, 445
improper listings, 95
in rem proceedings, 126
inactive licenses, 36–37, 439
income
  active, 450
  borrower's
    FHA underwriting, 241
    Freddie Mac underwriting, 240–241
    VA underwriting, 242–243
  effective gross, 294, 448
  exempt, 368, 450

net operating (NOI), 292, 349
  portfolio, 369, 451
incurable defects, 291, 449
index leases, 150, 444
index plus a margin, 208, 446
industrial property, 6, 339–340
ineffective licenses, 38, 439
innocent (unintentional) misrepresentation, 178
inspections, 270–271
installment sales contracts, 190, 451
insulation
  asbestos, 329–330
  defined, 450
  overview, 314
  R value, 314, 323–324, 450
  urea-formaldehyde foam, 329, 450
insurance
  companies, 218
  loan
    homeowners', 272–273
    Section 203(b) loan program, 227–231
    Section 245 graduated payment loan
      program, 228
    special terms for veterans, 227–228
  title, 141–142
intentional misrepresentation, 178
interest
  calculating, 402
  deferred, 209, 446
  defined, 446
  mortgages, deducting from, 372
  rates
    Section 203(b) loan program, 229
    VA loans, 233
  reversionary, 118, 442
interior lots, 328, 450
intermediation, 216, 447
Internal Revenue Service (IRS), 11, 154
interpleaders, 67, 440
interpreting market conditions, 387–388
Interstate Land Sales Full Disclosure
  Act, 99
investigations, complaint, 80
investments
  business brokerage
    expertise, 357
    versus real estate, 356
    sale of businesses, 357
    valuation of businesses, 357–358
  calculating
    cost and price, 353–354
    price and commissions, 345–353
  real estate
    advantages/disadvantages, 341–343
    expertise, 337
    goals, 340
    price problems, 354–356
    property investment analysis, 343–345
    property types, 338–340
involuntarily inactive licenses, 37, 439
irrevocable consent to service forms, 20, 438
IRS (Internal Revenue Service), 11, 154

J

jalousie windows, 315–316
Johnson v. Davis, 189
joint tenancy, 120, 442
joint ventures, 73
joists, 316, 322
judgment liens, 154–155
judicial foreclosure, 203–204
junior mortgages, 203
just value, 363, 451

K

key lots, 328, 450
knobs, 325

L

laches, doctrine of, 101, 135, 398, 443
land
    acquisition and subdivision, 10
    defined, 442
    feudal versus allodial systems,
        107–108
    versus site, 283
landlords
    defined, 118
    lease requirements, 100–102
law of agency, 43–44
lead, 188, 330–331
leased property, 108, 117, 442
leasehold, 147, 442, 444
leasehold estates, 118, 442
leases
    assignment, 152
    basic principles of, 147
    contract rent, 150
    economic rent, 150
    essentials of, 151
    graduated, 149–150, 444
    gross, 148, 444
    ground, 149, 444
    index, 150, 444
    net, 148, 444
    overview, 146
    percentage, 148–149, 444
    proprietary, 126, 442
    residential dwelling units, 99–102
    sale and leaseback arrangements,
        209–210
    sandwich, 150, 444
    security deposits, 150–151
    subletting, 150, 152, 444
    termination of, 151–152
legal descriptions, 161, 444
legally registered brokerage entities, 69
legally sufficient complaints, 79, 440
lender-funded buydowns, 208
lending practices, 209–210
lessees, defined, 118
lessors, defined, 118

letters of guidance, 81, 441
leverage, 341–342, 407, 450
licensees
    complaints against, 80–83
    responsibilities, 44–48
    specialty areas, 6
licenses
    defined, 438
    versus registrations, 23, 69–73
licensing law, 147
licensure
    applications for, 19
    brokers/broker associates, 18–19, 23–24
    categories of, 15–16
    defined, 23
    disciplinary procedures, 79–80
    easements, 143–144
    examination for, 19–20
    exemptions, 24–26, 36
    FREC and DRE, 31–39
    nonresident, 20
    postlicense education, 21–22
    renewal, 21–22, 36
    sales associates, 16–17, 24
    state laws, 22–23
    status of, 36–37
    via mutual recognition, 20–21
    violations, 84–87
lien theory, 197–202, 446
liens
    categories of, 155–156
    deficiency judgment, 155, 204
    defined, 444
    judgment, 154–155
    mechanic's, 154
    mortgage, 153
    priority of, 156
    tax, 153–154
    transfer of encumbered title, 156
life estates, 116–117, 442
life estates pur autre vie, 116, 442
like-for-like trades, 377, 451
limited confidentiality, 55, 439
limited liability companies (LLCs), 72, 440
limited liability partnerships (LLPs), 71, 440
limited partnerships, 70, 440
limited representation, 54, 439
lines of credit, 207, 446
linkage, 344
liquidated damages, 185–186, 189, 445
liquidation analysis, 356, 450
liquidity, 343, 450
lis pendens
    defined, 444, 446
    judicial foreclosure, 203
    mechanic's liens, 154
listing contracts, 186–187
litigation, escrow dispute, 67–68
LLCs (limited liability companies),
    72, 440
LLPs (limited liability partnerships),
    71, 440

loan discount, 222
loans. *See also* Department of Veterans Affairs (VA)
　　loans; Federal Housing Administration (FHA);
　　mortgages
　adjustable rate, 207–208, 210
　amortized
　　defined, 446
　　history of, 220
　　versus other loans, 210
　　overview, 205–206
　applications, 245, 272
　appraisal requirement, 243
　assumptions of, 235–239, 270
　blanket, 207, 210
　bridge, 217
　budget, 206
　buydown, 208, 210
　charges
　　discount points, 245
　　fixed costs, 244–245
　　overview, 243–244
　　variable costs, 244
　conforming, 239, 447
　construction
　　defined, 208–209
　　supply factors, 386
　conventional, 223–227, 406
　discounting, 221–223
　Fannie Mae, 219–221, 239
　Freddie Mac, 220, 239–241
　Ginnie Mae, 219–220
　graduated payment, 207
　home equity, 207, 446
　insurance
　　for homeowners, 272–273
　　Section 203(b) loan program, 227–231
　　Section 245 graduated payment loan program, 228
　　for veterans, 227–228
　maximum amount
　　Section 203(b) loan program, 229
　　VA loans, 232
　open-end, 207, 210
　package, 206, 210
　PITI, 206, 446
　problems, 352–353
　processing, 230
　purchase money, 206, 210
　recourse, 155, 444
　reverse annuity, 209–210
　sale and leaseback arrangements,
　　209–210
　selecting lenders, 272
　shared equity/participating, 209
　straight, 205, 210, 447
　wraparound, 208, 447
loan-to-value ratio (LTV), 209, 223–224, 447
local governments, role in real estate business, 11
local planning agencies, 396–397
lots
　defined, 161, 445, 450
　types of, 325–328
LOW PAIN mnemonic, 46

loyalty, 45–46
LTV (loan-to-value ratio), 209, 223–224, 447

M

mansard roofs, 323, 450
manufacturing property, 5
market analysis, 300–304
market data approach, 285–287
market knowledge, 7
market value, 279
marketable title, 139, 444
math formulas, 402–407
mechanical systems/equipment
　cooling systems, 319
　electrical system, 320–321
　heating systems, 318
　hot water system, 320
　overview, 317
　plumbing systems, 319–320
　sewers/septic tanks, 320
mechanic's liens, 154
mediation, 67, 440
meeting of the minds, 177, 445
metes and bounds, 161–163, 445
mills, 367, 451
minimum property requirements (MPRs), 230
minorities, 95–97
MIP (mortgage insurance premium), 227
mistakes, 179
mixed-use property, 5, 340
MLSs (multiple-listing services), 300
monthly maintenance, 126–127, 442
monuments, 162, 445
mortgage bankers, 217, 447
mortgage brokers
　defined, 448
　licensure, 9
mortgage companies, 217, 448
mortgage insurance premium (MIP), 227
mortgage liens, 153
mortgage markets. *See also* Department of Veterans Affairs
　　(VA) loans; Federal Housing Administration (FHA)
　assumptions, 235–239
　disintermediation, 216
　FDIC, 216
　Federal Reserve System, 215
　FHLB, 215
　intermediation, 216
　loans
　　charges, 243–245
　　conventional, 223–227
　　discounting, 221–223
　　history of, 220–221
　　loan-to-value ratio (LTV), 223
　　primary, 216–218
　　qualifying/underwriting, 239–243
　　secondary, 218–220
mortgage relief, 378
mortgagees, 199, 446
mortgagee's title insurance, 141–142
mortgages. *See also* loans

mortgages. *See also* loans (*Continued*)
  acquiring property with, 200–201
  adjustable rate (ARMs), 207
  brokers, 217
  calculating loans, 406
  changing loan balance, 201–202
  companies, 217
  deducting interest, 372
  defined, 195, 446
  elements of, 199–200
  first, 203
  junior, 203
  parties to, 199
  purchase money (PMMs), 218, 448
  second, 203
  senior, 203
  subject to mortgage transaction, 202
  wraparound, 200
mortgagors, 199, 446
motels, 339
MPRs (minimum property requirements), 230
multiple licenses, 36, 439
multiple-listing services (MLSs), 300
municipal bonds, 218
mutual agreements, 177–179
mutual recognition agreements, 20–21, 438

N

naked title, 196
name recognition, 7
National Association of Realtors (NAR), 11, 97
natural breakeven, 148–149
negative amortization, 207, 446
net leases, 148, 444
net operating income (NOI), 292, 349
net worth, 241
new money, 253
No Brokerage Relationship Notices, 52
NOI (net operating income), 292, 349
nolo contendere, 16, 438
nonconventional loans
  FHA, 227–228
  VA, 232–235
nonfreehold estates, 117–119
nonrepresentation
  defined, 51–53, 439
  disclosure requirements, 52–53
nonresident licensure, 20
nonresidential sales transactions, 57
notices of noncompliance, 80, 441
novation, 181, 445

O

obedience, 45
office buildings, 339
Office of Thrift Supervision, 215, 448
open-end loans, 207, 210
open-market operations, 215, 448
option contracts, 176, 184–185, 445
"OR" "EE" rule, 11

origination fees, 244, 448
ostensible partnerships, 70–71, 440
outside dimensions, 306
over-improvement, 284, 449
owners associations, 125, 442
owner's title insurance, 141
ownership
  community
    condominiums, 124–126
    cooperatives, 126–128
    overview, 123–124
    planned-unit development (PUD), 128–129
    resort time-share developments, 129
  forms of
    concurrent, 119–121
    partitioning of, 122
    sole, 119
    special interests, 122–123
  real property
    classification of, 107–108
    composition of, 110–111
    fixtures, 111–114
    types of estates, 114–119
ownership interest, 114, 117
ownership test, 376

P

package loans, 206, 210
panic selling, 92
partially amortized loans, 210
partitioning, 122, 442
partnerships, 69–71, 440
party wall easements, 143
passive income, 369, 451
payments
  balloon, 205, 210, 446
  down
    calculating, 224–225
    FHA loans, 241
    VA loans, 232
penalties
  administrative, 32–33, 84–85
  civil, 86
  criminal, 85–86
percentage leases, 148–149, 444
percolation tests, 323
personal easements in gross, 143
personal property, 109, 135, 442
personalty, 109, 442
physical deterioration, 290, 307
pitch, 323
PITI (principal, interest, taxes, insurance) loans, 206, 446
places of public accommodation, 97, 441
planned-unit development (PUD), 128–129
planning
  history of, 393–394
  private land-use controls, 398–399
  public land-use controls
    building codes, 398
    developments of regional impact, 398
    local planning agencies, 396–397

master plans, 396
   nonconforming use, 395
   special exceptions, 396
   variances, 395–396
   zoning ordinances, 394–395
plat maps of subdivisions, 10, 438
platform framing, 313–314
plot plans (plot maps), 323
plottage, 284–285, 449
plumbing systems, 319–320
PMI (private mortgage insurance), 223–225, 448
PMMs (purchase money mortgages), 218, 448
point of beginning (POB), 162, 445
point of contact information, 65, 440
portfolio income, 369–370, 451
post-and-beam framing, 314
post-and-beam roofs, 316–317
postlicense course, 18
postlicense education, 17–19, 21–22, 36
potable water, 323
power-of-sale clause, 196, 447
prepayment clause, 198, 447
prepayment penalties, 198, 447
price to control, 201, 237
pricing
   versus appraisal, 277–278
   income approach to, 291–295
   problems, 354–356
   of real estate, 384–386
   replacement cost, 304–308
prima facie, 33, 439
primary mortgage market, 216–218, 448
principal, interest, taxes, insurance (PITI) loans, 206, 446
principal meridians, 163, 445
principals (clients), 44–46, 439
principle of substitution, 449
private land-use controls, 398–399
private lenders, 218
private mortgage insurance (PMI), 223–225, 448
probable cause, 80–81, 441
professional organizations, 11
progression, 285, 449
promissory notes, 197–198, 447
property. *See also* real property
   defined, 442
   personal, 109, 135, 442
   rental, 68, 117
   residential, 5, 338–340
property management, 8–9, 438
property reports, 99, 441
property taxes
   disclosures, 188, 366
   grievance process, 364
   prorating, 263–265
proprietary leases, 126, 442
proprietary real estate schools, 38
prorating, 261–265, 402–403, 448
public accommodation, 97
public land-use controls
   building codes, 398
   developments of regional impact, 398
   local planning agencies, 396–397

master plans, 396
   nonconforming use, 395
   special exceptions, 396
   variances, 395–396
   zoning ordinances, 394–395
public records, 140
PUD (planned-unit development),
   128–129
purchase money loans, 206, 210
purchase money mortgages (PMMs), 218, 448
purchase price, calculating, 402

Q

qualifying buyers
   appraisal, 243
   credit history, 242
   documentation, 242–243
   FHA guidelines, 241
   Freddie Mac guidelines, 239–240
   maximum loan amount, 243
   VA guidelines, 241–242
quantity survey method, 289–290
quasi-judicial responsibilities, 32
quasi-legislative responsibilities, 32
quiet enjoyment, 138, 444
quitclaim deeds, 138–139, 444

R

R value, 314, 323–324, 450
radon, 188, 329
rafters, 316, 323
ranges, 164–165, 445
Rayner v. Wise Realty Co. of Tallahassee, 189
real estate. *See* real property
real estate agents, 3. *See also* agency
real estate brokerage, 5–7, 438. *See also* brokerage
real estate business
   appraisal, 9
   brokerage, 5–7
   development and construction, 10
   example forms, 434–437
   financing, 9
   national economy and, 4–5
   professional organizations, 11
   professions that rely on, 3–4
   property management, 8–9
   role of government, 10–11
   sales process, 7–8
Real Estate Education and Research Foundation, 39
real estate market
   economic characteristics of, 384–387
   interpreting conditions, 387–388
   physical characteristics of, 383
Real Estate Recovery Fund, 34, 86–87
Real Estate Settlement Procedures Act (RESPA),
   97–98, 274, 441
real property
   composition of, 110–111
   defined, 108–109, 442
   description methods

real property (*Continued*)
  basic math relationships, 166–168
  government rectangular surveys, 163–166
  metes and bounds, 161–163
  recorded plats, 161
fixtures, 111–114
inspections, 270
ownership
  classification of, 107–108
  community, 123–129
  concurrent, 119–122
  estates, 114–119
  partitioning, 122
  sole, 119
  special interests, 122–123
showing, 7
taxes
  calculating, 263–265, 403–404
  capital gains, 375–377
  deductions, 370–374
  exchanges, 377–378
  installment sales, 377
  on sale of, 374–375
types of, 338–340
valuation
  appraisal process, 285
  assemblage versus plottage,
    284–285
  concepts of, 279–280
  cost approach (reproduction),
    287–291
  deducting depreciation,
    307–308
  elements of, 280–281
  gross rent multiplier (GRM), 295
  income approach, 291–295
  market analysis, 295–304
  market data approach, 285–287
  physical characteristics of land, 281–282
  principles (theorems) of value, 282–284
  reconciliation process, 295
  regression versus progression, 285
  replacement cost pricing, 304–308
reasonable period, 179
recommended order, 82, 441
reconciliation, 278, 295, 449
reconveyance clause, 196, 447
record keeping, 8, 57
recorded plats, 161
recording titles, 140
recourse loans, 155, 444
redlining, 97, 441
registration
  corporations, 71–72
  defined, 23, 438
  entities not permitted, 72–73
  versus licensure, 23, 69–73
  limited liability company, 72
  partnership, 69–71
  sole proprietorship, 69
regression, 285, 449
regular documentation, 242

remaindermen, 116, 442
rental property, 68, 117
replacement cost, 287, 304, 449
rescission of contracts, 182, 185, 445
reserve requirements, 215, 448
residential construction
  environmental hazards, 329–332
  exterior construction, 313–317
  lots, 325–328
  mechanical systems/equipment, 317–321
  terminology, 321–325
Residential Lead-Based Paint Hazard Reduction
    Act of 1992, 330
residential property, 5, 338–340
residential sales, 50, 57, 439–440
residential transactions, 4–5, 438
resort time-share developments, 129
RESPA (Real Estate Settlement Procedures Act), 97–98,
    274, 441
restrictive covenants, 10, 438
retail establishments, 339
return of investment, 337, 450
return on investment, 337, 450
reverse annuity loans, 209–210
reversionary interest, 118, 442
revocation, 38, 441
ridgeboards, 323
right of rescission, 126
right of survivorship, 121, 442
roofs, 316–317, 323
Rule 61J2-26.002, 20, 438

S

S&Ls (savings and loan associations), 217
sale and leaseback arrangements, 209–210
sales associates
  defined, 438
  designated, 57, 439
  licensure, 16–17, 24
sales comparison approach, 285, 449
sales process, 7–8
sandwich leases, 150, 444
sashes, 325
savings and loan associations (S&Ls), 217
scarcity, 281
second mortgages, 203
secondary mortgage market, 218–220, 448
second-degree misdemeanors, 33
Section 203(b) loan program
  appraisal, 230–231
  cash investment, 229
  closing costs, 230
  discount points, 230
  escrow (trust) accounts, 230
  interest rate, 229
  loan amount, 229
  loan insurance, 228–229
  loan processing, 230
  maximum term, 230
  overview, 227
  restrictions, 231

Section 245 graduated payment loan
     program, 228
sections, 165–166, 445
security deposits, 150–151
seller financing, 208
sellers, 47
seller's market, 387, 451
senior mortgages, 203
separate property, 124, 442
septic tanks, 320
service industries, 397, 452
servient estates, 142
seven-business day right of rescission,
     99, 441
sewers, 320
shake roofing, 325
shared equity loans, 209–210
sheathing, 323–324
shell, 325
shingles, 325
signage
   broker's offices, 64
   local planning agency, 397
sills, 324
Single Agent Notice disclosure form, 54
single agents, 53–54, 57, 440
single-hung windows, 315–316
single-purpose properties, 287
site, versus land, 283
site plans, 397
situs, 282, 449
slabs, 325
slate, 325
soil pipes, 324–325
sold signs, 274
sole ownership, 119
sole plates, 325
sole proprietorships, 69, 440
solid sheathing, 324
special agency, 49–50, 440
special assessment taxes, 154, 451
special exceptions, 396, 452
special flood hazard areas, 452
special ownership interests, 122–123
special warranty deeds, 138, 444
special-use properties, 287
specific liens, 156, 444
speculative homes, 10
square foot method, 289
state broker license examinations, 18
state government, role in real estate business, 11
state transfer taxes, 253–261, 403
Statute of Frauds, 173, 183, 445
Statute of Limitations, 186, 445
statutory law, 43
statutory life estates, 117, 443
statutory redemption, 204, 447
steam heating systems, 318
steering, 92, 96, 441
straight loans, 205, 210, 447
straight loans (term loans), 205, 210, 447
studs, 325

subdividing, 10, 98
subdivision plats, 397
subject property, 285, 302, 449
subject to the mortgage, 202, 447
subleases, 150, 152, 444
subordination clause, 203, 447
substitution principle, 282–283
subsurface rights, 111
summary (emergency) suspension, 82, 441
supply and demand principle, 280–281, 283–284,
     384–387, 451
surface rights, 110–111
surveys, 163–166, 271, 444
surviving spouse exemption, 365
swing loans, 217

T

T lots, 328, 450
takeout loans, 208, 447
taking back mortgages, 206
tax bases, 367, 383, 451
tax liens, 153–154
tax rates
   capital gains, 377
   defined, 451
   property, 367
tax shelters, 342, 450
taxable income, 370, 451
taxable value, 365, 451
taxes
   federal income, 369–370
   real property
      ad valorem, 363–368
      calculating, 263–265, 403–404
      capital gains, 375–377
      deductions, 370–374
      exchanges, 377–378
      immunities/exemptions, 365–366
      installment sales, 377
      liens, 153–154
      on sale of, 374–375
   state transfer, 253–261, 403
Taxpayer Fairness Act of 1997, 376
tenancy at sufferance, 118–119, 443
tenancy at will, 118, 442
tenancy at will (estates at will), 118, 442
tenancy by the entirety, 121, 443
tenancy in common, 120–121, 443
tenants, defined, 118
term
   Section 203(b) loan program, 230
   VA loans, 233
term loans (straight loans), 205, 210, 447
terminating contracts, 181–182
terraces, 127
third parties, 47
third-degree felonies, 33
tiers, 164, 445
time limits, 189
time-shares, 25, 129, 443
title companies, 4

title opinion, 140, 444
title theory, 195–197, 447
titles
    actual notice, 140
    closing computations, 265–269
    closing statements, 249–261
    constructive notice, 140
    defined, 444
    insurance, 141
    methods of transfer, 133–134
    mortgagee's insurance, 141–142
    overview, 139–140
    owner's insurance, 141
    prorating, 261–265
    public records, 140
    recording, 140
    between signing and closing, 269–274
    sold signs, 274
    Torrens land titles, 140–141
    transfer of encumbered, 156
Torrens system, 140–141, 444
township lines, 164, 445
tract homes, 10
trade names, 64, 440
Transaction Broker Notice disclosure form, 55
transaction brokers, 54–56, 440
transfer taxes, 11
transferability, 281
transitioning agency relationships, 56
TRIM (truth-in-millage), 368, 451
triple net, 148
trusses, 316, 325
trust accounts. See escrow accounts
trusts, 73
truth-in-millage (TRIM), 368, 451

U

underground storage tanks, 331, 450
underwriting
    appraisal(s), 243
    credit history, 242
    documentation, 242–243
    FHA, 241
    Freddie Mac guidelines, 239–241
    maximum loan amount, 243
    risk, 209–210
    VA guidelines, 241–242
unenforceable contracts, 174, 184, 445
Uniform Standards of Professional Appraisal
        Practice (USPAP), 9, 277–278,
        438, 449
unilateral contracts, 174–176, 445
unintentional (innocent) misrepresentation, 178
unintentional misrepresentation, 178
unit-in-place method, 289
universal agency, 48–49, 440
unlimited liability, 70
urban planning. See planning
urea-formaldehyde foam insulation, 329, 450
use test, 376
use variances, 395–396

USPAP (Uniform Standards of Professional Appraisal
        Practice), 9, 277–278, 438, 449
utility, 280–281

V

VA loans. See Department of Veterans Affairs
        (VA) loans
vacancy rate, 284, 388, 451
valid contracts, 174, 445
valuation, property
    appraisal process, 285
    appraisal versus pricing, 277–278
    assemblage versus plottage, 284–285
    concepts of, 279–280
    defined, 449
    elements of, 280–281
    market data approach, 285–287
    physical characteristics of land, 281–282
    principles (theorems) of value, 282–284
    problems, 349–351
    regression versus progression, 285
variable costs, 244
variances, 395–396, 399, 452
verification of deposit (VOD) form, 242
verification of employment (VOE) form, 242
Veterans Administration. See Department of Veterans
        Affairs (VA) loans
veteran's liability, 234
violations
    administrative penalties, 32–33, 84–85
    civil penalties, 86
    criminal penalties, 85–86
    housing
        advertising, 96
        blockbusting, 94–95
        improper listings, 95
        poor treatment of minorities, 95–97
        redlining, 97
        steering, 96
    overview, 83–84
    Real Estate Recovery Fund, 86–87
    revocation/suspension of broker's license, 84
VOD (verification of deposit) form, 242
VOE (verification of employment) form, 242
void contracts, 174, 445–446
void, defined, 439
void licenses, 37–38
voidable contracts, 174, 182, 446
voltages, 320–321
voluntary inactive status, 37, 439
voluntary life estates, 116–117

W

warm air heating systems, 318
water heating systems, 318
water supplies, 319–320
windows
    air-conditioning units, 319
    defined, 449–450
    types of, 315–316

wraparound loans, 208, 447
wraparound mortgages, 200

Y

yield, calculating, 406
yield maintenance, 198

Z

zoning
   history of, 393–394
   ordinances, 111, 452

private land-use controls,
      398–399
public land-use controls
   building codes, 398
   developments of regional impact, 398
   local planning agencies, 396–397
   master plans, 396
   nonconforming use, 395
   ordinances, 394–395
   special exceptions, 396
   variances, 395–396